D0843215

Clinical Psychiatry and the Law

Second Edition

Clinical Psychiatry and the Law

Second Edition

By

Robert I. Simon, M.D.
Clinical Professor of Psychiatry,
Director, Program in Psychiatry and Law,
Georgetown University School of Medicine,
Washington, DC

DISCARDED

American
Psychiatric
Press, Inc.

Washington, DC
London, England

BOWLING GREEN STATE
UNIVERSITY LIBRARIES

Note: The authors have worked to ensure that all information in this book concerning drug dosages, schedules, and routes of administration is accurate as of the time of publication and consistent with standards set by the U.S. Food and Drug Administration and the general medical community. As medical research and practice advance, however, therapeutic standards may change. For this reason and because human and mechanical errors sometimes occur, we recommend that readers follow the advice of a physician who is directly involved in their care or the care of a member of their family.

Books published by the American Psychiatric Press, Inc., represent the views and opinions of the individual authors and do not necessarily represent the policies and opinions of the Press or the American Psychiatric Association.

Copyright © 1992 Robert I. Simon, M.D.
ALL RIGHTS RESERVED
Manufactured in the United States of America on acid-free paper.
95 94 93 92   4   3   2   1
First Edition

American Psychiatric Press, Inc.
1400 K Street, N.W., Washington, DC 20005

Library of Congress Cataloging-in-Publication Data

Simon, Robert I.
      Clinical psychiatry and the law / by Robert I. Simon. — 2nd ed.
      p. cm.
      Includes bibliographical references and index.
      ISBN 0-88048-401-2
      1. Psychiatrists—Malpractice—United States. 2. Psychiatrists—Legal
status, Laws, etc.—United States. 3. Insanity—Jurisprudence—United
States. 4. Psychotherapist and patient—United States. I. Title.
      [DNLM : 1. Malpractice—United States.   2. Psychiatry—United
States—legislation. WM 33 AA1 S5c]
      KF2910.P753S48 1991
      344.73'041—dc20
      [347.30441]
      DNLM/DLC   91-31031
      for Library of Congress   CIP

British Library Cataloguing in Publication Data
A CIP record is available from the British Library.

To my mother, Elizabeth Simon,
who lovingly laid down the law

And ye shall know the truth, and the truth shall make you free.

John 8:32

With purity and with holiness I will pass my life and practice my art . . . may it be granted to me to enjoy life and the practice of the art respected by all men.

The Oath of Hippocrates

Contents

Acknowledgments

The second edition of *Clinical Psychiatry and the Law* required the dedicated support of a number of people. Susan Breglio, my secretary, deciphered the manuscript festooned with endless arrows with remarkable intuition and patience. I very much appreciate and count upon her steadfastness and unique skills.

David Berthiaume, J.D., provided legal assistance in editing the second edition. His legal review of the manuscript ensured the accuracy of the legal commentary and citations.

I want to thank Dilip V. Jeste, M.D., Professor of Psychiatry and Neuroscience, University of California, San Diego, for his excellent assistance in the clinical review and updating of the chapter on tardive dyskinesia.

I am also greatly indebted to Gary R. Schoener, Executive Director of the Walk-In Counseling Center in Minneapolis, Minnesota, for his expert review of the sexual misconduct chapter.

The chapter on electroconvulsive therapy was critiqued by Frank M. Moscarillo, M.D., a respected colleague and friend, to whom I express my thanks.

Finally, I want to recognize my wife's grace and good humor while listening to me renounce, yet one more time, any intention of writing another book.

Preface

This book is intended to be used as a guide to the clinical management of legal issues for psychiatrists, psychologists, social workers, psychiatric nurses, and other mental health professionals entrusted with the care of emotionally and mentally disturbed patients. Accordingly, I have adopted the use of clinical vignettes to introduce each chapter. I have attempted to weave the vignette through the discussion that follows in each chapter and present it in a question-and-answer format. The clinical vignettes are fictitious. Like a dream, they contain the inevitable "day residues" of my own clinical experiences as well as the clinical experiences that colleagues have shared with me. The patients and therapists depicted in the vignettes are totally a creation of my own imagination and do not describe any real persons, living or dead.

I have left the fuller explication of psychiatric and legal issues surrounding the rare clinical situation to the current textbooks on forensic psychiatry. I have not attempted to touch upon the area of forensic psychiatry proper—that is, the application of psychiatry to legal issues for legal ends. The purpose of this book is to facilitate the clinical management of legal issues so that good patient care will be enhanced. The book's objective is medical, not legal.

This book is written primarily for psychiatrists. Because of the divergent professional backgrounds of readers who might find this book of interest, I have tried to use applicable professional titles in the text that recognize these differences. This task has been difficult because of the considerable overlap in patient care among the various mental health disciplines. When writing on matters of potential interest to all readers, I have used the generic designation *mental health professional.* When presenting clinical material of relevance to both medical and nonmedical practitioners directly involved in patient care, I have tried to consistently use the generic term *therapist.* In order to avoid monotonous repetition, I have sometimes varied the term therapist with *clinician* and *practitioner.*

Some readers might rightfully argue with my arrangement of chapters under certain major topic headings. For example, the chapter on involuntary hospitalization falls under the topic heading of "Patient Rights." With the robust liberty rights of patients surrounding involuntary hospitalization, this chapter seems to reasonably fit in the general category of patient rights. Similarly, the chapter on defensive psychiatry is included under "The Doctor-Patient Relationship." This makes sense because of the potentially adverse effects of defensive practices upon the therapeutic alliance. Many chapters overlap a number of topic areas. I ask the readers' indulgence with the inevitable problems of categorization.

In a number of chapters I make general references to the *Diagnostic and Statistical Manual of Mental Disorders* (DSM). Because the DSM undergoes periodic revision and only general references are made to the DSM in this book, I have refrained from citing the current edition.

Mental health professionals frequently point out to their patients the maladaptive aspects of denial that prevent a more adaptive accommodation to reality. Mental health professionals are not immune from this problem, particularly regarding legal requirements governing the practice of their profession. The denial of these requirements inevitably leads to blind spots that can be clinically and legally disastrous. Although therapists do not need to be lawyers, they must realistically practice within the law. A clear knowledge of legal issues relevant to clinical practice is essential to diminish fears of legal entanglement with patients—that often interfere with good clinical practice. In fact, the personal and career problems arising from the fear of malpractice suits have become so widespread that many support groups are being formed for physicians and their families.

There are three fundamental spheres of influence that affect the practice of mental health professionals: the therapist's professional, moral, and legal duty to provide competent care to patients; the patient's right of self-determination to receive or reject such care; and the decisions and directives of courts, legislatures, and nongovernmental agencies that regulate professional practice. Effective psychiatric treatment must encompass the tension between clinical practice and legal requirements.

For example, the imposition of the *Tarasoff* duty upon therapists in an ever-increasing number of jurisdictions has been viewed with much alarm. Because of the liability consequences, many therapists have resisted accepting this as a professional duty. They have viewed it as an external, unwarranted intrusion by the law into their professional practices. Thus, the moral principles underlying the duty to protect potential victims from violence by mental patients are often overlooked. Few therapists would disagree with the need to protect an endangered third person if the therapist believes that his or her patient intends to do physical harm. What initially appears to be a conflict between the therapist's duty to maintain the confidentiality of patients and the law's requirement to safeguard the citizenry can be viewed with less rancor when the commonality of underlying moral concern for the safety of fellow human beings by both the law and therapists can be appreciated.

Furthermore, patient rights movements, the ascendancy of the informed-consent doctrine, the right to refuse treatment, and the right to treatment all overlap and may appear to conflict with the mental health practitioner's duty to provide a reasonable standard of care. Judicially imposed duties, however, are not necessarily in conflict with good clinical practice. Preoccupation with the law causes therapists to discharge their duties to patients in legally formalistic ways that may interfere with the all-important therapeutic alliance. An iatrogenic liability neurosis can take hold of the therapist's professional judgment, producing an Alice-in-Wonderland view of patient care and management. Does not the psychiatrist who prescribes homeopathic doses of medication in the vain hope of helping the patient without risking any harm abrogate his or her moral, professional, and legal duty to provide good clinical care to the patient? Is not the patient unnecessarily exposed to harm from homeopathic dosages without the possibility of receiving any benefit? Thus, the patient continues to suffer and remains disabled.

Shame and guilt may accompany defensive practices, causing practitioners ultimately to disdain themselves and their work. For instance, the therapist may be legally correct in following the dictates of a confidentiality statute that prohibits warning endangered third parties; however, the therapist is eschewing good clinical practice in not warning an intended victim if it is clear that a patient constitutes a significant threat of harm and warning is the only option available. The therapist can be legally right but professionally and morally wrong.

As a matter of fact, it is the rare legal problem in the psychiatric treatment of patients that cannot be productively addressed through the use of good clinical practice and knowledge of pertinent legal issues. The key is to never lose sight of the primary duty of the therapist: to render good clinical care to the patient. The therapist has a professional and moral duty in providing care for patients that transcends standards imposed by the law or regulatory agencies. I do not impute a moral superiority to the therapist's professional duty that transcends the law's authority. Legal standards, however, are fixed at a minimum level by necessity. The professional and moral duty of the therapist regarding patients is set at a maximum level. The difference represents the gulf that exists between the human condition and the human spirit.

In regard to the law, clinicians should have a clear working knowledge of the relevant legal requirements governing professional practice. For example, some courts have considered what is not documented as not being done. Maintaining an adequate clinical record can be crucial in the defense of a malpractice claim. This bit of legal knowledge can go a very long way in easing the anxieties of therapists who fear the possibility of being second-guessed by plaintiffs' experts in a court of law. Yet it is truly astounding how infrequently mental health professionals keep records that can be considered even minimally acceptable.

Whenever a legal issue arises in clinical practice, every opportunity should be taken to turn it to therapeutic account for the patient. When the patient is to be informed about the risks of tardive dyskinesia before administering neuroleptic medication, the process of informing should be used to enhance the therapeutic alliance with the patient. Can warning an endangered third party be done in such a way that includes the patient's participation so as to preserve the therapeutic alliance? If not, can the damage be contained by a very discreet warning? Maintaining good clinical practices while discharging legal duties is an integral part of the professional standard of patient care.

The traditional rule of tort law that a person has no duty to come to the aid of another in distress, to which *Tarasoff* and its progeny are a distinct exception, is probably an unacceptable position for most psychiatrists and psychotherapists. The therapist does not act in these situations strictly from an obligation to meet the law's requirements. Long before *Tarasoff* and its progeny, therapists protected others who were endangered by their patients or sought involuntary treatment for violent patients when all else failed. Moreover, long before confidentiality statutes were enacted, most practitioners maintained and indeed still maintain a level of confidentiality that far exceeds any current statutory requirements.

I have cited a large number of legal cases in this book. I have attempted to summarize the essential elements of these cases for the psychiatric practitioner. All cases are cited for the reader who wishes to review the original cases. In a number of instances, reference is made to legal commentators who provide additional analysis. I have included a glossary of legal terms in Appendix 3 for the clinician who may be unfamiliar with certain legal language used in the text. Appendix 4 contains common terms and abbreviations used in legal citations.

The biblical epigraph to this book, from John 8:32, "And ye shall know the truth, and the truth shall make you free," can be applied at two fundamental levels to clinical practice. At the most basic level, a knowledge of the duties of the therapist, the rights of the patient, and the legal and regulatory duties imposed upon therapists and their clinical practice will allow for a more positive treatment experience for both patient and therapist. Hopefully, a comfortable familiarity with the law will diminish defensive practices that can inhibit good quality care. At the highest level, the clinician must understand the overriding truth that professional concern for the patient is the fundamental law.

The legal regulation of mental health practitioners and their interventions will undoubtedly increase in the years ahead. The necessity for practitioners to possess a working knowledge of relevant legal requirements governing clinical practice is now an unavoidable reality. Legally knowledgeable therapists are in a much better position to provide quality care. Ignorance of the law makes the law appear like an unmanageable monster rather than a workable partner, thus diminishing professional gratification.

As a lifelong dedication, the practice of medicine should be enjoyed. Knowledge rather than ignorance of the legal requirements governing psychiatric practice should significantly help to diminish malpractice fears and uncertainties that threaten personal and professional well-being. The words of Hippocrates from centuries past are particularly applicable today: "May it be granted to me to enjoy life and the practice of the art respected by all men."

Robert I. Simon, M.D.

Foreword

The recent intensification of the legal regulation of psychiatric practice has been overwhelming for many clinicians. Areas of concern have expanded from confidentiality to type of treatment to the specifics of the doctor-patient relationship. Recent developments in mental health legislation, including patients' rights, the right to treatment, and the right to refuse treatment, have been confusing to many practitioners. The increase in litigation in malpractice cases has discouraged many psychiatrists from continuing in practice or from beginning a private practice. Some have been afraid to take on particular kinds of patients or to become involved in forensic psychiatric matters.

Dr. Simon has updated an outstanding book to help all of us understand the impact of these legal incursions on our practices. He writes in a most readable fashion, asking pertinent questions following a relevant and practical case presentation. His responses to these questions are important guidelines for busy practitioners. His method of presenting this information is well suited to the clinical needs of psychiatric practitioners.

Dr. Simon covers the total clinical psychiatric spectrum in his many chapters devoted to problem areas in psychiatric treatment. His knowledge of the law is broad and his clinical experience deep. He takes a very complicated clinical situation that has the potential for complex legal difficulties and clarifies, simplifies, and illustrates the problem, the solution, and methods for prevention. Other books provide theoretical presentations of medicolegal and forensic psychiatric issues. Some are good textbooks for students in law schools or for residents in the field of forensic psychiatry. Dr. Simon's helpful book is for practitioners who need to have clear but ready answers to the many clinical problems that arise in their practices.

In sum, this book is a comprehensive approach to the many potential and actual problems facing mental health clinicians. It is not merely a guide, but a thorough and complete presentation of the current issues, with in-depth discussion and appropriate recommendations. This edition of *Clinical Psychiatry and the Law* is a necessary addition to the practitioner's library to be read and re-read frequently, as needed, to help the clinician understand and respond to the current legal changes that affect us all.

Robert L. Sadoff, M.D.
Clinical Professor of Psychiatry,
The University of Pennsylvania School of Medicine; and
Lecturer in Law, Villanova University School of Law

Introduction

J ust what is malpractice in psychiatry? How is a standard of care established? How is a causal nexus established between an alleged injury and a breach of the standard of care? These are not easy questions to answer, but they are coming before the courts with increasing frequency. Malpractice litigation, we hear, is becoming as much a nightmare to psychiatrists as it has been for neurosurgeons and obstetricians.

A certain role behavior is expected of a professional. In any negligence action, the complainant must establish *1)* a duty on the part of the defendant to conform to a certain standard of conduct, *2)* a dereliction of that duty, and *3)* a reasonably close causal connection between the professional's conduct and the resulting injury. In a malpractice action (the term *malpractice* meaning professional negligence) the law traditionally has looked to the profession itself to set out the standard of care. The law entrusts the defendant's peer group with the responsibility of establishing the appropriate role-expectation behavior. The "respectable minority rule" allows a physician to defend against a malpractice suit by showing that where there are different schools of medical thought about a particular matter, the treatment did accord with the practices of a respectable minority of practitioners within the profession.

As a general rule, consequently, the complainant must present expert testimony in order to establish a malpractice. A generation ago there was a "conspiracy of silence," that is, a reluctance of doctors to testify against their professional colleagues. This conspiracy of silence was overcome in some cases by the doctrine of *res ipsa loquitur* (the thing speaks for itself) or by an exception carved into the hearsay rule for learned treatises. A generation ago, because of the refusal to testify, lawsuits were actually brought against doctors for "conspiracy to obstruct the ends of justice." Another alleviating measure was to allow the expert witness to come from a different locality. With these developments, this conspiracy of silence became a thing of the past. At present, nothing is easier than to obtain an expert witness, as is evident by experts' advertising their services.

The controversy today in psychiatric malpractice cases is not over getting an expert, but over the elusive nature of the standard of care, and the causal nexus between a deviation from the standard of care and the alleged harm. The task of demarcating a standard of care in psychiatry may seem, in the words of one court, much like trying to nail a jellyfish to the wall. Given the various schools of therapy, can a single or consistent standard be enunciated? Is the daily practice of psychiatry ad hoc or eclectic? Does every psychiatrist write his or her own script, as critics say? If no standard can be agreed upon, a number of law commentators have argued that strict liability, or liability without fault, should be imposed, just as for different reasons it has been imposed on a manufacturer producing a defective product. Indeed, in cases of alleged negligent discharge of a patient, the courts have cited product liability cases in holding the doctor or hospital liable for injuries sustained by a person assaulted by the patient. My colleague, Dr. Elliot Luby, Director of the Harper Hospital Department of Psychiatry, said at a recent meeting of directors of hospitals:

> In reviewing recent malpractice cases, it is becoming apparent that the courts are holding us responsible for the conduct of our patients for months and even longer after they are discharged. It is as though they were applying products liability principles to psychiatric treatment. Once the patient is treated, the courts seem to hold us to a standard of predicting dangerousness over an extended period of time.

For lack of standards, or otherwise, will the courts apply the doctrine of strict liability, expressed or implied, to various areas of psychiatric practice? Given the litigious nature of the times, and the search by many lawyers for a solvent or insured defendant, it behooves professionals to set out their standards clearly and to record in each case their observance of these standards, just as manufacturers are doing with the appointment of safety committees. The analogy of patient to product may be tenuous, but there is a parallel.

Protecting against liability in the everyday practice of psychiatry has become more difficult than ever before. Traditional legal theories of liability have been expanding in ways that simply were not foreseen only a decade earlier. Also, because we live in a very litigious society, the therapist is more vulnerable to suit from unhappy patients and to ever-increasing malpractice insurance costs. The issue of discharge, of course, is only an illustration of matters that have involved the psychiatrist in litigation. Any aspect of the professional's work, as well as reporting duties imposed by law, can be the subject of a claim of professional negligence. Some say the therapist today is expected to be, at one and the same time, both a confidant and a cop. In many states the legislature or the courts have mandated the reporting of child abuse, elder abuse, and the dangerousness of a patient. The doctor traditionally has had the duty to contain contagious diseases; the psychiatrist nowadays also has the duty to contain dangerous individuals. The psychiatrist also has a duty to prevent suicide. A new law on the horizon—already enacted in Minnesota but rejected in California—requires therapists who are informed by a patient of sexual involvement with a prior therapist to make a report to the licensing board. A number of states have enacted legislation making it a criminal offense for a therapist to have sexual relations with a patient.

These and other laws place therapists in a bind because they involve an erosion of confidentiality. To preserve the confidentiality of his patients, Dr. Marc

Hollender, at the 1963 annual meeting of the American Psychiatric Association (APA), said, "I do not keep any records at all. Very candidly, I do not want any records that could ever be subpoenaed into court, and records could not be subpoenaed if they do not exist." Today, that recommendation would be foolhardy. Whatever its use in treatment, a record today is essential not only in accreditation but also as a legal document. In the case of litigation, the record may be the doctor's best friend or worst enemy. The courts usually assume that what has not been recorded has not been done or has not been considered. The lawyer plays the game not of what's there but of what's not there. Owing to a patient is "the duty to keep accurate records to insure that details are recorded properly and that sufficient data is present to evaluate the care of the patient." By and large, judge and jury do not second-guess the doctor—they do not pretend to practice medicine—but rather, relying on expert opinion, they impose liability when the doctor's judgment was not based on an adequate history. Documentation, therefore, may discourage an incipient lawsuit or may be the bulwark of a defense. Moreover, whatever the practitioner may think about the therapeutic need for a consultation, the fact of a consultation would indicate an observance of standard of care.

In ordinary affairs, we always ponder: "What is the accepted convention?" and "What happens next?" Professional persons especially must be concerned about the acceptability of their work and its consequences. The public expects more of them. The practice of psychiatry, like any practice, must fulfill expectations, and there are legal consequences. When a patient dies, the case as treatment ends, but it may be the beginning as a case in litigation. Is it a suicide for which the doctor will be held responsible?

Suits involving the use of psychotropic medications are becoming more common. Although their use may avert a suicide or alleviate the symptoms of mental illness, they may result in untoward side effects. A study of claims filed in the last decade against psychiatrists insured by the professional liability insurance program sponsored by the APA showed that 20% of the claims involved drug reactions. Like other physicians, a psychiatrist who uses medication faces two kinds of legal challenges: 1) failure to obtain the informed consent of the patient or a proxy consent, and 2) negligence in prescribing the medication. The need for record keeping in these matters goes without saying, but the controversy remains over how to satisfy the elements of an informed consent. The doctor is legally obliged to disclose and explain to the patient the nature of the ailment, the nature of the proposed treatment, the probability of success, alternative methods of treatment, and the foreseeable risk. The complainant may need to establish through expert testimony that the accepted practice is for the doctor to have informed the patient of the particular risk or hazard involved.

The question arose not long ago of whether a program on medical malpractice should qualify for Continuing Medical Education credit. The objection that "the legal aspects of medicine deal with the business aspects of medicine rather than the practice of medicine" has not prevailed, and quite rightly so. There is, to be sure, an inevitable connection between law and medicine. Doctors, like it or not, are always performing a legal function. Writing a prescription, for example, is in the nature of a legal document. A doctor does not have to go to law school, as a number have done, but it is important for the doctor to know something about the law. As Dr. Emanuel Tanay once put it, the doctor facing the law is like a displaced person who must learn something about new terrain. With knowledge, there is power. Today's psychiatrists, feeling intimidated by the law, often refrain from the use of medication or electroconvulsive therapy, and they are reluctant to engage hospital patients in work activities. Imagining legal liabilities, they forego good clinical judgment.

In litigation, to establish a standard of care, the lawyer or expert turns to any standards or principles set out by the professional organization as well as to any rules of a regulatory agency. The APA's declaration that sexual activity between a therapist and patient cannot be condoned under any circumstances is cited in any case of this type. Its publications on tardive dyskinesia and electroconvulsive therapy are used in these cases to set out a standard of care. Every hospital should have a "written, rehearsed, and approved" set of guidelines for secluding and restraining patients, according to an APA task force report. On diagnoses, the lawyer or expert turns to the most recent edition of the APA's *Diagnostic and Statistical Manual of Mental Disorders* (DSM), notwithstanding the caveat in the DSM that it is not designed for legal purposes. A substantial percentage of the sales of the DSM, we may note, has been to lawyers. In a recent issue of *Trial,* the monthly publication of the Association of Trial Lawyers of America, a lawyer began an article, "Trying a Trauma Case," with these words: "An attorney trying a case involving a psychic injury or mental disorder caused by trauma should be familiar with the *Diagnostic and Statistical Manual of Mental Disorders.*"

Given the division of opinion among members of a large organization, especially one as divided as psychiatry, position statements or guidelines rarely find consensus, and hence they appear infrequently. What, for example, is the role for multiple medications in the treatment of schizophrenia? One psychiatrist says: "No role. Stick with one drug, adjust it up or down until effective. If ineffective change to a different drug." Another psychiatrist says: "If we assume the etiology of schizophrenia to be related with multiple complex interrelated biochemical processes, then multiple medications affecting them in different ways would be a logical way of managing this illness." Still another says: "No medication. It merely masks the problem."

With the growing role of law in the practice of psychiatry, a number of issues or duties have developed raising the question of whether the law in these areas would defer to the profession in setting the standard of care. Given that treatment of choice clashes with reimbursement systems, the necessity of enunciating standards of care is increasingly apparent. By and large, the legal literature has been polemical in arguing for the imposition of standards by the law. In a landmark decision, Federal District Judge Frank M. Johnson, in 1971 in *Wyatt v. Stickney,* set minimum standards as a matter of constitutional law for adequate treatment of the institutionalized mentally ill. Testifying in the case, Dr. Karl A. Menninger denounced this "computer method" of setting standards of care.

In large measure, however, the profession remains in mastery on standards of care. On the use of seclusion or restraint, the U.S. Supreme Court in 1982 in *Youngberg v. Romeo,* a case involving an institution for developmentally disabled individuals, acknowledged that there are occasions when it is necessary to restrain the movement of residents in order to protect them as well as others from violence. The Court noted that the state may not restrain residents except when and to the extent "professional judgment" deems it necessary to ensure such safety or to provide needed training. Dr. Alan A. Stone, a former president of the APA, says in the foreword to *The Psychiatric Uses of Seclusion and Restraint* (edited by Dr. Kenneth Tardiff) that the book "should demonstrate to courts and other lawmakers that they can look to responsible psychiatrists for expert guidance even when rights and needs are in potential conflict." In a review of the book, Dr. Robert L. Sadoff, a leading forensic psychiatrist, writes:

> This book now becomes *the* guide for courts in cases of legal conflict. Should an individual or hospital be sued for negligent or improper use of seclusion or restraint, the courts will most certainly look to this book as the official guideline for the standard of care in this aspect of treatment of psychiatric patients.

On the duty to protect third persons from the acts of potentially violent patients, as set out in the now famous 1976 case of *Tarasoff v. Regents of the University of California,* the California Supreme Court defined that duty with latitude for professional judgment by the therapist:

> When a therapist determines, or pursuant to the standard of his profession should determine, that his patient presents a serious danger of violence to another, he incurs an obligation to use reasonable care to protect the intended victim against such danger. The discharge of this duty may require the therapist to take one or more of various steps depending upon the nature of the case. Thus it may call for him to warn the intended victim or others likely to apprise the intended victim of danger, to notify the police, or [to] take whatever steps are reasonably necessary under the circumstances.

In fulfilling this duty, the therapist is charged with determining the likelihood of future violence and acting only when that likelihood is high. On this assessment of dangerousness, the court in *Tarasoff* holds the therapist to a presumed professional standard of care in prediction. The court deferred to standards of the profession. It said, "The therapist need exercise that reasonable degree of skill, knowledge, and care ordinarily possessed and exercised by members of [that professional specialty] under similar circumstances." Yet, there is no professional standard for predicting future violence, as many psychiatrists have attested.

Just about any credible publication may be cited in the courtroom, in direct or cross-examination, in an attempt to establish a standard of care. It need not carry the imprimatur of a professional association. For example, the *Physician's Desk Reference,* a publication by a commercial house using information provided by manufacturers, is regularly cited on the use of medication. A lawyer or expert may turn to articles in professional journals, although they are not written for or in the context of litigation. The articles on malpractice in the law journals, by and large, are expository of legal theories, often contentious, and usually thin on the reality of practice.

In 1989 the APA, through its American Psychiatric Press, published the monumental 3,000-page, four-volume *Treatment of Psychiatric Disorders* (prepared by the Task Force on Treatment of Psychiatric Disorders). The prepublication infighting spilled a lot of professional blood. Those opposing an "official treatment manual" believe it will spur malpractice suits against psychiatrists. They say it will provide contentious or dissatisfied patients and their attorneys with "ammunition" in the form of an allegedly authoritative checklist of standards against which treatment will be measured in a courtroom. A clinician doing something other than what the "official treatment manual" says will have a difficult time justifying it.

The treatment efforts of psychiatrists may well be graded by this manual not only for malpractice or professional competency questions but also for reimbursement. Because payment for health care nowadays comes mainly by way of a third-party payer, or insurance company, and is distributed among a variety of health service providers, evaluation and regulation of practice are increasingly being done by the payers. Reimbursement policy influences what will be treated, how it will be treated, and who will do the treating. In making such an assessment, the third-party payer looks to authoritative guidelines. The treatment manual was generated, in large measure, to satisfy the health care payer.

Public concern about the efficacy and cost-effectiveness of psychiatric services has also resulted in increased regulation from peer review organizations and licensing boards. They too will be using the manual. In the case of involuntary treatment in a mental hospital or correctional facility, the guidelines likely will be considered "mainline" (permissive) therapy.

Those who claim that psychiatry is a science say practice protocols should be published because they can be justified by current knowledge about the treatment of mental illness. Those who say that psychiatry is an art, on the other hand, claim that knowledge about human behavior is too limited, and behavior too varied, to enunciate guidelines, and that it is hazardous to practitioners to do so. These critics claim that a supposedly authoritative work would restrict their professional freedom.

A number of psychiatrists launched a petition drive aimed at compelling the APA to cancel publication of the work. In the end, the APA issued a disclaimer, saying that the book is not official policy, but rather an "approved" task force report. In the disclaimer the APA states that the work contains information on evolving knowledge, does not encompass all approaches, is not intended to impose rigid methods, and leaves final assessment up to the practitioner. It will nonetheless be offered as "state of the art" in the courtroom.

Dr. Robert I. Simon's book *Clinical Psychiatry and the Law* is a welcome contribution to the literature. On psychiatric malpractice this book is unrivaled, a rarity: a wonderful marriage of theory and practice. Each of the 24 chapters begins with a case vignette, born of practice, followed by pertinent questions and answers that sharpen the issues. Open the book anywhere, and the reader will find an interesting discussion.

Each case example illustrates the many complex legal and therapy choices involved in that chapter's topic. Dr. Simon's analysis of legal precedents is sound and clearly presented. The most common examples of potential problem areas, which touch virtually every psychiatrist, are thoughtfully probed. Most important, Dr. Simon exposes areas of common everyday practice that unwittingly carry the potential for serious trouble. For instance, one common mistaken assumption is that the legal rights and duties between a physician and patient are reciprocal. On the contrary, however, this is not the case. A patient has the unilateral right to terminate treatment at any time, whereas the therapist may never simply abandon the patient at any time. Even when a patient has not paid his or her bill or shown up for an appointment, termination is not appropriate. Often such conflicts of interest between a psychiatrist's interest in his or her fee and the duty of service to the patient will arise. Certainly the duty of service must prevail, particularly when a patient is in need of further care.

Several serious problems may result after a patient referral. The practice of sending a patient to a different specialist must be accepted as a fact of life. As Dr. Simon states, no therapist is able to deal effectively with all of the vast array of psychiatric difficulties. When referring a patient, however, the therapist must give proper notice; otherwise a claim of abandonment may ensue. Also, care must be given to the handling of the patient's records and of keeping all extraneous information out of the report. Liability for invasion of privacy or even defamation may result from an improper disclosure of the contents.

Practitioners of unique or innovative therapy procedures suffer from peculiar legal dilemmas. The use of "implosive" therapies and confrontational treatment practices often causes a patient to be overwhelmed both physically and emotionally and may lead to a court appearance on a claim of intentional or negligent infliction of emotional distress. As usual, Dr. Simon clearly explains the relevant legal concepts in this area through the case study method. In this area, as in all others, reliance by the therapist on instincts or good faith as to what is "in the best interests" of the patient is not enough. The more unconventional the therapy, the more likely it will be found that emotional harm was substantially foreseeable.

As a corollary, a psychiatrist may be liable for negligence in failing to adequately explain the risks that are likely to befall a patient under a particular treatment modality. The law on "informed consent" is not at all clear in most cases, but the case study method used here helps enormously in pinning down this amorphous concept in specific factual surroundings. In certain areas, obtaining informed consent is particularly necessary, but also troublesome. In some cases, particularly those involving electroconvulsive therapy, written consent that explains all the aspects of the treatment procedure may not be enough.

In addition, and perhaps most helpful of all, Dr. Simon provides insightful advice as to how to avoid these various legal problems. Particularly in the areas of informed consent and the least-restrictive alternative, documentation is essential. In restraining a patient, a psychiatrist's judgment will be given more serious consideration if a written record has been made indicating that a risk-benefit analysis was undertaken at the time. Alternatives must be considered and reasons given as to why they were rejected.

Perhaps no area of the law relating to psychiatric malpractice is more controversial than liability imposed on a physician due to his or her inability to predict the dangerousness of a patient. Damages increasingly are being granted in this area against therapists who fail to protect injured third parties or who fail to prevent a patient from injuring himself or herself. A prediction of dangerousness must not be made without some hesitation, however, because liability may ensue for restricting the freedom of a truly nondangerous patient or for exposing the patient's condition to third parties, thus breaching doctor-patient confidentiality standards and ruining the therapeutic alliance. Because this area of the law is rather confused and rapidly changing, it is important to understand its impact in the widest possible array of circumstances. That perspective is what Dr. Simon has provided here.

Clinical Psychiatry and the Law is an incisive book, one that provides a clear guide for practice and a solid foundation for recognizing, analyzing, and—ultimately—resolving complex problems. It makes superb reading from cover to cover, and at the same time it is useful for reference on particular points. This book serves, all at once, as a reference manual for the practitioner of both psychiatry and law, a guidebook for reform, and a solid presentation of theory. The first edition was widely used in courses on law and psychiatry. In a creative way, Dr. Simon educates the psychiatrist about the law's interaction with psychiatry and educates the lawyer about psychiatry. With this book, the arguments urging strict liability in psychiatry for lack of standard of care are deflated.

For the court or for the clinic, this book provides a ready source of information on standard of care. However, given that the court is open to even frivolous suits, the clinician might ask, "Of what value is *any* book in preventing a suit?" To be sure, no book can provide asylum, and to seek it would be as futile as a dog chasing a bird. However, in ameliorating the risk of litigation or an adverse judgment, it is best to follow an old adage: An ounce of prevention is worth a pound of cure.

Physical injury or death generates the high verdict claims in litigation. The most frequent claim is for patient suicide, but these claims are usually easily defendable and have not resulted, generally speaking, in large judgments. The relative frequency of various types of claims appears to be changing with the times, as certain treatments, such as electroconvulsive therapy, are made safer or are abandoned, while others, such as psychotropic medications, become linked with deleterious side effects. Improper treatment, either involving the dispensing of drugs or the decision not to dispense drugs, accounts for a great number of claims.

The overall number of claims against psychiatrists, however, has stayed fairly steady over the last decade, and the insurance premium rates for psychiatrists still remain the lowest of all medical specialties. The surgeon's chances of being sued are 12 in 100, while the psychiatrist's are 4 in 100. However, it appears that claims against psychiatrists may be rising. This increasing number of suits may be due, in part, to a more open attitude about psychiatric treatment, increased expectations of its efficacy, the increased use of medication, the emphasis on patients' rights in court decisions and the popular literature, the emergence of new legal duties out of the therapist-patient relationship, and the publicity of several large verdicts. A recent article in a leading newspaper carried the headline, "Why Not Sue a Psychiatrist?"

Dr. Simon brought to the task of writing this book a profound knowledge of the field. He is a highly respected and experienced practitioner in general and forensic psychiatry. Observing the pitfalls that his colleagues have fallen into, Dr. Simon has set out to post warning signs. He has conducted seminars in various parts of the country for psychiatrists and lawyers, in which didactic instruction is mixed with good practical advice in actual cases. He has a reputation for being eager to instruct, and his serious preoccupation with the legal aspects of psychiatry is tempered by a quick mind and a ready wit. Dr. Simon is a consultant to psychiatrists, professional associations, and mental health institutions in managing psychiatric-legal problems. He is the author of, among other writings, *Concise Guide to Psychiatry and Law for Clinicians* as well as the coauthor (with Dr. Robert L. Sadoff) of *Psychiatric Malpractice: Cases and Comments for Clinicians.* Dr. Simon has also edited a three-volume work entitled *American Psychiatric Press Review of Clinical Psychiatry and the Law.* In his writings, Dr. Simon pays close attention to detail and accuracy. He is Clinical Professor of Psychiatry at the Georgetown University School of Medicine in Washington, D.C., and director of its Program in Psychiatry and Law.

Dr. Simon has given us a book on psychiatric malpractice that is thoroughly stimulating, amazingly informative, always readable, and spiced here and there with a bit of humor. *Clinical Psychiatry and the Law* is a most helpful work. It is an illuminating source on the standard of care in the practice of psychiatry.

Ralph Slovenko, LL.B., Ph.D.
Professor of Law and Psychiatry,
Wayne State University
Detroit, Michigan

Section I:

The Psychiatrist-Patient Relationship

Chapter 1

Creation of the Psychiatrist-Patient Relationship

Mr. May, a 27-year-old single man, is seen for a pre-employment psychiatric evaluation by Dr. Olin. The pre-employment health questionnaire, completed by Mr. May, indicates that he has suffered from periods of anxiety since the death of his father 2 years ago.

Mr. May is an only son who has two younger sisters. His father, a laborer, appeared to resent his son's academic achievements. Mr. May remembers as a child his father saying to him, "You're only a laborer's son, so don't think you're going to be a big shot someday." Mr. May experienced considerable guilt over his academic achievements, feeling that his success made his father resentful.

Dr. Olin surmises that Mr. May has suppressed his feelings of resentment toward his father throughout his childhood, developing a reaction formation of compliance and dutiful behavior. Mr. May describes the outbreak of brief panic episodes after his father's death from cancer 2 years ago. It was just prior to his father's death that he was accepted into a doctoral program.

Mr. May is a very friendly, conscientious person whom Dr. Olin finds appealing as a prospective employee. Dr. Olin has always tried to use the opportunity of the pre-employment interview to be of some therapeutic assistance to applicants whenever possible. In his current position as director of corporate health services, Dr. Olin misses treating patients as he once did in his private psychiatric practice. Thus Dr. Olin makes the following interpretation to Mr. May: "Do you think that the anxiety you have experienced since your father's death may have to do with some guilt feelings toward your father?" Mr. May begins to explore this issue but becomes extremely anxious. He begins to sweat profusely. His hands shake violently, and he feels as if he will pass out. Dr. Olin keeps a supply of benzodiazepines in his office. Noting Mr. May's extreme distress, he quickly obtains a glass of water and gives Mr. May a 10-mg diazepam tablet. Within half an hour, Mr. May is slightly more comfortable. Dr. Olin terminates the interview and gives Mr. May 10 diazepam tablets (10 mg each) to take home. Dr. Olin recommends to Mr. May that if panic attacks recur, he should see a therapist. Mr. May leaves feeling very shaken.

That evening, a panic attack occurs. For the first time, Mr. May experiences deep feelings of despondency tinged with self-destructive ideas. He calls Dr. Olin but is unable to reach him. Mr. May decides to wait until the next morning. He feels slightly better the next day. Three days later, another severe attack of panic and depression occurs in the evening. Dr. Olin again cannot be reached. Mr. May is very frightened by the emergence of self-destructive thoughts. The next day he does reach Dr. Olin, who informs Mr. May that he is not his doctor but saw him only for the pre-employment interview. Dr. Olin recommends that Mr. May call a psychiatrist, but Mr. May is not able to obtain an appointment for another week. Three days later Mr. May attempts to hang himself but is fortuitously discovered by the landlord and admitted to the hospital. After 6 weeks of hospitalization for a major depressive episode, he is discharged. Shortly thereafter, Mr. May files a $500,000 suit against Dr. Olin for negligent treatment and abandonment.

What is the legal basis of the psychiatrist-patient relationship?

An essential element in any malpractice claim is the existence of a duty owed by the defendant (e.g., psychiatrist, physician) to the injured party (e.g., patient). The idea of duty typically invokes two questions. First, there is the inquiry as to whether one has a "duty to act" at all for the benefit of another. Second, once a duty has arisen, there is the question of the "nature" of that duty. The first question relates to the *existence* of a duty and addresses whether there is some legally recognized "relationship" between the two parties creating a duty of care on the part of one party for the benefit of the other (1).

The legal basis of the psychiatrist-patient relationship is founded on the contract or the "undertaking" theory (2). The most common type of legal relationship between psychiatrist and patient is initiated by contract, either express or implied. For example, when a psychiatrist agrees to accept a fee in exchange for the rendering of professional services to an individual, a contract may be created with accompanying rights and liabilities (3). In instances in which a specific agreement as to the terms of treatment is reached between the patient and the psychiatrist, an express contract may have arisen. Courts may infer that an implied contract exists based upon the surrounding conduct of the parties, such as when the patient consents to treatment and the psychiatrist agrees to provide it. Thus, the contract created is based upon a fiduciary, not a financial, relationship (4).

Circumstances arise in professional practice that do not always fit into the traditional contract model, yet a duty of care is still created on the part of the provider (e.g., physician). For example, an unconscious patient requiring medical treatment may be treated without the patient's knowledge or consent or a patient may be treated free of charge. Despite the absence of an agreement or contract between the two parties in those situations, a professional relationship giving rise to a duty of care may also have been created. If the psychiatrist-patient contact caused the patient to have a reasonable expectation of treatment, or if the psychiatrist undertook to treat the patient, the courts will generally imply a relationship. Thus, under the "undertaking" theory, even if a patient is treated without charge, the psychiatrist remains liable for any negligence committed during the course of diagnosis and treatment. The legal basis for this theory is set forth in Section 323 of the *Restatement (Second) of Torts:*

> One who undertakes, gratuitously or for consideration, to render services to another which he would recognize as necessary for the protection of the other's person or things, is subject to liability to the other for physical harm resulting from his failure to exercise reasonable care to perform his undertaking, if
> (a) his failure to exercise such care increases the risk of harm
> (b) the harm is suffered because of the other's reliance upon the undertaking. (5)

Regardless of the basis of the formation of the psychiatrist-patient relationship, unless specifically stated, there is no implied warranty or guarantee of a specific outcome or result. What is created, however, is the promise to provide an acceptable standard of care. For example, in *Servais v. Philbrick* (6), no enforceable contract of warranty arose when a physician, prior to performing an arteriogram, "expressly assured" the patient that the procedure would be "routine." The court concluded that such statements were too vague to ascertain whether both parties understood and were agreeing to the same thing. Thus, the physician's assurances did not constitute an express warranty of care or result.

Bianco (7) advises that a physician who wishes to avoid undertaking treatment of the patient

> must politely, emphatically, and clearly inform his patient that he is not undertaking to treat and, where advice is given, the advice should be no more than a recommendation to find other medical assistance while at the same time avoiding any detailed query concerning the patient's past medical history or present illness.

However, psychiatrists who perform evaluations of acutely mentally ill patients may not be able to remain aloof from the patient in crisis. Some immediate intervention that will create a psychiatrist-patient relationship may be ethically and clinically necessary.

Must psychiatrists accept all persons who seek their help?

According to the Council on Ethical and Judicial Affairs of the American Medical Association (AMA) in "Current Opinions" (8), a physician is not required to accept every patient who requests treatment. The "no duty" rule states that a psychiatrist who is self-employed and not required by the policies of others to accept patients owes no legal (9) or ethical (10) duty to enter into a professional relationship with a patient. Moral obligations have not been transformed into legal obligations (11). There is common law precedent holding that no duty is owed by one individual to come to the aid of another or to accept every patient who seeks professional services (12). Moreover, commentators have correctly recognized that medical practice is essentially a private enterprise, consistent with individualism and independence (13).

Thus, the law recognizes that a doctor may limit his or her engagement to treat a patient to one particular treatment or procedure, to the terms of his or her availability, or to any other aspect of his or her contact and professional services (14). But in order for such conditions to be enforceable, they must be understood and accepted by the patient. It should also be noted that if a physician cannot or will not provide treatment to a particular patient, he or she has an ethical, if not legal, duty to refer that patient to another health care provider. This is especially true in cases involving potential emergencies (15). Failure to exercise reasonable care in making such a referral may result in liability for patient abandonment (16).

The AMA's Council on Ethical and Judicial Affairs (17) states the official AMA position concerning creation of the physician-patient relationship:

PHYSICIAN-PATIENT RELATIONSHIP: RESPECT FOR LAW AND HUMAN RIGHTS. The creation of the physician-patient relationship is contractual in nature. Generally, both the physician and the patient are free to enter into or decline the relationship. A physician may decline to undertake the care of a patient whose medical condition is not within the physician's current competence. However, physicians who offer their services to the public may not decline to accept patients because of race, color, religion, national origin, or any other basis that would constitute illegal discrimination. Furthermore, physicians who are obligated under preexisting contractual arrangements may not decline to accept patients as provided by those arrangements.

Clinically, the psychiatrist who is free to do so may wish to undertake a brief period of evaluation, but not necessarily accept the patient for treatment—at least not immediately. To avoid creating the expectation that a doctor-patient relationship for treatment purposes is or has been established, the psychiatrist must expressly notify the patient, making it clear that no treatment will be rendered, and provide a description of what the evaluation will include. On completion of the evaluation, a decision by both the therapist and the patient can be made concerning the advisability of treatment.

What is the psychiatrist's duty in situations where emergency care might be needed by a nonpatient?

An extension of the normal "no duty" rule is that a physician has no legal obligation to provide emergency medical care unless the doctor, for example, an emergency room physician, is under a contractual obligation to do so. Essentially, the "no duty" rule provides that no tort liability can be imposed for nonfeasance, or failing to aid one in peril. Moral obligation alone does not impose a duty to aid another. Liability can be imposed only if one fails to exercise reasonable care or commits an act that injures another (18). Notwithstanding the law, the Council on Ethical and Judicial Affairs of the AMA (19) advises, "The physician should, however, respond to the best of his ability in cases of emergency where first aid treatment is essential."

When the psychiatrist undertakes to gratuitously render assistance to the person "at the wayside," good Samaritan statutes enacted in some form by all states (20) can be raised as a defense to a negligent action. However, the professional act or omission must be performed in "good faith" and cannot amount to gross negligence (21). Good Samaritan laws in some states cover the physician who is not licensed in the state where the emergency assistance occurred (22). It is noteworthy that emergency assistance need not necessarily be rendered in a public setting in order for the good Samaritan defense to apply. For example, although most good Samaritan statutes apply only to services rendered at the scene of an emergency or accident, some state statutes (23) and court decisions (24) have applied good Samaritan immunity to emergency treatment provided in a hospital setting where the defendant had no preexisting relationship with the patient and the physician's hospital duties did not require response to the emergency.

In order for the good Samaritan provider to be held liable for services rendered in an emergency, there must be evidence of gross negligence. Bianco (7) states that gross negligence is found when a physician fails to exercise even the slightest degree of care in the face of a clear and present danger. He offers the example of the physician who comes upon an accident victim sprawled on the highway who has sustained a head injury from impact with the windshield. The physician, without even a brief examination, moves the victim's injured head, whereupon the accident victim complains of weakness and numbness in all extremities. The physician may be held liable for gross negligence because of the expectation that every physician is or should be aware that a head injury may be associated with a cervical spine injury and that special care must be taken prior to moving the victim. If the same accident victim, however, suffers from acute respiratory distress and the physician's reasonable attempts to clear it by chin lift and cardiopulmonary resuscitation fail, leading to quadriplegia, the legal standard to be applied is that of ordinary negligence.

Once a psychiatrist has decided to render aid, that person is obligated to exercise reasonable care under the particular facts and circumstances. Therefore, the applicable standard is that of the degree of skill, care, and knowledge an ordinary practitioner would exercise under the circumstances imposed by the emergency. This duty of "due care" includes the duty not to abandon the rescue and to use whatever reasonable means are available to continue the rescue effort without placing oneself in jeopardy. The psychiatrist must either wait until competent medical assistance arrives or accompany the victim to the hospital and into the hands of competent medical care. A good Samaritan, acting in good faith, does not send the trauma victim a bill for services. In fact, most good Samaritan statutes specifically bar the defense if the health care provider bills the victim (25).

Halleck (26) maintains that the ethical psychiatrist should come to the rescue of the accident victim. However, psychiatrists who are accustomed to practicing their profession in the quiet of their offices may no longer possess even rudimentary medical or first-aid skills. Thus they may decide to refrain from rendering aid to trauma victims unless immediate lifesaving actions are necessary. This failure to act is not created out of a fear of legal liability but rather out of the psychiatrist's desire to avoid any potential further harm to the victim. The oft-heard tale that a psychiatrist is a physician who is afraid of blood may contain a certain kernel of truth. Some psychiatrists, in fact, may be unable to function satisfactorily in an accident-trauma situation. Psychiatrists, when asked about aiding accident victims, present a very wide spectrum of attitudes on this subject.

How is the psychiatrist-patient relationship created?

Whether a psychiatrist-patient relationship legally exists is a factual determination. Generally speaking, if the existence of such a relationship is disputed, the courts will determine whether the patient entrusted care to the psychiatrist and whether the psychiatrist indicated acceptance of that care. Most often, a psychiatrist-patient relationship is created knowingly and voluntarily by both parties. However, not infrequently, a professional relationship is established with a patient unwittingly. No professional duty of care is owed a patient unless a psychiatrist-patient relationship exists. Once that relationship is established, duties attach and the psychiatrist can be held liable for damages that are proximately caused by any breach of duty.

Although the law imposes no duty on physicians to take a prospective patient, at times it seems that courts are quick to establish a doctor-patient relationship. Several examples are instructive (see Table 1-1). Giving advice, making interpretations, or prescribing medication during the course of an independent medical evaluation may create a doctor-patient relationship (27). Providing care to an unexamined individual over the telephone and a person's having the expectation that he or she is accepted for treatment also may create a doctor-patient relationship (28). Similarly, certain acts by a physician, such as offering to prescribe medication over the telephone, have been construed to constitute a "continuation of treatment" for purposes of determining the date of accrual of a medical malpractice claim (29). Accepting an appointment to treat a patient may create an implied agreement with a duty to provide a specific medical service for a certain time and date (30). Thus a formal psychiatrist-patient relationship may arise as a result of acceptance by the psychiatrist or his or her staff of an appointment to see the patient for a specific problem. If a physician is aware that a patient is relying upon his or her directions, concern, and occasional advice, even if there have not been actual treatment visits for over a year, "a continuous course of treatment" may still be upheld (31).

On the other hand, courts have held that there must be fairly distinct evidence of doctor-patient contact or reasonable patient reliance on a physician's promises or acts in order to find that a duty of care based on a doctor-patient relationship was owed. For example, in *Clanton v. Von Haam* (32), a Georgia court found that a telephone call did not establish a doctor-patient relationship. The patient, after having been seen in an emergency room for increasing numbness in her legs, telephoned the emergency room again when her symptoms worsened. The physician who had originally examined her had gone home. The patient called another physician who had treated her in the past for another condition. He refused to make a house call, indicating he would see her in the morning. She later became paralyzed. The patient sued, claiming the physician knew or should have known that her condition was critical and, in the absence of medical intervention, would result in paraplegia. The court stated that the fact the physician previously treated the patient for an unrelated condition, returned her call, and listened to her symptoms did not create a physician-patient relationship. Nor did the physician's advice to see him the next morning create a physician-patient relationship. The court noted that the patient never relied upon any medical advice from the doctor and was not dissuaded from obtaining other medical help. In *Bass v. Barksdale* (33), no doctor-patient relationship was found where the sole contact between the doctor and patient consisted of the doctor's signing a prescription form on behalf of another physician.

Occasionally, a new patient who calls for an appointment will want to engage the therapist in a lengthy discussion. This should be tactfully discouraged.

TABLE 1–1.   Actions by therapists that may create a doctor-patient relationship

  1. Giving advice to prospective patients, friends, and neighbors
  2. Making psychological interpretations
  3. Writing a prescription or providing sample medications
  4. Supervising treatment by a nonmedical therapist
  5. Having lengthy phone conversation with a prospective patient
  6. Treating an unseen patient by mail
  7. Giving a patient an appointment
  8. Telling walk-in patients that they will be seen
  9. Acting as a substitute therapist
 10. Providing treatment during an evaluation

Clearly, the telephone should be avoided in making diagnoses or initiating treatment (34). Similarly, physicians should be mindful that their acts and opinions, even when expressed to a patient or colleague as a gratuitous gesture intended to be helpful, may create some duty of care even when it was not contemplated. For instance, allowing one's name to be used in order that a patient can be admitted to a hospital (35) was found in at least one case to be sufficient grounds to allow a lawsuit to go forward. On the other hand, merely giving an informal opinion to a colleague about a case without the benefit of having any contact with the patient or without having reviewed any of the patient's records has been found to be insufficient grounds for a doctor-patient relationship to be established (36).

In *Rainer v. Grossman* (37), the plaintiff suggested that a medical school professor's opinion expressed during a teaching conference that surgery was indicated made the professor liable for malpractice. The court declined to find liability, stating the following:

> Presumably every professor or instructor in a professional school hopes, expects or foresees that his students will absorb and apply in their own careers at least some of the information he imparts. Does he thereby assume a duty of care and potential liability to those persons who may ultimately become clients or patients of those students? We think not.

Traditionally, a psychiatrist's duty of care was limited only to persons with whom a psychiatrist-patient relationship had been established. However, judicial decisions holding therapists liable to nonpatient third parties have increased in recent years. Thus family members involved in the therapy of a "basic patient" may assert a relationship with the therapist or claim an expanded duty to nonpatient third parties. This issue is quite separate from the therapist-patient relationship established with all members in formal family or group therapy. Should any doubt exist, the therapist must make clear to family members who are seen in conjunction with the patient's treatment that no therapist-patient relationship exists with them. Family members who require individual psychiatric attention should be referred to another therapist.

A circumscribed duty of care can also be extended to third parties wholly unrelated to either the patient or the therapist in those instances in which the patient poses a threat of danger to someone in society. In these situations courts have recognized that a "special" relationship exists between the psychiatrist and the "victim" of the patient's dangerous conduct if the psychiatrist has the right or ability to control the conduct of his or her potentially dangerous patient (38). The landmark case *Tarasoff v. Regents of the University of California* (39), and the many cases and statutes that followed it (40), are excellent illustrations of this "extraordinary" extension of duty.

Can the innocent or gratuitous offering of advice to friends or colleagues establish a legally recognized doctor-patient relationship?

Often psychiatrists are asked by friends, neighbors, or colleagues for advice about their problems. The key in these situations typically is whether the contact (e.g., giving advice) created a reasonable expectation in the person seeking information that professional services were being provided. To avoid this dilemma, psychiatrists, as well as other therapists, should make clear in these situations that in listening or giving advice, they are doing so only as friends. The practice of prescribing psychoactive drugs or giving medication to such individuals also may create a doctor-patient relationship with responsibility for liability if the recipient suffers an adverse reaction. Psychiatrists who wish to provide some form of treatment, whether professional advice or medication samples, to friends, neighbors, or colleagues must understand that in doing so they are likely creating a duty of care to these individuals.

Radio and television shows, newspaper and magazine columns, and large groups with special interests often invite therapists' views and opinions. Therapists who engage in informational and educational activities directed toward the general public must make clear that they are speaking about general principles only and are not specifically advising individuals in the audience. Otherwise, a duty of care may be found. The American Psychiatric Association (APA) offers guidelines for psychiatrists who make radio and television appearances (41).

Third-party requests for treatment may also create a duty of care. In instances in which parents ask a therapist to treat their child and the therapist accepts, a duty of care is owed to the child. Psychiatrists may owe duties to third parties even if a therapist-patient relationship does not exist when, during the course of an evaluation, the therapist discovers a danger to others such as child abuse, contagious disease, or threats of violence.

What is the psychiatrist's potential legal liability in conducting an independent medical evaluation?

Third parties, such as employers and insurance companies, sometimes engage psychiatrists to examine patients for diagnostic purposes only. Two scenarios typically arise. One involves the nonemployee psychiatrist who is independently hired by a company, agency, or some other third party to evaluate an employee or potential employee's health, suitability for employment, or on the job injuries, or for some other purpose. The second scenario involves psychiatrists who are employed by companies to examine employees or conduct preemployment psychiatric examinations. In both situations, when performing evaluations that are not intended or reasonably construed to be "therapeutic," no therapist-patient relationship is normally created or legally implied (42).

Similarly, independently hired psychiatrists and psychologists employed by the company must not exceed the scope of their employment or role. Any advice or treatment that is rendered, no matter how innocent or gratuitous, is likely to establish a doctor-patient relationship (43). For example, in *Licht v. Hohl Machine & Conveyor Company* (44), a physician hired to examine a company employee in a worker's compensation dispute was held to be subject to a third-party action when he advised the employee to cease taking an anticoagulant drug. The employee, relying on the examining physician's advice, did so and developed phlebitis. The court, in denying the physician's request for dismissal of lawsuit, held that the "physician had gone beyond his engagement as examiner on behalf of the insurance company by undertaking to give the employee direct medical advice."

In worker's compensation examinations and other third-party evaluations, the duty of the examining psychiatrist is limited to the needs of the carrier or agency requesting the evaluation (45). Accordingly, the examinee, if reinjured after being cleared to return to work, usually cannot sue the examining physician because the defendant's duty of care was to the employer and not the employee (46).

In independent psychiatric evaluations, the examinee does not come voluntarily but is required to do so by arrangement with a third party. Nevertheless, although it should be clear that the usual psychiatrist-patient relationship is not being created, the psychiatrist owes the examinee a duty of care in performing the evaluation in a reasonable manner whereby no physical or psychological harm is caused to the examinee (47). This duty, however, does not extend so far as to include using reasonable care and holding one liable for failing to diagnose a patient's condition. For example, in *LoDico v. Caputi* (48), a New York court failed to recognize a cause of action against an examining physician for the State Insurance Fund when he certified an employee as being capable of returning to work but negligently failed to detect a brain-stem tumor. The court concluded that when a physician conducts an examination of an injured employee "solely for the purpose of rating the injury for the employer's insurance carrier in a worker's compensation proceeding" and does not otherwise treat the person being examined, there can be no liability for failing to diagnose a patient's brain tumor.

Although the psychiatrist employed by a company is typically not subject to suit by the employee for a negligently performed evaluation, the employer may be liable for the negligent acts of the psychiatrist-employee under the doctrine of *respondeat superior* (49), and the "company doctor" may be contractually liable to the *company* for any resulting damages.

Forensic psychiatric experts who conduct independent medical examinations are unlikely to be successfully sued for malpractice by the litigant when a doctor-patient relationship does not exist. In *Tolisano v. Texon* (50), Dr. Meyer Texon, a cardiologist, examined Samuel Tolisano to see if his heart condition precluded testifying before a grand jury. Dr. Texon found that testifying was "without significant risk to his life." Tolisano appealed a judge's decision requiring his testimony but died 7 weeks later while the appeal was pending. Tolisano's wife commenced a wrongful death suit against Dr. Texon. The New York State Court of Appeals accepted the position stated in the *amicus curiae* filed by the Medical Society of the State of New York and dismissed the suit against Dr. Texon. The medical society claimed that, as a matter of law, a non-treating physician owes an examinee no duty of care concerning the opinion rendered to a third party. The court agreed that no doctor-patient relationship existed.

What is the psychiatrist's potential legal liability in conducting a court-ordered examination?

Therapists who examine litigants at the request of the court are often immune from liability, even if negligent (26). In *Seibel v. Kemble* (51), for example, the Hawaii Supreme Court held that court-appointed psychiatrists were entitled to the same absolute immunity from suit that is also accorded to judges and other judicial officers. In this case, a man started weekly sessions with a psychiatrist shortly after he was charged with kidnapping, sodomy, and rape. Several months later, the treating psychiatrist and two other psychiatrists were appointed to serve on a sanity commission. The commission, after examining the man, reported to the court that he was suffering from compulsive neurosis with a passive-aggressive personality. They stated that, with treatment, he probably would not be a danger to himself or others. The court entered an acquittal on the grounds of mental disease, disorder, or defect that excluded responsibility. He was released on condition that he continue treatment with his psychiatrist.

Ten months later, he killed a woman. Even though one of the psychiatrists on the sanity commission was the defendant's treating psychiatrist with a clearly established doctor-patient relationship, the court granted absolute immunity from suit. Pointing to the uncertainty in the diagnosis and treatment of mental illness, and in the prediction of future behavior, the court stated that if court-appointed psychiatrists were not given the freedom to make difficult decisions, more persons would be institutionalized because of fear of possible adverse consequences and liability. The court held that the psychiatrists were "advisors or arms of the court" and served as an integral part of the judicial process. Thus, the psychiatrists were entitled to absolute immunity.

Similarly, psychiatrists appointed by the court in civil commitment cases generally are protected from liability. The reason for granting such immunity is to permit psychiatrists, like judges, to make commitment decisions without fear of a malpractice suit. However, when psychiatrists involuntarily hospitalize their own patients, liability claims may be possible for negligence or intentional torts due to the existing duty of care. In those instances in which a psychiatrist-patient relationship exists, a court is less inclined to grant immunity based on the theory that the psychiatrist owes a greater responsibility to his or her own patient than to an individual examined exclusively for the purpose of involuntary hospitalization (52).

What salient clinical and legal issues are raised in the clinical vignette?

The clinical vignette at the beginning of this chapter illustrates how easily a pre-employment psychiatric interview can legally become a treatment relationship. Giving advice, making interpretations, and providing medications, even from a sample supply, may create a doctor-patient relationship with attendant duties and liabilities. Dr. Olin confuses his role as an evaluator with that of a treater. In his eagerness to be helpful, he makes therapeutic interpretations to Mr. May that the applicant is psychologically unprepared to accept, precipitating an unexpected, severe regression. Dispensing medication to Mr. May further underscores the shift to a treatment relationship.

Once a doctor-patient relationship is created, the psychiatrist cannot unilaterally terminate the relationship without reasonable notice. Even if notice is given, the psychiatrist must be available for emergencies for a reasonable period of time. Mr. May's claim of abandonment is based on the theory that Dr. Olin created a duty of care for Mr. May and then unilaterally terminated the relationship, thus abandoning his patient. As pointed out earlier, courts have found a doctor-patient relationship to exist based upon much less evidence of therapeutic intervention than that provided by Dr. Olin.

Dr. Olin should have at least made himself available to the patient by providing phone numbers where he could be reached. If he was unable to treat Mr. May directly, he should have helped Mr. May find competent help without delay. The unavailability of Dr. Olin throughout the patient's psychiatric crisis is an abrogation of even ordinary professional concern. It also is potentially legally actionable. (A detailed discussion of abandonment can be found in Chapter 18.)

As hard as psychiatrists may try to maintain an evaluatory stance toward a patient initially, it may not be possible in actual clinical practice. The psychiatrist usually does not know how sick an outpatient will be when the patient is seen for the first time. Patients with severe personality disorders may rapidly develop intense transferences that require immediate psychiatric attention. Some patients are floridly psychotic or may present clinical situations in which danger to self or others threatens. The therapist may decide that the best clinical course for the patient is to intervene and forego an initial evaluation period. But what if the therapist does not want to accept the patient for treatment? Therapists often feel helpless and trapped when confronted with a patient in a crisis that requires immediate attention. Therapists who do not want to accept the patient for help should attempt to find immediate competent treatment for the patient. In some instances, this may require accompanying the patient to a hospital or emergency room. The possibility exists that the therapist who remains indifferent to the patient's immediate crisis can be sued for performing a negligent evaluation. Professional concern for the patient in a crisis dictates that the patient be directed to immediate help.

Some psychiatrists may find litigation concerns to be an additional incentive to see a prospective patient for a period of evaluation. An unknown patient seen in the absence of a therapeutic alliance, perhaps having unrealistic expectations, harboring discontents, and possibly being litigious, may create a high liability potential. Psychiatrists have become increasingly vulnerable to suits by patients seen for a short period of time, even after a single visit (53). For example, a significant number of persons who commit suicide have recently been seen by a physician. In a study by Roy (54), 17% of 70 outpatients committed suicide on the same day as seeing a psychiatrist, 34% 2 days after seeing a psychiatrist, and 41% within a week of their psychiatric appointment. In Barraclough's study (55), half of the patients who committed suicide had seen a psychiatrist during the previous week.

When the psychiatrist supervises the work of another psychotherapist, does a treatment relationship also arise between the supervisor and the patient?

Official professional guidelines, theories of legal liability, and employment relationships generally determine whether a treatment relationship arises between a supervisor and a patient whose care is being supervised. The APA's "Guidelines for Psychiatrists in Consultative, Supervisory, or Collaborative Relationships With Nonmedical Therapists" (56) states that the psychiatrist is responsible for the patient's diagnosis and treatment plan and for the supervision of the nonmedical therapist to ensure that the treatment plan is properly administered with suitable adjustments to the patient's condition. The guidelines do not specify the frequency of supervision. Thus the psychiatrist, when supervising the nonmedical therapist, is responsible for the patient as if the patient were his or her own (56). The guidelines explicitly state: "Psychiatrists remain ethically and medically responsible for the patient's care as long as the treatment continues under his or her supervision" (p. 1490). The guidelines do not represent official policy. They should be viewed as a "living document" to be adapted to local custom and practice.

For psychiatrists supervising other psychiatrists, psychiatric residents, or interns, the situation is somewhat different. If an intern or resident is treating the psychiatrist's patient, the resident or intern may be considered a "borrowed servant," whereupon the psychiatrist will be held vicariously responsible for any negligence that leads to harm. Interns and residents treating their own patients, but supervised by a psychiatrist, may themselves incur direct liability, while the psychiatrist may be held vicariously liable when supervisory control has been exercised.

The determination of vicarious liability may depend on the disparity in training and experience between supervisor and supervisee. The narrower the training gap, the less likely is the imposition of vicarious liability if the supervisee is treating his or her own patients. For example, a psychiatrist that supervises other graduate psychiatrists may be viewed as an "independent contractor." The supervisor that serves solely as an independent contractor will not, therefore, generally bear liability for acts of negligence committed by the supervised psychiatrist. Because of the considerable independence and freedom of action that physicians possess in the practice of medicine, it is unlikely that one psychiatrist will be viewed as the "servant" of the other. Although not strictly consultative, the supervisory relationship between graduate psychiatrists appears to be closer to the consultative model, even though it occurs on a continuing basis.

Under the doctrine of *respondeat superior,* or vicarious liability, the supervisor may be responsible for the acts and omissions of the training psychotherapist who is treating the patient. According to Cohen and Mariano (57):

> In too many training institutions today, psychotherapist supervision is set up on a pro forma once-a-week or once-a-month basis . . . which . . . is too low. If some harm or injury befalls the patient of the student psychotherapist because the supervisor improperly failed to take into account the specific and unique needs of the patient and the supervisee, then it would seem that the doctrine of respondeat superior would be applicable.

The doctrine of *respondeat superior* originated from the master-servant relationship (58). The one with the right of control is ultimately responsible for the torts of one's servant who is acting within the scope of the employment. Under the doctrine of *respondeat superior,* vicarious liability may be imposed on the individual therapist or institution for negligent acts committed by employees under the defendant's supervision (59). Liability for a subordinate's negligence exists only if the professional has the right or the ability to control the subordinate's actions. Even in the absence of an employer-employee relationship, a therapist exercising extensive control over the employee of another employer may be liable for negligence of the subordinate under the "borrowed servant" doctrine. However, if a subordinate substantially deviates from the assigned work and becomes engaged in a "frolic and detour," the employer will no longer be held liable.

The psychiatric team concept has gained considerable popularity in treating patients. The team may contain a psychiatrist, a psychologist, a social worker, and other mental health professionals, which concomitantly increases the liability of individual members (57). Psychiatrists may be held liable under the doctrine of joint and several liability for the negligent acts of partners, even though they have never seen the patient. Vicarious liability also may be imposed for the negligent acts of employees committed within the scope of their employment. The issues surrounding the legal liabilities of supervision are discussed in greater detail in Chapter 21.

References

1. See generally, Annotation, What constitutes physician-patient relationship for malpractice purposes, 17 ALR4th 132–160 (1982)
2. King JH: The Law of Medical Malpractice. St Paul, MN, West Publishing, 1977, p 3
3. Ibid, p 2
4. American Medical Association: Medicolegal Forms With Legal Analysis. Chicago, IL, American Medical Association, 1991
5. RESTATEMENT (SECOND) OF TORTS § 323 (1965)
6. 380 SE2d 496 (Ga Ct App 1989)
7. Bianco EA: The physician-patient relationship. Legal Aspects of Medical Practice 11:1, 1983
8. American Medical Association, Council on Ethical and Judicial Affairs: Current Opinions. Chicago, IL, American Medical Association, 1989, 9.06
9. Smith JT: Medical Malpractice: Psychiatric Care. Colorado Springs, CO, Shepard's/McGraw-Hill, 1986, pp 21–23
10. American Psychiatric Association: The Principles of Medical Ethics With Annotations Especially Applicable to Psychiatry. Washington, DC, American Psychiatric Association, 1989, Section 6
11. Yania v Bigan, 397 Pa 316, 155 A2d 343 (1959) [defendant not liable for ignoring pleas of drowning man]; Hurley v Eddingfield, 156 Ind 416, 59 NE 1058 (1901) [physician not liable for refusing to answer call of dying person]
12. See, e.g., Hiser v Randolph, 617 P2d 774 (Ariz Ct App 1980); Oliver v Brock, 342 So 2d 1 (Ala 1976); Hoover v Williamson, 203 A2d 861 (Md 1964); Duke Sanitarium v Hearn, 13 P2d 183 (Okla 1932); Pearson v Norman, 106 P2d 361 (Colo 1940); Childers v Frye, 158 SE 744 (NC 1931)
13. King JH: The Law of Medical Malpractice. St Paul, MN, West Publishing, 1986, pp 10–11
14. See, e.g., Sendjar v Gonzalez, 520 SW2d 478 (Tex Civ App 1975); Osborne v Frazor, 425 SW2d 768 (Tenn Ct App 1968)
15. Walters P: Ethical issues in the prevention and treatment of HIV infections and AIDS. Science 239:597, 1988
16. Stevens GE: Malpractice liability of a referring physician. Medical Trial Technique Quarterly 32:121–129, 1985
17. American Medical Association, Council on Ethical and Judicial Affairs: Current Opinions. Chicago, IL, American Medical Association, 1989, 9.12
18. Keeton WP, Dobbs DB, Keeton RE, et al: Prosser and Keeton on Torts, 5th Edition. St Paul, MN, West Publishing, 1984, § 56
19. American Medical Association, Council on Ethical and Judicial Affairs. Chicago, IL, American Medical Association, 1989, 8.11

20. See generally Annotation, Construction and application of "good Samaritan" statutes, 68 ALR4th 294 (1989); Good Samaritan law bars malpractice action against physician who responded to call for intraoperative assistance. Medical Liability Reporter 10:272–273, 1988; Comment, "Good Samaritan laws" legal disarray: an update. Mercer Law Review 38:1439, 1987

21. Rodriguez v New York City Health & Hospitals Corp, 32 Misc 2d 705, 505 NYS2d 345 (Sup Ct 1986)

22. Klein JI, Macbeth JE, Onek JN: Legal Issues in the Private Practice of Psychiatry. Washington, DC, American Psychiatric Press, 1984, p 11

23. ALASKA STAT §§ 08.64.336, 09.65.090; TEX CIV PRAC & REMEDIES CODE ANN § 74.001, 74.002 (Vernon)

24. Kearns v Superior Court, 204 Cal App 3d 1325, 252 Cal Rptr 4 (1988); Clayton v Kelly, 183 Ga App 45, 351 SE2d 865 (1987); Higgins v Detroit Osteopathic Hospital Corp, 398 NW2d 520 (Mich App 1986); Burciaga v St John's Hospital, 187 Cal App 3d, 232 Cal Rptr 75 (1986)

25. See, e.g., ALA CODE § 6-5-332; CONN GEN STAT § 52-557b; DEL CODE ANN tit 16, § 6801; GA CODE ANN §§ 31-11-8 and 51-1-29; HAW REV STAT § 663-1.5 and 663-1.6

26. Halleck SL: Law in the Practice of Psychiatry. New York, Plenum, 1980, p 59

27. Newman A, Newman K: Physician's duty in independent medical evaluations. Legal Aspects of Medical Practice 17:8–9, 1989

28. O'Neill v Montefiore Hospital, 11 AD2d 132, 135–36, 202 NYS2d 436, 439–40 (1960)

29. Shane v Mouw, 323 NW2d 537 (Mich Ct App 1982)

30. Lyons v Grether, 218 Va 630, 329 SE2d 103 (1977)

31. Shumway v DeLaus, 152 AD2d 951, 543 NYS2d 777 (1989)

32. 340 SE2d 627 (Ga App 1986)

33. 671 SW2d 476 (Tenn App 1984)

34. See, e.g., Hamil v Bashline, 307 A2d 57 (Pa Super 1973)

35. Giallanza v Sands, 316 So 2d 77 (Fla Dist Ct App 1975)

36. Ingber v Kandler, 128 AD2d 591, 513 NYS2d 11 (1987)

37. 31 Cal App 3d 539, 107 Cal Rptr 469 (1973)

38. See generally RESTATEMENT (SECOND) OF TORTS § 315 (1965)

39. 17 Cal 3d 425, 131 Cal Rptr 14, 551 P2d 334 (1976)

40. Bisbing SB: Recent legal developments and psychiatry, in American Psychiatric Press Review of Clinical Psychiatry and the Law, Vol 2. Edited by Simon RL. Washington, DC, American Psychiatric Press, 1991, pp 327–379

41. Official actions: guidelines for psychiatrists working with the communication media. Am J Psychiatry 134:609–611, 1977

42. Lotspeich v Chance Vought Aircraft, 369 SW2d 705 (Tex Civ App 1963)

43. Keene v Wiggins, 69 Cal App 3d 308, 138 Cal Rptr 3 (1977); Coss v Spaulding, 126 P 468 (Utah 1912)

44. 551 NYS2d 149 (App Div 1990)

45. Craddock v Gross, 504 A2d 1300 (Pa Super Ct 1986)

46. Ferguson v Wolkin, 131 Misc 2d 304, 499 NYS2d 356 (Sup Ct 1986); Craddock v Gross, 504 A2d 1300 (Pa Super Ct 1986)

47. Beadling v Sirotta, 197 A2d 857 (NJ 1964)

48. 129 Ad2d 361, 517 NYS2d 640 (1987), appeal denied, 71 NY2d, 528 NYS2d 829, 52 NE2d 149 (1988)
49. See, e.g., Lotspeich v Chance Vought Aircraft, 369 SW2d 705 (Tex Civ App 1963); see also Johnston v Sibley, 558 SW2d 135 (Tex Civ App 1963)
50. 550 NE2d 450, 551 NYS2d 197 (1989)
51. 631 P2d 173 (Haw 1981)
52. Davis v Tirrell, 110 Misc 2d 889, 443 NYS2d 136 (Sup Ct 1981)
53. Paddock v Chacko, 522 So 2d 410 (Fla Dist Ct App 1988), review denied, 553 So 2d 168 (Fla 1989)
54. Roy A: Risk factors for suicide in psychiatric patients. Arch Gen Psychiatry 39:1089–1095, 1982
55. Barraclough B: Suicide prevention, recurrent affective disorder and lithium. Br J Psychiatry 121:391–392, 1972
56. Guidelines for psychiatrists in consultative, supervisory, or collaborative relationships with nonmedical therapists. Am J Psychiatry 137:1489–1491, 1980
57. Cohen RJ, Mariano WE: Legal Guidebook in Mental Health. New York, Free Press, 1982, p 315
58. Keeton WP, Dobb DB, Keeton RE, et al: Prosser and Keeton on Torts, 5th Edition. St Paul, MN, West Publishing, 1984, § 69, pp 499–500
59. Reisner R: Law and the Mental Health System. St Paul, MN, West Publishing, 1985, p 56

Chapter 2   # The Psychiatrist as a Fiduciary: Avoiding the Double Agent Role

---

Mr. Lewis, age 33, has been undergoing insight psychotherapy three times per week for the past year with Dr. Robbins for episodic anxiety and depression. These symptoms usually occur in relation to his work as junior associate in a law firm. When working with a certain senior partner, anxiety and depressive symptoms erupt that interfere considerably with his ability to function. Ironically, Mr. Lewis was hired by this senior partner, who saw "great promise" in him.

In his work with Mr. Lewis, Dr. Robbins tries to understand the conflict behind his patient's symptoms. Mr. Lewis is the oldest of three sons. His father was an extremely successful multimillionaire businessman who was greatly admired and respected in the community. Mr. Lewis remembers his father as being very strict and principled, demanding top performance from his sons both academically and athletically. The patient recalls the adoration his mother held for his father and their very close relationship. The patient's parents frequently took long trips to other countries. A live-in housekeeper took care of the children during these absences. Mr. Lewis remembers having prolonged temper tantrums before and after these trips.

Mr. Lewis admired and envied his father intensely. In his academic work, Mr. Lewis tried to equal his father's achievements, but frequently would "block" during exams. Consequently, he was not able to utilize fully his high intellectual capacities. When the patient's father died 2 years ago, he was left an inheritance of two million dollars. Shortly after his father's death, Mr. Lewis began experiencing more anxiety and depression in connection with work.

After a year of therapy, Mr. Lewis is able to see that he holds intense ambivalent feelings toward the senior partner in his law firm. He also is aware that he envies this partner's legal acumen and financial success. When he is asked to prepare briefs on major cases litigated by the senior partner, Mr. Lewis experiences increased symptoms of anxiety and depression. Mr. Lewis is faintly aware of angry feelings toward his boss at these times.

Dr. Robbins, utilizing dynamic insight psychotherapy, is able to help the patient begin to connect some of his current conflicts with earlier childhood expe-

riences and feelings, particularly with regard to his father. The patient maintains an idealizing transference toward Dr. Robbins, which appears to be a defense against his feelings of envy and anger. Mr. Lewis's symptoms abate only slightly.

In addition to his practice of psychiatry, Dr. Robbins from time to time puts together real estate syndications. When he learns that his patient is looking for opportunities to invest some of his inheritance, Dr. Robbins informs his patient about his real estate syndications. He has two $10,000 limited partnerships left on a promising resort condominium project. Mr. Lewis buys a partnership for himself and one for his wife. Six months later, the entire syndication is sold at a huge profit, returning to Mr. Lewis $125,000 for each partnership purchased.

Mr. Lewis is extremely pleased with the investment profits. His symptoms at work improve, but he notices increased anxiety and depression surrounding his therapy sessions. He finds it more difficult to come to therapy and occasionally misses sessions altogether. The therapy becomes stalemated. Mr. Lewis leaves after 2 years of therapy with thinly disguised feelings of an oedipal triumph. However, his symptoms at work recur and become much worse. Mr. Lewis considers filing a lawsuit for negligent treatment.

What is the legal meaning of the term *fiduciary*?

Legally, the term *fiduciary* refers to "a person [or institution] having [a] duty, created by his undertaking, to act primarily for another's benefit in matters connected with such undertaking" (1). More broadly, it refers to any relationship in which one person is under a duty to act for the benefit of another. Fiduciary relationships may be formal, as with a banker and an investor or a guardian and a ward, or informal, as with an adult and a child or an aged parent. Fiduciary relationships are usually created when confidence placed in one person is accepted by the other. Merely respecting another person's judgment or trusting an individual's character does not give rise to a fiduciary relationship. A fiduciary relationship arises, therefore, whenever confidence, faith, and trust are reposed on one side, and domination and influence result on the other (2). Fiduciary relationships may be personal, domestic, moral, or social.

Persons acting as a fiduciary are not permitted to use the relationship for their personal benefit, except with the full knowledge and consent of the other person:

> Out of such a relation [fiduciary relationship], the law raises the rule that neither party may exert influence or pressure upon the other, take selfish advantage of his trust, or deal with the subject-matter of the trust in such a way as to benefit himself or prejudice the other except in the exercise of the utmost good faith and with the full knowledge and consent of that other, business shrewdness, hard bargaining, and astuteness to take advantage of the forgetfulness or negligence of another being totally prohibited as between persons standing in such a relation to each other. (1)

The person giving such consent must be mentally competent and free from any undue influence before the courts will consider the consent valid. Courts tend to carefully scrutinize transactions between individuals in fiduciary relationships, especially when there is a claim of abuse, exploitation, or undue influence by the dominant individual at the expense of the individual in a submissive position.

How have courts defined the fiduciary responsibility that psychiatrists owe their patients?

Psychiatrists as physicians must treat their patients at all times with good faith, with trust, and in strict confidence. The psychiatrist, as a fiduciary, must not use the patient for his or her personal benefit. This responsibility is "implicit" in the doctor-patient relationship and is a fundamental part of the general "duty of care." The special vulnerability of the patient rather than the special powers of a profession gives rise to a fiduciary duty.

Both the common law (3) and medical ethics (4) have affirmed that once a physician enters a professional relationship with a patient, a position of special trust and confidence is created that requires the physician to act in good faith and in the patient's best interests. Because of the physician's special training and knowledge, but particularly because of "the ignorance and helplessness of the patient regarding his [or her] own physical condition," the physician-patient relationship is considered a fiduciary relationship (5).

For example, in *Omer v. Edgren* (6), a lawsuit was brought against a psychiatrist for alleged sexual exploitation of a patient. The Washington Court of Appeals noted that

> Washington also has characterized the relationship between physician and patient as fiduciary: "The physician-patient relationship is of fiduciary nature. The inherent necessity for trust and confidence requires scrupulous good faith on the part of the physician [citations omitted].

This holding has been echoed by other courts in cases in which psychiatrists have violated the trust and confidence of their patients (7).

Do psychiatrists owe a duty of neutrality to their patients as part of their fiduciary role?

One way for psychiatrists to ethically and legally fulfill their role as a fiduciary and to avoid conflicts of interest is to maintain a position of "neutrality." In general, the duty of neutrality is an independent legal formulation. This duty, however, also parallels Freud's abstinence principle, which stated that psychiatrists must refrain from gratifying themselves at the expense of patients (8, 9). A corollary of this principle is that the psychiatrist's main source of gratification should arise from participating in the psychotherapeutic process. The only material satisfaction received is payment for the therapist's services.

The duty of neutrality is based on the legal concept of the fiduciary relationship, which requires mental health professionals to act in the patient's best interest through a position of personal neutrality. This neutrality should not be confused with impersonal attitudes or the psychoanalytic therapist's technical position of neutrality that is equidistant between reality and the patient's superego, ego, and id. Although such a position does militate against self-serving interventions in psychoanalysis, it also serves other important treatment purposes in psychoanalytic therapy.

Not infrequently, psychiatrists may need to support a patient's defenses, mitigate a harsh conscience, or help a patient to better define reality. These are all legitimate treatment interventions for the needs of specific patients. The duty of neutrality refers not to these technical issues but rather to therapists' curbing any tendencies to manipulate and exploit patients for their own personal gain. Neutrality, however, does not preclude an interactive relationship between therapist and patient. Nevertheless, the duty to neutrality is a fundamental underlying principle to the establishment of treatment boundary guidelines (10).

What ethical-legal problems are raised by the clinical vignette?

Dr. Robbins uses his psychotherapeutic position to strike a business deal with his patient. This is a clear example of transference exploitation. Although the patient is overtly grateful for his windfall profits, an unspoken price is paid in damage to the therapeutic relationship and process. For example, the patient's gratitude toward the psychiatrist is in direct conflict with his strong rivalrous tendencies toward authority figures. As a result, anxiety and depression intensify in the therapeutic situation. Mr. Lewis is able to use his gratitude unconsciously as a defense against his hostile, rivalrous feelings toward the psychiatrist. The therapeutic stalemate develops as a direct consequence of the psychiatrist's shift into the role of businessman-entrepreneur, which is similar to the profession of the patient's father. This self-serving business intrusion into the patient's therapy distorts the transference by making the psychiatrist appear more like the father in reality. Leaving the treatment unimproved reflects, on one level, the patient's triumph over the psychiatrist-father not only by making money through the therapy but by defeating the therapist in his therapeutic endeavors. Clinically, however, the patient's deep-seated feelings toward his father and authority figures in general remain unresolved and exacerbated.

Mental health professionals cannot serve two masters. A psychiatrist must choose between being a physician and being a business partner, social acquaintance, personal advisor, or some other nontreatment-related role. When therapists leave their position of neutrality, they violate their fiduciary trust position with patients. This violation inevitably results in compromised treatment and could result in malpractice claims for negligent psychotherapy.

How is double agentry defined in the clinical practice of psychiatry?

In psychiatry, double agentry occurs when a psychiatrist has a conflict of interest that interferes with the fiduciary responsibility to act solely in the best interest of the patient to whom a duty of care is owed. The opportunities to assume a double agent role in clinical practice are more numerous than generally realized. The practice of psychotherapy bristles with moral dilemmas (some of which are described later in this chapter).

It should be noted that the conflict of interest may be stated or unstated. When the conflict of interest is stated, the patient or evaluee is presumably put on proper notice. However, instances arise when even though the patient or evaluee is aware of the psychiatrist's conflict of interest, coercion is present that nullifies this knowledge. For example, in Section 4 of the *Opinions of the Ethics Committee on the Principles of Medical Ethics With Annotations Especially Applicable to Psychiatry* (11), an opinion is given regarding the potential ethical conflicts of a student health psychiatrist who sees some patients for treatment and other patients for administrative reasons. The opinion states that a classic example of double agentry exists if an administrative opinion is rendered upon a patient with whom the psychiatrist has a therapeutic contract. The psychiatrist cannot adequately serve both the university and the student-patient at the same time. Even if a student consents to an administrative report after a period of psychotherapy, the conflict of interest is not resolved if the consent is not given freely but is coerced (e.g., administrative exigencies). The opinion further states that the psychiatrist should clearly define his or her role with the student in advance of treatment.

The problem of conflicting loyalties should be a major concern to psychiatrists (12). It is also a common concern for other mental health professionals, lawyers, bankers, accountants, and a host of other professionals serving in a fiduciary capacity. In a report by The Hastings Center (13) entitled "In the Service of the State: The Psychiatrist as Double Agent," the problem of double agentry was studied from the perspective of the psychiatrist's conflicting loyalties when simultaneously serving the patient and an agency, institution, or society. For example, for the military psychiatrist, the loyalty to the soldier (patient) versus the military's best interests poses a potential double agent role. Prison psychiatrists are often confronted with the choice of having to serve the interests of their prisoner patients, prison officials, or society. School psychiatrists must balance the interests of the student, the parents, and the school administration. Psychiatrists working in mental institutions must manage the conflicting duties to their patients with those of the institution and society. With the emergence of the *Tarasoff* doctrine of duty to warn and protect endangered third parties, the preservation of the patient's confidentiality conflicts with society's needs to be protected from harm. But as noted in the Hastings report, what has traditionally been called double agentry is, in fact, multiple agentry with conflicting responsibilities and confused loyalties due to undefined purposes and contradictory goals.

In this chapter, double agentry has been broadened to include those actions of mental health professionals in which the therapist's interests come before the patient's best interests. Direct conflicts between the therapist's personal interests and a patient's treatment needs are not so often discussed in professional literature as are the more traditional conflicts of loyalty with external agencies. Yet psychotherapists are no better or worse than other human beings. Although they possess skill and have received training in understanding and treating emotionally disturbed individuals, the best training available will not protect against character deficiencies that may lead some therapists to exploit their patients.

Psychotherapists also typically possess powerful value systems that make it a struggle for some to remain therapeutically neutral. Should these values be made explicitly known to patients as a kind of *Miranda* warning? If so, patients would have a clearer idea of the therapist's interests and objectives and would not be subject to hidden value agendas. For example, the clinical vignette illustrates a manipulation of the transference for the advancement of the psychiatrist's entrepreneurial agenda.

All psychiatrists should seriously consider three fundamental recommendations of the Hastings report in dealing with the problems of double agentry (13):

1. Separate functions should be assigned to mental health professionals who manage different roles.
2. Following an informed-consent model, patients need to be informed of the treatment objectives and methods as well as the therapist's priorities and any personal agendas.
3. Mental health professionals must assume active "responsibility to clean our own house."

As an example of the last recommendation, Section 2 of *The Principles of Medical Ethics With Annotations Especially Applicable to Psychiatry* states, "A physician shall deal honestly with patients and colleagues, and strive to expose those physicians deficient in character or competence, or who engage in fraud or deception" (11).

What are some common examples of double agentry found in clinical practice?

Double agentry can occur when a mental health professional writes an article about a patient, conducts research using therapy patients, or becomes an expert witness in a lawsuit involving a patient whom he or she has treated (14). Several case examples are instructive.

In *Roe v. Doe* (15), a psychiatrist was sued by a former patient when she tried to capitalize on their therapeutic relation by publishing a book in which she reported verbatim information from the therapy, including the patient's thoughts, feelings, and fantasies. In concluding that no valid patient consent for the disclosure existed, the court admonished the defendant, stating, among other things, that

> a physician who enters into an agreement with a patient to provide medical attention impliedly covenants to keep in confidence all disclosures made by the patient concerning the patient's physical and mental condition as well as matters discovered by the physician in the course of the examination or treatment. . . . such is particularly and necessarily true of [the] psychiatric relationships. (15)

Obtaining or using information obtained in therapy for nontherapeutic purposes, whether during or following treatment, is fraught with ethical and legal dilemmas. For example, can informed consent be obtained if the patient has not seen the manuscript? When writing about patients, does the therapist prolong treatment to obtain material? Are interpretations skewed by the need to develop certain material of interest to potential readers? Did note taking done for the purpose of the book inhibit the treatment process? Finally, does disclosing negative information about the patient violate the therapist's ethical and legal obligation not to harm the patient (14)?

Therapists may attempt the difficult task of trying to disguise the patient's identity. Sometimes, the only disguise that is attempted is to withhold the patient's name. Often too much disguise undermines the scientific veracity of a case, turning the patient into the therapist's fictional fantasy. Of course, publishing research and clinical studies that support new discoveries is a professional obligation. However, the conflict that exists between treatment and research obligations may disrupt the fiduciary relationship with the patient. Thus, no matter how well disguised the material appears to be, it should be discussed with the patient and written permission should be obtained prior to publication.

Forensic examinations requested by an attorney or the court may present similar conflicts (14). Although the trial record is public, approval must be granted by defendants for the use of the information obtained by mental health professionals so as not to breach the fiduciary relationship. Psychiatrists must never attempt to obtain information from defendants for law enforcement personnel by converting a psychiatric examination into a criminal investigation. With court-ordered examinations, the interviewer must advise the defendant that information gathered during the course of the interview is not confidential because a report will be rendered to the court.

In those instances in which the examination is requested by an attorney, the report's confidentiality is protected pursuant to the attorney-client privilege until the attorney decides to utilize the information. If the examiner intends to publish the information, the accused is often not told that the information will be used for an article or book. The forensic examiner's unstated, hidden agenda of writing a book may lead to an attempt to seek material that is thrilling and that will make sensational copy rather than best serve a legal defense. If the defendant is executed, will that ensure higher book sales? Thus, the examiner's literary ambition may interfere with the best possible legal defense for the client (14).

Psychiatrists working in managed care settings face major ethical concerns and potential serious double agent roles (16). "Negative" incentives to cut costs at the expense of diminished quality of care constitute a major threat to the fiduciary commitment to patients (17). A 1987 report from The Hastings Center, entitled "New Mental Health Economics and the Impact on the Ethics of Psychiatric Practice" (18), recognizes the conflicting responsibilities that psychiatrists experience between serving patients and institutions simultaneously. The report underscores the psychiatrist's primary responsibility to the patient by stating that "the new reimbursement schemes share the financial risk with the provider and may incentivize the psychiatrist to take a clinical approach that is not entirely in the patient's best interest" (p. 9).

Therapists who exploit their patients sexually violate egregiously their fiduciary trust relationship with the patient. In *Roy v. Hartogs* (19), the court held that the psychotherapist-patient relationship was a fiduciary relationship analogous to a guardian-ward relationship. The court further stated that "there is a public policy to protect a patient from the deliberate and malicious abuse of power and breach of trust by a psychiatrist when the patient entrusts to him [or] her body and mind." Interestingly, prior to the initiation of sexual contact, Dr. Hartogs was having the plaintiff run errands, do light office work, and perform other tasks (20). Clearly, the sexual contact was but one of several conflicts of interest that existed in the exploitation of the doctor-patient relationship.

In *Hrebec v. Van Dooren* (21), a double agentry–sexual exploitation occurred when a female psychiatrist was alleged to have committed numerous acts of malfeasance with her female patient, including making sexual advances. The plaintiff maintained that the defendant allowed the patient to have regular social contact with the psychiatrist's family and friends. This allegation was supported by evidence that the defendant accepted gifts from the plaintiff and allowed the plaintiff to stay at her home for 7 months.

Stone (22) feels that emphasis upon the fiduciary relationship removes the patient consent issue raised by the defendant in sexual misconduct cases. Whether the patient had a capacity to consent becomes irrelevant.

Another form of double agentry may occur when a patient who has been sexually abused by a therapist is referred to another therapist for treatment. The subsequent therapist with forensic interests or unstated moral vendettas may convert the treatment relationship into a forensic case, encouraging a suit and initiating ethical and licensure proceedings against the former therapist. The patient who sought treatment should be offered the choice of treatment or forensic advocacy, but the latter should not be misrepresented to the patient as treatment. It must be remembered that patients who were sexually abused in a prior therapy have already experienced a devastating deception through a conflict of interest by the previous therapist.

Finally, the use of "insider information" obtained from the patient for the personal advantage of the therapist occurs with disturbing frequency. A clear example of double agentry occurred when a psychiatrist used a stock tip obtained from a bank executive's wife during the course of therapy to turn a large profit (23). The psychiatrist ran afoul of the Securities and Exchange Commission. Ultimately, he pled guilty and was fined $150,000, given a 5-year suspended sentence, placed on 5 years probation, and required to perform 3,000 hours of community service.

Is it ever appropriate for the psychiatrist to become involved in a business deal with a patient?

No. In the clinical vignette, Dr. Robbins involves his patient in a business deal. Unfortunately, such exploitations are common. More frequently, however, the therapist is seduced by a business deal offered by the patient. Experience reveals that double-agentry breaches of fiduciary trust cut through all schools of psychiatric treatment and occur at all levels of training. Honesty and integrity in the practice of one's profession appear to reflect innate character and are something that can be learned only to a limited degree.

Therapists who become involved in business dealings with patients may later be accused of undue influence when purchasing valuable goods or property from the patient at below-market value, or when the patient leaves the witting therapist a large amount of money in a will (24). Litigation is usually aimed at voiding the business contract or will. Although monetary damages against the therapist are not usually sought, the burden of proof is on the patient to show that undue influence occurred.

In the *Opinions of the Ethics Committee on the Principles of Medical Ethics* issued by the American Psychiatric Association (APA) (11), two clinical situations are discussed that bear directly upon the subject matter of this chapter:

Question: Is it proper for a psychiatrist to advise a patient to make an investment from which the psychiatrist receives a finder's fee?

Answer: Clearly, no. Section 2, Annotation 2 (APA) [*Principles of Medical Ethics*] states:

> The psychiatrist should diligently guard against exploiting information furnished by the patient and should not use the unique position of power afforded him/her by the psychotherapeutic situation to influence the patient in any way not directly relevant to the treatment goals.

It would be a strange form of psychotherapy that included giving advice about investments, let alone the fact that offering such advice would obviously constitute exploitation of the treatment relationship. (March 1978) [*Opinions,* Section 2-I, p. 11]

The other situation discussed in the *Opinions* concerns accepting bequests:

Question: My patient of almost 5 years has a terminal illness. With my assistance she has been able to more effectively deal with her approaching death. She has no family and wishes to bequeath her estate to me. Would it be ethical for me to accept?

Answer: It would not be advisable for you to knowingly permit yourself to be the beneficiary. To do so gives the appearance of impropriety and raises the possibility of exploitation of the therapeutic relationship. We advise you to encourage your patient to make this gift to a trust, foundation, educational situation, or public charity whose purposes are consistent with the patient's wishes. (January 1983) [*Opinions,* Section 1-D, p. 6]

Psychiatrists who have accepted large bequests from patients have been accused of exerting undue influence (25).

In the clinical vignette, if Mr. Lewis had lost his money by investing in Dr. Robbins's real estate syndicate, legal action could have been brought to recover his original monies on the basis of undue influence exerted by the therapist. Even assuming that Mr. Lewis had obtained expert investment advice from his psychiatrist, the business deal vitiated the therapy. Dr. Robbins placed greater importance on his real estate investment than on the patient's therapy and welfare by contaminating the therapy with a business deal.

Must psychiatrists avoid social contacts with both current and terminated patients?

Mental health professionals who treat patients may themselves feel isolated and lonely, and seek out the friendship and companionship of current and past patients. Although overtly nonsexual, such an intrusion into nontreatment-related aspects of a patient's life may be confusing, upsetting, gratifying, or reassuring to the patient. Regardless of the patient's initial experience or response, attempting to establish social relationships with former patients is another example of double agentry. "Once a patient—always a patient" is a sound principle that allows patients to go about their lives free from the influence of their therapists. However, exceptions to this dictum do exist. For example, in various training institutes, students or candidates who undergo therapy may, upon graduation, establish a collegial and social relationship with their former therapists.

One of the personal deprivations of psychiatric practice, in contrast to other medical specialties, is the prohibition against socializing with current and former patients. A useful distinction can be made between maintaining a friendly interest in former patients and striking up a social relationship with them.

From time to time, therapists receive letters from former patients. These contacts provide important follow-up data. Although these communications often contain manifest or latent psychological overtones in relation to the therapist, the human response is to answer these letters unless clearly contraindicated. "Once a patient—always a patient" should not become an inhuman dictum.

Initially a social relationship with a patient may represent the beginning of more serious treatment boundary violations. There are scores of lawsuits against psychiatrists (26), psychologists (27), social workers (28), pastoral counselors (29), and unlicensed counselors (30) in which ""extracurricular socializing" culminated in some form of sexual relations.

In addition to legal sanctions, recent changes in the APA's code of ethics reflect a growing concern about the ramifications of extracurricular doctor-patient relationships, even after the professional relationship has technically terminated. For example, in 1988 the APA Assembly approved an amendment to *The Principles of Medical Ethics With Annotations Especially Applicable to Psychiatry*, stating that "sexual involvement with former patients generally exploits emotions deriving from treatment and therefore almost always is unethical" (31).

In addition to post-therapy concerns, in the *Opinions of the Ethics Committee on the Principles of Medical Ethics* (32), the following issue is raised that presents a different twist on the problem of socializing with patients:

Question: In the reverse of the usual, a "social relationship" turns into a professional relationship. Is this worthy of an investigation?

Answer: Yes. What is the nature of this "social relationship" and does it continue now that a professional relationship has occurred? Was the psychiatrist treating this person honestly in accepting clinical responsibility under the circumstances? And, what is the nature of the professional relationship? Some advice? Comfort in a crisis? Medications? Formal psychotherapy? Was there a treatment contract including a fee? Answering these questions through investigation should lead to a decision whether or not a possible ethical violation has occurred.

What conflict of interest roles may develop for therapists in patient billing and payment?

Self-serving interventions may also occur with respect to billing and fees (33). Most therapists explain their fees at the beginning of treatment so that patients can either agree, disagree, or enter into negotiations for a mutually agreed-upon fee. However, double agent roles can arise over billing for missed appointments or through discounting or inflating bills.

Therapists are free to bill their services at rates they have established in an agreement with their patients. Billing for missed appointments may be appropriate if the patient is advised of this practice at the onset of the treatment relationship. The APA (34) provides ethical guidelines concerning billing for missed appointments. These guidelines, however, state that one must treat the patient "always with the utmost consideration for the patient and his/her circumstances." If the therapist charges for phone conversations, for preparing reports, or for completing lengthy insurance forms, the patient should be informed of this policy in advance. In *Current Opinions of the Judicial Council* (35), the AMA states that "the attending physician should complete without charge the appropriate 'simplified' insurance claim forms as part of his [or her] service to the patient to enable the patient to receive his [or her] benefits. A charge for more complex forms may be made in conformity with local customs."

Legal commentators state that charges for missed sessions should not be represented as treatment sessions to third-party payers, as doing so could be interpreted as misrepresentation (36). Some therapists feel that they do not want to place themselves in the position of the patient's conscience; hence, they inform the patient that conflicts with the insurance carrier over payments for missed appointments will need to be handled by the patient. But therapists should make clear on the bill that all appointment times are reserved. Some therapists stipulate conditions on the bill, such as "sessions reserved, 50 minutes each" (37). Other therapists indicate all missed appointments directly on the billing statement even if patients object. In this way, patients' feelings are addressed as treatment issues. In any case, failure to clarify billing procedures with third-party payers may raise the question of collusion with the patient against an insurance carrier.

When a patient has insurance but is unable to pay his or her own portion of the bill, "discounting" of the bill occurs if the therapist accepts no payment or a smaller amount from the patient (38). The effect of this practice is to nullify the insurance company's position that services are unlikely to be overly or inappropriately used when patients pay their part for the therapy. In most instances, insurance companies are responsible for a percentage of the psychiatrist's usual and customary fee. When the psychiatrist accepts the insurance reimbursement as payment in full, but collection of the copayment from the patient is possible, the insurer is actually paying 100 percent of the fee. Insurance carriers consider this practice to be fraudulent because the physician is pocketing their "overpayments."

"Inflating" bills refers to charging the insurance carrier a higher fee than the therapist is actually charging the patient. When this happens, the therapist pockets the difference or applies it to the patient's portion of the fee. Double agent roles are certain to adversely affect therapy. Moreover, such practices may be exposed in court, and the therapist's credibility can be severely undermined if the patient chooses to file a lawsuit.

In *Feiler v. New Jersey Dental Association* (39), a suit was brought against a dentist by the New Jersey Dental Association that challenged the dentist's practice of submitting to insurance carriers the actual patient charge and representing it as his usual and customary charge. This charge would be accurate only if the dentist charged his patients the insurance copayment amount. Because the dentist had already promised his patients that he would not seek their portion of the charge, his statements to the carrier overstated the patient charges and the usual and customary fees. The court concluded that these billing practices represented unfair competition and required the defendant to include on all statements either the total amount he intended to collect or a statement of the amount he would bill the patient upon receiving the carrier's payment. This case, however, addresses only the situation in which a practitioner did not intend to collect patient copayments. The case did not address the practice of billing the full amount but waiving or not pressing the patient who has become impecunious for payment.

In *Metropolitan Life Insurance Company v. Ditmore* (40), the United States Court of Appeals for the First Circuit reinstated an insurance company's lawsuit against a psychiatrist for damages for overpayments allegedly resulting from fraudulent claims. The insurance company charged the psychiatrist with making three types of statements amounting to misrepresentations: *1)* listing himself as the "attending physician" when the therapy was actually conducted by nonmedical therapists; *2)* indicating services rendered as "psychotherapeutic sessions" without specifying whether the sessions were individual or group; and *3)* charging $100 per session regardless of the kind or duration of the sessions.

The trial court granted summary judgment in favor of the psychiatrist. The psychiatrist admitted to the allegations but pointed out that the state statute permitted delegation of medical services and that insurance claim forms were general and did not call for specific information. However, the court stated that "partial disclosures and half truths are under some circumstances tantamount to misrepresentations of the fact." The appellate court remanded the case for trial after concluding that a genuine issue of material fact existed as to whether the psychiatrist's statements amounted to misrepresentations. As a result of this case, both insurance carriers and the courts will carefully scrutinize the billing practices of psychiatrists (41).

Some patients undergoing treatment may become unable to pay their bills. These same patients may also need to continue their treatment. To continue treatment, a patient may offer to barter cars, jewelry, property, or other valuable items. However, the coin of the realm must literally always be money as the only medium of exchange when accepting payment from patients. Patients who desperately feel they need treatment, or who experience intense transference feelings, often are unable to render an arms-length assessment of the monetary value of their possessions.

Slovenko (42) discusses the problem of therapists' accepting paintings, poetry, sculpture, and other valuable items under the concept of bailment of property. Bailment is defined as the delivery of personal property by the bailor (patient) to a bailee (therapist) for a specified purpose with an express or implied agreement of the parties that when the purpose is accomplished, the property will be returned to the bailor, kept until reclaimed, or disposed of according to agreement. An appropriate reason for the therapist to receive such property is for use as grist for the therapy. When the treatment relationship is concluded, these items should be returned.

Similarly, therapists should tactfully refuse large gifts from patients, and, if possible, the opportunity should be taken to investigate the meaning of the gift in the service of the treatment. This is not easily accomplished, because some patients will feel devastated by having their gifts questioned. Small gifts given by patients at the termination of therapy should be accepted graciously and are best left unanalyzed. A good rule to follow is that compensation for one's services is the fee received and the professional gratification derived from conducting competent therapy.

The AMA has issued guidelines for physicians when accepting gifts from industry, as formulated by the AMA's Council on Ethical and Judicial Affairs (43). The guidelines state that physicians should accept gifts of only "minimal value" that are related to their work and that "entail a benefit to patients." For example, acceptable items might include pens, notepads, or books. As stated in the guidelines, "Textbooks, modest meals and other gifts are appropriate if they serve a genuine educational function." Cash payment should never be accepted. Physicians should not accept any gift "with strings attached" that might, for example, imply a change in prescribing practices. The guidelines also address protecting physicians from undue influence by pharmaceutical companies through subsidized Continuing Medical Education activities.

Physicians long have struggled with what has appeared to be an inherent conflict of interest between the patient's interest and the pecuniary aspects of treatment. The physician determines treatment interventions while at the same time deriving income from serving the patient. What distinguishes the professional from the nonprofessional is that the physician "is first and foremost dedicated to serving the patient's interest" (44). Thus economic benefits accruing to the physician are not necessarily in conflict with acting in the patient's best interest. To the conscientious, dedicated physician, the patient's interest is intrinsic. Money is part of the transaction but extrinsic to the central concerns about the patient's welfare. Furthermore, physicians have a tradition of providing *pro bono* service to the economically disadvantaged.

Psychiatrists and other mental health professionals cannot serve two masters. Psychiatrists must be diligent in maintaining their roles as physicians. The guiding ethical principle of beneficence requires that our patients' best interests come first. When psychiatrists abandon a position of concerned neutrality, they may violate their position of trust and beneficence toward patients. The inevitable result is compromised treatment and increased exposure to malpractice claims for negligent psychotherapy (45).

References

1. Black HC: Black's Law Dictionary, 6th Edition. St Paul, MN, West Publishing, 1990, p 625
2. Ibid, p 564
3. Lockett v Goodill, 430 P2d 589 (Wash 1967)
4. American Psychiatric Association: The Principles of Medical Ethics With Annotations Especially Applicable to Psychiatry. Washington, DC, American Psychiatric Association, 1989
5. Miller v Kennedy, 11 Wash App 272, 522 P2d 852, 860 (1974), aff'd, 85 Wash 2d 151, 530 P2d 334 (1975); Hunter v Brown, 4 Wash App 899, 484 P2d 1162 (1971), aff'd, 81 Wash 2d 465, 502 P2d 1194 (1972)
6. 38 Wash App 376, 685 P2d 635 (1984)
7. Roy v Hartogs, 81 Misc 2d 350, 366 NYS2d 297 (1975); Mazza v Huffaker, 61 NC App 176, 300 SE2d 833 (1983)
8. Furrow BR: Malpractice in Psychotherapy. Lexington, MA, DC Heath, 1980, p 31
9. Freud S: Observations on transference-love (1915), in the Standard Edition of the Complete Psychological Works of Sigmund Freud, Vol 12. Translated and edited by Strachey J. London, Hogarth Press, 1958, pp 159–171
10. Simon RI: Treatment boundary violations: clinical, ethical, and legal considerations, in Forensic Psychiatry: A Comprehensive Textbook. Edited by Rosner R. New York, Van Nostrand Reinhold (in press)
11. American Psychiatric Association: Opinions of the Ethics Committee on the Principles of Medical Ethics With Annotations Especially Applicable to Psychiatry. Washington, DC, American Psychiatric Association, 1989
12. Weinstein HC: Perspectives on dual loyalties in the practice of psychiatry, in American Psychiatric Press Review of Clinical Psychiatry and the Law, Vol 3. Edited by Simon RI. Washington, DC, American Psychiatric Press, 1992, pp 153–220
13. The Hastings Center: In the Service of the State: The Psychiatrist as Double Agent (Special Supplement). Hastings-on-Hudson, NY, The Hastings Center, 1978
14. Slovenko R: The hazards of writing or disclosing information in psychiatry. Behavioral Sciences and the Law 1:109–127, 1983
15. 93 Misc 2d 201, 400 NSY2d 668 (Sup Ct 1977)
16. Sabin JE: Psychiatrists face tough ethical questions in managed care setting. Psychiatric Times 6(9):1, 10–11, 1989
17. May WE: Patient advocate or secret agent? JAMA 256:1784–1787, 1986
18. The Hastings Center: New Mental Health Economics and the Impact on the Ethics of Psychiatric Practice. Briarcliff Manor, NY, The Hastings Center, April 16–17, 1987
19. 81 Misc 2d 350, 366 NYS2d 297, 299 (1975)
20. Freeman L, Roy J: Betrayal. New York, Stein & Day, 1976

21. No 86-2-03320-9, Pierce Cty Cir Ct (Wash Jan 1988)
22. Stone AA: Law, Psychiatry, and Morality. Washington, DC, American Psychiatric Press, 1984, p 198
23. Northrup B: Psychotherapy faces a stubborn problem: abuses by therapists. Wall Street Journal, October 29, 1986, p 1
24. Halleck SL: Law in the Practice of Psychiatry. New York, Plenum, 1980, pp 38–39
25. Chicago analyst charged with impropriety. Psychiatric Times 5(6):21, 1988
26. See, e.g., Barton v Achar, No 86-0873, Portland Cty Cir Ct (Ore 1988); Gray v Wood, No F2-1670, Dane Cty Patients Compensation Panel (Wisc February 1, 1984); Mazza v Huffaker, 61 NC App 170, 300 SE2d 833 (1983)
27. See, e.g., Commerce Bank v Hite, No LA-1957, Va Bch Cir Ct (VA 1986); Carmichael v Carmichael, CV Nos DR-5289-88 and DR-37-89, DC Super Ct (Oct 20 1989)
28. See, e.g., Cosgrove v Lawrence, Nos A-350-86T5 and A-352-86T5, NJ Super Ct (App Div March 10, 1987); Rowe v Bennett 514 A2d 802 (Me 1986)
29. See, e.g., Destefano v Grabrian, CA No 84CV0773, El Paso Cty Dist Ct (Colo July 1984)
30. See, e.g., Benetin v Carney, No 82-2-02722-7 (Seattle Dist Ct Wash Jan 1984); Doe v Roe, No 344,601 Norwalk Dist Ct (CA 1987)
31. Assembly endorses adversarial ethics hearing rules. Psychiatric News 23(23):1, 12, 1988
32. American Psychiatric Association: Opinions of the Ethics Committee on the Principles of Medical Ethics With Annotations Especially Applicable to Psychiatry. Washington, DC, American Psychiatric Association, 1989, Section 2-NN, p 22
33. Simon RI: Psychiatric Interventions and Malpractice: A Primer for Liability Prevention. Springfield, IL, Charles C Thomas, 1982, pp 62–63
34. American Psychiatric Association: The Principles of Medical Ethics With Annotations Especially Applicable to Psychiatry. Washington, DC, American Psychiatric Association, 1989, Section 2, Annotation 6
35. American Medical Association, Council on Ethical and Judicial Affairs: Current Opinions of the Judicial Council. Chicago, IL, American Medical Association, 1989, Section 104, 6.06
36. Klein JI, Macbeth JE, Onek JN: Legal Issues in the Private Practice of Psychiatry. Washington, DC, American Psychiatric Press, 1984, pp 59–60
37. Simon RI: Psychiatric Interventions and Malpractice: A Primer for Liability Prevention. Springfield, IL, Charles C Thomas, 1982
38. Robitscher J: The Powers of Psychiatry. Boston, MA, Houghton Mifflin, 1980, p 438
39. 199 NJ Super 363, 489 A2d 1161 (1984)
40. 729 F2d 1 (1st Cir 1984)
41. American Psychiatric Association Legal Consultation Plan Newsletter, Summer 1985, pp 6–7
42. Slovenko R: Psychiatry and the Law. Boston, MA, Little, Brown, 1973, pp 415–417
43. American Medical Association, Council on Ethical and Judicial Affairs: Gifts to physicians from industry. JAMA 265:501, 1991
44. American Medical Association: Reports of the Judicial Council, December 1984. JAMA 253:2424–2425, 1985
45. Simon RI: The psychiatrist as a fiduciary: avoiding the double agent role. Psychiatric Annals 17:622–626, 1987

Chapter 3   # The Unduly Defensive Psychiatrist and the Provision of Substandard Care

---

Dr. Kane hospitalizes a 43-year-old attorney because of increasing depression over the past 6 months. Therapeutic dosages of different tricyclic antidepressants given over a sufficient amount of time prove ineffective. The addition of lithium to enhance the response to antidepressants does not help. The patient's symptoms of anorexia, weight loss, psychomotor retardation, and early morning waking intensify. A monoamine oxidase inhibitor (MAOI) is started but is equally ineffective. Electroconvulsive treatment is not tried because of the patient's adamant refusal. The refusal appears to be competent.

Because the depression remains refractory, Dr. Kane obtains a consultation from an expert psychopharmacologist. The consultant, who is European trained, recommends use of a combination of a tricyclic antidepressant and an MAOI to be administered simultaneously. He feels that the concern over giving these two medications together is greatly exaggerated. It has been utilized for some time with considerable success in Europe in properly selected patients and with proper precautions. Dr. Kane checks the recommended tricyclic antidepressant in the Physician's Desk Reference *(PDR) and finds the following statement under contraindications: "It should not be given concomitantly with monoamine oxidase inhibitors. Hyperpyretic crises, severe convulsions, and deaths have occurred in patients receiving tricyclic antidepressants and monoamine oxidase inhibitors simultaneously." Dr. Kane also consults the psychiatric literature. Some careful studies suggest that the use of a tricyclic-MAOI combination is of value in treating refractory depression. These studies state that although this treatment combination should not be used routinely, it has a definite place with selected patients under expert supervision and that the hazards are overemphasized.*

Dr. Kane decides not to follow the consultant's recommendation for using a tricyclic-MAOI combination because of his fear of a malpractice action should serious side effects occur. Given the clearly stated contraindications in the PDR, Dr. Kane worries he would be defenseless should legal liability arise.

Instead, he decides to try the patient on a newer tetracyclic antidepressant com-
bined with supportive-expressive psychotherapy. When the patient's depression
continues to remain unchanged after 2 months, he is transferred to a long-term
psychiatric facility for continued treatment.

What is defensive medicine?

The definition of defensive medicine is difficult to articulate because of the
complexity of the issue. Generally, however, defensive medicine refers to any
act or omission by a physician that is performed not for the benefit of the patient
but solely to avoid malpractice liability or to provide a legal defense against a
malpractice claim (1).

It is not unusual for psychiatrists to feel that the law is weighted in favor of
the patient because of the numerous court decisions that have strongly emphasized patients' rights and civil liberties (2). However, the unduly defensive psychiatrist perceives that every patient is a potential malpractice case, all the
while feeling "belegaled" (3). Legally uninformed psychiatrists often see little
danger, but their denial may make them even more vulnerable to a claim of
malpractice.

Defensive psychiatry comes in two forms, positive and negative, with some
psychiatrists practicing both (4). The terms *positive* and *negative* do not refer to
value judgments but rather to acts of commission and omission, respectively.
The "positive" defensive psychiatrist orders procedures and treatments to prevent or limit liability. These actions may or may not accord with generally accepted clinical care. For example, a psychiatrist was appalled by his own
defensive requirement that the family of his patient sign an exculpatory letter
that would release the psychiatrist from legal liability after the family refused
the psychiatrist's defensive recommendation of hospitalization. The psychiatrist said that he learned the important lesson of putting the patient's best interests ahead of "selfish fear" (5). The "negative" defensive psychiatrist avoids
procedures or treatments out of fear of a lawsuit even when the patient might
benefit from these interventions. This latter course is particularly unconsciona-
ble and possibly legally disastrous. In the clinical vignette, Dr. Kane rejects a
potentially helpful treatment recommended by an expert consultant in psychopharmacology. Although Dr. Kane referred to the PDR, his primary concern
was avoiding a malpractice lawsuit rather than basing treatment upon the clinical needs of the patient.

Defensive practices do not necessarily shield against malpractice suits. On
the contrary, in the pursuit of defensive psychiatry, a patient may receive substandard treatment that is, in fact, harmful. At a minimum, defensive practices
generally are expensive and largely ineffective (6). A far more devastating consequence of practicing defensive medicine is that the fear of malpractice leads
to fear of patients. The patient is viewed as an adversary. The fiduciary relation-

ship between therapist and patient, in which the therapist is an unequivocal ally of the patient, becomes eroded. Countertransference reactions to the patient stirred up by a fear of being sued may contain retaliatory fears the therapist experienced toward childhood authority figures, thus further adversely affecting clinical judgment (7).

Are all defensive practices inappropriate?

No. Given the current legal climate, only the most naive physician would not consider taking appropriate defensive measures when treating certain patients. The single most important step that a psychiatrist can take to limit the risk of exposure to a malpractice claim is to maintain adequate patient evaluation and treatment records. For instance, it is foolhardy to ignore careful documentation of risk-benefit assessments made in the course of treating suicidal or violent patients, particularly because adequate record keeping is consistent with good clinical care. Poor or absent record keeping may be the result of a defensive fear that treatment notes could be used against the psychiatrist in court. On the other hand, responding defensively to the current litigious climate by maintaining overly detailed, voluminous notes could eventually create a spurious standard of care in record keeping. The difficulty is to know when and how to appropriately practice defensive medicine and, at the very least, to be certain that patients are not harmed by such measures.

Some defensive practices are rooted in the best conservative traditions of medicine and are not necessarily overreactions to the fear of litigation. The fundamental rule, *first do no harm,* is quintessentially defensive. It originates in the basic ethical principle of beneficence that expresses deep concern for the patient's welfare (8). For example, appropriate consultation represents good clinical practice when determined by the clinical needs of the patient while only secondarily providing a shield from litigation. In comparison, the *unduly* defensive psychiatrist tends to put his or her own litigation worries first in the course of attending the patient (9).

What are some of the more common examples of inappropriate defensive practices in psychiatry?

Electroconvulsive therapy (ECT) may be withheld for treatment of severe psychotic or refractory depression by an unwarranted fear of a lawsuit. Thus, because of the high morbidity and mortality rates associated with severe depression, the patient may be deprived of a lifesaving treatment by an unwarranted fear of suit. In fact, the number of lawsuits involving ECT is quite low (10). In the American Psychiatric Association Professional Liability Program, psychiatrists who use ECT do not pay higher insurance premiums.

Minor tranquilizers may be prescribed when it is obvious that a patient needs a neuroleptic, such as in agitated, psychotic elderly patients. Ayd (11) speaks of undertreatment by physicians who practice defensive medicine in prescribing homeopathic doses of medication, hoping to help but trying to do no harm. Such prescribing practices deny patients access to effective and safe treatment modalities. While not only prolonging the patient's suffering and disability, prescribing of homeopathic doses frequently exposes patients to the risks but not the benefits of the prescribed drug. Paradoxically, the chances of being sued for negligent treatment are thereby increased.

What can the clinician do to minimize inappropriate defensive practices?

The psychiatrist is a physician, not a litigant. The psychiatrist's primary concern must always be the welfare of the patient. Whenever possible, the clinician should attempt to turn legal requirements to the patient's therapeutic advantage. This is not to imply that laws should be violated if doing so might benefit the patient. In order to turn legal requirements to clinical account, the clinician should have a clear working knowledge of the relevant legal requirements governing professional practice. For instance, some courts have considered what is not documented as not being done. Even this tiny bit of legal knowledge can go a long way toward easing the anxieties of therapists who fear being second-guessed by plaintiffs' expert witnesses in a court of law. Yet, it is truly astounding how often mental health professionals fail to keep minimally acceptable records.

The clinician should discharge legal requirements in a clinically supportive manner. For example, when the patient is to be informed about the risks of tardive dyskinesia before receiving neuroleptic medication, the clinician should disclose the necessary information in such a way as to enhance the therapeutic alliance with the patient. When confidentiality must be breached because of an emergency (12) or a court order (13), or in the course of civil litigation (14), the therapist must deal with the treatment consequences of the breach with the patient. Treatment disclosures made by the psychiatrist in court may be especially psychologically injurious to an unprepared and unsuspecting patient (15). The psychiatrist should have a full and open discussion with a patient concerning the content of the psychiatrist's testimony. Distracting anxiety may arise when legal issues complicate patient treatment and interfere with the clinician's ability to provide good clinical care.

Similarly, warning or protecting endangered third persons should be done out of a professional and moral concern for the patient and the intended victim, not only from a legal concern about being sued for breach of confidentiality. The traditional rule of tort law that a person has no duty to come to the aid of another in distress, to which *Tarasoff* and its progeny are distinct exceptions, probably is an unacceptable position for most psychiatrists and psychotherapists. The therapist does not act in these situations because of an obligation to meet the law's requirements. Long before *Tarasoff*, therapists protected others who were endangered by their patients, and sought involuntary treatment for violent patients when all else failed. And long before confidentiality statutes were enacted, most practitioners maintained and still maintain a level of confidentiality that far exceeds any current statutory requirements.

The fear of malpractice, to the extent that it leads to inappropriate defensive practices, may itself create paradoxical legal liability consequences. The unduly defensive psychiatrist is unaware of a fundamental truth: that in addition to an ethical (moral) and professional duty, psychiatrists possess an affirmative legal duty to provide a reasonable standard of care for their patients (16). This is the psychiatrist's duty alone and cannot be abrogated or delegated to others. The law and lawyers cannot treat patients. Gutheil and Mills (17) provide instances of court-mandated treatments that are ludicrous.

Two polarized unduly defensive reactions tend to be seen in response to an exaggerated fear of malpractice suits: *1)* counterphobic attitudes, or *2)* passive compliance. Counterphobic fears of malpractice expressed by a "damn the torpedoes" or "the devil with the law" approach may lead to an insensitivity to patients' rights and prerogatives. These approaches also can invite lawsuits. An example of this attitude occurs when a physician overrides a competent patient's objections to taking psychotropic medication despite the presence of informed-consent requirements that exist in every state. On the other hand, the passive, overcompliant practitioner adheres compulsively to legal rituals and formalisms, distracted from the care of the patient by the vain hope of securing safety from malpractice claims. This practitioner may feel compelled to make a declaration to all new patients about his or her duty to warn any endangered persons of threats made against them that arise in the course of the patient's treatment.

Ultimately, the psychiatrist must recognize that the risk of being sued is an inevitable consequence of practicing medicine. The clinician should concentrate on providing good clinical care to patients while also obtaining good liability insurance.

Despite adequate liability insurance, why do many psychiatrists and other physicians so fear malpractice suits?

There is more than a kernel of truth to the defensive practitioner's fears of a lawsuit when one realizes that even a frivolous claim can destroy a psychiatrist's practice, profession, and even his or her personal life (18). The psychological and physical stress of seemingly endless interrogatories, depositions, conferences, and consultations with attorneys can be extremely wearing, leaving little time for family life or anything else for that matter. Other burdensome worries that beset the practitioner include the threat to one's reputation, the time away from practice, the distracting effect of litigation on one's ability to listen to patients, and the fear that the policy limits of liability coverage may be exceeded or that the liability insurance may not cover the claim.

Charles et al. (18) assessed the impact of malpractice litigation on physicians' personal and professional lives by randomly sampling the Chicago Medical Society membership. After evaluating the responses of physicians who had and had not been sued, they found changes in the professional, emotional, and behavioral reactions of both groups to the threat and actuality of litigation. Physicians who were sued reported that they were significantly more likely to stop seeing certain types of patients, would consider early retirement, and would discourage their children from undertaking a medical career.

In the powerful book *Defendant* (19), Drs. Sara Charles and Eugene Kennedy describe the ordeal of four years of malpractice litigation that culminated in a trial. Psychiatrists who read this book will understand why their colleagues are so concerned about becoming enmeshed in malpractice litigation.

What areas of patient care are likely to evoke defensive attitudes and behavior?

Nearly all areas of psychiatric practice present an opportunity for legal liability. One major area of defensive concern is the management and treatment of the dangerous patient. Any therapist who has lost a patient through suicide knows that it can be a personally devastating experience. Guilt, sorrow, anger, self-recrimination, deflation of professional confidence, and a resolve never again to treat a suicidal patient are common reactions. A malpractice suit may follow even though the psychiatrist is not at fault (20, 21). This seems like cruel and unusual punishment to many psychiatrists, leading some of them to refuse to treat patients who manifest the slightest hint of suicidal ideation or behavior.

This situation applies equally to therapists treating patients who threaten others. In jurisdictions where a duty to warn or to protect endangered third parties exists, psychiatrists may refuse to treat these patients if they can be identified ahead of time, or perhaps give *Miranda*-type warnings concerning therapists' duty to disclose. Unfortunately, such defensive practices may vitiate the therapeutic relationship before it gets started. Furthermore, overly defensive therapists may have such a low litigation fear tolerance that either they are unable to work with the violent fantasies of their patients or they end up prematurely warning others and destroying the relationship with the patient.

The fear of being sued for medical certification of patients is also another defensive practice concern. The standards for involuntary hospitalization have undergone considerable change, with a resulting increase in the protection of the civil liberties of patients. Patients are required to be hospitalized according to the least-restrictive alternative. Because of the law's emphasis on the dangerousness criterion, many psychiatrists feel unduly pessimistic about being able to hospitalize their patients involuntarily, or fear being sued for wrongful commitment and false imprisonment if they do (22). Consequently, patients in need of involuntary hospitalization and treatment and who meet the substantive standards for involuntary hospitalization may remain inadequately treated because of undue fears of legal entanglement with the patient. As Halleck (20) points out, a malpractice suit for involuntarily hospitalizing a patient is extremely unlikely if an adequate examination is performed, the letter of the law is followed, and the procedure is free from malice.

Lebensohn (23), in his insightful paper "Defensive Psychiatry, or How to Treat the Mentally Ill Without Being a Lawyer," emphasizes that psychiatrists do intuitively apply a least-restrictive analysis to their interventions with patients. This is largely true except for unduly defensive psychiatrists, who hospitalize dangerous patients for excessive periods of time. Thus the suicidal patient may be hospitalized too long, engendering feelings of hopelessness that in fact may encourage suicide. The least-restrictive alternative is generally misunderstood and misapplied in psychiatric practice. This subject is examined further in Chapter 15.

Can psychiatrists legally prescribe medication for unapproved uses?

Prescribing an approved medication for an unapproved use does not violate federal law (24). "Off label" prescription of medications is at the discretion of the physician once a drug has been approved. The psychiatrist is not restricted by indications and labeling approved by the Food and Drug Administration (FDA). Restrictions apply only to the manufacturer's representations in advertising. The FDA in 1961 established regulations to provide a package insert for all prescription drugs (25). All drugs must contain adequate information concerning use, dosages, method of administration, frequency, duration, relevant risks, contraindications, side effects, and precautions in prescribing the drug. The FDA evaluates only the use that the drug company wants to place in the insert, thus not precluding other specific uses not included in the insert. Failure to describe a particular use may mean only that the FDA has not been requested to review those data. Usually this is because the pharmaceutical company does not believe a market exists for a specific use, thus not justifying a need to prove its effectiveness to the FDA. The FDA abides by the principle that good medical practice requires a physician to prescribe medication according to the best information available. However, the physician who deviates from the package insert may have to explain such a departure should a lawsuit arise.

Few psychiatrists appreciate the treatment latitude they possess in regard to the PDR (26) and the drug insert, but rather perceive FDA guidelines as absolutely authoritative (4). Could this be a symptom of defensive psychiatry? A psychiatrist may prescribe a drug for a use that is not yet approved by the FDA. For example, no drug is presently approved by the FDA for the treatment of aggression (27). Yet a number of drugs, including neuroleptics, benzo-diazepines, beta blockers, and anticonvulsants, and lithium are used effectively to treat violence. Furthermore, the use of anticonvulsants and calcium channel blockers are not approved by the FDA for the treatment of mood disorders (28). However, the psychiatric literature and clinical experience validate the useful-ness of these drugs in the clinical management of violent and mood-disordered patients, respectively.

As recommended in the clinical vignette, a tricyclic-MAOI combination may be prescribed for refractory depression. The decision to prescribe for nonap-proved uses should be based on sound knowledge of the drugs backed by firm scientific rationale and sound medical studies. The psychiatrist should have texts or journal articles to substantiate the fact that the decision to prescribe for a nonapproved use was based on the sound practice of psychiatry. For example, alprazolam was recently approved by the FDA for the treatment of panic disor-der (29). Nevertheless, psychiatrists have used this drug safely and effectively in the treatment of this condition for years based on scientific studies in the psychiatric literature.

The standard for obtaining informed consent is correspondingly heightened when a medication is prescribed for an unapproved use. The patient or guardian must be informed that he or she will be taking a drug for use that has not been approved by the FDA and should be warned of all possible, reasonably foresee-able risks. Although a consent form may provide added protection, the nature of the disclosure should be recorded in the patient's chart. Whether the disclosure is given orally or provided in a consent form, the chart notes should also contain an assessment indicating whether the information was understood by the pa-tient, that consent was freely given, and the rationale for using a medication for unapproved purposes. This procedure should also be followed when prescribing at higher than recommended doses.

In the clinical vignette, Dr. Kane's fears of being sued prevented him from exercising professional discretion that varied from recommended guidelines. The FDA does not have the power to control psychiatrists or dictate the practice of psychiatry, particularly when it comes to prescribing drugs. The use of a drug, once marketed, is the responsibility of physicians, and the drug is pre-scribed at their sole discretion.

Can psychiatrists legally prescribe unapproved drugs?

The prescription of an unapproved drug technically violates the law. Under 21 U.S.C. § 355, to "introduce or deliver for introduction into interstate com-merce" an unapproved drug is a violation of the law (24). A classic example arose with clomipramine in the treatment of obsessive-compulsive disorder. Prior to its approval in the United States in February 1990, clomipramine was approved for use in the treatment of obsessive-compulsive disorder only in Canada and some other countries. The psychiatric literature in this country and other countries supported the treatment of obsessive-compulsive disorder with clomipramine. No untoward consequences were expected because the side-effect profile was similar to those of other tricyclic antidepressants. Patients had to go to Canada to obtain clomipramine or receive it from the pharmaceutical company under an official humanitarian protocol.

Generally, it is the policy of the FDA not to prosecute physicians who prescribe legitimate drugs approved in other jurisdictions (24). However, the risk of malpractice is increased should the patient be harmed by a drug not approved by the FDA as safe and effective.

What is the medicolegal significance of the PDR or drug insert?

The PDR is published privately by a commercial firm (26). The publisher compiles, organizes, and distributes product descriptions prepared by the manufacturers' medical departments or consultants. The FDA requires that products having official package inserts must be reported in the PDR in the identical language appearing on the circular. For products without official package inserts, the publisher emphasizes to manufacturers the necessity of comprehensive reporting of all information necessary for informed prescribing. However, FDA conclusions regarding the safety of a drug as described in the PDR and in the drug insert are not binding on psychiatrists and represent only one element of rebuttable evidence that may be presented in a malpractice action (30).

Typically, manufacturers' drug inserts, the PDR, and other recognized treatises or authorities will be presented by one of the litigants as establishing that the standard of care was or was not breached. Cases in which the PDR or a drug insert is offered as evidence of a breach of the standard of care have had mixed results. For example, in *Callan v. Nordland* (31), an elderly woman was being treated with Azulfidine (sulfasalazine) for intestinal colitis. After developing various side affects from the medication, the defendant prescribed neomycin sulfate as a substitute. The subsequent prescription was filled at the pharmacy with Mycifradin, the generic equivalent of neomycin sulfate. Approximately 14 months after neomycin sulfate was substituted, the plaintiff began to experience a loss of hearing. The lawsuit alleged that the defendant was negligent in prescribing neomycin sulfate for a prolonged period as a treatment for colitis and offered as evidence the PDR's warning that Mycifradin may cause deafness. The court allowed the PDR reference into evidence, and the plaintiff was eventually awarded $250,000. The use of the PDR as evidence and the jury award were affirmed on appeal.

In *Ramon v. Farr* (32), a slightly different result occurred. A malpractice action alleged birth defects from the injection of Marcaine (bupivacaine) 1 hour before a child's birth. The fact that the PDR and the manufacturer's package insert indicated that the use of Marcaine as a paracervical block was not recommended without further research was used as evidence to support the plaintiff's claims. The court rejected the plaintiff's contention that this information constituted *prima facie* evidence of the defendant's negligence. Instead, the court ruled that this information did not establish the standard of care but was to be considered by the court as additional evidence, along with the expert testimony, to be weighed in determining whether there had been a breach in the duty of care.

It is in the best interests of drug companies to protect themselves by disclosing all potential risks associated with a particular drug. Thus, with the manufacturer's having disclosed all known information, the manufacturer's insert tends to shift responsibility to the physician who prescribes the medication. This shifting of responsibility is known as the "learned intermediary" defense. This defense states that physicians, not drug companies, are responsible for warning patients about a drug's possible side effects (33). Generally, courts have ruled that it is virtually impossible for a manufacturer to comply with the duty to directly warn a patient because it is difficult for the manufacturer to directly reach the patient. This defense, however, has been successfully challenged in some jurisdictions (34, 35).

Another problem associated with manufacturers' brochures is that they may be outdated, having been written before all known indications and risks were discovered. Furthermore, the psychiatrist should know that the package insert lists almost all the side effects ever reported in drug trials, even ones not produced by the drug (36). That is, side effects found in similar drugs also are reported. Moreover, the side effects of many drugs reported in the package insert are not weighted for probability of occurrence in the course of clinical practice. Patients who wish to read the PDR or rely on package insert information should be so informed. Finally, the dosage requirements may be antiquated because pharmaceutical companies may no longer hold patents on a particular medication. They may be unwilling to embark on additional research to further establish the drug's safety and efficacy at higher dosage levels. For example, although imipramine is commonly prescribed to inpatients and outpatients at 300 mg per day, the package insert continues to state that outpatients should not be prescribed more than 225 mg per day (37).

The FDA does not consider its regulations to be legal documents, admissible as establishing the breach of the standard of care (25). Rather, although the guidelines are to be considered relatively authoritative and indicative of a standard of care, physicians are free to prescribe according to their best knowledge and judgment. The legal significance of the package insert or PDR, therefore, can vary with each medication, the facts of a given case, and the jurisdiction in which a physician resides. Courts are typically willing to declare that a departure from a manufacturer's use or dosage recommendations establishes a *prima facie* case of negligence rebuttable by the physician (24). A *prima facie* case exists when the evidence in the case is "such as will prevail until contradicted and overcome by other evidence" (38). Thus, in *Mulder v. Parke Davis & Co.* (39), the Minnesota Supreme Court stated that deviations from drug manufacturer recommendations for use, precautions, and dangers represented *prima facie* evidence of negligence. In addition, the court stated that the physician must disclose his or her reasons for such a deviation, leaving the issue to be settled by the trier of fact.

Although the PDR is frequently used by attorneys in court, it would be a professional error for treating psychiatrists to regard the PDR as establishing the standard of care and as a constraint upon their clinical judgment. Psychiatrists are solely responsible for making informed decisions, taking into account their own clinical training, experience, and judgment as well as the relevant professional literature. They also must be prepared to justify their decisions based on professional standards. Because the PDR is not a textbook of psychiatry, patient care may be compromised if clinicians see the PDR as their primary source of professional guidance. Furthermore, the FDA and the American Medical Association have taken the position that prescription for nonapproved indications or at higher than recommended doses should be based upon a physician's discretion (40).

In the clinical vignette, Dr. Kane certainly could consider prescribing the tricyclic-MAOI combination because the expert consultation, the psychiatric literature, and the approval for such use in Europe clearly indicated a sound, scientific basis for such a treatment in properly selected patients (41). If his patient had been injured by this combination treatment, a *prima facie* case against Dr. Kane could have been rebutted on the basis that he sought a competent consultation and investigated the relevant scientific literature, which in this case supported such a treatment intervention for the patient's severe, refractory depression.

The point here is not to promote combined tricyclic-MAOI therapy for refractory depression. This treatment also might have been ineffective. The issue presented is that Dr. Kane placed himself in a therapeutic straitjacket as a result of unwarranted malpractice fears. By avoiding a potentially promising intervention out of a fear of malpractice, Dr. Kane continued to provide treatment that was ineffective, thus subjecting his patient to long-term hospitalization, heavy financial costs, and the possibility of chronicity. The irony of such a defensive approach is that it may itself induce legal claims of substandard care and injury to the patient. Unduly defensive practices may backfire, laying the groundwork for legal liability. The best strategy remains the full exercise of the psychiatrist's professional discretion to provide the best possible care to one's patient. Intimidated psychiatrists provide weak and ineffective treatment (23). Although such treatment may conform to the letter of the law, it frequently avoids or underutilizes risky, though proven, therapeutic methods that could shorten illness and relieve needless suffering.

References

1. Hallagan JB, Hallagan LF, Hirsh HL: Second opinions: physician's friend or foe? Legal Aspects of Medical Practice 12:1, 1984
2. See, e.g., Casewell v Secretary of Health and Human Services, No 77-0488-CV 8 (WD Mo Feb 8, 1983); O'Connor v Donaldson, 422 U.S. 563 (1975); Wyatt v Stickney, 325 F Supp 781 (M D Ala 1971), aff'd in part and remanded in part, 503 F2d 1305 (5th Cir 1974)
3. Rappeport JR: Editorial: "Belegaled." Bull Am Acad Psychiatry Law 5(1):iv–vii, 1977
4. Simon RI: Coping strategies for the defensive psychiatrist. International Journal of Medicine and Law 4:551–561, 1985
5. Kalman TP: I'm through practicing like a coward. Medical Economics 64(3):52–55, 1987
6. Harris JE: Defensive medicine: it costs, but does it work? JAMA 257:2801–2802, 1987
7. Meyerson AT: Countertransference and recent changes in the law. Journal of Psychiatry and Law 6:371–376, 1978
8. Luce JM: Ethical principles in critical care. JAMA 263:696–700, 1990
9. Simon RI: Clinical philosophy for the (unduly) defensive psychiatrists. Psychiatric Annals 17:197–200, 1987
10. Simon RI: Ethical and legal issues in neuropsychiatry, in American Psychiatric Press Textbook of Neuropsychiatry, 2nd Edition. Edited by Hales RE, Yudosky SC. Washington, DC, American Psychiatric Press, 1992, pp 773–805
11. Ayd FJ Jr: Prescribing mistakes which invite lawsuits. Psychiatric Times 3(1):6, 10, 1986
12. See, e.g., Tarasoff v Regents of University of California, 17 Cal 3d 425, 131 Cal Rptr 14, 551 P2d 334 (1976)
13. See, e.g., Anderson v Glismann, 577 F Supp 1506 (D Colo 1984)
14. See, e.g., In re Lifschutz, 2 Cal 3d 415, 85 Cal Rptr 467, P2d 557, 829 (1970)
15. Strasburger LH: "Crudely, without any finesse": the defendant hears his psychiatric evaluation. Bull Am Acad Psychiatry Law 15:229–233, 1987
16. Simon RI: Psychiatric Interventions and Malpractice: A Primer for Liability Prevention. Springfield, IL, Charles C Thomas, 1982, p 6
17. Gutheil TG, Mills MJ: Conceptualizations, legal fictions and the manipulation of reality. Bull Am Acad Psychiatry Law 10:17–28, 1982
18. Charles SC, Wilbert JR, Franke KJ: Sued and nonsued physicians' self-reported reactions to malpractice litigation. Am J Psychiatry 142:437–440, 1985
19. Charles SC, Kennedy E: Defendant. New York, Free Press, 1985
20. Halleck SL: Law in the Practice of Psychiatry. New York, Plenum, 1980
21. See, e.g., Paddock v Chacko, No 84-7298, (Orange Cty Dist Ct Fla 1986), rev'd 522 So 2d 410 (Fla App 1988), review denied, 553 So 2d 168 (Fla 1989); Rudy v Meshorer, 146 Ariz 467, 706 P2d 1234 (1985)
22. See, e.g., Taylor v Herst, 537 A2d 1163 (Me 1988); Carter v Landy, 163 Ga App 509, 295 SE2d 177 (1982)
23. Lebensohn ZM: Defensive psychiatry, or how to treat the mentally ill without being a lawyer, in Law and the Mental Health Professions. Edited by Barton WE, Sanborn CJ. New York, International Universities Press, 1978, pp 19–46

24. American Psychiatric Association Legal Consultation Plan Newsletter, August 1984, p 1
25. Hirsh HL: The medicolegal significance of the package insert. J Fam Pract 4:1141–1143, 1977
26. Physicians' Desk Reference, 46th Edition. Montvale, NJ, Medical Economics Company, 1992
27. Managing aggression in elderly patients. APA 90 Clinical Perspectives, 3(5):9–10, 1990
28. Schatzberg AF, Cole JO: Manual of Clinical Psychopharmacology, 2nd Edition. Washington, DC, American Psychiatric Press, 1991, pp 166–169
29. Alprazolam first drug to receive FDA approval for treatment of panic disorder. Psychiatric News 26(1):12, 1991
30. Food and Drug Administration: Clinical testing for safe and effective drugs: investigational drug procedures (DHEW Publ No DA-74-3015). Rockville, MD, Food and Drug Administration, 1974
31. 114 Ill App 3d 196, 448 NE2d 651 (1987)
32. 770 P2d 131 (Utah 1989)
33. See, e.g., Reyes v Wyeth Laboratories, 498 F2d 1264 (5th Cir), cert denied, 419 U.S. 1096 (1974); Percival v American Cyanamid Co, 689 F Supp 1060 (D Okla 1987)
34. Kirk v Michael Reese Hosp & Medical Center, 136 Ill App 3d 945, 483 NE2d 906 (1985), rev'd on other grounds, 117 Ill 2d 507, 513 NE2d 387 (1987), cert denied, 485 U.S. 905
35. Brushwood DB, Simonsmeier LM: Drug information for patients: duties of the manufacturer, pharmacist, physician and hospital. J Leg Med 7:279–340, 1986
36. Schatzberg AF, Cole JO: Manual of Clinical Psychopharmacology, 2nd Edition. Washington, DC, American Psychiatric Press, 1991, p 5
37. Schatzberg AF, Cole JO: Manual of Clinical Psychopharmacology, 2nd Edition. Washington, DC, American Psychiatric Press, 1991, pp 7–8
38. Black HC: Black's Law Dictionary, 6th Edition. St Paul, MN, West Publishing, 1990, p 1189
39. 288 Minn 332, 181 NW2d 882 (1970)
40. Archer JD: The FDA does not approve uses of drugs (editorial). JAMA 252:1054–1055, 1984
41. Feighner JP, Herbstein J, Damlouji N: Combined MAOI, TCA, and direct stimulant therapy of treatment-resistant depression. J Clin Psychiatry 46:206–209, 1985

Chapter 4

Confidentiality in Clinical Practice

Mr. Davidson, a 29-year-old married car dealer, has been in twice-a-week individual psychotherapy with Dr. West for the past 2 years. He is being treated for recurrent symptoms of anxiety and depression. Prior to coming into treatment, the patient was addicted to heroin. He also was involved in selling drugs on a large scale. As a young child, he was severely physically abused by his father, who died in a car accident when Mr. Davidson was 6 years old. Three years prior to entering treatment, Mr. Davidson developed hepatitis and was hospitalized. At that time, his heroin addiction was discovered. After recovering from the hepatitis, he entered a drug rehabilitation program, gave up drugs, and changed his life-style. He completed college, receiving a degree in business administration. He married shortly thereafter and started a very successful automobile dealership. After the birth of his son, Mr. Davidson noticed a marked intensification of symptoms of anxiety and depression that he had not experienced for many years.

During the second year of therapy, Mr. Davidson reveals that 7 years ago, he killed a competing drug dealer who was trying to take over his territory. Another individual was found guilty for the murder and given life imprisonment without the possibility of parole. This information surfaces in the therapy only after Dr. West, responding to her patient's concerns about confidentiality, reassures her patient repeatedly that everything said in the therapy is strictly confidential and that no records are kept.

After hearing about the murder, the false arrest, and conviction of another man, Dr. West understands more clearly the origins of some of her patient's symptoms. Moreover, she does not feel that she has a duty to report past criminal acts or correct the errors of the judicial system. Dr. West feels comfortable maintaining a strict treatment position toward Mr. Davidson while trying to help him come to his own decision about an appropriate course of action. Dr. West believes the fact that Mr. Davidson discussed the murder and the arrest of an innocent person is a very positive therapeutic development. Much of the treatment from this point on centers on the patient's thoughts and feelings about the murder, the falsely imprisoned man, and the connections between his relationship with his father and his father's death.

As more specific information emerges about the murder, Dr. West finds it more difficult to deal with the crime strictly as a treatment matter. The murder was very sadistic. She checks old newspaper accounts and compares them with the details revealed by her patient. She becomes convinced that such knowledge of a crime could be possessed only by someone who had committed it. Dr. West becomes concerned about her duty to the falsely imprisoned man. Will she be considered an accessory after the fact by withholding information? Dr. West experiences internal pressure to accelerate the treatment process.

Mr. Davidson is involved in an automobile accident in which he is struck from behind by another vehicle. He receives a severe whiplash injury and a moderate concussion that significantly interfere with his normal living. He becomes depressed. He sues, alleging physical and emotional injuries with loss of income because of his work restrictions. The attorney for the defendant discovers Mr. Davidson's psychotherapy from written interrogatories. Dr. West receives a subpoena from the defendant to appear in court with her patient's records. Dr. West wonders with her patient if guilt is impelling him to become a litigant, thereby exposing his secret in a court of law. Mr. Davidson becomes alarmed and, on advice from his attorney, refuses to sign a consent for release of information. Dr. West engages her own attorney. Mr. Davidson's attorney files a motion to quash the subpoena. The court dismisses this motion. Dr. West prepares for the trial.

What is the difference between confidentiality and privilege?

Confidentiality refers to the ethical duty of the psychiatrist not to disclose information obtained in the course of evaluating or treating the patient to any other individual or party without the express permission of the patient. Confidentiality exists because of the physician-patient relationship. The duty of confidentiality also protects against unauthorized disclosure of information. If statutory regulation or public policy is violated, a legal action may result. Moreover, if information is negligently disclosed that directly damages the patient, a lawsuit for professional negligence may be brought.

In the law, the term *privilege* is confusing because it may have two entirely different meanings, depending on the legal context. Privilege usually refers to testimonial privilege. Statutorily, testimonial privilege provides that a physician, with certain exceptions and lacking the consent of the patient, cannot be examined in certain legal proceedings about confidential information obtained during treatment. Testimonial privilege belongs to the patient, not to the physician or therapist. It stems out of the *privata lex,* meaning a special favor for an individual or group (1). In the vignette, Mr. Davidson attempts to assert testimonial privilege by refusing to consent to a subpoena of his psychiatric records.

The other meaning of privilege is the privilege to disclose, referring to a statement or disclosure that the law has chosen to shield from liability that would otherwise be actionable (2). When used in this fashion, the term refers to the *exceptions* to testimonial privilege. In this book, privilege refers to testimonial privilege and is so specified. When quoting legal commentators who use privilege to mean an exception to confidentiality, the dichotomous use of the term privilege unavoidably appears.

What are the ethical and legal obligations of psychiatrists to maintain patient confidentiality?

Physicians have had an ethical duty to maintain the confidentiality of their patients since the time of Hippocrates. The Hippocratic oath states:

> Whatsoever things I shall see or hear concerning the life of men, in my attendance on the sick or even apart therefrom, which ought not to be raised abroad, I will keep silence thereon, counting such things to be as holy secrets. (3)

The Principles of Medical Ethics With Annotations Especially Applicable to Psychiatry (4) states: "Confidentiality is essential to psychiatric treatment. This is based in part on the special nature of psychiatric therapy as well as on the traditional ethical relationship between physician and patient" (Section 4, Annotation 1).

The American Psychiatric Association (APA), in its "Position Statement on Confidentiality" (5), sets forth some examples in which common sense and good judgment, after careful evaluation of the patient and the issues, could lead to a decision to break patient confidentiality. The situations presented include: *1)* a patient will probably commit murder and the act can be stopped only by the psychiatrist's intervention; *2)* a patient will probably commit suicide and the act can be stopped only by the psychiatrist's intervention; and *3)* a patient who is charged with serious responsibilities, such as an airline pilot or bus driver, shows marked impairment of judgment.

Aside from statutory disclosure requirements and judicial compulsion, no legal obligation exists to provide information, even to law enforcement officials (6). In *State v. Miller* (7), the Oregon Supreme Court held that the ethical obligation of a psychotherapist rarely justifies disclosure of a patient's confidence to police and "never justifies" a full disclosure in open court. In this case, Jerry Lee Miller, by phone, told a receptionist at Dammasch State Hospital that his problem was "murder." The receptionist called the local sheriff's department and the psychiatrist on duty, who spoke with Miller for about 15 minutes. The police traced the call and arrested Miller. The Supreme Court did not allow into evidence some of the preliminary, incriminating statements made by Miller to the receptionist and the psychiatrist.

The psychiatrist has an ethical obligation to maintain confidentiality. Confidentiality is an ethical issue until it is breached. A breach of this ethical obligation may result in a legal action based on the following theories: breach of implied contract, breach of a fiduciary duty, invasion of right to privacy, and malpractice (8).

Under an implied contract theory to maintain confidentiality, courts have found a cause of legal action in the implied contractual relationship between doctor and patient to maintain confidential information gained from the patient. In *Doe v. Roe* (9), monetary damages were awarded to a patient when a book was written about the patient's treatment by her psychiatrist. Written on the patient's oral consent, the book revealed intimate fantasies, feelings, and memories. The patient's anonymity was maintained. The court stated that when providing medical treatment, a physician impliedly covenants to keep in confidence all disclosures made by the patient about physical and mental matters as well as the findings discovered in the course of the examination, particularly in the course of psychiatric treatment.

In *Horne v. Patton* (10), a physician, ignoring the clear instructions of the patient, released confidential information that resulted in the patient's losing his job. The court held that the physician was liable on an implied covenant of confidentiality, based on public knowledge that physicians have a professional obligation to maintain confidentiality. Also, the court recognized that unauthorized release of medical information constitutes an invasion of privacy.

In *MacDonald v. Clinger* (11), the court found that a fiduciary duty beyond a mere contract existed to maintain confidentiality. The patient claimed that the psychiatrist had revealed intimate information to the patient's wife that led to a deterioration in his condition, marriage, and employment. Under a fiduciary duty of confidentiality theory, the breach-of-contract limitation of damages for economic losses resulting directly from the breach was circumvented to permit recovery for psychic trauma secondary to the deterioration of his marriage and loss of employment.

The *MacDonald* court defined invasion of privacy as an unwarranted disclosure of the patient's private affairs to the public that has no legitimate interest in receiving such information and that causes the patient mental distress and humiliation. When this theory is applied, public disclosure of confidential information is required, rather than disclosure to a small group or to an individual (12).

In *Alberts v. Devine* (13), a Methodist minister under psychiatric treatment claimed that the psychiatrist, without authorization, responded to questions from the minister's superiors about his mental condition. The minister also alleged that the superiors informed other church officials and otherwise publicized their opinions about the minister's mental condition. The Supreme Judicial Court of Massachusetts ruled that the patient was entitled to a civil remedy against a physician who made an out-of-court disclosure of confidential information arising from the physician-patient relationship. The court supported its conclusion by noting that the traditional rules of ethics within the medical profession protect confidentiality. The court added that public policy concerns found in state evidence and licensing statutes protect the patient's right to confidentiality. The court also held that the patient could sue the third party who intentionally induced the psychiatrist to breach confidentiality.

Liability may occur when confidentiality statutes are violated. Statutes in a number of states contain rules for the maintenance of confidentiality (14). Confidentiality statutes also define procedures for disclosure, including the confidentiality rights of minors and parents. A number of jurisdictions permit direct access by patients to their records for the purposes of inspection or copying. Some states permit indirect access by the patient's attorney, physician, or next of kin, but not by the patient. Therapeutic privilege to withhold information usually exists when the doctor can establish that the information would be detrimental to the patient. Many statutes provide an exception to the release of mental health records to protect patients from being psychologically traumatized by the reading of their own mental health records (15).

Confidentiality statutes usually spell out provisions for penalties and potential liability for their violation. If such statutes exist, psychiatrists should become familiar with the rules governing confidentiality and disclosure. For example, the Illinois Mental Health and Developmental Disabilities Confidentiality Act (16) provides for disclosure, with the patient's consent, to a superior, a treatment team member, a record custodian, or a peer review member. Attorneys or patient advocates consulted by a therapist may have access to records as well (14).

In addition to the comprehensive mental health information statutes, state statutes that are essentially privilege statutes proscribe extrajudicial disclosures except under certain circumstances. These statutes do not specify patient remedies or physician penalties for improper disclosures (2). State licensing and certification statutes may incorporate a code of ethics of professional organizations governing the maintenance of patient confidentiality (17). Courts may rely on public policy requirements for the maintenance of confidentiality based on state licensing laws, professional ethical standards, and the Hippocratic oath (11).

In *Shaw v. Glickman* (18), the court stated that warning an endangered third party would have violated the physician-patient privilege statute that permits disclosures only in judicial proceedings. Most courts, however, have taken the position that privilege statutes are applicable only to judicial proceedings and that licensing statutes are strictly administrative and do not provide a legal basis for a lawsuit. To the extent that these statutes set forth public policy, support is present for litigation based on unauthorized disclosure (14).

How is testimonial privilege defined? What is the scope of this privilege?

Every state has enacted a physician-patient or psychotherapist-patient privilege statute. Privileged information usually includes not only the patient's direct communications but information gained through examination, treatment, and the physician's diagnosis and conclusions (19).

For the treating psychiatrist, the law on testimonial privilege applies to both criminal and civil proceedings unless the statute creating the privilege limits its application. For instance, criminal prosecutions and worker's compensation proceedings frequently are excluded from privilege. Many of the medical privilege statutes are inapplicable to a homicide prosecution when disclosure relates directly to the fact of the homicide or its immediate circumstances (6). Furthermore, privilege covers only the content of communications, not the existence of a treatment relationship. Under a discovery demand, the identity of the treating psychiatrist can be revealed.

The physician-patient privilege protects the privacy of the doctor-patient relationship. Privilege prevents a physician from being compelled to testify about confidential communications unless consent is obtained from the patient. Privilege is established by statute, underscoring the principle that freedom of communication between physician and patient is sufficiently important to be free from forced disclosure. No physician-patient privilege is recognized in common law. There is no federal privilege statute. Civil actions and proceedings in federal courts are governed by the state law on privilege (20).

In *Doe v. United States* (21), the United States Court of Appeals for the Ninth Circuit ruled that the psychotherapist-patient privilege does not extend to federal court criminal proceedings. The court held that federal law, which is based upon the common law, does not recognize either a psychotherapist-patient privilege or a physician-patient privilege in criminal cases. The justices stated, "If such a privilege is to be recognized in federal criminal proceedings, it is up to Congress to define it, not this court." Thus, the psychiatrist of a patient involved in a federal criminal case can be subpoenaed and ordered to testify before a grand jury or at trial.

In *Doe,* the mother claimed that her baby died of sudden infant death syndrome. The FBI and a federal grand jury were investigating the possibility of murder. The mother had received psychiatric treatment since the death of her baby. A motion to quash a subpoena for her psychiatric records was denied.

In *People v. Wharton* (22), currently pending before the California Supreme Court, a treating psychologist and psychiatrist testified as prosecution witnesses against their patient in a death penalty trial, despite vigorous defense objections. The patient had physically abused and threatened to kill a female companion. A *Tarasoff* warning was issued to the female companion, who made no effort to protect herself. She was killed by the patient shortly thereafter.

The legal issue in this case involves the applicability of the therapist-patient privilege statute. In particular, does issuing a *Tarasoff* warning waive psychotherapist-patient privilege in a later criminal trial? If a *Tarasoff* warning is admissible at trial, how deeply can the prosecution delve into the patient's psychiatric history to gain incriminating information? If the California Supreme

Court affirms *Wharton,* psychotherapists acting as witnesses for the prosecution may set a legal trend for other states.

Privilege statutes are not uniform, but vary from state to state. Some statutes protect all communications between doctor and patient, whereas others take a narrow view of privilege that protects information only directly related to treatment of the patient. For psychiatrists, the scope of the privilege is very broad because treatment requires that the patient be able to say anything. Privilege may not exist for personal relationships, court-ordered examinations, or employment and insurance examinations.

In a number of states, privilege is considered to be "polluted" if third parties are privy to the disclosures (23). An Illinois statute, however, protects communications between family members of the patient and the psychiatrist (16). Cases have been decided in favor of privilege, as well as against, in litigation between family members (23). Because state statutes vary considerably on the issue of privilege and third parties, therapists should familiarize themselves with the rulings in their jurisdiction or consult with legal counsel. If privilege is "polluted" by the presence of third parties, the psychiatrist should inform the patient, spouse, or couple before evaluation or therapy begins, especially if a couple appears to be headed for a legal battle.

Nonphysician providers who are supervised by psychiatrists are not likely to be covered by a physician-patient privilege. For staff members who are considered the physician's agents, privilege has usually been extended (24). As a result, a secretary acting within the scope of his or her employment may be considered the psychiatrist's agent (25).

Although the requirements for privilege apply to licensed physicians and surgeons, a number of states have enacted psychotherapist-patient privilege statutes applicable only to psychiatrists and licensed psychologists (26). The psychotherapist-patient privilege is usually limited. The privilege usually applies only when a therapist-patient relationship exists. In addition, only communications of a professional nature are protected. Third persons present during the communication between the therapist and the patient may be compelled to testify (15).

A number of states have enacted separate privilege statutes for professional groups such as physicians, psychologists, social workers, and marriage counselors. Some states do not have privilege statutes covering social workers or marriage counselors. A number of these statutes are ambiguous, and the scope and availability of privilege in various contexts may be difficult to determine (17).

Shuman and Weiner (27) found that the existence of psychotherapist-patient privilege is consequential to only a small percentage of individuals who might consider therapy. Furthermore, the privilege will impact only a small percentage of judicial proceedings. The authors state that both the opponents and the proponents of psychotherapist-patient privilege overstate their cases.

When patients have requested psychiatrists to testify and they refuse, psychiatrists have been held in contempt of court and jailed briefly (26). In two separate cases, psychiatrists were held in contempt for refusing to reveal information when the privilege was waived by the patient and the patient's mental and emotional status was at issue (28, 29). The court ruled in each instance that the state statute required disclosure of information relevant to the patient's mental and emotional condition. In a Pennsylvania child custody case, however, the psychiatrist refused the judge's request for records of the patient and was vindicated by the State Supreme Court on appeal (30).

A legally competent adult may execute a valid waiver of privilege. If the patient has been adjudicated incompetent, the legal guardian possesses the right of waiver. A guardian *ad litem* may be appointed by the court *just* for legal proceedings involving a mentally incapacitated patient who has not yet been adjudicated incompetent. Parents or guardians have the right to waive for a minor child, although older adolescents defined as mature or emancipated minors may possess the right under certain circumstances.

What are the exceptions to testimonial privilege?

So many exceptions exist to privilege that it is often considered illusory. The main exceptions involve involuntary hospitalization proceedings, court-ordered examinations, criminal proceedings involving the patient, will contests, child custody disputes, child abuse proceedings, a legally required report, and the patient-litigant exception by which the patient raises his or her mental or emotional condition as an element of a claim or defense in a legal proceeding. In the clinical vignette, the court applied the patient-litigant exception when it dismissed Mr. Davidson's motion to quash the testimony of Dr. West and prevent the treatment records from being presented to the court.

In *Novak v. Rathnam* (31), the court ruled that the testimony of a therapist attempting to establish the defense of insanity at the defendant's murder trial was a waiver of the psychiatrist-patient privilege for the later civil trial for the wrongful death of the victim. Most jurisdictions have held that a waiver of the therapist-patient privilege in a prior proceeding waives privilege in a subsequent proceeding.

Some courts may protect privilege fully in child custody cases, relying instead on an independent psychiatric examination. Slovenko (23) notes other exceptions: "To obtain information required by the public interest or to avoid fraud" (p. 62), actions on insurance policies, medical reports for treatment of venereal disease, gunshot wounds, child abuse, communications made in premeditation of a future crime or fraud in criminal prosecution. To this list have been added examinations on behalf of third parties (forensic evaluations), hospital records, group therapy, investigation of the doctor, fee collection, and discovery procedures (32). Slovenko feels that other aspects of the law such as relevancy, materiality, and need more effectively protect confidentiality.

How can psychiatrists be certain that they are obtaining a valid authorization to release information?

A valid, informed authorization for the release of information protects a psychiatrist ethically and legally (33). State law and mental health confidentiality statutes generally specify the requirements for a valid authorization. Statutes may forbid release of certain information even when the patient consents, as with information supplied to third-party payers.

Consent should be obtained in written form. This creates a permanent record of the fact and the scope of the consent. Patients need to be able to make a considered judgment about the impact of their decision. Written forms do possess this advantage. A sample consent form is contained in Appendix 2.

Blanket consents should be avoided (34). Instead, consent should be given for a specific release of information. The purpose and any limitation should be specified. The form should have a place to indicate whether a one-time or continuing consent is being given. Patients also should be informed on the form that they have the right to revoke consent at any time, as well as a right to inspect and copy any information authorized for release.

The Principles of Medical Ethics (4) states: "The continuing duty of the psychiatrist to protect the patient includes fully apprising him/her of the connotations of waiving the privilege of privacy" (Section 4, Annotation 2). Psychiatrists should satisfy themselves that the patient understands the kind of information requested and the type of information in the record. Whenever possible, the patient should be allowed to see all information that will be released to others as well as the opportunity to be the final decision-maker on release. The information can be provided to the patient in an addressed envelope without a stamp. The intent is not to save money but to emphasize to patients their responsibility and consent in releasing such information. The walk to the mailbox has produced a change of heart in some patients in regard to releasing certain information. If the patient does not wish to know the content of the disclosure, the psychiatrist should assess if the request is competent and record the patient's wish in the medical record.

The APA Task Force on Confidentiality (35) states that psychiatrists are most concerned about statutory requirements of disclosure and judicial compulsion. Apart from these requirements, there is no other legal requirement to provide information. By far, the most frequent occasions for release of information are by patients themselves when they authorize disclosure by the psychiatrist for insurance, employment benefits, welfare benefits, driver's licenses, or even charge accounts (36). Often, however, psychiatrists needlessly reveal the identity of patients in correspondence involving the peer review process, even though the latter is set up to maintain patient anonymity.

The situation is entirely different when an evaluation is being performed for a third party, as in court evaluations, preemployment interviews, or disability evaluations. Unless a treatment relationship has been established between therapist and patient, a duty of confidentiality does not arise. For example, at the very beginning of the examination, the person being examined is told that the examination is being made at the request of a third party. Quite apart from legal constraints, the individual should be told at the outset that information obtained is not confidential and that the individual will not be given a report by the psychiatrist. The report will be sent directly to the interested third party. Consent is implied when the individual proceeds with the evaluation. *The Principles of Medical Ethics* (4) states:

> Psychiatrists are often asked to examine individuals for security purposes, to determine suitability for various jobs, and to determine legal competence. The psychiatrist must fully describe the nature and purpose and lack of confidentiality of the examination to the examinee at the beginning of the examination. (Section 4, Annotation 6)

The psychiatrist's duty to protect confidentiality remains even when blanket consent forms are signed. Again, according to the *Principles of Medical Ethics*:

> Ethically the psychiatrist may disclose only that information which is relevant to a given situation. He/she should avoid offering speculation as fact. Sensitive information such as an individual's sexual orientation or fantasy material is usually unnecessary. (Section 4, Annotation 5).

Do psychiatrists have a duty to maintain the confidentiality of minors?

The "law of adolescence" is evolving. Historically, the legal status of all minors from ages 7 to 17 was considered the same. Currently, the rights of a 15- to 17-year-old are not the same as those of a 7-year-old. In addition, all states allow young people to consent to treatment for venereal disease. Most states permit young people to secure birth control devices without parental notification. States are beginning to lower the age of medical consent from 18 to 14 or 15 (37).

As best can be determined, no lawsuits for civil damages or criminal charges have been brought against physicians who have beneficially treated a minor over age 15 for any condition on the consent of the minor. Because of an alarming rise in venereal disease, alcohol and drug abuse, and teenage pregnancies, "enabling laws" have been passed by states providing minors with access to medical care without parental approval.

The general rule is that confidentiality follows the legal ability to consent to treatment. Mental health confidentiality statutes usually provide a definition of who is a young minor. If a child is under age 12, the APA suggests relying on parental consent (26). With young minors, the parents or guardians are the legal decision-makers. Thus, parents have a right to know about the course of treatment as well as the diagnosis and prognosis. Obviously, revealing confidential information must be done cautiously so that damage is not done to the treatment or to the child's relationship with caregivers.

States require the reporting of child abuse, and some states require reporting the *suspicion* of child abuse. Most states, however, do not require such a report unless the professional sees both the allegedly abused child and the alleged abuser. The psychiatrist is fully protected by the reporting statute from suit for breach of confidentiality in these cases. A number of state statutes have criminal penalties for not reporting. However, prosecution for not reporting child abuse is rare. In the first appellate decision of its kind, the California Supreme Court in 1976 held a hospital and a physician liable for failure to report suspected abuse of a minor (38). A few states exempt the physician from reporting child abuse if the physician is attempting to deal with the child abuse by counseling (39).

When releasing medical records or testifying about treatment, one parent's consent is generally sufficient. If divorce or custody litigation is taking place, parents may disagree about waiver of confidentiality. The therapist should wait before releasing confidential information until the court has ruled on the validity of the waiver. In the absence of a court ruling, the therapist should consult state law requirements. In some jurisdictions, the state may require an attorney to represent the interest of the child regarding waiver of confidentiality. If a minor is too young to personally exercise the privilege, courts may appoint a guardian to act in the best interests of the child. Under such circumstances, the parents, neither alone nor together, may agree or refuse to waive the privilege on the child's behalf (40).

After a divorce is final, usually one parent is granted custody of any minor children. The custodial parent holds the health care decision-making power. Psychiatrists may be asked to perform an examination or evaluation of a minor child at the request of a noncustodial parent. However, psychiatrists who perform such examinations expose themselves to legal action. Although no court has found a psychiatrist liable for failure to obtain the custodial parent's consent prior to examination or evaluation, such decisions appear likely (41). Court decisions as well as statutory interpretations of the term "parent" have limited the use of that word to the parent awarded custody under a divorce decree's term (42, 43). Before performing an evaluation or examination upon a minor child, the psychiatrist should obtain the consent of the parent with legal custody.

As minors are able to consent to treatment independently and legally, they are able to control disclosure of medical information. Usually from age 14 to 15, minors may be considered "emancipated minors" when not living at home. Also, self-supporting minors, or "mature minors," have been judged by physicians to possess sufficient maturity to understand and consent. Consent of a parent is never required in a genuine emergency. A fourth category of unemancipated minors can in all states be treated for venereal disease without consent or knowledge of parents for the protection of the community.

Relying on parental consent alone for these groups is insufficient. When disclosures are made to interested third parties, consent of both the patient and the parents may be advisable. In addition to distinguishing between these four categories, the risk of treatment is an important consideration that enters into treatment interventions provided without parental consent and knowledge. In psychiatry, the use of psychoactive drugs increases the risk of treatment. Not only are adverse drug effects possible side effects, but also important activities such as educational performance, sports activities, or newly learned driving skills may be impaired. Thus, the risk of treatment and the maturity of the minor are crucial issues to be weighed in proceeding with or without parental consent.

Regardless of whether the minor patient has consent rights, every effort should be made to preserve confidentiality for the sake of the treatment. The conflicting interests of the minor's independent right to confidentiality with the parents' need to have information for making reasonable treatment and confidentiality decisions are always present. *The Principles of Medical Ethics* (4) are sensitive to these conflicting interests: "Careful judgment must be exercised by the psychiatrist in order to include, when appropriate, the parents or guardian in the treatment of a minor. At the same time the psychiatrist must assure the minor proper confidentiality" (Section 4, Annotation 7).

In psychiatric practice, the parents of minors undergoing treatment will often need to be involved to some degree. The problems of minor children are often inextricably wound together with those of their parents. Ground rules for confidentiality must be set out from the beginning of treatment. For the most part, the therapist may choose to avoid disclosure as much as possible, perhaps encouraging the child and parents to improve communications with each other. The parents must live with the child from day to day, and often the parents feel the psychic pain of their child's emotional disturbance. Almost all parents have some useful knowledge of the child and of the family's psychologic dynamics. Thus, they are a source of essential information to the therapist.

Economic reality rather than legal theory may determine the right to confidential information. Therapists or hospitals will often be unwilling to treat a minor patient without the signature of a financially responsible person. When the parent receives an itemized bill or statement from a therapist or insurance provider, privacy can no longer be maintained. If parents do not consent to nonemergency treatment of a minor, the parent is not responsible for payment of care. Some state statutes make this explicit (37).

What defenses exist to a legal action for unauthorized disclosures?

Psychiatrists have been sued for unauthorized release of information to patients' employers (44), to insurers (45), to defendants in personal injury cases

(11), to spouses (11), and in books (9). Psychiatrists have raised various defenses in these cases. When a valid consent is obtained, the psychiatrist is legally and ethically protected (4).

The consent, however, must be given competently, knowingly, and voluntarily. Because of the influence of the transference in psychiatric treatment, voluntariness of consent needs to be considered. In *Doe v. Roe* (9), the psychiatrist's allegation that consent was obtained for a book about the patient met with the following derisive comment from the court: "This defense is without substance. Consent was sought while the plaintiff was in therapy. It was never obtained in writing. . . . I need not deal with the value of an oral waiver of confidentiality given by a patient to a psychiatrist during the course of treatment." Clearly, under these circumstances consent should be obtained in writing. Also, consideration should be given to obtaining a consultation from a psychiatrist or attorney to discuss the confidentiality issue with the patient and to determine if consent is competent, knowing, and voluntary.

The defense of an overriding public interest may be used under certain circumstances. The public interest defense is carefully scrutinized for possible self-interest. In *Doe v. Roe* (9), the public interest defense (i.e., educational contribution to the medical profession) appeared to be self-serving. Careful risk-benefit analysis should be conducted when unauthorized disclosures are made in the service of public interest.

Allegations of unauthorized disclosure also may occur in the course of warning endangered third parties. The competing interests of confidentiality and warning are discussed in Chapter 13. If a therapist suspects that a patient is abusing a child, a number of child abuse statutes require reporting of such a suspicion. Some statutes also provide for the reporting of psychological abuse. The actual consequences for the therapy make such reporting a highly problematic matter. Reporting of contagious disease, epilepsy, and gunshot wounds are just some of the other reporting requirements contained in many statutes.

The defense of the lack of a statute addressing the particular right of confidentiality was raised during the course of *Alberts v. Devine* (13) discussed above. The court held that the lack of statute was no bar to recognizing a nonstatutory remedy. The court also noted that other courts had established a similar duty of confidentiality.

Breaching confidentiality in the interest of protecting the patient may occur. Although a psychiatrist does not have a legal duty to warn others of a patient's possible suicide attempt, good clinical practice may require such an action. *The Principles of Medical Ethics* (4) is very clear on confidentiality and protecting the patient or the community from danger: "Psychiatrists at times may find it necessary, in order to protect the patient or the community from imminent danger, to reveal confidential information disclosed by the patient" (Section 4, Annotation 8).

Courts rarely support the gratuitous invoking of "protecting the patient or community" in order to make unauthorized disclosures to spouses or family members. In *MacDonald v. Clinger* (46), the court stated: "Disclosure of confidential information by a psychiatrist to a spouse would be justified whenever there is a danger to the patient, the spouse; otherwise, information should not be disclosed without authorization." This is sound advice to follow.

Whenever psychiatrists who practice in jurisdictions having mental health confidentiality statutes abide by these statutes, or disclose confidential information as required by reporting statutes, a defense against legal claims of unauthorized disclosure is present. Psychiatrists also may be vulnerable to ethical complaints filed by patients with the District Branch and the APA over unauthorized disclosures. Justified claims may result in reprimand, suspension, or expulsion from these organizations. In a number of states, licensing statutes contain confidentiality requirements whose breach may lead to suspension or revocation of the psychiatrist's license (24).

How is confidentiality most commonly breached?

One of the most common but most indefensible ways in which confidentiality is breached is by "loose lips." Sargent (47) describes this syndrome and provides a very credible psychological interpretation for its continued prevalence among psychiatrists. Because secrets confer power on their guardians, the temptation exists to display that power. The psychiatrist's stock-in-trade is secrets. Lacking the technological skills of the surgeon and the wonder drugs of the internist, psychiatrists depend on their unique knowledge of the mind and the secrets entrusted to them to impress others. When yearning for recognition, the temptation to reveal confidential patient information can be very great. Thus, at one time or another, many psychiatrists have been chagrined by an "inadvertent" disclosure of confidential information.

Weiss (48) compared patients' expectations with those of physicians concerning the likelihood that a breach of confidentiality might occur. Weiss questioned patients, medical students, house officers, and senior physicians about the chances of confidentiality lapses. Although patients mostly believed that confidentiality was not breached, a significant number of medical students and physicians at each level believed that lapses were common. Although psychiatrists generally are acutely sensitive to confidentiality issues, constant vigilance is required to prevent unauthorized release of any confidential patient information.

How should the psychiatrist proceed when receiving a subpoena to testify about a patient?

When a psychiatrist is subpoenaed to testify about a patient, conflicting ethical and legal issues immediately arise. Physician-patient or psychotherapist-patient privilege statutes may allow patients to prevent a treating psychiatrist from disclosing information in court obtained during the course of treatment. In the case of *In re "B"* (49), the Pennsylvania Supreme Court ruled that a patient's constitutional right to privacy protects confidential communications made in psychotherapy.

As an ethical matter, *The Principles of Medical Ethics* (4) states: "A psychiatrist may release confidential information only with the authorization of the patient or under proper legal compulsion" (Section 4, Annotation 2). The psychiatrist should also explain to the patient the possible impact of testimony or disclosure of the psychiatric record upon his or her treatment or possibly on the outcome of the lawsuit. When presented with a subpoena, the psychiatrist should question the subpoena on behalf of the patient to protect the confidentiality of the information gathered during psychotherapy. The standard professional liability policy usually covers the costs of legal services when responding to a subpoena relating to a psychiatrist's practice.

A subpoena by itself is not "proper legal compulsion." The subpoena merely compels the psychiatrist to appear, not to testify (24). A subpoena may be issued by various governmental authorities and administrative agencies. Not all of these agencies have the power to issue subpoenas, but this does not necessarily prevent them from trying to compel testimony (50). Attorneys have an absolute right to obtain a subpoena without a judge's prior review by merely attesting to a belief that certain individuals have information that is relevant to the issue at court. There are two basic types of subpoenas: *1) subpoena duces tecum,* which requires the physician to bring medical records, and *2) subpoena ad testificandum,* which requires only the attendance of the physician, usually for testimony. Trying to avoid being served a subpoena is both unrealistic and unethical. Psychiatrists should not deny reality when it is essential that they know their own rights and the rights of patients in the legal matter at hand.

After receiving a subpoena, the psychiatrist must still regard all information obtained during the course of therapy as privileged from testimonial disclosure until the issue has been reviewed and properly resolved by legal authority. The subpoena often will be accompanied by a signed consent form from the patient. The psychiatrist may testify and provide records if the consent complies with state law requirements and is a competent, informed consent. The psychiatrist is ethically obligated to provide only information that is relevant to the issue at court. The pursuit of irrelevant information should be directly questioned by the testifying psychiatrist. An appeal to the judge by either the patient's attorney or the psychiatrist may be necessary. In a deposition, irrelevant, sensitive information should not be provided without a court order or specific consent by the patient (24).

When no consent form accompanies the subpoena, the psychiatrist should ascertain whether consent will be forthcoming. If the patient fails to give consent, the patient's attorney or the psychiatrist may file a motion to quash the subpoena on the basis of protection under physician-patient privilege and the duty to maintain confidentiality. The court will rule on the motion, settling the question of whether or not the psychiatrist must testify or turn over records.

If there is no motion to quash, the psychiatrist must appear at the deposition or trial. When the psychiatrist is asked to testify, the physician-patient privilege should be raised, and the court should be requested to rule on this issue. If the court rules that the psychiatrist must testify, the psychiatrist must do so or risk a contempt-of-court citation. A similar procedure should be followed in depositions. If necessary, attorneys at the deposition will arrange for a court resolution of the issue (24, pp 37–39).

In the vignette, Dr. West receives a subpoena to testify and produce her patient's records at the trial. Mr. Davidson's attorney files a motion to quash the subpoena, but the court dismisses the motion. At the time of trial, Dr. West intends to inform the court that she does not keep written records. Because Dr. West is not on trial, the absence of a written record will probably not be used as a basis for impeaching her credibility and testimony. Mr. Davidson is extremely concerned that information about the murder, wrongful arrest, and imprisonment of another person not be disclosed at trial. Dr. West explains to her patient that she will testify to only relevant information for the legal issue at hand. Should an irrelevant line of inquiry develop, she and the patient's attorney will request a ruling from the judge on the relevancy issue. On further consideration, Mr. Davidson decides to settle the matter out of court, and Dr. West is greatly relieved. If the judge permitted the attorney for the other side to pursue a line of inquiry that would develop damaging information revealed in the therapy in order to discredit the patient, Dr. West felt she could not have perjured herself if asked directly about her patient's former criminal activities.

What should the psychiatrist's position be toward the patient who reveals the commission of a crime during the course of psychotherapy?

For past crimes, the law does not require the psychiatrist to report criminal offenses, unless they involve treasonous activities (23). Many state reporting laws require the reporting of individuals who have sustained gunshot wounds. In addition, some psychiatric patients confess to crimes they have never committed. Unless the therapist is certain that the patient has recently committed a heinous crime that may be repeated or that the patient may be a serial murderer, the mere revealing of a crime should be managed initially as a treatment issue. If a patient confesses to having committed a serious crime in the past, the therapist's response should be that the revelation is grist for the therapeutic mill. The psychiatrist is not a prosecutor and should not confuse treatment with an adversarial role. Also, the psychiatrist should not worry that he or she will be considered an accessory to a crime for not reporting it. An accessory to a crime participates directly in some aspect of the commission of a crime. If the conflict for the patient is whether or not to confess the crime to the authorities, the optimal approach remains psychotherapeutic.

Grossman and Slovenko (32) take a somewhat different view. If a patient is known to have committed a crime during the course of therapy, the crime demonstrates that therapy has not afforded protection to society. They feel that "the obligation to protect society has priority over the ethics of confidentiality" (p. 9) and that ethical considerations, as well as the law, require the notification of authorities. A distinction is made between ongoing investigation of a crime, a threatened crime, and a crime committed in the relatively distant past. Grossman and Slovenko state: "Reporting a past crime does not avert an imminent danger or protect society" (p. 9). They find no ethical basis for making such a disclosure unless an innocent person is serving time for the crime. For example, a patient who claims rape and identifies a rapist confesses in therapy that she in fact consented to the sexual activity. They conclude that this behavior should be regarded as criminal.

Future crimes are another matter. A future crime exception to the privilege not to disclose confidential information does exist. Rule 27 of the Uniform Rules of Evidence adopts the future crimes exception as applied to physicians (51). In a number of states, therapists are required to reveal a patient's intent to commit a future harmful act or crime (52). The duty to disclose knowledge of impending harm has been imposed by courts adopting a *Tarasoff*-type duty to warn endangered third persons. Child abuse statutes in every state require the protection of children.

In *State v. Andring* (53), the court disagreed with the state argument that the Minnesota reporting statute completely abrogated the physician-patient privilege. In child abuse cases, the court held that the primary purpose of reporting is to protect children, not to punish offenders. The court adopted a narrow construction of the statute, holding that patient-physician privilege is abrogated only to the extent of permitting evidentiary use of the information in the required report (i.e., identity of child, parent, or guardian; nature and extent of injuries; name and address of the reporter). The court noted that many abused children return to their homes, and the interests of the child are best served by a law that encourages rehabilitation of child abusers.

Whether future crimes should be reported remains a matter of judgment. No regulation can specify for the psychiatrist what may or may not be divulged. If the psychiatrist holds a reasonable belief that the patient intends to seriously harm another but does not act, a suit for monetary damages may be forthcoming. How does one define harm? Should it be defined primarily in terms of physical harm? Can embezzlement be a severely harmful and damaging act? Even a legalistic distinction between an intended act that would constitute a misdemeanor and one that would constitute a felony is not helpful because the psychological consequences for a victim in either case could prove harmful.

As a matter of clinical practice, the *Tarasoff* decision has not drastically changed reporting practices of psychiatrists. Endangered persons and law enforcement authorities were discreetly informed of serious impending danger for years before the *Tarasoff* decision. As mentioned earlier, the APA "Position Statement on Confidentiality" (5) states that confidentiality may be broken, after careful evaluation of the patient, when the patient appears intent upon murder or suicide, or when the patient represents a danger to the public and can be stopped only by the psychiatrist.

A few states have enacted immunity provisions for mental health professionals who breach confidentiality in order to protect a third party endangered by the patient. Usually, a specific threat must be made against an identifiable victim or class of victims (54). AIDS patients who represent a danger to others raise complex issues surrounding the maintenance of confidentiality. The APA has published confidentiality and disclosure guidelines in the management of AIDS patients (55).

Most psychiatrists probably would not disclose future crimes to intended victims or authorities unless the possibility of serious physical or mental harm exists. A clinical approach is recommended that attempts to maintain confidentiality in order to deal with the future crime issue therapeutically. Such an approach encourages development of the therapeutic alliance, which may act as a brake on antisocial behavior. Ignoring the law or its outright contravention risks professional and legal jeopardy, especially if the psychiatrist's duty is defined.

What clinical and legal dilemmas confront Dr. West in the clinical vignette?

In the vignette, Dr. West decides that she has no duty to report either the murder confessed by her patient or the fact that an innocent man was imprisoned. Dr. West does not feel she has a duty to correct the injustices of society. She is not a judge and prefers to handle her patient's revelation as a treatment issue, letting the patient make the ultimate decision. As Dr. West becomes increasingly convinced that her patient actually did commit a vicious murder, however, she finds it difficult to view the crime strictly as a treatment issue. Reality intrudes and she becomes concerned that she could be an accessory to the continued imprisonment of an innocent man. Even if the patient decides to make a confession after 6 additional months of treatment, would that justify 6 more months of imprisonment of an innocent man? Could even one day of unnecessary imprisonment be justified when the possibility exists of serious harm or even death in prison? Dr. West believes she could be criminally charged as an accessory to the original crime. Moreover, could the prisoner sue her if her patient confesses at a later time, contending that Dr. West withheld information critical to his innocence and release?

A fundamental question is raised about the treatment of patients such as Mr. Davidson. Can patients who continue to lie be treated? Patients who persist in lying despite continued psychotherapeutic interventions probably suffer from malignant character disorders with severe anomalies of conscience. Such patients usually are not responsive to most current methods of psychotherapy and should be terminated from treatment. Continued treatment of the patient who lies, particularly when he or she commits crimes, places the therapist in the untenable position of either appearing to ignore the criminal acts or taking on the role of a police officer toward the patient. No treatment can take place under these circumstances. On the other hand, Mr. Davidson's situation is different because his criminal activities were in the past and were not continuous. The issue of lying remains a fundamental impediment to his treatment, raising insurmountable transference and countertransference problems.

What would constitute an appropriate treatment resolution of Mr. Davidson's case? From the patient's perspective, perhaps the treatment goal would be learning to live with the guilt of the murder and the false imprisonment of another without turning himself in to the police. The goal of treatment for the psychiatrist might be nothing short of a full confession and imprisonment of the patient. Such a critical disparity of treatment goals between patient and therapist would doom the therapy.

As a general legal principle, a person has no duty to come to the aid of another unless there is a special relationship giving rise to that duty. Does Dr. West owe a duty to come to the aid of the imprisoned man? If Dr. West withdraws from the case immediately, does that absolve her of such a duty even though she still possesses vital information? If she gives the patient an ultimatum that he must confess, might she become a victim of the patient's violence?

Dr. West assured her patient that all communications in therapy are absolutely confidential. This position ignores reality, because the psychiatrist's duty to maintain confidentiality does not negate other responsibilities that the psychiatrist has to the patient, third persons, the profession, and society. A noted psychiatrist favors a *Miranda*-type warning similar to the requirement that police must advise suspects of their rights, including that anything they say may later be used against them: "All you say is confidential; but, just in case some very major antisocial behavior comes up, I would report it" (6 [p. 1989]). The chilling effect of *Miranda*-type warnings on psychotherapy is very real. Trust, rather than absolute confidentiality, is the cornerstone of psychotherapy (6).

Dr. West does not have a legal duty to come to the aid of the falsely imprisoned person. Consequently, no basis for a legal action exists against Dr. West by the imprisoned man should he be exonerated. Furthermore, no patient has the right to exploit a confidential relationship to entrap the psychiatrist as a participant in criminal activity (6). The crime of accessory after the fact occurs only if one assists another involved in a crime. Dr. West's fear of being considered an accessory to the original crime is unfounded. She cannot realistically be considered to have assisted her patient in concealing a crime.

What is the crime of misprision? How do the crimes of misprision and accessory after the fact differ?

The crime of misprision, a misdemeanor, is defined as the active or passive concealment of a felony from the prosecuting authorities by one not guilty of those crimes (56). Dr. Samuel Mudd was considered to be an accessory by making it possible for Booth to escape after his assassination of President Lincoln. Conceivably, Dr. West could be found guilty of misprision of a felony.

Slovenko (1) states that "prosecution for accessory after the fact and especially for misprision seems to be as rare as a dodo bird." Appelbaum and Meisel (57) found that the federal statute governing misprision of a felony consistently has been interpreted as requiring more than a mere failure to report. The federal definition of misprision requires an affirmative act of concealing evidence, so that misprision becomes equivalent to the crime of being an accessory after the fact (58).

Appelbaum and Meisel (57) find state law more complex. Few states have broad-based misprision statutes, and those that exist are rarely interpreted by the courts. States without statutes have tended to reject misprision as a common-law crime, finding it inimical to our judicial system. Only South Dakota has a strict felony misprision statute. Physicians can be held liable if they conceal a crime or do not disclose knowledge of the crime. States with limited misprision statutes require the reporting of confessions of treason, child abuse, or other violent crimes committed by patients. Some misprision statutes require citizens to distinguish between felonies and misdemeanors and to report felony crimes.

Questions about patients from law enforcement personnel may present special problems. Lying would be considered an act of concealment, placing the psychiatrist in a questionable legal position. A response can be made indicating that information cannot be provided without breaching the confidentiality of the therapist-patient relationship and incurring liability. Although the law in this area is unclear, a therapist acting in good faith would probably not be held liable for warning law enforcement authorities of a dangerous patient. Nevertheless, such a possibility exists, as the following case demonstrates.

Kevin Young, 20 years of age, was voluntarily admitted to a Baltimore hospital after threatening the life of then President-elect Ronald Reagan. He told various doctors that his mission in life was to kill Reagan. Because such threats are a clear violation of the federal criminal code, the psychiatrist notified the Secret Service. The patient was arrested and transferred to a federal prison for evaluation. Eventually, the charges were dropped and he was released. Mr. Young subsequently filed suit against the medical staff and hospital alleging unlawful disclosure of confidential information. He cited the Maryland privilege statute that prohibits disclosure of information contained in medical records without the patient's authorization (59).

Mr. Young claimed a breach of confidentiality, violation of a contractual relation, mental anguish, and the possession of a criminal arrest record. The court certified the matter to mandatory nonbinding arbitration as provided by Maryland's Health Care Malpractice Claims Act. One would expect the issue to be moot because the federal code requiring reporting threats against the president of the United States supersedes any confidentiality statutes.

A majority of states have enacted criminal codes that have a provision on obstructing justice that would supersede any misprision statute. "Obstructing justice" covers such matters as intimidating witnesses and concealing a crime (1). In the absence of criminal codes containing a provision on obstructing justice, the issue of whether or not to report the patient's crime and the false imprisonment of another is more an ethical rather than a legal concern. Because most states have enacted these codes, legal consultation is advisable. Dr. West acted wisely in retaining an attorney. Reviewing her state's statute would clarify whether she is in violation of the criminal codes by withholding information about a crime. On the other hand, even if her patient is a clear and present danger to others, disclosure by Dr. West without statutory compulsion could raise the possibility of liability for breach of confidentiality.

What are some of the special confidentiality issues that arise in the course of psychiatric hospitalization?

Psychiatrists do not appear to protect confidentiality as carefully when caring for patients in the hospital as compared with outpatient treatment. The reasons for this disparity go beyond the necessity of involving family and other medical and nonmedical mental health practitioners. Severely ill psychiatric patients can induce sufficient anxiety to interfere with the professional judgment of the psychiatrist in maintaining confidentiality.

The psychiatrist should obtain the competent patient's permission before speaking to the patient's family. When this is not possible, a note should be recorded explaining the reasons for not obtaining the patient's permission. Maintaining confidentiality in the hospital is a complex issue because of the needs of various staff members to have information in order to develop evaluation and treatment plans. Psychiatrists should not assume they possess carte blanche authorization when speaking to hospital staff members about all matters revealed by the patient. Information should be provided that will enable the staff to function effectively on behalf of the patient. It is often unnecessary to disclose intimate details of the patient's mental life. As a rule, the staff spends more time with the patient than does the psychiatrist, allowing trust to develop between staff and patient. Under these circumstances, patients may choose to reveal more information about themselves.

Kernberg (60) suggests an approach for the maintenance of confidentiality with hospitalized borderline patients that appears applicable to many hospitalized patients. He finds it helpful for the psychotherapist to receive routinely a full report from the staff concerning the patient's interactions. In addition, he believes the therapist should share this information with the patient in an attempt to integrate it. The therapist informs the patient that all information will be kept confidential except for specific issues that will need to be explored with the hospital team. Specific authorization from the patient should be obtained before doing so. Kernberg explicitly informs the patient that he will not feel bound by confidentiality under circumstances involving threats to the patient or lives of others. Even under these circumstances, he would continue the policy of sharing the information to be divulged with the patient first.

Another problem with confidentiality arises when the psychiatric hospital is affiliated with a medical school and has training responsibilities. Halleck (61) states that often students participate in diagnostic and treatment conferences, even though these students have no professional involvement with the patient. When consent is not obtained, the psychiatrist is at risk for malpractice. He recommends that the psychiatrist obtain consent in advance before individuals not directly involved in the patient's care are permitted to interview the patient or attend a treatment or evaluation conference. According to Halleck:

> The patient has an absolute right to refuse participation in a teaching conference where he is on display before a large number of individuals who are not directly involved with his care. The patient also has a right to refuse to see anyone not officially connected with the hospital or not directly involved in his care or treatment and to refuse to see social workers and to forbid them from reviewing his records.

Also, no constructive purpose is served by divulging the patient's name during a conference.

As a general rule, communication between doctor and patient loses privileged status if it takes place in front of a third party (23). The presence of a third party is said to "pollute" confidentiality. Some statutes include nurses and attendants within the privileged class. The problem arises in the hospital during community meetings and group therapy sessions. If there is any reason to suspect that a patient may be facing legal proceedings, the patient should be told that information given in the presence of third parties has not always been accorded confidential status by the courts. In the "therapeutic community," if treatment decisions are made within the patient group, there is no privacy of discussion between the therapist and the patients. A number of state statutes provide confidentiality for group therapy (62). However, complex legal questions arise about privileged communication in any group therapy situation. Can patients be subpoenaed to testify against other patients who admit involvement in illegal activities? Can the patient prevent the therapist from disclosing incriminating information in court? There are no reported instances in which members of a group have been compelled to testify concerning confidences revealed in group therapy (63).

Although the presence of third parties has been found by some courts to pollute privilege (14), other courts have found to the contrary, particularly in those cases in which the third party is necessary or advances treatment. In *Yaron v. Yaron* (64), privilege was upheld in a family therapy situation. In *State v. Andring* (53), the Minnesota Supreme Court concluded that communications should be privileged if third persons are necessary and customary participants in treatment and the communications serve the purpose of aiding treatment. The court concluded that privilege extended to group therapy because every participant has a physician-patient relationship with the attending professional and, "in the group therapy setting, the participants actually become part of the diagnostic and therapeutic process for co-participants."

Group therapy remains an uncertain area, with little assurance that privilege will be upheld (65). Although considerable uncertainty exists in this area, the psychiatrist's general duty to maintain confidentiality remains unaffected. At least two jurisdictions, through statutes, require the maintenance of confidentiality among group members (66, 67).

What confidentiality issues arise in psychiatric writing?

Psychiatrists, unlike nonpsychiatric physicians, are obliged to disguise their clinical data in order to avoid recognition of the patient (68). Psychiatrists may have to suffer harm to the value of their data in order to protect the patient. Without the patient's being adequately disguised, consent of the patient is required for publication. If the psychiatrist does not obtain the patient's consent, he or she may be subject to legal liability and ethical charges if the subject of the writing is recognized. *The Principles of Medical Ethics* (4) states that "clinical and other materials used in teaching and in writing must be adequately disguised in order to preserve the anonymity of the individuals involved" (Section 4, Annotation 3).

In *Roe v. Doe* (69), the court found that the patient had not consented to a book's being written about herself. Obtaining valid consent of a patient in psychiatric treatment is never easy, even when given in writing. In *Roe,* the court doubted whether a valid consent could be given because of the therapist's influence over the patient. Moreover, if the patient gives consent without having reviewed the book or article, informed consent may not be possible. Consultation with another psychiatrist after the patient has had an opportunity to read the work should be considered.

When publishing a book, two important interests are pitted against each other: confidentiality and publication (68). In general medicine, this conflict is minimal as compared with psychiatry, because in the latter discipline, all the data are sensitive and personal. Psychiatrists are entitled to protection when writing in a nonsensational manner and when the patient remains anonymous and disguised (69). The disguise should be sufficient so that even a close friend cannot recognize the patient's true identity. In obtaining consent, the law distinguishes between a retrospective waiver and a general prospective waiver. The latter usually is obtained in medical and psychiatric practice, although this form of waiver, even when written, may not stand up to court scrutiny. The more the hazards are unknown, the less likely a prospective waiver will be considered valid because of the lack of informed consent. Psychiatrists, like other physicians, need to write in order to further understanding of mental illness by both professionals and lay persons. Fear of being sued, however, may be sufficient to chill scientific and educational writing in the mental health profession.

Must confidentiality be maintained when the therapist turns over the patient's bill to a collection agency or attorney?

There are no ethical principles that forbid therapists from using collection agencies or the courts to collect bills. The physician-patient privilege is not held as a bar from suing the patient to collect rightful fees. The ethical and legal obligations to protect the patient's confidentiality continue even though the patient breaches the treatment contract by not paying the bill. Patients may not want therapists to reveal their status as patients and may sue for breach of confidentiality when disclosure of such information is made to a collection agency or in a court proceeding. In litigation between the doctor and patient, however, privilege does not apply. This is true whether the litigation involves bill collection or malpractice.

Whenever possible, therapists should try to use other means in recovering fees rather than collection agencies or the courts. If the patient is unresponsive, the therapist may decide to bring suit or employ a collection agency. The patient should be informed that such actions will take place if the bill is not paid within a specified period of time. When using a collection agency or suing, the therapist is ethically and legally obligated to reveal only essential information for the purpose of fee collection. Essential information includes the patient's name and the amount owed. Itemized bills should be general, indicating "office visits" rather than the type of therapy.

Some states have enacted laws that outline the specific steps that must be followed when referring an account to a collection agency. These laws also include the information that may be revealed. For example, the District of Columbia Mental Health Information Act (70) requires that a psychiatrist not turn over a patient's account to a collection agency or lawyer until the patient receives "written notification that the fee is due and has failed to arrange for payment . . . within a reasonable time after such notification." If recourse to a collection agency or lawyer is taken, the act states that disclosure should include only "administrative information," such as the patient's name, age, sex, address, and identifying number; dates and character of the sessions (individual or group); and fee (70).

If collection is pursued, the therapist should select a reputable collection agency that does not harass patients or use abusive tactics. Therapists themselves must not harass patients with threats of criminal prosecution or threats of disclosure of false information to ruin a credit reputation. In addition, therapists should not threaten to contact the debtor's employer before obtaining a judgment, disclose information about the debt, or use other harassing tactics (24). Although contrary to the law in various jurisdictions, such tactics also may lead to a lawsuit based on the intentional infliction of emotional distress, or they may be the basis of an ethical complaint.

Therapists also must not withhold services they are legally and ethically required to provide in order to put pressure on patients for payment. Even though the American Medical Association sanctions the charging of interest on overdue accounts if patients are properly informed of such charges, this practice appears to be an unseemly commercialization of the therapist-patient relationship. Whether or not interest is paid, overdue accounts place the therapist in the position of a moneylender with all the attendant transference and countertransference problems occasioned by patients who continue to come for treatment without paying.

References

1. Slovenko R, personal communication, October 1985
2. King JH: The Law of Medical Malpractice. St Paul, MN, West Publishing, 1986, p 187
3. Osler W: The Evolution of Modern Medicine. New Haven, CT, Yale University Press, 1922, pp 63–64
4. American Psychiatric Association: The Principles of Medical Ethics With Annotations Especially Applicable to Psychiatry. Washington, DC, American Psychiatric Association, 1989
5. American Psychiatric Association: Position Statement on Confidentiality. Washington, DC, American Psychiatric Association, 1978
6. Slovenko R: Forensic psychiatry, in Comprehensive Textbook of Psychiatry IV, Vol 2. Edited by Kaplan HI, Sadock BJ. Baltimore, MD, Williams & Wilkins, 1985, pp 1960–1990; see p 1986
7. 709 P2d (1985); cert denied, Miller v Oregon, 475 U.S. 1141 (1986)
8. Perlin ML: Mental Disability Law: Civil and Criminal, Vol 1. Charlottesville, VA, Michie, 1989, pp 106–107
9. 93 Misc 2d 201, 400 NYS 2d 668 (NY Sup Ct 1977)
10. 291 Ala 701, 287 So 2d 824 (1973)
11. 84 AD2d 482, 446 NYS2d 801 (NY App Div 1982)
12. Prosser WL: Law of Torts, 4th Edition. St Paul, MN, West Publishing, 1971, p 117
13. 395 Mass 59, 479 NE2d 113, cert denied, Carroll v Alberts, 474 U.S. 1013 (1985)

14. Klein J, Onek J, Macbeth J: Seminar on Law in the Practice of Psychiatry: Confidentiality and Privilege. Washington, DC, Onek, Klein, and Farr, 1984, p 42
15. Reisner R, Slobogin C: Law and the Mental Health System, 2nd Edition. St Paul, MN, West Publishing, 1990, p 293
16. ILLINOIS ANN STAT ch 91-1/2, § 801-817 (Smith-Hurd Supp 1985)
17. Reisner R, Slobogin C: Law and the Mental Health System, 2nd Edition. St Paul, MN, West Publishing, 1990, p 278
18. 45 Md App 718, 415 A2d 625 (Md Ct Spec App 1980)
19. Ferguson v Quaker City Life Ins Co, 129 A2d 189 (DC 1957)
20. Fed R Evid 501
21. In re Grand Jury Proceedings, 867 F2d 562, (9th Cir), cert denied, Dee v U.S., 110 S Ct 265 (1989)
22. Case No 161315, Santa Barbara County Superior Court, decided July 22, 1987; California Supreme Court Case No S0047691/Crim 26408
23. Slovenko R: Psychiatry and Law. Boston, MA, Little, Brown, 1973, p 355
24. Klein JI, Macbeth JE, Onek JN: Legal Issues in the Private Practice of Psychiatry. Washington, DC, American Psychiatric Press, 1984; see p 33
25. Reisner R, Slobogin C: Law and the Mental Health System, 2nd Edition. St Paul, MN, West Publishing, 1990, p 265
26. Sloan JB, Hall B: Confidentiality of psychotherapeutic records. J Leg Med 5:435–467, 1984
27. Shuman DW, Weiner MS: The privilege study: an empirical examination of the psychotherapist-patient privilege, in Therapeutic Jurisprudence: The Law as a Therapeutic Agent. Edited by Wexler DB. Durham, NC, Carolina Academic Press, 1990, pp 75–119
28. In re Lifschutz, 2 Cal 3d 415, 467 P2d 557, 85 Cal Rptr 829 (1970)
29. Caesar v Mountanos, 542 F2d 1064 (9th Cir 1976), cert denied, 430 U.S. 954 (1977)
30. Sadoff R: Pennsylvania psychiatrist vindicated in refusing judge's request for records. Legal Aspects of Medical Practice 7:38–39, 1979
31. 119 Ill App 3d 847, 457 NE2d 158 (Ill App Ct 1985), rev'd, Novak v Rathnam, 106 Ill 2d 478, 478 NE2d 1334 (1985)
32. Grossman M, Slovenko R: Confidentiality and testimonial privilege, in Psychiatry, Vol 3. Edited by Cavenar JO. Philadelphia, PA, JB Lippincott, 1985, pp 1–18
33. Slovenko R: Accountability and abuse of confidentiality in the practice of psychiatry. Int J Law Psychiatry 2:431–454, 1979
34. American Psychiatric Association: Official action: model law on confidentiality of health and social service records. Am J Psychiatry 136:137, 1979
35. American Psychiatric Association: Confidentiality: A Report of the Conference on Confidentiality of Health Records. Washington, DC, American Psychiatric Association, 1975
36. Slovenko R: Psychotherapy and confidentiality. Cleveland State Law Review 24:375, 1975
37. Holder AR: Minors' rights to consent to medical care. JAMA 257:3400–3402, 1987
38. Landeros v Flood, 131 Cal Rptr 69, 551 P2d 389 (1976)
39. ME REV STAT ANN tit 22:4011(L) (1986); 62 Maryland Op Att'y Gen 157 (1977); or MD REV STAT § 40.225, 40.295 (1986)
40. Nagle v Hooks, 296 Md 123, 460 A2d 49 (1983)

41. Kuder A: Legal alert: treatment and consent. Washington Psychiatric Society Newsletter, Summer 1986, pp 8–9
42. Gary v Gary, 631 SW2d 781 (Tex Ct App 1982)
43. TEXAS FAM CODE ANN § 14.08(C)(I) (Vernon 1990)
44. Hopewell v Adebimpe, 130 PHL J 107 (Pa Ct Com Pl 1981)
45. Hammonds v Aetna Casualty & Surety Co, 243 F Supp 793 (N D Ohio 1965)
46. 84 AD2d 482, 446 NYS2d 801 (NY App Div 1982)
47. Sargent DA: Viewpoint: loose lips. Psychiatric News 20(20):2, 16, 1985
48. Weiss BD: Confidentiality expectations of patients, physicians, and medical students. JAMA 247:2695–2697, 1982
49. 482 Pa 471, 394 A2d 419 (1978)
50. Marvit RC: You and the law—problem areas. Psychiatric News 17(7):12–13, 1982
51. Brooks AD: Law, Psychiatry, and the Mental Health System. Boston, MA, Little, Brown, 1974, p 1094
52. Melton GB, Petrila J, Poythress NG: Psychological Evaluations for the Courts. New York, Guilford, 1987, p 47
53. 342 NW2d 128 (Minn 1984)
54. Brakel JS, Parry J, Weiner BA: The Mentally Disabled and the Law. Chicago, IL, American Bar Foundation, 1985, pp 592–596
55. American Psychiatric Association, Ad Hoc Committee of the Board on AIDS Policy: AIDS Policy: Confidentiality and Disclosure. Washington, DC, American Psychiatric Association, December 10, 1987
56. Perkins RM, Boyce RN: Criminal Law. New York, Foundation Press, 1982
57. Appelbaum PS, Meisel JD: The obligation to report patients' criminal acts. Bull Am Acad Psychiatry Law 14:221–230, 1986
58. U.S. v Farrar, 38 F2d 515 (D Mass), aff'd U.S. v Farrar, 281 U.S. 624 (1930)
59. Young v Sheppard and Enoch Pratt Hospital, No 139/328/82-L-598 (Cir Ct Baltimore Cty 1983)
60. Kernberg O: Borderline Conditions and Pathological Narcissism. New York, Jason Aronson, 1975, pp 209–211
61. Halleck SL: Law in the Practice of Psychiatry. New York, Plenum, 1980, p 34
62. COLO REV STAT § 12-43-218 (1990); COLO REV STAT § 13-90-107 (1990); KANSAS STAT ANN § 65-5602 (1989); LA REV STAT ANN § 37-2714 (West 1990); NM STAT ANN § 61-31-24 (1978)
63. Brakel JS, Parry J, Weiner BA: The Mentally Disabled and the Law. Chicago, IL, American Bar Foundation, 1985, pp 573–574
64. 83 Misc 2d 276, 372, NYS2d 518 (1975)
65. Slovenko R: Group psychotherapy: privileged communication and confidentiality. Journal of Psychiatry and Law 5:405–466, 1977
66. COLO REV STAT § 13107 (1973)
67. DC CODE ANN § 6-2003 (1981)
68. Slovenko R: The hazards of writing or disclosing information in psychiatry. Behavioral Sciences and the Law 1:109–127, 1983
69. 420 U.S. 307 (1975)
70. DC CODE ANN § 6-2001, et seq (1981)

Chapter 5

Protecting the Confidentiality of the Clinical Record: A Life-and-Death Matter

Mr. Grant, a 55-year-old businessman, dies suddenly under suspicious circumstances. At the time of his death, he was being treated with twice-a-week psychotherapy by Dr. Bellows, a psychiatrist. Mr. Grant suffered a depression secondary to recent business reversals. The depression was interfering with the patient's ability to concentrate, causing difficulties with his business partners, who noticed that Mr. Grant had become indecisive. While previously Mr. Grant was a very successful businessman, his productivity recently had markedly diminished. Disputes broke out with his business partners over his diminished ability to function effectively. Six months prior to his death, Mr. Grant had separated from his wife of many years. The divorce proceedings promised to be acrimonious.

Dr. Bellows started his patient on a tricyclic antidepressant because Mr. Grant displayed vegetative signs of depression and occasional unbidden suicidal thoughts. These symptoms improved after a month of taking the antidepressant. However, Dr. Bellows became concerned when Mr. Grant increased his alcohol intake significantly. The patient was warned about the possible dangerous interaction between alcohol and antidepressant medication. Mr. Grant was able to cut his drinking back but only for short periods.

The therapy sessions were utilized by Mr. Grant to talk about his depression and rage at his business partners. He accused a senior partner of embezzlement. Mr. Grant felt that certain irregularities in the company's finances had surfaced at the same time that this same partner bought a very expensive foreign car. In addition, he was certain that another partner profited from fraudulently misrepresenting to wealthy investors a limited partnership that eventually went bankrupt. Dr. Bellows, who keeps meticulous records, noted in detail the comments made by his patient.

Six months after starting therapy, Mr. Grant is found at home dead in bed. There are no antidepressants left in his medication bottle. Liquor bottles are found strewn about his apartment. The partners of the business firm hold key life insurance policies on each other in case of untimely death. Because the circumstances of Mr. Grant's death are unclear, the insurance carrier is unwilling to make payment on the life insurance policy until a final decision is reached as to the cause of Mr. Grant's death. Attorneys for the partners request and, under threat of a subpoena, receive Mr. Grant's psychiatric records from Dr. Bellows. Because of the trauma surrounding the death of his patient, Dr. Bellows is eager to avoid any more personal turmoil and readily provides the records. He is worried and intimidated by the subpoena. The state confidentiality statute prohibits such a disclosure. Mr. Grant's former business partners are outraged when they discover accusations of embezzlement and fraud written about them in the medical records. They threaten Dr. Bellows with a suit for defamation of character.

Do psychiatrists have a duty to maintain confidentiality after a patient's death?

After Mr. Grant's death, Dr. Bellows releases his patient's detailed psychiatric records to the attorney of the patient's former partners. The duty to maintain confidentiality of patient records that existed in life follows the patient in death, unless a specific court decision or statute in a particular jurisdiction provides otherwise. The American Psychiatric Association's *Opinions of the Ethics Committee on the Principles of Medical Ethics With Annotations Especially Applicable to Psychiatry* (1) presents the following question and answer asked by a psychiatrist on this very point:

> **Question:** Can I give confidential information about a recently deceased mother to her grieving daughter?

> **Answer:** No. Ethically, her confidences survive her death. Legally this is an unclear issue varying from one jurisdiction to another. Further, there is a risk of the information being used to seek an advantage in the contesting of a will or in competition with other surviving family members.

Many patients feel they have horrible secrets that they must hide at all costs. If the confidentiality of their therapy were to cease to exist after their death, many patients would be deterred from treatment. This is particularly true if death seems imminent, as in the patient considering suicide or patients with terminal illnesses.

Many occasions arise in which information is requested after a patient's death. As a general rule, written authorization should be obtained from the executor or administrator of the deceased patient's estate before releasing a *copy* of the medical records. If the estate has been settled and an executor or administrator no longer exists, a *copy* of the medical records should be released only to properly appointed legal representatives.

For a variety of reasons, psychiatrists often decide to disclose confidential information after the patient's death despite ethical and legal strictures to the contrary. In the vignette, the question of the cause of death for life insurance payment purposes is the reason for requesting the patient's record. Criminal investigations, will contests, the Internal Revenue Service, and families seeking information about the patient as part of their grieving are not uncommon reasons for postmortem requests for information. When a patient commits suicide, family members may request a meeting with the treating psychiatrist to try to understand the suicide. This is a very stressful time for the family and the psychiatrist. The psychiatrist may feel defeated, guilty, and defensive. The family invariably feels guilt, anger, and blame. In an effort to exculpate himself or herself, the psychiatrist may reveal too much information. Releasing to the family additional painful details of the patient's life that are not relevant to the inquiry must be avoided. The immediate priority should be to console the family and assist them in their grief. The psychiatrist should not refuse to see the family unless litigation has been threatened or instituted by the family against the psychiatrist.

If the psychiatrist feels compelled to reveal confidential information after the patient's death, legal risks may be minimized by providing just enough information for the task at hand. Details of the patient's therapy are rarely, if ever, required. Relevancy is the guiding rule. Also, revealing information about third parties learned from the patient may be legally dangerous. Slovenko (2) points out that the dead or their survivors cannot sue for defamation or the invasion of privacy because these are personal rights that die with the individual. Even if a person is defamed while alive, the cause of action under common law dies with the person. However, a legal cause of action may exist when words contained in a medical record independently reflect on and defame those living. Slovenko states that "one who divulges an allegation by another may find himself liable although he did not indicate his own belief in the truth of the statement" (p. 126). Unless privilege exists to make disclosures, mental health professionals are responsible for statements made, even though the views are purported to be those of the patient.

In the clinical vignette, Dr. Bellows keeps comprehensive psychiatric records that detail his deceased patient's inflammatory comments about his partners. Such comments about third persons are rarely, if ever, necessary for the purposes of record keeping (e.g., facilitating ongoing treatment, a record to be available in the future for other physicians, research, or legal purposes). A defamation suit against Dr. Bellows is possible.

Dr. Bellows released confidential records out of a desire to diminish the personal turmoil experienced as a result of the unexpected death of his patient. Moreover, he was intimidated by the threat of a subpoena that would have required him to turn over the patient's psychiatric record to the partner's attorney. Unless a state law provides otherwise, confidentiality must be preserved after the death of the patient just as it was in life. In Dr. Bellows's jurisdiction, confidentiality statutes prohibit unauthorized disclosure of medical information. As stated in the previous chapter, subpoena of the psychiatrist or the patient's records is not by itself sufficient legal compulsion to breach confidentiality.

Furthermore, the physician-patient privilege does not expire upon the patient's death. Privilege continues after death and may be claimed by the deceased patient's next of kin or legal representative. Privilege seeks to protect the patient from embarrassment, which could extend to family members after the patient dies (3). Before releasing any information, Dr. Bellows should have sought the advice of legal counsel. Psychiatrists must be careful not to make unauthorized extrajudicial or statutorily prohibited disclosure of patient records unless the disclosure is justified by overriding public interest. A majority of states have enacted legislation subjecting physicians to loss of their licenses for the unauthorized release of medical records. In addition, such a release could constitute the basis for a lawsuit.

Dr. Bellows also violated an ethical obligation to maintain confidentiality. The APA, in *The Principles of Medical Ethics With Annotations Especially Applicable to Psychiatry* (4), states: "A psychiatrist may release confidential information only with the authorization of the patient or under proper legal compulsion" (Section 4, Annotation 2).

A major controversy was raised when disclosures were made by the treating psychiatrist following the death of a famous American poet, Anne Sexton. This case underscores many of the complex legal and ethical issues surrounding after-death release of confidential information (5).

The American Psychiatric Association's "Guidelines on Confidentiality" are explicit concerning disclosure of information by a psychiatrist after the death of a patient:

Psychiatrists should remember that their ethical and legal responsibilities regarding confidentiality continue after their patients' deaths. . . . In cases in which the release of information would be injurious to the deceased patient's interests or reputation, care must be exercised to limit the released data to that which is necessary for the purpose stated in the request for information. (6)

Is the privacy of psychotherapeutic records legally protected?

Courts and legislatures have become more sensitive to the protection of the constitutional rights to privacy. However, the United States Supreme Court has not specifically addressed the issue concerning a right to privacy as applied to psychotherapeutic records. Each state has statutory provisions governing the confidentiality of mental health records. But federal or state statutes have not provided clear or comprehensive protection of treatment records (7). Furthermore, state privilege statutes provide numerous exceptions. Court decisions interpreting these statutes have not delineated useful guidelines for the patient or the mental health professional.

The extent to which psychotherapy has been undermined by a lack of clear guidelines on the privacy of psychotherapeutic records by the courts and legislatures is not known. However, the courts have held that the disclosure of information to an insurance company for the purpose of establishing coverage constitutes a total waiver of the right to confidentiality of all medical records (7). Such rulings can have only a chilling effect on the psychotherapeutic process. The message for psychotherapists is clear: they cannot rely upon courts and legislatures to protect the confidentiality of psychotherapeutic records. The most prudent protection is discrete record keeping.

What clinical and legal issues are present in maintaining the clinical record during the patient's life and after the patient's death?

Clinically, keeping a record during the course of the patient's treatment serves a number of purposes. Review of the record between sessions as well as the exercise of summarizing treatment sessions permits a better understanding of the patient and the treatment process. If the patient interrupts or terminates treatment but later decides to return, the previous record will prove helpful in refreshing the therapist's memory. Accurate record keeping can also help resolve billing disputes. However, the need to maintain clear records has increased because of the need to maintain quality assurance—for accreditation, for financial reimbursement, and for legal purposes (8).

Some courts have concluded that what is not recorded has not been done (9, 10). Generally, in the absence of corroborating records, an assertion in court that certain actions were taken is a question for the factfinders who must consider the issue of proof. When an adequate record exists, the possibility of proving that an action (e.g., treatment or procedure) was taken is significantly enhanced.

A patient's record should document major management and treatment decisions. Medication records should accurately reflect the amount of medication prescribed, instructions given for taking the medication, and any warnings issued to the patient regarding risks associated with a medication. The record should also contain the risk-benefit assessments considered in making important treatment interventions. Informed consent obtained from the patient and any waivers of confidentiality should be recorded. Noncompliance with psychiatric treatment, including failure to take psychoactive drugs, is also important to note. Significant phone conversations with patients should be made part of the medical record. The treatment record that accurately portrays the reasoning behind treatment interventions or noninterventions, particularly when careful risk-benefit analyses are being conducted, will be the psychiatrist's best ally should litigation arise. Errors in psychiatric diagnosis and treatment are not, per se, actionable. Good records can go a long way in showing that, although an error was made, the psychiatrist used reasonable skill and diligence in arriving at a treatment decision.

Usually, no useful purpose is served by noting the patient's fantasies, derogatory opinions of others, or any other information not directly relevant to documenting treatment decisions. When a record of intimate details is necessary for supervision of student psychotherapists or analysts, these records probably should not be kept after their educational and research functions have been served. A consistent policy of destroying these records is an option. Medical records can be disposed of by burning or shredding. Confidentiality must be maintained during this process. The destruction can be certified and the certificate kept permanently. However, a certificate of destruction is not a legal requirement. State law may forbid destruction of records when the intent is to prevent disclosure at a judicial proceeding. If the psychiatrist discloses at a judicial hearing that records are routinely destroyed, the presence of a consistent policy will tend to negate questions about credibility.

Writing self-serving statements in a record in the hope of exonerating oneself should a lawsuit arise is foolhardy and useless. Both the record and the psychiatrist will be subjected to searching cross-examination. The discrepancy between testimony developed in court and self-serving information recorded in the psychiatric record may deal a severe blow to the psychiatrist's credibility.

As noted earlier, the laws concerning access to a deceased patient's record vary considerably from state to state. Clinicians need to know the law in their state. Generally, states that permit patients access to their medical records also usually allow access by a specified third party (e.g., next of kin, executor, or administrator). Appropriate court documentation should be received prior to any release to other parties of the deceased patient's medical records.

Do psychiatric patients have a legal right to gain access to their records?

Psychiatrists also must realize that the psychiatric record can become an iatrogenic factor in exacerbating a patient's condition, particularly if it contains damaging or frightening information. Many states allow patients access to their records. The actual record maintained by the psychiatrist is the physical property of the psychiatrist. The information contained in the record, however, belongs to the patient. The original record should never be relinquished to the patient. Only a copy of the record should be provided.

The rules governing patients' access to their own records are complicated and vary considerably in each jurisdiction. When a lawsuit is filed against a psychiatrist, every state permits the patient to subpoena the records. In this instance, only a copy of the record should be provided.

A number of states have enacted patient-access statutes permitting patients to have access to medical records in the absence of litigation, after the payment of administrative costs such as photocopying charges (11). Some jurisdictions make a distinction between mental health records and other medical records. Access to records may also depend on who is making the request (i.e., patient, next of kin, or legal representative) and the reason for the access request. A minority of jurisdictions permit direct access by the patient's attorney, physician, or near relative but not by the patient. Many states provide an exception for the release of mental health treatment records on the grounds that the psychological welfare of the patient might be impaired by knowledge of the contents of the record.

In *Bartlett v. Danti* (12), the Rhode Island Supreme Court held that the provision of the State Confidentiality of Health Care Information Act exempting confidential health care information from compulsory legal process violated the Rhode Island Constitution. The act was amended, defining situations in which physicians may be compelled to testify or produce evidence regarding a patient's medical condition. Medical information was defined as privileged rather than confidential.

A few states have passed statutes expressly prohibiting the release of mental health records to anyone except under court order (13). Most state statutes protect institutional records independently of the therapist's obligation to maintain confidentiality (11). This is frequently the case in state hospitals for the mentally ill and retarded. However, some states treat state hospital records as nonprivileged public documents or privileged under government privilege statutes that are subject to waiver by the government without the patient's consent (14).

The federal government, however, encourages access to records. Under the Federal Privacy Act of 1974, all patients receiving medical care under the federally administered Medicare program, all patients in Veterans Administration hospitals, and recipients of Social Security or Supplemental Security Income benefits have access to their records (15).

The therapist should be present in order to answer questions whenever a patient wishes to inspect the clinical record. The patient may become very distressed during the course of reading the clinical record, requiring the assistance of the therapist. The therapist also should be present to prevent any alteration of the record.

Can psychiatric records be compelled during Medicaid fraud and other investigations?

In general, courts have held that Medicaid fraud investigators do not have unlimited access to psychiatrists' medical records (16). Before a subpoena is issued, investigators usually will need to show how the records are relevant to their investigation.

In *Commonwealth v. Kobrin* (17), a Massachusetts grand jury issued a subpoena to a psychiatrist directing that all records of his Medicaid patients be made available. The psychiatrist disclosed the names of his Medicaid patients and the time spent for each therapy session. At the request of his patients, however, the psychiatrist invoked the psychotherapist-patient privilege recognized by Massachusetts statute, and refused to release those portions of the Medicaid patients' records that revealed diagnosis and treatment. Subsequently, the psychiatrist was held in contempt. The claim of privilege was rejected on the grounds that Medicaid laws require records to be kept and disclosed when requested by the Medicaid agency or fraud control unit.

On appeal, the Supreme Judicial Court of Massachusetts (18) ruled that substantial portions of Medicaid patients' psychiatric records are protected from disclosure by the psychotherapist-patient privilege. The court established rules for determining which portions of psychiatric records may be disclosed. The state may discover "the times and lengths of patient appointments, fees, patient diagnoses, treatment plans and recommendations, and somatic therapies." Blood tests, drug prescriptions, electroconvulsive therapy, and "observations on objective indicia of emotional disturbance" are also discoverable. On the other hand, portions of the record that contain "patients' thoughts, feelings, and impressions, or contain the substance of the psychotherapeutic dialogue" are protected from disclosure. When the state seeks the psychiatrist's records in a legal proceeding, a judge shall review the records, dividing them into disclosable and undisclosable portions. The court observed that the state and federal Medicaid statutes require disclosure only of those records that are "necessary fully to disclose the extent of the services provided." This standard, it concluded, does not support "the wholesale assault on privacy" made by the state in this case.

Records can conceivably be obtained through a search warrant. The psychiatrist who is confronted with a search warrant should not resist the search or officers executing it. Remedies are available to contest the search warrant, but these can be exercised only after the records have been seized. Patients whose records have been seized should be notified immediately so that they may assert their rights (19).

In *Hawaii Psychiatric Society v. Ariyoshi* (20), a psychologist, together with the Hawaii Psychiatric Society, challenged the constitutionality of a statute that authorized issuance of administrative search warrants to obtain the records of Medicaid recipients. In granting a preliminary injunction, the court concluded that a high probability existed that the statute had violated constitutional prohibitions against invasion of privacy and unreasonable searches.

There is a division of opinion on the issue of compelled disclosure of information in judicial or administrative investigations of physicians. The disclosure requirements depend on the type of case. As a rule, courts require that certain safeguards be established so that only information required for the purposes of the investigation will be examined (21). However, despite the ruling in *Kobrin,* inroads are being made to gain access to the medical records of nonparty patients on the basis of anonymity (22). Factual information compiled by peer review committee and hospital incident reports is also becoming discoverable (23). Approximately half the states have laws making all peer review reports privileged. A number of states have "qualified" peer review confidentiality, allowing attorneys access to factual materials but not to the opinions and conclusions of individual participants (24).

Subpoenas may be issued by various governmental authorities and administrative agencies. Not all of these agencies have the legal power to issue subpoenas. However, this does not necessarily prevent them from attempting to compel testimony (25). Records may be obtained illegally either through unauthorized inspection or by being stolen. For example, through bank records it was discovered that Daniel Ellsberg, author of the *Pentagon Papers,* was receiving psychiatric treatment from Dr. Lewis Fielding. This led to the infamous break-in of Dr. Fielding's office during the Watergate era. Mental health records must be kept in a safe place and available only to authorized personnel. Psychiatrists can be held liable for unauthorized disclosure by employees.

Should psychiatrists maintain two separate sets of records in order to prevent legal discovery?

Therapists sometimes keep two separate sets of records: one set for diagnosis, prognosis, and treatment decisions and the other set for the therapist's speculations and the fantasies and intimate details of the patient's life. Although the American Psychiatric Association, in its "Model Law on Confidentiality of Health and Social Service Records" (26), recognizes this distinction, only two jurisdictions permit dual records (27, 28). The Illinois statute (27) segregates personal notes, which are defined as follows: *1)* information disclosed to the therapist in confidence by other persons on condition that such information would never be disclosed to the recipient or other persons; *2)* information disclosed to the therapist by the recipient that would be injurious to the recipient's relationships to other persons; and *3)* the therapist's speculations, impressions, hunches, and reminders. No court has allowed such a distinction, and the work product privilege that protects attorneys' records has not been applied to medical practice. Slovenko (29) warns against the practice of keeping two sets of records. Concealment of records is a violation of the law. Instead of using illegal means, Slovenko advises, the psychiatrist should exercise "extreme caution" when writing in the patient's record.

How long should medical records be kept? How should medical records be managed when the therapist dies?

State laws and administrative regulations in a number of states require that patient records be kept. Some state regulations and statutes specify the number of years that medical and hospital records must be held. Moreover, state licensing and certification laws may incorporate record-keeping guidelines and principles of a state or national professional organization.

Records should be kept until the relevant statute of limitations has lapsed (30). These statutes of limitations usually require that a suit be brought within 2 or 3 years from the time of the last treatment or from the time of discovery of the injury caused by the treatment. Therapists who retire should keep their records at least until the statute of limitations runs out. It should be noted, however, that the limitations period can be extended for minors or for incompetent patients. The statute of limitations will be tolled (i.e., suspended) when a person is under a legal disability at the time that the alleged injury arises. Legal disability is defined as the lack of legal capacity to perform an act. Thus, a minor or mentally incompetent person is considered to be incapable of initiating a lawsuit in his or her own behalf.

Professional organizations do not provide specific guidelines on record keeping. State licensing and certification laws may contain record-keeping requirements. Violations of these legal requirements may lead to suspension or loss of the practitioner's license. The statute of limitations for ethical charges filed by professional organizations or licensing authorities may be longer than the time established for legal actions. No time limit for filing ethical charges may exist in some states.

If the therapist should die during this time, family members may be left with the burden of handling patient records. The creation of a "professional will" spelling out clear instructions for the managing of confidential records may help expedite the transfer and treatment of patients (31). A number of alternatives are available. A colleague or medical society may be willing to store records and respond to patient requests in event of the death of the therapist. Charts may be sent to the patient's new therapist if the patient consents. A written understanding that the original record will be returned after being photocopied is essential. In the meantime, a copy of the medical record, complete with numbered pages, should be kept. Family members also could keep the charts and provide copies at the patient's expense. The same procedure should be followed when a practice is sold, including sending a blanket notice to all patients informing them when the successor will take over and requesting that patients wanting their records transferred to another doctor should make their requests in writing.

In what form must medical records be kept?

Medical records may be kept in written form, on microfilm, on audiotape, or on a computer disk. Although no specific recognition of computerized records may exist, there is no specific prohibition against their use. Confidentiality and access to these records must be carefully protected. Computerized systems may need to be modified according to state statutes. The use of computerized, voice-activated medical charts is becoming more commonplace in hospitals. Most statutes require the record to be signed. Some states require that the record be written in ink. A therapist will not usually be held liable for entrusting confidential reports to the secretary for typing (29). However, by extension, the secretary is under the same obligation to maintain confidentiality as the therapist.

What confidentiality precautions must be observed when sending or receiving information through a facsimile (FAX) machine?

The use of FAX machines to transmit medical data is becoming more common. Since this is a new development, little or no precedent has been set concerning the use of electronically transmitted mail. A major malpractice insurer (32) recommends that the following precautions be observed:

1. All FAXs should be photocopied to preserve their integrity.
2. The FAX cover sheet should indicate that the transmission is confidential. Instructions for the return of the documents should be provided in case the material arrives at a misdialed FAX machine.
3. Recipients of material sent by FAX should require that the original records be mailed for inclusion in the medical record.

Confirmation and confidentiality are essential when sending or receiving information via a FAX machine. The use of FAX machines does raise concerns about breaches of confidentiality. The sender cannot be certain who will see the confidential information at the receiving end. As in other situations, care must be used in handling and processing confidential medical information.

Must medical records be kept by psychiatrists?

In the clinical vignette, Dr. Bellows kept very detailed records. However, Dr. West in the previous chapter kept none. The problem with unnecessarily detailed records was demonstrated by the possibility that independent parties were defamed by statements included in Mr. Grant's record discovered posthumously. Whenever possible, detailed personal notes should not be allowed to leave the office. Instead, an attempt should be made to give the court a summary of the diagnosis, prognosis, progress of the patient, and specific difficulties encountered in the illness.

On the other hand, the practice of keeping no records of patient care places the psychiatrist in an extremely disadvantageous position should legal action arise. Properly kept medical records can be the psychiatrist's best ally in malpractice litigation. If no record is kept, numerous questions will be raised regarding the psychiatrist's competence and credibility. This failure to keep medical records may also violate state statutes or licensing provisions. Failing to keep medical records may arise out of the psychiatrist's concern that patient treatment information be totally protected. Although this is an admirable ideal, in real life the psychiatrist may be legally compelled under certain circumstances to testify directly about confidential treatment matters.

What are some of the confidentiality issues surrounding the psychiatric hospital record?

Hospital records are often read by an army of mental health professionals and trainees. Other physicians, nurses, nurses aides, paraprofessionals, dietitians, nursing students, social workers, social worker students, occupational and art therapists, clerks, ministers, administrators, medical students, and others may peruse the patient's hospital record. More and more patients read their own medical records. Seigler (33) demonstrated that an average of 75 staff members had access to a surgical patient's record during the course of a normal hospital admission. Hence, any thought that the hospital record is even a quasi-private document is an illusion.

Because so many persons are privy to the patient's record, confidentiality is considered "polluted" because persons other than the treating physician have access to the record (34). Thus some courts have held that the medical privilege does not protect the hospital record from subpoena. The majority of states have rectified this by enacting a statute which provides that the hospital records remain privileged. However, the privilege may be waived under the same conditions as the waiver of testimonial privilege (35). Information about the patient must, therefore, be entered very discreetly.

Gutheil (36) writes about the motivational use of paranoia to make psychiatric records more effective for forensic purposes, utilization review, and sound treatment planning. One format that can be used effectively for record keeping is the problem-oriented record as adapted to psychiatric practice and published by the American Psychiatric Association (37).

Any evidence of tampering with medical records taints the health care provider's credibility (38). The patient's record should not contain any alterations, additions, deletions, or substitutions without proper notations concerning the reasons for the change. If corrections are necessary to achieve accuracy, the original records should be left intact with a single line drawn in ink through the entire entries being corrected. An initialed notation with the date and time should be made along the side margin indicating that the entry was in error. Such a notation of correction should be entered in the record chronologically. Contemporaneously corrected errors in the medical record will dispel accusations of tampering and falsification.

References

1. American Psychiatric Association: Opinions of the Ethics Committee on the Principles of Medical Ethics With Annotations Especially Applicable to Psychiatry. Washington, DC, American Psychiatric Association, 1989, Section 4, Annotation K

2. Slovenko R: The hazards of writing or disclosing information in psychiatry. Behavioral Sciences and the Law 1:109–127, 1983
3. Thorèn J: The physician-patient privilege. Medical Trial Technique Quarterly 29:61–78, 1982
4. American Psychiatric Association: The Principles of Medical Ethics With Annotations Especially Applicable to Psychiatry. Washington, DC, American Psychiatric Association, 1989
5. Goldstein RL: Psychiatric poetic license? Postmortem disclosures on confidential information in the Anne Sexton case. Psychiatric Annals (in press)
6. American Psychiatric Association: Guidelines on confidentiality. Am J Psychiatry 144:1522–1526, 1987
7. Sloan JB, Hall B: Confidentiality of psychotherapeutic records. J Leg Med 5:435–467, 1984
8. Slovenko R: On the need for record keeping in the practice of psychiatry. Journal of Psychiatry and Law 7:399–440, 1979
9. Whitree v State, 56 Misc 2d 693, 290 NYS2d 486, 498–499 (1968)
10. Abille v United States, 482 F Supp 703, 708 (ND Cal 1980)
11. Brakel SJ, Parry J, Weiner BA: The Mentally Disabled and the Law. Chicago, IL, American Bar Foundation, 1985, pp 574–575
12. No 83-453-Appeal (RI Jan 14, 1986)
13. Bromberg J, Hirsh HL: Medical records and hospital reports. Medical Law 1:253–272, 1982
14. Reisner R: Law and the Mental Health System. St Paul, MN, West Publishing, 1985, p 244
15. Slovenko R: Forensic psychiatry, in Comprehensive Textbook of Psychiatry IV, Vol 2. Edited by Kaplan HI, Sadock BJ. Baltimore, MD, Williams & Wilkins, 1985, pp 1960–1990; see p 1982
16. Grand Jury Subpoena Duces Tecum, et al v Kuriansky, 69 NY2d 232, 505 NE2d 925, 513 NYS2d 359, cert denied, Y v Kuriansky, 482 U.S. 928 (1987)
17. 395 Mass 284, 479 NE2d 674 (1985)
18. Ibid
19. Berryhill LK: Search warrants (letter). Psychiatric News 17(13):2, 1982
20. 481 F Supp 1028 (D Hawaii 1979)
21. Grossman M, Slovenko R: Confidentiality and testimonial privilege, in Psychiatry, Vol 3. Edited by Cavenar JO. Philadelphia, PA, JB Lippincott, 1985, pp 1–18
22. Hirsh HL: The great wall about nonparty patients' medical records is crumbling. Medical Trial Technique Quarterly 31:434–450, 1985
23. Chandra v Sprinkle, 678 SW2d 804 (Mo 1984)
24. Cassidy R: Can you really speak your mind in peer review? Medical Economics, January 23, 1984, pp 246–262
25. Marvit RC: You and the law—problem areas. Psychiatric News 17(7):12–13, 1982
26. American Psychiatric Association: APA Model Law on Confidentiality of Health and Social Service Records. Am J Psychiatry 136:138, 1979
27. ILL STAT ANN 91-1/2, 802, § 2(4)(iii) (Smith-Hurd Supp 1985)
28. DC CDE § 6-2003
29. Slovenko R: Psychiatry and Law. Boston, MA, Little, Brown, 1973, p 69

30. Klein JI, Macbeth JE, Onek JN: Legal Issues in the Private Practice of Psychiatry. Washington, DC, American Psychiatric Press, 1984, p 53
31. Bies EB: Mental Health and the Law. Rockville, MD, Aspen, 1984, p 65
32. Princeton Risk Review 1:6, 1991 [Princeton Insurance Co, Princeton, NJ]
33. Siegler M: Sounding boards—confidentiality in medicine: a decrepit concept. N Engl J Med 307:1518–1521, 1982
34. Reisner R: Law and the Mental Health System. St Paul, MN, West Publishing, 1985, p 246
35. Novak v Rathman, 119 Ill App 3d 847, 457 NE2d 158 (1985), rev'd, Novak v Rathman, 106 Ill 2d 478, 478 NE2d 1334 (1985)
36. Gutheil TG: Paranoia and progress notes: a guide to forensically informed psychiatric record keeping. Hosp Community Psychiatry 1:479–482, 1980
37. American Psychiatric Association: The Problem-Oriented System in Psychiatry. APA Task Force No 12. Washington, DC, American Psychiatric Association, 1977
38. Hirsh HL: Will your medical records get you into trouble? Legal Aspects of Medical Practice 8:46–51, 1978

Section II:

Patient Rights

Chapter 6

The Right to Refuse Treatment and the Therapeutic Alliance

General Ward, an 88-year-old retired army general, is admitted to a nursing home from a hospital. He is diagnosed as suffering from congestive heart failure and primary degenerative dementia, presumptively of the Alzheimer's type. Dr. Pritchard, the psychiatrist who diagnosed and treated General Ward in the hospital, continues to follow her patient at the nursing home. Other than some initial confusion and agitation, General Ward makes a reasonably smooth transition to nursing home care. Dr. Pritchard sees her patient once every 2 weeks for about 15 minutes and occasionally adjusts his sleep medication. His family, consisting of two daughters and one son, visits weekly.

Gradually, General Ward begins to chafe at nursing home rules. He becomes involved in a power struggle with nursing personnel over toileting and where he will eat his meals. Agitation and suspicion increase. The patient claims that the nursing home director is attempting to drive him out by instructing the nursing personnel to harass him. Dr. Pritchard reassures her patient that no such effort is being mounted.

General Ward is receiving digitalis for his heart failure. The doctor orders a blood level determination for digitalis and obtains a medical consultation. One week later, the patient becomes extremely agitated, voicing ideas that the director of the nursing home is poisoning him. Dr. Pritchard explains to General Ward that tranquilizing medication is necessary for both his emotional and his physical condition. She starts to discuss side effects with General Ward, who interrupts her and adamantly refuses medications. The internist notes the beginnings of atrial fibrillation and expresses concern that the patient's cardiac status is becoming precarious. Dr. Pritchard talks to the family about starting haloperidol, a major tranquilizer, despite her patient's objection. The medication is tasteless and available in concentrate form. The patient's family reluctantly gives permission for the covert administration of haloperidol against their father's wishes, but fears his wrath if he discovers the medication. Dr. Pritchard is unaware of the statute in her state requiring judicial determinations of incompetence before neuroleptic medication can be initiated against a

95

patient's will. The statute does not empower the next of kin to consent to medical treatments.

Haloperidol concentrate is placed in General Ward's food. The patient becomes asymptomatic within a month's time. However, a nursing aide who befriends the patient harbors strong feelings against covert administration of medication. She tells General Ward that his food contains a major tranquilizer. He stops eating and drinking. The patient summons his family, Dr. Pritchard, and the nursing home director. In a rage, he threatens the doctor and the director with a lawsuit. His family is terrified and withdraw their consent for treatment. The patient's agitation and paranoid ideas of poisoning return, reinforced now by the fact of covert administration of medication. He becomes episodically physically violent, striking the nursing staff with his cane. He refuses to see Dr. Pritchard. The internist notes increasing signs of decompensating cardiac function. During brief uninvited encounters with the patient, Dr. Pritchard notes more confusion, forgetfulness, and disorientation for the day, date, and year. She advises the family to obtain an immediate court order for treatment, but they refuse, withdrawing totally from the situation.

Confronted with an emergency, Dr. Pritchard begins intramuscular administration of haloperidol at 0.5 mg four times a day. General Ward again improves but continues to refuse and resist medication. Dr. Pritchard decides to see her patient each day in order to develop a therapeutic alliance. Dr. Pritchard also asks the social worker at the nursing home to see the patient and notify General Ward's former military colleagues that the general is quite ill. Their visit is much appreciated by the patient and buoys his spirits. Dr. Pritchard tries to understand her patient's conflicts and defenses. Realizing that her patient, as a senior military officer, is very threatened by passivity and loss of control, she allows him more autonomy concerning where he takes his meals as well as toileting methods. Despite the severe strain placed on the doctor-patient relationship, Dr. Pritchard is able to gradually redevelop a relationship with her patient. She explains to him why the covert administration of medication was necessary. An agreement is struck between them about full and open discussions concerning administration of medications in the future. Dr. Pritchard once again explains the benefits and risks of neuroleptic treatment, including a general statement about diagnosis and expected outcome with and without medication. General Ward agrees to take one 0.5-mg haloperidol tablet at bedtime, which helps control his bouts of agitation and suspicion. Dr. Pritchard continues to visit her patient once a week.

How did the right to refuse treatment develop historically?

The right to refuse treatment is intimately connected with the doctrine of informed consent. In 1914, Justice Cardozo stated that "every human being of adult years and sound mind has a right to determine what shall be done with his own body, and a surgeon who performs an operation without his patient's consent commits an assault, for which he is liable for damages" (1). In *Rogers v. Commissioner of the Department of Mental Health* (2), the Massachusetts Supreme Judicial Court recognized as a long-standing matter that "every competent adult has a right to forgo treatment, or even cure, if it entails what for him are intolerable consequences or risks, however unwise this sense of value may be in the eyes of the medical profession."

By withholding consent, patients express their right to refuse treatment except under certain circumstances. In rare situations, courts have authorized treatment against the wishes of a competent patient. Generally, these cases involve situations where the life of a fetus is at risk, where a patient is encumbered or responsible for the care of dependent children and can be restored to full health through the intervention in question (most often, blood transfusion), and where a patient who has attempted suicide is otherwise considered to be a healthy individual. The right to refuse treatment also reflects the exercise of basic constitutional rights. As Stone (3) points out, the right to refuse psychiatric medication is not an isolated issue. Protection of individual autonomy includes not only the right to refuse emergency lifesaving treatment, but living wills, the right to die, manifold problems involving the rights of children, participation in experimentation, and other issues.

Stone (4) traces the more recent history of the right to refuse treatment to California, where psychiatrists devised radical methods of aversive conditioning in an attempt to control violent, mentally ill offenders. These individuals were forcibly administered succinylcholine, a curare-like drug, that paralyzed breathing and produced the terror of suffocation. This technique was directed toward controlling violence toward others and self (5). Apomorphine, used to induce vomiting, was another aversive technique used in a similar fashion (6). These cases were ultimately found to constitute cruel and unusual punishment, violating the Eighth Amendment of the United States Constitution. Meanwhile, in *Kaimowitz v. Department of Mental Health* (7), the court held that patients confined under the quasi-criminal, sexual psychopath statute had constitutional rights that protected them from having experimental psychosurgical procedures performed as a condition of release. Stone (4) states that from this class of quasi-criminal patients, the right to refuse treatment was extended to ordinary treatments, including neuroleptic treatment, in all mental hospitals.

Since the mid-1960s, civil libertarians have proffered a number of constitutional arguments supporting the right of legally competent patients to refuse treatment, based on the view that psychoactive medications are intrusive and potentially harmful (8). These arguments would impose liability for administering psychoactive medications to the refusing patient in a nonemergency. The courts have been reluctant to use traditional approaches to the right to refuse medication in the inpatient setting or "intrusive" treatment of incompetent outpatients. Instead, the courts have turned to constitutional theories to impose liability. If state action is present, suit is brought under 42 U.S.C. § 1983 as a constitutional tort. If a claim is brought against federal officials, litigants sue directly under the Fifth Amendment. Psychiatrists who have to treat patients in the real world have found many of these constitutional arguments interesting but not helpful clinically.

Under the First Amendment right to freedom of speech, it has been argued that when the psychiatrist acting as the state's agent administers psychotropic medications, particularly neuroleptics, the state interferes with the generation and communication of ideas.

Fourth Amendment protection from illegal searches and seizures has been applied to intrusive injections of psychoactive medications as violations of the sanctity of the person. Another theory is that the state, through involuntary psychiatric hospitalization and treatment, punishes deviance and thus deprives the individual of liberty, violating the Eighth Amendment right to freedom from cruel and unusual punishment. Hospitalization is analogized to penal incarceration and treatment to punishment (8).

The Fourteenth Amendment right to due process arises from the proposition that nonconsensual administration of psychoactive medications by the state represents deprivations of liberty. In a less plausible argument, the equal protection clause is applied to involuntary patients who contend that they are denied equal protection under the law because voluntary psychiatric patients are allowed to refuse medication and treatment in general.

The right-to-privacy principle enunciated by the United States Supreme Court derives not from any specific constitutional provision, but rather arises from the "penumbras" surrounding them. Involuntary treatment represents an abridgment of bodily control and autonomy, allegedly violating privacy rights.

The "least restrictive alternative" test is applied to state actions that are restrictive and could be accomplished by less drastic means. Thus the state is required to provide the least treatment necessary to gain a given therapeutic end. When involuntary hospitalization occurs, patients no longer lose their civil rights. In every state but Utah, a determination to hospitalize a patient involuntarily does not equate with an adjudication of incompetence. This subject is discussed in greater detail in Chapter 15.

To keep these issues in perspective, Freishtat (9) points out that the U.S. Supreme Court in *Mills v. Rogers* (10) did not reach the question of a federal constitutional right to refuse treatment, holding instead that the issue depends on the existence of state-guaranteed rights. Freishtat (9) further remarks that these state rights are difficult to obtain. Statutory grants of the right to refuse treatment are rare, and, in the absence of such grants, courts have declined to discover such a right. Furthermore, the right cannot be considered absolute because the courts are frequently required to limit individual liberty in response to the demands for an orderly society. Thus, the extent to which patients have the right to refuse treatment is circumscribed by the state's legitimate concerns and responsibilities. The significance for the clinician is that although the reasoning in *Rogers* may ultimately prove persuasive, that is not the case now and may never be.

What are some of the more recent legal developments in the civil law concerning the rights of the mentally ill to refuse medication?

The extent of the legal regulation of antipsychotic medication administration to mental patients is one of the most controversial mental health law issues. The debate centers around the right of involuntarily hospitalized patients to refuse antipsychotic medications and the intent of such a right. The right to refuse treatment has two separate but related legal functions. The first function is regulatory. Specifically, regulatory issues focus on overseeing the provision of responsible hospital, staff, and medical practices in the administration of neuroleptics that have a substantial risk of serious adverse side effects, both reversible and irreversible. Although psychiatrists tend to overlook this function, it would require a substantial blink at reality to deny that serious abuses of neuroleptic administration have been uncovered in institutional settings.

The other legal function is to allow mental patients more autonomy in treatment decisions and to facilitate the emergence of a more effective therapeutic alliance. This clinical dimension of the right to refuse treatment has not been sufficiently appreciated. The hope for good mental health care is that out of the ruins of restricted professional judgment created by the right-to-refuse-treatment movement, the flower of the therapeutic alliance will bloom.

State courts have become the major venue for the litigation of the rights of patients. Federal courts have moved away from the extension of individual rights derived from the federal constitution toward permitting states to define such rights (11). Appelbaum (12) divides judicial decisions on the right to refuse treatment into two basic models: treatment-driven and rights-driven. In the treatment-driven model, the right of the patient to refuse treatment is limited. The treating physicians' judgments concerning treatment are given priority. In the rights-driven model, the emphasis is placed upon the civil liberties of patients and the right to control their own care. Regardless of the model used, patients who refuse almost always get treated anyway.

A number of major cases have been litigated concerning the right to refuse treatment. In *Rennie v. Klein* (13), the Third Circuit held that mental patients involuntarily hospitalized in state institutions retain a qualified constitutional right to refuse neuroleptic medications that may have permanently disabling side effects. The competing liberty and treatment interests must be administered by the "least intrusive means," striking a proper balance between treatment efficacy and intrusiveness. The court found that New Jersey administrative procedures for involuntary administration of medication were adequate. In a life-threatening situation or emergency, a doctor may medicate the patient. Otherwise, unless the patient has been adjudicated incompetent, a treatment team and the medical director or designee may involuntarily medicate the patient as necessary only after an examination. The judge constructively transformed the right to refuse treatment into a right to obtain proper treatment. The Supreme Court then granted certiorari in *Klein*. The court ultimately vacated and remanded *Klein* to the Third Circuit, based on its intervening decision in *Youngberg v. Romeo* (14) (discussed later in this chapter). The Third Circuit reiterated the basic premise of the earlier decision that involuntarily hospitalized patients do have a constitutional right to refuse administration of neuroleptics (15, 16).

In *In re the Guardianship of Richard Roe III* (17), the Massachusetts Supreme Judicial Court ruled that when an incompetent outpatient refused neuroleptics, these drugs could not be administered by his father, the court-appointed guardian, without a court order. Roe, hospitalized after committing a criminal offense, was found incompetent. His father was appointed guardian. With discharge drawing near, the father sought permission to authorize medication for his son against the latter's will, fearing his son would stop taking medication and become violent. The probate judge, guided by the original *Mills v. Rogers* case authorizing guardians to consent on behalf of incompetent inpatients, granted permission. The guardian *ad litem* challenged this finding and succeeded in bringing the case before the Supreme Judicial Court. The ruling stated that the judge is responsible for rendering a substitute determination on behalf of the ward based on six factors in order to reconstruct the ward's decision had he remained competent: *1)* the expressed preferences of the ward, *2)* his religious beliefs, *3)* the impact upon his family, *4)* the consequences of refusal, *5)* the probability of side effects, and *6)* the treatment prognosis. The court stressed that the substantive and procedural requirements established in this case were not intended to apply to involuntarily hospitalized patients.

Gutheil and Mills (18) discuss the inherent conceptual difficulties caused by this and other legal rulings. For instance, if the judge finds that the "best interests" of the ward require one outcome but concludes that the ward's substituted judgment requires another, the substitute judgment prevails in the absence of an overriding state interest. Thus, if a person would make a foolish or unwise decision if competent, the judge must respect that same decision as if made by a competent person in similar circumstances. This raises serious questions about the policy value of this model. Most courts take the position that if there is any means of knowing what decision the patient would make under the given circumstances, that is the mandatory standard of decision making both legally and ethically. When it is not possible to gather enough information to determine what the patient would have decided, then the decision must be made according to the best interests of the patient.

Rogers v. Mills (formerly *Rogers v. Okin*) (19) is a complicated case that has wound its way through the courts since 1974. Originally, it was brought as a class action suit by psychiatric patients at Boston State Hospital, alleging constitutional deviations and other tort claims. The federal district court held that an objecting patient could not be medicated in the absence of an emergency unless he or she was adjudicated incompetent and a court-appointed guardian provided consent for treatment. On appeal, the Court of Appeals for the First Circuit (19) held that justification for overriding an individual's general constitutional right to refuse treatment was justified by the state's police power authority to commit mentally ill persons in order to protect others from harm. Involuntary medication could be justified only on this basis in an emergency.

Psychiatrists have objected to such definitions of emergency that do not take into account criteria for medical interventions but, in essence, transform the psychiatrist into a police officer who must administer medication to stop violence. The fact that many patients "treated" under the criteria for an emergency may be fully competent and violent, quite apart from their mental illness, is not considered. As a result, treatment becomes "chemical restraint" falling under the statutory provisions for restraint and seclusion and requiring the full panoply of protection under that statute.

The First Circuit fashioned its own definitions of an "emergency" based on a determination of whether "the need to prevent violence in a particular situation outweighs the possibility of harm [from medication] to the medicated individual" and also "the absence of reasonable alternatives." The procedures required to make this assessment were left to the district court on remand. The court noted that committed patients are often in "desperate" need of treatment but that before *parens patriae* authority could be utilized to treat them, a judicial determination of competency would be required. If the patient was found to be incompetent, the determination of whether medication should be given would require a substituted decision.

The Supreme Court granted the petition for certiorari (19). In June 1982, the Court (19) vacated the First Circuit judgment and remanded the case for review in light of the *Roe III* (17) decision. The First Circuit immediately certified the case directly to the Massachusetts Supreme Judicial Court.

In its latest incarnation, *Rogers v. Commissioner of the Department of Mental Health* (2), the Massachusetts Supreme Judicial Court ruled that mental patients, even when involuntarily hospitalized, have an important right to arrive at their own treatment decisions. As noted earlier, the court stated that it has long been recognized that "every competent adult has a right to forgo treatment, or even cure, if it entails what for him are intolerable consequences or risks, however unwise this sense of value may be in the eyes of the medical profession." The court held that physicians may override the patient's right to make a treatment decision only after a judicial determination is made that the patient is legally incompetent and the judge, using a substituted judgment procedure, establishes an approved treatment plan.

Veliz (20) did a follow-up study on the application of the *Rogers* decision at Bridgewater State Hospital, the largest forensic psychiatric hospital in Massachusetts. He found that more than 50% of a group of involuntarily hospitalized patients refusing neuroleptic medication were subsequently judged incompetent in the first court proceedings after the Massachusetts Supreme Judicial Court ruled that the right to refuse medication was a protected right. The court appeared to place less emphasis on issues related to mental status than did psychiatrists. Subsequently, in Massachusetts, only 3% of treatment refusals were upheld, while in Minnesota, which utilizes the medical model, astoundingly 25% of treatment refusals were upheld. This may be due to psychiatrists in Massachusetts appearing in court in unprecedented numbers to declare patients incompetent, arguing that the patient would have made a decision to take the recommended medications if competent.

In *Youngberg v. Romeo* (21), the U.S. Supreme Court held that involuntarily hospitalized patients possess substantive constitutional rights to be free from unnecessary bodily restraints, to have safe conditions in which to live, and to receive some degree of training and treatment. Romeo, a severely mentally retarded patient with an IQ between 8 and 10, suffered injuries on at least 63 occasions both by his own violence and from other residents reacting to him. He was physically restrained for portions of each day in the infirmary while recovering from a broken arm. His mother alleged that officials at the institution had failed to institute appropriate preventive procedures.

The Supreme Court stated that "the Constitution only requires that the courts make certain that professional judgment in fact was exercised." It ruled that it is not appropriate for federal courts to specify which of several professionally acceptable choices of treatment should be selected. Furthermore, the Supreme Court held that federal courts "must show deference to the judgment exercised by professionals" and that "interference by the federal judiciary with the internal operations of these institutions [for the mentally retarded] should be minimized." The Court also held that a treatment decision made by a "professional" is presumed to be valid and that "liability must be imposed only when the decision by the professional is such a substantial departure from accepted professional judgment, practice, or standards as to demonstrate that the person responsible did not base the decision on such a judgment" (21). Although not applicable directly to mental hospitals, the ruling in *Youngberg* provides substantial latitude for mental health practitioners in rendering reasonable care for the institutionalized mentally retarded.

In *Rivers v. Katz* (22), the highest court of New York ruled that under the due-process clause of the New York constitution, involuntarily hospitalized mental patients have a fundamental right to refuse antipsychotic medication (neuroleptics and lithium). Involuntarily hospitalized patients at Harlem Valley Psychiatric Center brought legal action against the Commissioner of the Department of Mental Health and other hospital officials, seeking to stop the nonconsensual administration of neuroleptic drugs. The court held that the patient's right to determine his or her course of treatment was paramount to the obligation that the physician has to provide medical care. The hospital officials contended that an involuntarily hospitalized mental patient was presumptively incompetent to exercise the right to refuse treatment.

The court reaffirmed the recent trend in the courts and among legal and psychiatric commentators recognizing that the need for involuntary hospitalization and the ability to make health care decisions bear no significant relationship. The court espoused a rights-driven basis for treatment refusal in ruling that the decision to overrule an involuntary mental patient's refusal of medications was a judicial rather than a medical function. Furthermore, four conditions must be met for the proposed treatment:

1. The patient's liberty interests must be recognized.
2. The patient's best interests must be considered.
3. The benefits of treatment must be clearly defined.
4. Less intrusive alternative treatments must be evaluated.

The court relied upon the common law presumption that an adult of sound mind has the right to control his or her treatment as well as the due-process clause of the state constitution.

Deland and Borenstein (23) conducted a retrospective study of the initial impact of the *Rivers v. Katz* decision. They compared the "best interests" approach in *Rivers* to the "substituted judgment" approach in *Rogers v. Commissioner of the Department of Mental Health* (2). *Rogers* turned out to be considerably more expensive in human resources, time, and money.

In *Riese v. St. Mary's Hospital* (24), the California Supreme Court let stand the appellate court decision in a case involving the right to refuse treatment. It is now legally impossible to involuntarily medicate patients who are not believed to be competent in a nonemergency without first waiting for a court to make a formal finding of incompetency. The effect of *Riese* upon inpatient psychiatric practice is discussed by Binder and McNiel (25).

In *Stensvad v. Reivitz* (26), a United States District Court in Wisconsin upheld the constitutionality of the state statute permitting involuntarily hospitalized patients to be medicated without their consent. In this case, a Wisconsin court committed Richard Stensvad after a jury verdict found him not guilty of first-degree murder by reason of insanity. The court found that protection inhered in the commitment process, holding that "an involuntary commitment is a finding of incompetency with respect to treatment decisions." The court ruled that Wisconsin statute allows commitment for "custody, care and treatment." Thus, antipsychotic drug therapy is within the province of the committing court. This ruling may signal a philosophical turnaround by an increasingly conservative federal judiciary that counters a long string of state judicial decisions expanding patients' right to refuse treatment.

The alternatives presented by the above cases for resolving the right of involuntary patients to refuse treatment have been studied by the American Psychiatric Association's Council on Psychiatry and Law (27). Four models for managing treatment refusal were proposed:

1. A judicial hearing at the time of commitment where competency and the right to refuse treatment would be resolved
2. Separate judicial hearings for commitment and treatment, the latter to be held after commitment
3. Administrative determinations of the right to refuse treatment through utilization of second opinions and hearings within the hospital
4. A model similar to that adopted by the California consent decree utilizing a single hospital to test procedures

Arkin (28) states that it would be a mistake to view litigations involving the right to refuse treatment simply as a dispute between civil libertarians and psychiatrists who follow the medical model. These cases are a manifestation of society's desire for an appropriate balance between state interests and the liberty interests of the mentally ill.

The right-to-refuse-treatment litigation has not provided a meaningful solution to the problem of involuntary medication. Despite considerable efforts by the courts, litigation cannot solve the problem. Judges do not possess the medical training necessary to decide such issues, nor can legal review respond promptly or flexibly to the constantly changing nature of illness and treatment practices. In *Rennie* (13), the Third Circuit recognized this problem when referring to judges "who have doffed their black robes and donned white coats." Independent review within the institution by a multidisciplinary team that contains qualified staff and supervisory personnel is a preferable alternative to court review (29).

Stone (3) sees patient incompetence as the central issue in overcoming any constitutional right to refuse treatment. The overcoming of a presumption of competency required in all these cases is based on sound policy reasons. He feels it would be politically unacceptable for psychiatrists to determine competence and then treat patients against their wishes. Once the presumption of competence is legally overcome, however, treatment should be expedited. According to Stone, a "legal system that orders people into mental hospitals and then orders psychiatrists not to treat them seems to make Kafka's vision of the law a reality."

The American Psychiatric Association (APA) (30) has created a "right to refuse medication" resource document to assist states that have not mandated judicial review of medication refusal. The guidelines apply to voluntarily and involuntarily hospitalized adult patients who do not consent to a proposed course of medication treatment.

What judicial decisions have dealt with the rights of mentally ill prisoners to refuse antipsychotic medication? What effect do these decisions have upon the involuntarily hospitalized mentally ill?

As civil suits brought by involuntarily hospitalized patients proliferated in the lower courts, suits were also brought by prisoners in the federal courts against nonconsensual treatment with antipsychotic medication.

In *United States v. Charters* (31), the defendant was charged with threatening the life of President Reagan in 1983. He was found incompetent to stand trial and subsequently confined to a federal correctional institution. The commitment was reviewed on five subsequent occasions by the federal district court. Charters was found each time to be incompetent to stand trial and dangerous. The court granted the government's motion to have Charters forcibly medicated. Charters appealed.

The Fourth Circuit Court of Appeals rejected the "exercise of professional judgment standard" articulated in *Youngberg v. Romeo* (14) as applied to antipsychotic medication cases. The court affirmed the right to freedom of thought and privacy reasoning of the decision making in the earlier *Rennie* and *Rogers* cases. Although the court limited its ruling to pretrial detainees, it clearly applied previous right-to-refuse case law to a criminal pretrial detainee (32). The court of appeals held that Charters was "improperly confined." On the medication issue, the court required that medication decisions be made by an independent arbiter such as a federal court.

However, in *Charters II* (33), the en banc decision reached a different conclusion. The Fourth Circuit found that the original trial court adequately protected the interests of Charters by applying the professional judgment standard to federal correctional personnel when the decision was made to medicate Charters. The court noted that legally confined persons retain constitutionally protected liberty interests in controlling the administration of antipsychotic medication. However, these interests must yield to legitimate government interests and statutory duty to attempt restoration of mental competency to patients in order to return them to a free society.

Thus, *Charters II* continued the trend where federal courts generally rule in favor of professional judgment whereas state courts usually decide in favor of the right to refuse treatment (11).

In *United States v. Watson* (34), a different result was reached. The defendant had a long psychiatric history of repeated assaults. Upon the filing of a petition by the United States, the district court ordered Watson committed for treatment with involuntary medication. Watson appealed. The Court of Appeals for the Eighth Circuit ruled that involuntary medication with psychotropic drugs should be allowed only to the extent required to prevent prisoners from harming others or themselves. The court of appeals rejected the government's position that federal prisoners could be medicated involuntarily based solely on the nonarbitrary exercise of professional judgment.

Finally, the recent U.S. Supreme Court case involving a federal prisoner, *Washington v. Harper* (35), clarifies the Court's position on the constitutional aspects of involuntary treatment. Ironically, the Court had not squarely faced the constitutional issues brought by involuntarily hospitalized patients for over a decade in various litigations involving the right to refuse treatment (36).

Walter Harper had been incarcerated in the Washington State Penitentiary following conviction for robbery in 1976. Following assaults, his parole was revoked and he was transferred to the Special Offender Center (SOC) for seriously mentally ill convicted felons. When Harper refused antipsychotic medication, the treating physician sought to medicate Harper involuntarily according to the SOC's policy. Harper filed suit in state court, alleging that his due-process rights under the constitution of the state of Washington and the United States Constitution were violated. The state trial court upheld the SOC's procedures. Three years later, on appeal, the Washington Supreme Court reversed and remanded the case to the trial court. The case was then appealed to the United States Supreme Court.

The Supreme Court ruled that a prisoner with a serious mental illness could be treated involuntarily with antipsychotic medication if the prisoner was a danger to himself or others and if treatment was considered to be in the inmate's best interest. On the procedural issue, the Court observed that a mentally ill prisoner's interests might be better served by permitting medical professionals, rather than judges, to make the decision to involuntarily medicate. The court ruled that the SOC's policy provisions for procedural rights during hearings for involuntary treatment of prisoners met constitutional prerequisites.

Although both *Watson* and *Harper* apply only to incarcerated psychiatric patients, *Harper* clarified the Supreme Court's position on the constitutional aspects of involuntary treatment. This case's influence on state law, at which level most of the right-to-refuse-treatment litigation will continue, is only advisory (36). The reasoning in *Harper* may nevertheless be persuasive in states that have not adopted rigorous substantive and procedural involuntary treatment standards. *Harper* supports the utilization of medical peer review using medical professionals within the institution to evaluate the medical need for involuntary medication. It is reasonable to expect that the Supreme Court would apply a similar analysis to the rights of civil patients to refuse medication (36).

What options does the psychiatrist have in managing the mentally ill patient who refuses to give consent to treatment?

The two basic options for managing the nonconsenting mentally ill patient are clinical and legal. The options are often combined, as illustrated in the clinical vignette. Whenever possible, the clinician should attempt to manage legal requirements in a clinically supportive manner that furthers the course of treatment.

The dilemma for psychiatrists can often be acute when facing a nonconsenting mentally ill patient in need of treatment. Psychiatrists have a moral, ethical, professional, and legal duty to diagnose and treat their patients with reasonable skill and care. Patients have a right to receive such care, but only if they give their permission. Competent patients (those maintaining minimal treatment decision capacity) may refuse treatment, even if the psychiatrist feels treatment is necessary. The law mandates that the decision to use treatments that are considered intrusive or potentially harmful requires the patient's permission. If mental capacity is lacking to make such a decision, a legally designated representative or a substituted judgment is required to express the patient's "best interest" (37). As will be discussed later, "substituted judgment" and "best interest" may actually be alternative, or even competing, models. Clinicians must remember that mental incapacity does not prevent treatment. It means only that substitute consent must be obtained.

Psychiatrists should not be immobilized in their professional judgment by remaining unfamiliar with the options available in managing nonconsenting mentally ill patients. Too often, ineffective or compromised treatments are provided in these situations that undermine the duty to provide reasonable skill in diagnosis and treatment of the patient. Thus, Stone (4) decries the fact that judicial decisions limiting access to the appropriate medical use of antipsychotic drugs encourage inappropriate treatment with minor tranquilizers. The minor tranquilizers not only may be ineffective but could be psychologically and physically addicting.

The psychiatrist must be aware of an evolution in the doctor-patient relationship as a result of increased patient rights, consumerism, and the possibility that newer treatment modalities may contain the possibility of serious adverse reactions. The patient is no longer a passive supplicant before the all-powerful god-physician. Many psychiatrists welcome the opportunity to come down from Olympus and join with their patients in sharing the often prodigious responsibilities for care and treatment. Accordingly, the nature of the fiduciary relationship has shifted from stewardship to collaboration. Today, part of the psychiatrist's fiduciary responsibility to act in the patient's best interest requires engaging the patient as an active partner in the decision-making process.

An important, although perhaps incidental, benefit derived from the cases involving the right to refuse treatment is that a working therapeutic alliance with patients is encouraged. When the patient lacks the mental capacity to consent, shared decision making continues through legally designated representatives of the patient or by substituted judgments of the court, except in actual emergencies.

Many psychiatrists are perplexed by the opposing doctrines of the right to refuse treatment and the right to treatment. In *Whitree v. State* (38), a New York court awarded $300,000 in damages to a patient because the hospital failed to provide drug therapy against the patient's wishes. The court ruled that "the [hospital's] reason for not using such drugs was that Whitree refused them. We consider such reasons to be illogical, unprofessional and not consonant with prevailing medical standards" (38). Some psychiatrists consider the right to refuse treatment as "one right too many" (39). Others feel that the patient has a "right to be free from psychosis" (40). On the other hand, Hoffman (41) states that the patient's right to refuse treatment is a "necessary complement" to the right to receive treatment when the common goal is the achievement of adequate treatment. Patients must be able to refuse inadequate or inappropriate treatments in their quest for appropriate treatment. As a consumer, the competent patient is "always right." The right to refuse treatment is intimately connected with the right to terminate treatment, as the successful patient asserts independence and autonomy.

The clinical vignette illustrates many of these issues. When Dr. Pritchard is unable to obtain the patient's consent for neuroleptic therapy, she obtains permission from his children. Good faith or proxy consents by the next of kin may be of dubious legal standing in a number of states. When General Ward became psychotically agitated, presenting both a psychiatric and a medical emergency, Dr. Pritchard treated her patient under an implied consent available in emergency situations. The emergency must be actual, presenting a clear danger to the patient. The term "emergency" must not be defined overly broadly as a means for clinicians to circumvent informed-consent requirements. The definition of an emergency also may be contained in state statutes governing informed consent and the right to refuse treatment.

At the beginning of General Ward's declining mental functioning, Dr. Pritchard could have requested that the family petition the court for a competency hearing for an adjudication of incompetence and the appointment of a guardian for the purpose of giving consent to treatment. This approach, however, is usually time consuming. Families also are frequently reluctant to psychologically accept the disability of a loved one, much less participate in a formal legal declaration of incompetency. Dr. Pritchard also had the option of petitioning the court directly for an adjudication of incompetence and the appointment of a temporary guardian for health care decisions. Petitioning the court directly by a physician for an adjudication of incompetence and the appointment of a guardian for treatment may not be a standard option available in all jurisdictions. The vast majority of states, however, permit initiation of guardianship proceedings by "any interested party" (42). Because of time constraints, a more practical option is to seek temporary guardianship. This mechanism is used when a non-life-threatening emergency arises that nevertheless requires prompt treatment. Procedural requirements are eased because of the need for expedited action. A majority of states provide a mechanism for temporary or emergency guardianship (43). Another option for clinicians is involuntary hospitalization of the patient, which is discussed further in Chapter 8. Depending on the jurisdiction, other options that may be available include decision making by institutional administrators, institutional committees, and treatment review panels; proxy decision making by the family; and advanced directives such as the use of durable power of attorney (see Table 6-1).

Gutheil et al. (44) propose a psychiatrist-attorney team in a collaborative approach to the evaluation of competency, treatment refusal, and vicarious decision-making issues. The authors point out that neither competency determinations nor the provision of quality care can be attained solely by relying on legal procedures. Without clinical guidance, "courts may unwittingly order incompetent patients to submit to less than optimal treatment."

Although not always possible, clinical management of a mentally ill patient's refusal is the most desirable course. Dr. Pritchard sees her patient more frequently in order to develop the therapeutic alliance. She involves the social worker and General Ward's military friends. She permits the patient to exercise more control over bodily routines and schedules, giving him a greater sense of command. Thus, Dr. Pritchard diminishes General Ward's fear of helplessness and dependency, while also raising his self-esteem. Gradually, the therapeutic alliance between the psychiatrist and patient is rebuilt. At the first opportunity, the patient's competent consent is obtained. Continued treatment restores General Ward's competence.

Whenever time and circumstances permit, every effort should be made to develop a working alliance with a nonconsenting patient. These patients frequently are very suspicious or even delusional. They may have long-standing trust problems that predate the current illness. Legal options for obtaining consent should not be used initially unless required by emergency, by the clear failure of clinical interventions, or by law. Every effort should be made to maintain the therapeutic alliance with the patient, even if the alliance is strained by legal interventions governing consent that are unwanted by the patient. Research studies show that 85% to 99% of patients who initially refused medica-

---

TABLE 6–1. Common consent options for patients lacking the mental capacity for health care decisions

Proxy consent of next of kin

Adjudication of incompetence, appointment of a guardian

Institutional administrators or committees

Treatment review panels

Substituted consent of the court

Advance directives (living will, durable power of attorney, health care proxy)

Statutory surrogates (spouse or court-appointed guardian)*

---

*Medical statutory surrogate laws (when treatment wishes of patient unstated).

tion eventually chose to take it (45). Most patients changed their minds because they came to believe that medication would help them. Usually, this change was the result of the clinical staff's spending considerable time with the patient discussing medication.

Courts have generally assumed that when patients refuse treatment, the decision is made autonomously. This theory was evaluated by Schwartz et al. (46). The opinions of 24 involuntarily medicated patients were reviewed. Seventeen patients felt that the staff's decision to override their original treatment refusal was correct. Moreover, the patients felt they should be treated against their will again, if necessary. Persistent refusers of medication were highly grandiose, denying their illness. The authors concluded that treatment refusal should be considered primarily a psychotherapeutic issue and, in most cases, should be subjected to clinical rather than judicial review.

Legal proceedings should not be initiated unless the clinical approach fails and the patient's psychiatric condition requires legal intervention for care and treatment. The immediate summoning of the law may be motivated by a desire to be rid of a difficult, demanding patient. Gutheil (47) describes how forensic psychiatric concerns can be utilized defensively by the trainee as a resistance to the treatment process. If clinical approaches fail, however, the psychiatrist can realistically inform the patient that the legal intervention will be initiated not out of an adversarial position but from concern for the patient's health. The ultimate decision is the court's responsibility. Thus, both doctor and patient are in the same uncertain situation, awaiting the decision of the court. Miller et al. (48) discuss the emergence of the "hospital lawyer" as a treatment resistance. With the emphasis on patients' rights and the blurring of the demarcation between civil and criminal systems of control and treatment, clinicians must be able to identify the treatment-resistive aspects of legal challenges in order to treat their patients more effectively.

The psychiatrist should look on the patient's refusal as a treatment issue. Too often, the issue of treatment refusal is seen as an extratherapeutic problem rather than grist for the therapeutic mill. Appelbaum and Gutheil (49) note the great emphasis placed on analysis of legal issues and new rulings in the psychiatric literature. They wonder about the absence of interest in treatment refusal as a clinical issue and note some of the clinical issues that lead to treatment refusal.

Patients may have concerns based on previous experience with adverse drug effects or from having observed other patients undergoing unpleasant or frightening side effects. In addition, the following all play a major role in drug refusal: transference problems, idiosyncratic perceptions of treatment, primary and secondary gain, the influence of family and friends, and staff conflicts. Acceptance of medication may represent a frightening fusion with the psychiatrist for the borderline or psychotic patient. The psychotic patient may fear poisoning when the issue of drug therapy is raised. Illness-based fears or delusions of being transformed into the opposite sex may cause the patient to seize on the fact that neuroleptics may cause difficulty in ejaculating. Patients who are manic or depressed may refuse medication based on their mood disorder. Other reactions to the psychiatrist over medication include the refusal to accept treatment based on the reenactment of early power struggles with parental figures. Countertransference reactions that lead to inconsistency with the patient, such as being late for patient appointments, not answering phone calls, or spending little time with the patient, may manifest themselves as treatment refusals. Patients may want to maintain a sick role that brings secondary gains or may not want to give up the internal gratifications that disabling symptoms may provide. Furthermore, the act of taking medication may confirm the patient's worst fears about having a mental illness. Family and friends may foster the patient's denial out of their own guilt feelings toward the patient's illness. Denial of illness is one of the main clinical reasons for medication refusal by patients (50).

Staff problems caused by the psychiatrist's poor relationship with collegues and co-workers may be communicated to the patient, undermining the trust in the psychiatrist. Hospitalized, regressed borderline and psychotic patients often split their relationships into good and bad. Such patients have been known to treat psychiatrists who suggest medication as bad psychiatrists while viewing psychiatrists who have a reputation of giving little or no medication as good. The staff may unconsciously pick up and play out this attitude toward medication and reinforce the refusal of these patients. Thus, the reasons for refusal are myriad. Whenever possible, the psychiatrist should attempt to maintain his or her treatment position vis-à-vis such refusals for the sake of the patient's therapy. Seeking legal solutions to treatment refusal initially preempts therapeutic clinical solutions.

Can the psychiatrist rely on the good faith consent of next of kin in treating patients believed to lack the capacity to give consent?

The statutes of every state define procedures for the judicial determination of competency and the establishment of guardianship. A petition is filed with the appropriate court for a declaration of incompetency and guardianship. Although some courts will appoint a general guardian to make all decisions, limited guardianship frequently is provided for the purpose of consent to treatment. In some jurisdictions the judge will be the substitute decision-maker.

Psychiatrists often find that the time required to obtain an adjudication of incompetence unduly delays necessary treatment. Families are often reluctant to face a formal court proceeding that finally labels another family member as incompetent, particularly if a breach in the relationship is feared. The common practice is to seek the consent of a spouse, parent, or relative when the refusing patient is believed to be incompetent.

Perr (29) notes the advantages in having the family as decision-maker. First, decision making by the family is a customary family responsibility. The family seeks to keep decision-makers imposed legally out of the process and avoids the inherent problems of career decision-makers. Second, the decision-making process is also quicker and less costly. However, ambivalent feelings conflict within the family and with the patient, and conflicting economic interests may make next of kin suspect as guardians. Also, relatives may not be available. Furthermore, next of kin may possess dubious competence or even less competence than the patient (51).

The President's Commission for the Study of Ethical Problems in Medicine and Biomedical and Behavioral Research (52) recommends that the relatives of incompetent patients be selected as proxy decision-makers for the following reasons:

1. The family is generally most concerned about the good of the patient.
2. The family will also usually be most knowledgeable about the patient's goals, preferences, and values.
3. The family deserves recognition as an important social unit to be treated, within limits, as a single decision-maker in matters that intimately affect its members.

Unless proxy consent by a relative is provided by statute or a recent judicial decision in the state where the psychiatrist practices, it is not recommended that good-faith consent by next of kin be relied upon in treating a patient believed to lack sufficient mental capacity for medical care decision making (37). Some courts have sanctioned such consent, when the relative providing consent supported the patient, despite the presence of statutory provisions for incompetency determinations (53, 54). Even under these circumstances, consent of relatives should not be relied on unless provided by statute or a recent judicial decision.

A number of states permit proxy decision making by statute, most as part of their informed-consent statute (55). Of these states, approximately half specify that another person may authorize consent on behalf of the incompetent patient or mention specific relatives. A few states indicate that the substitute should be a family member or mention only a guardian as a substitute decision-maker. In a number of other states, courts have addressed the issue of proxy consent in individual cases.

With the increasing civil libertarian emphasis in legislatures and courts affirming and protecting the rights of patients to determine their own treatment decisions, psychiatrists who decide on their own that the refusing patient is incompetent and who institute treatment run the risk of being sued. Because every state specifically defines who may substitute consent and under what circumstances, patients may later refer to these statutes should a lawsuit arise. As a result, statutory provisions will protect psychiatrists when they adhere to established procedures for determining competency.

In the vignette, Dr. Pritchard lacks knowledge of the state statutory procedures for adjudication of incompetence and substitute consent. Given the nature of General Ward's illness, particularly the diagnosis of dementia, she should have at least considered obtaining an adjudication of incompetence and temporary guardianship at the first refusal by her patient. Most states allow the director of the nursing home or institution or the physician to petition the court for a competency determination. If the family disagrees, they can challenge the determination in court.

Even if Dr. Pritchard had obtained an adjudication of incompetence and the appointment of a temporary guardian to give consent, her efforts would still need to be directed toward building a therapeutic alliance with her patient. Psychological understanding and support from the therapist may permit some cognitively or emotionally impaired patients to gain increased mental capacity with a concomitant ability to provide a minimally competent consent. Developing rapport in the course of assessment promotes confidence and enables patients to ask medical questions.

Recourse to legal means should never deter the psychiatrist from attending to the treatment alliance. On the other hand, if the psychiatrist is prevented from providing required treatment by the patient, the family, or the law, discharge is an option that may be considered. Reasonable time and assistance must be provided to the patient in finding another health care placement if discharge is implemented.

What is the risk of liability in relying on the consent of next of kin in treating a patient believed to lack sufficient capacity for health care decisions?

If the patient is later found to be competent and the relative to be without authority to consent, the psychiatrist may be held liable for performing an unauthorized treatment. In fact, a decision by a patient that seems irrational is not, by itself, an acceptable basis for a determination of incompetence. When in doubt concerning the patient's capacity to make a treatment decision that cannot be resolved by additional medical and psychiatric consultations, legal consultation may be necessary. Generally, when the patient regains mental capacity, legal action is unlikely when the next of kin and the patient have been on good terms (37). If the relative giving the consent has a hostile relationship with the patient, a lawsuit may result.

A possible defense for psychiatrists is that the treatment would not have been changed by the appointment of a guardian, because the same relative that gave consent would be appointed. Moreover, if the patient was competent and refused treatment, the treatment would not have taken place. Courts are reluctant to impose liability when a physician acts in good faith and uses good medical judgment in making a medical determination of mental incapacity and treatment, particularly if the treatment needs and the incapacity of the patient are clear. The risk of suit can be avoided by adhering to statutory procedures for the determination of incompetency and of substituted consent.

What standards are used by substitute health care decision-makers?

A debate continues about the theory of substitute decision making. Should the substitute decision-maker act in the patient's best interest (the "objective test"), or should he or she rely on what the patient would have decided if competent (the "subjective" or "substituted judgment" approach)? The increasingly utilized subjective test is difficult to implement for patients who have never been competent, who have made improvident or less-than-competent past decisions, or who have never openly stated choices to be implemented by others. Also, the values of substitute decision-makers can be easily substituted for the patient regardless of which test is utilized (56). Both the best interest and the substituted judgment standards lead to predictable biases by those who implement them. Use of the best interest standard leads to treatment of patients and sustaining life. Application of the substituted judgment standard favors treatment refusal and the upholding of civil liberties (57).

The substituted judgment standard has found considerable judicial favor. It is based upon the incompetent person's right to privacy translated into the medical context as the right to refuse treatment. The right to privacy is the constitutional expression of the autonomy Americans claim as free persons living in a free society. On this point, courts find authority and inspiration from J. S. Mill:

> The only purpose for which power can be rightfully exercised over any member of a civilized community against his will, is to prevent harm to others. His own good, either physical or moral, is not a sufficient warrant. He cannot rightfully be compelled to do or forebear because it will be better for him to do so, because it will make him happier, because in the opinion of others, to do so would be wise, or even right. (58)

What are advance medical directives? How can they be used in the treatment of psychiatric patients?

Legal commentators recommend the use of advance directives for health care decisions executed pursuant to a natural death act such as a living will or a durable power of attorney (55). These instruments are executed pursuant to durable power-of-attorney statutes as a method for individuals, while competent, to choose proxy health care decision-makers in the event of future incompetency. A living will can be written as a subset of a durable power-of-attorney agreement. Sample living wills and durable power-of-attorney agreements can be found in Appendix 2.

In the ordinary power of attorney created for the management of business and financial matters, the instrument is used by the person who may not be geographically present to conduct personal business. The power of attorney becomes null and void if the person creating it becomes incompetent. Recently, state legislators have recognized that people may want to indicate who should make important health care decisions for them in case they become incapacitated and unable to act in their own behalf. Thus, all 50 states have made it possible for individuals to create a *durable* power of attorney for health care—that is, a power of attorney that endures even if the competence of the creator does not (59).

Some acutely psychotic patients treated in an emergency may be expected to recover the capacity to consent within a few days. At that time, consent for treatment should be obtained directly from the patient. For the patient who continues to lack sufficient decision-making capacity, an increasing number of states provide administrative procedures authorized by statute that permit involuntary treatment of the incompetent, refusing mentally ill patient who does not meet current standards for involuntary hospitalization (60, 61). In most jurisdictions, a durable power of attorney by the next of kin provides consent through enacted durable power-of-attorney statutes (55). However, in some instances, this procedure may not meet judicial challenge. In order to rectify the sometimes uncertain status of the durable power of attorney as applied to health care decisions, a number of states have passed or are considering passing health care proxy laws. The health care proxy is a legal instrument akin to the durable power of attorney but specifically created for health care decision making (62) (see sample health care proxy in Appendix 2). Medical statutory surrogate laws authorize certain individuals, such as a spouse or court-appointed guardian, to make terminal treatment decisions when the patient has not stated his or her wishes in writing.

A durable power of attorney that is created just for health care decisions does not cover business or other kinds of decisions. It is much broader and flexible than a living will, which covers just the period of a diagnosed terminal illness, specifying only that no "extraordinary treatments" be utilized that would prolong the act of dying (63, 64). Currently, an effort is being made to tailor the living will into a psychiatric living will as an alternative to involuntary treatment (65). The legal sufficiency of such a document remains untested.

The living will, the health care proxy, and the durable power-of-attorney agreements are even more important now after the Supreme Court decision in *Cruzan v. Director of the Missouri Department of Health* (66). After *Cruzan*, clear and convincing evidence of an incapacitated person's directives concerning terminal illness is required. Anecdotal evidence of the person's wishes probably will be insufficient. Guidance for physicians concerning ethical standards and legal liability after *Cruzan* is available (67). The Patient Self-Determination Act that took effect on December 1, 1991, requires hospitals, nursing homes, hospices, managed care organizations, and home health care agencies to advise patients or family members of their right to accept or refuse medical care and to execute an advance directive (68).

With a durable power of attorney or health care proxy, one can give specific directions about what decisions should be made in particular circumstances in the event one becomes unable to make these decisions. How competence should be determined is not specified in most durable power-of-attorney statutes or health care proxy laws. Competence is usually determined by examination of two physicians with notation in the medical record concerning the patient's ability to understand the nature and consequences of the proposed treatment, the ability to make a choice, and the ability to communicate that choice.

The application of advance directives to psychiatric patients presents difficulties. The health care proxies or durable power of attorney has been dubbed a "Ulysses contract" (69). In mythology, Ulysses (from the Greek Odysseus) instructed his men to tie him to the mast of their ship as they passed by the enticing but fatal Sirens. Ulysses told his men not to untie him, no matter how much he demanded release. When Ulysses heard the seductive Sirens singing, he struggled to free himself but to no avail. He passed safely by the Sirens.

The classic example of this advanced directive arises when the manic-depressive patient who is asymptomatic draws up a durable power of attorney or health care proxy directing that "if I become manic again, administer lithium therapy, even if I strenuously object." When a manic episode recurs, the patient strenuously objects to treatment with lithium. The patient has not been adjudicated incompetent and cognitive functioning may not be obviously disrupted. The treating physician or institution does not have much choice but to honor the patient's right of refusal, even if the decision appears to be incompetently made. Only if the patient is grossly disordered and an immediate danger to self and others should the patient's refusal of treatment be temporarily overridden. Otherwise, it is better to seek a court order for treatment than risk legal entanglement with the patient by forcing the issue of the advance directive.

Although a durable power of attorney or health care proxy may be of limited value for bipolar and other recurrent disorders, it may be of considerable value in other conditions. For example, a durable power of attorney or health care proxy should be considered in patients with chronic progressive neurological and physical disorders that eventually may lead to mental incapacity (70). Overman and Stoudemire (71) provide legal and financial guidelines for families of patients with Alzheimer's disease.

What consent issues are involved in the treatment of a minor?

Minors have been traditionally considered by the law to be incompetent for most purposes, including the right to make treatment decisions (37). The mental health professional must obtain the consent of the parent or legal guardian. Statutory and judicial exceptions to this rule exist, however. Mental health professionals should acquaint themselves with the law in their jurisdictions.

In the involuntary hospitalization of minors, the U.S. Supreme Court, in *Parham v. J. R.* (72), held that in addition to prescribed state law procedures, the federal due-process clause requires review of a parental decision to commit a minor child by an independent and neutral physician. The Court rejected the claim that the due-process clause necessitates more rigorous procedural safeguards.

Exception exists for emergencies and in most states is an extension of that provided for adults. A few states narrowly apply this exception if the delay in treatment would result in death or serious injury (73). Exception for the physician's judgment is made in some states, allowing treatment if the delay in obtaining parental consent would, in the physician's judgment, endanger the health of the minor (37). Exception also exists for the emancipated minor who is no longer under parental control. Marriage or military service always emancipates a minor. Age, residence, financial independence, property ownership, pregnancy, and parenthood also will be considered by the court in determining the appropriate status. More than half the states, through emancipation statutes, give minors the right to make decisions concerning treatment if certain criteria are met (74).

The mature minor exception allows treating minors on their own consent when the minor demonstrates capacity to appreciate the nature, extent, and consequences of medical treatment (75). Although every state has not adopted the mature minor exception, physicians have not been held liable for treating minors over 15 years of age. Annas (76) states that "no court in recent history has found any health care provider liable for treating a minor over 15 years without parental consent, where the minor has consented to his own care."

References

1. Schloendorff v Society of New York Hospital, 211 NY 125, 105 NE 92, (1914), overruled, Bing v Thunig, 2 NY2d 656, 143 NE2d 3, 163 NYS2d 3 (1957)
2. 390 Mass 489, 495, 458 NE2d 308 (1983)
3. Stone AA: The right to refuse treatment. Arch Gen Psychiatry 38:358–362, 1981
4. Stone AA: Law, Psychiatry, and Morality. Washington, DC, American Psychiatric Press, 1984, pp 50–52
5. Mackey v Procunier 477 F2d 877 (9th Cir 1973)
6. Knecht v Gillman, 488 F2d 1136 (8th Cir 1973)
7. Civil Action No 73-19434-AW (Wayne Cty Cir Ct 1973)
8. Gutheil TG, Appelbaum PS: Clinical Handbook of Psychiatry and the Law. New York, McGraw-Hill, 1982, pp 91–94
9. Freishtat HW: Forensic update. J Clin Psychopharmacol 4:162–163, 1984
10. 457 U.S. 291 (1982)

11. Miller RD, Rachlin S, Appelbaum PS: Patients' rights: the action moves to state courts. Hosp Community Psychiatry 38:343–344, 1987
12. Appelbaum PS: The right to refuse treatment with antipsychotic medications: retrospect and prospect. Am J Psychiatry 145:413–419, 1988
13. 653 F2d 836 (3d Cir 1981) (en banc), vacated and remanded, 458 U.S. 1119 (1982), on remand, 720 F2d 266 (3d Cir 1983) (en banc)
14. 457 U.S. 307 (1982), on remand, Romeo v Youngberg, 687 F2d 33 (3d Cir 1982)
15. Perlin ML: Mental Disability Law: Civil and Criminal, Vol 2. Charlottesville, VA, Michie, 1989, p 312
16. Ibid, pp 319–320
17. 383 Mass 415, 421 NE2d 40 (1981)
18. Gutheil TG, Mills MJ: Legal conceptualization, legal fictions and the manipulation of reality: conflict between models of decision-making in psychiatry and law. Bull Am Acad Psychiatry Law 10:17–27, 1982
19. Rogers v Okin, 478 F Supp 1342 (D Mass 1979); aff'd in part, rev'd in part, and remanded, Rogers v Okin, 634 F2d 650 (1st Cir 1980); vacated and remanded, sub nom, Mills v Rogers, 457 U.S. 291 (1982); later proceeding, Rogers v Commissioner Department of Health, 390 Mass 489, 495, 458 NE2d 308 (1983)
20. Veliz JR: Medicine court: Rogers in practice. Am J Psychiatry 144:62–67, 1987
21. 457 U.S. 323 (1982), on remand, Romeo v Youngberg, 687 F2d 33 (3d Cir 1982)
22. 67 NY2d 485, 504 NYS2d 74, 495 NE2d 337 (NY 1986)
23. Deland FH, Borenstein NM: Medicine court, II: Rivers in practice. Am J Psychiatry 147:38–43, 1990
24. 243 Cal Rptr 241 (Cal App 1 Dist 1987)
25. Binder RL, McNiel DE: Involuntary patients' right to refuse medication: impact of the Riese decision on a California inpatient unit. Paper presented at the 22nd annual meeting of the American Academy of Psychiatry and the Law, Orlando, FL, October 1991
26. 601 F Supp 128 (WD Wis 1985)
27. Roth LH: The Council on Psychiatry and Law (official actions). Am J Psychiatry 142:412–413, 1985
28. Arkin HR: Forcible administration of antipsychotic medication. JAMA 252:2620–2621, 1984
29. Perr IN: The clinical considerations of medication refusal. Legal Aspects of Psychiatric Practice 1:5–8, 1984
30. American Psychiatric Association: Right to Refuse Medication Resource Document. Washington, DC, American Psychiatric Association, December 1989
31. 829 F2d 479 (4th Cir 1987)
32. Perlin ML: United States v Charters: rights of pretrial detainees to refuse medication. AAPL Newsletter 12(1):4–8, 1988
33. United States v Charters, 863 F2d 302 (4th Cir 1988) (en banc), cert denied, Charters v United States, 110 S Ct 1317 (1990)
34. 893 F2d 970 (8th Cir 1990)
35. 494 U.S. 210 (1990), cert denied, 110 S Ct 3243 (1990)
36. Appelbaum PS: Washington v Harper: prisoners' right to refuse antipsychotic medication. Hosp Community Psychiatry 41:731–732, 1990
37. Klein J, Onek J, Macbeth J: Seminar on Law in the Practice of Psychiatry. Washington, DC, Onek, Klein, and Farr, 1983

38. 56 Misc 2d 693, 290 NYS2d 486 (NY Sup Ct 1968)
39. Rachlin S: One right too many. Bull Am Acad Psychiatry Law 3:99–102, 1975
40. German JR: Involuntary treatment: its limitations. Bull Am Acad Psychiatry Law 3:66–69, 1975
41. Hoffman PB: The right to refuse treatment: a clinical perspective. Bull Am Acad Psychiatry Law 4:269–274, 1976
42. Brakel SJ, Parry J, Weiner BA: The Mentally Disabled and the Law, 3rd Edition. Chicago, IL, American Bar Foundation, 1985, pp 379–380
43. Ibid, pp 388-389
44. Gutheil TG, Bursztajn H, Kaplan AN, et al: Participation in competency assessment and treatment decisions: the role of a psychiatrist-attorney team. Mental and Physical Disability Law Reporter 11:446–449, 1987
45. Beck JC: Legal approaches examined in the right to refuse treatment. Psychiatric Times 6(11):14–15, 1989
46. Schwartz HI, Vingiano W, Perez CB: Autonomy and the right to refuse treatment: patients' attitudes after involuntary medication. Hosp Community Psychiatry 39:1049–1054, 1988
47. Gutheil TG: Legal defense as ego defense: a special form of resistance to the therapeutic process. Psychiatry 51:251–256, 1979
48. Miller RD, Maier GJ, Blanke FW, et al: Litigiousness as a resistance to therapy, in Therapeutic Jurisprudence: The Law as a Therapeutic Agent. Edited by Wexler DB. Durham, NC, Carolina Academic Press, 1990, pp 329–338
49. Appelbaum PS, Gutheil TG: Clinical aspects of treatment refusal. Compr Psychiatry 23:560–566, 1982
50. Beck JC: Right to refuse antipsychotic medication: psychiatric assessment and legal decision-making. MPDLR 11:368–372, 1987
51. Gutheil TG, Appelbaum PS: Substituted judgment and the physician's ethical dilemma, with special reference to the problem of the psychiatric patient. J Clin Psychiatry 41:303–305, 1980
52. President's Commission for the Study of Ethical Problems in Medicine and Biomedical and Behavioral Research: Making Health Care Decisions, Vol 1: A Report on the Ethical and Legal Implications of Informed Consent in the Patient-Practitioner Relationship. Washington, DC, Superintendent of Documents, October 1982
53. Anonymous v State, 236 NYS2d 88, 17 AD2d 495 (3d Dept 1963)
54. Farber v Olkon, 40 Cal 2d 503, 254 P2d 520 (1953)
55. Solnick PB: Proxy consent for incompetent nonterminally ill adult patients. J Leg Med 6:1–49, 1985
56. Roth LH: Informed consent and its applicability for psychiatry, in Psychiatry, Vol 3. Edited by Cavenar JO. Philadelphia, PA, JB Lippincott, 1985, pp 1–17
57. Robertson ED: Is "substituted judgment" a valid legal concept? Issues Law Medicine 5:197–214, 1989
58. Mill JS: On Liberty, in Great Books of the Western World. Edited by Hutchins R. 1953, p 267
59. Perlin ML: Mental Disability Law: Civil and Criminal, Vol 3. Charlottesville, VA, Michie, 1989, pp 608–609
60. Zito JM, Lentz SL, Routt WW, et al: The treatment review panel: a solution to treatment refusal? Bull Am Acad Psychiatry Law 12:349–358, 1984

61. Hassenfeld IN, Grumet B: A study of the right to refuse treatment. Bull Am Acad Psychiatry Law 12:65–74, 1984
62. New York State Department of Health: The Health Care Proxy Law: A Guidebook for Health Care Professionals. New York State Department of Health, January 1991
63. Mishkin B: Decisions in Hospice. Arlington, VA, The National Hospice Organization, 1985
64. Peters DA: Advance medical directives. J Leg Med 8:437–464, 1987
65. Psychiatric News 26(22):8, 12, 1991
66. 110 S Ct 2841 (1990)
67. Weir RF, Gostin L: Decisions to abate life-sustaining treatment for nonautonomous patients. JAMA 264:1846–1853, 1990
68. LaPuma J, Orentlicher D, Moss RJ: Advance directive on admission: clinical implications and analysis of the Patient Self-Determination Act of 1990. JAMA 266:402–405, 1991
69. T. G. Gutheil, M.D., personal communication, September 1985
70. Rosoff AJ, Gottlieb GL: Preserving personal autonomy for the elderly: competency, guardianship and Alzheimer's disease. J Leg Med 8:1–47, 1987
71. Overman W, Stoudemire A: Guidelines for legal and financial counseling of Alzheimer's disease patients and their families. Am J Psychiatry 145:1495–1500, 1988
72. 442 U.S. 584 (1979)
73. ND CENT CODE § 51417.1 (1981)
74. Holder AR: Minors' rights to consent to medical care. JAMA 257:3400–3402, 1987
75. Younts v St Francis Hospital & School of Nursing, Inc, 205 Kan 292, 469 P2d 330 (1970)
76. Annas GJ: The Rights of Hospital Patients. New York, Avon Books, 1975

Chapter 7

Informed Consent: Maintaining a Clinical Perspective

Professor Horvath, a 35-year-old, single assistant chairman of a university department of natural science, gradually becomes depressed after surgery for a ruptured vertebral disc. When he returns to teaching, he notices that he has difficulty concentrating. The professor has periods of uncontrollable crying. His fiancée, whom he plans to marry in 6 months, becomes alarmed when she discovers that the professor is spending most of his time in bed. She further observes that he is not eating properly, is disheveled most of the time, and is not taking care of himself. He finally stops going to work altogether. Formerly sexually active, he no longer has any interest in sex. Professor Horvath begins to express the belief that he has testicular cancer. When his fiancée discovers that he is making a will because he expects to die soon, she contacts Dr. Moore, a private psychiatrist in the community.

Dr. Moore visits Professor Horvath at his home and makes the diagnosis of a major depressive episode with psychotic features. He recommends immediate hospitalization. Professor Horvath neither accepts nor rejects the recommendation, stating, "What difference does it make, I will die soon of cancer." He eventually submits to voluntary hospitalization and perfunctorily signs the consent-for-admission form.

On mental status examination, Dr. Moore finds that cognitive functioning is intact with the exception of delusional thinking. The patient is profoundly depressed but not suicidal. Professor Horvath freely talks about his nihilistic delusion, expressing the belief that he has testicular cancer. He feels that his whole life has been an empty gesture. Therefore, his imminent demise is apt.

Because of the clinical picture of delusional depression, Dr. Moore decides to start the patient on a combination of an antidepressant and a neuroleptic, amitriptyline and thiothixene, respectively. He determines that Professor Horvath, although delusional, has sufficient cognitive capacity to understand information about diagnosis and treatment and to be able to make a rational choice. He informs his patient of the necessity for treatment with these medications, mentioning some of the more common side effects such as dry mouth, blurring of vision, constipation, dizziness, and extrapyramidal side effects. Be-

cause the state statute requires utilization of written consent forms for neuro-leptic medications, Dr. Moore prepares a written statement explaining the side effects he mentioned to the patient, leaving out the potential side effects of sexual dysfunction and tardive dyskinesia. Dr. Moore decides not to inform his patient about these particular side effects, fearing that this information will deter his patient from taking much-needed medications. He also informs his patient of the diagnosis of "depression, complicated by delusions of illness." As a scientist, Professor Horvath inquires about how the antidepressants work at a biochemical level. Dr. Moore explains the catecholamine hypothesis. Seeing an opportunity to develop an alliance with his patient, since they are both men of science, Dr. Moore encourages further questions along these lines.

Professor Horvath initially declines to take medication, stating that "there is no point in treating a man about to die." He expresses fears that the medication will damage his sexual functioning, depriving him of a "dying man's last chance to make love to his fiancée." His fiancée warns Professor Horvath that unless he accepts treatment, their engagement is off. Stating that the engagement is moot because of his imminent demise, the professor decides to begin medication so as not to "add to the grief that lies ahead" for his fiancée. Dr. Moore views his patient's ultimate willingness to accept a rational treatment plan as further evidence of competency to consent. Just to be safe, Dr. Moore decides to obtain a written consent from the patient's fiancée. A state statute permits consent for treatment only by immediate next of kin (i.e., parent, sibling, spouse). The patient has no immediate next of kin living.

What are the fundamental legal principles that underlie the informed-consent doctrine? What are the purposes of informed consent?

The primary purpose of the doctrine of informed consent is to promote individual autonomy and, secondarily, rational decision making (1). The basic principle underlying the doctrine of informed consent is patient self-determination founded on common law. The constitutional right of privacy also protects individual autonomy.

A legally competent individual possesses the right to determine what is to be done to his or her own body and cannot be forced to accept treatment. Justice Cardozo, in *Schloendorff v. Society of New York Hospital* (2), firmly established the principle of self-determination, stating that "every human being of adult years and sound mind has a right to determine what shall be done with his own body, and a surgeon who performs an operation without his patient's consent commits an assault, for which he is liable in damages." In this case, the surgeon removed a fibroid tumor despite the patient's insistence that "there must be no operation." The principle of self-determination derives from a basic tenet of American law: the right to privacy (3).

The second legal principle underlying the doctrine of informed consent is the fiduciary relationship. A person who has placed special trust and confidence in another requires the latter to act in good faith and in the sole interest of the person placing the trust or confidence (4). Because physicians possess special knowledge and must recognize the "ignorance and helplessness of the patient regarding his [or her] own physical condition," a fiduciary relationship is created (5). The fiduciary relationship imposes a duty on the physician to disclose all pertinent facts relating to the patient's condition and to the treatment recommendations (6, 7).

What are the basic elements of informed consent?

The basic elements of informed consent are competence, information, and voluntariness. *Competence* is a confusing term because it may be equated with legal competence or with a variety of medical definitions of mental capacity. One operational definition of competence is the mental capacity to decide in accordance with the patient's goals, concerns, and values (8). Some prefer the term *decision-making capacity* (8). Competence is usually analyzed into component elements. Lynn (8), for example, divides competence into three elements: maturity, ability to understand, and the ability to reason.

Various approaches and tests have been developed in an attempt to measure competency. The criteria used to define or measure competency are usually weighted in favor of cognitive functioning (9). This definition derives largely from the laws governing transactions (10). Clinical findings such as affective incompetence are not usually recognized by the law unless they significantly diminish cognitive capacity. As the clinical vignette pointed out, Professor Horvath's mental capacity was adversely affected by depression. A patient who feels hopelessly depressed may believe all efforts at treatment are doomed. Cognitive functioning may be reasonably intact but unusable when under the pernicious influence of a mood disorder. The affected patient may be able to *understand* the risks and benefits of a proposed treatment but may be unable to *appreciate* the benefits as well as the risks. Manic denial or severe depression may lead to an almost exclusive focus on the risks of treatment. Thus, treatment decision-making capacity may be severely impaired.

The need to provide *information* to the patient about the procedure or treatment being proposed is based on the fiduciary nature of the doctor-patient relationship. Based on knowledge and experience, doctor and patient are not on the same footing. The psychiatrist, as a fiduciary, acts solely in the patient's best interest. To do so, the psychiatrist must adequately inform the patient about treatment. Ethical concerns are expressed in the legal concept of the fiduciary relationship, which is rooted in respect for the dignity and autonomy of the patient (11). The courts, however, have been inconsistent in applying ethical, contractual, and fiduciary principles to informed consent.

One purpose of the informed-consent doctrine is to allow patients to be partners in making treatment determinations that accord with their own needs and values. Quite apart from any legal compulsion, the therapist who is sensitive to clinical and ethical issues will inform the patient of the risks and benefits of any proposed procedure or treatment, the diagnosis, and the prognosis with and without treatment, as well as the risks and benefits of alternative treatments available as part of the working therapeutic alliance. A paternalistic, controlling stance vis-à-vis the patient may have an adverse effect on the therapeutic alliance. Szasz and Hollender (12) used a mutual participation model to conclude similarly.

The paternalism–patient autonomy issue can become blurred, however, when risks and benefits are unknown or uncertain, or when the patient's competence is in question. Presented with a patient who is suffering acutely, psychiatrists as physicians are trained to alleviate the patient's suffering. Although preferable, it may not always be possible to wait for the patient's consent. The ethical aspects of clinical decision making under these circumstances may need to take precedence over legal concerns. The law should not be ignored but instead incorporated into the clinical decision-making process whenever possible.

Voluntariness appears to be particularly illusory in the practice of psychiatry. Knowledge of the patient's transference can be used subtly to manipulate compliance with the therapeutic agenda of the psychiatrist. Regressed patients can develop intense dependent relationships with the psychiatrist, making it very difficult for these patients to make autonomous treatment decisions. Although the therapist may have no intention other than to help the patient, coercion may nevertheless be present when the therapist, even "benevolently," threatens the patient. The psychiatrist who tells the patient, "I cannot discharge you from the hospital unless you promise to take your medication," may be expressing concern for the patient but is nevertheless acting coercively. The power that therapists possess with patients can never be totally avoided, but sensitivity to the maintenance of the therapeutic alliance will minimize coercive interactions.

Roth et al. (13) distinguish between external and internal factors that may prove coercive to mentally disabled persons. For instance, to what extent does institutionalization lead to dependency upon caregivers or create a dulling of vigilance and a pseudo-cooperation through a wish for discharge? Rewards and inducements, even attitude changes by the staff or psychiatrist, may be coercively manipulative. To what extent are patients "internally ready" to consent compulsively to treatment recommendations? Transference feelings can be manipulated to gain the patient's consent. On the other hand, therapists should not flinch from expressing their professional opinions about the most efficacious treatment or firmly stating what they think is in the best treatment interest of the patient. Although the line between coercion and patient autonomy can become indistinct, the patient is not well served by a "supermarket" approach to informed consent in which the patient chooses from a display case of procedures or treatments (14). The essence of informed consent is the development of the therapeutic alliance and trust through mutual participation of the therapist and the patient.

Malcolm (15) notes the subtle differences in the concepts of coercion and persuasion. Persuasion is defined as the physician's aim "to utilize the patient's reasoning ability to arrive at a desired result." On the other hand, coercion occurs "when the doctor aims to manipulate the patient by introducing extraneous elements which have the effect of undermining the patient's ability to reason."

In the clinical vignette, Professor Horvath only reluctantly agreed to take amitriptyline and thiothixene until his fiancée threatened to call off their engagement. Families can be very coercive in their attempts to pressure patients into consenting to psychiatric treatments. Employees are sometimes pressured into psychiatric hospitalization by employers under threat of termination of their employment. Therapists must be sensitive to avoid misalliances with third parties who attempt to coerce treatment. Therapists' fiduciary duty to enhance patient autonomy should complement the informed-consent doctrine in ensuring that patients' treatment decisions are made as voluntarily as possible.

What are the differences between the legal and clinical definitions of competency? Is competency a relative concept?

Legally, only competent patients may give consent to treatment. Patients are considered legally competent unless adjudicated incompetent or temporarily incapacitated by a medical emergency. An example of a legal definition of competency for health care decision making was rendered in *In re Schiller* (16). The court held that persons are competent to make treatment decisions if they are of "sufficient mind to reasonably understand the condition, the nature and the effect of the proposed treatment, attendant risks in pursuing the treatment, and in not pursuing the treatment." When psychiatrists treat patients who give an incompetent consent, they may incur the same legal responsibility as treating a competent patient who refuses treatment. In the clinical vignette, Professor Horvath was legally competent because he had not been adjudicated otherwise. Clinically, his depression interfered with his judgment and raised questions about his "medical or psychological capacity" to reach a reasonable decision concerning his treatment.

When therapists evaluate a patient's competency, they do so from the clinical perspective. Regardless of what test of competency is used, clinical factors such as the patient's psychodynamics, the accuracy of the historical data provided by the patient, the accuracy of the information provided to the patient, the stability of the patient's mental state, and the effect of the setting in which the consent is obtained may influence the evaluation of competency (17). Roth et al. (18) describe the basic elements in the various tests used to evaluate competency to consent to treatment. These include evidencing a choice, choice compared to that of a "reasonable" person, choice based on "rational" reasons, ability to understand, and actual understanding. Roth et al. conclude that the circumstances when competency is raised determine which elements of any given test will be overemphasized or understated. They comment, "The search for a single test of competency is a search for a Holy Grail. Unless it is recognized that there is no magical definition of competency to make decisions about treatment, the search for an acceptable test will never end."

Competency is not a scientifically determinable state. It is colored by personal value judgments and social policy. In addition, a clear-cut, comprehensive judicial standard of competency does not exist (19). The various legal tests of competency occur as a singular event and tend to be applied by predetermined rules and definitions in a procrustean fashion: the patient either fits or does not fit the test. In clinical practice, however, mental capacity is continuous but variable, particularly when impacted on by physical or mental illness. Treatment exigencies and the subjective biases of caregivers also significantly influence clinical competency assessments. The mental capacity to give consent is always clinically overdetermined. Thus, the determination of medical or psychological competence in psychiatric practice is not a single event but rather a continuous process.

Competency is a here-and-now contextual matter. The competence of a patient is determined in reference to the particular issue at hand. Patients are rarely so incompetent that they cannot make at least some decision about medical care. Even patients adjudicated incompetent by a court of law with appointment of a conservator or guardian may retain at least some capacity to make medical care decisions. Furthermore, only a minimal competency is necessary and maximal capacity is irrelevant. Mishkin (20) recommends distinguishing the terms *incompetence* and *incapacity*. Incompetence refers to a court adjudication, while incapacity indicates a functional inability as determined by a clinician.

A very basic level of decision-making capacity exists when the patient is able to understand the particular treatment choice proposed, to make a treatment choice, and to communicate that decision. The problem with this standard of decision-making capacity is that it obtains a simple consent from the patient rather than an informed consent because alternative treatment choices are not provided. A review of case law and scholarly literature on this issue reveals generally four standards for determining incompetency in decision making (1). In order of levels of mental capacity required, these standards include *1)* communication of choice, *2)* understanding of information provided, *3)* appreciation of one's situation and the risks and benefits of options available, and *4)* rational decision making. Psychiatrists generally feel most comfortable with a rational decision-making standard in determining incompetency. Most courts prefer the first two standards. An informed consent reflecting the patient's autonomy, personal needs, and values occurs when rational decision making is applied to the risks and benefits of appropriate treatment options provided to the patient by the clinician.

When the patient seems competent, a decision that appears irrational is not, by itself, a basis for a determination of incompetence (21). Persons who are fully competent nevertheless make foolish decisions. Legal advice may be needed if the competency issue cannot be resolved by additional medical and psychiatric consultation.

What are the standards for the disclosure of information?

The traditional professional standard defines the scope of the physician's duty to disclose: what a reasonable physician would disclose under like circumstances (22). In most jurisdictions, the patient is required to bear the burden of defining what the prevailing disclosure standard is and showing that the disclosure made to the patient deviated from that practice. In states that have enacted informed-consent statutes, there are a significant number that hold to the professional custom standard (23).

Since the early 1970s, an increasing number of courts have adopted the material-risk approach (reasonable-man standard). This standard imposes upon the physician a duty to disclose all the information that a reasonable patient would need in order to make an informed decision about a procedure or treatment. This approach is more consistent with the ascendance of patient autonomy. The major impetus for the reasonable-man standard was provided by two 1972 cases, *Canterbury v. Spence* (24) and *Cobbs v. Grant* (25). The *Canterbury* court, however, rejected a truly patient-oriented standard, the so-called "subjective lay standard" (what a particular patient would want to know). Furrow (26) proposes the subjective lay standard of informing for psychotherapy because professional opinions about risks and benefits appear to be so uncertain and diverse. If the reasonable-patient standard prevails, psychiatrists may be able to defend a claim of lack of disclosure on the ground that the patient, had he or she known the information, would have made the same decision.

The psychiatrist is not required to inform the patient of every conceivable risk. A material risk is one that "a reasonable person, in what the physician knows or should know to be the patient's position, would be likely to attach significance to in deciding whether or not to forgo the proposed therapy" (4). Whether a risk is material depends on the severity and probability of the risk, the likelihood of treatment success, and the availability of alternative, less dangerous treatments. If necessary treatment presents minimal risks, the duty to disclose is not as rigorous as when a treatment presents high risk and is dangerous or intrusive. When less dangerous but equally effective alternative treatments are available, the duty to disclose is heightened. For instance, if neuroleptic medication is prescribed for a patient's anxiety when a benzodiazepine would be equally effective, the increased risk of adverse side effects from the neuroleptic medication would require a full disclosure.

Malpractice defense attorneys have recommended the "1% rule" as a guideline for physicians (27). If a particular risk of injury has a chance of occurrence greater than 1%, the risk is considered material and needs to be disclosed. This "rule" applies only in jurisdictions that have indicated some percentage in specifying what constitutes a material risk. As in all aspects of the informed-consent doctrine, uncertainty and inconsistency reign. Courts have been inconsistent in deciding what is a major or minor risk.

Although the general trend of increased physician liability for adverse side effects of prescribed medication continues, a countertrend may be developing, as in the case of *Precourt v. Frederick* (28) in Massachusetts. In this case, an ophthalmologist administered prednisone to the patient after two separate surgeries. The patient developed aseptic necrosis of both hips from the steroid. The ophthalmologist gave no warning of side effects. Even though the defendant admitted that aseptic necrosis was a "prominent" complication of steroid use, the court ruled in favor of the physician, stating, "A physician is not required to inform a patient of remote risks." The court justified its conclusion by stating, "There must be a reasonable accommodation between the patient's right to know, fairness to physicians and society's interest that medicine be practiced in this commonwealth without unrealistic and unnecessary burdens on practitioners." The court attempted to treat the interests of individual patients, physicians, and society evenhandedly. Hopefully, *Precourt* will be the beginning of a countertrend away from holding physicians as guarantors of the health and safety of patients whenever drugs are prescribed.

Generally, doctors should provide patients with individualized information about the diagnosis, the nature and purpose of the proposed treatment, the risks and consequences of the proposed treatment, the probability that the proposed treatment will be successful, feasible treatment alternatives (including risks and benefits), and the prognosis if the proposed treatment is declined (see Table 7-1). Psychiatrists probably fulfill a subjective lay standard when informing

TABLE 7–1.   Informed consent: reasonable information to be disclosed

Although there exists no consistently accepted set of information to be disclosed for any given medical or psychiatric situation, as a rule of thumb, five areas of information are generally provided:
1. Diagnosis—description of the condition or problem
2. Treatment—nature and purpose of the proposed treatment
3. Consequences—risks and benefits of the proposed treatment
4. Alternatives—viable alternatives to the proposed treatment, including risks and benefits
5. Prognosis—projected outcome with and without treatment

their patients of the risks and benefits if they approach every patient in an individualized manner (29). Furthermore, patients usually are given ample opportunity to ask questions in the give-and-take format of therapy.

All states require informed consent by either case law or statute (15, 30). Many states have statutes requiring informed consent for treatment (31). The statutes may spell out instances when no consent is required beyond explaining the risks of anesthesia and surgery. For additional procedures, the state may specify what risks must be told to the patient and in what form (i.e., verbal or written). Under these statutes, only the disclosure of risks specified in the statute is deemed material as a matter of law (32). Some statutes make compliance to the guidelines voluntary. Most state statutes classify failure to obtain informed consent as negligence rather than battery (33).

In the clinical vignette, Dr. Moore was aware of his state's informed-consent statute, requiring written disclosures of the risks of neuroleptic treatment. Many practicing psychiatrists, however, may be either uninformed or misinformed concerning statutory informed-consent requirements in their state. Under these statutes, a violation of the patient's statutory rights may occur when treatment is prescribed without the patient's consent (34).

Mental health professionals who inform their patients on the basis of developing and maintaining the treatment alliance will more than likely meet the requirements of the material-risk standard. It certainly is not necessary to inform depressed patients about the dopamine hypothesis or the families of demented patients about the neuropathology of the nucleus basalis of Meynert in Alzheimer's disease. Providing too much information (overly informed consent) can be distressing and confusing to patients, and can lead to a malpractice suit (35). For certain patients with a scientific background, a level of informing in response to questions of causality may be necessary to create the therapeutic alliance. In psychiatry at least, the professional standard and material-risk standard of informing are beginning to move closer together as more psychiatrists appreciate the therapeutic importance of informing the patient as part of the treatment partnership (29).

What are the exceptions to the requirements for disclosure?

The most common exceptions to disclosure are incompetency, emergency, therapeutic privilege, and waiver.

Patients who are incompetent are defined by the law as being incapable of giving an informed consent. If consent is required, the psychiatrist must obtain consent from a substitute decision-maker. This subject is discussed in detail in Chapter 6.

Informed consent may be either expressed or implied. When expressed, the patient verbally agrees to treatment. On the other hand, if there is no explicit agreement between doctor and patient but the discussion or the conduct of the parties implies consent to participate in treatment, then implied consent is established. Implied consent also occurs when the current treatment is a necessary extension of the original treatment. The law implies consent in acute, life-threatening crisis situations requiring immediate medical attention and treatment. The law assumes that every rational person under these circumstances would want treatment. Consent is implied in an emergency if the patient cannot receive information or give consent, and when not enough time is available to obtain consent from a substitute decision-maker.

The definition of a medical emergency is open to debate. Generally, two situations constitute a medical emergency. First, the patient must be incapacitated and lack the mental capacity to make an informed choice. Second, the injury or disease is life-threatening and requires immediate treatment. State statutes and courts have defined medical emergency in both narrow and expansive terms (36). Clinicians who see acutely ill patients should know the legal definition of a medical emergency in their jurisdiction. At the time of an emergency, the provision of good clinical care to the patient is of primary concern.

In the vignette Dr. Moore decided not to inform his patient about the risk of tardive dyskinesia because he feared that Professor Horvath would reject the much-needed treatment. Therapeutic privilege allows a physician to withhold full disclosure of risks if it might have a serious detrimental effect on the patient's physical and psychological welfare (37). Thus, the more disturbed a patient is, the more likely it is that a reason may exist for not informing the patient. This is also true for the patient who is otherwise legally competent. In *Canterbury v. Spence* (24), the court stated, "It is recognized that patients occasionally become so ill or emotionally distraught on disclosure as to foreclose a rational decision, or complicate or hinder the treatment, or perhaps even pose psychological damage to the patient." In *Natanson v. Kline* (38), the court noted that a full disclosure of risks "could so alarm the patient that it would, in fact, constitute bad medical practice." In *Dooley v. Skodnek* (39), the court held that a jury could find in favor of a doctor who testified that he felt it was inadvisable to tell a patient about the risks of taking thioridazine because the patient already was acutely depressed.

Dr. Moore asserted therapeutic privilege by not informing the patient about the possible neuroleptic side effects of sexual dysfunction and tardive dyskinesia because he was concerned that his patient would unreasonably reject the much-needed medication. Failing to inform the patient because of the psychiatrist's fears that the patient will refuse treatment may not necessarily be recognized by the courts. The purpose of informed consent is circumvented when therapeutic privilege is used exclusively as a carte blanche for the provision of the clinician's treatment agenda. Therefore, the reasons for asserting therapeutic privilege should be carefully documented. The psychiatrist should consider disclosing the withheld information to next of kin and certainly to a legally designated substitute decision-maker.

Circumstances that justify the invocation of therapeutic privilege have been described in very sketchy terms. Moreover, the courts differ on the standard for invocation of therapeutic privilege. The courts also differ on the scope of therapeutic privilege. Courts relying on the material-risk standard favor narrowing the scope. Some courts still require disclosure of risk and consent to next of kin. Utilization of this exception to informed consent is plagued by uncertainty (4). The clinician should use this exception judiciously. Whenever therapeutic privilege is used, it circumvents the patient's autonomy and may have a chilling effect on the therapeutic alliance.

Therapeutic privilege is a qualification of the informed-consent doctrine that prevents suffering disproportionate to its benefits. As a defense, therapeutic privilege affects only the disclosure element of informed consent. The privilege can be invoked for disclosures to patients but not for disclosure to third-party authorizers of the patient's treatment. The less urgent the need for treatment, the less likely it is that therapeutic privilege will apply. Even when the therapeutic privilege is invoked, the physician is still required to disclose the basic elements of the procedure proposed and its inevitable consequences (40).

Frequently, psychiatrists believe that therapeutic privilege applies when the reason for nondisclosure is that the information may cause the patient to reject treatment. Although the doctrine of therapeutic privilege has been recognized by many courts and some statutes, not all courts have recognized it. Clinically, therapeutic privilege should be invoked after it is clear that disclosure could cause the patient to become so alarmed and distraught as to cause significant disruption of the patient's decision-making abilities or cause serious clinical regression. Should an alarm reaction occur, disclosure may again become possible if the patient and psychiatrist can resolve the reaction therapeutically.

On occasion, a patient may request not to be informed about a treatment or procedure. When patients voluntarily and knowingly make this request (i.e., realizing they have a right to this information and are competent), the request may be honored. A record should be made of the patient's waiver in the medical chart. A small number of cases and several state legislatures have recognized the role of waiver. However, the problems of definition and application of waiver remain (19).

Can informed consent for drug treatment be sought from psychotic patients? If so, should informed consent be obtained before treatment or some time after initiating treatment?

Roth (41) points out that, in accord with the developing doctrine of informed consent, psychiatrists should obtain consent for all treatments. Even if a patient is psychotic, this does not relieve the psychiatrist from attempting to obtain consent for treatment. Psychosis does not necessarily equate with an inability to consent. Some psychotic patients are quite capable of giving a valid consent to treatment. For those who are not able to consent, some form of substitute consent should be obtained. Furthermore, consent must be viewed as a continuing educational process rather than a singular ritualistic act in the service of defensive psychiatry.

When treating a psychotic patient, a major question is *when* and *if* to disclose the risk of tardive dyskinesia. Some psychotic patients cannot tolerate such information, particularly if it falls within their delusional system. Other psychotic patients do not blink when informed of tardive dyskinesia, appearing distressingly nonchalant. Individual circumstances must always be considered. Patients may initially refuse treatment recommendations as a way of dealing with their sense of helplessness. The vast majority of patients accept treatment recommendations even though they initially may refuse. Within 7 to 10 days after admission, most refusing inpatients accept treatment.

Tardive dyskinesia is usually, although not always, a late development in the course of neuroleptic therapy. Most cases do not develop for at least 3 months and usually not for 2 years (42). Therefore, some authors recommend withholding disclosure up to 3 months (43) or even a year (44). Some patients, however, may develop tardive dyskinesia after receiving relatively low doses of neuroleptics. The elderly, particularly elderly women, may develop tardive dyskinesia as early as a few weeks after beginning neuroleptic treatment. A more detailed discussion of informed consent and tardive dyskinesia can be found in Chapter 10.

For outpatients, it is generally preferable to obtain consent before initiating treatment. For some acutely disturbed hospital patients, a delay in starting drug therapy may be necessary until the therapeutic alliance has had time to develop. The managed care situation may not allow sufficient time for the therapeutic alliance to develop. Initially, these patients may not be able to provide valid consent when disclosure of side effects may seriously frighten them or possibly contribute to further regression. Furthermore, acutely disturbed patients may not be able to understand the information provided or weigh risks and benefits. In California, Title 9 of the administrative code requires that in nonemergency situations informed consent must be obtained before drug treatment of voluntary patients can be initiated (45).

When patients make an incompetent refusal or acceptance of drug treatment, proxy consent by relatives may be permitted in some jurisdictions. An increasing number of jurisdictions, however, are requiring an adjudication of incompetence and the appointment of a guardian to provide consent for treatment. In some jurisdictions, only the substituted consent of a judge is valid. Substituted consent by treatment review panels and other administrative bodies is discussed further in Chapter 6.

In addition to tardive dyskinesia, neuroleptic medications can cause other distressing side effects, although they may be acute and reversible. In the clinical vignette, Professor Horvath is very fearful that the medications prescribed might damage his sexual functioning. Some neuroleptics can produce sexual dysfunction by retarding or interfering with ejaculation. Dr. Moore is correct in withholding information that could have further distressed his patient psychologically. Withholding information that neuroleptic drugs might interfere with sexual functioning solely to prevent noncompliance would merely circumvent the patient's consent.

In a similar vein, Halleck (46) informs psychotic patients about the risks and side effects that he believes they can assimilate and that need to be known in order to allow patients to be effective participants in the treatment process. He informs his patients of immediate side effects such as autonomic and extrapyramidal reactions. Symptoms such as stuffy nose, dry mouth, blurred vision, constipation, postural hypotension, akinesia, dystonia, and akathisia also are revealed to the patient. The therapeutic alliance and compliance with the treatment are markedly enhanced when the patient is not surprised by potentially frightening side effects. Longer-range side effects such as depression, blood dyscrasia, sexual dysfunction, hepatitis, seizures, and, most important, tardive dyskinesia are discussed later when the patient can assimilate this information with less distortion in an atmosphere of trust. Halleck informs the relatives of acutely psychotic patients by using a printed list of all the risks and side effects of neuroleptic treatment.

Schizophrenic patients are known for their poor compliance with neuroleptic medications and a subsequent high relapse rate. Soskis (47), in a study of schizophrenic inpatients, suggests making treatment capital out of the readiness of these patients to share with the psychiatrist their reluctance to take medication as outpatients, thus offering an early warning system of detection and intervention to improve treatment compliance.

The Patient Medication Instruction (PMI) Program instituted by the American Medical Association (AMA) provides PMI information sheets for many medications commonly prescribed by physicians. PMIs for tricyclic antidepressants, lithium, neuroleptics, and benzodiazepines are available from the AMA. Each PMI sheet has dosage, precautions, and side effects in an easy-to-read format. Extraneous information is avoided. The patient is informed rather than alarmed. The PMIs are not intended as a substitute for information and instructions provided by the doctor, nor are they considered to be legal instruments of informed consent. The objectives of the PMIs are to increase drug compliance, reduce the risk of improper drug use, and decrease preventable, serious adverse reactions (48). The PMI is usually given to patients at the time the prescription is written. The legal significance of the PMI is unclear. PMIs may have the effect of increasing the physician's standard of care for drug therapy (49).

What are the advantages and disadvantages of written consent forms?

Although a few states specify by statute that a written consent form be utilized, ordinarily no legal requirement exists for a written consent form. Unfortunately, informed-consent statutes in some states do give written informed-consent forms the status of presumptive evidence of informed consent in the place of a continuing dialogue between doctor and patient. In *Hondroulis v. Schuhmacher* (50), the Louisiana Supreme Court held that the statutory presumption of the validity of a signed consent form could be rebutted by showing that the patient was not adequately informed of the material risks of a medical procedure. Other similar decisions in Florida (51) and Idaho (52) underscore the importance of not using blanket consent forms.

Nevertheless, the advantages of a signed, written disclosure form are two-fold: the patient cannot later say that adequate information was not provided, and the signed form establishes exactly what was disclosed and that the consent process took place (34). Whether consent is written or oral, studies have consistently shown that patients soon forget the information disclosed about a procedure or treatment (53). Furthermore, patient understanding of information contained in consent forms appears to be inversely proportional to the length of these forms (54). For the interested reader, sample consent forms are included in Appendix 2.

If consent forms are used, they should be included as part of the informing process. Without adding new information, the form should be considered a memorandum of agreement concerning the negotiations between the clinician and the patient. The form may be presented after negotiations are complete and the patient has consented to treatment. The consent form documents the existing consent rather than obtaining it, and is intended to protect the institution and the physician, not the patient (55).

The greatest disadvantage of written consent forms is that a particular hazard may be omitted. Sooner or later, the omitted hazard happens to a patient who then is able to prove beyond a shadow of a doubt that the warning of risks was not, in fact, complete and that the patient was not fully informed. In the vignette, Dr. Moore prepares a list of risks and benefits but leaves out the risks of tardive dyskinesia and sexual dysfunction. Unfortunately, consent forms are either all or nothing concerning the information that is to be provided. Moreover, written consent forms are not the appropriate place to assert therapeutic privilege.

Another major problem occurs when mental health professionals are lulled into a false sense of security because they possess a piece of paper containing the patient's signature. Consent forms have developed in specialties such as surgery, where a one-time treatment or procedure occurs. In the mental health specialties, informed consent can never be a singular event, but it must be part of a process that is intimately connected with the ongoing psychiatrist-patient relationship. Furthermore, consent forms may introduce an adversarial element into the relationship with the patient. Disturbed, suspicious patients may have a tenuous treatment alliance destroyed by the presentation of a form to sign. Also, written consent forms cannot adjust to the altered mental capacities of patients or promote understanding of the information provided if language difficulties are present. On the other hand, patients who have obsessive-compulsive traits or intellectualizing defenses may prefer a form that can be studied. Patients also may prefer written consent forms on reasonable grounds as well.

Foster (56) states that written documents afford the psychiatrist little protection and are looked upon with disdain by lawyers. The best means of protecting against an unjustified claim of lack of informed consent is for the clinician to write a note in the patient's record. The note should specify exactly the information imparted to the patient, the mental capacity of the patient to understand such information, the clinical indicators that the information was understood, and whether the patient's consent was voluntary. The obtaining of consent should not be delegated to nurses or other personnel. If any of the exceptions to obtaining consent are utilized, such as therapeutic privilege, then the reasoning for invoking the privilege should also be spelled out.

In the absence of any type of documentation, evidence that the psychiatrist obtained informed consent from the patient can be established by showing that the psychiatrist maintains a custom of informing patients of treatment risks. Rule 410 of the Federal Rules of Evidence (57) states, "Evidence of the habit of a person or of the routine practice of an organization, whether corroborated or not and regardless of the presence of eyewitnesses, is relevant to prove that the conduct of the person or organization on a particular occasion was in conformity with the habit or routine practice." In *Bloskas v. Murray* (58), a malpractice suit was brought against a physician for failure to inform the plaintiff of the risks of a total ankle replacement. The court permitted the physician to testify concerning his custom of informing patients about the risks associated with hip and knee replacement surgery to prove that he acted in accordance with this practice in informing the plaintiff of such risks.

Clearly, it is preferable to maintain a written record when obtaining a patient's consent. Relying upon establishing evidence of customary consent practices is tenuous at best.

Is informed consent necessary when therapists recommend psychotherapy to their patients?

Yes. All psychotherapies have risks and benefits that patients need to understand. In addition, an explanation should be given to patients concerning why a particular form of psychotherapy is being proposed.

Very few therapists warn patients of risks of a proposed method of psychotherapy, although the potential benefits may be extolled. Untoward transference reactions, regressive dependency states, and general worsening of a patient's clinical condition are some of the risks of psychotherapy (59). Moreover, prolonged nontherapeutic stalemates are not unusual.

Reisner and Slobogin (60) give two reasons why informed consent has been limited to the biomedical field. The first reason relates to the law of damages in which physical harm is required. In psychotherapy, where no physical damage can be demonstrated, the patient is unlikely to qualify for more than nominal damages when deprived of a right to give informed consent. In recent years, however, courts have demonstrated a marked tendency to compensate for non-physical injuries. Therapists may have an increased risk for liability under the informed-consent doctrine.

The second reason why informed-consent actions have not occurred against psychiatrists and psychologists for psychotherapy is the difficulty of proving that an injury was proximately caused by the psychotherapy. Nevertheless, Reisner and Slobogin predict that despite these difficulties, the concept of informed consent will be applied increasingly to the "nonmedical" treatment situation. As the scientific study of the treatment efficacy of psychotherapy moves forward, therapists will be expected to discuss with patients at the outset the qualitative and quantitative outcome data of alternative therapies.

Under classic tort theory, nonconsensual touching is a battery (61). The administration of drugs or electroconvulsive treatment, although therapeutic, is a battery when given without the patient's consent. Any unauthorized touching outside of ordinary social interaction constitutes a battery. Punitive and actual damages may be imposed because unauthorized touching is an offense to the dignity of the patient and an invasion of the right of self-determination. Because no touching occurs in purely talking therapies, no cause of action for battery is present (61).

Both the law and medical ethics impose a duty of loyalty and care to the patient based on the physician as a fiduciary (56). One of the pillars of the informed-consent doctrine rests on the fiduciary relationship between doctor and patient, requiring that the patient be adequately informed of any proposed treatments or procedures. With the application of the material-risk standard of informing, therapists are required to provide sufficient information so that the patient can make a knowledgeable decision. Providing insufficient consent may be actionable under negligence law. An action brought under negligence will have a longer statute of limitations as well as the availability of malpractice coverage.

The application of strict liability (i.e., when proof of negligence is not required) to the field of psychotherapy is recommended by Furrow (26). He describes the three standards of informing patients: *1)* the professional custom standard (what other therapists do); *2)* the objective lay standard (what a reasonable patient would want to know); and *3)* the subjective lay standard (what a particular patient would want to know). He recommends that the latter be used for psychotherapy because professional opinions about risks and benefits are so uncertain and diverse. In principle, most psychotherapists would agree that prospective patients should be permitted adequate time to ask questions about any of their specific concerns. This may be observed more in the breach than in actual practice.

What type of information is helpful in assisting patients to make an informed decision about psychotherapeutic treatment?

Slovenko (61) quotes Freud as advising against "lengthy preliminary discussions before the beginning of treatment." Freud felt that the patient should know of the difficulties and sacrifices of analytic treatment so that the patient would not be deprived "of any right to say later on that he had been inveigled into a treatment whose extent and implication he did not realize." Nevertheless, some psychodynamic therapists continue to express concern that sharing detailed psychological information about the assessment or the diagnosis may scuttle the fledgling psychotherapeutic process. The potential distorting effect of the doctrine of informed consent on the therapeutic process is discussed in some detail by Epstein (62) and Robitscher (63).

An initial period of evaluation allows the patient time to assess the therapist, the therapist's technique, and the interactional process between therapist and patient. A period of evaluation also allows the therapist time to make a reasonable diagnostic assessment. The nature of the patient's difficulties can be described in plain language using descriptive terms that form the basis of psychiatric nosology.

Anticipated benefits of treatment may be discussed along the lines of altering maladaptive defenses and resolution of underlying conflict, symptomatic relief, or crisis intervention, as best suits the patient's clinical situation. Obviously, no promises of cure can be made. For therapists who are prone to promising too much to patients, Freud's comment that the object of psychoanalysis is to substitute for neurotic misery ordinary human unhappiness should help temper therapeutic overzealousness. Bibring's (64) classification of psychotherapies according to the singular or combined use of catharsis, suggestion, manipulation, clarification, and insight can be a useful conceptualization for the therapist when explaining to the patient the methods to be used in any given psychotherapy. As treatment outcome studies become increasingly available, this information also can be shared with patients.

The risks of psychotherapy are more difficult to define when the evaluation reveals past regressive episodes occurring during a personal crisis. The psychiatrist may want to consider with the patient the possibility of such a recurrence during the course of long-term insight psychotherapy. A history of previous serious psychosomatic illnesses, marked dysfunctional periods, or intense transference reactions toward others should alert the therapist to a possible recurrence in the psychotherapeutic situation. Previous episodes provide indicia of potential risks to the patient. Although major life changes can occur as the result of long-term, intensive psychotherapy, specific events such as divorce or professional reverses that may seriously stress other family members often are not foreseeable risks. Life is uncertain at best. Unpredictable events or situations that are extremely traumatic may arise at anytime to destabilize a patient.

Prognostic statements should be made with great caution. In discussing prognosis, Freud used the example of the king who, in order to determine which of two subjects was bewitched, required each to be boiled. Presumably, the bewitched subject did not boil. Similarly, only after the patient has been "boiled" or treated over a period of time can the therapist have a more accurate assessment of the outcome.

Another analogy may be useful to the clinician. Long-term, intensive psychotherapy is like a journey taken with a guide over an uncharted territory to reach a destination that one is seeking. Because no maps exist, the way is often uncertain and sometimes treacherous. The traveler occasionally may encounter difficult, hostile inhabitants. Sometimes, the journey fails or never gets started beyond some initial forays. For those who successfully complete the journey, the experience results in a great sense of achievement, confidence, and a new personal perspective. Prospective travelers need the guide to explain the anticipated risks and benefits of the proposed journey. For some, the journey will be shorter and cover more familiar terrain. Sometimes the wisest course is just to stay at home or learn to appreciate the pleasures of one's own backyard.

Without treatment, the expected outcome of a particular mental disorder is extremely difficult, if not impossible, to determine. Many unforeseen life factors and the inherent course of any given mental disorder determine outcome considerations. Spontaneous remissions are not uncommon. Nevertheless, certain mental conditions such as phobic disorders or the schizophrenias have a recurrent or chronic course.

Alternative therapeutic modalities need to be discussed with patients. No longer can the psychiatrist recommend only one form of treatment. Hundreds of schools of psychotherapy exist. While therapists may not be competent in using more than a few basic treatment approaches, they should be up to date in their knowledge of the standard treatments used by competent, ethical therapists. Psychiatrists have an ethical and legal duty to stay abreast of new developments in their field. Psychiatrists should at least be able to explain such information intelligently to the patient. For example, the phobic patient can be treated by cognitive-behavioral therapy, psychodynamic therapy, medications, group therapy, or by a combination of therapeutic modalities. The therapist who primarily uses dynamic insight-oriented psychotherapy should be reasonably knowledgeable about the methods, indications, and contraindications of behavior therapy, cognitive therapy, and crisis intervention, to name just a few. Patients have a right to know about alternative therapies that may be reasonably expected to help their condition.

Psychoanalysts and other psychodynamic therapists have been almost totally immune from malpractice suits because of insurmountable technical and legal reasons. Patients dissatisfied with the lack of improvement after prolonged psychodynamic treatment may have found a way around these legal obstacles—a way provided by biological psychiatry. They may sue for malpractice because biological treatments were not administered. In *Osheroff v. Chestnut Lodge* (65), the plaintiff asserted that he was inappropriately treated with psychotherapy for depression, needlessly extending his hospital stay and causing him emotional and financial harms. This case, which was eventually settled, generated considerable controversy and discussion among mental health professionals and attorneys (66, 67, 68).

The American Psychiatric Association (APA) Task Force on Treatments of Psychiatric Disorders has published a three-volume work entitled *Treatments of Psychiatric Disorders* (69). As a consequence, psychiatrists can now inform themselves and their patients of available treatments for almost any psychiatric disorder. The book contains the following cautionary statement:

> This report does not represent the official policy of the American Psychiatric Association. It is an APA Task Force Report, signifying that members of the APA have contributed to its development, but it has not been passed through those official channels required to make it an APA policy document. **THIS REPORT IS NOT INTENDED TO BE CONSTRUED AS OR TO SERVE AS A STANDARD FOR PSYCHIATRIC CARE.**

Initially, the therapeutic alliance can be enhanced by discussing with the patient the length of sessions, cost, frequency of visits, vacation schedules, missed appointment policies, and confidentiality issues. Patients should give their informed consent to any waiver of confidentiality involving third-party payers. Patients need to understand that information about history, diagnosis, treatment, and prognosis may be requested by governmental agencies, insurance companies, or peer review committees. Psychiatrists should know that state laws enacted in the 1970s provide only a certain degree of protection for patients' records from legal discovery by peer review. Protection may not exist at all in antitrust or civil rights litigations. In some cases, malpractice actions or denial of staff privileges may lead to discovery of peer review records.

The patient should be informed that absolute confidential handling of personal data cannot be guaranteed once it leaves the therapist's office. In jurisdictions requiring the warning of endangered third persons by potentially violent patients, confidentiality may be breached. The issue that often arises is whether the patient should receive a *Miranda*-type warning concerning possible disclosure of the patient's violent intentions toward others. This problem is discussed in detail in Chapter 13. In short, informed consent in this context is a means of protecting patients from harmful disclosures. It also can be an important way for therapists to share with patients their dilemma over the duty to protect third parties from threatened harm (70). Thus, it may be possible that a mutually constructive action can be formulated without breaching confidentiality.

If the therapist is being supervised, should this fact be disclosed to the patient?

Another area of concern involves supervision of therapists. If the therapist will be supervised while treating the patient, consideration should be given to informing the patient. Informed-consent problems involving supervised cases and the attendant limitations on confidentiality may arise when patients are not informed of their actual status before beginning treatment (71). Although many therapists feel that it is unnecessary to inform patients of the supervised status of their therapy, this issue can no longer be shrugged off as lightly as in the past. Patients may be seeking a graduate psychoanalyst or psychiatrist and may not know that their therapist is in training or is a nonmedical therapist. Sometimes even medical students are passed off as "doctors" or fully trained therapists.

A strong case can be made that patients, as informed consumers, should no longer be kept ignorant of the training status of the therapist. Furthermore, important ethical and clinical issues are raised. Is the therapist deceiving the patient while in turn expecting honesty from the patient? Is not trust the mainstay of therapy? Is not the quest for truth one of the highest values shared between therapist and patient engaged in the therapeutic process? What countertransference issues are raised by "keeping a secret" from the patient? Could that adversely affect treatment?

A common apprehension of training personnel is that therapists-in-training will have their authority undermined or perhaps be perceived as needing help. The paradox of encouraging patients to seek help while denying a similar need in the therapist-in-training is indeed curious. Although patients need to have confidence in their therapists, it seems unnecessary to create an illusion of the omnipotent therapist to achieve that goal. Such an illusion precludes the reassuring idea that the patient may benefit from the experience and judgment of two therapists. No one will argue against the need for oversight and supervision of therapists-in-training. Supervision should be done with the knowledge and consent of the patient, except in instances when the patient does not want to know or might be unnecessarily burdened by such knowledge.

A concern expressed by some psychoanalysts is that informing patients of the presence of a supervisor will permit an external intrusion into the analysis that may skew the transference and offer a rallying point for intractable resistance (72). On the other hand, Robitscher (63) feels that giving patients detailed information will alter but not necessarily harm the therapeutic relationship. In speaking of psychoanalysis, Robitscher feels that a less omnipotent relationship between patient and analyst has numerous advantages: "This would lead to a different kind of psychoanalysis, but it would not necessarily be a worse kind of psychoanalysis."

At the start of treatment, patients should be given an opportunity to ask and receive answers to questions about psychotherapy even when aspects of the questions are overdetermined by psychological factors that are clearly treatment issues. Furthermore, informed consent is not a solitary event that occurs just at the beginning of treatment. It is a continuous process throughout the therapy. For example, recommending an increase in the frequency of visits or altering the goals of therapy may require that the patient receive additional information concerning diagnosis and prognosis before he or she can make a reasoned, informed decision.

Should therapists reveal to patients information about their professional background?

The professional background and credentials of the psychiatrist may be divulged upon a reasonable request for such information by the patient. Informed consumers of psychotherapy may rely on the information about the therapist's training to come to a reasonable treatment decision. Has the therapist been analyzed? Has the therapist been trained primarily in only one school of psychiatric treatment? Is the therapist proficient in using more than one treatment modality or will he or she recommend the same treatment for anyone who comes through the office door? An unvarying policy of revealing one's bona fides may not be appropriate for all patients. Although having some theoretical justification for the analytical psychotherapist, the practice of not displaying diplomas or certifications to maintain the psychiatrist's anonymity could be prejudicial to the patient's decision-making process (73).

Finally, should psychotherapists disclose any preferences they may have for the authority-directive or autonomy-insight models of psychotherapy? Will any of this information help the patient choose from the bewildering array of available psychotherapies? The question of whether therapists should divulge to prospective patients their value system as it pertains to their conduct of psychotherapy is discussed in Chapter 2.

What are the informed-consent requirements for innovative or experimental psychotherapies?

Innovative or experimental therapies require a full explanation of all foreseeable risks (74). In addition, written disclosures should be made and the patient's written consent obtained. Experimental therapies are discussed in further detail in Chapter 19.

What are the consent requirements for patients seeking voluntary hospitalization?

Voluntary admissions make up approximately 73% of the 1.6 million admissions to psychiatric care facilities in the United States (75). There is statutory authority for voluntary admissions in virtually every state (76). Most of these statutes attempt to encourage voluntary admission in the hope of aiding treatment. Individuals who voluntarily admit themselves are presumed to understand the conditions of admission as a matter of law. In a number of states, the patient seeking voluntary admission must possess the mental capacity to understand the nature and implications of his or her decision (77). State statutes generally place a greater emphasis on the appropriateness of the admission and, to a lesser extent, on the competency and the voluntariness of consent. Patients are required by hospitals to sign consent forms for admission. The admission forms are blanket forms of a very general nature. Blanks in the form may be filled in by administrative personnel who also witness the patient's signature. Such forms are not a record that a conversation between doctor and patient has taken place. Very disturbed, incompetent patients may sign these forms at the time of admission, although their consent may be clearly invalid. Most psychiatrists do not insist on the valid consent of a patient who is mentally disordered and is willing to seek psychiatric hospitalization and treatment. In at least one case, *Whitree v. State* (78), the court stated that failure to treat an incompetent patient when the patient refused treatment was "illogical, unprofessional and nonconsistent with medical standards."

In a recent United States Supreme Court case, *Zinermon v. Burch* (79), a mentally ill patient who was unable to give informed consent was permitted to go forward with a civil rights action against state officials who committed him to a state hospital using voluntary commitment procedures. The Court held that Florida must have procedures to screen all voluntary patients for competency and exclude incompetent persons from the voluntary admission process. For the few states requiring competent consent to voluntary admission, screening procedures must be created to exclude incompetent patients. Although the court did not directly address whether a voluntary patient must be competent to consent to admission, Appelbaum (75) feels that "*Zinermon* will refocus attention on the often-neglected process of voluntary admission" (p. 1060).

A very fine line exists between friendly persuasion and coercion of patients to accept hospitalization. Family members, employers, or other interested third parties may attempt to apply coercive pressures on the patient and the psychiatrist for psychiatric hospitalization. In these instances, psychiatrists may experience a split in their sense of duty to the patient. The psychiatrist must decide whether to pursue hospitalization of the patient or to sustain the patient's autonomy to make that decision. The more disturbed and incompetent the patient, the more the emphasis will be placed on treatment and less on autonomy.

When possible, and if the prospective patient desires, part of the informing process about hospitalization should allow for a visit to the ward. The prospective patient may wish to talk to the ward staff and make a direct appraisal. He or she should be informed of the rules and regulations governing the ward. In particular, the prospective patient should know whether the ward is locked or open. Sometimes certain patients currently residing on the ward may be psychologically threatening to the patient. Patients terrified of their own aggression may not be able to stay on a ward with openly abusive, aggressive patients. Direct observation of the ward and the inpatients by a prospective patient may invade their privacy. Thus, visits to the ward by prospective patients should be accomplished at a time when most patients are involved in groups and other activities.

In order to protect their civil rights, patients should be fully informed of the types of voluntary admission. Is it a pure or conditional voluntary admission? Pure or informal voluntary admission permits the patient to leave the hospital at any time. Only moral suasion can be used to encourage the patient to stay. Conditional voluntary admission contains the requirement that the patient will have to stay for a period of time after giving written notice of intention to leave. This provision is used when the patient appears to be a danger to self or others.

Although some psychiatric patients who have been literally dragged into a psychiatric hospital have later expressed gratitude for their enforced treatment, direct physical force in transacting a voluntary admission should be avoided. Under these circumstances, involuntary hospitalization should be considered if the patient meets applicable criteria. If the patient needs to be informed of involuntary hospitalization, threats of civil commitment when not actually intended as a course of action may be considered to be a fraud, a misrepresentation, and a violation of the patient's legal rights. For example, an appeals court ordered a new trial for a patient who alleged false imprisonment by her psychiatrist. The court held that a material issue of fact existed in the patient's apprehension of force or coercion used to keep her in a hospital by the threat of involuntary hospitalization (80).

In reality, the distinction between voluntary and involuntary admissions is not as clear as stated in statutory law. Patients are often induced or pressured into accepting voluntary admission. If voluntary admission were to be maintained as truly voluntary, involuntary admissions would likely increase. The situation is analogous to plea bargaining in criminal cases. The criminal justice system would have to accommodate an increased number of cases if the practice of plea bargaining was eliminated. Strict application of the informed-consent doctrine to voluntary patients would discriminate against patients temporarily lacking the mental capacity to provide a knowing consent or patients with partial mental incapacity who give a doubtful consent. This would produce considerable tension between empirical reality and the legal model.

Apart from *Zinermon*, relatively few cases have addressed the issue of informed consent for voluntary admission. In *In re Certification of William R.* (81), the court expressed disapproval for the procedure that admits an individual to a mental institution who makes no "positive objection," and thereby "shunts seniles into involuntary confinement without awareness by them of their plight and without their active approval or judicial surveillance."

In addition to voluntary admissions procedures, an increasing number of states permit nonjudicial hospitalization of nonprotesting persons. The District of Columbia statute provides a simple, nontraumatic admission process for those individuals who either do not recognize their need for hospitalization or are unwilling to seek admission but nevertheless sign a "no objection" statement when others initiate the admission process (82).

What malpractice risks surround the capacity to consent?

The fact that treatment was adequately performed, or even brilliantly performed, is irrelevant as a defense against a lack-of-informed-consent claim (33). Psychiatrists can be sued for battery when patients are treated without their consent. Battery is defined as nonconsensual touching (83). Malpractice insurance may not provide coverage for battery, an intentional tort. A negligence claim may be brought against the psychiatrist if the patient has been provided insufficient information and suffers harm. The standard of review depends on whether the court uses a professional or reasonable-man (patient) standard (33). The patient must prove that the lack of informing was the cause of the harm and that had adequate information been provided, the patient would have foregone the treatment. If the patient would have undertaken the treatment despite the deficient informed consent, no liability will incur. Civil rights actions also may be brought against psychiatrists working in federal and state facilities for treating nonconsenting, involuntarily hospitalized patients.

Psychiatrists must recognize that involuntary hospitalization does not always equate with a determination of incompetency that grants consent for treatment. In *Price v. Sheppard* (84), the Minnesota Supreme Court drew a line between nonintrusive treatment and intrusive treatment requiring court approval for civilly committed patients. Drug therapy was considered more intrusive than psychoanalysis and milieu therapy, but less intrusive than aversion therapy, electroconvulsive therapy, and psychosurgery. A number of states do not allow treatment of involuntarily hospitalized patients without a separate court hearing. If treatment is required, the court may substitute its own consent. This subject is discussed in greater detail in Chapter 6.

Competent patients should not be treated against their wishes except in an emergency. Patients whose competence is in doubt may consent readily to treatment. Irwin et al. (85) examined the ability of voluntary and involuntary patients who were psychotic to understand information about neuroleptic medication. Although most patients stated that they understood the information provided, objective ratings did not support their statements of comprehension. Impaired understanding was significantly associated with thought disturbance. Incompetent consent is usually not questioned because the treatment plan suggested by the psychiatrist is accepted. The more favorable the risk-benefit analysis for a proposed treatment, the more likely it is that the patient's refusal of that treatment will be judged incompetent. Accordingly, the tests used to evaluate the patient's competence should be more rigorous (61).

Paternalistic stances toward patients create legal vulnerability for the psychiatrist. In the clinical vignette, Dr. Moore determined that his patient had the mental capacity to give a valid consent based on his acquiescence to neuroleptic and antidepressant treatment, even though the patient's consent was coerced. Professor Horvath's cognitive functioning was gravely affected by depression. It is doubtful that Professor Horvath had the mental capacity to make either a competent acceptance or a refusal of treatment. Under these circumstances, substitute consent must be sought. To be prudent, Dr. Moore obtained the written consent of the patient's fiancée for treatment. However, her proxy consent may not be valid, because of the statutory provision that proxy consent can be given only by immediate family. Should difficulties arise later, the adequacy of consent may be questioned.

Nonconsenting psychotic patients who represent an acute threat of harm to themselves or others may be treated as emergencies under implied consent. In the clinical situation, competency to consent may be a "now it's here and now it isn't" phenomenon. Patients who have been incompetent may regain and maintain competence with rapid improvement in their clinical condition. As soon as the patient regains sufficient mental capacity to give a valid consent, it should be obtained. Patients who do not indicate a choice by either accepting or refusing treatment are assumed to be incompetent (46). The mute catatonic patient would fit into this category. A thorny problem is presented by patients who do not voice an acceptance or refusal of treatment but give nonverbal assent by following instructions for hospitalization and treatment. These patients may lack the mental capacity to consent to treatment. They should be monitored on a continuing basis for their capacity to provide a valid consent. If a therapeutic alliance develops, this may enhance the patient's psychological capacity to make a valid decision. In the clinical vignette, Professor Horvath follows the course of nonverbal assent to psychiatric hospitalization.

In some states, psychotic patients who appear to be incompetent and refuse treatment but are of no danger to themselves or others, may not be treated unless adjudicated incompetent. In an increasing number of states, nonjudicial administrative procedures that meet due-process requirements are being used for determining the need for involuntary medication (86, 87). Such patients present a serious dilemma for psychiatrists, because involuntary hospitalization is not an available treatment intervention unless the criteria for being gravely disabled are met. Patients presenting an acute danger to themselves or others may meet the criteria for involuntary hospitalization. In *Clites v. State* (88), the court grappled with informed-consent issues involving an institutionalized patient. (This case is reviewed in Chapter 10.)

In recent years, plaintiffs' attorneys alleging negligence in a procedure or treatment have been tacking on a separate complaint against the physician for failure to inform properly. This has increased the number of informed-consent cases before the courts. If the plaintiff has suffered an injury and cannot prove negligence, the courts have tended to permit the complaint to proceed on the basis of a failure to inform. As a result, the plaintiff has another chance to recover for injuries (33).

A variety of defenses exist in malpractice claims alleging lack of informed consent (76). These include *1)* common knowledge of the risk; *2)* waiver by patient; *3)* withholding of information to prevent psychological harm; *4)* a written, signed consent form; *5)* the fact that a reasonable, prudent person would have undergone treatment or procedure anyway; *6)* no expert medical testimony; and *7)* insubstantial risk.

How can mental health professionals maintain their clinical perspective vis-à-vis the evolving doctrine of informed consent?

Because of judicial decision making, the informed-consent doctrine has undergone significant changes over the past two decades. In a number of states, legislators have enacted informed-consent statutes. Although setting forth the requirements for obtaining informed consent, these laws do not pay sufficient attention to the manner in which the disclosure is made (89). The manner of disclosure is as critical as the content of disclosure. Thus, the current status of informed-consent law is incomplete and evolving (90).

As pointed out by Meisel et al. (90), what passes for a valid consent today may not be valid tomorrow. A valid consent in one jurisdiction may not be so in another. A valid consent in one specialty of medicine may not pass muster in another. The applicability of the doctrine of informed consent to the specialty of psychiatry is in an embryonic stage, and modifications that reflect the differences between psychiatry and other medical specialties will be necessary (91). In their comprehensive research effort, Lidz et al. (91) stated that "informed consent policy is not currently working in the settings that we studied, and on the basis of other studies we are performing, our conversation with colleagues, and our own knowledge of patients, we believe that it is not working very well in most other medical care settings either." Meisel and Roth (92) conclude:

> Despite the tomes that have been written about informed consent, the sad conclusion is that more than a quarter-century after the birth of the doctrine, we know almost nothing about its operation. Nevertheless, informed consent requirements will not disappear. The trend is clear that patient autonomy and decision making is a societal commitment that has been unequivocally made.

Because a basic theme underlying informed-consent law is uncertainty, legal commentary has been directed at making specific suggestions or "shoulds" to help psychiatrists combat legal liability (93). For instance, the psychiatrist should be the main person to discuss treatment with the patient. It is probably legally insufficient for a psychiatrist to send a nurse or a mental health paraprofessional to obtain consent. The psychiatrist should be available to answer questions from the patient about the proposed treatment. The information should be presented in an intelligible manner to the patient. The psychiatrist must affirmatively avoid false assurances of "no risk" as distinguished from expressing hope that the procedure or treatment will be successful. The psychiatrist should also explain risks to next of kin when exceptions are made as to informing the patient. Finally, the psychiatrist should make a clear record of the conversation with the patient and the patient's consent, so that later recollection will be facilitated.

Maintaining the therapist's clinical perspective is crucial amid so much uncertainty involving the informed-consent doctrine. Winslade (94) offers excellent advice to the clinician when stating that the law, like medicine, is uncertain. The Supreme Court decides many crucial issues by a five to four vote. Clinicians who think about treatment decisions primarily in terms of rules, either legal or medical, fail in their clinical responsibilities. Winslade adds that the psychiatrist who manifests respect for the personhood of the patient is not likely to suffer legal consequences whether the outcome of the treatment decision supports the values of physician paternalism or of patient autonomy. In both the law and the practice of medicine, rules can provide only minimum, necessary guidelines.

These guidelines provide an opportunity to make more sensitive, individualized decisions regarding the patient. Patients vary in their treatment needs and in their interaction with the psychiatrist. Decisions cannot be made on a consistent basis that follow either patient autonomy or medical paternalism. Winslade gives an example that goes to the heart of the matter. Suppose that hospital policies or state law permits involuntarily hospitalized patients to be treated against their wishes. To treat such nonconsenting patients may not be morally or clinically desirable. Rather, each patient must be considered individually. Thought must be given to the possible adverse effect on treatment goals when treatment is administered against the patient's consent.

In a similar vein, Gutheil et al. (95) point out that informed consent should be more than a legal formality serving narrow medicolegal ends. It can become a focal point for establishing the therapeutic alliance. Informed consent can become a powerful clinical tool by allowing patient helplessness to be supplanted by a degree of control as the patient becomes a participant with the therapist in the treatment process. The therapeutic use of informed consent enlists the patient in an active alliance that discourages simplistic blaming, and reduces the alienation toward the clinician that often produces malpractice claims.

Mental health professionals must practice within the law. A law degree is not a requirement for clinical practice and could conceivably be an impediment. Legal issues should be turned to clinical account whenever possible, not in an effort to circumvent or manipulate the law, but in the exercise of the psychiatrist's moral, ethical, and professional duty to provide the best possible care to the patient.

Often, the law has agendas that differ from the psychiatrist's. Slovenko (33) believes that the informed-consent doctrine was created to permit lawyers to add additional causes of action in malpractice suits, particularly in those instances in which a poor result occurred in the absence of negligence. For the clinician, informed consent is synonymous with the creation of trust. Both informing and working with the patient on arriving at a treatment plan are integral parts of building a trusting relationship. Without trust, there can be little effective treatment.

What are some of the informed-consent issues that arise in biomedical and behavioral research?

In psychiatry, biomedical research is aimed at discovering the physiological basis of mental disorders. Behavioral research is defined as scientific inquiry into factors motivating and determining human attitudes and behavior, without physically intruding on the subject (96).

Systematic human experimentation is regulated through self-regulation, statutory and administrative regulations, scientific peer review, local institutional review boards, and case law that defines the rights of research subjects (96). Regulatory guidelines promulgated by the U.S. Department of Health and Human Services (DHHS) currently exert the most significant influence on the conduct of research (97).

Reisner and Slobogin (96) discuss the special problems associated with behavioral research. In contrast to biomedical research, behavioral research may require deception of the subject concerning the nature and purpose of the experiment. Thus, strict application of the informed-consent doctrine would inhibit some behavioral research.

Behavioral research is not innocuous and may expose subjects to the risk of compensable psychological harm. Behavioral research that uses passive observation studies, surveys, and manipulation studies with and without overt deception may raise a number of litigation issues. Passive observation studies may lead to legal actions for invasion of privacy when the subject could be identified in the published study or if the study exposes the subject to embarrassment, legal liability, or financial loss. If the subject matter deals with sensitive personal matters, the researcher conducting a survey has a legal duty to protect the subject's anonymity. Studies that use deception obviously require special care on the part of the researcher.

Reisner and Slobogin provide two examples of behavioral research that could be legally actionable (96). In one experiment, researchers, studying the reactions of military recruits, flew to an altitude of 5,000 feet. The pilot was instructed to turn off the propeller, and the recruits were allowed to overhear communications that led them to believe the plane would crash-land. The reactions of the recruits were monitored by researchers. In another experiment, male subjects taking a personality test were told that the tests revealed they had latent homosexual tendencies. Some subjects experienced acute personal mortification but were eventually "dehoaxed" by the researchers. Both of these experiments exposed the researchers to liability for failure to obtain informed consent and for the intentional infliction of emotional distress.

In 1981, the DHHS issued regulations that are now in effect for all research subjects, including the mentally ill. These regulations require that subjects or their legally authorized representatives must give "legally effective informed consent" (97). There are eight disclosure requirements (97):

1. The fact and purposes of research
2. Reasonably foreseeable risks
3. Reasonably expected benefits
4. Appropriate alternatives
5. A statement about the maintenance of confidentiality
6. An explanation about possible compensation if injury occurs for research involving more than minimal risks
7. Information about how the subject can have pertinent questions answered
8. A statement about voluntary participation indicating that refusal to participate involves no penalties or loss of benefits

Given the work of Lidz et al. (91), the ability of mentally ill subjects to understand such a list of disclosure requirements is questionable. Lidz et al. found that mentally ill patients participating in research were not able to distinguish between the therapeutic and nontherapeutic goals of the research.

Roth and Appelbaum (98) reviewed pertinent data over the last decade involving informed consent to assess whether psychiatric patients are at special risk for participation in research. They found that the evidence is inconclusive. They recommend that before any conclusions are drawn that the mentally ill cannot understand or decide about participation in research, investigators should attempt "sustained, careful, and thorough" efforts to educate potential research subjects.

References

1. Appelbaum PS, Lidz CW, Meisel A: Informed Consent: Legal Theory and Clinical Practice. New York, Oxford University Press, 1987, p 84
2. 211 NY 125, 105 NE 92 (1914), overruled, Bing v Thunig, 2 NY2d 656, 143 NE2d 3, 163 NYS2d 3 (1957)
3. Olmstead v United States, 277 U.S. 438 (1928) (Cardozo dissenting), overruled, Katz v United States, 389 U.S. 347 (1967)
4. Miller LJ: Informed consent, I. JAMA 244:2100–2103, 1980
5. Miller v Kennedy, 11 Wash App 272, 522 P2d 852 (1974), aff'd per curiam, 85 Wash 2d 151, 530 P2d 334 (1975)
6. Natanson v Kline, 186 Kan 393, 350 P2d 1093 (1960)

7. Woods v Brumlop, 71 NM 221, 377 P2d 520, 524 (1962), overruled, Gerety v Deiners, 92 NM 396, 589 P2d 180 (1978)

8. Lynn J: Informed consent: an overview. Behavioral Sciences and the Law 1:29–45, 1983

9. Merz JF, Fischhoff B: Informed consent does not mean rational consent: cognitive limitations on decision-making. J Leg Med 11:321–350, 1990

10. Simon RI: Concise Guide to Clinical Psychiatry and the Law. Washington, DC, American Psychiatric Press, 1988, p 27

11. Roth LH: Informed consent and its applicability for psychiatry, in Psychiatry, Vol 3. Edited by Cavenar JO. Philadelphia, PA, JB Lippincott, 1985, pp 1–17

12. Szasz TS, Hollender MH: A contribution to the philosophy of medicine: the basic models of the doctor-patient relationship. Arch Intern Med 97:585–592, 1956

13. Roth LH, Appelbaum PS, Lidz CW, et al: Informed consent in psychiatric research. Rutgers Law Review 39:425–441, 1987

14. Roth LH, personal communication, July 1985

15. Malcolm JG: Informed consent in the practice of psychiatry, in American Psychiatric Press Review of Clinical Psychiatry and the Law, Vol 3. Edited by Simon RI. Washington, DC, American Psychiatric Press, 1992, pp 223–281

16. 148 NJ Super 168, 372 A2d 360 (1977)

17. Appelbaum PS, Roth LH: Clinical issues in the assessment of competency. Am J Psychiatry 138:1462–1467, 1981

18. Roth LH, Meisel A, Lidz CW: Tests of competency to consent to treatment. Am J Psychiatry 134:279–284, 1977

19. Meisel A: The "exceptions" to the informed consent doctrine: striking a balance between competing values in medical decision making. Wisconsin Law Review 2:413–488, 1979

20. Mishkin B: Determining the capacity for making health care decisions. Adv Psychosom Med 19:151–166, 1989 [Special issue: Issues in Geriatric Psychiatry. Edited by Billig N, Rabin PV.]

21. Benesch K: Legal issues in determining competence to make treatment decisions, in Legal Implications of Hospital Policies and Practices. Edited by Miller RD. San Francisco, CA, Jossey-Bass, 1989, pp 97–105

22. Winkjer v Herr, 277 NW 2d 579 (ND 1979)

23. Brakel SJ, Parry J, Weiner BA: The Mentally Disabled and the Law. Chicago, IL, American Bar Foundation, 1985, p 449

24. 464 F2d 772 (DC Cir), cert denied, Spence v Canterbury, 409 U.S. 1064 (1972)

25. 8 Cal 3d 229, 104 Cal Rptr 505, 502 P2d 1 (1972)

26. Furrow BR: Malpractice in Psychotherapy. Lexington, MA, DC Heath, 1980, pp 68–70

27. Gibbs RF: Informed consent: what it is and how to obtain it. Legal Aspects of Medical Practice 15(August):1–4, 1987

28. 395 Mass 689, 481 NE2d 1144 (1985)

29. Simon RI: Beyond the doctrine of informed consent: a clinician's perspective. Journal for the Expert Witness, The Trial Attorney, The Trial Judge 4(Fall):23–25, 1989

30. Brakel SJ, Parry J, Weiner BA: The Mentally Disabled and the Law. Chicago, IL, American Bar Foundation, 1985, p 448

31. Solnick PB: Proxy consent for incompetent nonterminally ill adult patients. J Leg Med 6:1–49, 1985

32. Meisel A, Kabnick LD: Informed consent to medical treatment: an analysis of recent legislation. University of Pittsburgh Law Review 41:407, 1980
33. Slovenko R: Misadventures of psychiatry with the law. Journal of Psychiatry and Law 17:115–156, 1989
34. Klein J, Onek J, Macbeth J: Seminar on Law in the Practice of Psychiatry. Washington, DC, Onek, Klein, and Farr, 1983
35. Ferrara v Galluchio, 5 NY2d 16, 152 NE2d 249, 176 NYS2d 996 (1958)
36. Swartz MS: What constitutes a psychiatric emergency: legal dimensions. Bull Am Acad Psychiatry Law 15:57–68, 1987
37. Sard v Hardy 281 Md 432, 379 A2d 1014 (1977)
38. 186 Kan 393, 350 P2d 1093 (1960)
39. 138 AD2d 102, 529 NYS2d 569 (NY App Div 1988)
40. Somerville MA: Therapeutic privilege: variation on the theme of informed consent. Law, Medicine and Health Care 12:4–12, 1984
41. Roth LH: Question the experts. J Clin Psychopharmacol 3:207–208, 1983
42. American Psychiatric Association: Tardive Dyskinesia (Task Force Report No 18). Washington, DC, American Psychiatric Association, 1979
43. Jeste DV, Wyatt RD: Guidelines for the use of neuroleptics in clinical practice. Psychiatric Annals 10:39–52, 1980
44. Sovner R, DiMascio A, Berkowitz D, et al: Tardive dyskinesia and informed consent. Psychosomatics 19:172–177, 1978
45. CAL ADMIN CODE tit 9, § 850–857 (1972). Subchapter 4, § 850–857 Community Mental Health Services under the Lanterman-Petris-Short Act. Article 5.5: Voluntary patients' right to refuse antipsychotic medications
46. Halleck SL: Law in the Practice of Psychiatry. New York, Plenum, 1980, p 94
47. Soskis DA: Schizophrenic and medical inpatients as informed drug consumers. Arch Gen Psychiatry 35:645–647, 1978
48. Mayberger HW, Moore JA: Patient medication instruction: an idea whose time has come. Legal Aspects of Medical Practice 11:1–4, 1983
49. Yacura M: The patient medication instruction (PMI) leaflet: regulatory and evidentiary ramifications. Medical Trial Technique Quarterly 31:499–519, 1985
50. 553 So 2d 398 (La 1988)
51. Public Health Trust of Dade County v Valcin, 507 So 2d 596 (Fla 1987)
52. Rook v Trout, 747 P2d 61 (Idaho 1987)
53. Robinson G, Merav A: Informed consent: recall by patients tested postoperatively. Ann Thorac Surg 22:209–212, 1976
54. Epstein, Lasagna: Obtaining informed consent: form or substance. Arch Intern Med 123:682, 1969
55. Holder AR: Books in review. American Medical News 19(October):35, 1984
56. Foster HH: Informed consent of mental patients, in Law and the Mental Health Professions. Edited by Barton WE, Sanborn CJ. New York, International Universities Press, 1978, pp 71–95
57. FED R EVID 410
58. 44 Colo App 480, 618 P2d 719 (Colo Ct App 1980), aff'd in part and rev'd in part, 646 P2d 907 (Colo 1982)
59. Hadley SW, Strupp HH: Contemporary views of negative effects in psychotherapy. Arch Gen Psychiatry 33:1291–1302, 1976

60. Reisner R, Slobogin C: Law and the Mental Health System, 2nd Edition. St Paul, MN, West Publishing, 1990, p 167
61. Slovenko R: Forensic psychiatry, in Comprehensive Textbook of Psychiatry IV, Vol 2. Edited by Kaplan HI, Sadock BJ. Baltimore, MD, Williams & Wilkins, 1985, pp 1960–1990; see p 1981
62. Epstein GN: Informed consent and the dyadic relationship. Journal of Psychiatry and Law 6:359–362, 1978
63. Robitscher J: Informed consent and psychoanalysis. Journal of Psychiatry and Law 6:363–370, 1978
64. Bibring E: Psychoanalysis and the dynamic psychotherapies. J Am Psychoanal Assoc 2:745–770, 1954
65. 490 A2d 720, 722 (Md App 1985)
66. Malcolm JG: Treatment choices and informed consent in psychiatry: implications of the Osheroff case for the profession. Journal of Psychiatry and Law 14:9–107, 1986
67. Klerman GL: The psychiatric patient's right to effective treatment: implications of Osheroff v Chestnut Lodge. Am J Psychiatry 147:409–418, 1990
68. Stone AA: Law, science, and psychiatric malpractice: a response to Klerman's indictment of psychoanalytic psychiatry. Am J Psychiatry 147:419-427, 1990
69. American Psychiatric Association Task Force on Treatments of Psychiatric Disorders: Treatments of Psychiatric Disorders, Vols 1–3. Washington, DC, American Psychiatric Association, 1989
70. Roth LH, Meisel A: Dangerousness, confidentiality, and the duty to warn. Am J Psychiatry 134:508–511, 1977
71. Simon RI: Psychiatric Interventions and Malpractice: A Primer for Liability Prevention. Springfield, IL, Charles C Thomas, 1982, pp 87–90
72. Simon RI: Psychiatric Interventions and Malpractice: A Primer for Liability Prevention. Springfield, IL, Charles C Thomas, 1982
73. Ibid, pp 112–114
74. Stone AA: The right to refuse treatment. Arch Gen Psychiatry 38:358–362, 1981
75. Appelbaum PS: Voluntary hospitalization and due process: the dilemma of Zinermon v Burch. Hosp Community Psychiatry 41:1059–1060, 1990
76. Brakel SJ, Parry J, Weiner BA: The Mentally Disabled and the Law. Chicago, IL, American Bar Foundation, 1985, pp 449–450
77. Ibid, pp 181–182
78. 56 Misc 2d 693, 290 NYS2d 486 (1968)
79. 494 U.S. 113 (1990)
80. Marcus v Liebman, 59 Ill App 3d 337, 375 NE2d 486 (Ill App Ct 1978)
81. 9 Misc 2d 1084, 172 NYS2d 869 (NY Sup Ct 1958)
82. DC CODE ANN § 21-513 (1981 & 1984 Supp)
83. Keeton WP, Dobbs DB, Keeton RE, et al: Prosser and Keeton on Torts, 5th Edition. St Paul, MN, West Publishing, 1984, p 46
84. 307 Minn 250, 239 NW2d 905 (1976)
85. Irwin M, Lovitz A, Marder SR, et al: Psychotic patients' understanding of informed consent. Am J Psychiatry 142:1351–1354, 1985
86. Hassenfeld IN, Grumet B: A study of the right to refuse treatment. Bull Am Acad Psychiatry Law 12:65–74, 1984

87. Zito M, Lentz SL, Routt WW, et al: The treatment review panel: solution to treatment refusal? Bull Am Acad Psychiatry Law 12:349–358, 1984

88. 322 NW2d 917 (Iowa Ct App 1982)

89. Andrews LB: Informed consent statutes and the decision-making process. J Leg Med 5:163–217, 1984

90. Meisel A, Roth LH, Lidz CW: Toward a model of the legal doctrine of informed consent. Am J Psychiatry 134:285–289, 1977

91. Lidz CW, Meisel A, Zerubavel E, et al: Informed Consent: A Study of Decision Making in Psychiatry. New York, Guilford, 1984

92. Meisel A, Roth LH: Toward an informed discussion of informed consent: a review and critique of the empirical studies. Arizona Law Review 25:265–345, 1983

93. Miller LJ: Informed consent, IV. JAMA 244:2661–2662, 1980

94. Winslade WJ: Informed consent in psychiatric practice: the primacy of ethics over law. Behavioral Sciences and the Law 1:47–56, 1983

95. Gutheil TG, Bursztajn H, Brodsky A, et al: Malpractice prevention through the sharing of uncertainty. N Engl J Med 311:49–51, 1984

96. Reisner R, Slobogin C: Law and the Mental Health System, 2nd Edition. St Paul, MN, West Publishing, 1990, pp 223–232

97. President's Commission for the Study of Ethical Problems in Medicine and Biomedical and Behavioral Research: Making Health Care Decisions: A Report on the Ethical and Legal Implications of Informed Consent in the Patient-Practitioner Relationship, Vol 1: Report. Washington, DC, Superintendent of Documents, October 1982

98. Roth LH, Appelbaum PS: Obtaining informed consent for research with psychiatric patients. Psychiatr Clin North Am 6:551–565, 1983

Chapter 8

Involuntary Hospitalization: Patient Rights and Professional Duties

---

Mr. Gilbert, a 21-year-old single artist, is initially evaluated in the emergency room of a general hospital because of feelings of depression alternating with rage and murderous impulses directed at his fiancée. The patient is examined by a psychiatrist, Dr. King, who discovers that the patient's symptoms emerged when Mr. Gilbert inadvertently learned that his fiancée had recently dated a former boyfriend. Further inquiry reveals that the patient had brief admissions to other hospitals in the past for similar symptoms, a juvenile police record for car theft and numerous assaults, a spotty work history, and periods of alcohol and drug abuse. Two months ago, he was admitted to another psychiatric facility after beating his fiancée with a beer bottle. He was intoxicated upon that admission.

Mr. Gilbert is not delusional, nor is there any evidence of a thought disorder. He is fully oriented. Dr. King calls the hospital where Mr. Gilbert was previously hospitalized and learns that the patient was diagnosed as suffering from an antisocial personality disorder. This information confirms Dr. King's own diagnostic impression. Because of the presence of murderous impulses and a call received by Dr. King from the patient's fiancée stating that she fears for her life, the patient is voluntarily admitted without protest to the psychiatric service under Dr. King's care.

Within 2 days of hospitalization, Mr. Gilbert feels in control of his anger. He no longer complains of depression. He refuses all medication and consistently turns away staff members with the stock phrase, "Leave me alone." Dr. King observes that no therapeutic alliance is developing. Mr. Gilbert tries to avoid Dr. King when he makes rounds on the ward. Mr. Gilbert has met and talked with his fiancée, and confidently states, "Everything is patched up." The patient's fiancée again contacts Dr. King and continues to express her fears about Mr. Gilbert's capacity to harm her. She is particularly concerned because she recently found a gun hidden in their apartment. Mr. Gilbert insistently presses for immediate discharge. He is found attempting to unlock the ward door.

155

Dr. King and his staff determine that a discharge now would be premature and possibly dangerous to the patient's fiancée. Mr. Gilbert signs papers to leave against medical advice. Dr. King's clinical judgment that the patient is not sufficiently recovered leads to a decision to seek an emergency commitment. Dr. King completes the emergency commitment form, stating that the patient suffers from an exacerbation of a severe character disorder with a DSM diagnosis of antisocial personality disorder. He needs continued hospitalization and crisis intervention therapy. The state commitment statute requires a recent overt act of violence (within 30 days) before the criteria of dangerousness can be met. An act of violence by the patient occurring 2 months prior to admission does not meet the statutory requirement of a recent overt violent act. Nevertheless, it is Dr. King's clinical judgment that the patient poses a high risk of violence to others, particularly his fiancée. In his risk assessment Dr. King considers his patient's past history of assaults, alcohol and drug abuse, and hospitalization for impulse control problems. The statute does not exclude antisocial personality disorder as a mental illness for involuntary hospitalization.

Mr. Gilbert is prevented from leaving the hospital pending his commitment hearing within 48 hours. During the probable cause hearing, a judge reviews the request for involuntary hospitalization but finds that Mr. Gilbert does not meet the statutory requirements for involuntary hospitalization. The patient is discharged. Three days later, Dr. King learns that Mr. Gilbert and his fiancée were killed in an automobile accident.

What have been the historical vicissitudes of civil commitment in the United States? What are some current trends?

In the United States, civil commitment took form during the first half of the 19th century under the legal principle of *parens patriae* (i.e., the state acts in the place of the parent). Patients could be involuntarily hospitalized solely on the grounds of mental illness, with the decision-makers being physicians and families rather than the courts. After the Civil War, public protests were made alleging abuses. Because of an increasing number of stories about wives being whisked away to mental institutions by malicious husbands and conniving physicians, procedural safeguards were developed. To determine if mental illness was present, many states required a jury trial and the exercise of the state's police power as part of parens patriae commitment. Between 1900 and 1920, and again after World War II, the so-called criminalization of commitment declined. Civil commitment procedures became "remedicalized." Procedural due-process requirements of notice, presence at hearings, and trial by jury were eliminated. Short-term emergency commitments were permitted under authority of the physician, with greater emphasis placed on voluntary admission. Civil commitment could be sought strictly on the need for treatment when illness interfered with the ability to obtain treatment. In the 1960s and 1970s, the state hospital came under attack as part of the upsurge in interest in patients' civil rights and autonomy. The psychiatric profession was viewed as abridging individual liberties.

Recent legislative changes and court decisions in most states have practically abandoned the parens patriae standard and have reinstated the police power criteria, utilizing dangerousness as the standard for involuntary hospitalization. The psychiatrist's power to commit without court review has been markedly limited, with patients granted broad procedural protection almost similar to that of criminal defendants (1). Based on the due-process clause of the Fourteenth Amendment, most states now require judicial hearings with notice to the patient, representation by counsel, and proof of mental disorder and dangerousness by at least clear and convincing evidence.

Although the predominant ethos of early commitment law involved parens patriae, there have always been provisions for police power commitments. Historically, however, the distinctions between these two justifications for involuntary hospitalization were blurred because even those individuals who were committed by reason of dangerousness were simultaneously being committed with the understanding that treatment would be provided. More recently, the balance in substantive justification for civil commitment has shifted toward police powers. Nevertheless, a substantial parens patriae component remains, not only in the commitments for danger to self or grave disability, but also in commitments involving danger to others. The prospect of provision of treatment for the latter is what really separates civil commitment from preventive detention.

Currently, there appears to be a growing movement among state legislatures to revise civil commitment statutes to respond to the treatment needs of the seriously mentally ill before they become a danger to themselves or society. An increasing effort by patient advocates, psychiatrists, and state legislators is being made to move away from the narrowly defined dangerousness standard as the primary standard for civil commitment. A middle ground is being sought between meeting the treatment needs of the severely mentally ill and preserving their legal rights.

For instance, a 1972 Wisconsin case, *Lessard v. Schmidt* (2), received considerable publicity for promulgating the narrow standard of dangerousness for civil commitment. Yet the *Lessard* decision received negligible judicial notice outside of Wisconsin (3). The publicity from this case misled many psychiatrists into thinking that imminent dangerousness based on a recent overt act was the only basis for commitment.

Actually, Hiday (4), in a study of over 1,000 commitment hearings in North Carolina following adoption of a strict dangerousness standard, found that the majority of commitments continued to be made based on parens patriae. If the statutory criteria were narrowly followed, including evidence of a threat or an overt act occurring within a week before the hearing, only 24% of the cases met the criteria. Miller (5) reports that subsequent statutory revisions have broadened the North Carolina criteria for dangerousness.

How does usage of the term *civil commitment* among psychiatrists differ from formal legal usage?

The term *civil commitment* is not used in this book in the strict legal sense to encompass both voluntary and involuntary commitment. Commitment statutes define the nature and conditions for both voluntary and involuntary hospitalization. Psychiatrists do not think of voluntary hospitalization as a commitment, even though patients who undergo conditional voluntary admission may be detained against their will for varying periods of time. When psychiatrists speak of involuntary hospitalization, they usually just say "commitment." In order not to confuse the reader, the terms *voluntary* and *involuntary* hospitalization are used whenever possible. The term civil commitment is used synonymously with involuntary hospitalization, except when referring to outpatient commitment.

What legal principles form the basis for civil commitment?

The power to hospitalize psychiatric patients against their will represents a marked departure from traditional Anglo-American jurisprudence that seeks to maximize individual autonomy. Civil commitment rests on two basic principles. The first principle is parens patriae, which has come under attack by civil libertarians. In Anglo-American law, this concept was derived from the power of English kings, who were viewed as fathers to their subjects and presumed to act in their subjects' best interests, particularly when the subjects were incapable of protecting themselves. Today, this principle is greatly muted. Some variant of parens patriae, however, remains in almost every statute permitting hospitalization of the nonconsenting "gravely disabled" or mentally ill.

The other basic principle underlying civil commitment is the state's police power. Individual states have always had the power under the United States Constitution to take those actions necessary to protect and maintain the safety of society. These "police powers" of the states are limited both by their state constitution and by the Fourteenth Amendment of the U.S. Constitution, which guarantees that all citizens will receive due process and equal protection under the law.

The state has the right to involuntarily hospitalize patients under two basic forms of commitment: criminal and civil. Criminal commitments are utilized for mentally ill patients found guilty of crimes or not guilty by reason of insanity. These individuals are sent by the court to a psychiatric facility rather than a prison. Thus, criminal commitments manifest the state's desire to treat the patient's psychiatric illness as a means of prevention of future crimes. In many states, such commitments are considered to be civil commitments but are not exactly like other civil commitments. They represent a hybrid form between civil and criminal commitments. In recent years, criminal commitments have become surrounded by extensive procedural protection such as the right to counsel, the right to a hearing, and the right to regular review. Even short-term commitments for the purpose of evaluating a patient's competency to stand trial or for criminal responsibility require such procedural protection.

As for civil commitments, the states' right to use police powers to commit individuals who are not found guilty of any crime has been markedly curtailed in the past decade. Civil commitment under police power principles rests on the assumption of dangerousness. In other words,individuals with mental illness are more likely to be dangerous and commit more crimes than the nonmentally ill. Under this rationale, a civil commitment constitutes a preventive detention (6).

Does the psychiatrist commit the patient when initiating involuntary hospitalization? What types of commitment may be utilized, and what procedures must be followed?

It is extremely important for mental health professionals to understand that they do not make long-term commitment decisions about patients. Commitment is a judicial decision that will be made by a judge, jury, or commission. Clinical decisions surrounding civil commitment are difficult enough without laboring under the illusion of having judicial responsibility. Historically, psychiatrists did have the power to commit. Recently, the psychiatrist's discretion in long-term civil commitment has been abolished. When mental health professionals file an emergency commitment, however, a clerk or magistrate may proceed without further question. In some states, filing an emergency commitment is unnecessary, and the patient can be held for a number of days.

Ensminger and Ligouri (7) find that the commitment hearing itself may have therapeutic significance. The hearing allows for confronting the patient with reality and educating the family about the patient's problems. In addition, the hearing is a unique opportunity for mental health professionals to observe family dynamics and to advise the judge accordingly.

State laws vary substantially regarding procedures and types of commitment. Most states provide for short-term emergency hospitalization until a hearing has been held. Most states have a short "hold period" of 48 to 72 hours, particularly if the state requires a probable-cause hearing. Longer holding times under emergency commitment may occur if provisions exist for formal hearings. Probable-cause hearings determine whether substantial evidence exists to show that the patient meets the standards for involuntary hospitalization. If sufficient evidence is found, the patient may continue to be hospitalized until the formal hearing. The basis for emergency commitment is that the patient suffers from a mental illness and presents a danger to others or self. Some states require that there be a recent overt act, that the danger be imminent, or that the danger present a risk for substantial harm (8).

Procedures for initiating commitment vary considerably from state to state. A report or form is usually required stating the reasons for emergency hospitalization, with a description of the patient's statements and behavior. Some states require a statement to the effect that least-restrictive alternatives have been pursued and are not available or appropriate. No general rules dictate who must file a petition, where it should be filed, or how the patient is to be taken into custody (9). Police officers, next of kin, psychiatrists, other physicians, psychologists, social workers, or even "interested parties" may file a petition for emergency hospitalization. In circumstances in which the therapist is concerned about endangering the treatment alliance with the patient, next of kin may be requested to petition for involuntary hospitalization.

A number of states provide for short-term commitment in addition to emergency commitment. The times specified for emergency, short-term, and long-term commitment vary considerably from state to state. Generally, short-term commitment is for a longer period than emergency commitment. Although greater procedural protection is required, the hospital or psychiatrist rather than the court is responsible initially for the hospitalization decision. Substantive standards for short-term commitment may not be as stringent as standards for long-term commitment. Short-term commitments are usually not utilized by states that hold probable-cause hearings. In the clinical vignette, the judge dismissed the petition for civil commitment of Mr. Gilbert during the probable-cause hearing.

For long-term commitment, all states require judicial or administrative determinations (10). Long-term commitment procedures vary considerably, although the requirement of the substantive criteria of mental illness and dangerousness is usually followed. Indeterminate hospitalization has given way to periodic review for continued involuntary hospitalizations. Such reviews are usually conducted by the court that held the original hearing. Reviews may be conducted every 3, 6, or 12 months.

The minimum standard of proof required for long-term commitment was decided by the United States Supreme Court in *Addington v. Texas* (11). The Court determined that the standard of "clear and convincing evidence" was constitutionally required. This represents a midway position (75% certainty) between "a preponderance of the evidence" in civil cases (51% certainty) and the "beyond a reasonable doubt" standard in criminal cases (95% certainty). These percentages are given for the purpose of discussion only, because the law does not set out a percentile. States that have a "beyond a reasonable doubt" standard for civil commitment are not prevented from continuing to maintain and uphold that standard.

Halleck (12) points out the inconsistency in limiting the psychiatrist's discretion to influence long-term commitment decisions while giving psychiatrists almost total discretion over release of involuntarily hospitalized patients at any time. He theorizes that society's intense concerns with civil liberties and a sense that hospitalized patients have undergone beneficial treatment account for this discrepancy. Sadoff (13) suggests that when courts assume control over involuntary hospitalization, the courts should logically assume responsibility for the patient's release, thus protecting the psychiatrist from the risk of suit if released patients harm themselves or others.

Psychiatrists must not confuse their discretionary freedom to release committed patients under civil statutes with requirements governing release responsibilities for patients who have been criminally committed. The latter require a court order for release from the committing court. Psychiatrists have been sued when patients under criminal commitment are released without court approval and harm another person (14). Juveniles and mentally retarded persons committed by court order also require a court order for discharge. According to some statutes, dangerous patients can be discharged only by written consent of designated hospital authorities on examination and guarantee of proper supervision by reputable persons (15). In those instances in which families or other interested parties oppose discharge, the discharge may be stayed until such persons have been allowed to present their reasons why the patient should be detained. This subject is discussed in greater detail in Chapter 14.

Minors may be hospitalized under "voluntary" provisions, although these provisions vary considerably from state to state. In Maryland, a parent or legal guardian may voluntarily hospitalize a minor in a private hospital when the minor suffers from a "mental disorder which is susceptible of care or treatment." In addition, Maryland permits admission of a minor to a public child or adolescent unit by the parent for only 20 days (9). In some states, a minor is given some discretion over the "voluntary" admission. If minors refuse to consent where their consent is statutorily required, the parent may initiate civil commitment. In *Parham v. J. R.* (16), the U.S. Supreme Court held that in addition to prescribed state law procedures, the federal due-process clause requires review of a parental decision to commit a minor child by an independent and neutral physician. The court rejected the claim that the due-process clause necessitates more rigorous procedural safeguards.

What other civil commitment alternatives exist to involuntary hospitalization?

Outpatient civil commitment is one alternative for the pressing problem of the homeless mentally ill who may be in dire need of treatment and care. Outpatient civil commitment, however, works only for a minority of patients. The "revolving door" patient, regardless of residence, is the person for whom outpatient commitment may be most beneficial.

Miller (17) conducted a national survey of state mental health directors and state attorney generals on the use of outpatient commitment in their states. The survey revealed that in two-thirds of the jurisdictions that permit outpatient commitment this procedure was used as an alternative to inpatient commitment in fewer than 5% of commitments. Miller concluded that unless states obtain more input from clinicians who are involved in treating both inpatients and outpatients, outpatient commitment will continue to be an underutilized and ineffective intervention.

All states permit some form of involuntary outpatient commitment (18). The states usually apply involuntary outpatient commitment in one of three ways: as a conditional release, as a dispositional alternative to hospitalization, or as a preventive commitment.

Another means of assisting the "revolving door" patient is through newly enacted preventive commitment statutes (19). Although often included under outpatient commitment, preventive commitment is more specialized. The purpose of preventive commitment is to prevent predictable deterioration in an individual's mental condition that will lead eventually to involuntary hospitalization. In contrast to involuntary hospitalization, preventive commitment requires lower commitment standards and fewer procedural protections. Preventive commitment differs from outpatient commitment by providing less-restrictive alternatives to hospitalization. Preventive commitment also differs from conditional release, because a conditional release requires compliance with an individual treatment plan. Under conditional release, the patient remains on the hospital rolls until the commitment period has ended. The increasing popularity of preventive commitment is related to *1)* concerns about the patient who resists least-restrictive alternative treatment, *2)* concerns about mentally disordered homeless persons, *3)* a backlash among mental health professionals to legal overregulation of the mental health system, and *4)* demands by patient advocacy groups allied with mental health professionals for easing of commitment standards.

Preventive commitment statutes have the following criteria in common: the existence of mental illness, the likelihood that the patient will meet the standards for involuntary hospitalization, and determination of whether the mental illness will prevent voluntary treatment. Only a few states have enacted these statutes, but more states are considering such legislation.

What recognized clinical approaches should be followed in initiating involuntary hospitalization?

Recognized clinical approaches to civil commitment that maintain the traditional treatment role of psychiatrists include performing a careful examination of the patient, abiding by the requirements of the law, and ensuring that sound clinical reasoning motivates the certification of the mentally ill patient. In *Stowers v. Wolodzko* (20), a husband in the midst of a marital conflict called a psychiatrist to come to his home and examine his wife. The psychiatrist and a colleague arrived without explaining to the wife the purpose of their visit. The plaintiff, a homemaker, was forcibly dragged from her home, taken to a private hospital, and denied the right to write or receive letters, use the phone, or consult with her attorney. She attempted to refuse treatment but was forced to submit to intramuscularly and orally administered medications. The psychiatrist was held liable for false imprisonment and assault and battery for actions taken pursuant to the temporary commitment. The plaintiff was awarded $40,000 for her 11-day detention.

Spouses sometimes call psychiatrists to their homes for the purpose of involuntarily hospitalizing a mate. House calls may be indicated for certain patients (21). Although the call to the psychiatrist by a spouse may not be motivated by malice or cunning, care must be used in making an adequate examination. In one instance, two psychiatrists who were called by a husband observed a woman through a closed window before signing commitment papers. This examination would hardly be considered acceptable. The American Psychiatric Association, in *The Principles of Medical Ethics With Annotations Especially Applicable to Psychiatry* (22), states: "The psychiatrist may permit his/her certification to be used for the involuntary treatment of any person only following his/her personal examination of that person" (Section 7, Annotation 4). The less opportunity the psychiatrist has to observe and speak to the patient, the more questions will be raised about whether the psychiatrist conducted an adequate personal examination.

Psychiatrists who respond to the call of one spouse to examine the other at their home may need to be concerned about trespass. Psychiatrists also should consider their personal safety in entering a household when uninvited by one of its members. Ordinarily, the consent of one in lawful possession is a sufficient defense against a claim of trespass. If the spouse lives separately, however, the psychiatrist has no right to enter uninvited.

TABLE 8–1.   Typical substantive criteria for involuntary hospitalization

- Mentally ill
- Dangerous to self or others
- Unable to provide for basic needs

Miscellaneous criteria (in conjunction with one or more criteria above)
- Gravely disabled (unable to care for self to the point of likely self-harm)
- Refusing hospitalization
- In need of hospitalization
- Danger to property
- Lacks capacity to make rational treatment decisions

Note.   Criteria are statutorily determined and vary from state to state.

What are the substantive standards for long-term commitment? How can psychiatrists preserve their traditional clinical roles in adhering to such standards?

To varying degrees, involuntary hospitalization represents the exercise of the state's parens patriae and police powers. Mental illness and dangerousness are the fundamental substantive requirements for civil commitment (see Table 8-1). State statutes, however, are not uniform in their definition of mental illness. Although a few statutes (23) specifically define psychiatric disorders that qualify, most are indefinite. Epilepsy or alcoholism may be included, whereas antisocial personality may not (24). Some statutes apply an impairment requirement. The psychiatric disorder must substantially impair the patient's functioning so that care, treatment, and protection are required (25). Most Axis I and Axis II diagnoses from the *Diagnostic and Statistical Manual of Mental Disorders* (26) meet the statutory definitions of mental illness unless specifically excluded. Psychiatrists should be prepared, however, for legal challenges to the sufficiency of their evidence substantiating a patient's mental illness and, particularly, their diagnosis of dangerousness.

As discussed above, procedures for involuntary hospitalization have gone through several cycles of recriminalization and decriminalization since the mid-1800s. Real changes in substantive standards are a relatively new phenomenon. Recently, a shift toward police power has occurred through judicial decisions and legislative enactments. All state statutes require a finding of dangerousness or grave disability in addition to mental illness. The dangerousness standard refers to either dangerousness to self or to others as the most common basis for long-term commitment. Definitions of dangerousness vary considerably, including "substantial physical harm to others" (27), "imminent or immediate" harm to others (28), and serious physical injury to others (29). The Iowa statute (29) specifies emotional as well as physical harm to others. A significant number of state statutes include the requirement of a recent overt act or threat of violence. Dangerousness to self incorporates a blend of parens patriae and police powers and is a part of every state statute.

In a few states, posing a danger to property may be sufficient. The threat of harm to physical property is not usually considered a justification for civil commitment. In *Suzuki v. Yuen* (30), the district court held that a Hawaii statute that allowed commitment of a mentally ill individual who was dangerous only to property was unconstitutional. The statute permitted deprivation of liberty on the basis of threatening harm to any property. The court ultimately held that a standard of "substantial property damage" would be an adequate basis for involuntary commitment.

Other criteria that will justify commitment include persons who are gravely disabled or who lack the ability to care for themselves and are in need of treatment (31). Most states have such a provision, which is a pure expression of parens patriae. In *O'Connor v. Donaldson* (32), the U.S. Supreme Court explicitly declined to address the question of whether a state can compel confinement of persons for the sole purpose of treatment. As a result, there is no constitutional barrier to involuntary hospitalization of the nondangerous mentally ill person (33). The definition of "gravely disabled" varies to include neglect that threatens the person's life (34) or the inability to provide for basic needs such as food, clothing, or shelter (35).

The number of involuntary hospitalizations has not changed drastically over the years even though more restrictive substantive standards have been required. The category of "gravely disabled" has permitted many patients to be involuntarily hospitalized by psychiatrists. A smattering of states have additional requirements such as refusal of voluntary admission, a treatable patient, the person's inability to make a rational decision about treatment, and hospitalization as the least-restrictive alternative. The latter has little to do with the treatment needs of the patient, but represents a balancing of liberty interests against the restrictions imposed on a dangerous patient. A number of statutes have been redrafted to broaden commitment provisions to allow commitment when deterioration is likely (36). The statutes have specifically adopted the wording of the American Psychiatric Association Model Law (37).

Psychiatrists may have difficulty maintaining their traditional clinical roles because of great pressure to certify patients on the basis of dangerousness, whether treatable or not. In the past, psychiatrists involuntarily hospitalized patients who were dangerous, but the dangerousness was often incidental to the need for treatment of a psychiatric illness. When psychiatrists are pressured to certify persons on the basis of dangerousness, they are placed in the role of society's police officer. This double-agent role may ultimately destroy the trust of the patient and make the possibility of treatment outside of the institution difficult.

A model state law of civil commitment has been approved by the American Psychiatric Association (37). The model law attempts to address the pressing problems surrounding involuntary hospitalization. The model law would permit commitment of mentally ill persons who lack the capacity to make an informed treatment decision but who refuse treatment. Usually, these patients suffer from a mental disorder treatable at the facility where they are involuntarily hospitalized consistent with the principle of the least-restrictive alternative. They would suffer substantial mental or physical deterioration if not treated.

How can psychiatrists maintain an appropriate clinical stance when assessing the dangerousness criterion for involuntary hospitalization?

The statutory definitions of the dangerousness requirement are often vague and reflect the value judgments of the statute's authors. As is now widely known, not only are psychiatrists unable to predict dangerousness, but they also may err on the side of overprediction. Furthermore, dangerousness is often situational or reflects an interaction between the individual and the environment, defying predictability. Eisenberg et al. (38) stress that the psychiatric literature is preoccupied with procedural, substantive, and statistical issues surrounding civil commitment, and little attention is paid to the clinical aspects of commitment. Hoffman (39) points out "there is virtually no case law on point for a variety of clinical situations" and that most "existing state mental health statutes incompletely reflect contemporary legal and psychiatric understanding."

Beigel et al. (40) studied 40 psychiatrists who were asked to rate dangerousness to self or others. The case study consisted of 16 patients described by case history. Psychiatrists were asked to recommend a course of action. Half the psychiatrists were given the state statute defining dangerousness to use in responding. Psychiatrists who used the statute summary were less consistent in predicting dangerousness than psychiatrists who did not refer to it, especially when the patient had a history of violence. The authors explained that the psychiatrists who reviewed the law changed their initial impressions of patient dangerousness when they found the patient did not fit the legal criteria for dangerousness. The other psychiatrists went with their "gut" impressions. Beigel et al. concluded:

> There seems to be no question that focusing on the law tends to influence some clinicians away from their own clinical judgments, turning them more into legal decision makers. When some clinicians seem to ignore the law and make their decisions based on clinical criteria, while others choose to use legal criteria, relatively low reliability results in the group that was given the law to use. (40)

Legal criteria for dangerousness determined by social policy and political issues can adversely influence the most competent psychiatrist's clinical assessments of potential violence. This should not be understood to mean that psychiatrists should ignore, fudge, or attempt to manipulate statutes for their own treatment agendas. Rather, psychiatrists often become mesmerized by statutory definitions of dangerousness that cripple their clinical judgments. Eisenberg et al. (38) discuss the different ways that the commitment process can be turned to clinical account through maintaining or enhancing the therapeutic alliance.

The fit between mental illness and dangerousness is loose. One study (41) indicated that in the early stages of mania, patients are frequently violent. Drug abuse, alcohol abuse, organicity, or other conditions that loosen impulse control are often implicated in dangerous behavior. Monahan (42) notes that the first step in increasing the accuracy of prediction of rare events such as violence lies in identifying populations with higher than ordinary base rates of violent behavior. Empirically verified predictors of future violent acts include a history of previous violence (by far the most valid measure of future dangerousness), age

in the late teens and early twenties, male gender, black race, lower socioeconomic class, history of opiate or alcohol abuse, low IQ, and residential and employment instability (43). Race as a factor in violence has been disputed (44).

The assessment of the risk of violence has to be tailored to the individual at
hand. Professional standards for the prediction of violence do not exist. The
psychiatrist's focus must be on the presence or absence of a diagnosable, treatable mental illness because the ability to diagnose dangerousness is so problematic. When using DSM criteria, standards for diagnosis that have been tested by
interrater reliability trials are used. The *kappa* coefficients of agreement for
Axis I and Axis II diagnostic classes for adults (18 and older) indicate reasonably high levels of agreement for many of the major diagnostic categories. Diagnosis and treatment are the proper métier of psychiatrists, and they prove
more reliable than any prediction of dangerousness. Persons who are dangerous
but not diagnosably mentally ill are the responsibility of the police, not the psychiatrist. Whenever the law permits, psychiatrists should avoid outright predictions of dangerousness and instead focus on why a particular patient is more
likely to commit a dangerous act than the average person (12). Attorneys argue
that psychiatrists should have a very limited role in determining dangerousness
and that it should be decided entirely in the courtroom (45). Ennis and Emery
(46) state:

> Because statutory definitions of dangerousness are usually vague, it is easy for
> mental health professionals to call people dangerous. As we noted, many profes-
> sionals consider dangerousness a mere technicality, a magic word that must be ut-
> tered in order to get patients the treatment they need!

In fact, psychiatrists sometime label prospective patients "dangerous" in
order to achieve parens patriae purposes.

How can the psychiatrist minimize damage to the doctor-patient relationship when initiating involuntary hospitalization?

Appelbaum (47) highlights three issues of paramount importance to the clinician participating in the commitment process: assessing patients' suitability for
commitment, assessing the degree to which involuntary hospitalization is a
threat to the therapist-patient relationship, and managing conflicts that arise between legal and ethical issues.

Assessment difficulties arise from the almost universal requirement that a
prediction of dangerousness to self or others be made prior to commitment. (Assessing the risk of violence rather than the prediction of dangerousness is
discussed in Chapters 12 and 13.) The assessment of another form of dangerousness, grave disability, has received much less attention in the literature than
overt dangerousness. The psychiatrist is on firmer ground when predicting the

ability of the patient to care properly for himself or herself during acute psychotic episodes or when the patient suffers from advanced forms of senile dementia.

There may be a disjunction between the presence of certain severe mental disorders and the ability to take day-to-day care of oneself. Some chronic schizophrenic patients manage their lives reasonably well in the presence of hallucinations, delusions, and thought disorder. Assessment of functional ability for this group should be focused on survival tasks. Can the patient manage food, finances, clothing, and shelter requirements? Is an adequate support system in place? Are any changes occurring in the environment that are potentially or actually destabilizing?

The decision to commit a patient can be a threat to an enduring psychiatrist-patient relationship. Once a treatment relationship has been damaged or destroyed, the patient's subsequent treatment relationships may be adversely affected. For this and other reasons, treatment and administrative roles have been kept separate in some mental health institutions. The psychiatrist is spared the dual role of serving both the needs of society and the needs and interests of the patient.

Attempting to work with the healthy side of the patient may help preserve at least the rudiments of a therapeutic alliance even in the face of a florid psychosis. Keeping the patient informed of, and hopefully even involved with, the decision-making process may serve to sustain the alliance. Approximately 25% of patients who are involuntarily hospitalized refuse treatment on admission. However, clinical experience demonstrates that within 7 to 10 days after admission, most patients will agree to treatment. This initial period of treatment refusal may reflect, in part, a temporary absence of the treatment alliance.

Accountability in the commitment process also favors not taking the commitment decision away from the treating psychiatrist. Abusing the commitment process and harming the patient are much less likely to happen when commitment is initiated by the treating psychiatrist. Can psychiatrists and judges who evaluate the patient on a one-time basis and then walk away have the same sensitivity as the patient's therapist to the long-term psychological consequences of involuntary hospitalization for the patient?

Turning to ethical and legal conflicts surrounding commitment, statutes governing commitment require psychiatrists to predict specific kinds of future harm, encouraging error on the side of liberty over confinement (47). This view may conflict with the clinician's perceived ethical responsibility to protect patients from harm and to provide critical treatment. An attempt should not be made to certify patients who could benefit from hospitalization but do not meet commitment criteria. Although clinicians should not become mesmerized by the law, neither should they take it into their own hands. In doubtful situations in which the psychiatrist has reason to believe the patient may be dangerous but is uncertain about this conclusion, erring on the side of commitment appears to be justified. Appelbaum (47) recommends that in these situations psychiatrists rely on their instincts as physicians in determining which course is in the patient's best interest. Appelbaum adds that the courts should temper clinical biases through legal scrutiny. It is this author's opinion that on those rare occasions when adherence to a legal requirement might prevent provision of critical care to the patient, the psychiatrist must first act as a physician.

Stone's (48) proposed "thank you theory" of civil commitment captures the essence of the clinical approach. It asks the psychiatrist to focus inquiry on illness and treatment while asking the law to guarantee treatment before intervening in the name of parens patriae. Stone feels that moral and legal justification for the doctrine of parens patriae can be achieved if the three essential ingredients of reliable criteria are present: diagnosis of illness, incompetent refusal, and a decent institution. Stone's "thank you theory" divests civil commitment of a police function. Dangerousness is returned to the province of criminal law. Only the mentally ill, treatable and incidentally dangerous patient would be confined in mental health systems, prompting a thank you from an ultimately grateful patient.

What important clinical-legal issues are illustrated by the vignette?

When dangerousness is the overriding criterion for involuntary hospitalization, patients suffering from severe character disorders come to inhabit psychiatric hospitals. Many of these patients are not treatable by current psychiatric modalities. Patients who need treatment but are not "dangerous" are discharged to join the armies of street people. Frequently, the character-disordered individual will terrorize hospital staff and other patients as he or she is shuttled back and forth from jails to hospitals for criminal offenders.

Mr. Gilbert was diagnosed as an antisocial personality disorder. In certain jurisdictions a diagnosis of antisocial personality disorder will not meet the mental illness criteria for initiating involuntary hospitalization. The initial decision to admit Mr. Gilbert relied on the presence of depression and murderous impulses. The decision to seek commitment was based on the patient's continued need for treatment and the belief that he still posed a danger to his fiancée.

Although an act of violence occurred 2 months prior to admission, Dr. King was not deterred from seeking involuntary hospitalization of his patient. Dr. King sought to admit Mr. Gilbert in violation of the statute, which requires a violent act within 30 days. The 30-day criterion does not correspond with clinical reality. Previous violence is more important than an arbitrarily imposed time frame noting when the violence occurred. The clinician should not abrogate clinical judgment to the law, although he or she should remain knowledgeable and respectful of the law. Thus, Dr. King stayed with his clinical judgment, allowing the judge to make the legal decisions. The decision to pursue involuntary hospitalization of Mr. Gilbert was not based on a treatment agenda hidden behind an allegation of dangerousness, nor was it used primarily as a risk-management technique. Dr. King was genuinely concerned about violence directed at the patient's fiancée because of the history of frequent violent episodes and depression in the past. Furthermore, Dr. King and his staff cannot be held legally liable for the judge's decision. When the court denies the petition for commitment, psychiatrists should make certain that they introduce into the record their concerns about potential violence.

In *Jacobs v. Taylor* (49), the Court of Appeals of Georgia held that the psychiatrist could not be found liable for failing to control the patient or protecting three victims who were killed when the decision not to commit the patient was made by a judge based on the psychiatrist's evaluation.

Sadoff (50) states that dangerousness may be a current overriding commitment issue for the law. However, he feels that it should not in fact be the issue for psychiatrists:

> Psychiatrists should be concerned primarily with the best interests of the patient as a patient. The psychiatrist's concern is the mental illness or disability of the patient. Another part of their concern is the manifestations of the illness in terms of behavior, whether violent, self-destructive or self-negating. The law may interpret the clinical medical statements of psychiatrists in any way it chooses in order to justify its disposition or decision. These decisions are not medical or psychiatric, however, but rather legal, based on clinical psychiatric input.

Some psychiatrists feel that they should not be called on to treat patients with severe character disorders who are potentially violent. There may be some merit in this position if proper facilities and appropriately trained personnel are not available. However, psychiatrists have long treated patients with severe character disorders through crisis intervention techniques, often hospitalizing these patients for brief periods. Dangerousness is often situational and brief. Few persons are continually dangerous. Character disorder diagnoses are clearly defined in the DSM. Furthermore, these patients often represent a significant volume of psychiatrists' outpatient practice. To say that psychiatrists do not and cannot treat some of these individuals is to blink at reality. Because long-term treatment approaches are often not suitable for patients with severe character disorders in crisis, psychiatrists and hospitals who receive these patients should become proficient in short-term crisis management and specialized treatment techniques (51).

What legal liabilities have been imposed on psychiatrists when involuntarily hospitalizing patients?

The most common legal actions against psychiatrists who participate in civil commitment proceedings are malicious prosecution, false imprisonment, assault and battery, and civil rights actions (52). According to Klein and Glover (53), these suits allege that decisions or recommendations by psychiatrists to hospitalize patients involuntarily were unreasonable. In *Daniels v. Finney* (54), the court held that there was insufficient evidence presented by expert testimony to establish a negligent diagnosis. The court required the plaintiff to establish that the defendant psychiatrist did not have reasonable cause to believe that the patient was mentally ill. In *Mezullo v. Maletz* (55), the court concluded that even if the defendant psychiatrist acted with malice and bad faith, he was protected in his capacity as a court witness by an absolute privilege because of the court's need for frank medical testimony.

In *Marcus v. Liebman* (56), a patient brought an action for false imprisonment against a psychiatrist. The appellate court held that a material issue of fact existed for the jury as to the reasonableness of the patient's apprehension of force or coercion used to keep her in the hospital. In addition, the court held that a cause of action for false imprisonment was established by the threat of committing a voluntarily hospitalized patient to a state hospital. The patient alleged that she was forced to rescind her request to be released as a voluntary inpatient because she was threatened with involuntary hospitalization.

Psychiatrists must not use the threat of involuntary hospitalization to coerce patients into accepting treatment or procedures when the psychiatrists have no real intention of petitioning for commitment. If the psychiatrist expects to seek involuntary hospitalization for the patient, the patient should be informed of this intention. Not to do so may deal a severe blow to the patient's trust and may adversely affect future treatment efforts.

Psychiatrists must be certain that they spend sufficient time with the patient to ensure an adequate examination. In *James v. Brown* (57), for example, the court held that too brief an examination was conducted to arrive at a proper diagnosis.

On a state by state basis, courts have held that psychiatrists who participate in commitment proceedings are immune from malpractice suits (58). For example, in *LaLonde v. Eissner* (59), the Massachusetts Supreme Judicial Court held that a court-appointed psychiatrist was entitled to absolute immunity in performing quasi-judicial services in conducting the evaluation. Courts reason that psychiatrists who perform evaluations for the judicial system such as making decisions surrounding commitment should do so without fear of legal liability (60). A large number of states have immunity provisions in their commitment statutes for good-faith actions. When a psychiatrist-patient relationship already exists, courts in some jurisdictions may be less willing to cloak the commitment process with immunity for the psychiatrist (61). The treating psychiatrist has more knowledge and responsibility for the patient than does the psychiatrist examining the patient solely for the purpose of civil commitment.

Often, physical confinement is the physical injury alleged as the cause of action for false imprisonment. The patient, however, does not have to be physically injured during confinement. Damages will be available even without physical injury.

When the plaintiff can show that the psychiatrist did not perform an adequate psychiatric examination, liability often will be assessed. In *Maben v. Rankin* (62), a woman was forcibly abducted, hospitalized, and given electroconvulsive therapy when her husband said she needed treatment. The psychiatrist was found liable for failing to conduct an adequate examination. In *Whitree v. State* (63), a patient confined in a state hospital for 12 years was awarded $300,000 in damages when the court found that an adequate psychiatric examination was never performed.

One of the two substantive prongs of all commitment statutes is the requirement of mental illness. People who are dangerous, but not mentally ill, do not qualify. To ensure adequacy in diagnosis, psychiatrists should consider utilizing the diagnostic criteria contained in the most recent edition of the DSM. By adhering to officially approved diagnostic criteria, a standard reference can be used that helps dispel allegations of caprice or malice in diagnosing mental illness. This procedure is also an effective antidote to the temptation to fudge the mental illness standard in order to get around a perceived legal impediment to involuntary hospitalization. Generally, courts are willing to defer to psychiatric diagnoses as long as the litigation issue requires assessing whether a given individual poses a danger to self or others (64). On the other hand, courts generally are not hesitant in overturning a commitment order if statutory procedural guidelines are not carefully followed. Legal commentators state that the inflexibility of statutory guidelines has the advantage of providing less opportunity for errors in judgment and subsequent legal liability (64). They advise avoiding exposure to liability by following the strict letter of the commitment law, no matter how trifling such details may appear.

Psychiatrists also have been sued for alleged errors in diagnosing dangerousness (65). The ability of psychiatrists to predict dangerousness outside of specific contexts is significantly below 50%. Should the psychiatrist fail to initiate commitment of potentially violent patients who then injure themselves or others, liability for damages may arise. If they do commit a patient and that commitment later appears inappropriate, a lawsuit for wrongful commitment may be filed in those jurisdictions where good-faith immunity is not provided by statute.

Under these circumstances, psychiatrists should follow their clinical judgment about the treatment needs of mentally ill, potentially violent or violent patients based on careful examination and risk-benefit analysis. Patients can expect to benefit from involuntary hospitalization if they suffer from a treatable mental illness and if appropriate hospitals and adequately trained personnel are available. In contrast, the risks of hospitalization include inducing dependency and other stigmata of institutionalization. The benefits of not involuntarily hospitalizing the patient include avoiding interruption of the treatment, enhancing the therapeutic alliance, and promoting patient autonomy. The risks of not hospitalizing the patient include the potential of harm to self and others as well as further deterioration of the patient's psychiatric condition.

Dangerousness, the second substantive prong of commitment statutes, is vaguely defined in state statutes and often shaped by societal and political issues that influence legislators. Psychiatrists should not be distracted or deterred from their traditional diagnostic and treatment roles by assuming quasi-legal roles as interpreters of statutory language. Although statutory definitions need to be understood and followed as a guide to the commitment of patients, preoccupation with statutory language is not a productive activity for the psychiatrist. Legal scrutiny should be left to lawyers and judges.

Psychiatrists should be reassured that involuntary hospitalization is a valid intervention for appropriate patients. Controlled studies have found that patients are mostly appreciative, in retrospect, for the care they were given. One controlled study found involuntary patients to be no less satisfied with the outcome of hospitalization than voluntary patients (66). Another controlled study revealed that involuntarily committed patients functioned as well as voluntary patients after discharge, despite being more severely ill at the time of admission (67). Clinical experience also is consistent with the findings of these studies that involuntary patients, for the most part, will achieve significant short-term gains and will be appreciative of the intervention. When involuntary hospitalization has been appropriately undertaken, patient gratitude has been, by far, the more common experience than patient dissatisfaction that leads to litigation.

Do commitment statutes require involuntary hospitalization of persons under certain defined circumstances?

No. Commitment statutes are permissive (68). In other words, the statutes enable mental health professionals and others to seek involuntary hospitalization for persons who meet certain substantive criteria. The duty to seek involuntary hospitalization is a standard-of-care issue. Patients who are mentally ill and pose an imminent, serious threat to themselves or others may require involuntary hospitalization as a primary psychiatric intervention.

In *Petersen v. State* (69), the court specifically acknowledged the psychiatrist's duty to commit patients *under certain circumstances* in the state of Washington. A patient was involuntarily detained when the hospital staff discovered that he was suffering from hallucinations and delusions. The patient had a history of abusing phencyclidine and other drugs. He was diagnosed as suffering from a schizophrenic disorder and given thiothixene. On expiration of the emergency detention period, the psychiatrist petitioned and obtained an additional 14 days of hospital stay. The psychiatrist testified that the patient was gravely disabled by drug abuse and remained a danger to himself. On the day before expiration of the last detention period, the patient was given a pass. He was observed that evening spinning his car in circles on the hospital grounds. Nevertheless, the patient was discharged the next day after the psychiatrist concluded that the patient had recovered from his drug-induced psychosis. Five days later, the patient struck the plaintiff's car while traveling at 50 to 60 miles per hour while running a red light. The patient was under the influence of drugs. The plaintiff claimed that the psychiatrist's failure to try to extend the commitment was the direct cause of her injuries. The jury awarded damages of $250,000.

The court scrutinized the steps the psychiatrist should have followed to protect the public from the patient. While stating that the psychiatrist "failed to petition the court for a 90-day commitment," the court made no mention of other interventions that could have been utilized. The court held that the psychiatrist was liable for not petitioning for commitment.

Although this case involves a psychiatrist practicing at a state hospital, the holding applies to psychiatrists at private hospitals in the state of Washington (70). The decision places an increased burden on psychiatrists practicing in this state to initiate commitment proceedings. *Petersen v. State* (69) represents a further extension of *Tarasoff* liability to a duty to protect unidentified victims, even when they are unintentionally harmed.

In 1986, the U.S. District Court in North Carolina held that "a psychotherapist judgment rule" would be applied to evaluate the "good faith independence and thoroughness" of a decision not to seek commitment (71). Liability would not be imposed for "simple errors of judgment." In this case, a patient seen irregularly in outpatient treatment for posttraumatic stress disorder killed one person and wounded others in a shooting spree. Shortly before the shootings, 15 psychiatrists at a VA hospital staff meeting unanimously concluded that the patient could not be committed under North Carolina law despite threats of violence. The patient was subsequently convicted of first-degree murder.

In the civil case, the court said, "What society in general desires and expects psychotherapists to do when considering whether a patient should be involuntarily committed is to actively consider the public interest and to use their professional judgment in light of that interest" (71). The court ruled that the doctors did perform this duty.

On appeal, the Fourth Circuit affirmed the lower court's summary judgment for the defendants (71). The court agreed with the psychiatrists who argued that controlling the patient through commitment would destroy the psychiatrist's potential for constructive influence over the patient, "while warnings to threatened third persons may well remain unknown to the patient or appear . . . as not necessarily attributable to the physician. Initiation of involuntary commitment proceedings threatens the patient's constitutionally protected liberty interest, while warnings to third persons . . . does [sic] not."

In *Schuster v. Altenberg* (72), the Wisconsin Supreme Court ruled that a complaint alleging failure to seek commitment of a patient was legally sufficient, remanding the case to the trial court. The court (72) stated:

In the instant case, if it is ultimately proven that it would have been foreseeable to a psychiatrist, exercising due care, that by failing to warn a third person or by failing to take action to institute detention or commitment proceedings someone would be harmed, negligence will be established.

This opinion establishes in Wisconsin an affirmative duty to commit. In this case, a manic-depressive patient on psychotropic medications crashed into a tree at 60 mph within an hour of treatment. The patient died, leaving her 17-year-old daughter paraplegic. The trial court found the decedent 80% contributorily negligent, the plaintiff 20% negligent, and the defendant psychiatrist not negligent (73).

What are the rights of involuntarily hospitalized patients?

Almost every state specifies the rights of psychiatric inpatients in its mental health code. Mental health codes normally contain two parts: admission and discharge of patients, and the rights of patients in institutions (74). Patients in psychiatric facilities retain a variety of rights based on general state laws and federal statutory law (75). In certain instances, the patient's rights will emanate from the U.S. Constitution itself. The Fourteenth Amendment, however, requires that constitutional rights attach only in those cases in which the patient asserts these rights against an action *by the state or one of its entities.* As a result, if the administration of a psychiatric facility is within the ambit of "state action," the facility's care and treatment of the mentally ill will be subject to constitutional restraints (75). In cases in which the state "has exercised coercive power or has provided such significant encouragement, either overt or covert, that the choice must in law be deemed to be that of the state" or if "the private entity has exercised powers that are traditionally the exclusive prerogative of the state" (76), a sufficient nexus between the state and private hospital may be established.

As states continue to encourage and facilitate the role of private facilities in providing care and treatment to the mentally ill, these facilities will be subject to constitutional limitations and restraint. In particular, constitutional rights permit freedom to generate and communicate ideas and freedom of speech (First Amendment), freedom from illegal search and seizure (Fourth Amendment), freedom from cruel and unusual punishment (Eighth Amendment), and rights to due process and equal protection (Fourteenth Amendment). All of these rights have been asserted in the right to refuse treatment and are discussed in detail in Chapter 6.

The right to treatment has been championed in three major cases: *O'Connor v. Donaldson* (32), *Wyatt v. Stickney* (77), and *Youngberg v. Romeo* (78). These court decisions held that involuntarily hospitalized persons have a "right to treatment" or, for those persons developmentally disabled, "a right to habilitation." In some jurisdictions, the right to treatment has been provided by legislative action. The judicially mandated right to treatment also has been imposed on the basis of constitutional principles. Such judicial mandates have produced increases in state expenditures for the improvement of psychiatric institutions. Although treatment may be vaguely defined, the *Wyatt* court defined minimally acceptable treatment in great detail (i.e., the number of square feet of floor space required per patient and the number of cooks that must be employed in the kitchen).

The right to treatment is not a guarantee of treatment for all patients. It applies only to involuntarily hospitalized patients. The right to treatment has never been judicially extended to outpatients or voluntary hospital patients. States, at their own discretion, are free to determine the provision or limitation of services (79). Furthermore, there is no guarantee of optimal treatment. Courts have required only minimal constitutionally required standards. Similarly, no guarantee of effective treatment can be judicially mandated where none exists, nor can the provision of treatment be so closely monitored that only the most efficacious is provided. Not infrequently, the right to treatment of involuntary patients collides with the rulings on the right to refuse treatment. Patients are not guaranteed their choice of treatment. A single accepted form of treatment has been generally deemed sufficient by the courts.

Until recently, the U.S. Supreme Court had not recognized a right to treatment, although lower federal courts have recognized such a right (80). In *Youngberg v. Romeo* (78), however, a limited right to treatment was recognized. Although not recognizing a right to treatment directed toward improving or curing the patient's disorder, the Supreme Court held that a patient had a constitutional right to treatment sufficient to protect the liberty interests of patients while institutionalized.

A majority of states recognize the right of inpatients to refuse treatment. Even though the patient is involuntarily hospitalized, the hospitalization does not negate a presumption of competence. In a number of states, patients involuntarily hospitalized who refuse medication require a separate court hearing for an adjudication of incompetence and the provision of substitute consent by the court. Recently, persons hospitalized under criminal commitment have been accorded the right to refuse treatment (81). The courts have found that patients' constitutional right to due process is "adequately protected by the exercise of professional judgment" within the medical peer review process of the institution. The right to refuse treatment is discussed in detail in Chapter 6.

Hospitalized patients possess other rights. Patients possess rights of visitation, although these rights can be temporarily suspended for proper cause relating to the patient's care and treatment. For example, if a patient becomes agitated by a visitor, the hospital has the right to restrict visits. Hours of visitation can be regulated so that the hospital can properly conduct its work.

Free communications of hospitalized patients through mail, telephone, or visitors are considered a right, unless protection of the patient or others requires supervision of communications. Some state statutes explicitly grant permission to hospitals to censor communications (82). For example, if it is suspected that the patient is receiving contraband through the mail, the mail may be opened in front of the patient. Most states permit unrestricted communications to clergy, lawyers, and government officials.

The right to privacy includes allowing patients to have secure locker space, private toilet and shower facilities, and minimum square footage of floor space. Protection of confidentiality is also included. Many of these requirements were specified in *Wyatt* and are becoming increasingly accepted. The respect for patient's inviolability is a major element in proper treatment.

Economic rights include the right to have and spend money and to handle one's own financial affairs. In most jurisdictions, involuntarily hospitalized patients do not lose their civil rights, such as the right to manage their own money. If the patient's illness leads to profligate spending, mental health professionals may be found negligent. If the patient's incapacity to manage his or her own financial affairs appears more than short term, guardians or conservators should be appointed.

Involuntarily hospitalized patients have been required to work as a form of cheap labor, although this work often has been euphemistically termed "therapeutic labor." The Thirteenth Amendment's ban against involuntary servitude has been held by some courts to prevent the utilization of uncompensated labor. Thus, hospitalized patients must be paid for their work in certain jurisdictions unless it is truly therapeutic labor (i.e., work not connected with maintenance of the hospital).

"Patient rights" are not absolute and often must be tempered by the clinical judgment of the mental health professional. Inevitably, disputes over perceived or real violations of patients' rights arise. In some jurisdictions, a civil rights officer or ombudsman is mandated by statute to mediate these disputes. The ombudsman is not required to resolve disputes, but rather he or she is designated to help the patient find the proper forum for making complaints or for bringing the patient's complaint before appropriate officials (83). (For a comprehensive discussion of the rights of the mentally disabled, the reader is referred to Perlin [84].)

References

1. Appelbaum PS, Gutheil TG: Clinical Handbook of Psychiatry and the Law, 2nd Edition. Baltimore, MD, Williams & Wilkins, 1991, pp 46–47
2. 349 F Supp 1078 (E D Wis 1972), vacated and remanded, 414 U.S. 473 (1974), 379 F Supp 1376 (E D Wis 1974), vacated and remanded on other grounds, 421 U.S. 957 (1975), aff'd, 413 F Supp 1318 (E D Wis 1976)
3. Slovenko R: Misadventures of psychiatry with the law. Journal of Psychiatry and Law 17:115–156, 1989

4. Hiday VA: Reform commitment procedures: an empirical study in the courtroom. Law and Society Review 11:652–666, 1977
5. Miller RD: Involuntary Civil Commitment of the Mentally Ill in the Post-Reform Era. Springfield, IL, Charles C Thomas, 1987, p 28
6. Appelbaum PS, Gutheil TG: Clinical Handbook of Psychiatry and the Law, 2nd Edition. Baltimore, MD, Williams & Wilkins, 1991, p 47
7. Ensminger JJ, Ligouri TD: The therapeutic significance of the civil commitment hearing: an unexplored potential in therapeutic jurisprudence, in The Law as a Therapeutic Agent. Edited by Wexler DB. Durham, NC, Carolina Academic Press, 1990, pp 245–260
8. MD HEALTH–GEN CODE ANN § 10-626(a) (1990)
9. Klein J, Onek J, Macbeth J: Seminar on Law in the Practice of Psychiatry: Dangerous Patients. Washington, DC, Onek, Klein, and Farr, 1984, p 35
10. Ibid, p 38
11. 441 U.S. 418 (1979)
12. Halleck SL: Law in the Practice of Psychiatry. New York, Plenum, 1980, p 125
13. Sadoff RL: New malpractice concerns for the psychiatrist. Legal Aspects of Medical Care 6:31–35, 1968
14. Semler v Psychiatric Institute of Washington, DC, 538 F2d 121 (4th Cir 1976), cert denied, Folliard v Semler, 429 U.S. 827 (1976)
15. Slovenko R: Psychiatry and Law. Boston, MA, Little, Brown, 1973, p 213
16. 442 U.S. 584 (1979)
17. Miller RD: Commitment to outpatient treatment: a national survey. Hosp Community Psychiatry 36:265–267, 1985; Miller RD: Involuntary civil commitment, in American Psychiatric Press Review of Clinical Psychiatry and the Law, Vol 2. Edited by Simon RI. Washington, DC, American Psychiatric Press, 1991, pp 95–172
18. McCafferty G, Dooley J: Involuntary outpatient commitment: an update. MPDLR 14:277–287, 1990
19. Stefan S: Preventive commitment: the concept and its pitfalls. MPDLR 11:288–302, 1987
20. 386 Mich 119, 191 NW2d 355 (1972)
21. Psychiatric house calls benefit certain patients, reduce need for hospitalization. Psychiatric News 25(16):7, 1990
22. American Psychiatric Association: The Principles of Medical Ethics With Annotations Especially Applicable to Psychiatry. Washington, DC, American Psychiatric Association, 1989
23. VA CODE ANN § 37.1-1 (1984)
24. Johnson v Noot, 323 NW2d 724 (Minn 1982) (en banc), superseded by statute, Enebak v Noot, 353 NW2d 544 (Minn 1984)
25. MICH COMP LAW ANN § 330.1400a (West 1980)
26. American Psychiatric Association: Diagnostic and Statistical Manual of Mental Disorders. Washington, DC, American Psychiatric Association
27. CAL WELF & INST CODE § 5304 (West 1984)
28. MICH COMP LAWS ANN § 330 (West 1979)
29. IOWA CODE ANN § 229.1(2)(a) (West 1985)
30. 617 F2d 173 (9th Cir 1980)
31. Miller RD: Involuntary Civil Commitment of the Mentally Ill in the Post-Reform Era. Springfield, IL, Charles C Thomas, 1987, pp 41, 192

32. 422 U.S. 563, (1975), remanded, Donaldson v O'Connor, 519 F2d 59 (5th Cir 1975)
33. Hermann DHJ: Civil commitment: statutory developments and contemporary practice. Paper presented at the 15th annual meeting of the American Academy of Psychiatry and the Law, October 1984
34. KAN STAT ANN § 59-2902 (a)(2) (1983)
35. CAL WELF & INST CODE § 5008(h) (West 1984)
36. TEX HEALTH & SAFETY CODE ANN § 5547-50 (Vernon 1984); WASH REV CODE ANN § 71.05 (1982); PA STAT ANN tit 50, § 7100 (Purdon 1978); NC GEN STAT § 122-58 (1981)
37. Stromberg CD, Stone AA: Statute: a model state law on civil commitment of the mentally ill, in Issues in Forensic Psychiatry. Washington, DC, American Psychiatric Press, 1984, pp 57–180
38. Eisenberg GC, Barnes BM, Gutheil TG: Involuntary commitment and the treatment process: a clinical perspective. Bull Am Acad Psychiatry Law 8:44–55, 1980
39. Hoffman P: The right to refuse treatment: a clinical perspective. Bull Am Acad Psychiatry Law 4:269–270, 1976
40. Beigel A, Berren MR, Harding TW: The paradoxical impact of a commitment statute on prediction of dangerousness. Am J Psychiatry 141:376–377, 1984
41. Ionno JA: Prospective study of assaultive behavior in female psychiatric inpatients, in Assaults Within Psychiatric Facilities. Edited by Lion J, Reid W. New York, Grune & Stratton, 1983, pp 71–80
42. Monahan J: Clinical Prediction of Violent Behavior. Rockville, MD, National Institute of Mental Health, 1981, pp 63–67
43. Simon RI: Concise Guide to Clinical Psychiatry and the Law. Washington, DC, American Psychiatric Press, 1988, pp 99–121
44. Tardiff K: A model for the short-term prediction of violence potential and related research, in Current Approaches to the Prediction of Violence. Edited by Brizer DA, Crowner M. Washington, DC, American Psychiatric Press, 1989, pp 1–12
45. Ennis BJ, Emery RD: Commission on the Mentally Disabled, American Bar Association: suggested statute on civil commitment. MDPLR 2:127–159, 1977
46. Ennis BJ, Emery RD: The Rights of Mental Patients. New York, Avon, 1978
47. Appelbaum PS: Civil commitment, in Psychiatry, Vol 3. Edited by Cavenar JO. Philadelphia, PA, JB Lippincott, 1985, pp 1–18
48. Stone AA: Mental health and law: a system in transition (Publ No ADM-76-176). Rockville, MD, National Institute of Mental Health, 1976
49. 190 Ga App 520, 379 SE2d 563 (GA Ct App 1989)
50. Sadoff RL: Indications for involuntary hospitalization: dangerousness or mental illness? in Law and the Mental Health Professions. Edited by Barton WE, Sanborn CJ. New York, International Universities Press, 1978, pp 297–309; see p 307
51. Applebaum PS: Hospitalization of the dangerous patient: legal pressures and clinical responses. Bull Am Acad Psychiatry Law 12:323–330, 1984
52. Fishalow SE: The tort liability of the psychiatrist. Bull Am Acad Psychiatry Law 3:191–230, 1975
53. Klein JI, Glover SI: Psychiatric malpractice. Int J Law Psychiatry 6:131–157, 1983
54. 262 SW2d 431 (Tex Ct App 1953)
55. 331 Mass 233, 118 NE2d 356 (1954)
56. 59 Ill App 3d 337, 375 NE2d 486 (Ill App Ct 1978)

57. 637 SW2d 914 (Tex 1982)
58. Perlin ML: Mental Disability Law: Civil and Criminal, Vol 3. Charlottesville, VA, Michie, 1989, p 71
59. 405 Mass 207, 539 NE2d 538 (1989)
60. Enberg v Bonde, 331 NW2d 731 (Minn 1983)
61. Davis v Tirrell, 110 Misc 2d 889, 442 NYS2d 136 (1981)
62. 55 Cal 2d 139, 10 Cal Rptr 353, 358 P2d 681 (1961) (en banc)
63. 56 Misc 2d 693, 290 NYS2d 486 (1968)
64. Levin RB, Hill EH: Recent trends in psychiatric liability, in American Psychiatric Press Review of Clinical Psychiatry and the Law, Vol 3. Edited by Simon RI. Washington, DC, American Psychiatric Press, 1992, pp129–150
65. Davis v Lhim, 335 NW2d 481 (Mich App 1983), remanded on other grounds, 422 Mich 875, 366 NW2d 7 (1985), on rem, 147 Mich App 8, 382 NW2d 195 (1985), rvsd sub nom Canon v Thumudo, 430 Mich 326, 422 NW2d 688 (1988), 211, 215
66. Spensley J, Edwards DW, White E: Patient satisfaction and involuntary treatment. Am J Orthopsychiatry 50:725–727, 1980
67. Gove WR, Fain T: A comparison of voluntary and committed psychiatric patients. Arch Gen Psychiatry 34:669–676, 1977
68. Appelbaum PS, Zonana H, Bonnie R, et al: Statutory approaches to limiting psychiatrists' liability for their patients' violent acts. Am J Psychiatry 146:821–828, 1989
69. 100 Wash 2d 421, 671 P2d 230 (1983) (en banc)
70. American Psychiatric Association Legal Consultation Plan Newsletter 3:2–3, 1984
71. Currie v United States, 644 F Supp 1074 (MD NC 1986), aff'd, Currie v United States, 836 F2d 209 (4th Cir 1987)
72. 144 Wis 2d 223, 424 NW2d 159 (1988), rev'd and remanded
73. Schuster v Altenberg, 86-CV-1327 (Cir Ct Racine Cty 1990)
74. Slovenko R: Forensic psychiatry, in Comprehensive Textbook of Psychiatry IV, Vol 2. Edited by Kaplan HI, Sadock BJ. Baltimore, MD, Williams & Wilkins, 1985, pp 1960–1990; see p 1978
75. Reisner R: Law and the Mental Health System. St Paul, MN, West Publishing, 1985, p 430
76. Blum v Yaretsky, 457 U.S. 991 (1982)
77. 325 F Supp 781 (MD Ala 1971), aff'd in part and remanded in part, and remanded sub nom, Wyatt v Aderholt, 503 F2d 1305 (5th Cir 1979)
78. 457 U.S. 307 (1982)
79. Appelbaum PS, Gutheil TG: Clinical Handbook of Psychiatry and the Law, 2nd Edition. Baltimore, MD, Williams & Wilkins, 1991, pp 89–90
80. Bies EB: Mental Health and the Law. Rockville, MD, Aspen, 1984, pp 149–151
81. United States v Charters, 863 F 2d 302 (4th Cir 1988); see also, United States v Watson, 893 F2d 970 (8th Cir 1990); Washington v Harper, 494 U.S. 210 (1990), cert denied, 110 S Ct 3243 (1990)
82. Appelbaum PS, Gutheil TG: Clinical Handbook of Psychiatry and the Law, 2nd Edition. Baltimore, MD, Williams & Wilkins, 1991, p 94
83. Gutheil TG, Appelbaum PS: Clinical Handbook of Psychiatry and the Law. New York, McGraw-Hill, 1982, pp 95–96
84. Perlin ML: Mental Disability Law: Civil and Criminal, Vol 2. Charlottesville, VA, Michie, 1989

Section III:

Somatic Therapies

Chapter 9

Drug Therapy and the Varieties of Legal Liability

Mr. Ellis, a 33-year-old truck driver, is admitted to the psychiatric service of a general hospital from the emergency room. He suffers from severe agitation and persecutory delusions of a week's duration. The patient spent 20 hours a day driving for the 2 weeks before the outbreak of his psychotic symptoms. The history also reveals that for the past 6 months, Mr. Ellis consumed two six-packs of beer each evening. Results from physical and laboratory examinations are normal.

Dr. Brock, the admitting and treating psychiatrist, starts Mr. Ellis initially on haloperidol, 5 mg four times a day. She increases the dosage to 10 mg four times a day when the patient's extreme agitation and anxiety do not respond to the lower dosage. Because Mr. Ellis is so agitated and delusional, Dr. Brock decides not to inform her patient of the risks of neuroleptic treatment because this information could be psychotically interpreted, leading to the rejection of urgent treatment. With daily supportive therapy, group therapy, and haloperidol, 40 mg a day, the patient improves rapidly by the fifth day of hospitalization. He is anxious to leave the hospital and return to work. Dr. Brock is reluctant to discharge Mr. Ellis so soon, but she agrees to the discharge if the patient will continue to take 40 mg of haloperidol per day. Dr. Brock makes arrangements to see her patient at the first available appointment in 2 weeks. Because Mr. Ellis is concerned about side effects, Dr. Brock explains the possibility of developing anticholinergic, autonomic, and extrapyramidal side effects, but reassures the patient that these reactions are unlikely because they did not occur earlier. Dr. Brock prescribed 60 10-mg haloperidol tablets, an amount sufficient to provide medication until the next appointment.

Six days after discharge, Mr. Ellis is brought to the emergency room in a state of extreme muscular rigidity. He manifests an elevated temperature of 39.3°C, excessive salivation associated with difficulty swallowing, labile blood pressure, a pulse rate of 180 per minute, profuse sweating, dyspnea, and urinary incontinence. The patient was found immobile at home by a friend after neighbors had not seen him for 2 days. Laboratory analysis reveals a white blood cell count of 18,000/mm³ and a creatinine phosphokinase level of 1,040 IU/ml. The EEG shows diffuse metabolic encephalopathy. A neurologist consultant makes the diagnosis of neuroleptic malignant syndrome and immediately transfers Mr. Ellis to the intensive care unit. Treatment with diazepam, diphenhydramine, and benztropine mesylate is given in conjunction with physical therapy, which produces a gradual recovery over a period of 3 weeks.

What clinical issues are raised in the vignette by Dr. Brock's drug management of the patient?

Patients who are discharged from a hospital on high levels of neuroleptic medication after an acute psychotic episode require close psychiatric supervision. Leaving Mr. Ellis medically unsupervised for 2 weeks while he is taking very substantial levels of haloperidol is a highly questionable practice. Dr. Brock should have attempted to extend the patient's hospital stay in order to evaluate the patient's condition on lower levels of medication prior to discharge.

Neuroleptic malignant syndrome (NMS) is reported to be a relatively rare complication of neuroleptic treatment (1). However, the cases that do occur may not be correctly diagnosed. Because NMS is a very serious complication that is fatal in about 20% of cases (2), it is imperative that it be recognized and treated early. Furthermore, NMS can develop at any time, even though the patient has been taking a neuroleptic uneventfully for some time (3, 4). Additional anticholinergic, autonomic, and extrapyramidal side effects may also develop that can lead to noncompliance with treatment, causing relapse, rehospitalization, or other untoward consequences.

In addition to monitoring for NMS, the psychiatrist in the vignette needed to recognize and consider other issues concerning the prescription of medication. For example, providing Mr. Ellis with 60 10-mg haloperidol tablets appears to be excessive. Dr. Brock knew the patient for less than a week. Did a therapeutic alliance develop during this time that would provide some assurance that the medication would be taken as prescribed? Had the alcohol issue been dealt with effectively? What assurance did Dr. Brock have that her patient would not drive or drink while taking the medications? Should Mr. Ellis have been referred to an outpatient alcohol program? The best disposition, short of longer hospitalization, would be to see the patient frequently after discharge or to refer the patient to a colleague who can provide that service. Mr. Ellis presented too many difficult and challenging clinical problems at the time of discharge that should not have been allowed to go unsupervised for 2 weeks.

What informed-consent issues arise in Dr. Brock's treatment of Mr. Ellis in the vignette?

Physicians, with certain very narrow exceptions, have a duty to obtain a patient's informed consent before proceeding with a proposed treatment or course of action. In this case, Dr. Brock initially chose to exercise one of those exceptions known as "therapeutic privilege" and did not inform Mr. Ellis about the risks and benefits of neuroleptic treatment. Her rationale was that psychotic misinterpretation of such information could lead to refusal of much needed treatment. However, as noted in Chapter 7, therapeutic privilege may not be used solely to induce treatment compliance in the patient. Therapeutic privilege has been narrowly defined by most courts (5) and statutes (6). Informing a patient of the risk associated with a particular treatment may upset the patient and foreclose rational decision making. In addition, it may have a significantly adverse psychological impact on the patient. These two situations have been recognized by some courts as appropriate times for the invocation of therapeutic privilege (7, 8).

When Mr. Ellis asked about side effects, Dr. Brock could have taken this opportunity to obtain a competent, informed consent. Given Mr. Ellis's history of alcohol intake, the patient should have been warned about the possible adverse consequences of mixing alcohol with haloperidol on his ability to drive a truck. Without such warnings that are clearly documented in the patient's medical record, Dr. Brock could be held liable for injuries from an accident involving her patient. Liability would occur if it can be proven that the failure to warn about the adverse effects of mixing medication and alcohol proximately caused the accident.

How have courts ruled in cases in which a patient, after taking medication prescribed by a physician, negligently operated a motor vehicle that caused injury to others?

In a number of cases, courts have held that an accident resulting from a therapist's failure to warn the patient not to drive is a breach of the duty of care owed to patients. This duty even extends toward injured third parties despite the absence of a therapist-patient relationship. The duty is owed to persons foreseeably in the general field of danger (i.e., other drivers and pedestrians) (9). The duty to inform, however, does not extend so far as to require that a therapist affirmatively prevent a patient from driving.

These principles were affirmed in *Gooden v. Tips* (10), where the court ruled that a physician has a legal duty to take reasonable steps to reduce the likelihood of injury to third parties caused by a patient under the influence of a prescribed intoxicating drug. In this case, the plaintiff was a pedestrian injured by a woman driving under the influence of methaqualone prescribed by her physician. The physician had failed to warn the patient not to drive after taking this drug. The court found that a duty of reasonable care exists where harm resulting to an injured third party was a reasonably foreseeable consequence of the physician's failure to warn the patient not to drive. As previously noted, this duty may exist, in the absence of a doctor-patient relationship, to the injured third party. The court held that the duty is owed to any person foreseeably in the general field of danger. However, the court stated that this duty to warn does not include a duty to control or affirmatively prevent the patient from driving.

In *Wilschinsky v. Medina* (11) the New Mexico Supreme Court ruled that pursuant to the state's Medical Malpractice Act, a third-party nonpatient who was injured in a car accident with a physician's patient 70 minutes after an office visit could maintain an action of medical negligence against the physician. Specifically, the court held that the physician's injection of the patient with drugs that were known to affect judgment and driving ability created a duty on the part of the doctor to adequately warn the patient about the side effects in question. Because it was foreseeable that the patient might drive, this duty of care also extended to the driving public, since the public could be affected by a patient impaired by the prescribed medications.

Similarly, in *Welke v. Kuzilla* (12), a Michigan appeals court ruled that a physician owed a duty to a third party who had been killed in an auto accident by a patient who was under the influence of medication prescribed by the physician. The court based liability on the principle that an individual owes no duty to protect another individual who is endangered by a third party *unless* the first individual has some special relationship with either the dangerous person or the potential victim. In this case, the court reasoned that the defendant owed a duty to the decedent by virtue of his special relationship with the patient-driver whom he had injected with medication on the evening prior to the accident. This "special relationship" was predicated on the fact that administering medication that is likely to impair a patient's ability to drive posed a foreseeable risk of danger to third parties (e.g., the driving public). Accordingly, the physician's failure, in this case, to inform his patient to refrain from driving because of the potential adverse effects upon the patient's driving ability was held to be the proximate cause of the plaintiff's death.

An accident that results following a physician's failure to inform a medicated patient about the risks of driving while taking the medication, however, will not automatically result in actionable liability. In *Stebbins v. Concord Wrigley Drugs* (13), a lawsuit was brought against a pharmacy and a doctor for failing to advise a patient not to drive while taking the antidepressant imipramine, which resulted in an accident with the plaintiff. The plaintiff's failure to establish a causal relationship between the patient's ingestion of the drug and the accident defeated the claim. The defendant, for example, submitted an affidavit from another doctor, which the plaintiff did not contradict, concluding that the drug dosage was insufficient to have caused drowsiness the day the accident occurred.

In *Duvall v. Goldin* (14), the plaintiffs suffered injury when their car was hit by the psychiatrist's patient after the patient suffered an epileptic seizure. The plaintiffs claimed that because the psychiatrist had knowledge concerning the patient's epilepsy, the psychiatrist breached his duty to third parties by failing to prescribe or continue the patient on anticonvulsant medications. Additionally, it was alleged that the psychiatrist failed to instruct the patient not to drive a car after discontinuing his medication. The court, relying on the *Tarasoff* duty to warn endangered third parties, held that the psychiatrist breached his duty to protect individuals endangered by the conduct of his epileptic patient.

In *Kirk v. Michael Reese Hospital and Medical Center* (15), the plaintiff, a passenger in an automobile driven by a discharged patient, was injured after the patient received an injection of fluphenazine decanoate and orally administered chlorpromazine prior to discharge. Upon discharge, the patient drank an alcoholic beverage, shortly after which an accident resulted and the passenger was injured. The court held that the drugs "diminished [his] mental and physical abilities, which caused [him] to lose control of the automobile." However, the court stressed that even though the hospital had a duty to warn the patient about the adverse effects of the medications, the duty did not extend to controlling the patient or preventing the patient from driving. Such a duty to warn arises only if physicians, hospitals, or pharmaceutical manufacturers knew or should have known of the adverse effects of the medications.

Similarly, in *Cartier v. Long Island College Hospital* (16), the plaintiff was struck while standing on a sidewalk by a car driven by a patient who had received treatment at an outpatient alcohol treatment program. The patient had been drinking heavily and apparently blacked out while driving. The plaintiff brought suit against the hospital responsible for the alcohol treatment center and the physicians who worked at the clinic, alleging that the patient was an alcoholic dangerous to the public. Furthermore, the plaintiff alleged that the defendants should have notified the Department of Motor Vehicles (DMV), requested the DMV to revoke their patient's driver's license, prevented the patient from driving, and taken other steps to prevent the incident. The court rejected the plaintiff's argument, however, holding that the defendants had no duty to the public to take actions to prevent the patient from driving. The court stated that the "relationship between [the patient] and defendants was not one which required defendants to control [the patient's] conduct as [the patient] merely attended the hospital's outpatient clinic and had not been admitted to the hospital." The court made clear that it is common knowledge that one should not drive while intoxicated. This case, however, is distinguishable from cases in which drugs with side effects not known to patients are given by the physician, on grounds that patients are not familiar with all potential side effects that a medication might cause.

Generally, have courts found a duty to warn or protect to prevent automobile accidents?

Felthous (17) cites five additional major automobile accident cases involving the duty to warn and protect: *Hasenei v. United States* (18), *Petersen v. State*

(19), *Cain v. Rijken* (20), *Schuster v. Altenberg* (21), and *Naidu v. Laird* (22). All of these cases, except *Cain v. Rijken*, are discussed in Chapter 13. In *Cain v. Rijken,* the Supreme Court of Oregon held that a community mental health provider had a duty to supervise the patient's conduct to protect the public. Paul Rijken, the patient, recklessly drove his car at 70 miles per hour in a 35 mile per hour zone. He drove through two red traffic lights, collided with a vehicle at an intersection, and killed the driver. Mr. Rijken had previously been found not guilty by reason of insanity on criminal charges involving the reckless operation of a vehicle.

In commenting upon these five cases, Felthous notes that courts collectively are not establishing consistent, coherent law. Plaintiffs allege a wide variety of nonclinical duties, such as relying heavily on the duty to warn, that foster the potential for courts to find "duties and liabilities that are diffuse and unclear." Felthous recommends that if warning or reporting is desired as a matter of public policy, then the clarity and consistency of statutory law would be preferable over inconsistent court decisions.

How common are malpractice suits based on the psychiatrist's improper use of psychoactive medication? What are the litigation trends in this area?

In medicine generally, drug-induced reactions are the most common cause of malpractice claims. Of all hospital admissions, it is estimated that 2% to 5% are caused by adverse reactions, while 5% to 30% of hospitalized patients experience an adverse drug reaction during the course of their hospital stay (23).

One study reported prescribing errors committed by physicians that occurred in a tertiary-care teaching hospital (24). The authors reviewed 289,411 medication orders written during a 1-year period; 905 prescribing errors were detected and averted. A total of 57.7% of these errors were rated as having potential for adverse consequences. As expected, first-year residents made more errors than experienced physicians. The most common errors were overdosing, issuing prescriptions with missing information, and giving insufficient amounts of a drug. Most errors happened between noon and 4 P.M. The fewest errors occurred between 8 P.M. and midnight. A total of 6.7% of the errors involved giving a drug to a patient who was allergic to the drug. The study concluded that a significant risk exists to patients from medication errors.

The experience of the American Psychiatric Association (APA) through its professional liability insurance program reveals that improper treatment is the most common complaint (25). Thirty-five percent of cases fall into this broad category. However, this category also includes failure to diagnose, failure to choose or execute proper treatment, and undue familiarity.

Some of the most common areas of liability for drug treatment include lack of informed consent, excessive dosage of medication, inappropriate indications for medication, failure to properly monitor a patient's response to medication, failure to properly intervene when undesirable side effects occur, and tardive dyskinesia. (Tardive dyskinesia is discussed separately in Chapter 10.)

Psychiatrists who treat patients without obtaining informed consent risk liability. The patient must have the mental capacity to understand information presented about diagnosis, risks (including side effects), and benefits of treatment; alternative forms of therapy that may also be effective; and the consequence of not receiving any treatment. The patient must give consent freely (26).

Clinical situations do arise, however, in which the psychiatrist may need to exercise therapeutic privilege and not inform a patient concerning certain aspects of treatment. When a patient lacks mental capacity or the psychiatrist exercises therapeutic privilege, consent should be obtained from next of kin (27). However, psychiatrists must realize that in some states, "good faith" or the proxy consent of relatives is insufficient, requiring the consent of a legal guardian or the substituted consent of the court (28). Consent may be obtained in written form, but it should also be independently documented that the patient understood the information given and that no coercion was present. Informed consent does not insulate a doctor who has been negligent in the care of a patient. It only protects against risks that may occur had a "reasonable person been informed of them and rejected the proposed treatment" (29).

The American Medical Association (AMA) now publishes a patient medication instruction (PMI) form for many classes of psychoactive medications. These forms provide useful information to patients in a format that is highly readable and easily understandable. As part of their consent procedures with patients, a number of psychiatrists have found the PMI useful. In addition, physicians have been advised to inform patients of the following when prescribing a drug (30):

1. Drug name
2. Whether the action of the drug is to treat the disease or to relieve symptoms
3. How to determine if the medication is effective and what to do if it is not
4. When and how to take the drug (e.g., before or after meals)
5. How long to take the drug
6. An explanation of side effects important to the patient and what to do should they occur
7. Possible effects on driving, working around machinery, including a) the proper precautions to observe and b) any interactions with other drugs and alcohol

Obtaining informed consent for the use of investigational drugs is an absolutely necessary and rigorous process, requiring that the patient be informed of all foreseeable risks associated with taking the medication and the possibility that unforeseeable risks may occur. Malpractice insurance may not cover or may provide only limited coverage for psychiatrists who work with investigational drugs (31). Obtaining the informed consent of patients being treated for mental disorders is a complex issue that is discussed in detail in Chapter 7.

What is the standard by which a psychiatrist's use of medication will be judged? How is this standard established?

A physician's actions are evaluated by how the ordinary and prudent psychiatrist would act under the same or similar circumstances (32). Legal commentators note that limited case law exists which specifies that the use of certain drugs given under particular circumstances is considered negligence (33). Generally, reference will be made to medical standards as expressed in expert testimony, the professional psychiatric literature, drug manufacturers' recommendations, and the *Physicians' Desk Reference* (PDR). Thus the legal risks of drug therapy can be determined by the psychiatrist through reference to traditional sources of medical information. However, the enactment of statutory regulations establishing guidelines for prescribing medication will also influence the standard of care with respect to providing drug therapy. For example, the Omnibus Budget Reconciliation Act of 1987 regulates the use of psychotropic drugs in long-term health care facilities receiving funds from Medicare and Medicaid (34). The Health Care Financing Administration (HCFA) guidelines for neuroleptic drugs include *1)* documentation of the psychiatric diagnosis or specific condition requiring neuroleptic use; *2)* prohibition of neuroleptics if certain behaviors alone are the only justification; *3)* prohibition of prn neuroleptic use; and *4)* gradual dose reductions of neuroleptics combined with attempts at behavioral programming and environmental modification (35). A more complete discussion of how the standards of professional practice are formulated can be found in Chapter 24.

What clinical and legal issues surround the inappropriate administration of psychoactive medications?

Most claims resulting from the inappropriate administration of medication allege that the psychiatrist failed to perform or obtain an adequate physical examination and failed to obtain a medical history before prescribing psychoactive drugs. An adequate history is the primary, initial intervention of the psychiatrist. Medical, drug, and psychiatric histories are necessary to establish a working diagnosis. Factors that could modify drug treatment, such as previous responses to medications as well as the responses of family members to certain drugs, are essential information that must be obtained. Speaking with relatives or friends to obtain additional information may be necessary with certain patients. Allergic reactions to medications particularly must be noted.

Although some psychiatrists do perform their own physical examinations, most psychiatrists who use psychodynamic psychotherapy generally avoid physically touching the patient. Even though the physical examination is considered by patients to be an essential aspect of a physician's function, the situation is different in psychiatry. Among the many possible psychological complications that could arise from physical examination of the psychiatric patient prior to psychotherapy, untoward positive and negative transference complications loom as the most serious. Nevertheless, when psychiatrists decide to prescribe a psychoactive medication for the patient, they must assure themselves of the patient's physical health.

If questions remain after obtaining the patient's medical history, consultations with a general physician or specialist may be necessary. Reliance solely on interns and, particularly, psychiatric residents in the inpatient setting for the performance of medical evaluations of psychiatric patients may present some difficulties. With the explosive growth of medical knowledge, even a psychiatric resident can be rapidly out of touch with current medical developments. The intern often lacks experience and requires supervision. Many psychiatrists feel that their medical skills have atrophied beyond the ability to conduct a reasonable medical investigation of the patient.

In *Watkins v. United States* (36), a military physician prescribed 100 5-mg diazepam tablets for an airman with anxiety. The physician did not obtain a history or check the records of the base clinic that would have indicated that the airman had recently been treated for a psychotic episode and depression. Two days later, the airman had an automobile accident that was caused by the effects of taking diazepam. The court ruled that by prescribing diazepam, under the circumstances, the physician's conduct fell below the required standard of care.

Similarly, in *United States v. 1328 North Main Street, Dayton, Ohio* (37), a search warrant for the search of a physician's office for improper prescription practices was upheld because of considerable evidence that controlled substances were being prescribed without any proper physical examination.

The duty to properly examine a patient not only involves performing or obtaining a physical examination if clinically indicated but also extends to obtaining a patient's medical and psychiatric history and an assessment of current functioning. The failure to conduct or obtain such an examination before prescribing medication to certain patients can have disastrous consequences. For instance, in *Shaughnessy v. Spray* (38), a patient being treated for heroin and morphine addiction died of an overdose of propoxyphene hydrochloride capsules that had been prescribed by his physician without the benefit of a physical or psychiatric history. The estate of the plaintiff claimed that had an adequate history been taken, it would have revealed the decedent's suicidal tendencies, which would have necessitated hospitalization and close monitoring of any medication treatment. A jury returned a verdict for the plaintiff and awarded $250,000.

In *Hirschberg v. State* (39), a patient was admitted to a state hospital after ingestion of a large amount of aspirin. No physical examination was conducted because the patient arrived after normal operating hours. The patient died of salicylate poisoning. Among other things, the court found that no informed judgment was made in the absence of a careful examination. Drugs were prescribed contrary to the orders of a qualified physician. No precautions were taken against the foreseeable risks of side effects such as cardiac arrhythmias or shock. The physician also ignored the warning signs of toxicity. A medical specialist was not called, and salicylate blood tests were not ordered. The court held the state hospital liable for medical malpractice.

Halleck (40) points out that psychiatrists can be held liable for failing to diagnose organic conditions. According to Halleck, psychiatrists have a clear responsibility to search out organic causes of psychological illness, either by performing their own examination or by referring the patient to a competent specialist. As more understanding is gained about the intimate connection between mind and body, the obligation to be certain that the patient's physical condition is properly evaluated will correspondingly be heightened. Psychiatrists, at a minimum, should be able to take the patient's pulse and obtain sitting and standing blood pressures. Familiarity with conducting a basic neurological examination is important in providing the psychiatrist the ability to evaluate extrapyramidal and dyskinetic reactions arising from psychotropic medications.

In *Gitlin v. Cassell* (41), the court ruled that a patient could bring a malpractice suit against a psychiatrist for failure to warn of the dangers associated with medication prescribed for the patient by another physician. The patient was a cigarette smoker who for more than 10 years had been taking birth control pills prescribed by her internist. The patient started having headaches, eventually suffering a left middle cerebral artery thrombosis. The court heard evidence that the psychiatrist failed to take an accurate medication history. Moreover, the psychiatrist failed to make the connection between a higher risk of developing a stroke and the patient's smoking, the history of taking contraceptives, and the onset of headaches.

Prescribing neuroleptics for patients who are not psychotically depressed or who suffer from neurotic anxiety may be another example of medicating inappropriately. However, the clinical needs of the patient are determinative. Psychoactive medications that are usually indicated for one type of psychiatric disorder may be empirically useful for a nonindicated disorder in certain patients. For example, the work of Hollister et al. (42) indicates that neuroleptics may be useful in certain depressive subtypes.

The use of multiple medications, or polypharmacy, has been much disparaged as a "shotgun" approach to treatment of patients that may significantly increase the possibility of serious side effects. Nevertheless, under certain circumstances, some patients may benefit from such a regimen. Polypharmacy has become synonymous with negligent or inappropriate treatment, but judicious use of medication combinations in selected patients can be clinically useful. Prusoff et al. (43) demonstrated the benefits of a neuroleptic-tricyclic combination in the treatment of schizophrenic patients with secondary depression. Such a combination also may prove necessary in the treatment of delusional depressions. In bipolar disorders, when proper precautions are observed, good clinical practice may include various combinations of antidepressants, lithium, anticonvulsants, calcium channel blockers, and adjunctive sleep medications. A significant number of patients are treatment-resistant to a single drug therapy.

The use of multiple medications becomes clinically inappropriate and potentially actionable when there is not a reasonable *medical* explanation for the use of each medication and when complications due to possible adverse drug interactions have not been evaluated. However, the art and science of psychopharmacology and psychiatric diagnosis have not progressed to the point where dogmatic positions can be taken about the drug treatment of patients. Psychiatrists should document any reasons for deviating from recognized guidelines in prescribing medication through a risk-benefit assessment. The specific treatment needs of the patient should also be adequately documented.

Nevertheless, psychiatrists may be held liable if they prescribe a medication considered inappropriate under currently acceptable standards of diagnosis and treatment of mental disorders (44). For example, in *Merril v. Florida Department of Health and Rehabilitative Services* (45), a mother sued a training center for the excessive and inappropriate use of psychotropic medication that caused the death of her son. While at a training center for the retarded, the plaintiff's son was given diazepam. This was followed by administrations of 100 mg of chlorpromazine and 400 mg of methyprylon. An expert for the claimant testified that the synergistic effect of the two psychotropic medications with the diazepam resulted in the patient's death. A jury agreed and awarded the mother $200,000.

In another case, *Stewart v. Bay Minette Infirmary* (46), summary judgment for a hospital and emergency room physician was reversed on the basis of an autopsy report that a patient's death was likely caused by an idiosyncratic, but foreseeable reaction to the ingestion of multiple drugs (pentazocine, promethazine, oxycodone-acetaminophen, and cyclobenzaprine) prescribed by the defendant. Plaintiff's expert opined that these medications taken with the alcohol and diazepam ingested by the patient, which the defendant knew of, along with the defendant's knowledge of the patient's experience with drugs and alcohol, should have signaled to the defendant that complications could arise.

In *Mulder v. Parke Davis & Co.* (47), the Minnesota Supreme Court held that

> where a drug manufacturer recommends to the medical profession 1) the conditions under which its drug should be prescribed; 2) the disorders it is designed to relieve; 3) the precautionary measures which should be observed; and 4) warns of the dangers which are inherent in its use, a doctor's deviation from such recommendations is *prima facie* evidence of negligence if there is competent medical testimony that his patient's injury or death resulted from the doctor's failure to adhere to the recommendations. Under such circumstances, it is incumbent on the psychiatrist to disclose the reasons for departing from the procedure recommended by the manu-

facturer. . . . [I]t will ordinarily be a jury question whether the doctor has justified or excused his deviation.

Thus nonapproval of a drug for a certain disorder, (e.g., anticonvulsant for bipolar mood disorder) is only one factor that the courts may consider. Other factors in determining the appropriate standard of care include clinical experience, the scientific literature, expert testimony, and any approvals in other countries.

Psychiatrists must be careful not to addict or contribute to the addiction of patients (48). For example, in *Reid v. Jones* (49), a 26-year-old woman sued her psychiatrist for the negligent treatment of her nervous disorder on the grounds that she had become addicted to amphetamines that had been prescribed for nearly $1\frac{1}{2}$ years. Rejecting the psychiatrist's contention that his selection of medication was proper and his prescription practices were consistent with the standard of care, the court awarded the plaintiff $75,000.

The use and abuse of benzodiazepines in clinical practice is becoming the subject of increasing litigation (50) and can result in disciplinary actions (51). Clinicians must remain knowledgeable and aware of the appropriate prescription methodologies for these drugs (52). To assist psychiatrists, the APA has issued a task force report with guidelines on the use of benzodiazepines (53).

In *Doe v. Axelrod* (54), a group of plaintiffs sought the court's declaration that a proposed state regulation requiring strict prescription control procedures for benzodiazepines was unconstitutional and invalid. The Commissioner of Health, David Axelrod, M.D., argued that such strict control of benzodiazepines was required because of "over-prescription," harmful effects, and illegal distribution of these drugs. The appellate court affirmed the lower court injunction holding that the issues raised in this dispute should be settled at trial.

An attempt to impose social control on mentally ill patients through "chemical straitjackets" is another inappropriate indication for psychoactive medication. This is especially inappropriate when the objectionable behavior is not directly the result of a psychiatric illness. This type of situation often occurs in nursing homes, where strong-willed, difficult elderly residents who are not accustomed to the constraints of institutional living annoy staff or interfere with staff functioning. For the severely agitated elderly patient with dementia and psychosis, a neuroleptic may be lifesaving. However, abuse of neuroleptic medications occurs when they are prescribed to squelch objectionable behavior that is a long-standing aspect of the patient's personality rather than the symptom of a treatable mental illness. In addition, psychoactive drugs should never be used as a form of punishment (55). Although chemical restraints raise deprivation of liberty issues that can result in a civil rights suit, malpractice actions are much more likely.

A much less appreciated form of inappropriate administration of medication occurs when homeopathic doses are prescribed in the spirit of defensive medicine. Such practices deny a patient safe and effective clinical care. At the same time, they may expose the patient to the risks but none of the benefits of treatment, while prolonging the disability and suffering of the patient. Rather than avoiding suits, defensive homeopathic prescribing may actually invite legal action (56).

Another major problem area is the failure to prescribe psychotropic drugs for patients when they are clearly indicated. Patients suffering from severe, incapacitating depressions or severe anxiety disorders should be informed that drugs are available that may produce rapid relief. Subjecting such patients to long-term psychotherapy without first providing this information is a disservice to the patient and is potentially legally actionable (57).

Outdated drugs must be disposed of in an appropriate manner. Throwing outdated drugs in the garbage or in the dumpster outside one's office can potentially cause major legal problems (58). For example, outdated drugs or drug samples carelessly disposed of may fall into the hands of children or individuals who may use or sell the drugs. The requirements of the Drug Enforcement Agency (DEA) for disposal of controlled substances must be followed. The DEA demands strict compliance with its specific instructions. Failure to comply with these standards could result in a loss of license.

Finally, psychiatrists practicing in a managed care setting must not use medications inappropriately as a means of manipulating managed care reviewers. For example, in the treatment of inpatients, psychiatrists must resist any temptation to give medication that would otherwise not be given in order to convince managed care reviewers of the need for inpatient care (59).

What are the clinical and legal issues surrounding the administration of medications that exceed recommended dosages?

Some severely mentally ill patients may require the administration of psychoactive medications that exceed dosage guidelines. The reasons for making such a decision must be clearly documented in the patient's record. The patient should be made aware that drug guidelines are being exceeded. Generally, if very high levels of medication are required, the patient may need to be hospitalized until a safer maintenance level can be achieved. The Food and Drug Administration (FDA) and the AMA have taken the position that prescribing higher-than-recommended doses remains at the physician's discretion.

Because drug tolerance may vary considerably from patient to patient, appropriate drug dosages may be difficult to assess. For instance, a young, acutely psychotic male may require 40 mg of haloperidol per day for management, whereas an agitated, demented elderly patient may need only 0.5 mg of haloperidol per day to provide necessary treatment. Therefore, it is difficult to ascertain when the patient has received an inappropriate dose. For example, in *Moon v.*

United States (60), a patient taking 20 mg of fluphenazine per day for a number of days while hospitalized drowned on an outing. The testimony of a forensic pharmacologist indicated that doses in excess of 20 mg per day should be administered only with precautionary measures based on manufacturer's recommendations and the PDR. A private psychiatrist stated that when more than 20 mg per day of fluphenazine is given, vital signs should be checked frequently and a daily examination should be conducted for side effects. Based upon a review of the professional literature, the hospital physicians testified that the dosage of fluphenazine was not excessive. The court, while acknowledging that a serious dispute over the appropriate dosage of fluphenazine existed, held that the drug treatment provided the patient was within allowable standards and was, therefore, not negligent.

As noted earlier, the decision to prescribe medication exceeding normal therapeutic limits should be done with the utmost care and consideration for the patient's psychiatric needs and possible consequences. Psychiatrists encounter problems in prescribing excessive medication if either no reasonable medical rationale exists for such a prescription or there is little or no monitoring of the patient's condition. For example, in *Dooley v. Skodnek* (61), $1 million was awarded to a woman who became blind after taking excessive doses of thioridazine (Mellaril), despite repeated complaints of deteriorating vision. Similarly, in *Fitrak v. United States* (62), a Veterans Administration (VA) extended care facility was found liable for the death of a woman who originally sought treatment for gastrointestinal trouble. While at the VA she became psychotic and was treated with lithium. Appropriate lab work was never ordered, nor was the woman monitored until she reached a fatal level of lithium toxicity. Her estate was awarded in excess of $100,000.

Psychiatrists who prescribe a large amount of medication, particularly tricyclic antidepressants, to a known suicidal patient risk causing harm to the patient and then possibly being sued should the patient commit suicide. These problems exist because the psychiatrist often prescribes medications that are capable of being abused to patients with conditions that predispose to misuse and abuse. For instance, in *Argus v. Scheppegrell* (63), the Louisiana Supreme Court held that a physician supplying prescriptions for controlled substances in excessive amounts to a teenager addicted to drugs could be held liable for the patient's suicide. The court noted that the use of medication to commit the suicide was a consequence that the defendant should have foreseen.

Appelbaum and Gutheil (64) point out that focusing on the dispenser, rather than the patient, inappropriately shifts responsibility to the psychiatrist, producing an illusion of control. They state that life bristles with opportunities for self-destruction, including obtaining medication from other sources. Thus liability should not automatically result when determined patients circumvent all precautions to kill themselves. This includes overdosing with prescribed psychoactive medication.

On the other hand, prescribing less than the minimum lethal dose of medication may assure the suicidal patient of the psychiatrist's concern and effort to apply external supportive structure. Patients who represent a risk of suicide from drug overdose should be seen frequently. Although important, issuing smaller amounts of medication may not be the central issue. The emphasis with the patient should be on strengthening the therapeutic alliance. This ultimately provides the greatest hope to the patient. The mere prescribing of medication apart from a working doctor-patient relationship does not meet generally accepted standards of good clinical care. Such a practice will diminish the efficacy of the drug treatment itself or may lead to the patient's failure to take the prescribed medication. Fragmented care, in which the psychiatrist functions *only* as a prescriber of medication while remaining uninformed about the patient's overall clinical status, will likely be considered substandard care and could lead to a malpractice action.

Often, a real danger to patient care is created from the patient's failure to renew his or her prescriptions. Thus prescriptions that require frequent renewal may lead to noncompliance. For some patients, the risk of suicide is not actually lessened by prescribing small amounts. In addition, with neuroleptics, the prescription of what might appear to be a lethal dose to the ordinary patient may only be a single dose for a chronic patient who is on long-term maintenance therapy. The psychiatrist should note these differences in the patient's medical record, including the fact that tolerance to the toxic effects of neuroleptics develops quickly.

Patients who appear suicidal should not be prescribed barbiturates or glutethimide for sleep. Other less dangerous medications such as benzodiazepines should be considered. Moreover, medications in high doses should not be used in lieu of hospitalization if hospitalization is indicated for the suicidal patient.

Psychiatrists covering for the treating psychiatrist sometimes receive requests from patients for large amounts of drugs. Unless a large volume of medication is specifically recommended by the treating psychiatrist, the covering psychiatrist should prescribe only enough medication for the patient until the treating psychiatrist returns. If the treating psychiatrist will be away for a long period of time, the covering psychiatrist should consider seeing the patient first hand. This will allow for adjustments in the amount of medication according to the patient's clinical needs.

Psychiatrists generally do not make a practice of turning over their patient records to the covering physician. While a brief history, including diagnosis and treatment, is usually provided either orally or in writing, the absent psychiatrist's patients basically remain unknown to the covering psychiatrist. Some patients might seriously regress during the absence of their treating psychiatrist. Therefore, reviewing prescriptions by telephone must be done with great care. In some clinical instances, renewal of medications may require an appointment with the patient.

What are the clinical and legal issues surrounding the monitoring of side effects of psychoactive medications?

The standard of care for prescribing medication requires that psychiatrists have a duty to possess that degree of skill and learning ordinarily possessed and used by members of the psychiatric profession in good standing engaged in prescribing, dispensing, and administering medication in the same or similar circumstances (44). Warning the patient of potential side effects, continued monitoring of the patient, and treating undesired side effects in a timely manner fall within this duty. Clinically, as part of the working alliance with their patients, psychiatrists should inform patients of the possible side effects of medication, encouraging them to notify the psychiatrist if side effects arise that are of concern. Open communication about potential problems with medications enhances the therapeutic process through the establishment of trust and reduces the problem of patient noncompliance.

Psychiatrists may be found liable for failing to diagnose treatable side effects or complications of psychiatric treatment. When the patient is under reasonable supervision, side effects or complications that arise from medications may be effectively treated by diminishing the dose, discontinuing the drug, or adding another treatment. The acute anticholinergic, autonomic, and extrapyramidal side effects of neuroleptic and antidepressant medications can be quite disabling. If left unattended, patients may develop serious injury (65) or, at the least, become noncompliant with drug therapy, which itself may be harmful.

According to FDA regulations, the PDR and drug information inserts must list all reported side effects. Obviously, informing the patient of each and every possible side effect is unreasonable, and even potentially harmful if the patient becomes unduly frightened. However, certain basic side effects or drug interactions are sometimes overlooked and can result in patient injury.

For instance, in *Macholz v. Banas* (66), a 62-year-old homemaker was prescribed amitriptyline for various psychiatric problems from 1962 to 1978. In 1978 she informed the defendant physician that she was experiencing head tremors. He advised her to continue taking the amitriptyline. At trial the central issues were whether the continued use of the medication was the proximate cause of the tremors and whether the medication should have been discontinued when the tremors were first noticed by the plaintiff. In countering the defendant's argument that the tremors were of "unknown origin," the plaintiff's expert offered into evidence the PDR, which contained a warning that head tremors were a known adverse effect of amitriptyline. The plaintiff's expert stated that the defendant had a duty to inform the plaintiff of this side effect and to closely monitor her for it.

In *Christy v. Saliterman* (67), the plaintiff was able to argue successfully that the psychiatrist should have evaluated the patient before prescribing paraldehyde and should have advised the patient that the paraldehyde could have undesirable side effects. The patient, who was not warned of the soporific qualities of paraldehyde, fell asleep in a chair while smoking and set himself on fire, suffering serious burns.

Patients must be warned about driving or working around dangerous machinery if the medications they are taking produce drowsiness or slow reflexes. Similarly, the patient must be warned of the dangers of mixing alcohol with psychoactive drugs. Patients taking monoamine oxidase inhibitors should be warned against ingesting food and drinks that contain tyramine or taking interactive drugs (68). It is remarkable to observe how often these rudimentary warnings are not given despite the clear legal consequences that may arise (69).

The proper monitoring of psychotropic medications requires that patients not be allowed to stay on prolonged drug therapy without improvement. Re-evaluation of the patient's diagnosis, of the indications for any given drug regimen, and of dosage levels of the drug is necessary when patients remain refractory to treatment. Generally, psychotropic medications should be withdrawn gradually, particularly if the drugs have been taken for more than a few months. Sudden withdrawal syndromes can occur that have severe sequelae and possibly serious legal consequences.

In monitoring medication, it is not necessary that the psychiatrist obtain serum blood levels for antidepressants as a matter of course (70). Drug plasma monitoring, however, can provide objective evidence substantiating the need for high doses of antidepressants in certain patients while indicating that the drug plasma levels are not in the toxic range. If toxicity from a tricyclic antidepressant is suspected, a plasma level for that drug may prove helpful. Furthermore, medication compliance can be monitored by obtaining blood levels. When carbamazepine is used in the treatment of psychiatric disorders, regular serum level and hematological monitoring is necessary.

When clinicians use the recently approved antipsychotic drug clozapine, the drug manufacturer will not distribute the drug unless the patient undergoes weekly blood tests for the early detection of agranulocytosis. In addition, a confidential national master file is maintained to ensure that patients who have previously experienced serious side effects with clozapine are not prescribed the drug again (71). This carefully structured clozapine monitoring program appears, at least in part, to reflect very serious concerns about possible product liability litigation for fatal agranulocytosis (72).

Neuroendocrine markers such as the dexamethasone suppression test (DST) or the thyrotropin-releasing hormone (TRH) test are not required to be performed on depressed patients in order to comply with the standard of care. At present, it is premature to rely upon radioreceptor assays in monitoring neuroleptic drugs. The value of these blood tests in psychiatry is still controversial (73). Psychiatrists may wish to order these tests when clinical conditions warrant but should not do so from any sense of legal compulsion. Obviously, monitoring lithium levels when the therapeutic and toxic levels are relatively close is extremely important, particularly if patients are on low salt diets or are taking diuretics. Neurotoxicity from lithium therapy does not necessarily parallel lithium levels. Utilizing good clinical judgment rather than relying solely on laboratory reports remains essential.

The medical consequences of prolonged lithium therapy are imperfectly understood. Thyroid dysfunction is not an uncommon consequence of lithium therapy and should be closely monitored. Thyroid insufficiency developed in 10% of patients undergoing lithium therapy in one study (74). Thyroid insufficiency appears to be a much more significant risk than renal disease. However, appropriate renal studies should be performed on patients receiving lithium for long periods of time as part of a general medical surveillance. The potential legal liability arising from serious medical complications due to unmonitored long-term lithium therapy remains a distinct possibility.

Finally, proper monitoring cannot occur unless prescriptions are written legibly. If the psychiatrist's handwriting tends to be unreadable, the prescription should be printed. To prevent drug-abusing patients from altering the number of tablets or pills described, this number should be spelled out. The pharmacist should be instructed to label all medications. Directions for taking the medication should be specific rather than "sig: as directed." Unlabeled medications may be difficult to identify by emergency room personnel should the patient require emergency care.

What other salient medicolegal issues surround the prescribing of drugs in psychiatric practice?

Supervision of nonmedical personnel who dispense psychoactive medications is essential. In *Tucker v. Hutlo* (75), a prisoner was administered powerful psychotropic medications by other prisoners and untrained personnel without his consent and without proper supervision. The patient became virtually paralyzed, lying for long periods in bed and developing huge bedsores that became infested with maggots. The patient almost died. Officials at the hospital denied any liability, but the state agreed to a settlement of $518,000.

Psychiatrists should avoid prescribing medication for an unseen patient. Psychiatrists who work in clinics may be asked to prescribe medications for patients seen by nonmedical therapists. It is not enough to receive reports about these patients from the nonmedical therapists. These therapists are not trained in psychopharmacology, and their reports cannot be relied upon to form a clinical opinion about prescribing psychoactive drugs to the patient. Psychiatrists who prescribe medication are responsible for such treatment even though another provider is primarily responsible for the overall care of the patient. Under these circumstances, psychiatrists remain highly vulnerable to malpractice actions arising from the improper supervision of patients who develop serious or fatal reactions to medications.

Nonmedical therapists must be careful not to recommend unilateral discontinuance of the medication that patients are receiving from physicians. If any questions arise, a call to the prescribing physician should be made following a discussion with the patient. Cohen (76) reports a case in which a psychologist told the patient that medication was no longer required. The patient subsequently discontinued medication, with disastrous consequences (including the loss of employment).

Ayd (77) warns of the problems of ordering medication as needed (i.e., prn). He states that the safety for such an order depends on assumptions and knowledge that may or may not accompany a prn order. Physicians must carefully consider the need for prescribing potent medications prn for newly admitted patients, particularly those patients who have not been examined or whose histories are unknown and for whom no diagnosis has been established. The language of such orders must leave as little as possible to chance. Interpretation of orders should not be left to the discretion of staff members who may lack the required experience and knowledge in administering medications that require frequent monitoring and expert interpretation of side effects.

In large hospitals or institutions, the psychiatrist may not be able to personally see each patient. The psychiatrist may write prescriptions for drugs covering a period of many months that are dispensed by nurses or by mental health aides. The only medically acceptable solution is for the psychiatrist to see the patient each time before a prescription is written. If this absolutely cannot be done, the reasons for failing to do so should be carefully documented. The "blind" prescribing of powerful psychoactive drugs to an unseen patient is an unacceptable practice and fraught with very serious legal consequences.

Psychiatrists sometimes authorize a prescription for a person unknown and unseen who lives some distance away and who does not have nearby medical services available. Presumably this would be done on a one-time basis as a humanitarian gesture, allowing time for the patient to find medical care. This too, however, is a dangerous clinical practice. In many states, prescribing for unseen persons is a violation of the medical code. For example, the Michigan Medical Practices Act (78) states that a physician should not prescribe medication for a patient not personally seen, nor should the medication be administered and monitored by someone who is not a physician. In these situations, malpractice is established by demonstrating the breach of the statutory standard of care.

The practice of seeing a patient once a year or every 6 months while providing refills in the interim is also highly questionable. Studies have repeatedly shown that compliance with drug treatment by mentally ill patients is often poor (79). A significant number of schizophrenic patients, despite supervision, do not take their medication consistently. They may spit out, regurgitate, hide, or discard their pills. Patients taking psychoactive medication need to be seen as frequently as their clinical needs require. These patients should not be allowed to go unsupervised for excessive lengths of time (80).

In monitoring patient treatment compliance, Ulmer (81) recommends that one sheet of the medical chart be labeled "compliance information." The careful documentation of compliance and noncompliance behavior of the patient may prove to be a useful part of clinical practice. Moreover, if litigation arises, this information would likely be invaluable to developing a malpractice defense. For example, patient noncompliance, which would include apprising the doctor of the development of any adverse effects, may be a mitigating factor if the patient sues the therapist (82). Soskis (83) found that schizophrenic inpatients readily shared their reluctance to take medication with an interviewer, offering an avenue for detection and intervention to improve outpatient compliance.

The psychological issues surrounding patient compliance and noncompliance with prescribed medications are complex and need to be fully explored with the patient. Threatening patients by various means to take medications is coercive, circumvents their informed consent, and impairs the development of the doctor-patient relationship. Threats also may prevent the exploration of the psychological meanings of patient noncompliance with treatment recommendations. Paranoid patients may feel that by ingesting drugs they are being poisoned or malevolently controlled. Side effects may confirm these fears. For some patients, continuing to take medications despite having no further symptoms of illness may be an unwelcome reminder of their past illness and may lead to noncompliance. Furthermore, taking medications from the psychiatrist may symbolize feared dependency or the gratification of frightening wishes for fusion that must be denied through noncompliance.

On the other hand, some patients are noncompliant when the psychiatrist suggests discontinuing medications. Medications may become transitional objects that allow the patient to feel continuously connected with the psychiatrist. Discontinuing medications may arouse severe separation anxiety. For these reasons, medications should be dispensed in the context of a therapeutic alliance with the patient that allows for exploration with the patient of the manifold psychological meanings surrounding the taking of drugs.

Do psychiatrists have an ethical and legal duty to keep abreast of psychopharmacological developments in psychiatry?

Yes, particularly if the psychiatrist prescribes psychotropic medications or treats patients psychotherapeutically who might also benefit from psychotropic drugs. Some dynamically trained psychotherapists have avoided acquiring knowledge or skill in administering drug therapy. They, as well as nonmedical therapists, may ask a medical colleague to prescribe medications for a patient. This practice introduces an artificial split into the intimate connection between treating the patient by medication and treating the patient by psychotherapy. Fragmentation of the therapeutic process should be avoided, if possible. Ostow

(84) also disagrees with fragmented treatment practices because the data obtained from psychotherapy are necessary for proper administration of drug therapy. In addition, to understand the patient, drug effects must be distinguished. Furthermore, the patient's transference may be split, and divided treatment is doubly expensive (85).

Psychiatrists have an ethical and legal duty to keep abreast of scientific developments in their specialty. Particularly in the burgeoning area of psychopharmacology, psychiatrists who prescribe medications need to keep pace with new developments. Psychiatrists can no longer afford to be therapeutically one dimensional—that is, knowledgeable in only one method of treatment. However, the psychiatrist who is unfamiliar with a specific treatment modality should avoid its use. Lesse (86), speaking about the treatment of depression, states that "those who treat severe depressions should have the broadest possible knowledge of the limitations of various psychotherapeutic techniques. Similarly, they should have an intimate knowledge of the benefits and limitations of the antidepressant drugs." Thus, in *Osheroff v. Chestnut Lodge* (87), the plaintiff alleged that his major depression was inappropriately treated by intensive psychotherapy, unnecessarily prolonging his hospitalization and suffering. Following transfer to another hospital and the initiation of antidepressant medication, the plaintiff improved rapidly. This case, which was eventually settled, is discussed extensively in the literature (57).

The fear of litigation should not deter the psychiatrist from prescribing clinically indicated and FDA-approved medications that may be embroiled in public controversy. Staying abreast of research and developments in psychopharmacology should help minimize defensive psychiatric practices in these instances. For example, a number of suits have been filed claiming that fluoxetine caused suicide or violence toward others in patients taking this medication. Currently, studies show no clear relationship between any specific antidepressant and the emergence of suicidal or violent ideation or behavior (88). Psychiatrists must be guided by their clinical experience, the treatment needs of the patient, and a continuing knowledge of developments in the field of psychiatry in order to provide appropriate care to patients.

What are the clinical and legal issues surrounding therapeutic and generic substitution?

The psychiatrist is professionally and legally responsible for the selection of the appropriate medication for the patient. To pursue a consistent prescribing and monitoring policy, the psychiatrist should be aware of the clinical and legal issues surrounding therapeutic and generic substitution.

The Drug Price Competition and Patent Term Restoration Act of 1984 (89) authorized the FDA to approve generic versions of drugs found to be safe and effective. Recently, however, controversy has arisen surrounding the quality control, safety, and efficacy of generic drugs (90). Generic drugs that contain the same active ingredients as established brand-name drugs may not necessarily possess the same clinical efficacy because of differential dissolution, absorption, and distribution rates in the human body (91). Thus, although not necessarily of inferior quality, the clinical efficacy of generic drugs on patients may vary significantly. Therapists may become confused when patients report continued symptoms due to the lack of therapeutic efficacy of a generic drug. Although cost-saving is important, reducing the patient's suffering in the shortest amount of time with an effective medication is essential.

The FDA's "Orange Book" (92) states: "An FDA evaluation of therapeutic equivalence in no way relieves practitioners of their professional responsibilities in prescribing and dispensing such products with due care and with appropriate information to individual patients." The "Orange Book" lists over 8,000 multisource drug products. Bioavailability or therapeutic drug equivalence has been evaluated for 80% or approximately 5,000 products. The FDA allows plus or minus 30% deviation in *in vivo* testing approval of a generic drug (93).

Controversy exists concerning the appropriateness of the FDA's standards for establishing generic interchange (94). This raises an important question. Must psychiatrists inform patients who are taking generic drugs that these medications may be ineffective or that unknown, adverse reactions might occur? Psychiatrists should consider making such disclosures because of the wide variability in bioequivalence (at least 30%). In order to discourage noncompliance, patients should be informed about the different color and shape of the generic drug that is substituted (93). Whether generic or brand name, the well-selected drug that achieves maximal therapeutic efficacy in the shortest time will be cost-saving in the long run.

The repeal of antisubstitution laws and the enactment of drug product selection (DPS) laws (i.e., generic substitution) have taken place in all 50 states, the District of Columbia, and Puerto Rico. Substitution standards vary from state to state. For example, 12 states require mandatory *generic* substitution, while the remainder leave this decision to the prescriber (95).

Generic substitution allows the pharmacist to substitute a drug with identical chemical ingredients. Less than half of the generic substitution laws provide that every prescription form contain two separate signature lines: 1) substitution permissible or 2) dispense as written (96). Only when the physician signs the generic "substitution permissible" line may the pharmacist substitute a less expensive drug with the same active ingredients. More than half of the DPS laws stipulate that the prescriber must expressly indicate "Do not substitute" in some manner when prohibiting generic substitution. Three states allow this decision to remain optional (96).

Drug product selection laws apply only to generic substitution. Therapeutic interchange ("therapeutic substitution") permits, or may even require, pharmacists to dispense a chemically different product that has the same therapeutic effect unless the physician enters a positive objection. Most state statutes are silent on the issue of therapeutic interchange. Wisconsin and Illinois prohibit the practice except in hospitals (95). Only the state of Washington has given therapeutic interchange explicit legislative approval but requires the prescriber's prior consent (95).

For over 30 years, many hospitals have adopted the formulary system in which physicians and pharmacists agree to therapeutic interchange according to a preselected list of drugs. Thus, if alprazolam is prescribed, diazepam might be substituted. Authority for therapeutic interchange flows from medical practice acts that delegate authority for drug substitution to pharmacists. *Therapeutic interchange* rather than therapeutic substitution is the correct term because of mutual agreement between physicians and pharmacists to implement the hospital formulary system. Many hospitals, as a precondition for granting hospital privileges, require physicians and dentists to execute a blanket authorization permitting therapeutic interchange from the hospital formulary.

Until recently, therapeutic interchange did not occur outside of hospital settings. Currently, however, health maintenance organizations (HMOs) and other managed care programs are utilizing therapeutic interchange. In 1988, 30% of HMOs throughout the country had therapeutic formularies (95). By 1991, Medicare plans to automatically require generic substitution when brand name drugs are not specifically prescribed. Accordingly, states are likely to modify their DPS statutes to conform to the federal law governing Medicare.

Despite the recent controversy surrounding the quality control and efficacy of generic drugs, the FDA (97) makes the following recommendation:

> Despite recent reports of problems in the generic drug industry and FDA's regulation of that industry, FDA recommends that physicians continue to consider prescribing generic drugs so that pharmacists can select lower cost generic alternatives to brand-name products when appropriate. This recommendation is based on FDA laboratory testing of more than 2,500 samples of the top 30 prescribed generic drugs and intensive FDA inspection of 36 of the largest generic drug firms and 12 contact laboratories that test samples of generic drugs for bioequivalence.

References

1. Lazarus A, Mann SC, Caroff SN: The Neuroleptic Malignant Syndrome and Related Conditions. Washington, DC, American Psychiatric Press, 1987, pp 7–8
2. Caroff SN: The neuroleptic malignant syndrome. Psychopharmacol Bull 24:25–29, 1988
3. Levenson JL: Neuroleptic malignant syndrome. Am J Psychiatry 142:1137–1145, 1985
4. Mueller PS: Neuroleptic malignant syndrome: a review. Psychosomatics 26:654–662, 1985
5. Cowman v Hornaday, 329 NW2d 422 (Iowa 1983)

6. ALASKA STAT § 09.55.556 (1976); DEL CODE tit 18 § 6852 (1981)
7. Canterbury v Spence, 464 F2d 772 (DC Cir), cert denied, 409 U.S. 1064 (1972)
8. Pardy v United States, 783 F2d 710 (7th Cir 1986)
9. Fitzer v Forlaw, 435 So 2d 839 (Fla App 1983)
10. 651 SW2d 364 (Tex App 1983)
11. 108 NM 311, 775 P2d 713 (1989)
12. 144 Mich App 245, 375 NW2d 403 (1985)
13. 164 Mich App 204, 416 NW2d 381 (1987)
14. 139 Mich App 342, 362 NW2d 275 (1984)
15. 136 Ill App 3d 945, 483 NE2d 906 (1985), rev'd, 117 Ill2d 507, 513 NE2d 387 (1987), cert denied, 485 U.S. 905 (1988)
16. 111 App Div 2d 894, 490 NYS2d 602 (1985)
17. Felthous AR: The duty to warn or protect to prevent automobile accidents, in American Psychiatric Press Review of Clinical Psychiatry and the Law, Vol 1. Edited by Simon RI. Washington DC, American Psychiatric Press, 1990, pp 221–238; see pp 237–238
18. 541 F Supp 999 (D Md 1982)
19. 100 Wash 2d 421, 671 P2d 230 (1983)
20. 300 Or 706, 717 P2d 140 (1986)
21. 144 Wis 2d 223, 424 NW2d 159 (1988), rev'd, Schuster v Altenberg, 86-CV-1327 (Cir Ct Racine Cty, 1990)
22. 539 A2d 1064 (Del Sup 1988)
23. Drug induced disease called a "double-barreled" liability. Clinical Psychiatry News 12(1):12, 1984
24. Lesar TS, Briceland LL, Delcoure K, et al: Medication prescribing errors in a teaching hospital. JAMA 263:2329–2334, 1990
25. Risk of malpractice suit for psychiatrists may be rising. Clinical Psychiatric News 12(12):1, 18, 1984
26. King JH: The Law of Medical Practice in a Nutshell, 2nd Edition. St Paul, MN, West Publishing, 1986, pp 154–173
27. Canterbury v Spence, 464 F2d 772, 789 (DC Cir), cert denied, 409 U.S. 1064 (1972), citing Fiorentino v Wenger, 26 App Div 2d 693, 272 NYS2d 557, 559 (1966), appeal dismissed, 276 NYS2d 639 (1966), reversed on other grounds, 280 NYS2d 373, 227 NE2d 296 (App Div 1967)
28. Klein JI, Glover SI: Psychiatric malpractice. Int J Law Psychiatry 6:131–157, 1983
29. Cheung v Cunningham, 214 NJ Super 64a, 520 A2d 832 (1987), reversed on other grounds, 111 NJ 573, 546 A2d 501 (1988)
30. What should we tell patients about their medicines? Drug Ther Bull 19:74, 1981
31. Fishalow SE: The tort liability of the psychiatrist. Bull Am Acad Psychiatry Law 3:191–220, 1975
32. Colten RJ: The professional liability of behavioral scientists: an overview. Behavioral Sciences and the Law 1:9–22, 1983
33. Klein JI, Macbeth JE, Onek JN: Legal Issues in the Private Practice of Psychiatry. Washington, DC, American Psychiatric Press, 1984, pp 7–8
34. Hendrickson RM: New federal regulations, psychotropics, and nursing homes. Drug Therapy (Suppl), August 1990, pp 101–105

35. Health Care Financing Administration: Medicare and Medicaid: requirements for long-term care facilities. Final rule with request for comments. Federal Register 54(February 12):5316–5336, 1989
36. 589 F2d 214 (5th Cir 1979)
37. 713 F Supp 1495 (SD Ohio 1988)
38. No A7905-02395, Multonamah Cty Cir Ct (Ore Feb 16, 1983)
39. 91 Misc 2d 590, 398 NYS2d 470 (1977)
40. Halleck SL: Law in the Practice of Psychiatry. New York, Plenum, 1980, pp 66–67
41. 107 App Div 2d 636, 484 NYS2d 19 (1985)
42. Hollister LE, Overall JE, Johnson MH, et al: Amitriptyline, perphenazine and amitriptyline combination in different depressive syndromes. Arch Gen Psychiatry 17:486–493, 1967
43. Prusoff BA, Williams DH, Weissman MM, et al: The treatment of secondary depression in schizophrenia: double-blind placebo-controlled trial of amitriptyline added to perphenazine. Arch Gen Psychiatry 36:566–575, 1979
44. Bies EB: Mental Health and the Law. Rockville, MD, Aspen, 1984, p 163
45. No 83-11951, Dade Cty Cr Ct (Fla 1985)
46. 501 So 2d 441 (Ala 1986)
47. 288 Minn 332, 181 NW2d 882 (1970)
48. Sarno GG: Physician's liability for causing patient's drug addiction, in Proof of Facts, 2nd Edition. New York, Bancroft-Whitney, 1979, pp 589–632
49. No 829211, King Cty Cir Ct (Washington March 1979)
50. Ray v Rhoades, No 254551 Sacramento Cty Cir Ct (CA April 1978)
51. Kollmorgen v State Board of Medical Examiners, 416 NW2d 485 (Minn Ct App 1987)
52. Woods JH, Katz JL, Winger G: Use and abuse of benzodiazepines. JAMA 260:3476–3480, 1988
53. American Psychiatric Association: Benzodiazepine Dependence, Toxicity, and Abuse (Task Force Report). Washington, DC, American Psychiatric Association, 1990
54. 136 AD2d 410, 527 NYS2d 385, modified, 73 NY2d 748, 536 NYS2d 44, 532 NE2d 1272 (1988), later proceeding, 144 Misc 2d 777, 545 NYS2d 490 (1989)
55. Knecht v Gillman, 488 F2d 1136 (8th Cir 1973)
56. Carter v Dunlop, 138 Ill App 3d 58, 484 NE2d 1273 (1985)
57. Malcolm JG: Treatment choices and informed consent in psychiatry: implications of the Osheroff case for the profession. Journal of Psychiatry and Law 14:9–107, 1986
58. Brooten KE: Outdated drugs can cause headaches. Private Practice, December 1988, pp 19–20
59. Managed care has created new liability concerns. Clinical Psychiatry News 18(11):7, 1990
60. 512 F Supp 140, 146 (D Nev 1981)
61. 138 AD2d 102, 529 NYS2d 569 (1988)
62. No CU81-0950 USDC (ED NY 1985)
63. 472 So 2d 573 (La 1985), cert denied, 494 So 2d 331 (La 1986)
64. Appelbaum PS, Gutheil TG: Clinical Handbook of Psychiatry and the Law, 2nd Edition. Baltimore, MD, Williams & Wilkins, 1991, pp 191–192

65. Dovido v Vasquez, No 84-674 15th Jud Cir Ct, Palm Beach Cty (Fl April 4, 1986)
66. No 83-175F, Erie Cty Sup Ct (NY 1986)
67. 288 Minn 144, 179 NW2d 288 (1970)
68. Anonymous v anonymous psychiatrist. Medical Malpractice: Verdicts, Settlements & Experts 4(December):60, 1988
69. Sarno GG: Liability of physician, for injury to or death of third party, due to failure to disclose driving related impediment. American Law Review 4th 43:153–171, 1986
70. American Psychiatric Association Task Force on the Use of Laboratory Tests in Psychiatry: Tricyclic antidepressants: blood level measurements and clinical outcome. Am J Psychiatry 142:155–162, 1985
71. Two new psychiatric drugs. FDA Drug Bulletin 20(1):9, 1990
72. Salzman C: Mandatory monitoring for side effects: the "bundling" of clozapine. New Engl J Med 323:827–829, 1990
73. American Psychiatric Association Task Force on the Use of Laboratory Tests in Psychiatry: The dexamethasone suppression test: an overview of its current status in psychiatry. Am J Psychiatry 144:1253–1262, 1987
74. Myers DH, Carter RA, Burns BH, et al: A prospective study of the effects of lithium on thyroid function and on the prevalence of antithyroid antibodies. Psychol Med 15:55–61, 1985
75. No 78-0161-R (ED VA filed Sept 8, 1978)
76. Cohen RJ: Malpractice: A Guide for Mental Health Professionals. New York, Free Press, 1979, p 219
77. Ayd FJ: Problems with orders for medication as needed. Am J Psychiatry 142:939–942, 1985
78. MICH COMP LAW § 333.1801 et seq
79. Kane JM: Compliance issues in outpatient treatment. J Clin Psychopharmacol 5(suppl):22–27, 1985
80. Kane JM: Schizophrenia: somatic treatment, in Comprehensive Textbook of Psychiatry V, Vol 1. Edited by Kaplan HI, Sadock BJ. Baltimore, MD, Williams & Wilkins, 1989, pp 777–792; see pp 790–792
81. Ulmer RA: Patient noncompliance documentation: tactic for successful medical malpractice prevention and defense. Medical Trial Technique Quarterly 28(Spring):361–374, 1982
82. Tisdale v Johnson, 177 Ga App 487, 339 SE2d 764 (1986)
83. Soskis DA: Schizophrenic and medical inpatients as informed drug consumers. Arch Gen Psychiatry 35:645–647, 1978
84. Ostow M: Is it useful to combine drug therapy with psychotherapy? Psychosomatics 20:731, 1979
85. Slovenko R: Malpractice in psychiatry and related fields. Journal of Psychiatry and Law 9:5–64, 1981
86. Lesse S: Editorial comment. Am J Psychother 19:105, 1965
87. 490 A2d 720, 722 (Md App 1985)
88. Mann JI, Kapur S: The emergence of suicidal ideation and behavior during antidepressant pharmacotherapy. Arch Gen Psychiatry 48:1027–1033, 1991
89. 15 U.S.C. § 355 (1984)
90. FDA studies generic samples in wake of growing scandal. Psychiatric Times 6(10):1, 53, 1989

91. Chien CP, Okeya BL: Bioequivalence of generic psychotropic drugs. Carrier Letter, No 90, June 1983

92. Food and Drug Administration: Approved Drug Products With Therapeutic Equivalence Evaluations, 7th Edition. Rockville, MD, Food and Drug Administration, 1987

93. Nightingale SL, Morrison JC: Generic drugs and the prescribing physician. JAMA 258:1200–1204, 1987

94. Barone JA, Byerly WG: Determination of bioequivalence of psychotropic drugs and concerns involving product interchange. J Clin Psychiatry 47(9, suppl):28–32, 1986

95. Schutte JE: Who's deciding whether to overrule your prescriptions? Medical Economics, March 6, 1989, pp 50–55

96. Rea AJ: Generic substitution laws: how much control do you have? Legal Aspects of Medical Practice 15:1–4, 1987

97. FDA Drug Bulletin, April 1990, p 4

Chapter 10

Tardive Dyskinesia: Reducing Legal Liability Through Risk-Benefit Analysis

Dr. Matthews has treated Mrs. Stone, a 59-year-old married woman, for the past 5 years for a recurrent manic-depressive disorder. Three times during this period she was hospitalized for 4 to 6 weeks. Between hospitalizations, the patient received twice-a-week psychotherapy without medication. During the hospitalizations, lithium therapy was extremely effective in terminating manic episodes. With each subsequent hospitalization, Mrs. Stone manifested increasing reluctance to take lithium because it left a "metallic taste" in her mouth. Neuroleptic medications were required initially for a few weeks until the patient's manic symptoms subsided. Tardive dyskinesia, although a possible complication of neuroleptics, was not discussed because of the short duration of neuroleptic therapy. Also, Dr. Matthews did not want to alarm the patient. Over the years, the patient became almost phobic about being stuck with a needle to have blood drawn for lithium levels. Furthermore, she feared hospitals and the taking of any medication. After her last hospitalization, she refused lithium maintenance therapy.

During the past 3 weeks, Mrs. Stone again has become manic, spending money frivolously, talking nonstop, and threatening to divorce her husband of many years. Through Mrs. Stone's husband and the therapeutic alliance, Dr. Matthews prevails upon Mrs. Stone to enter the psychiatric service of a general hospital. Mrs. Stone adamantly refuses to take lithium, stating it will form "salt deposits in my brain that will cause depression." Because Mrs. Stone is enjoying her elation, she does not feel the need for any medication. Her husband threatens to leave her if she refuses medication. Mrs. Stone compromises. She agrees to take haloperidol, 3 mg four times a day. Again, Dr. Matthews does not inform Mrs. Stone about tardive dyskinesia, a potentially serious complication of neuroleptic treatment. Given her fear of taking medications, Dr. Matthews is concerned that his patient will become noncompliant. Furthermore, he plans to use haloperidol for only a short time. He informs Mrs. Stone about the possibility of dry mouth, constipation, and blurred vision. Mr. Stone, however, is in-

formed of the risk of tardive dyskinesia associated with neuroleptic therapy. He gives his consent for treatment. The consent is noted in the patient's medical chart.

Within 3 weeks, Mrs. Stone is considerably improved. The only symptom that remains is rapid speech. Dr. Matthews decides to maintain Mrs. Stone on halo-peridol rather than jeopardize her clinical condition by changing to an alternative treatment. When Mrs. Stone develops bradykinesia and hand tremors, Dr. Matthews begins benztropine mesylate, 2 mg a day, which produces mild improvement. Mrs. Stone is discharged from the hospital. She is seen once per week as an outpatient.

After 10 weeks, the maintenance dose of haloperidol is lowered to 2 mg four times a day because the patient is now almost totally asymptomatic. The patient manifests mild worm-like movements of the tongue with occasional lip smacking and pursing of the lips. Dr. Matthews becomes alarmed and discontinues the haloperidol and benztropine mesylate immediately. The tongue and lip movements become more pronounced. A neurological consultation reveals withdrawal-onset tardive dyskinesia.

What do psychiatrists need to know about tardive dyskinesia in order to properly inform patients?

Tardive dyskinesia (TD) is a movement disorder similar to other disorders such as Huntington's disease. A wide spectrum of movement disorders can occur, including tardive dystonia and tardive akathisia. The prevalence of TD has been reported in the range of 15% to 30% of patients who take neuroleptic medication (1). In 15% to 25% of patients who develop TD, the condition is severe and persistent (2).

The risk of developing TD is approximately 4% to 7% per year of neuroleptic usage. If the patient's age is 55 to 60, the incidence rises to 15% per year, with a prevalence of 50% in patients who have been chronically treated with neuroleptics (3). TD is characterized by a combination of involuntary movements involving the tongue, lips, extremities, and, in some instances, the trunk of the body. Respiratory muscles also may be affected. TD often begins insidiously and may be initially detectable as wormlike contractions of the tongue. In some patients, frequent blinking or tic-like movements of the lips or face are harbingers of TD. Later manifestations include obvious protruding, curling, and twisting tongue movements; pouting, sucking, smacking, and puckering lip movements; retraction of mouth corners (bridling); bulging of the cheeks; and chewing and lateral jaw movements. Involuntary swaying movements of the trunk as well as abnormal postures, expiratory grunts, and noises on respiration may occur. In patients over 50, oral-facial dyskinesias usually appear first and are the most conspicuous feature of this disorder (4).

Every movement disorder is not TD. Acute, reversible neurological disorders occur regularly with patients taking antipsychotic drugs. These disorders usually can be treated by decreasing the dose of major tranquilizers or adding an antiparkinsonian agent. The differential diagnosis in evaluating TD includes, but is not limited to, the following (4):

- Transient acute dyskinesias associated with neuroleptics (withdrawal dyskinesias)
- Stereotyped movements of schizophrenia
- Spontaneous oral dyskinesias of advanced age or senility
- Oral dyskinesias related to dental conditions or prostheses
- Huntington's chorea
- Gilles de la Tourette's syndrome
- Wilson's disease
- Fahr's syndrome
- Postencephalitic and encephalitic syndromes
- Rheumatic chorea (St. Vitus' dance)
- Drug intoxications
- Brain tumors
- Central nervous system complications secondary to metabolic disorders

Although TD appears to be more commonly associated with high-dose and long-term treatment or total exposure to neuroleptics, severe and persistent cases can sometimes occur after only a relatively short course of low-dose treatment (5). As a rule, however, the development of TD is unlikely when the *total* time of exposure to neuroleptics is under 3 months (6). In the elderly, however, TD may develop within 1 to 3 months after initiating neuroleptic treatment. The established connection between TD and neuroleptic drugs is based on widely replicated epidemiologic studies. For example, data developed over a 10-year period at Hillside Hospital indicate that the proportion of patients treated with neuroleptics who developed TD increased approximately 4% for each year of neuroleptic therapy (7).

Tardive dyskinesia may occur in any diagnostic group. Patients manifesting extreme degrees of emotional instability or affective disorders may be at particular risk (8). Patients with unipolar depressions and organic mental disorders are thought to be at higher risk for developing TD following neuroleptic treatment than are chronic schizophrenic patients (3). Irreversible TD is more likely to occur in the elderly, particularly elderly women (9). Severe and persistent cases also occur in children and adolescents (10). Less than one-third of TD cases persist. About one-third persist but improve, while approximately 40% of TD cases remit completely within 3 to 6 months of stopping neuroleptic treatment (1).

The onset of TD may be either overt (maintenance onset) or covert (withdrawal onset). In the former, abnormal movements begin while the patient is on maintenance doses of neuroleptics. In the latter, the dyskinesia is apparent only when reducing the dose or withdrawing the patient from the drug. Unfortunately, neuroleptics may mask the very disorder they cause. Maintenance-onset TD is usually more severe and persistent. When clinically indicated, drug discontinuation can be useful in uncovering TD at an early, reversible stage. Although elderly patients often appear unaware of involuntary movements, younger patients may be mortified sufficiently to withdraw from social contacts. Disfigurement is an important risk of neuroleptic treatment, providing a basis for significant monetary damages to be awarded.

There is no "safe" neuroleptic or any published evidence that any particular neuroleptic is more or less safe or harmful in causing TD (4). Thus the claims that low-potency neuroleptics are safer while high-potency neuroleptics are more likely to cause TD lack any current factual basis. Clozapine, recently introduced for the treatment of intractable types of schizophrenia, is rarely associated with the development of TD (11). The relatively high incidence of agranulocytosis associated with this drug, however, precludes its use as a first-line antipsychotic agent (12). Other psychotropic drugs, including amphetamines, lithium, antidepressants, phenytoin, metoclopramide, antihistamines, and L-dopa, are also reported to induce dyskinesias resembling TD (13).

The prognosis of patients with TD is less clear. Gardos and Cole (14) argue that TD is a variable disorder and that the concept of irreversibility needs to be reexamined. They base their views on a review of the literature suggesting that the first signs of TD can be reversed by discontinuing neuroleptic treatment. Moreover, they point to reports of long-established cases that show improvement and the variability of this disorder over time. In assessing TD, these authors point out that extensive fluctuation in movement severity is influenced by the time of day, arousal level, and dosage of medications. Risk factors include age, sex, neuroleptic exposure (although no conclusive proof exists that continual neuroleptic treatment worsens prognosis), prior brain damage or "soft signs" of organicity, and the nature of the psychiatric disorder. Patients with mood disorders, especially depression, appear at greater risk for TD. Although severe dyskinesia may develop rapidly and go on to a malignant course, patients who develop mild to moderate TD rarely progress to severe disease.

In assessing the benefits of neuroleptic treatment against the risk of TD, what clinical factors should be considered?

Neuroleptic drugs have been found repeatedly to be the best treatment available for most forms of schizophrenia. Neuroleptics have been credited with the remarkable decrease in the number of public mental hospital patients from more than 500,000 in 1955 to well below 200,000 in the late 1970s (15). This success, however, led to a much broader use of major tranquilizers at high doses, for prolonged periods, and for conditions such as neurotic anxiety or character disorders in which neuroleptic efficacy was not established. The American Psychiatric Association (APA) Task Force Report on Tardive Dyskinesia (4) is now dated, but many of the recommended guidelines for the avoidance and management of TD are still sound. The most recent guidelines for management of TD from the soon-to-be-published updated APA Task Force Report on Tardive Dyskinesia (Spring 1992) are given in Table 10–1.

Careful diagnosis is the cornerstone of rational treatment. The failure to use rigorous diagnostic criteria for schizophrenia has caused neuroleptics to be prescribed to patients suffering from affective disorders, personality disorders, and acute psychoses of unspecified origins. The synonymous use of schizophrenia with psychoses, in general, has further blurred diagnostic categories. The APA's DSM (16) specifies criteria for the definitive and differential diagnosis of schizophrenia. In addition to the diagnosis, the patient's past history (including response to neuroleptic treatment), a risk-benefit analysis of the psychopharmacological intervention contemplated, and a determination of whether the neuroleptics will be prescribed short term (less than 6 months) or long term are of considerable importance to rational therapy.

Although the APA Task Force on TD defined long-term treatment as longer than 6 months, most authorities would use 3 months of neuroleptic treatment as the threshold duration of neuroleptic administration for inducing TD (17). In the elderly, TD has been described even after 1 to 3 months of treatment.

TABLE 10–1. Recommendations for Prevention and Management of Tardive Dyskinesia

1. Review indications for neuroleptic drugs; consider alternative treatments when available.
2. Educate the patient and his or her family regarding benefits and risks. Obtain informed consent for long-term treatment, and document it in the medical record.
3. Establish objective evidence of the benefit from neuroleptics, and review it periodically (at least every 3–6 months) to determine ongoing need and benefit.
4. Utilize the minimum effective dosage for chronic treatment.
5. Exercise particular caution with children, the elderly, and patients with affective disorders.
6. Examine the patient regularly for early signs of dyskinesia, and note them in the medical record.
7. If dyskinesia does occur, consider an alternative neurologic diagnosis.
8. If presumptive tardive dyskinesia is present, reevaluate the indications for continued neuroleptic treatment and obtain informed consent from the patient regarding continuing or discontinuing neuroleptic treatment.
9. If a neuroleptic is continued, attempt to lower the dosage.
10. If dyskinesia worsens, consider discontinuing the neuroleptic or switching to a new neuroleptic. At present, clozapine may hold some promise in this regard, but it is important to stay alert to new research findings.
11. Many cases of dyskinesia will improve and even remit with neuroleptic discontinuation or dosage reduction. If treatment for tardive dyskinesia is indicated, utilize more benign agents first (e.g., benzodiazepines and tocopheral), but keep abreast of new treatment developments.
12. If movement disorder is severe or disabling, consider obtaining a second opinion.

Source. With permission, from *Tardive Dyskinesia: A Task Force Report of the American Psychiatric Association.* Washington, DC, American Psychiatric Association, 1992, pp 250-251. +Copyright 1992

Indications for short-term and long-term neuroleptic treatment are discussed in the APA Task Force guidelines (4) and other sources (18). Short-term (less than 6 months) administration is justifiable in many cases of acute psychotic episode, severe mania or agitated depression, and certain organic mental disorders. In general, scientific support exists for long-term (greater than 6 months) use of neuroleptics in the treatment of schizophrenia, paranoia, childhood psychosis, and certain neuropsychiatric disorders such as Tourette's syndrome and Huntington's chorea (4). Clinical experience shows that certain unstable borderline patients can maintain reasonable stability or stay out of the hospital only while on maintenance neuroleptics (19). These patients usually have not responded to alternative treatments. In fact, some seriously disturbed patients who do not fit the criteria for neuroleptic treatment may be able to function only with long-term neuroleptic treatment. In this clinical situation, revision of the psychiatric diagnosis may be necessary. Generally, neuroleptics are indicated for the treatment of acute psychotic episodes in patients with borderline personality disorder. There are no established long-term indications for the neuroleptic treatment of borderline personality disorder. Official guidelines, however, cannot replace sound clinical judgment.

Clinical pragmatism and the specific treatment needs of patients cannot always conform to official guidelines. Some elderly patients with severe dementia and violent agitation require maintenance neuroleptics to prevent injury to themselves and others or to prevent physical exhaustion and death from constant agitation. In these cases, the lowest possible dose of neuroleptic should be given for the minimum necessary time (20).

The APA guidelines recommend discontinuation of neuroleptic medications, when appropriate, for hospitalized chronic schizophrenic individuals and selected outpatients to detect withdrawal TD and to evaluate the necessity of further treatment (4). Many studies emphasize the importance of uninterrupted neuroleptic therapy of chronic schizophrenic patients in maintaining remission and preventing exacerbations (15). When adequate aftercare programs do not exist and close follow-up is not possible, interrupting treatment in order to evaluate for TD is not without risk. Interruption of treatment must be weighed against the risk that severe regression in the patient's condition may cause intense personal suffering or tragedy. According to Jeste (17), the issue of drug holidays is still unresolved. Studies have shown that drug holidays either have no effect on the prevalence of TD or may be associated with an increased frequency of persistent TD. Currently, no hard scientific data exist showing that drug holidays prevent TD.

In addition to obtaining a patient's informed consent, another fundamental part of any drug therapy regimen is the implementation of a careful risk-benefit analysis. With regard to the use of neuroleptics and the concern for TD, the risk-benefit analysis should consider the following:

1. Is the disorder one for which neuroleptics are clearly indicated?
2. If neuroleptics are indicated, are they indicated for short-term (less than 3 months) or long-term use?
3. Are alternative, equally effective therapies available?
4. Does the patient present significant risk factors such as older age, female sex, mood disorder, sensitivity to acute extrapyramidal side effects, or an organic mental syndrome?
5. Is the patient a candidate for clozapine or other nonneuroleptic antipsychotic drugs (e.g., carbamazepine)?

The risks and benefits of both prescribing and not prescribing neuroleptic medications must be evaluated. The clinician must not fall into the defensive trap of considering only the risks of neuroleptic treatment.

The value of the risk-benefit analysis is aptly illustrated when applied to the clinical vignette. Dr. Matthews prescribed haloperidol to a manic-depressive patient undergoing a manic episode. His patient was successfully treated with lithium previously. Because of Mrs. Stone's delusional beliefs about lithium, Dr. Matthews started and maintained his patient on a neuroleptic instead. Although neuroleptic drugs often are used during the initial treatment of a manic episode until lithium begins to take effect, long-term maintenance neuroleptic treatment for most manic-depressive patients is not indicated (21, 22). As Mrs. Stone recovered, Dr. Matthews should have placed the patient on lithium and discontinued the haloperidol. She had four risk factors to be assessed in considering continued neuroleptic use: advancing age, female gender, previous neuroleptic treatment, and a diagnosis of an affective disorder. Careful risk-benefit analysis would have favored only the short-term use of haloperidol until an alternative therapy such as lithium could be instituted.

On what legal grounds may psychiatrists be sued by patients who develop TD secondary to neuroleptic treatment?

If consent is lacking, liability may arise based on two legal theories: the intentional tort of battery (nonconsensual touching) and negligence (23). The failure to warn of the risk of TD may be the basis of a suit. The suit may be brought as a battery, because the failure to inform about TD is tantamount to treatment without consent. In addition, a negligence claim could be made on the basis of the information a "reasonable physician" would convey or the information a "reasonable patient" would need to know in order to make an informed decision. Because professional liability insurance ordinarily does not cover intentional torts (battery), most claims are brought under negligence theory. Obtaining informed consent does not prevent a suit alleging negligence. By consenting to treatment, the patient is not consenting to negligence (23).

If Dr. Matthews' patient decides to sue, her attorney could bring a suit for negligence and one for lack of informed consent. The attorney would contend that Dr. Matthews maintained Mrs. Stone on neuroleptic medication too long for the treatment of her affective disorder. Lithium should have been prescribed at the earliest opportunity, because it had been effective on previous occasions. The attorney will contend also that the use of anticholinergics such as benztropine mesylate exacerbated Mrs. Stone's TD, even though anticholinergics may only unmask TD. The attorney would allege that her age and sex presented increased risk factors for the development of TD. Although a complication of neuroleptic treatment, the presence of TD is not by itself presumptive evidence of negligence. Before negligence can be proven, it must be demonstrated that the TD was the proximate result of negligent care and treatment.

Any discussion of legal liabilities for TD must take into account the doctrine of informed consent. Given Mrs. Stone's psychotic, delusional condition at the time of admission, she clearly made an incompetent refusal of lithium. Furthermore, she was not informed of the risk of TD, nor did she give consent to neuroleptic treatment. Her attorney will make these consent issues the basis for a negligence suit. The proxy consent given by her husband may or may not provide a defense, depending on the legal sufficiency of the proxy consent in the jurisdiction. Dr. Matthew's assertion of therapeutic privilege would likely be easily overcome by the attorney because therapeutic privilege cannot be invoked solely to circumvent the patient's consent.

Allegations of negligent care and treatment by patients who develop TD may occur when neuroleptics are prescribed at improper levels, for excessive lengths of time, and for inappropriate conditions. Failure to reduce or discontinue neuroleptics or provide drug holidays to unmask TD may be alleged as evidence of negligence. The undetected presence of TD or the failure to diagnose and monitor this complication may incur liability.

Because current knowledge of TD is sketchy, the proof of negligence can be very difficult. Because of the uncertainties about the diagnosis and treatment of TD, several standards of care may exist (24). If an authoritative treatise or a governmental, hospital, or statutory regulation exists concerning the care and management of patients taking neuroleptics, violations of such standards may be argued as evidence of negligence, despite the standard-of-care controversies that exist in the professional literature.

Establishing the causation of TD may present difficulties when etiology rests upon multiple factors. A variety of toxic, infectious, neurological, medical, and dental conditions may produce or mimic TD. Preexisting movement disorders must also be excluded. Often, the length of time required for TD to manifest itself can raise significant doubt concerning causality. Early dyskinesias may not be the same as tardive dyskinesias. Furthermore, the psychiatrist need not conclude that neuroleptics are contraindicated in the future care of a patient who has had any dyskinesia (25). In summary, consultation and the documentation of the clinical reasoning behind continued neuroleptic treatment represent good clinical practice.

In the case of Mrs. Stone, the relatively long-term treatment of her manic episode with a neuroleptic when previous lithium therapy was effective may represent a substandard level of care. Neuroleptics often are extremely useful in the initial management of manic episodes until lithium treatment takes effect. As noted earlier, long-term neuroleptic maintenance therapy of affective disorders is not recommended unless lithium or anticonvulsants are contraindicated or the affective symptoms are part of a schizophrenic disorder.

A breach-of-contract action may ensue if the psychiatrist promises a result or cure that does not take place. Promising no side effects from neuroleptics or the successful treatment of TD may bring about a suit for breach of contract, even though the treatment was not negligent. Fraud occurs if the psychiatrist willfully misrepresents information about procedures or treatment to the patient, or falsely and deliberately conceals negligence or disease (24). Patients should be told that they have TD, unless their psychological welfare contraindicates disclosure. Patients rarely complain of mild symptoms of TD. Information about TD must not be withheld from patients because of fear of a possible lawsuit.

Strict liability is the imposition of legal responsibility for harm done even though there is no proof of negligence. According to this standard, the mere occurrence of TD would be actionable. Whatever the prevailing standards, courts may impose strict liability based on judicially construed standard of care using the rule of reasonable prudence (26). Klein and Glover (27) note that in *Clites v. State* (28), the court decision was tantamount to holding the psychiatrist strictly liable for the plaintiff's TD. Damages in the amount of $750,000 were awarded. The Iowa Court of Appeals concluded that a state facility was negligent in administering major tranquilizers to control the violent behavior of a mentally retarded patient without first obtaining the patient's or guardian's informed consent.

How frequently should the patient who is taking neuroleptics be monitored?

The frequency of monitoring a patient on neuroleptics is generally a matter of clinical judgment. Patients should be monitored according to their clinical needs and their susceptibility to TD. For example, a young schizophrenic patient on low doses of neuroleptics may need drug monitoring less frequently than an elderly female patient with dementia on the same doses of neuroleptics. The incidence of TD is thought to increase with the dose and duration of neuroleptic therapy. The APA Task Force (4) recommends reevaluation and documentation of indications and response to neuroleptics at least every 3 to 6 months, with attempts made to reduce the dose. The Task Force also recommends that patients be "regularly" examined for signs and symptoms of TD. No stock answer can be given to the question of exactly how often a patient who is taking neuroleptics should be seen for follow-up visits.

Patients receiving high doses of neuroleptics, patients undergoing prolonged neuroleptic treatment, and elderly patients (especially women) receiving neuroleptics should be seen more frequently. Seeing the patient once every 6 months or less while continuing to renew neuroleptic medications by phone or mail is not good clinical practice. Early detection of TD, usually through a brief, simple examination, may catch this disorder at a reversible stage. Patients with mild dyskinesia rarely complain or are aware of the TD. Family members, however, are usually quick to notice the involuntary movements. Physicians may misdiagnose TD as another illness, thus prolonging the patient's exposure to neuroleptics (29). Neuropsychiatric consultation should be obtained when in doubt about the diagnosis and management of TD. The routine use of the Abnormal Involuntary Movement Scale (AIMS) has been helpful in the early detection of TD (30). Munetz and Benjamin (31) suggest that the benefits outweigh the disadvantages of having nonphysicians screen for TD using the AIMS in community mental health centers.

When prescribing medications that are associated with increased risks, are the requirements for obtaining informed consent correspondingly more rigorous?

The greater the risk of any treatment, the greater the obligations to disclose even relatively remote risks, especially if alternative treatments are available that present lesser risks or a greater probability of success (32). If a neuroleptic is prescribed when a benzodiazepine might be equally successful in treatment of a disorder, then more detailed informing of risks of neuroleptic treatment is necessary. Alternative approaches to the use of high-dose neuroleptic therapy are being developed to try to reduce the incidence of TD. Some of the alternative treatments include low-dose neuroleptic treatment; the concomitant use of electroconvulsive therapy; the administration of benzodiazepines, allowing for reduction of dosages of neuroleptics in agitated, acutely psychotic patients; and the addition of carbamazepine to neuroleptics in the management of violent, assaultive psychotic patients.

The administration of neuroleptic drugs raises constitutional issues and is considered by civil libertarians to be an invasive, drastic treatment almost on par with electroconvulsive therapy and psychosurgery (33). Procedural safeguards that include rigorous informed consent for "invasive" treatments have been actively litigated (34, 35, 36, 37). The consent requirement may also vary according to the standard of informing in each jurisdiction (38). The "reasonable man" standard (also known as the material-risk standard) states that the psychiatrist must generally disclose to the patient all that an average, reasonable patient would consider material to the decision whether to accept or forego the proposed treatment or procedure (39). Generally, patients need to know about the risks and benefits of the proposed treatment, the diagnosis, the risks and benefits of alternative treatments, the possibility of no treatment, and the prognosis. Traditionally, the scope of disclosure was determined by "what a reasonable medical practitioner would disclose under the same or similar circumstances" (40). This standard was referred to as the "medical community standard" or "reasonable physician standard." According to this standard, if psychiatrists or other physicians in the community did not normally provide certain information regarding a procedure, than the failure to disclose this information typically could not be raised later as a basis for liability (41).

Either by statute or by case law, all states require informed consent (42). The "reasonable patient" standard is gaining ground rapidly (43). In jurisdictions with this standard, disclosure of TD risk is required unless the patient chooses *not* to be informed of the risks of the procedure. Competent patients have a right *not to be told* of the risks of treatments. In addition, in jurisdictions following the "reasonable patient" standard, the physician has a duty to disclose the risk of refusing the recommended procedure (44).

Because the incidence of TD is quite low with less than 3 months of neuroleptic treatment, some authors feel it is not a material risk at the outset of treatment and need not be disclosed. Schatzberg and Cole (45) recommend waiting 4 to 6 weeks after neuroleptic treatment has begun with an acutely psychotic patient before discussing the subject of TD. They feel that informing such a patient before starting the treatment is impractical and will unnecessarily provoke anxiety. TD, however, can begin after a few weeks of neuroleptic treatment if the patient has taken neuroleptics in the past. The consequences can be permanent and disabling. Consequently, the clinician may find it necessary to inform the patient before initiating treatment.

To bolster a TD malpractice action against a psychiatrist for failing to obtain informed consent, plaintiffs' attorneys often point out that physicians have been on notice about TD since 1973. Psychiatrists were first informed of TD through the *FDA Drug Bulletin* (46), a publication that is sent to all physicians who have a drug prescription number. Second, legal liability can attach for failing to obtain a patient's informed consent prior to initiating treatment unless an emergency existed or therapeutic privilege was legitimately asserted. If TD develops several years later, the failure to obtain informed consent at the initiation of treatment could cause serious problems should litigation arise.

Many chronically mentally ill patients are mobile and may have been taking neuroleptics prescribed by a number of physicians for some time. These patients may not be able to provide an accurate medication history. Delaying the obtaining of informed consent may further extend the period of the patient's cumulative intake of neuroleptics without a valid consent. Generally, the law favors the obtaining of consent before any medications are given (47, 48).

Full disclosure, with certain exceptions, is the optimal standard medically and ethically. Statutory requirements setting *minimal* standards for obtaining informed consent exist in a number of jurisdictions (49). Exercising a risk-benefit analysis for any treatment or procedure is not exclusively the domain of physicians. The essence of the informed-consent doctrine is to allow patients, whenever possible, to collaboratively make their own informed risk-benefit assessments.

In addition to the requirement of informing, valid consent must be competently given without being coerced. As in the clinical vignette, when family members threaten patients who do not comply with medical recommendations, informed consent may be vitiated. Competent patients possess the right to refuse treatment. Patients who lack health care decision-making capacity require substitute consent by others. This issue is discussed in Chapters 6 and 7.

Should a psychotic patient be informed about the risk of TD before neuroleptic treatment is started?

Often, the patient who requires neuroleptic treatment may not possess sufficient mental capacity to understand explanations about TD. Paranoid patients may distort the information or include it in their delusions. It is one thing to comprehend dry mouth and constipation but quite another matter to comprehend the involuntary movements of TD, as even professionals are uncertain about the extent of this clinical disorder. As Slovenko (32) points out, much of the knowledge about TD is disputed. Among the disputed elements of TD are its etiology, pathology, incidence, course, and treatment. He quotes Beauteille's comments in 1818 about Huntington's chorea as applicable to TD: "Everything is extraordinary in this disease; the name is ridiculous, its symptoms peculiar, its character equivocal; its cause unknown, and the treatment problematical."

For this reason, only information about TD that is definitely known should be supplied to patients. Too much information may cause sensory overload and contribute to an incompetent consent or refusal of neuroleptic treatment. The decision by a patient who lacks mental capacity but nevertheless accepts treatment may go unquestioned because it accords with the clinician's treatment recommendations. Moreover, incompetent acceptance of treatment is the least questioned because it accords with the psychiatrist's therapeutic intent. The idea that the psychiatrist always knows what is best for the patient may lead to an unquestioned acceptance of an incompetent consent.

On the other hand, the presence of psychosis does not necessarily mean that the patient cannot give a valid, informed consent to treatment. The law presumes that a person is competent unless judicially determined to be incompetent or unless the person has been incapacitated by a medical condition or emergency. The mere fact that a person is being treated for a mental illness (50) or is being institutionalized (51) *does not* automatically render him or her incompetent. Accordingly, a psychiatrist has a duty to make a reasonably complete and fair disclosure of the risks of treatment and to obtain, in most situations, a psychiatric patient's informed consent prior to the imposition of treatment (52).

A psychotic patient with TD may be able to consent competently to the risk of continuing neuroleptic treatment. Competency to consent aside, continued neuroleptic treatment may be the best clinical course in accord with the overall treatment needs of the patient, even though a lawsuit may later materialize. Psychotic patients with TD who have an acute exacerbation or who require maintenance therapy may need continued neuroleptic therapy. Elderly patients with severe TD (i.e., life-endangering exhaustion) may require emergency neuroleptic therapy to suppress TD symptoms. The risks of continuing neuroleptic treatment when TD is already present include masking the severity of the TD or possibly converting a reversible case into an irreversible one. Management guidelines for the continued drug treatment of patients with TD include alternative low-dose neuroleptics, the use of non-neuroleptic antipsychotics, and the selected use of experimental drugs (11).

Roth (53) recommends that when restarting drugs with patients already manifesting TD, or who begin to manifest such symptoms, no delay is justified in obtaining informed consent in the absence of an emergency. Jeste and Wyatt (54) provide the clinician with guidelines for informing such patients. The patient's understanding of this information should be assessed over time and a consent obtained from a legally authorized individual or another substitute decision-maker if the patient is unable to comprehend the information provided about TD. When the patient needs to continue neuroleptic therapy in the presence of TD, a confirming second opinion should be obtained. Research data suggest that before meaningful consent for medication can be obtained, the information must be repeated often within the context of a collaborative doctor-patient relationship (55).

Should the psychiatrist require patients to sign consent forms that disclose the risk of TD when proposing neuroleptic medications?

For optimal protection, the written consent form is considered by some to be mandatory, particularly for patients receiving long-term neuroleptic treatment. (A sample consent form for neuroleptic treatment can be found in Appendix 2.) Souvner et al. (56) use two consent forms. One form is given to patients who have been on maintenance neuroleptic treatment for longer than a year; the other is offered to patients who develop signs of TD but clinically require continued neuroleptic treatment. Although no negative effects on treatment compliance were reported, a major geriatric facility that used these forms over a number of years experienced occasional noncompliance when family members became frightened by the detailed written description of TD symptoms (57).

Patients who read package inserts will find a class warning about the risk of TD when taking neuroleptics. Simply providing the patient a package insert will not meet a doctor's duty of obtaining informed consent. Doctors also have a duty to make sure that their patients *reasonably understand* what they are reading or being told. Therefore, if a psychiatrist decides to use a Food and Drug Administration insert as part of an informed-consent procedure, he or she must take the time to explain its contents in language that the patient can understand.

The APA Task Force Report on Tardive Dyskinesia (4) recommends against the routine use of written consent for maintenance use of neuroleptics. The report distinguishes between invasive surgical, diagnostic, and experimental procedures in which written consent is necessary, and the consent needed for established pharmacological treatments. In addition, written forms introduce a potentially detrimental, adversarial feature into the psychiatrist-patient relationship. Also, using consent forms would create a precedent for requiring written consent for a widely accepted, nonexperimental treatment. The APA Task Force recommends careful documentation of the discussion about risks and benefits of prolonged neuroleptic treatment with the patient or family.

In the study by Munetz et al. (55), many chronic schizophrenic patients who were informed about TD in an ambulatory clinic were not able to "understand, retain and/or process the necessary information in order to make a rational decision about treatment." The patients' knowledge was distorted by their mental state. Patients did not appear to learn much from formal procedures that involved the reading and signing of consent forms. Based on these findings, the authors recommend repeated informal sharing of information within the therapeutic relationship.

Although some psychiatrists feel more secure with a consent form that also includes the signature of a family member under such circumstances, it is important for clinicians to avoid legal rituals and formalisms. The compulsive reliance on forms results in "formed consent" rather than a true consent. The therapeutic alliance between psychiatrist and patient can be enhanced by a non-threatening, ongoing explanation of risks and benefits of treatment. Some patients may require additional time to develop a trusting relationship before they are able to adequately understand what the psychiatrist is recommending. Furthermore, the psychological support within the therapeutic alliance may help restore enough mental capacity to permit the patient to conduct a risk-benefit analysis sufficient to give a valid consent to treatment. Consent should be renewed periodically, especially for both inpatients or outpatients on high doses of neuroleptics. There are no "official" rules or good data to specify how frequently consent should be renewed.

In the clinical vignette, did Dr. Matthews obtain the competent consent of his patient for neuroleptic treatment? Was therapeutic privilege properly asserted?

Dr. Matthews accepted the patient's consent for haloperidol treatment as competently given even though it was probably incompetent because of delusional thinking and the coercion applied by the husband. "Good faith" or proxy consents by family members may not be legally sufficient to overcome the patient's right to refuse treatment in a growing number of jurisdictions, especially if the patient has not been adjudicated incompetent. Dr. Matthews was prudent to note in the medical chart the patient's verbal consent to neuroleptic treatment provided by the husband. Slovenko (58) states:

> Generally, there is no authority in law for a spouse to give consent in the treatment of the other spouse, nor is there authority for consent of a parent in the case of an adult child, or vice versa. There is authority in law only for the consent of a parent in the care of a minor child. However, as a matter of common practice, one finds this kind of proxy consent. It is a good idea on all consent forms to have the signature of the closest family member in the event that the competency of the patient may be challenged. While there may be no legal authority for the giving of the consent, it would be said that there would be no causal nexus for failure to have a legally appointed guardian. If a legal guardian were to be obtained, it would more than likely be the closest family member who has signed the consent form. As a consequence, it would not be said that the failure to appoint a guardian resulted in a lack of consent.

Nevertheless, both voluntary and involuntary psychiatric patients who appear to make an incompetent acceptance or refusal of neuroleptic medication will require the consent of a substitute decision-maker. Psychiatrists who are cavalier in overriding a patient's refusal of medication or who assume competence merely because of patient compliance leave themselves open for lawsuits. Competent patients must not be treated against their will. If the patient is a clear danger to self or others, an implied emergency consent for treatment may exist. At the earliest opportunity, however, the patient's consent for neuroleptic treatment should be obtained. Exceptions to informed consent and substitute decision-makers is discussed at length in Chapters 6 and 7.

Dr. Matthews asserted therapeutic privilege by not informing Mrs. Stone of the risk of TD. The courts have stated that therapeutic privilege may be asserted if informing the patient would likely worsen the patient's condition or increase the risk of the treatment recommended (39, 59, 60). Therapeutic privilege may not be used by the psychiatrist to circumvent the patient's right to refuse treatment or to induce compliance with treatment, as occurred with Mrs. Stone. Because some courts may not recognize therapeutic privilege, or are quite skeptical of its use, it is prudent to obtain consent from relatives or a legal guardian. Although Dr. Matthews obtained Mr. Stone's consent, he still may be vulnerable to a claim of a lack of informed consent because the husband's proxy consent may not be legally sufficient. Moreover, lithium was effective in prior treatments of the patient and is presumably a safer alternative than haloperidol, thus raising the requirements for a more rigorous informing of risks associated with neuroleptic therapy.

What is the current status of TD litigation?

As noted in the previous chapter, medication-related treatment represents the greatest potential for injury to psychiatric patients. Not surprisingly, it is a major source, along with suicide, of malpractice actions against psychiatrists and psychiatric facilities (61). Foremost among the plethora of side effects that a patient might suffer as a consequence of taking neuroleptic medication for an appreciable length of time is the development of TD.

Because the use of properly prescribed neuroleptics has such therapeutic promise for a significant percentage of psychiatrically ill patients who might otherwise have no chance of improvement, the use of these agents in psychiatric practice is quite high (62). Since the development of chlorpromazine in the early 1950s, the use of neuroleptics as a major treatment for the severely psychiatrically disabled has been well documented and acknowledged. Heralded as one of the primary reasons for the tremendous reduction in the average length of stay of patients in state institutions, neuroleptic medications have been viewed by many as a major treatment breakthrough. As was later discovered, this class of drugs could have severe, adverse side effects. Accordingly, trying to balance the advantages and disadvantages of this class of drugs has been neither easy nor consistent. As noted by Guttmacher (63):

> During the three decades of experience with these drugs there have been cycles in prescribing practices. We have vacillated between high-dose, aggressive treatment and more moderate courses of medication. Increasing awareness of serious toxicity, such as tardive dyskinesia and neuroleptic malignant syndrome, has recently led to a movement back to more temperate use.

The swing back to more "temperate" and "moderate" uses of neuroleptic medication has not been followed by all practitioners. Despite the availability of clinically sound guidelines for the use of neuroleptic medication and the prevention and management of TD (64), the development of TD continues to occur with unacceptable regularity. Allegations of negligence involving neuroleptic medication that results in tardive dyskinesia are conceptually no different than those made in any other medication-related malpractice action.

In *Clites v. State* (28), the Iowa Court of Appeals awarded $750,000 in damages when it concluded that a state facility for the mentally retarded negligently used major tranquilizers. Timothy Clites, a mentally retarded male, was admitted at age 17 to the state residential facility. From age 18 to 23, major tranquilizers were prescribed to control his violent behavior. At age 23, TD was diagnosed. The patient suffered mild to moderate TD involving facial and oral musculature. The court found that the state facility did not follow "industry" standards because it *1)* failed to follow up on the patient with regular visits by a physician, including consultation with other specialists, physical examination, and performance of tests; *2)* failed to provide drug holidays to evaluate the patient's condition while drug free; *3)* failed to respond to the patient's TD and change his treatment; *4)* prescribed polypharmacy, which was not appropriate for his clinical status; and *5)* prescribed major tranquilizers for the convenience and expedience of the facility, rather than for treatment.

The court also ruled that informed consent was not obtained because the risks of neuroleptic treatment were not explained to the parents, even though they knew he was receiving medication. The court relied on traditional negligence law to establish standards for prescribing neuroleptics that apply to both voluntary and involuntary patients (65).

This decision has been criticized because of the court's erroneous clinical conclusions. The court issued a blanket condemnation of polypharmacy, incorrectly concluding that antiparkinsonian drugs acted with neuroleptics to mask symptoms of TD and that the use of two neuroleptics had more effect than a higher dosage of either alone (2).

In *Faigenbaum v. Cohen* (29), a large judgment was awarded when the court found that Dr. Cohen caused Mr. Faigenbaum's mother to have TD and subsequently suffer brain damage. The patient, Anita Katz, manifested classic TD symptoms after her physician prescribed neuroleptic medications. After misreading her symptoms, Dr. Cohen advised her to seek medical care for what he thought were signs of an inherited disease—Huntington's chorea. According to the court, neuroleptic treatment was poorly monitored. In addition, the diagnosis of TD was missed by several psychiatrists and a consulting neurologist, leading to a continuation of neuroleptic treatment amid severe dyskinetic movements and the strenuous objections of her family. The psychiatrist who examined Mrs. Katz exclaimed that she suffered from "one of the worst cases of tardive dyskinesia I've ever seen." The victim was awarded $1,000,000, plus interest, which came to $1,350,000. Subsequently, the malpractice claim against the hospital was reversed by the appeals court on the grounds of governmental immunity (66).

In *Hedin v. United States* (67), a United States District Court in Minneapolis ordered the Veterans Administration (VA) to pay Mr. Hedin economic damages of $691,653 and general damages (i.e., pain and suffering, mental anguish, emotional distress, humiliation, and physical disability) of $1,500,000. His ex-wife received a loss-of-consortium award of $30,000. The government admitted negligence. The patient was taking 600 mg of chlorpromazine per day as an outpatient and did not see a VA physician for 17 months. Prescriptions were filled through the mail. The patient was found to have continuous, uncontrollable, spasmodiclike muscle movements of his mouth, face, trunk, and extremities that were totally disabling. The court described the TD as "severe, medically irreversible, and totally disabling."

In *Barclay v. Campbell* (68), however, a different result was achieved. Mr. Barclay was treated with neuroleptic medication prescribed by Dr. Campbell. The evidence was undisputed that Dr. Campbell failed to warn the patient about the risk of TD associated with neuroleptic medication. After developing TD, the patient sued, alleging negligent prescription of neuroleptics and negligent failure to disclose their risks. The trial court granted Dr. Campbell's motion for a partial directed verdict on the issue of informed consent and submitted the case to the jury on the remaining allegations of negligence. The jury found Dr. Campbell not negligent in his treatment of the patient.

On appeal, the Texas Court of Appeals affirmed the trial court's decision, basing its finding on the Texas Medical Liability Act of 1977. Section 6.07a(2) of the Texas Medical Liability Act provides that even when the defendant is presumed negligent in failing to disclose a risk requiring disclosure under the act, no negligence can be found if it "was not medically feasible because it would probably cause him [the patient] to refuse the treatment, no matter how minimal the risk and how great the countervailing risk of refusing the medication" (68). The appeals court agreed with the defendant and three defense experts who testified that because of the patient's age, the dosage, and the duration of antipsychotic treatment, the risk of developing TD was low. The court held that the plaintiff "did not have the reactions of a reasonable person" and that disclosure of risks was not medically feasible because it might have led to noncompliance with treatment. The decision was reversed by the Texas Supreme Court. The court held that a subjective standard was applied to the plaintiff rather than the objective "reasonable person standard" as required by the Texas act governing informed consent (68).

In *Frasier v. Department of Health and Human Resources* (69), a 62-year-old schizophrenic woman with TD sued the state of Louisiana for failure to obtain informed consent for the administration of neuroleptic medication. The trial court held that during a "life-threatening" emergency, no consent was necessary. The plaintiff had refused to eat and take her medication. The court noted that a written consent to hospitalization, which was an adequate consent to the use of antipsychotic medication, was signed by the plaintiff. The court found that the patient's daughter provided informed consent to the continued use of the medication. The trial court's verdict was upheld on appeal.

As is common in many medication-related negligence lawsuits, the failure of doctors to inform patients of the adverse effects of neuroleptics and to obtain their informed consent to proceed with drug therapy can result in a lawsuit (70). In what is probably the largest TD award to date, a head injury patient who developed TD from the unconsented use of loxapine sued her psychiatrist, her neurosurgeon, and the drug manufacturer (71). The plaintiff alleged that the manufacturer failed to give adequate warnings for the safe use of loxapine, that his physicians failed to obtain his informed consent, and that they failed to warn him or his family of the possible side effects of loxapine. A jury held the manufacturer completely liable and awarded the plaintiff $2,695,000 in damages, of which $500,000 were punitive damages. No negligence was found on the part of the physicians. The verdict and damage award were upheld on appeal.

In *Headley v. Hanneken* (72), a 62-year-old female was awarded $300,000 when she was not informed of the possibility of developing TD from the administration of thiothixene.

The failure to detect early signs of TD and medically intervene in order to prevent further development is another important area of negligence in TD cases. For example, in *Rosenbloom v. Goldberg* (73), the plaintiff consulted a physician complaining of chest tightness, faintness, flushing of the face, and dry mouth. In January 1975, a combination of perphenazine and amitriptyline was prescribed. For the next 2 years the plaintiff continued to take the medication. In April 1977, the doctor observed that the plaintiff had developed very noticeable involuntary, spasticlike movements of the face, jaw, and neck. Even though the plaintiff had intermittently complained of these problems, the doctor never took them seriously, stating that these problems would come and go. The plaintiff was subsequently diagnosed to have TD and forced to resign his job of 3 years as a government clerk. The plaintiff sued his physician, alleging that he had been negligent in prescribing the drug, allowing medication refills without properly examining the plaintiff, failing to warn of the side effects, and failing to detect and properly treat his neurological symptoms when they first were reported to him. Prior to trial, the parties settled for $500,000.

A patient's recovery from initial TD symptoms will not necessarily safeguard a negligent psychiatrist from a successful lawsuit. For instance, in *Urbani v. Yale University School of Medicine* (74), a 15-year-old plaintiff suffered from TD allegedly caused by the use of perphenazine, thioridazine, and benzotropine mesylate. The plaintiff complained that his doctors did not pay attention to early signs of TD such as his difficulty in walking, and failed to intervene in a timely manner. Although the plaintiff eventually recovered, the parties settled the case for approximately $30,000.

In *Snider v. Harding Hospital* (75), a 35-year-old teacher was admitted to a hospital because of an acute psychotic episode. She was treated with thiothixene in December 1982. The drug was continued after discharge in February. The plaintiff stopped taking thiothixene in July when she experienced several abnormal movements of the head, face, neck, and extremities. She was later diagnosed as having developed tardive dyskinesia. The plaintiff sued the prescribing psychiatrist and psychiatric hospital, alleging that they should have discontinued or reduced the amount of drug after her psychosis cleared up. The defendants denied the allegations, stating that they were not negligent but that the plaintiff suffered from a conversion reaction and not tardive dyskinesia. The parties settled for $800,000.

A similar result occurred in *Collins v. Cushner* (76). A family practitioner treated a patient complaining of chronic anxiety with trifluoperazine for 6 years, including a 29-month period without a single treatment session. When the plaintiff complained of jerky arm movements, the defendant abruptly took the plaintiff off the medication for 2 months and then restarted the medication at a higher dose. A lawsuit was brought, alleging that the defendant had ignored product information warnings regarding the use of the drug in the treatment of anxiety. The claim linked the long-term use of neuroleptics by females of the plaintiff's age to the development of tardive dyskinesia. A $125,000 settlement was agreed upon.

What are some of the legal defenses that have been successfully asserted in TD lawsuits?

Not all lawsuits involving TD result in large judgments or even in verdicts for the plaintiff. In fact, of 31 published and unpublished TD-related actions, approximately half were found for the defendant (77). Unpublished cases have very little precedential value in the law. Settled cases before a trial verdict have no precedential value. Moreover, the vast majority of important TD litigation has come in the context of equity rather than malpractice cases (e.g., injunction, mandatory relief such as *Rennie v. Klein* [78]).

There are a number of defenses that can and have been raised in TD malpractice cases that have either mitigated the defendant's liability or barred it altogether. Although strictly procedural and having nothing to do with negligence, the most common defense is that the plaintiff failed to file within the statute of limitations. In a 1989 federal lawsuit, *Bolen v. United States* (79), a medical malpractice action filed by a patient who developed TD from long-term trifluoperazine use was dismissed. The court held that the statute of limitations had expired and that the physicians in Idaho in 1965 could not be held responsible for knowing that long-term use of trifluoperazine could lead to TD.

In 1962, the plaintiff was successfully treated by the VA for anxiety with low doses of trifluoperazine. The plaintiff claimed that between 1963 and the early 1970s, he continued taking the drug without any medical monitoring. In 1972, he began to develop early symptoms of TD. Some doctors believed that the plaintiff might have TD. He was referred to a neurologist. A psychiatrist testified that he probably informed the plaintiff he did have TD by 1973. The plaintiff was subsequently hospitalized twice for treatment of the TD. In 1975, the plaintiff filed a claim against the VA that was rejected by the VA the following year. The plaintiff denied receiving notice of the VA's determination. Approximately 11 years later, the plaintiff filed a Federal Tort Claims Act (FTCA) action in federal court against the VA.

Federal Tort Claims Act actions, like civil suits in every state, have a statute of limitations requiring timely filing of a claim within a specified period of time either upon the plaintiff (actually) learning that malpractice had been committed or when such a determination should have been made using reasonable diligence (80). The court held that the plaintiff did not meet the FTCA's 2-year statute of limitations because he first received notice of TD in early 1974 but did not file his claim until the latter part of 1976. Moreover, the court held that the standard of care in Idaho in 1965 had not been breached because of the paucity of information about TD. Furthermore, the doctor closely monitored the plaintiff's condition the first few months that he prescribed trifluoperazine.

In some cases, a patient may develop TD despite reasonable medical efforts. As long as the defendant's treatment is consistent with the applicable standard of care, there will generally be no finding of liability, even when there is a bad result (e.g., TD). For instance, in *Riviera v. NYC Health and Hospitals Corporation* (81), a 39-year-old plaintiff developed TD after 7 years of treatment with chlorpromazine. Five or six months before this medication was withdrawn, the plaintiff exhibited torticollis. The plaintiff argued that he had incurred torticollis on an intermittent basis until the chlorpromazine was withdrawn and chlordiazepoxide was successfully substituted. The defendant countered that the plaintiff had exhibited only one incidence of torticollis in the 6 months that the chlorpromazine was taken and that this incidence was due to stress. The defendant argued, and the jury agreed, that the plaintiff was properly treated by the successful substitution of chlordiazepoxide when early signs of TD began to appear.

The plaintiff bears the burden of proving all four elements of malpractice in order to succeed on a claim of negligence. A failure to prove the elements will result in a judgment for the defendant. Sometimes, proving that the defendant's actions were the proximate cause of the plaintiff's developing TD can be a major stumbling block. For example, in *Babbitt v. Fisher* (82), the defendant-psychiatrist failed to properly diagnose the plaintiff's TD. The patient's reaction to molindone, however, was not found to be the proximate cause of his injuries. Similarly, in *Tisdale v. Johnson* (83), summary judgment was granted in favor of the defendant-psychiatrist. The plaintiff had failed to inform the doctor of side effects she was experiencing until it was too late for him to effectively treat them. The court noted that the plaintiff has a duty to exercise ordinary care for her own protection by keeping her physician informed of problems she might be having with prescribed treatment.

What is the outlook for TD litigation?

Unless there are a significant number of TD cases being secretly settled and going unreported, the anticipated flood of litigation reported by numerous commentators has not developed yet (84). "Yet" is the operative word with regard to future TD litigation. TD appears in approximately 15% to 33% of chronically treated patients (85). Estimates suggest that no less than 3 million people are currently taking neuroleptics and that over 900,000 new patients receive neuroleptics each year (1). Thus, the potential for new TD cases each year is staggering.

The fact that there are currently few published TD lawsuits in the case literature is *not* reliable evidence that patients are not developing TD as a result of poor clinical practices. On the contrary, there is considerable potential for a significant rise in the number of TD actions, especially as the civil rights of the institutionalized mentally ill are actively defended. Often, TD suits may end up in decisions for the defense because of the expiration of the statute of limitations or other available defenses.

Some psychiatrists and other physicians continue to minimize the seriousness of TD while clinging to the unreasonable belief that neuroleptics are very safe, despite warnings from the APA Task Force Report on Tardive Dyskinesia (4) and continual warnings and guidelines from numerous publications and presentations (86). Given the six- and seven-figure monetary damages already awarded in a number of TD cases, attorneys can be expected to litigate these cases more vigorously in the future.

References

1. Jeste DV: Madness, movements, and malpractice: what a mess! Paper presented at the 21st annual meeting of the American Academy of Psychiatry and the Law, San Diego, CA, October 1990
2. Smith JT, Simon RI: Tardive dyskinesia revisited: a major public health crisis. Medical Trial Technique Quarterly 31:342–349, 1985
3. Lohr JB, Wisinewski A, Jeste DV: Neurological aspects of tardive dyskinesia, in Handbook of Schizophrenia, Vol 1: Neurology of Schizophrenia. Edited by Nasrallah H, Weinberger DR. Amsterdam, Elsevier, 1986, pp 97–119
4. Tardive dyskinesia: summary of the Task Force Report of the American Psychiatric Association. Am J Psychiatry 137:1163, 1165, 1980
5. Moline RA: Atypical tardive dyskinesia. Am J Psychiatry 132:534–535, 1975
6. Jeste DV, Wyatt RJ: Understanding and Treating Tardive Dyskinesia. New York, Guilford, 1982
7. Kane JM, Woerner M, Lieberman JA, et al: Tardive dyskinesia and drugs. Drug Development Research 9:41–51, 1986
8. Rosenbaum KM, Niven RG, Hanson MP: Tardive dyskinesia: relationship with primary affective disorder. Diseases of the Nervous System 38:423–427, 1977
9. Davis JM, Barter JT, Kane JM: Antipsychotic drugs, in Comprehensive Textbook of Psychiatry V, Vol 2. Edited by Kaplan HI, Sadock BJ. Baltimore, MD, Williams & Wilkins, 1989, pp 1591–1626; see pp 1623–1624
10. Schatzberg AF, Cole JO: Manual of Clinical Psychopharmacology, 2nd Edition. Washington, DC, American Psychiatric Press, 1991, pp 319–320
11. Lieberman JA: Neuroleptic-induced movement disorders and experience with clozapine in tardive dyskinesia. J Clin Psychiatry Monograph 8(1):3–8, 1990
12. Marder SR, Van Putten T: Who should receive clozapine? Arch Gen Psychiatry 45:865–867, 1988
13. Thach BT, Chase TN, Bosma JF: Oralfacial dyskinesia associated with prolonged use of antihistaminic decongestants. N Engl J Med 293:486–487, 1975
14. Gardos G, Cole JO: The prognosis of tardive dyskinesia. J Clin Psychiatry 44:177–179, 1983

15. Jeste DV, Wyatt RJ, Matthysse S: Neuroleptics and tardive dyskinesia: quo vadis? J Clin Pharmacol 2:303–304, 1982
16. American Psychiatric Association: Diagnostic and Statistical Manual of Mental Disorders. Washington, DC, American Psychiatric Association
17. Dilip Jeste, M.D., personal communication, July 1990
18. Schooler N, Kane J: Research diagnosis for tardive dyskinesia. Arch Gen Psychiatry 39:486–487, 1982
19. Soloff P, George A, Nathan R, et al: Progress in pharmacotherapy of borderline disorders: a double-blind study of amitriptyline, haloperidol, and placebo. Arch Gen Psychiatry 43:691–697, 1986
20. Doongaji DR, Jeste DV, Jape NM, et al: Tardive dyskinesia in India: a prevalence study. J Clin Psychopharmacol 2:341–344, 1982
21. Hirschfeld RMA, Goodwin FK: Mood disorders, in American Psychiatric Press Textbook of Psychiatry. Edited by Talbott JA, Hales RE, Yudofsky SC. Washington, DC, American Psychiatric Press, 1988, pp 430–431
22. Goodwin FK, Jamison KR: Manic-Depressive Illness. New York, Oxford University Press, 1990, p 717
23. Slovenko R: Misadventures of psychiatry with the law. Journal of Psychiatry and Law 16:115–156, 1989
24. Wettstein RM: Tardive dyskinesia and malpractice. Behavioral Sciences and the Law 1:85–107, 1983
25. E Gershon, personal communication, January 1985
26. Peters VM: The application of reasonable prudence to medical malpractice litigation: the precursor to strict liability? Law, Medicine and Health Care 1:21–45, 1981
27. Klein JI, Glover SI: Psychiatric malpractice. Int J Law Psychiatry 6:131–157, 1983
28. 322 NW2d 917 (Iowa Ct App 1982)
29. Faigenbaum v Cohen, Wayne County Circuit Court, No 79-904-736 (NM Mich May 1982)
30. Munetz MR, Schulz CS: Screening for tardive dyskinesia. J Clin Psychiatry 47:75–77, 1986
31. Munetz MR, Benjamin S: Who should perform the AIMS examination? Hosp Community Psychiatry 41:912–915, 1990
32. Slovenko R: On the legal aspects of tardive dyskinesia. Journal of Psychiatry and Law 7:295–331, 1979
33. Appelbaum PS, Gutheil TG: Clinical Handbook of Psychiatry and the Law, 2nd Edition. Baltimore, MD, Williams & Wilkins, 1991, pp 97–104
34. Rogers v Okin, 478 F Supp 1342 (D Mass 1979), aff'd in part, rev'd in part, Rogers v Okin 634 F2d 650 (1st Cir 1980), vacated and remanded, Mills v Rogers, 457 U.S. 291 (1982), on remand, Rogers v Okin, 738 F2d 1 (1st Cir 1984)
35. Rennie v Klein, 653 F2d 836 (3d Cir 1981) (en banc), vacated and remanded mem, 458 U.S. 1119 (1982), on remand, 720 F2d 266 (3d Cir 1983) (en banc)
36. Wyatt v Hardin, No 3195-N, 1 MDLR 55 (MD Ala Feb 28, 1975, modified July 1, 1975)
37. Kaimowitz v Department of Mental Health for the State of Michigan, Civil Action No 73-19434-AW (Mich Cir Ct Wayne Cty, July 10, 1973)
38. Rosoff A: Informed Consent: A Guide for Health Care Providers. Rockville, MD, Aspen, 1981, pp 75–185

39. Canterbury v. Spence, 464 F2d 772 (DC Cir 1972), cert denied, Spence v Canterbury, 409 U.S. 1064 (1972)
40. Natanson v Kline, 186 Kan 393, 350 P2d 1093 (1960); Aiken v Clary, 396 SW2d 688 (Mo 1965)
41. Young v Yarn, 136 Ga App 737, 222 SE2d 113 (Ga Ct App 1975)
42. Malcolm JG: Informed consent in the practice of psychiatry, in American Psychiatric Press Review of Clinical Psychiatry and the Law, Vol 3. Edited by Simon RI. Washington, DC, American Psychiatric Press, 1992, pp 223–281
43. Hook v Rothstein, 281 SC 541, 316 SE2d 690 (SC Ct App 1984), cert denied, 283 SC 64, 320 SE2d 35 (SC 1984); Otwell v Bryant, 497 So 2d 111 (Ala 1986); Arena v Gingrich, 84 Or App 25, 733 P2d 75 (1987), aff'd remanded, 305 Or 1, 748 P2d 547 (1988); Festa v Greenberg, 354 Pa Super 346, 511 A2d 1371 (Pa Super Ct 1986)
44. Truman v Thomas, 27 Cal 3d 285, 165 Cal Rptr 308, 611 P2d 902 (1980)
45. Schatzberg AF, Cole JO: Manual of Clinical Psychopharmacology, 2nd Edition. Washington, DC, American Psychiatric Press, 1991, p 6
46. FDA Drug Bulletin, May 1973
47. Miranda v Arizona, 384 U.S. 436 (1966)
48. Dunham v Wright, 423 F2d 940 (3rd Cir 1970)
49. Meisel A, Kabnick LD: Informed consent to medical treatment: an analysis of recent legislation. University of Pittsburgh Law Review 41:407, 1980
50. Wilson v Lehman, 379 SW2d 478 (Ky 1964)
51. Rennie v Klein, 462 F Supp 1131 (D NJ 1978), Rennie v Klein, 653 F2d 836 (3d Cir 1981) (en banc), vacated and remanded mem, 458 U.S. 1119 (1982), on remand, 720 F2d 266 (3d Cir 1983) (en banc)
52. Rivers v Katz, 67 NY2d 485, 495 NE2d 337, 504 NYS2d 74 (1986) [psychopharmacotherapy]; Pickle v Curns, 106 Ill App 3d 734, 435 NE2d 877 (Ill App 1983) [ECT]
53. Roth LH: Question the experts. J Clin Psychopharmacol 3:207–208, 1983
54. Jeste DV, Wyatt RD: Guidelines for the use of neuroleptics in clinical practice. Psychiatric Annals 10:39–52, 1980
55. Munetz M, Roth LH, Cornes CL: Tardive dyskinesia and informed consent: myths and realities. Bull Am Acad Psychiatry Law 10:77–88, 1982; see p 87
56. Souvner R, Dimascio A, Berkowitz D, et al: Tardive dyskinesia and informed consent. Psychosomatics 19:172–177, 1978
57. D Patel [former Medical Director, the Hebrew Home of Greater Washington, Rockville, MD), personal communication, July 1984
58. R Slovenko, personal communication, March 1985
59. Sard v Hardy, 281 Md 432, 379 A2d 1014 (1977)
60. Natanson v Kline, 186 Kan 393, 350 P2d 1093 (1960)
61. Suicide, drugs hot areas for malpractice litigation. Clinical Psychiatric News, 16(5):1, 15, 1988
62. Parry HJ, Balter MB, Mellinger GD, et al: National patterns of psychotherapeutic drug use. Arch Gen Psychiatry 28:769–783, 1973
63. Guttmacher LB: Concise Guide to Somatic Therapies in Psychiatry. Washington DC, American Psychiatric Press, 1988, p 16
64. Jeste D, Wyatt RJ: Therapeutic strategies against tardive dyskinesia. Arch Gen Psychiatry 39:803–816, 1982

65. American Psychiatric Association Legal Consultation Plan, Fall 1981, pp 9–10
66. Faigenbaum v Oakland Medical Center, 143 Mich App 303, 373 NW2d 161 (Mich Ct App 1985), aff'd, Hyde v Univ of Mich Board of Regents, 426 Mich 223, 393 NW2d 847 (1986)
67. No 583-3 (D Minn December 27, 1984) as amended (January 3, 1985), appeal dismissed per stipulation, No 85-5057-MN (8th Cir May 21, 1985)
68. 683 SW2d 498 (Tex Civ App 1985), rev'd 704 SW2d 8 (Tex 1986)
69. 500 So 2d 858 (La 1986)
70. Paterson RM: Drugs In Litigation: Damage Awards Involving Prescription and Non-prescription Drugs. Charlottesville, VA, Michie, 1989
71. American Cyanamid Co v Frankson, 732 SW2d 648 (Tex Ct App 1987)
72. No ST81-151, Marion Cty Super Ct (OH March 1984)
73. No 29798, Suffolk Cty Super Ct (Mass 1984)
74. No 85-46EBB (D Conn 1986)
75. No 84-CV-06-3582, Franklin Cty Ct Comm (Columbus, OH August 1988)
76. No 48751, Montgomery Cty Cir Ct (MD October 20, 1980)
77. Bisbing SB, Smith JT: Tardive dyskinesia: a growing malpractice threat. Paper presented at the 18th annual meeting of the American Academy of Psychiatry and Law, Ottawa, Canada, October 1987; SB Bisbing, personal communication, October 1990
78. 653 F2d 836 (3d Cir 1981) (en banc), vacated and remanded mem, 458 U.S. 1119 (1982) on remand, 720 F2d 266 (3d Cir 1983) (en banc)
79. 727 F Supp 1346 (DC Idaho 1989)
80. 28 U.S.C. § 2401(b)
81. No 27536/82, New York Sup Ct (NY 1988)
82. No C-78-7201, Salt Lake City Cir Ct (UT December 1979)
83. 177 Ga App 487, 339 SE2d 764 (Ga App 1986)
84. Baker B: Expect a flood of tardive dyskinesia malpractice suits. Clinical Psychiatry News 12(1):3, 35, 1984; Tardive dyskinesia malpractice suits may be rising. Clinical Psychiatry News 15(12):13, 1987; Wettstein RM, Appelbaum P: Legal liability for tardive dyskinesia. Hosp Community Psychiatry 35:992–993, 1984
85. Kane JM, Woerner M, Weinhold P, et al: A prospective study of tardive dyskinesia development: preliminary results. J Clin Psychopharmacol 2:345–349, 1982
86. Gualtieri CT, Sprague RL: Preventing tardive dyskinesia and preventing tardive dyskinesia litigation. Psychopharmacol Bull 20:346–348, 1984

Chapter 11

Electroconvulsive Therapy and the Acutely Psychotic, Nonconsenting Patient

Mr. Brooks, a 55-year-old attorney, is hospitalized on the psychiatric ward of a general hospital after his wife found him attempting to hang himself in the attic. His law firm partnership was recently dissolved as a result of long-term disagreements between the partners. Mr. Brooks is convinced that he was cheated by his partners. He believes that they "stole" his clients after the dissolution of the law firm.

At the time of admission, Mr. Brooks is extremely depressed and agitated. Dr. Evans, his admitting psychiatrist, learns of a 30-pound weight loss during the past 2 months and constant pacing punctuated by increased bouts of physical violence toward his wife. He has been unable to sleep more than 2 to 3 hours for the past 2 weeks. Mr. Brooks is difficult to interview because of his agitation and suspicion that Dr. Evans is in collusion with his former partners. Dr. Evans makes a preliminary diagnosis of a major depressive episode with delusional features. He obtains permission from Mr. Brooks to talk to his wife. Dr. Evans discovers that his patient has had minor depressive episodes in the past and tends to be a suspicious person. Mr. Brooks has never suffered as severe a depression before nor exhibited any violence or persecutory ideas.

Dr. Evans wants to begin treatment with a tricyclic antidepressant, but Mr. Brooks flatly refuses. The patient's agitation increases dramatically, followed by several episodes of head banging, knocking over furniture, and pushing other patients. The patient is found by the staff looking for overhead pipes to hang himself. After concluding that his patient poses a serious threat of danger to himself, Dr. Evans places Mr. Brooks in restraints in a seclusion room. He is concerned that Mr. Brooks could physically exhaust himself and perhaps suffer a heart attack. A medical consultation is requested. The patient is found to have a mitral valve prolapse with enlargement of the left ventricle. Otherwise, he is in good physical condition. The cardiac findings are not considered to be a contraindication to electroconvulsive therapy (ECT).

Dr. Evans confers with a psychiatric consultant who recommends ECT. He

*familiarizes himself with a recently enacted state statute that contains the re-
quirements governing administration of ECT. The statute specifies that proxy
consent may be provided by a relative if the patient gives an incompetent acceptance or refusal of ECT after examination and recommendation of ECT by two
physicians. If proxy consent by relatives is withheld or not available, the determination of the patient's competency must be made by the court. Implied consent for emergency administration of ECT is expressly prohibited. Dr. Evans
also reviews the hospital's ECT policies.*

*At this point, ECT is considered to be the quickest and most effective inter-
vention both by Dr. Evans and the psychiatric consultant. They also agree that
immediate treatment is necessary. The anticipated benefits of ECT far outweigh
cardiac risks or other possible complications of this procedure. After explanation of the diagnosis, prognosis, risks, and benefits, Mr. Brooks becomes agitated and shouts, "You doctors are in a conspiracy with my partners and are
going to kill me anyway. So kill me with shock treatment and get it over with."*

*Dr. Evans concludes that his patient is incompetently consenting to treat-
ment based on his severe depression and delusional beliefs. Although very concerned, Mr. Brooks' wife is afraid to give permission for ECT because of her
husband's expressed views of the therapy as murder. She always has deferred
to her husband's wishes. Because Dr. Evans considers his patient's deteriorating condition to be an emergency, he determines to go forward with ECT.*

*Dr. Evans decides to obtain a court determination of competency to consent
to ECT as required by statute. Dr. Evans is very concerned that legal procedures to obtain consent might unduly delay critically needed treatment. Dr.
Evans petitions the court to determine Mr. Brooks' capacity to consent to ECT.
The next day, the court hears the case at 9 A.M. Mr. Brooks is brought to court in
restraints. He is in imminent danger of critically exhausting himself but cannot
be taken out of restraints because of an intense drive to injure himself. He
shouts and struggles during the hearing. Because of his psychotic state, the
court returns the patient to the hospital by 10 A.M. while it continues deliberations. The court determines that Mr. Brooks is incompetent to consent to ECT
and appoints a nonrelative guardian for the purpose of making health care decisions. The guardian finds it impossible to meet with Dr. Evans and the patient
until the next day at 11:00 A.M. The guardian does not want to provide consent
over the phone.*

*On evaluating his patient's condition on return to the hospital and finding
him nearly moribund, Dr. Evans determines that life-saving ECT must be given.
He is very worried that his patient might not live long enough for consent to be
obtained the next day. He considers emergency use of neuroleptics to gain time
but decides that drug therapy probably would be too little, too late. It also might
endanger Mr. Brooks's clinical condition. Dr. Evans initiates treatment with
the full knowledge that he is proceeding in violation of the statute. He feels he
would rather have a live patient than remain legally correct. After the first ECT*

treatment is given, Mr. Brooks becomes less agitated. When the guardian arrives the next day, he is informed that Mr. Brooks has received an initial ECT treatment. The guardian gives consent for ECT after a brief visit with the patient. Mr. Brooks is given eight ECT treatments and makes a dramatic recovery.

What are the recognized indications for ECT?

The American Psychiatric Association (APA) Task Force on ECT (1) makes specific nonbinding recommendations for the use and administration of ECT. The Task Force states that primary indications for ECT include major depression, mania, schizophrenia, and other functional psychoses of significant clinical severity when alternative forms of treatment are not appropriate or effective.

The APA guidelines may be used by the plaintiff to establish a prima facie case of negligence (2). Official guidelines, however, can never be a substitute for sound psychiatric judgment. A Massachusetts study on the provision of ECT indicates that the administration of ECT varies widely from guidelines published by the APA Task Force on ECT (3). Yet, malpractice suits in this area are rare.

Because of the emergency presented by the condition of his patient, Dr. Evans decided that ECT was the only reasonable, effective alternative. The selection of ECT by Dr. Evans was appropriate for a major depression with delusional features, especially because the patient flatly refused an earlier suggestion for drug therapy. Experienced clinicians know that ECT is one of the few lifesaving treatments available for certain psychiatric emergencies. Patients in catatonic furor, who may exhaust themselves to the point of death, have had their lives saved by ECT. Mr. Brooks' malignant depression impelled him to seek self-destruction every waking second, presenting a serious psychiatric emergency.

With the possible exception of an acute myocardial infarction, cardiac problems do not present a contraindication to ECT. In the clinical vignette, left ventricular enlargement secondary to mitral valve prolapse was not considered a contraindication to ECT. A risk-benefit analysis should be recorded in the patient's chart, including careful evaluation of any concurrent medical risks found on medical consultation. Although medical conditions may represent only relative rather than absolute risks to ECT treatment, medical consultation is recommended because the psychiatrist's skills at physical examinations and medical evaluation may have atrophied.

ECT may be far safer for elderly patients with delusional depression who are not able to tolerate antidepressants or antipsychotic medications. ECT still remains an extremely important treatment modality for carefully selected patients (4). As more depressed patients who are resistant to drug therapy are discovered, ECT has enjoyed a renaissance. Patients with delusional depressions or schizoaffective disorders; severely depressed, medically ill elderly persons; and patients who have not responded to antidepressant medication may be candidates for ECT. Moreover, ECT avoids the possibility of the development of tardive dyskinesia in those cases in which alternative treatment approaches would necessitate use of neuroleptics.

Some severely depressed patients who begin to improve may be able to garner enough energy to attempt suicide with their antidepressant medications. Such patients may be more safely treated with ECT. Too often, severely depressed patients who are resistant to drug therapy are denied ECT and remain at high risk for suicide.

The question of whether an anesthesiologist should be present to administer anesthesia during ECT is still controversial (5). Practices vary in different parts of the country and even within the same city. The APA Task Force on ECT recommends that local policies governing pre-ECT evaluations should include an anesthetic evaluation based upon the clinical needs of the patient (1). An anesthetic evaluation would consider anesthetic risks and recommendations about medications and anesthetic technique.

Whatever the merits of the arguments, the cost of a medical evaluation prior to ECT and the presence of an anesthesiologist may make the treatment unavailable to many elderly patients and persons from lower socioeconomic classes. Obviously, the cost of ECT should not be placed ahead of patients' clear need for this treatment. If ECT is attempted with a patient who is at high risk, the direct assistance of an anesthesiologist may be needed, at least for the first few treatments.

The National Institute of Mental Health (NIMH) convened a consensus conference on ECT (6). The Consensus Conference on ECT considered the scientific evidence and agreed to answer questions about the indications for ECT, risks, adverse effects, the effectiveness of ECT for specific mental disorders, and methods for the administration of ECT. The goal of the conference was to maximize benefits and minimize risks, and also to suggest directions for future research.

The conference concluded that ECT is the most controversial treatment in psychiatry. It is demonstrably effective for a narrow range of severe psychiatric disorders such as delusional and severe endogenous depression, manic disorders, and certain schizophrenic syndromes. The conference also acknowledged significant side effects, especially acute confusional states and persistent memory deficits for events during the months surrounding ECT treatment. The conference recommended that careful risk-benefit analysis be conducted by both physician and patient.

With the ascendance of managed care, pressure will be exerted to treat patients with the most effective treatments that produce the shortest hospital stays. Because ECT may be 90% effective for severe endogenous or delusional depressions, the temptation may exist to broaden the use of ECT for less clear indications—perhaps inappropriately.

When is ECT absolutely prohibited?

ECT must never be used for political reasons or for punishment. ECT should not be used to provide an electrical straitjacket for violent behavior. Relative medical contraindications exist in the presence of brain neoplasm because of the possibility of increased intracranial pressure during the induced seizure (7). State statutes and courts may bar ECT for those under age 12 or for individuals diagnosed as suffering from mental retardation (8). In *Wyatt v. Hardin* (9), the court prohibited ECT for anyone under age 18 or the use of any regressive, multiple, or depatterning ECT. For underfunded public institutions with inadequate facilities and inadequately trained personnel, no patient should receive ECT unless the minimum standards established by the APA Task Force on ECT are met (4).

What is the extent of ECT regulation by legislative and other regulatory bodies?

With the advent of the patient's rights movements in the 1960s and 1970s, ECT became a symbol of patient abuse and repression. In 1967, legislators in Utah passed statutes regulating ECT. By 1983, 26 states had passed ECT-regulating statutes, and at least 6 other states established agency regulations governing ECT (8). Winslade et al. (8) concluded that the *Wyatt v. Hardin* decision impeded physician decision making among the 15 most populous states where legal regulation of ECT was studied from 1981 to 1983.

Legislative and other regulatory decisions regarding the medical aspects of ECT include numerous indications and contraindications for its use. Provisions are made for consultation and review, medical procedures required before and during treatment, regulation of the frequency of treatment, and specific record-keeping requirements (8). Furthermore, the Joint Commission on Accreditation of Healthcare Organizations (JCAHO) considers ECT a special treatment procedure, requiring hospitals to have written informed-consent policies concerning the use of ECT and to obtain the written consent of patients (10). Violation of JCAHO and hospital policies governing psychiatric treatment can provide ammunition for the allegation of negligent treatment. The overregulation of ECT in public institutions, however, may create a situation in which poor patients may not have equal access to ECT when it is clinically indicated (11).

The APA Task Force on ECT recommends that informed consent should be obtained from the patient except when the patient's capacity to give consent is lacking (1). In the latter instance, local and state laws governing consent for treatment of patients lacking the capacity to consent should be followed.

Many judicial and legislative decisions regarding ECT consent procedures attempt to deal with the problem of how to manage the incompetent patient. Requirements range from informal hospital evaluations to formal court procedures. Thus competency determinations may be permitted by doctors, lawyers, or judges.

The APA Task Force on ECT recommends that specific information be provided to the patient (1) (see Table 11-1). The Task Force also recommends that a formal consent document be used that ensures the provision of at least a minimum amount of information to the patient. Sample ECT consent forms are contained in the Task Force report (1) and in Appendix 2 of this book.

The NIMH Consensus Conference on ECT (6) recommends repeating the consent procedure because of the relatively rapid therapeutic efficacy of ECT, the likelihood of enhanced judgmental capacities after initial treatment, the changing risk-benefit assessment for the patient if adverse effects increase with repeated treatments, and the fact that short-term memory deficits may erase the memory of the earlier consenting transaction. While the recommendation of a repeated consent procedure is consistent with the current legal doctrine of informed consent and laudably attempts to foster the patient's autonomy, clinically it may be impractical for many patients.

By producing confusion and memory loss, ECT may undermine the continuing consenting capacity of the patient. To persist with continued efforts to transact consent may be burdensome and bewildering to a patient who has an induced acute organic brain syndrome superimposed on a severe psychiatric illness. Moreover, what if the patient refuses further ECT once having given a competent consent? Should the patient's decision be immediately honored, especially in the presence of confusion, memory loss, and the original psychiatric illness? Should the psychiatrist suspend clinical judgment and turn the treatment decision over to the patient, who may be unable to make the necessary

---

TABLE 11–1. Recommended information to be provided to patients considered for ECT

1. Description of ECT procedures including:
   a. When, where, and by whom.
   b. Range of number of treatments.
   c. Brief overview of ECT technique.
2. Reason for recommendation of ECT, including reasonable treatment alternatives.
3. Therapeutic benefits may be transitory.
4. Likelihood and severity of risks associated with anesthesia, muscular relaxation, and seizure induction.
5. Consent for ECT implies consent to perform appropriate emergency interventions, if necessary.
6. Consent is voluntary and can be revoked at any time.
7. Questions about ECT may be asked at any time.
   a. Whom to contact.
8. Restrictions on patient behavior prior to, during, and following ECT.

Source. Adapted from American Psychiatric Association: *The Practice of Electroconvulsive Therapy: Recommendations for Treatment, Training, and Privileging* (Task Force Report), Washington, DC, American Psychiatric Association, 1990. Reprinted with permission.

decisions of an informed consumer? Can the patient's family provide proxy consent for the patient?

For informed-consent purposes, ECT bears certain similarities to surgery. There is induction by anesthesia, a period of unconsciousness, application of a treatment procedure for a serious illness, and a postprocedure period of recovery. ECT should be looked upon as a unitary procedure, even though a series of treatments are given. The surgeon does not stop after making the incision or exposing the diseased organ to awaken the patient to ask for additional consent. The analogy to surgery, while not perfect, may help keep the informed-consent issue for ECT in perspective. It does not make clinical sense to obtain a renewed consent for each ECT treatment unless some compelling clinical problem intervenes between treatments, such as a complication that significantly increases the risk of further ECT.

State statutes vary widely in the amount of information required to inform the patient. California and Illinois statutes demand more disclosure than most other states and parallel the earlier ECT Task Force recommendations. Both states require full disclosure of risks and benefits. Some states may not require that any specific information be provided, but only that the patient has a right to refuse ECT. Is the distinction between the right to refuse ECT and the requirement for informed consent a distinction without a difference? Is it easier to get around a patient's faint reluctance to receive ECT than to demonstrate that the patient has a sufficient understanding to provide consent? Some states may not allow ECT to be used like other medical procedures, even under life-threatening circumstances, unless there is full compliance with regulatory procedures (8). Thus, due-process requirements in some states obviate the implied consent that is usually presumed in genuine emergency situations, leading to unnecessary suffering or even death.

California (12) specifies that ECT cannot be administered to involuntary patients unless a variety of requirements are met: *1)* documentation in the medical record by the attending physician of the need for ECT; *2)* a committee of at least two other physicians to review the record and concur as to need for ECT; *3)* the written, informed consent of the patient; *4)* verification of the capacity of the patient to consent by the patient's attorney or court-appointed public defender; and *5)* a full-scale evidentiary hearing in court if the patient's capacity is in question. When a determination is made by the court that the patient is not competent to consent, the statute permits ECT treatment on consent of a responsible relative, guardian, or conservator.

The Food and Drug Administration (FDA) exerts control over ECT through its ability to regulate medical devices. While ECT is currently classified in the Class III category (high-risk devices), the FDA is considering reclassifying ECT devices in Class II (requires submission of a premarket approval application to FDA listing acceptable safety and performance standards). The FDA has proposed reclassification of ECT only for the treatment of major depression with melancholia (13). The APA maintains that sufficient information is available to classify ECT devices in Class II (11).

Which major court decisions have affected the use of ECT?

In *Wyatt v. Hardin* (9), a federal court forbade certain uses of ECT and established 14 rules to severely restrict its use.

The first judicial standard in the country for determining competence of a patient to consent to or refuse ECT was enunciated by a California appellate court (14). The court interpreted the provisions of the recently enacted California statute that provides detailed procedural safeguards for the administration of ECT on voluntary or involuntary patients. The court ruled that before an order can declare that a patient lacks the capacity to consent to or refuse ECT, "clear and convincing evidence" must be presented to the court.

In *Lillian F. v. Superior Court,* the conservator claimed that the standard of proof needed to prove the patient's incapacity in court was "proof by a preponderance of the evidence," which is the standard of proof for most civil cases. The patient claimed that the conservator was required to prove the patient's incapacity "beyond a reasonable doubt," which is the standard in criminal cases. The court concluded that the rights at issue were more fundamental than those in a typical civil proceeding. Unlike criminal proceedings, however, the state was interested in assuring appropriate treatment of the patient. The court opined: "To use the much more difficult standard of beyond a reasonable doubt in such a hearing [as the patient sought] would frustrate the purpose of the [ECT statute] and effectively condemn a gravely disabled person to life in a mental institution."

In *Price v. Sheppard* (15), a civilly committed minor patient was given ECT without the consent of the minor's guardian. The court held that if a patient is incompetent to give or refuse consent or if the responsible guardian refuses consent, an order must be obtained from the court authorizing the prescribed treatment before more intrusive forms of treatment can be implemented. Furthermore, a guardian *ad litem* shall be appointed to represent the interests of the patient, and in an adversary proceeding the court shall determine the necessity and reasonableness of the prescribed treatment.

Although the patient in *Price* was a minor, the court's reasoning, which limits the authority of the state to impose ECT without either judicial authorization or the guardian's consent, applies equally to adult patients (16). Unless otherwise specified to the contrary by judicial decision or statute, the prescription of ECT for a civilly committed patient refusing treatment should be authorized by court order. *Price v. Sheppard* (15) is one of a limited number of appellate decisions that recognize a constitutional limitation of the use of ECT. Whether the constitutional holding of the *Price* court will achieve general acceptance is still in doubt (16).

Finally, in *In re Matter of Alleged Mental Illness of Kinzer* (17), a Minnesota court extended protections provided for involuntarily hospitalized mental patients by holding that an order authorizing ECT must be time-limited. That is, the order cannot authorize future ECT.

Must psychiatrists strictly follow the legal regulations governing the administration of ECT, even when clinical judgment runs contrary to the letter of the law?

In the vignette, Dr. Evans found himself confronted by a serious medicolegal dilemma. The patient's wife refused to provide a proxy consent for ECT. Thus, by statute, the court had to decide the competency of Mr. Brooks to consent to ECT. In addition, Dr. Evans was faced with an acutely suicidal patient who constituted a serious danger to himself, requiring immediate treatment. Dr. Evans perceived a direct conflict between, on the one hand, his duty to treat and, on the other, a statute that did not provide for implied consent for the use of ECT in emergency situations. He determined that the immediate welfare of his patient had to take precedence over a blind adherence to the letter of the law. He was fully aware that legal consequences might ensue but opted to take that chance and treat his patient.

The author does not recommend that psychiatrists violate the law in providing treatment to patients. For the most part, psychiatrists are not usually faced with head-on conflicts with the law. As Appelbaum (18) aptly states: "It is the exceptional legal problem in psychiatric treatment that cannot be most successfully addressed by the application of common sense and good clinical care, in the context of a clear knowledge of relevant legal requirements." The case in the vignette, however, is an example of clear conflict between professional duty and the law. What is the best way to proceed?

Dr. Evans could have consulted with an attorney familiar with mental health law. In addition, careful documentation of the reasons for proceeding with ECT on an emergency basis would be crucial. Rarely will psychiatrists find themselves in conflict with the law when representing the best treatment interests of their patients. The clinician may also choose to seize this opportunity to challenge the legal system to reexamine current laws that may be interfering with good clinical practices. *The Principles of Medical Ethics With Annotations Especially Applicable to Psychiatry* (19) states: "A physician shall respect the law and also recognize a responsibility to seek changes in those requirements which are contrary to the best interests of the patient" (Section 3).

In the above situation, administering emergency ECT for sound clinical reasons and in the best interests of the patient provided a strong measure of protection against liability. Mr. Brooks could allege a lack of informed consent for the initiation of ECT. The state statute could be used as evidence for a prima facie case against Dr. Evans. In that event, Dr. Evans would be required to contradict and overcome evidence presented by the plaintiff. A negligence suit would be unlikely because of a lack of damages. An intentional tort for battery could be brought. Malpractice insurance usually does not cover intentional torts. In a patient emergency, psychiatrists must remember that they are physicians first, not litigants, and proceed accordingly.

Given the same clinical facts in the vignette, some psychiatrists might regard treating an incompetent patient with ECT in disregard of a statutory consent requirement to be morally, professionally, and legally wrong. Instead, additional efforts could be made at gaining Mrs. Brooks's proxy consent or waiting in order to obtain a judicial determination of consent. In the meantime, Mr. Brooks could be restrained in a quiet room with constant one-on-one supervision. Neuroleptic medications could be given to quiet the patient and prevent exhaustion. Potential serious cardiac side effects would need to be closely monitored. In an emergency, implied consent for use of neuroleptic treatment usually exists.

Other psychiatrists might decide not to attempt to treat Mr. Brooks in the absence of a proxy consent from the family. While observing the precautions of close observation and control of the patient, the psychiatrist could transfer the patient to another psychiatrist willing to care for the patient or seek involuntary hospitalization. This view implies that ECT given in the face of family opposition or lack of support is antitherapeutic. Risk-management concerns also might dictate that no treatment be given under circumstances that could invite liability. Some psychiatrists do not wish to expose themselves to the anxieties of potential or actual litigation that could disrupt their personal and professional lives for years to come.

No matter what decision is made, it should be carefully thought out and documented. Consultation should be sought with other psychiatrists. Legal consultation should not be ignored when dealing with difficult medicolegal dilemmas. Dr. Evans pursued one particular treatment course in dealing with a direct clinical-legal conflict. Because there are few straight roads in psychiatric treatment and management, a number of avenues of approach exist that are consistent with good clinical practice.

What malpractice allegations have been made against psychiatrists using ECT?

ECT is no longer a frequent source of malpractice claims against psychiatrists. Less than 1% of malpractice claims filed against psychiatrists involve ECT (20).

Five major areas of liability have been litigated in the courts. The negligent administration of premedication such as sedatives or muscle relaxants is one major area of litigation. A Florida court (21) found a psychiatrist negligent in not using a muscle relaxant before administering ECT. The APA Task Force on

ECT recommends administration of a muscle relaxant. In *Pettis v. State* (22), the physicians were not found negligent for failing to use succinylcholine during the course of ECT. The physicians, however, were found negligent for administering ECT after the patient had already suffered fractured vertebrae during the first treatment.

A second area of liability is the administration of ECT without conducting an adequate pretreatment examination (23). Third, physicians have been held liable when their negligent administration of ECT causes a patient to suffer fractures or other injuries. The psychiatrist should respond diligently with adequate examinations and tests to any complaints of pain or injury by the ECT patient. The fourth major area of litigation is the significant number of lawsuits that have been brought for lack of post-ECT supervision of the patient. Patients who have been confused and disoriented have fallen down stairs, fallen out of bed, or injured themselves in other ways. The fifth major area of liability involves failure to obtain competent informed consent for ECT.

The ECT consent form is often a derivative of the surgical consent form because ECT patients undergo a temporary period of unconsciousness and amnesia (24). Documenting that the patient was provided with and understood written information describing post-ECT memory loss and confusion is critical. Although no conclusive scientific evidence exists that permanent memory loss results from ECT, malpractice cases have been brought alleging such an outcome (25).

Patients who do not consent to ECT or give an incompetent consent may sue for battery or for violation of their civil rights without proving physician injury resulting from ECT (11). Patients who claim a lack of informed consent must prove that ECT caused an injury and that they would have refused ECT if warned in advance of the risk of the injury that occurred.

In *Mitchell v. Robinson* (26), the defendant-physician testified that because of the patient's mental and emotional state, the informed consent provided at a conference could not be remembered years later. Again, the need for contemporaneous documentation of consent to ECT is essential.

As previously discussed, implied consent for ECT in emergency situations may not exist in all jurisdictions. Also, exercising therapeutic privilege to withhold explanations that might alarm the patient, causing refusal of treatment or increasing the risks of treatment, may not apply to the ECT patient. If challenged, "good faith" consents by family members may be legally insufficient. Many psychiatrists continue to rely on the proxy consent of relatives for ECT when confronted with the patient's incapacity to consent. Unless case law or statutory provisions permit proxy consent for ECT, it may be necessary to obtain the written consent of a court-appointed substitute decision-maker.

California (27) and Massachusetts (28) require consent for ECT by a guardian as opposed to a relative. Consent is required for adult patients who have not already been involuntarily hospitalized. Court decisions and legislative regulation in many states require actual adjudication of the patient's capacity to consent for ECT.

Consent can be withdrawn up until the moment of injection of the anesthetic (29). False assurances of cure and safety must not be made (30). Unrealistic promises may lead to a breach-of-contract action. In a life-threatening emergency, consent may not be required at all in some jurisdictions.

The doctrine of *res ipsa loquitur* ("the thing speaks for itself"), which creates a presumption of negligence, does not apply to injuries resulting from ECT (31). Fractures, cardiac arrests, or other injuries alone will not result in liability because these results may occur during ECT without imputing negligence (24, 30). Liability will depend on the plaintiff's being able to show that standard practices in the administration of ECT were not followed. On the other hand, in *Dohmann v. Richard* (32), the court stated that ECT is not considered to be within the category of nondangerous and ordinary medical treatment. The court held that ECT does not fall within the line of cases that require injured persons to mitigate their damages (i.e., those cases in which the patient has a duty to use ordinary care to minimize damages). Customarily, the plaintiff is not allowed to let the meter run indefinitely on the defendant.

In *Woods v. Brumlop* (33), the patient was told that no harm could result from ECT treatments. At trial, the psychiatrist was found negligent for not informing the patient about the risks of ECT. The patient sustained a fracture. The appeals court in *Brumlop* reversed the judgment on an evidentiary rule.

Can psychiatrists be sued for not administering ECT?

Psychiatrists can be sued for acts of omission that cause harm to patients and that fall below the standard of care. For some psychiatric patients, ECT is the only effective treatment. This is particularly true when ECT has been an effective treatment for the patient in the past for a similar condition and other treatments have failed.

In *Gowan v. United States* (34), the guardian of a patient who attempted suicide 5 days after discharge from a hospital alleged that the defendants failed to use ECT. The court held that failure to require ECT was not malpractice because it was not used previously and was not available at the hospital.

To maintain clinical perspective, psychiatrists should consider the risk of *not* using ECT when it is clearly indicated for a patient and when other appropriate interventions have been tried (35).

How have sociopolitical pressures on legislatures and courts influenced the availability of ECT?

The courts and legislatures are becoming the decision-makers concerning the very existence of ECT, particularly in response to public concerns about the safety of this procedure. Psychiatrists are no longer in full control of a treatment proven to be highly effective for carefully selected patients. Taub (11) concludes that ECT may be overregulated because the law has not kept pace with advances in knowledge and procedures concerning ECT. Unfortunately, some patients who might benefit from ECT may be deprived of an effective and safe treatment.

One such effort to prohibit ECT took the form of a referendum by the city of Berkeley, California. Berkeley made the administration of ECT a criminal offense punishable by a fine of up to $500 and 6 months in jail (36). This regulation was subsequently held to be unconstitutional. The city of Berkeley appealed to the California Court of Appeals, which held that the administration of ECT is not within the jurisdiction of a municipality. The appellate decision clarified the limits of public authority in limiting medical treatments (37). The city council voted to take the case to the California Supreme Court. The California Supreme Court declined to hear the appeal, thus invalidating the city's law. The Berkeley City Council then voted to cease any further attempts at banning ECT. What is not clear is whether some other more traditional form of public action, such as an ordinance or a statute enacted by an elected representative banning ECT, might have been upheld.

In legal developments to counter this trend, the Association for Convulsive Therapy (ACT) filed a lawsuit in the Superior Court of California attempting to have the state's law governing ECT declared unconstitutional (38). The suit foundered when the litigants ran out of money.

In Vermont, an anti-ECT bill failed, but the proponents vow to continue the fight (39).

In the latest California initiative against the use of ECT, the San Francisco Board of Supervisors passed a resolution repudiating ECT and urging that its use be restricted (40). The resolution has no legal force. New legislation is currently being proposed in the California General Assembly to further restrict ECT. Involuntary ECT would be greatly curtailed. ECT for minors under 16 years of age would be prohibited. Before treatment, it would be required that patients be informed orally and in writing that they have the right to speak with a patient rights advocate at any time.

ECT is already severely limited legislatively in California. In 1974, California enacted the strictest ECT statute to date (41). A recent set of regulations governing ECT procedures was appended to the so-called 1974 ECT statute so that it could be made more specific. The regulations limit ECT treatment to 15 times in a 30-day period. The maximum number of treatments per year is 30. A problem immediately arises, however, because any seizure counts as a treatment. Usually, the minimum duration required for effective therapy is a grand mal seizure of 25 seconds. Seizures of shorter duration have questionable therapeutic benefit. The law is so restrictive that ECT is facing extinction in northern California, and a significant decline in its use has taken place in the southern part of the state.

Should the level of competency to give a valid consent for ECT be higher than that required for administration of neuroleptic medication?

An argument can be made that a heightened level of competency is required to consent to ECT because an electrical current is passed through the brain, causing temporary memory loss, confusion, and disorientation. Thus, ECT is considered by many psychiatrists to be both physically and psychologically more invasive than neuroleptic medication. Currently, there is no evidence to support allegations that ECT produces brain damage (42). Because the mind is altered, an interference with First Amendment rights of freedom of expression and privacy, particularly to form one's own thoughts, has been alleged (43). A similar argument has been made against the use of neuroleptics, but somewhat less stridently. These concerns also are reflected in the APA Task Force on ECT recommendation that adequate information be provided patients before administration of ECT (1). The previous Task Force guidelines have been adopted by statute in some states. Current Task Force guidelines will likely be incorporated into new statutes as well.

The mental capacity of the patient to understand the rather complicated information must be reasonably high. For instance, the NIMH Consensus Conference on ECT (6) recognizes the presence of "acute confusional states and persistent memory deficits for events during the months surrounding the ECT treatment." When psychiatrists inform patients of this side effect, they may wish to explain in nontechnical language certain aspects of ECT administration that may affect memory. For example, the electrical current may be given in the form of the traditional sine wave or by brief pulse. With the latter, there is less confusion and memory loss, but the treatment may not be as effective (44). Similarly, electrodes may be applied bilaterally or unilaterally to the nondominant hemisphere. Less confusion and memory loss may be anticipated with unilateral application of ECT, but the treatment may not be as effective as bilateral application (45). Initial bilateral electrode placement usually is recommended for very severely ill patients, delusionally depressed patients, patients with severe inanition, and patients in whom no benefit has occurred after five to seven treatments with unilateral placements (46). ECT monitored by electroencephalography to assure the presence of an adequate seizure produced equivalent results in both unilateral and bilateral electrode placements (47). No apparent memory loss could be documented in nondominant unilateral ECT.

These considerations and the higher standard of informing for ECT patients recommended by the APA Task Force on ECT appear to require a higher level of competency to understand such information. Yet the patient who is the most appropriate candidate for ECT is the most severely ill and the least likely to be able to provide competent consent. Thus, judicial determinations of capacity to consent with the appointment of a guardian to provide consent, as well as statutory provisions for proxy consent of relatives in some jurisdictions, are more common with this class of patients (48).

In the clinical vignette, Dr. Evans very successfully treated a severely mentally ill patient who required emergency psychiatric intervention. Along the way, he may have violated state statutes governing the administration of ECT. The patient's consent for ECT appeared to be incompetent, even though it was congruent with Dr. Evans' treatment plan. Under these circumstances, patients who experience poor results or injuries may bring suit. Outright violation of regulations governing administration of ECT may help establish a prima facie case against the psychiatrist.

How has the term intrusiveness been applied to psychiatric treatments by the courts? How helpful have the proposed criteria for intrusiveness been to the psychiatric clinician in selecting treatments like ECT?

Court decisions and legal commentators have distinguished between intrusive and nonintrusive treatments. The intrusive therapies have been subject to special regulation and control. Violation of First Amendment rights have been raised when treatments allegedly interfere with freedom of expression, such as the ability to hold or formulate one's own ideas (43). According to Reisner (16), intrusiveness in psychiatry concerns physical interference with the patient in order to alter thought or behavior processes. To determine the intrusiveness of psychiatric treatments, Shapiro (49) proposes six criteria. Both physical and psychological invasion are part of the treatment:

● The extent to which the effects of the therapy on mentation are reversible
● The extent to which the resulting psychic state is "foreign," "abnormal," or "unnatural" for the person, rather than simply a restoration of his or her prior psychic state (closely related to "magnitude" or "intensity" of the change)
● The rapidity with which the effects occur
● The scope of the change in the total "ecology" of the mind's functions
● The extent to which one can resist acting in ways impelled by the psychic effects of therapy
● The duration of change

The problem with this formulation is that it is one-sided. If mental illness is substituted for therapy, then the intrusiveness of the mental disorder can also be evaluated by the same criteria. To what extent is the mental illness reversible? Is it a foreign, abnormal, or unnatural state for the person in question? With what rapidity did the mental disorder occur? What is the effect of the mental disorder on the patient's total functioning? What is the extent to which the patient can resist the influence of the mental disorder on thinking and behavior? What is the duration of the mental illness?

Applying these criteria to psychiatric treatments without also considering the intrusive, damaging aspects of a mental disorder blinks at reality. No reasonable risk-benefit calculus concerning treatment interventions can take place if only the risks of treatment are considered. Risk-driven treatment decisions do not properly serve patients, because the severity of the patient's illness and the benefits of the proposed treatment are not given equal emphasis. Such decisions often lead to the provision of substandard care and possible malpractice litigation. Treatment invasiveness and efficacy may overlap. Implementing Shapiro's criteria of intrusiveness (see above) could deprive severely ill patients who are in need of treatments such as ECT.

For example, which treatment is more intrusive for a 75-year-old man with congestive heart failure suffering from a major depressive disorder—a benzodiazepine with antidepressant effects, a tricyclic antidepressant, or ECT? Applying Shapiro's six criteria, the effects of ECT on "mentation" are generally reversible and less likely to lead to a prolonged unnatural psychic state compared with the confusion and drowsiness produced in elderly persons by benzodiazepines or tricyclic antidepressant medications. Tricyclic antidepressants also can produce serious cardiac complications in elderly persons with heart disease. ECT alone is more likely to have a circumscribed effect on mental functioning by producing a more rapid remission of depressive symptoms and causing fewer serious mental and general physical side effects. If this analysis is correct, then ECT is likely to be a less intrusive treatment than medications for this elderly depressed patient.

The concept of the least-restrictive alternative has been applied largely to the issue of outpatient versus inpatient status. An increasing number of states, however, have applied the least-restrictive alternative to treatment as well (50). As the above clinical example demonstrates, the treatment needs of patients can be so different that the least-restrictive alternative does not readily apply itself to the treatment needs of individual patients and may not constitute good medical practice. The clinician is more concerned with the most therapeutic alternative. The long-established dictum in medical practice of *primum non nocere*—first do no harm—contains the principle of using the least drastic means to achieve a therapeutic result.

Legal formulations of intrusiveness often are not helpful to the clinician in making reasonable decisions about the selection of psychiatric treatments. Legal scholars do not treat patients. The absence of clinical knowledge and experience leads to seriously flawed conclusions that may adversely affect the health care needs of patients. Language such as "the scope of the change in the total ecology of the mind's functions" is too vague and metaphysical to be of value to the clinician.

The most invasive of all psychiatric treatments is psychosurgery. Psychosurgery is rarely used at present and has become clouded by ethical and legal issues. Although cingulotomies are still being performed in some medical centers on suicidal patients suffering from intractable obsessive-compulsive disorder (51), nevertheless, the clinical indications for this procedure remain vague and the procedure is rarely recommended today. State legislation has placed significant restrictions on the use of psychosurgery (52). In addition, courts have intervened to set controls on the use of this procedure (9, 42). In 1974, the United States Congress established a National Commission for the Protection of Human Subjects of Biomedical and Behavioral Research (Public Law 93-384). The commission investigated the use of psychosurgery from 1968 through 1972 and made recommendations to Congress. The commission recommended the establishment of a national psychosurgery advisory board to oversee the preoperative and postoperative clinical data on patients undergoing psychosurgery. The commission was also intended to ensure a valid informed consent, determine the appropriateness of patients selected for psychosurgery, and enforce specific procedural recommendations for minors, prisoners, involuntarily hospitalized patients, and patients with appointed legal guardians.

Compared to ECT, how clinically invasive are other psychiatric treatments?

Although some legal commentators have focused exclusively on the intrusiveness of physical or organic psychiatric treatments, the potential for unwanted or unintended invasion into the sanctity of the individual's intrapsychic life remains quite high with the psychological therapies. The psychiatric interview itself, particularly in the forensic context, creates the possibility of self-incrimination when the individual divulges to the mental health professional information that would not be revealed anywhere else.

Nonpsychodynamic therapies that do not attempt to plumb the patient's unconscious are probably the least intrusive. Behavioral, relaxation, and supportive therapies contain the lowest potential for intrusion. Good supportive psychotherapy, however, requires a thorough psychodynamic understanding of the patient. Therapies that use manipulation, suggestion, and abreaction can be highly intrusive. The primary use of clarification as the method of choice in Rogerian therapy appears to render this treatment one of the least intrusive psychotherapeutic modalities.

The psychodynamic therapies, particularly psychoanalytic therapy, appear to possess the highest potential for unwanted or unintended intrusion into the patient's unconscious mental life. The therapist is allowed to enter the internal mental world of the patient at the deepest levels. Mishandling of transference and countertransference and overzealous interpretation can overwhelm the patient's defenses. The psychodynamic therapies are designed to be "intrusive" in a controlled fashion. Unwanted or unintended psychic intrusion can be markedly reduced when the therapist works directly with the patient's resistances and other defenses. Furthermore, respect for patients' defenses by therapists makes psychodynamic therapies the least coercive. On the other hand, exploitation of patients' transferences can be exceedingly coercive as well as intrusive. Unbridled therapeutic ambition is the handmaiden of psychic intrusion. In some ways, the invasive potential of physical therapies such as drugs and ECT is more circumscribed than that of certain psychological therapies.

References

1. American Psychiatric Association: The Practice of Electroconvulsive Therapy: Recommendations for Treatment, Training, and Privileging (Task Force Report). Washington, DC, American Psychiatric Press, 1990
2. Stone v Proctor, 259 NC 633, 131 SE2d 297 (1963)
3. Benedict AR, Saks MJ: The regulation of professional behavior: electroconvulsive therapy in Massachusetts. Journal of Psychiatry and Law 15:247–275, 1987
4. Fink M: ECT: for whom is its use justified? J Clin Psychopharmacol 4:303–304, 1984
5. Pearlman T, Loper M, Tillery L: Should psychiatrists administer anesthesia for ECT? Am J Psychiatry 147:1553–1556, 1990
6. National Institute of Mental Health Consensus Conference on ECT: Electroconvulsive therapy. JAMA 254:2103–2108, 1985
7. Weiner RD: Electroconvulsive therapy, in Comprehensive Textbook of Psychiatry V, Vol 2. Edited by Kaplan HI, Sadock BJ. Baltimore, MD, Williams & Wilkins, 1989, pp 1670–1678; see p 1677
8. Winslade WJ, Liston EH, Ross JW, et al: Medical, judicial, and statutory regulation of ECT in the United States. Am J Psychiatry 141:1349–1355, 1984
9. Wyatt v Hardin, No 3195-N, 1MDLR 55 (MD Ala Feb 28, 1975, modified July 1, 1975)
10. Joint Commission on Accreditation of Healthcare Organizations: Consolidated Standards Manual. Chicago, IL, Joint Commission on Accreditation of Healthcare Organizations, 1988, p 72
11. Taub S: Electroconvulsive therapy, malpractice, and informed consent. Journal of Psychiatry and Law 15:7–54, 1987
12. CAL WELF & INST CODE § 5326.7 (West 1984)
13. Limited reclassification of ECT devices proposed. Psychiatric Times 8(1):21, 1991
14. Lillian F v Superior Court (Santa Clara Valley Medical Center), 160 Cal App 3d 314, 206 Cal Rptr 603 (1984)
15. 307 Minn 250, 239 NW2d 905 (1976)
16. Reisner R: Law and the Mental Health System. St Paul, MN, West Publishing, 1985, pp 460–461
17. 375 NW2d 526 (Minn Ct App 1985)
18. Appelbaum PS: Tarasoff and the clinician: problems in fulfilling the duty to protect. Am J Psychiatry 142:425–429, 1985; see p 429
19. American Psychiatric Association: The Principles of Medical Ethics With Annotations Especially Applicable to Psychiatry. Washington, DC, American Psychiatric Association, 1989

20. Slawson PF: The clinical dimension of psychiatric malpractice. Psychiatric Annals 14:358–363, 1984
21. McDonald v Moore, 323 So 2d 635 (Fla Dist Ct App 1975)
22. 336 So 2d 521 (La Ct App 1976), rev'd on other grounds, 339 So 2d 855 (La 1976)
23. Collins v Hand, 431 Pa 378, 246 A2d 398 (1968)
24. Lebensohn ZM: Defensive psychiatry, or how to treat the mentally ill without being a lawyer, in Law and the Mental Health Professions. Edited by Barton WE, Sanborn LJ. New York, International Universities Press, 1978, pp 19–46
25. Rice v Nardini, Ca 703-4, Docket No 78N-1103 (DC 1976)
26. 334 SW2d 11 (Mo 1960), overruled Aiken v Clary, 395 SW2d 668 (Mo 1965)
27. CAL WELF & INST CODE § 5326.7 (West 1984)
28. 104 CMR § 3.09(2) (1986)
29. Halleck SL: Law in the Practice of Psychiatry. New York, Plenum, 1980, p 99
30. Johnston v Rodis, 151 F Supp 345 (D DC 1957), reversed on other grounds, 251 F2d 917 (DC Cir 1958)
31. Slovenko R: Psychiatry and Law. Boston, MA, Little, Brown, 1973, pp 409–410
32. 282 So 2d 789 (La Ct App 1973)
33. 71 NM 221, 377 P2d 520, (1962), overruled, Gerety v Demers, 92 NM 396, 589 P2d 180 (1978)
34. 601 F Supp 1297 (D Or 1985)
35. Simon RI, Sadoff RL: Psychiatric Malpractice: Cases and Comments for Clinicians. Washington, DC, American Psychiatric Press, 1992
36. MDLR 6:366, 1982
37. Freishtat HW: Electroconvulsive therapy: no ban in Berkeley. J Clin Psychopharmacol 5:52–53, 1985
38. Group files lawsuit to protect ECT in California. Clinical Psychiatry News 15(7):8, 1987
39. Vermont anti-ECT bill fails; proponents vow fight. Clinical Psychiatry News 13(5):8, 1985
40. San Francisco adopts resolution to stop use of ECT. Psychiatric News 26(March 1):1, 4, 1991
41. CAL WELF & INST CODE §§ 5000–5404.1 (West 1984)
42. Tenebaum J: ECT regulation reconsidered. MDLR 148:151, 1983
43. Kaimowitz v Department of Mental Health for the State of Michigan, Civil Action No 73-19434-AW (Wayne Cty Cir Ct 1973)
44. Squire LR, Zouzounis JA: ECT and memory: brief pulse versus sine wave. Am J Psychiatry 143:596–601, 1986
45. Sackeim HA, Decina P, Kanzler M, et al: Effects of electrode placement on the efficacy of titrated, low-dose ECT. Am J Psychiatry 144:1449–1455, 1987
46. Abrams R, Taylor MA, Faber R, et al: Bilateral versus unilateral ECT: efficacy in melancholia. Am J Psychiatry 140:463–465, 1983
47. Horne RL, Pettinati HM, Sugerman AA, et al: Comparing bilateral to unilateral electroconvulsive therapy in a randomized study with EEG monitoring. Arch Gen Psychiatry 42:1087–1092, 1985
48. Winslade WJ: Electroconvulsive therapy: legal considerations and ethical concerns, in American Psychiatric Press Review of Psychiatry, Vol 7. Edited by Frances AJ, Hales RE. Washington, DC, American Psychiatric Press, 1988, pp 513–525

49. Shapiro MH: Legislating the control of behavior control: autonomy and the coercive use of organic therapies. Southern California Law Review 47:237, 256, 1974, n 51
50. Brakel SJ, Parry J, Weiner BA: The Mentally Disabled and the Law. Chicago, IL, American Bar Foundation, 1985, pp 456–457
51. Jenike MA, Baer L, Ballantine T: Cingulotomy for refractory obsessive-compulsive disorder: a long-term follow-up of 33 patients. Arch Gen Psychiatry 48:548–555, 1991
52. R Slovenko, personal communication, May 1985

Section IV:

Violent Patients

Chapter 12

Clinical Risk Management of the Suicidal Patient

Mr. Walters, a 33-year-old accountant, has been in twice-a-week psycho-therapy for recurrent depression for the past 6 months with Dr. Williams, a psychiatrist. Dr. Williams makes the diagnosis of dysthymic disorder. No anti-depressant medication is prescribed because of an absence of vegetative signs of depression. Mr. Walters has had suicidal ideation associated with previous depressions, but only once did he make a "suicidal gesture" by taking 10 diaz-epam tablets. The patient also suffers from Crohn's disease, which has worsened during the past 3 months. A paternal grandfather committed suicide. An uncle on his mother's side was hospitalized for recurrent depressions. His sister, who is 3 years younger, has an alcohol abuse problem.

Although Mr. Walters is having difficulties getting along with associates at his accounting firm, Dr. Williams determines that the primary precipitant of his depression involves marital problems. The patient moves out of his home and into an apartment just before entering treatment. Although no legal papers are signed, he and his wife discuss a trial separation. She wants to have children, whereas he has become interested in another woman. Two weeks prior to hos-pitalization, the relationship with the other woman ends quite suddenly. Mr. Walters' depression worsens. He is preoccupied with obtaining a gun to end his life. His ability to work falls off dramatically. He has great difficulty sleeping past 2 A.M. He loses 10 pounds. Overcome with feelings of despair and worth-lessness, Mr. Walters voluntarily enters the psychiatric service of a general hospital on the recommendation of Dr. Williams and the strong support of his wife.

Immediately upon Mr. Walters' admission at 1 A.M., Dr. Williams is called by the psychiatric nurse on duty. His last office appointment with Mr. Walters was 3 days prior to admission. He orders oxazepam, 10 mg, to induce sleep and advises the nurse to observe the patient at her discretion, depending on his clin-ical condition. After his office hours conclude at 5 P.M. the next day, Dr. Williams sees Mr. Walters at the hospital. He speaks with the staff concerning the patient's history. Mr. Walters states that his suicidal ideation has "dimin-

ished." Accordingly, Dr. Williams does not order any direct supervision of the patient. Instead, he prescribes a program of daily group therapy run by the third-year psychiatric resident and supervised by Dr. Williams, who is the attending psychiatrist. In addition, the psychiatrist writes in the admission note that he will provide the patient with daily, individual psychotherapy. He observes in his note that the patient appears to be only mildly depressed but attributes the decrease in intensity of suicidal ideation to the relief of being hospitalized. Dr. Williams makes an admission diagnosis of major depressive episode. He orders doxepin, 150 mg, to be given at bedtime because of the patient's poor appetite and the continuing sleep disturbance.

Because of the pressure of his office schedule, Dr. Williams is not able to see his patient daily. Initially, he comes in on Monday, Wednesday, and Friday for 45-minute sessions. Later, Dr. Williams cuts back the 45-minute sessions to 20 minutes. He decides to rely on the reports of the resident conducting the group therapy and on the nursing staff. The patient is not able to use the full sessions productively, and much time during the sessions is spent in silence. In a progress note, Dr. Williams records that Mr. Walters specifically requests the maintenance of strict confidentiality, and that this includes not disclosing any information to his wife.

Mr. Walters appears to improve rapidly from his depression, although he continues to keep to himself. He refuses to take any more medication. A psychiatric technician on the night shift who was previously acquainted with Mr. Walters writes in the nursing notes that the patient cryptically alludes to having purchased a gun recently. On further questioning by the technician, the patient is unwilling to discuss the matter. Dr. Williams and the resident are not in the habit of consistently reading the nurses' notes. They do not notice this particular entry. Somehow, this incident is not verbally communicated to Dr. Williams by the nursing staff. The resident suggests more privileges and responsibility for the patient, who appears to be considerably less depressed.

On the 10th day of hospitalization, Mr. Walters requests a brief pass to go home to pick up some reading materials. The nursing staff express some concern to Dr. Williams about the appropriateness of such a pass. Mr. Walters has not developed any relationships with the staff or other patients during his hospital stay. Dr. Williams and the staff agree that his increased interest in reading, which is the patient's main activity on the ward, is a positive sign. Dr. Williams sees Mr. Walters for 20 minutes. He makes a note that the patient "now appears ready to have a pass" but does not ask him about suicide intent. He also notes that the "patient appears markedly improved with no overt signs of depression. The patient smiles frequently and appropriately." A 6-hour pass is granted to Mr. Walters, who goes directly home and kills himself with a shotgun he recently purchased. Six months later, his wife brings a malpractice suit against Dr. Williams alleging negligent treatment and management of her deceased husband.

Did Dr. Williams exercise reasonable care in the evaluation and management of the patient's suicide risk?

Whether or not Dr. Williams deviated from a reasonable standard of care in his treatment of Mr. Walters will be determined in a court of law, after hearing the testimony of experts for both the defendant and plaintiff. The clinician who carefully documents his or her thinking processes during the care of the patient will be in a better position to neutralize any after-the-fact second-guessing by the plaintiff's expert. The plaintiff's expert might make the following criticisms of Dr. Williams' care, although the points are not necessarily valid and may reflect the emphasis of the plaintiff's expert:

1. Dr. Williams admitted his patient as a psychiatric emergency. Failing to attend to the patient until 16 hours after admission was substandard psychiatric care.
2. He failed to place the patient on suicide precautions or order adequate supervision and frequent checks of his patient both at the time of admission and after the initial hospital examination. He inappropriately left the care and supervision of a suicidal patient to the discretion of the nursing staff.
3. He violated his own treatment recommendation of daily individual psychotherapy without adequate explanation.
4. The three patient visits a week were insufficient because of the emergency need for hospitalization and the presence of a substantial risk of suicide.
5. He turned the treatment of his patient over to a third-year resident, relying upon the resident's and nursing staff's care and management. Even though the resident was supervised, proper evaluation and control of the suicidal risk presented by the patient were not provided.
6. The absence of a therapeutic alliance was demonstrated by the need for the wife's intervention in persuading her husband to follow Dr. Williams' recommendation of hospitalization, the patient's refusal to take prescribed medication, and the presence of long silences in therapy that led to a cutback in therapy time. The significance of the absence of a therapeutic alliance was missed or ignored. It should have been recognized that no meaningful treatment was taking place and a consultation obtained.
7. Dr. Williams failed to read the nurses' notes containing the statement about the patient's cryptic remark concerning a recent gun purchase.
8. He did not perform a suicide risk assessment concerning the patient's readiness for a pass. Furthermore, Dr. Williams did not ask the patient directly about suicidal intent.
9. The patient's treatment and supervision were fragmented throughout his hospital stay. No attempt was made at a unified team approach, nor was a patient treatment and management conference held with the staff. Finally, Dr. Williams apparently failed to communicate directly with the staff concerning the suicidal potential of his patient.

The expert for the plaintiff will conclude that the whole tenor of the evaluation, treatment, and control of Mr. Walters fell far below a reasonable standard of care and was the proximate cause of his suicide. More important, the report of the plaintiff's expert will underscore the point that deficiencies in care existed throughout Mr. Walters' hospitalization, not just surrounding the decision to render a fatal pass.

In addition to prescribing antidepressant medication, would the direct participation of Dr. Williams in his patient's group therapy have been sufficient for the evaluation and management of the patient's suicide risk?

Hospitalized patients usually present complex, difficult management and treatment problems that require a thorough knowledge of each patient. Whenever a patient is psychiatrically hospitalized, the patient requires careful supervision and management. Does the suicidal patient need to be placed on suicide precautions (i.e., constant one-on-one supervision) or will patient observation suffice (i.e., 15-minute checks)?

Definitions of suicide precautions and observation may vary from hospital to hospital. The clinician should have a clear understanding of how these terms are being used. Moreover, powerful drugs can be prescribed that necessitate close supervision for both clinical efficacy and side effects. Of all patients admitted to a psychiatric hospital, suicidal patients generally require the closest supervision and management.

Clinical experience demonstrates that one of the best indicators of a patient's suicidal intent is the status of his or her interpersonal relationships. When Dr. Williams was unable to establish a working relationship with his patient, an ominous situation existed requiring immediate attention. Furthermore, the psychiatrist cannot rely solely on medications to the exclusion of an ongoing doctor-patient relationship and the therapeutic alliance. With antidepressant medications, a lag period of 4 to 6 weeks before reaching full therapeutic efficacy requires the active presence and support of a viable treatment relationship. In addition, group therapy cannot replace individual patient evaluation and management. The needs of other, more vocal patients may command attention in the group process and shift the focus away from the critically determinative intrapsychic experiences of a withdrawn, suicidally depressed patient.

How often should a patient hospitalized for psychiatric care be seen by the treating psychiatrist?

Psychiatric practice lacks standards regarding frequency of patient visits. The frequency of visits by the psychiatrist treating the patient in the hospital varies according to the clinical needs of the patient. Because of the hospitalization of a patient, the psychiatrist is on notice that serious problems exist requiring close and frequent supervision. Adequate treatment cannot be given to psychiatric inpatients if they are seen infrequently by the treating psychiatrist, even in the presence of a treatment team or trained nursing staff. Unless otherwise provided by hospital policy, the treating psychiatrist bears full responsibility for the care and management of the patient. This responsibility cannot be delegated to others. If the psychiatrist cannot meet the patient's treatment needs adequately, the patient should be referred to another psychiatrist or hospital that can provide the necessary care.

Because of the complexity and severity of the patient's clinical condition, Dr. Williams did not spend sufficient time with the patient gathering the necessary clinical data required to make a critical risk-benefit decision before issuing the patient a pass. Progress notes should contain risk-benefit assessments whenever the clinician considers a major intervention such as a change of hospital floors, pass, or discharge.

How often should a progress note be written?

Each time the patient is seen, a note should be recorded concerning the patient's clinical course, treatment interventions, and general management. The problem-oriented record as adapted to psychiatric practice is a useful guide for record keeping (1). Some courts have taken the position that if treatment has not been recorded, it has not been done (2, 3). Dr. Williams's progress notes were too infrequent, insufficient, and vague to be of any use in his defense. Good record keeping is one of the best clinical risk management techniques available to the psychiatrist.

Psychiatrists occasionally have been advised to exclude any reference to suicidal ideation or behavior from the patient's chart on the theory that liability cannot be assigned if there is no notice of the patient's self-destructive tendencies. Will following such advice provide a defense in a malpractice action after a successful suicide?

No. On the contrary, it exposes psychiatrists to legal mayhem (4). Apart from being dishonest and probably fraudulent, exclusion of vital data about the patient as a defense in a malpractice suit is the ostrich theory of legal survival. The best way for the clinician to proceed is to duly note the patient's suicidal ideation and behavior while clearly indicating the treatment and supervision the patient is receiving. Risk-benefit notes should be written whenever the psychiatrist plans any significant change in the approach to treating or supervising the patient.

Is a psychiatrist more vulnerable to a lawsuit for a suicide that takes place in a hospital or on pass from the hospital than when an outpatient commits suicide?

It is more difficult for the psychiatrist to supervise a patient out of the hospital. As Fishalow (5) indicates, foreseeability is critical in determining negligence. The opportunities to control and anticipate suicide are greater in the hospital setting, although hospitalization obviously does not guarantee against suicide. Often the hospitalized patient will put the psychiatrist "on notice" by a prior attempt or by exhibiting suicidal ideation or behavior on the ward. Because a suicidal patient can be placed on suicide precautions, one would expect from the psychiatrist a higher level of awareness and subsequent diligence in reducing the likelihood that the patient will commit suicide. Some courts have reasoned that when an outpatient commits suicide, the therapist will not be held to have breached a duty to safeguard the patient from foreseeable self-harm because of the difficulty in controlling the patient (6). In general, the courts assess whether suicide risk was recognized and whether the psychiatrist adequately balanced the risk of suicide against the benefit of more control.

For the outpatient at suicide risk, treatment remedies may include a number of psychotherapeutic and pharmacological interventions. Seeing the patient more frequently may strengthen the suicide-inhibiting therapeutic alliance. The clinician needs to be readily available to the patient and monitor closely any medications given. Ultimately, the patient may require hospitalization. Involuntary hospitalization may be a final option for the suicidal patient who meets the substantive criteria for mental illness and dangerousness. Liability might arise for the suicide of an outpatient if there is gross error in deciding not to seek involuntary hospitalization of the patient (7).

Although a duty to inform others of the patient's suicidal intentions generally does not exist, the psychiatrist may determine that part of the care of the suicidal patient requires mobilization of family members or close friends to provide a support system. *The Principles of Medical Ethics With Annotations Especially Applicable to Psychiatry* (Section 4, Annotation 8) permits breaking confidences in order to protect the welfare of the patient (8). Some state confidentiality statutes permit waiving of privileged communications when the patient is in danger of causing self-harm (9).

What is the purpose of risk-benefit analysis in the clinical management of the suicidal patient?

One purpose of risk-benefit analysis is to permit the psychiatrist to evaluate systematically the balance of clinical factors favoring or opposing the treatment intervention under consideration. Both sides of the issue must be considered. For example, in the clinical vignette, the risks and benefits of not issuing a pass should have been considered along with the risks and benefits of a pass. Neither was done. A risk-benefit evaluation also allows the psychiatrist more therapeutic latitude with the suicidal patient, and protects against fears of malpractice suits.

Psychiatrists sometimes fear a malpractice action when treating a suicidal patient and overly restrict the patient to his or her therapeutic detriment. To protect themselves, psychiatrists must not defensively "lock up" suicidal patients, promoting despair and hopelessness. In this era of open-door policies in psychiatric hospitals, courts recognize that suicidal patients cannot be treated like maximum security prisoners. When allowing the improving suicidal patient more freedom, recording risk-benefit assessments surrounding increased privileges also frees psychiatrists from undue fears of a lawsuit. Risk-benefit notes enable psychiatrists to exercise greater clinical discretion while also acting as an excellent risk management tool. The record should reflect what sources of information were consulted, what factors went into the clinical decision, and how the factors were balanced in the risk-benefit assessment (10).

In the clinical vignette, careful evaluation of Mr. Walters would have indicated that even though the patient reported a decreased intensity of suicidal preoccupations, the quintessential therapeutic alliance was missing. The resident and the nursing staff found no evidence of the existence of a therapeutic alliance or fundamental treatment progression, even though the patient's depression appeared moderately improved. Furthermore, the possibility that a gun was hidden away at home markedly increased the risk of suicide, countering any possible therapeutic benefit that a pass might provide.

In instances when the clinician has used reasonable care in evaluating and managing the suicidal patient and the patient injures or kills himself or herself anyway, the medical judgment would be considered to be in error, but not negligent, if the risks were reasonably considered (11). When the psychiatrist's records prove that reasonable care and management were provided, the mainstay defense of the exercise of professional judgment can be used in a malpractice suit following a patient's suicide (12). The knowledge that every mistake is not necessarily negligence is essential information for psychiatrists. Armed with this knowledge, they can provide the best possible treatment for their patients without having to live in constant fear of litigation.

The perfunctory note written by Dr. Williams before issuing the pass did not contain any reasonable risk-benefit assessment. When a risk-benefit analysis is noticeably absent, the court is unable to evaluate the complex issues involved in the assessment of suicide risk. Courts are then encouraged to fasten onto only one objective fact concerning the case while ignoring the complexities of evaluation and treatment that exist with every suicidal patient.

What risk-benefit assessments must be made before issuing a pass or discharging a patient from the hospital?

In the clinical vignette, Dr. Williams made no record of any reasonable risk-benefit analysis before providing a pass for his patient. The court must assess whether the risk of suicide was foreseeable to the doctor and, if so, whether Dr. Williams reasonably concluded that the benefits of a pass outweighed the risks. Dr. Williams will not be able to submit his records in his own defense because the plaintiff's attorney will take the position that what was not recorded was not done.

Discharging a patient from the hospital may be a more difficult decision than that of admission. At the time of a pass or discharge, the patient's anxiety about separating from the security of the hospital and facing the burdens and responsibilities of outside life may precipitate a crisis. The psychiatrist should evaluate this issue very carefully (see Table 12-1). Although keeping the patient hospitalized may lessen the chance of suicide and diminish the psychiatrist's anxiety, resumption of the patient's life-style as soon as possible can be tremendously reassuring and therapeutic to the patient. Although "throwing the key away" may prevent suicide for the present, it may only increase hopelessness and suicidal resolve.

TABLE 12–1. Suicidal patients: pass and discharge considerations

Analysis of benefits of release versus risk
    Determined by direct evaluation.
    Consultation with all appropriate staff.
    Review of patient's current and past course of hospitalization.
Evidence of posthospitalization self-care ability
    Can patient function without significant affective and cognitive impairment?
Capability of and accessibility to obtaining assistance
    Is patient physically and emotionally able to employ others for support?
Remission of illness
    What remains unchanged and can be dealt with as an outpatient?
Control by medication
    Can side effects be tolerated and managed outside hospital, and will patient comply with treatment?
Support system
    Do family or significant others exist and are they stabilizing or destabilizing?
Timing of proposed release
    Does staff adequately know the patient?
    Has the patient adequately been acclimated to the therapeutic milieu, with sufficient time allowed to develop meaningful relationships?
    Has sufficient time elapsed to evaluate the effectiveness of treatment?
Therapeutic alliance
    Will the patient continue to work with the psychiatrist?

Adapted, with permission, from Simon RI: *Concise Guide to Clinical Psychiatry and the Law.* Washington, DC, American Psychiatric Press, 1988, p. 88. Copyright 1988, American Psychiatric Press.

For suicidal patients requiring greater restrictions, the situation is complicated by court directives that require highly disturbed patients to be treated by the least-restrictive means (13). The psychiatrist can easily feel trapped at this point. The tension between promoting individual freedom and protecting a person from self-injury is a basic conflict encountered in the ethical and legal aspects of clinical management of suicidal patients (14). Nevertheless, clinical judgments based on the treatment needs of the patient must be determinative. In *Johnson v. United States* (15), the court noted that an "open door" policy creates a higher potential for danger. The court went on to say:

> Modern psychiatry has recognized the importance of making every effort to return a patient to an active and productive life. Thus, the patient is encouraged to develop his self-confidence by adjusting to the demands of everyday existence. Particularly because the prediction of danger is difficult, undue reliance on hospitalization might lead to prolonged incarceration of potentially useful members of society.

The clinician must understand that an open-door policy cannot be applied in stock fashion to all psychiatric patients. Autonomy in the hospital setting must bear a rational nexus with the patient's diagnosis, clinical condition, and level of functional mental capacity.

Before the improving suicidal patient is allowed on a pass or is discharged, the psychiatrist needs to consider a number of factors (16):

1. The current level of risk versus anticipated benefits for and against pass or discharge as determined by direct evaluation, reports of other staff members, and the record of the patient's current and immediate past hospital course.
2. Evidence of the ability of the patient to take care of himself or herself while out of the hospital. Can the patient function without significant cognitive and affective impairment?
3. The ability to receive assistance. Is the patient too isolated to employ others for help?
4. Remission of illness. What remains unchanged, and can it be dealt with on an outpatient basis?
5. Control by medication. Can side effects be tolerated outside of the hospital, and will the patient take his or her medication?
6. Support system. Does family exist, and if so, is it stabilizing or destabilizing?
7. Is the pass being issued too soon? Have the psychiatrist and staff given themselves sufficient time to get to know the patient, to allow the patient to adjust to the hospital milieu, to allow medication to work, and to see if meaningful relationships develop? Passes should be viewed by staff as a "therapeutic assignment" (17). Staff should carefully document the ratio-

nale and duration of the pass. For example, whom will the patient be with during the pass, who will accompany the patient from the hospital, and what are the goals to be achieved? What are the reasons for the timing and duration of the pass?

8. Therapeutic alliance. Will the patient continue to work with the psychiatrist? The therapeutic alliance is a critical indicator of the patient's subsequent adjustment outside of the hospital. Serious second thoughts should arise before allowing a patient to go out on pass or be discharged if the therapeutic alliance is not in place and working. Patients who do not form working relationships with their therapist, staff members, or other patients may be at an increased risk for self-destructive behavior if discharged. In the clinical vignette, Mr. Walters was discharged at a time when he had withdrawn from all relationships.

Should Dr. Williams have breached his duty of confidentiality in order to try again to enlist the help of the patient's wife in attempting to avert suicide?

If Dr. Williams felt that the participation of Mrs. Walters continued to be necessary, he should have raised that as a treatment issue, even though Mr. Walters initially demurred. Dr. Williams may be second-guessed by the plaintiff's experts in not continuing to enlist the wife's support, particularly so that she could accompany her husband on his pass. The competent patient's request for the maintenance of confidentiality must be honored unless the patient is a clear danger to self or others.

The Principles of Medical Ethics (8) states: "Psychiatrists at times may find it necessary, in order to protect the patient or the community from imminent danger, to reveal confidential information disclosed by the patient" (Section 4, Annotation 8). Thus, if Dr. Williams determined that his patient was suicidal and that his wife's participation was critical in preventing it, ethically he could have informed the patient of his decision to break confidentiality and recorded his reasons in the patient's chart. At this critical point, the possible damage to the therapeutic alliance becomes a secondary issue, although still in need of attention.

When the patient who lacks mental capacity gives an incompetent refusal to speak to family or others, confidentiality should be honored for the sake of the therapeutic alliance unless compelling reasons exist to breach confidentiality. The reasons for breaching confidentiality should be noted in the patient's chart.

If the psychiatrist suspects that the patient is suicidal, does the psychiatrist have a legal duty to inform third parties such as family members?

The legal duty to warn or inform third parties exists in some jurisdictions only if the danger of physical harm is threatened toward others, not toward the patients themselves (18). Psychiatrists do have a professional duty to take appropriate preventive measures to keep patients from harming themselves. For example, communicating with family members about specific aspects of the patient's case, attempting to ameliorate pathological family interactions with the patient, or mobilizing family support are among the therapist's options. Statutory waiver of confidential information is provided in some states when a patient seriously threatens self-harm (9). Before breaking confidence in order to solicit the support of others, the matter should be discussed with the patient.

What indicators do therapists usually consider in assessing suicide risk?

There are no pathognomonic indicators of suicide. The assessment of suicide risk usually is based on more than one risk factor. Generally, a number of risk factors of varying significance must be assessed together. Some of the more commonly relied upon clinical indicators of increased suicide risk include the following:

1. The lack of a therapeutic alliance with the therapist
2. Recent discharge from a psychiatric hospital (within 3 months)
3. Severance of formerly meaningful relationships and failure to substitute new ones
4. Unstable living circumstances
5. Unemployment
6. Presence of severe depression with feelings of despair, hopelessness, and worthlessness; and the presence of psychosis, particularly if command hallucinations are present
7. Epidemiologic data, for example, patient in a population with elevated suicide base rates (e.g., single or divorced)
8. Prior suicide attempts, particularly a recent attempt—an idea has become an act
9. Impulsivity (e.g., violence, driving, money)
10. Remission of a psychotic episode but continuance of secondary depression. Studies show that 25% to 40% of patients who experience an acute schizophrenic disorder will have a depressive episode (19).
11. Special situational factors
12. Advancing age, personal losses, or physical illness, particularly if the latter is chronic
13. High lethality potential of the method used to attempt suicide
14. Behavior indicative of a finalized decision to die (e.g., making final personal arrangements, giving away valued possessions, cutting off relationships, peace, calm, "happiness")
15. Presence of a specific plan
16. Availability of lethal means

17. A family history of suicide
18. Chronic alcoholism
19. Drug addiction
20. Human immunodeficiency virus (HIV) diagnosis
21. Age group 15–24
22. Mental incompetency
23. Not living with a child under 18 years old

Fawcett and co-workers (20, 21) report data from an ongoing prospective investigation of suicide risk in patients with major affective disorders identifying statistically significant risk factors associated with early suicide. Early suicide is defined as suicide occurring within 1 year of the diagnosis of a major affective disorder. The risk factors are as follows:

1.   Panic attacks
2.   Psychic anxiety (pure affect of anxiety in contrast to somatic anxiety, e.g., headaches, constipation, gastrointestinal distress)
3.   Anhedonia (loss of pleasure and interest)
4.   Alcohol abuse
5.   Depressive turmoil (rapid switches of mood from depression to anxiety to anger or vice versa accompanied by agitation and perturbation)
6.   Diminished concentration
7.   Global insomnia

Furthermore, as demonstrated by Fawcett et al. (21), the suicide risk factors for individuals with major affective disorders who committed suicide within 1 year of assessment were different from the suicide risk factors found among individuals who committed suicide with 2 to 10 years of assessment. In the former group, the anxiety-related symptoms of panic attacks, psychic anxiety, global insomnia, diminished concentration, alcohol abuse, and loss of interest and pleasure were significantly more severe. The more traditional suicide risk factors such as hopelessness, suicidal ideation, suicidal intent, and a history of previous suicide attempts were not associated with short-term suicide but were significantly associated with long-term suicide. Thus, clinical interventions directed at treating anxiety-related symptoms in patients with major affective disorders may significantly diminish a number of short-term suicide risk factors.

Simon (22) presents a detailed discussion of suicide risk factors and a method for their use in assessing patients at suicidal risk.

What is the significance of the therapeutic alliance in assessing suicide risk?

Patients who still maintain their personal relationships and who have a working alliance with their therapist, combined with a strong religious and cultural conviction against suicide, present a diminished risk for suicide. Older depressed patients with families will frequently be heard to say that they do not want to burden or shame their children with such an act.

In the clinical vignette, one of the most significant risk factors for suicide was the absence of a therapeutic alliance. The therapeutic alliance is defined as the conscious task-oriented collaboration between therapist and patient in which the therapist's aim is to form an alliance with the patient for the purpose of mutual exploration of the patient's problems (23). The therapeutic alliance also contains unconscious and affective elements.

An example of one kind of therapeutic alliance occurs when splitting of the patient's treatment perceptions into an observing and an experiencing part takes place. The observing part is allied with the therapist when the patient asks such questions as "Can I understand why I feel suicidal?" or "Will you be available to me if I can't control myself?" The presence of a therapeutic alliance is a bedrock indicator of the patient's willingness to seek help and sustenance during serious emotional crises. It is one of the most important nonverbal statements indicating a desire to live.

The therapeutic alliance with the suicidal patient reflects the willingness of the healthy part of the patient's personality to work with the therapist based upon a life-affirming statement such as "*I* believe *you* can help *me* learn to cope better and be happier." This is the antithesis of hopeless feelings that impair the therapeutic alliance, as when the patient says, "There is no hope for the relief of my unendurable pain; I am going away" (24). The therapeutic alliance can be used by clinicians as a here-and-now indicator of the patient's suicidal state. If the alliance does not develop for reasons that lie primarily within the therapist, or because of some idiosyncratic therapist-patient interaction, then the presence or absence of other sustaining object relations can be determinative. Therapist-patient impasses need to be addressed directly. If a stalemate persists, the patient should be seen in consultation or referred elsewhere if possible.

There are patients who, because of their illness, may not be able to form or sustain a working alliance. Borderline patients can rapidly fluctuate in and out of a working alliance. Schizoid patients may have great difficulty in reaching out to anyone. Paranoid patients tend to treat any close relationship with extreme fear. Nonetheless, unless determined to commit suicide, even these patients usually maintain at least a modicum of a relationship with someone. The paranoid patient usually tries to find one person to trust. In the hospital, members of the staff are extremely important in providing sustaining relationships at the time of a suicidal crisis.

There are some notable exceptions to the general rule that the presence of an ongoing, meaningful relationship is relatively antithetical to suicide. The nature and quality of the relationship must be assessed. Some patients may develop intense relationships based on strong feelings of anger. In the presence of a borderline personality disorder, splitting defenses may turn the rage meant for others toward oneself. Idealization of the object is maintained, but the self is suicidally devalued (25). Psychotic fusing and merging with a hated person may lead to suicide. Patients with sustained relationships may make a suicide pact with their partner or induce the other to join in a double suicide. Social isolation, dominance, and aggression seem to characterize persons who form suicide pacts (26).

An important clinical caveat against too heavy a reliance upon the therapeutic alliance in assessing suicide risk occurs with certain depressed patients. During the treatment session, the patient may manifest a working therapeutic alliance. After leaving the therapist, the patient may not be able to internalize the alliance because of depressive symptomatology. Unless the therapist assesses with the patient the status of the therapeutic alliance when the patient is outside of the session, the therapist may falsely assume that a viable, ongoing therapeutic alliance exists with the patient that minimizes suicide risk. This clinical phenomenon often accounts for the bewilderment of therapists following a patient's suicide with whom it was thought that a working therapeutic alliance existed (27).

How much reliance should the clinician place on a suicide prevention contract with the patient?

Some therapists attempt to formalize the alliance by a verbal or even a written contract with the patient stating that the latter will call upon the therapist if serious doubts about control of suicidal impulses arise. These contracts have no legal force. Although some patients may accept such a contract, many state they cannot be sure that if self-destructive impulses strike, they can or will want to call. The problem with the patient contract against suicide is that it may falsely ease the therapist's concern and lower vigilance without having any appreciable effect on the patient's suicidal intent. Frequently, such contracts reflect the therapist's attempt to control the inevitable anxiety associated with treating suicidal patients.

In *Stepakoff v. Kantar* (28), the psychiatrist thought he had a "solid pact" with a manic-depressive patient to contact him if the patient felt suicidal. In combination with the patient's defense mechanisms, the psychiatrist felt that the patient was unlikely to commit suicide. The patient committed suicide anyway.

Some therapists gauge the patient's suicidal intent by a willingness or unwillingness to formalize the alliance into a contract (23). Contracts against suicide may be useful in certain instances by reaffirming the therapeutic alliance, but their limitations should be understood. The suicide prevention contract never should be used in place of a comprehensive assessment of suicide risk (29). Therapists need to remember that the only sure way to prevent the personal agony experienced when a patient commits suicide is never to take patients.

What is the significance of a prior suicide attempt in assessing current suicide risks?

Of those who commit suicide, 9% to 33% have made previous attempts (30). If everyone who attempted suicide could be prevented from attempting it again, suicides would still continue at a high rate.

In the vignette, Mr. Walters made a previous "gesture" by taking 10 diazepam tablets. Should this gesture have placed Dr. Williams on notice that his patient was at increased suicide risk? Placing significant clinical weight on the distinction between a gesture and an attempt can be perilous, particularly if the act occurred in the distant past. Without question, some suicide attempts can be identified as gestures, because the patient does not have the slightest intention of killing himself or herself. When the therapist learns of previous attempts from the patient, unconscious distortion or retrospective falsification may convert a genuine attempt into a gesture. On the other hand, a suicide attempt may reflect the need to manipulate individuals or situations or serve as a call for help or attention. Individuals who continually make suicide gestures may misjudge and "accidentally" kill themselves.

Upon proper authorization, medical and psychiatric records should be obtained regarding previous diagnoses, treatments, or suicidal acts. If possible, the psychiatrist should call the therapist who previously treated the patient. With patient permission, family members may need to be interviewed to determine the gravity of past suicide attempts. Did the patient intend to die? Did he or she expect to be found in time? Was there some obvious manipulation or secondary gain? Was the patient overtly depressed?

Weisman and Worden (31) have devised a risk-rescue rating in suicide assessment as a descriptive and quantitative method of assessing the lethality of suicide attempts. For example, a patient who takes a few minor tranquilizers and immediately calls the physician is at low risk and high rescue. The patient who makes superficial slashes on the unit with a razor but remains alone is at low risk and low rescue. A high-risk, high-rescue patient attempts hanging in the presence of a friend. The high-risk, low-rescue situation occurs, for example, when the patient buys a hose to fit a car exhaust and waits for everyone to leave the house. The hypothesis underlying the suicide risk rating is that the lethality of the method of suicide, defined as the probability of inflicting irreversible damage, may be expressed as a ratio of factors influencing risk and rescue. Risk-rescue rating correlates with the level of treatment recommended, the subject's sex, and whether the subject lived or died. Taken by itself, the risk-rescue rating is not a predictive instrument. When considered along with other factors, such as explicit intention to die, prior history of mental illness, and availability of family and community support, the risk-rescue rating can be used to assist in individualized suicide assessment.

Courts and juries may place greater emphasis than clinically warranted on previous suicide attempts when assessing liability. To the layperson, the clinician has been placed on notice by a prior overt self-destructive act. The jury may reason, "Once a suicide attempt, always a suicide risk."

What can the therapist do to reduce legal liability when treating the suicidal patient?

The thought of suicide is entertained by almost everyone at some point in life, thus making it more difficult for therapists to evaluate. One suicide occurred every 20 minutes in the United States from 1970 to 1980. Patients who commit suicide may visit a physician within a few months of their death complaining of symptoms of depression (32). Although 30,000 persons a year are reported to attempt suicide, the actual number may be 8 to 10 times that many.

Whereas the goal of the therapist is the preservation of life, the patient may seek only to die. For some human beings, the freedom to terminate one's own life is a fundamental solace. Nietzsche, in *Beyond Good and Evil,* said: "The thought of suicide is a great consolation: by means of it one gets successfully through many a bad night." As a result, little therapeutic alliance may exist, preventing the therapist from "beneficially" intervening with certain patients.

Theories of negligence involving suicide can be grouped into three broad categories: *1)* failure to properly *diagnose* (assess the risk of suicide); *2)* failure to *treat* (use reasonable treatment interventions and precautions); and *3)* failure to *implement* (treatment is negligently carried out) (33) (see Table 12-2). The most difficult cases to defend occur when suicide is correctly "diagnosed" but the clinician does not act appropriately to control the patient.

In the clinical vignette, the assessment of suicide risk was not performed adequately by Dr. Williams when he considered the pass for his patient. There is no evidence that the patient was asked directly about suicidal intent. Evaluating the risk of violence to the patient or others must be a routine part of every mental status examination. Evaluation should be done not only at the time of admission but at other critical junctures during the course of hospitalization. Ongoing assessment of the suicide risk posed by Mr. Walters should have been performed through daily interviews by Dr. Williams and the hospital staff. Furthermore, adequate control of the patient required evaluation immediately or shortly after admission. Patient observation every 15 minutes should have been ordered until Dr. Williams and the staff became more familiar with the treatment and protective needs of the patient. At each phase, when consideration was given to granting more freedom to the patient, a risk-benefit assessment should have been made and recorded.

In *Abille v. United States* (10), a psychiatrist failed to maintain contemporary notes, orders, or other records that adequately explained the management decisions for a patient who committed suicide. The psychiatrist transferred the patient from suicide status to a status appropriate for less dangerous patients. At the time of the transfer, no notation was made by the psychiatrist explaining the transfer, even though he usually made such notes. This note taking also was required by hospital regulations. The court acknowledged that a reasonable psychiatrist might have determined that the patient could be reclassified with safety; but without notes, there was concern that the decision was made negligently. *Abille* underscores the court's need to know the decision-making process of the psychiatrist in a recorded form. A psychiatrist's best friend in court

---

TABLE 12–2. Civil liability for the suicide of a psychiatric patient: causes of action and defenses

---

Inpatient (hospital) liability

Diagnosis
   Unforeseeable suicide: failure to properly assess
   Foreseeable suicide:
     a) Failure to properly document
     b) Improper diagnosis or assessment
Treatment (foreseeable suicide)
   Failure to supervise properly
   Failure to restrain (high-risk patient)
   Premature release (e.g., pass)
   Negligent discharge
   Unjustified freedom of movement
Defenses
   Compliance with accepted medical practice
   Lack of reasonable knowledge of suicidality
   Justifiable allowance of freedom of movement (e.g., "open ward")
   Reasonable physician's decision regarding diagnosis or course of treatment
   Intervening acts or factors (e.g., third parties)
   Extraordinary circumstances precluding or circumventing reasonable precautions or restraint

Outpatient psychotherapist liability

Diagnosis
   Unforeseeable suicide: negligent diagnosis
   Foreseeable suicide: improper diagnosis
Treatment
   Negligent treatment (e.g., supervision, abandonment, referral)
   Failure to control (e.g., hospitalize)
Defenses
   Compliance with standard of care
   Diagnosis of suicidality not reasonable
   Intervening acts
   Extraordinary circumstances

Source. From Smith J, Bisbing S: *Suicide: Caselaw Summary and Analysis.* Potomac, MD, Legal Medicine Press, 1988

is a carefully documented medical record that contemporaneously documents the provision of reasonable clinical care.

The clinician should specifically evaluate the patient's competence to participate in decisions involving more freedom (34). Another concern is whether the patient has the mental capacity to consider the risks and benefits of giving or withholding information. Mr. Walters withheld his suicidal intent. Although he "smiled frequently" before receiving his pass, this may have represented some measure of relief and calm derived from his secret decision to kill himself. As patients recover from depression, they may have more energy to carry out suicide while hiding their intent. For this reason, the assessment of hopelessness is particularly important toward the end of the patient's hospital stay and at discharge. Continued hopelessness in the presence of regained energy may enable the patient to commit suicide.

Gutheil (34) recommends informing the patient, "If you don't level with me, I can't help you." The clinician should assess the patient and decide whether the patient is competent to weigh the risks. Patients who are not competent represent greater risk, requiring more conservative management. Gutheil feels that for the "many competent but duplicitous suicidal patients encountered in practice, this competence assessment strikes at the specious view of the patient as a pseudochild, whose suicide must have been the result of the clinician's negligent care." The courts generally recognize that no amount of precautions can provide absolute assurance that the patient will not commit suicide (35).

Ordinarily, good clinical practice is a sound defense against legal liability. In general, the baseline for decision making in court is the general standard of care for psychiatric malpractice (i.e., the care and skill customarily exercised by the average qualified psychiatrist). This standard was affirmed by the Massachusetts Supreme Judicial Court in *Stepakoff v. Kantar* (28). In Massachusetts, the general standard of care will be interpreted broadly to include the relatively unusual case of suicide.

In *Stepakoff,* the plaintiff alleged that Dr. William Kantar knew or should have known that her husband was suicidal and that Dr. Kantar negligently failed to inform the patient's wife or to make appropriate arrangements for the protection of her husband. As a result, according to the plaintiff, the patient committed suicide. The state high court held that the psychiatrist did not owe the patient a specific legal duty to safeguard him from himself. The psychiatrist's legal obligation to the patient was to treat him according to the standard of care and skill of the average psychiatrist. Beyond that standard, the psychiatrist did not have a duty to take reasonable preventive measures after diagnosing the patient as suicidal. Thus, the court affirmed the "best judgment" standard over the reasonableness standard. The court stated that the duty owed by a psychiatrist to a suicidal outpatient was no different from that imposed on other physicians to other patients. As will be seen later, some courts have gone beyond the general standard of care toward a "strict liability" standard.

Perr (36) points out that considerations in risk management for the hospitalized suicidal patient include "adequate and timely records, documentation of decisions (particularly involving privileges), clear hospital policies and procedures, and adherence to those policies." He describes the key judgment points for increased suicide potential as the time of admission, the precautions or procedures used to minimize suicide, and changes in management that accord with the patient's clinical status.

Although the psychiatrist may not have deviated from or failed to render reasonable care to a patient who ultimately commits suicide, juries may nevertheless decide retrospectively in favor of the family of the deceased. Psychiatrists cannot guarantee control over the behavior of their patients. Suicide has multiple causes and may not be simply the result of misdiagnosis or improper prescribing of medications. The causes of suicide need to be studied further so that more effective interventions can be made. Courts sometimes have trouble understanding that psychiatrists are ordinary mortals struggling with the conundrum of suicide.

Why is the comprehensive assessment of suicide risk of critical importance both clinically and as a risk management technique?

The evaluation of suicide risk by the practitioner is one of the most complex, difficult, and challenging clinical tasks in psychiatry. Patient suicides are all too common in the clinical practices of psychiatrists. The clinician must know how to conduct a competent suicide risk assessment. In short, there are only two types of clinicians: those who have had patient suicides and those who will.

Suicide is a rare event with low specificity (high false-positive rates). Providing a reasonable standard of care in *assessing* suicide risk preempts the very problematic issue of *predicting* the actual suicide occurrence for which standards do not exist. Murphy (37) points out that it is not possible to predict suicide in the general population. Only persons in groups or classes that have been shown to be statistically at "high risk for suicide" can be identified (38).

The inability to predict suicide was demonstrated by Pokorny (39), who in a prospective study of 4,800 consecutive patients, attempted to identify which psychiatric patients would commit suicide. Twenty-one items were used to identify a subsample of 803 patients as suicide risks. Sixty-seven committed suicide during the 5-year follow-up period. Only 30 of the 67 suicides were patients in the 803-patient subsample. Thirty-seven (over 50%) were not identified at risk. Furthermore, 766 of the 803 at-risk patients did not commit suicide. The overprediction of suicide risk and the high number of "missed" or undetected suicides are consistent with the results of other "future behavior prediction" research (40).

The legal standard of *reasonableness* in assessing and treating suicidal patients preempts the thorny dilemma of "violence prediction" by judging professionals not on the absolute accuracy of their determinations but on whether their suicide risk assessment *process* was clinically reasonable (41). Psychiatrists experience inevitable tension due to concerns of over-restricting a patient's freedom of movement versus not providing enough safeguards for the patient's immediate welfare. This dilemma can be relieved by implementing a suicide risk-benefit analysis each time a significant procedural decision is made (e.g., initial determination of risk, consideration for day pass, consideration for more freedom of movement) (42).

When a risk-benefit analysis is noticeably absent, a court will have difficulty evaluating the appropriateness of the decision-making process in assessing the risk of suicide. Clinicians should have all suicide assessments recorded in the patient's chart *at the time of evaluation.* For the outpatient who continues to be suicidal, an assessment should be made at each patient visit.

What is the "weather forecast" model of suicide risk assessment?

The weather forecast model is a time-driven suicide risk assessment method. Because time attenuates assessment reliability, the weather forecast model is applicable to the assessment of suicide risk. Short-term risk assessments, like weather forecasts, are much more accurate than long-term assessments. In the short term, the parameters that influence future occurrences can be specified with greater precision.

Psychiatrists cannot *predict* when or if a patient will actually commit suicide. At best, only the degree of suicide risk can be assessed after an adequate psychiatric evaluation of the patient. As time passes, the ability to specify both psychological and environmental determinants of behavior diminishes. As a result, assessment accuracy becomes progressively less reliable beyond the immediate short term (e.g., 24–48 hours). Thus, assessment of suicide risk is a here-and-now determination regarding a specific psychiatric intervention being considered by the clinician. Every suicide is a unique event that defies easy analysis, even in retrospect. Accordingly, patients undergoing a suicidal crisis should be seen frequently and the suicide risk assessed from session to session. Here-and-now suicide risk assessment requires close monitoring of the patient concerning major clinical decisions (e.g., hospitalization, pass, discharge). Like a weather forecast, suicide risk assessment is time-driven and needs to be updated frequently. The clinician must remember that the systematic assessment of suicide risk is good clinical practice and, only secondarily, a risk management technique.

Before an adequate suicide risk assessment can be done, the clinician must obtain a complete psychiatric history and conduct a thorough mental status examination. Records of prior psychiatric treatment also should be reviewed. Frequently, obtaining the actual records will require considerable time. The clinician should attempt to call previous treaters if the patient or guardian provides a competent authorization to release information. Even if the patient refuses to produce an authorization, former caregivers may nevertheless decide to provide clinical information for the sake of the patient's treatment. Also, past psychiatric history may be provided when an emergency exists on the basis of the emergency exception to consent.

Assessing suicide risk involves three separate steps (Tables 12-3 and 12-4):

TABLE 12–3. Assessment of suicide risk

Risk factors	Facilitating suicide	Inhibiting suicide
Short-term*		
Panic attacks		
Psychic anxiety		
Loss of pleasure and interest		
Alcohol abuse		
Depressive turmoil		
Diminished concentration		
Global insomnia		
Recent discharge from psychiatric hospital (within 3 months)		
Long-term		
Therapeutic alliance—ongoing patient		
Other relationships		
Hopelessness		
Psychiatric diagnoses (Axes I and II)		
Prior attempts		
Specific plan		
Living circumstances		
Employment status		
Epidemiologic data		
Availability of lethal means		
Suicidal ideation: syntonic or dystonic		
Family history		
Impulsivity (violence, driving, money)		
Drug abuse		
Physical illness		
Mental competency		
Specific situational factors		

Rating system: L = low factor; M = moderate factor; H = high factor; 0 = nonfactor.
Note. Clinically judge as high, moderate, or low the potential for suicide within 24–48 hours from assessment of suicide.
*Short-term indicators are risk factors found to be statistically significant within 1 year of assessment.
Source. Reprinted, with permission, from Simon RI: "Clinical risk management of suicidal patients: assessing the unpredictable," in *American Psychiatric Press Review of Psychiatry and the Law, Vol. 3.* Edited by Simon RI. Washington, DC, American Psychiatric Press, 1992. Copyright 1992, American Psychiatric Press.

1. Identifying patients with certain clinical and epidemiologic risk factors associated with suicide
2. Assessing the overall risk of suicide based on the rating of specific risk factors
3. Implementing preventive interventions that bear a logical nexus to the overall suicide risk assessment

No one suicide risk variable can be counted upon exclusively in the assessment of suicide potential. Instead, the clinician should consider all of the relevant risk factors and weigh them accordingly. Suicide risk factors are not listed in order of clinical importance in Table 12-3. This determination depends upon the patient's clinical presentation. In a crisis, when consultation is desired but unavailable, the suicide risk assessment and intervention tables can be completed in lieu of consultation.

In addition, Table 12-3 can be used as a patient self-assessment instrument to evaluate suicide risk. The psychiatrist also completes an assessment. The findings are compared and discussed with the patient. Retrospective patient self-assessment using Table 12-3 (e.g., rating of suicide risk a week or a month prior to current assessment) can be used to track the recent history of suicide developments and to compare it with the patient's current assessment. Also, repeated assessments by the psychiatrist over time may provide a useful baseline and subsequent clinical profile of suicide risk status. The clinician, however, should not rely solely upon the patient's self-assessment of suicide risk in the evalua-

TABLE 12–4. Assessment of suicide risk and psychiatric intervention options

Suicide risk	Psychiatric interventions
HIGH	Immediate hospitalization
MODERATE	*Consider* Hospitalization Frequent outpatient visits Reevaluate treatment plan frequently. Remain available to patient.
LOW	Continue with current treatment plan.

Note. Tables 12-3 and 12-4 represent only one method of suicide risk assessment and intervention. The purpose of these tables is heuristic, encouraging a systematic approach to risk assessment. The therapist's clinical judgment concerning the patient remains paramount. Given the fact that suicide risk variables will be assigned different weights according to the clinical presentation of the patient, the method presented in these tables cannot be followed rigidly.
Source. Reprinted, with permission, from Simon RI: "Clinical risk management of suicidal patients: assessing the unpredictable," in *American Psychiatric Press Review of Psychiatry and the Law, Vol. 3.* Edited by Simon RI. Washington, DC, American Psychiatric Press, 1992. Copyright 1992, American Psychiatric Press.

tion of suicide risk potential. It is not likely that the patient will be able to assess risk factors such as, for example, diagnosis, epidemiologic data, and the state of the therapeutic alliance.

What are the more common legal defenses asserted in suicide lawsuits?

Simon and Sadoff (43) discuss the legal defenses available to psychiatrists who are sued following a patient's suicide. The most common defenses include the following:

1. Exercise of reasonable professional judgment and compliance with the standard of care
2. That determination of suicide was not reasonable
3. Justified allowance of movement ("open door" policy)
4. Intervening acts
5. Governmental immunity

As noted above, the use of reasonable professional judgement is a mainstay defense. The credibility of this defense depends upon compliance with the standard of care as documented by the doctor's own records (12). For example, in *Centeno v. City of New York* (12), the court ruled that the decision to release a patient from the hospital and place him on convalescent outpatient status during which time he committed suicide was not negligent but an act of reasonable medical judgment.

If after adequate psychiatric evaluation, no evidence of a foreseeable suicide risk is found, courts have held in favor of the clinician. For example, in *Wilson v. State* (44), the court held that no liability could be imposed for granting grounds privileges to a patient who later committed suicide. The court reasoned that there was no foreseeable evidence that the patient was suicidal. The defendant knew the patient's history through prior treatment records, and nothing in his current behavior indicated that the patient was contemplating suicide.

Foreseeability must be distinguished from preventability. A suicide may not be foreseeable but, in hindsight, may have been preventable. Experts who testify in suicide cases should not confuse these two important but fundamentally different concepts.

In recent years, the more liberal open-door policy has evolved in the treatment and management of suicidal patients. The open-door policy is one aspect of the greater autonomy accorded all patients in general and psychiatric patients in particular. Some courts have not imposed liability because of the reasonableness of the decision to implement the open-door policy with certain patients. These courts have viewed the open-door policy, when reasonably used as an extension of professional judgment, as a viable treatment approach. For instance, in *Johnson v. United States* (15), a discharged patient committed suicide after killing his brother-in-law and wounding his wife. While the court noted that an open-door policy creates a higher potential for danger, it went on to say the following:

> The court is aware that some psychiatrists adhere to the older, more custodial approach. However, it has been proved to the court's satisfaction that the open door policy and the judgement balancing test are an accepted method of treatment. Therefore, no liability can arise merely because a psychiatrist favors the newer over the older approach.

The clinician must understand that an open-door policy cannot be applied in a stock fashion to all psychiatric patients. Autonomy in the hospital setting must bear a rational nexus to the patient's diagnosis, clinical condition, and level of functional mental capacity.

Robertson (45) identifies two other defenses, contributory and comparative negligence, that can serve as either a complete or a partial bar to defendant liability. The theory of *contributory negligence* states that if the plaintiff was negligent to any degree, he or she is barred from recovery. Because of the harshness of this rule, only a few states still use contributory negligence. The modern trend has been toward *comparative negligence,* which reduces the plaintiff's recovery by a percentage of his or her fault. In a comparative negligence statute, an accident victim receiving a $1,000 award who was 20% at fault would recover only $800.

Despite the provision of reasonable care in the management of a suicidal patient, an unforeseen or extraordinary circumstance may arise that enables the patient to commit suicide. When this occurs, a clinician can argue that the unforseen event *supersedes* the care or lack of care provided by the defendant. For example, in *Paddock v. Chacko* (46), a Florida appeals court concluded that the psychiatrist was not liable for self-inflicted injuries of a patient he had seen only once. The patient placed herself in her parents' care and custody. The parents disregarded the psychiatrist's recommendation that their daughter be hospitalized. The parents' unwillingness to heed the psychiatrist's recommendation represented a "superceding" factor that intervened between the patient's injuries and the psychiatrist's care.

The concept of the least-restrictive alternative also may be a valid defense in suicide litigation. Particularly in the case of patients involuntarily hospitalized, a number of states require that patients be treated in the least-restrictive treatment environment consistent with their clinical needs (47).

Governmental immunity is another common defense in suicide cases. It is an expression of the traditional legal principle that federal and state governments cannot be sued without their consent. Professionals employed by federal, state, or municipal agencies or facilities may be protected from liability by some form of governmental immunity (48). Whether absolute or qualified, governmental immunity is governed by statute.

To what extent is suicide a function of psychiatric illness?

Suicide is the result of complex, multiple factors including diagnostic (psychiatric and medical), constitutional, occupational, environmental, social, cultural, existential, and chance factors. Although there is a loose fit between diagnosis and suicide, suicide rarely occurs in the absence of psychiatric illness. Adult suicide studies indicate that more than 90% of suicide victims were mentally ill before their deaths (49, 50, 51); 30% to 70% of suicide victims were suffering from depression. The fit is closest with affective disorders, for which there is a lifetime suicide mortality rate of 15%. In the clinical vignette, Mr. Walters' hospital diagnosis was major depressive episode and a medical disorder, Crohn's disease. His grandfather committed suicide and an uncle had a recurrent affective disorder.

The factor of chance may also be critical. A patient may be determinedly suicidal for only a few seconds, minutes, or hours during the course of a psychiatric illness. If the suicidal patient comes upon an unlocked window, new construction, or a lethal instrument carelessly left about, the patient may take advantage of a chance opportunity. If such a situation is suspected, constant one-to-one supervision or even restraint may be necessary until the critical time of lethality passes.

Acute and chronic suicidal states bear some relation to psychiatric diagnosis. Acutely suicidal patients often suffer from a major affective or schizophrenic illness requiring immediate hospitalization and treatment. The suicide risk will pass with the remission of the acute or recurrent episode of illness. The clinician is on notice to act quickly and affirmatively to hospitalize and supervise these patients appropriately.

Chronically suicidal patients are often treated as outpatients and suffer from personality disorders, particularly borderline personality disorder. These patients may require psychiatric hospitalization from time to time when their suicidal impulses undergo exacerbation because of some life crisis. The chronic suicidal state of these patients appears to be related to problems in managing rage secondary to unstable self-esteem regulation, which is often triggered by some interpersonal crisis. Such patients may use the possibility of suicide as a comforting means of escape and control. At times of crises, these patients may present real suicide risks. If not hospitalized, they should at least be seen frequently and their medication monitored very closely. The patient's support system should be mobilized, and the psychiatrist needs to be readily available. Both the patient and the therapist must be able to tolerate a certain level of chronic suicidal ideation in order to continue the work of therapy.

Although suicide occurs across the spectrum of psychiatric disorders, it is seen most often with affective disorders and chronic alcoholism. Schizophrenic disorders are also associated with a higher suicide risk. Neurotic depressive patients have a low suicide rate compared with psychotic depressive patients. Examining suicide as a psychopathological event is always good clinical practice because it allows for appropriate treatment and supervision of the patient who is experiencing deep psychological pain.

Can epidemiologic data be useful to the clinician in assessing suicide risk?

The use of base rates for given populations may be of limited value in increasing the clinician's level of suspicion for suicidal behavior. For example, the base rate of suicide for the general population, including children, is 10 to 15 per 100,000 (52). The suicide rate in the psychiatric hospital population is 40 to 50 per 100,000 or 1% of the total of 30,000 admissions per year (30). Within this population, those patients with a history of previous attempts have a 9% to 33% successful suicide rate. One-third (or approximately 100) of these hospital cases are litigated. In general, the suicide rate for a given psychiatric hospital is proportional to the types of patients admitted. Facilities that admit acutely ill patients, particularly those suffering from acute schizophrenia, have higher suicide rates (53). Not surprisingly, suicide risk is reported to be higher in the psychiatric emergency room subset (32).

Patients diagnosed as suffering from affective disorder, schizophrenia, or alcohol and drug abuse are at greater risk for suicide, at a rate of 180 per 100,000 (52). For patients over 65 and for divorced persons, the suicide rates are 247 and 662 per 100,000, respectively (30). Predictably, physical illness and social isolation are important factors. Men die three to four times more frequently from suicide than women, although the latter attempt suicide three to four times more frequently than men. Racially, the suicide rate is higher among white individuals (except in young adults) (52). In Perr's sample of 32 suicides, 43.8% were in the 15- to 24-year age group (36). Thus, a specific population that is at increased risk for suicide can be identified that should raise the clinician's level of suspicion. Mr. Walters was separated, white, physically ill, and hospitalized for depression. Epidemiologically, this placed him in a high-risk category.

Although epidemiologic analysis or the use of suicide scales and checklists can be helpful, the groups used to develop these modalities are not always representative of an individual who comes from a special population, such as Mr. Walters (a middle class, professional, white outpatient). Paradoxically, findings among studies show differing age, sex, and clinical factors in the prediction of suicidal behavior. Furthermore, because suicide is a rare event, even highly sensitive epidemiologic methods using base-rate data will include far too many false positives to be useful predictively (54). For example, patients with affective disorders have a lifetime suicide rate of 15%. Thus, 85% of this group, even when depressed, do not commit suicide.

Identification of individuals who will commit suicide is not currently feasible through the use of measures and instruments (55). Although suicide rating scales are useful in the gathering of important clinical data, nothing can take the place of sound clinical judgment that is based upon a comprehensive suicide assessment. Profiles of high-risk groups that are identified from statistical data can help focus clinical response to individual patients. Furthermore, the high suicide base rates for certain psychiatric disorders can be used as a suicide prevention factor. Patients and family members who are informed of increased suicide base rates associated with their psychiatric disorder may be encouraged to obtain early treatment when faced with future recurrences. Not all patients, however, can tolerate such information, nor can they use the data constructively.

Psychoendocrine assessment of suicidality has been reported (56). Urinary norepinephrine-to-epinephrine level ratios were significantly lower in a group of male psychiatric inpatients with a history of suicide attempts compared with those without such a history. Fawcett (20) reported metabolic studies demonstrating high levels of 24-hour urinary 17-hydroxycorticosteroid in prospectively studied high-risk patients. Replication data from initial studies suggest that patients with levels greater than 10 mg may be at risk for suicide. According to Winchel et al. (57), low ranges of cerebrospinal fluid 5-hydroxyindoleacetic acid (5-HIAA) concentration may enhance the importance of this biologic marker as a risk factor in suicide. Further work needs to be done to determine the predictive value of these biologic findings. The therapist should place greater weight on the individual patient and the immediate clinical evaluation.

Should the psychiatrist rely on the mental health staff for the management of the hospitalized patient?

Psychiatrists are responsible for the diagnosis, treatment, and management of their hospitalized patients. If control is turned over to other mental health professionals, adequate supervision must be provided. In jurisdictions where psychologists have hospital privileges and are allowed to treat inpatients, psychiatrists still may be required to provide supervision. The supervising psychiatrist may be held jointly responsible for any legal liability. Pro forma supervision, without direct examination and follow-up of the patient, can be legally disastrous.

Can the psychiatrist be held liable for the negligence of other mental health professionals? What is the hospital's legal responsibility for the negligence of the mental health staff?

Under the doctrine of *respondeat superior* ("let the master respond"), psychiatrists may be held monetarily responsible for the negligence of others working under their control and direction. The doctrine of vicarious liability means that the one who controls the conduct of treatment pays money damages to the successful plaintiff (58). Psychiatrists should exercise firm control and supervision over mental health professionals who work directly with their patients. While many nonmedical therapists and paraprofessionals provide excellent treatment to patients, the training and experience of some of these individuals may be insufficient. Therapists, including psychiatrists, are not born with an intuitive knowledge of how to treat psychiatric patients. All therapists must be adequately trained and supervised.

Cohen and Mariano (59) discuss vicarious liability for associates and assistants of the psychiatric team. Although there is no case law on this point yet, as the concept gains popularity and the number of members on the team grows, the potential liability of individual team members will probably increase. On a related issue, the court in *Durflinger v. Artiles* (60) held, among other things, that when a physician is employed by a state mental hospital and participates in a hospital team recommendation concerning discharging a committed patient, the physician has a duty to use reasonable and ordinary care and discretion in making such a recommendation. The court noted that this duty is owed to the patient and the public.

In the vignette, Dr. Williams relied upon the nurse's discretion in providing appropriate supervision at the time of the patient's admission. It was clinically inappropriate for Dr. Williams to turn over to the nursing staff his personal responsibility for supervision and control of the patient. Furthermore, primary treatment of Mr. Walters was provided by a third-year resident. Close supervision of the resident's treatment of the patient was necessary by the attending physician, Dr. Williams.

Psychiatrists are required to exercise close supervision and control, particularly when they assign duties that they know may be beyond the competence of other mental health professionals. If the hospital staff members are negligent in their duty to the patient, liability also may be imposed on these individuals and the hospital. For instance, the psychiatric technician who was aware that Mr. Walters might have purchased a gun should have directly reported this information to the head nurse. She, in turn, should have reported it immediately to Dr. Williams. Overlooking such a critical note about a patient who later commits suicide may amount to a case of *res ipsa loquitur* ("the thing speaks for itself"), similar to that of a surgeon leaving a sponge in the abdomen of the patient.

Nurses and other mental health professionals, while employees of the hospital, may become the "borrowed servants" of the psychiatrist when they are temporarily under the psychiatrist's control. Under the "borrowed servant" doctrine, the hospital might attempt to shift liability to the psychiatrist. In effect, the hospital would argue that these employees acted beyond the scope of their duties when working for the psychiatrist.

Hospitals themselves also may become liable for patients' suicide, particularly if these hospitals violate their own standards of care (61). The Joint Commission on Accreditation of Healthcare Organizations (JCAHO) (62) promulgates standards for hospitals that provide care for psychiatric patients. In addition, most hospitals have established their own standards. Once hospitals and accrediting organizations establish policies that address specific subjects, these may be admissible as evidence of the legal standard of care (63). Non-official guidelines for "suicide-proofing" psychiatric units have been proposed (64). Of course, no psychiatric unit can be made "suicide-proof."

Fishalow (5) notes several factors that hospitals must consider in caring for the suicidal patient:

1. No precise calibration of patient behavior to a corresponding level of vigilance exists. The passage of time dilutes the significance of prior attempts; moreover, there is a somewhat questionable distinction between threats and actual attempts.
2. Watchfulness may be relaxed if the patient's condition improves—but not merely for the sake of expediency.
3. The hospital must maintain its facilities and equipment so that hazards are not created.
4. If staff ratios are insufficient, this may be evidence of negligence.
5. Courts will often find negligence if it can be proven that the hospital violated its own precautionary rules.
6. If a mistake is found to be an honest error of judgment within a physician's discretion, liability will not usually be assigned.

Why does the patient's "volitional act" of suicide not break the liability claim against the psychiatrist?

When patients kill themselves, are they not the agents of their own deaths regardless of negligence? In negligence actions arising out of attempted or actual suicide, the patient or a representative must establish that the psychiatrist's acts or omissions were the proximate cause of the suicide. A patient's "volitional act" of suicide may be considered an intervening force, thus relieving the psychiatrist of liability if it was unreasonable to have foreseen the patient's act. For instance, after conducting a thorough assessment of a patient, including reviewing any past records and consulting with other knowledgeable sources, a psychiatrist could reasonably conclude that the patient does not represent a suicide risk. If the patient were to commit suicide, without warning or reasonable sign of intent, then the death would likely be considered "unforeseeable." The patient's unexplained behavior could be considered an "intervening cause," thus severing the chain of causation between the psychiatrist and the patient's injury.

Moreover, a patient may be considered *contributorily negligent* if he or she fails to participate reasonably in treatment and that failure is the proximate cause of injury or death. For example, in *Skar v. City of Lincoln, Nebraska* (35), the patient failed to cooperate in any manner, preventing the psychiatrist from obtaining a case history or from assessing the actual suicide risk. The patient injured his spine after attempting to jump out of a window. The court refused to hold the psychiatrist liable for the patient's injuries, stating that the patient has a duty to cooperate with the psychiatrist to the extent he is able.

In *Weathers v. Pilkinton* (65), the majority opinion of the Court of Appeals of Tennessee held that a patient's suicide was an independent intervening cause unless the patient "did not know and understand the nature of his suicidal act and, therefore, did not have willful and intelligent purpose to accomplish this." A wrongful death action was brought against a physician who allegedly failed to take appropriate steps to prevent his patient from committing suicide. The trial judge held that the suicide of the patient was an independent intervening cause and directed a verdict for the physician. The appeals court affirmed.

Beahrs (66) states that psychiatric patients incur legal duties in the health care context. Specific duties that arise from patients' specialized role in their own health care include the provision of accurate and complete information and the cooperation with treatment within the boundaries of informed consent. General duties that apply to all citizens but are particularly applicable to the mental health context include respect for the physical integrity of oneself, others, and their property, and obeying the law.

Because of psychiatric impairment, there are limits to how much responsibility the law will impute to a patient. Such limits are illustrated in the case of *Cowan v. Doering* (67). In *Cowan,* the trial judge refused to submit to the jury the question of the patient's contributory negligence for her own injuries. The patient, diagnosed as having a borderline personality disorder, jumped from her hospital window. She sued, contending that her physician was negligent for not ordering a "suicide watch." The experts all agreed on her diagnosis, but differed in their opinion concerning whether the patient made a genuine attempt or a manipulative gesture to gain attention. The jury awarded the plaintiff $600,000 in compensatory damages, and this decision was affirmed on appeal. The court noted that suicidal patients whose judgment is adversely affected by mental illness cannot have their conduct judged by the standards of care and risk assessment of rational adults. The physician had a duty to prevent or at least guard against the patient's suicidal act, including anticipating irrational behavior such as jumping from a window (68).

From a risk management perspective, psychiatrists should not look to the suicidal patient's "volitional" act as a defense in a malpractice suit. The psychiatric patient's mental impairment almost always voids the psychiatrist's defense of contributory negligence. Conducting timely, contemporaneously recorded suicide risk assessments combined with appropriate clinical interventions provides the best malpractice defense.

What is the legal standing of family members in bringing a malpractice suit?

In the vignette, Mrs. Walters brought a suit against Dr. Williams for the suicide of her husband. Ordinarily, only the patient with whom the psychiatrist has established a doctor-patient relationship can file a malpractice claim. No duty is owed to any family members. However, wrongful death statutes that allow survivors to recover money damages for a death caused by another person's wrongful act exist in every state (69). The right to sue for wrongful death belongs to individuals who suffer financial or other loss because of the patient's death.

Families also may bring malpractice suits under the Federal Tort Claims Act when the decedent was employed by the United States government and the government is accused of wrongdoing. This federal statute permits the government to be sued like any citizen in similar circumstances and is an exception to the doctrine of sovereign immunity.

In some lawsuits, are psychiatrists being held to a "strict liability" standard in the prevention of suicide?

The doctrine of strict liability states that the defendant is, in fact, legally responsible for the harm done even when there is no proof of carelessness or fault. Strict liability usually is applied to manufactured products. Unfortunately, some courts appear to have applied a form of "strict liability" to psychiatrists when patients have killed themselves. These courts seem to believe that the psychiatrist creates the patient (analogous to the manufacturing of a product) and is responsible for the destruction of the patient (analogous to when a manufactured product breaks) (25).

In malpractice claims, negligence must be proven. In the past, courts have not looked at the psychiatrist as an insurer or guarantor of results (70). Nevertheless, some courts have refused to defer to a psychiatrist's judgment about adequate precautions taken to prevent suicide. An after-the-fact review by these courts may find that the psychiatrist recognized the risk but underestimated its seriousness (70). The rationale of imposing liability on psychiatrists for the suicides of their patients suggests that the clinician should be held responsible only for the deaths of those patients whom a reasonable practitioner would have regarded as posing a substantial risk of suicide. Juries often cannot make the distinction between a high and low suicide risk (70). Retrospectively, every patient who commits suicide seems to have been a high risk. Thus, a type of "strict liability" is established through hindsight bias.

The presence of recorded risk-benefit assessments that substantiate good clinical practices may not necessarily prevent the application of "strict liability" analysis to patients' suicides. Risk-benefit analysis, while highly recommended, cannot provide a foolproof risk management shield. Psychiatrists cannot predict with certainty how the patient may respond to any given treatment intervention. Many treatments, including therapeutic passes, provide no guarantee of effectiveness. Furthermore, excessive restriction of the patient may itself be antitherapeutic, thus increasing liability for wrongful treatment.

Perr (30) points out that psychiatrists are unable to predict violent events accurately. This is recognized by the American Psychiatric Association, by a number of courts, and by lawyers who criticize the dangerousness requirement contained in many civil commitment statutes. Retrospective second-guessing of psychiatric treatment can lead to a finding of liability whenever a patient commits suicide. Drukteinis (71) points out that the broadening of liability on the basis of simple direct causation is not in line with modern psychiatric thinking that views suicide as a complex psychodynamic, social, cultural, situational, and biochemical event. He feels that such broadening becomes a convenient means of shifting the guilt of survivors who want to protect the reputation of their family members.

If a psychiatrist's patient commits suicide, the likelihood of a lawsuit against the psychiatrist exists. The majority of these cases are legally defensible, however, if an adequate suicide risk assessment was performed, recorded, and reasonably clinically implemented.

What are the circumstances under which iatrogenic or treatment-induced suicide may occur?

Talking therapies, including psychodynamic psychotherapy, are not without their risks (4). Patients who are improperly diagnosed or selected for a particular psychotherapy may undergo regression, with subsequent suicide attempts (72). Wild therapists, innovative or regressive therapies, sexual seduction of patients by therapists, malignant countertransferences, and the provision of suicidal patients with lethal amounts of medication may facilitate or cause suicide in vulnerable patients. Swenson (73) cites breach of confidentiality, directives for actions that result in suicide, and the fostering of symbiotic dependency followed by abrupt termination as iatrogenic suicide factors within the therapeutic process.

Stone (74) presents clinical case material demonstrating that psychotherapy can precipitate suicide or suicide attempts. When presented with the malignant insight that his or her reality situation is empty of any possible gratification, the patient may seek suicide. The patient is confronted with "an intolerable introject" when defensive wish-fulfilling fantasies are breached. The final step occurs when the therapist offers the possibility of symbiotic gratification and then withdraws it.

Inexperienced or improperly supervised mental health professionals may get in over their heads in attempting to treat suicidal patients. Suicidal patients can induce intense anxiety in both experienced and inexperienced therapists that may lead to precipitous abandonment of these patients with disastrous consequences. For these and other reasons, therapists who work with suicidal patients need to have the security of their own support system.

Psychiatrists who practice in managed health care settings must base their treatment interventions on the best interests of the patient. Curtailment or discontinuance of treatment of a suicidal patient based solely on administrative or cost-efficiency reasoning may lead to the provision of ineffective treatment or to abandonment of the patient. If the patient then attempts or actually commits suicide, the cost-cutting actions may be determined by a court to be the proximate cause of an iatrogenic suicide.

What are some of the risk management aspects of suicide aftercare?

In the aftermath of suicide, the psychiatrist has a number of responsibilities in providing aftercare (75). From a risk management perspective, certain steps should be taken after a suicide occurs (76). Suicide aftercare often presents conflicting concerns and roles for the clinician. The psychiatrist should ensure that the patient's records are complete, be available to assist grieving family members, and consult with colleagues and an attorney to protect against a claim of malpractice. The patient's records must also be brought up to date. To avoid any suggestion of impropriety, all entries made after the incident should be so dated. Rough notes should be kept. Self-serving, exculpatory statements and lengthy entries where previously briefer notations were made must be avoided.

If a conflict exists with another professional's notes (e.g., nurse's notes) that are believed to be in error, a meeting with that professional, that person's supervisor, and other physicians involved in the case should be considered. If litigation has been threatened or initiated, this meeting should also include the psychiatrist's attorney. The discrepancies or differences should be discussed to see if they can be honestly reconciled. If they can be reconciled, the corrections should be made. A jointly prepared memorandum that fully describes the circumstances should be signed by all parties and placed in the files. The memorandum will likely be made available to the plaintiff via discovery if litigation should arise. Thus, it is extremely critical to be forthright and make no effort to conceal any deliberations or discussions that are held.

Conversations with family members are appropriate and can allay grief and assist family members in obtaining help. Care must be exercised not to reveal confidential information about the patient and to avoid making self-incriminating or transparently self-exonerating statements. Such statements may further distress the family and provide a spur to litigation. Moreover, the ownership of the patient's records is typically governed by state law, which should be adhered to accordingly.

The psychiatrist should consult with an attorney before making any oral or written statements to other providers or before releasing patient records. Information necessary for the proper care and follow-up of a patient should be immediately provided. A detailed account of the suicide incident in question or statements apportioning responsibility should not be made before consultation with an attorney. For instance, details revealed to the hospital about the incident may later be used as evidence against the psychiatrist if the hospital attempts to shift responsibility for the incident.

A complete and candid reporting of the adverse incident should be made immediately to the malpractice defense attorney or insurance carrier, even if no suit is mentioned. A detailed report will likely be helpful in obtaining the best possible defense or settlement.

The survivors of suicide are at increased risk of suicide themselves (77). Moreover, they are more vulnerable to physical and psychological disorders. Gutheil (78) has noted that a postsuicide family outreach mode by the clinician is crucial for the devastated family members following a suicide. This recommendation, which is based primarily on humanitarian concerns for survivors, also, incidentally, may have a powerful risk management aspect. Gutheil points out that "bad feelings" combined with a bad outcome often lead to litigation. The individuals who lived with the patient before the suicide not only currently experience intense emotional pain but also shared it with the patient before death. Thus, a number of lawsuits are filed because of the clinician's refusal to apologize or express, in any way, feelings of condolence, sympathy, and regret for the patient's death.

In Massachusetts, an "apology statute" exists that renders various benevolent human expressions such as condolences, regrets, and apologies "inadmissible as evidence of an admission of liability in a civil action" (79). Such statutes may also exist in other jurisdictions.

Attorneys advise clinicians in two very different ways on the issue of suicide aftercare. Following a bad outcome, some attorneys recommend that the case be sealed and no communication be established with the family, except through the attorney. Other attorneys encourage *judicious* communication, consultation, or even treatment of family members. If this approach is taken, the psychiatrist should concentrate on addressing the feelings of the family members rather than the specifics of the patient's care. This situation is quite similar to any other grief-related therapy or consultation. Although clinicians may fear that such contact will increase the risk of a lawsuit, the value of such consultation in healing grief and decreasing the risk of a lawsuit is great enough for clinicians to consider providing such a humanitarian approach to the survivors of patient suicide.

References

1. American Psychiatric Association: The Problem-Oriented System in Psychiatry (Task Force Report No 12). Washington, DC, American Psychiatric Association, 1977
2. Whitree v State, 56 Misc 2d 693, 290 NYS2d 486, 498–499 (1968)
3. Abille v United States, 482 F Supp 703, 708 (ND Cal 1980)

4. Simon RI: The practice of psychotherapy: legal liabilities of an "impossible" profession, in American Psychiatric Press Review of Clinical Psychiatry and the Law, Vol 2. Edited by Simon RI. Washington DC, American Psychiatric Press, 1991, pp 3–91
5. Fishalow SE: The tort liabilities of the psychiatrist. Bull Am Acad Psychiatry Law 3:191–230, 1975
6. Speer v United States, 512 F Supp 670 (ND Tex 1981), aff'd, Speer v United States, 675 F2d 100 (5th Cir 1982)
7. Slovenko R: Forensic psychiatry, in Comprehensive Textbook of Psychiatry IV. Edited by Kaplan HI, Sadock BJ. Baltimore, MD, Williams & Wilkins, 1985, p 1986
8. American Psychiatric Association: The Principles of Medical Ethics With Annotations Especially Applicable to Psychiatry. Washington, DC, American Psychiatric Association, 1989
9. FLA STAT ANN § 3490.014 (West Supp 1988)
10. Abille v United States, 482 F Supp 703 (ND Cal 1980)
11. Katz v State, 46 Misc 2d 61, 258 NYS2d 912 (1965)
12. Centeno v City of New York, 48 AD2d 812, 369 NYS2d 710 (NY App Div 1975), aff'd 40 NY2d 932, 358, 389 NYS2d 837, 258 NE2d 520 (1976)
13. Halleck SL: Law in the Practice of Psychiatry. New York, Plenum, 1980, p 70
14. Amchin J, Wettstein RM, Roth LH: Suicide, ethics, and the law, in Suicide Over the Life Cycle. Edited by Blumenthal SJ, Kupfer DJ. Washington, DC, American Psychiatric Press, 1990, pp 637–663
15. 409 F Supp 1283 (MD Fla 1976), rev'd, Johnson v United States, 576 F2d 606 (5th Cir 1978), cert denied, 451 U.S. 1018 (1981)
16. Klein JI, Macbeth JE, Onek JN: Legal Issues in the Practice of Psychiatry. Washington, DC, American Psychiatric Press, 1984, pp 23–24
17. Remeikis G, Wise TN, Mann LS, et al: Use of passes on a general hospital psychiatric unit. Hosp Community Psychiatry 38:988–989, 1988
18. Bellah v Greenson, 81 Cal App 3d 614, 146 Cal Rptr 535 (Cal Ct App 1978)
19. Katz SE: Commentary on "Characterization of schizophrenic patients who commit suicide." Intelligence Reports in Psychiatric Disorders 3:9, 1984
20. Fawcett J: Predictors of early suicide: identification and appropriate intervention. J Clin Psychiatry 49(10, suppl):7–8, 1988
21. Fawcett J, Scheptner WA, Fogg L, et al: Time-related predictors of suicide in major affective disorder. Am J Psychiatry 147:1189–1194, 1990
22. Simon RI: Clinical risk management of suicidal patients: assessing the unpredictable, in American Psychiatric Press Review of Clinical Psychiatry and the Law, Vol 3. Edited by Simon RI. Washington, DC, American Psychiatric Press, 1992, pp 3–63
23. Karasu TB: Psychoanalysis and psychoanalytic psychotherapy, in Comprehensive Textbook of Psychiatry V, Vol 2. Edited by Kaplan HI, Sadock BJ. Baltimore, MD, Williams & Wilkins, 1989, pp 1442–1461; see p 1449
24. Shneidman ES: Definition of Suicide. New York, John Wiley, 1985, p 126
25. Gutheil TG: Medicolegal pitfalls in the treatment of borderline patients. Am J Psychiatry 142:9–14, 1985
26. Traits of people who formulate suicide pacts. Clinical Psychiatry News 13(3):12, 1985
27. J Fawcett, personal communication, January 1991
28. 393 Mass 836, 473 NE2d 1131 (1985)

29. Simon RI: The suicide prevention pact: clinical and legal considerations, in American Psychiatric Press Review of Clinical Psychiatry and the Law, Vol 2. Edited by Simon RI. Washington, DC, American Psychiatric Press, 1991, pp 441–451

30. Perr IN: Suicide liability: a clinical perspective. Legal Aspects of Psychiatric Practice 1:5–8, 1984

31. Weisman AD, Worden JW: Risk-rescue rating in suicide assessment. Arch Gen Psychiatry 26:553–560, 1972

32. Roy A: Risk factors for suicide in psychiatric patients. Arch Gen Psychiatry 39:1089–1095, 1982

33. Simon RI: Concise Guide to Clinical Psychiatry and the Law. Washington, DC, American Psychiatric Press, 1988, p 83

34. Gutheil TG: Malpractice liability in suicide. Legal Aspects of Psychiatric Practice 1:1–4, 1984

35. Skar v City of Lincoln, Nebraska, 599 F2d 253 (8th Cir 1979)

36. Perr IN: Suicidal litigation and risk management: a review of 32 cases. Bull Am Acad Psychiatry Law 13:209–219, 1985; see p 209

37. Murphy G: Clinical identification of suicide risk. Arch Gen Psychiatry 27:356–359, 1972

38. Cross CK, Hirschfeld RM: Epidemiology of disorders in adulthood: suicide, in Social, Epidemiologic and Legal Psychiatry. Edited by Cavenar JO. New York, Basic Books, 1986, pp 246–258

39. Pokorny A: Prediction of suicide in psychiatric patients. Arch Gen Psychiatry 40:249–257, 1983

40. Melton GB, Petrila JD, Poythress NG, et al: Psychological Evaluations for the Courts. New York, Guilford, 1987, pp 197–204

41. Simon RI: Concise Guide to Clinical Psychiatry and the Law. Washington, DC, American Psychiatric Press, 1988, pp 86–87

42. Ibid, p 87

43. Simon RI, Sadoff RL: Psychiatric Malpractice: Cases and Comments for Clinicians. Washington, DC, American Psychiatric Press, 1992

44. 112 AD2d 366, 491 NYS2d 818 (NY App Div 1985)

45. Robertson JD: The psychiatrist in the courtroom: suicide litigation—the trial of a suicide case, in American Psychiatric Press Review of Clinical Psychiatry and the Law, Vol 2. Edited by Simon RI. Washington, DC, American Psychiatric Press, 1991, pp 423–441

46. 522 So 2d 410 (Fla Dist Ct App 1988), review den, Paddock v Chacko, 553 So 2d 168 (Fla 1989)

47. Perlin ML: Mental Disability Law: Civil and Criminal, Vol 1. Charlottesville, VA, Michie, 1989, pp 349–350

48. Reisner R, Slobogin C: Law and the Mental Health System, 2nd Edition. St Paul, MN, West Publishing, 1990, pp 95–100; see, e.g., Miller v State, 731 SW2d 885 (Mo Ct App 1987)

49. Dorpat TL, Ripley HS: A study of suicide in the Seattle area. Compr Psychiatry 1:349–359, 1960

50. Robins E, Murphy GE, Wilkinson RH, et al: Some clinical considerations in the prevention of suicide based on a study of 134 successful suicides. Am J Public Health 49:888–899, 1959

51. Barraclough B, Bunch J, Nelson B, et al: A hundred cases of suicide: clinical aspects. Br J Psychiatry 125:355–373, 1974
52. Buda M, Tsuang MT: The epidemiology of suicide: implications for clinical practice, in Suicide Over the Life Cycle. Edited by Blumenthal SJ, Kupfer DJ. Washington, DC, American Psychiatric Press, 1990, pp 17–37
53. Lion JR: Violence and suicide within the hospital, in Modern Hospital Psychiatry. Edited by Lion JR, Adler WN, Webb WL. New York, WW Norton, 1988, pp 291–299
54. Murphy GE: On suicide prediction and prevention. Arch Gen Psychiatry 40:343–344, 1983
55. Pokorny AD: Prediction of suicide in psychiatric patients. Arch Gen Psychiatry 40:249–257, 1983
56. Ostroff RB, Giller B, Harkness L, et al: The norepinephrine-to-epinephrine ratio in patients with a history of suicide attempts. Am J Psychiatry 142:224–227, 1985
57. Winchel RM, Stanley B, Stanley M: Biochemical aspects of suicide, in Suicide Over the Life Cycle. Edited by Blumenthal SJ, Kupfer DJ. Washington, DC, American Psychiatric Press, 1990, pp 97–126
58. Keeton WP, Dobbs DB, Keeton RE, et al: Prosser and Keeton on Torts, 5th Edition. St Paul, West Publishing, 1984, Chapter 12, 69
59. Cohen RJ, Mariano WE: Legal Guidebook in Mental Health. New York, Free Press, 1982, p 315
60. 234 Kan 484, 673 P2d 86 (1983)
61. Lucy Webb Hayes National Training School v Perotti, 419 F2d 704 (DC Cir 1969)
62. Joint Commission on Accreditation of Healthcare Organizations: Consolidated Standards Manual. Chicago, IL, Joint Commission on Accreditation of Healthcare Organizations, 1988
63. Darling v Charleston Community Memorial Hospital, 33 Ill 2d 326, 211 NE2d 253 (1965), cert denied, 383 U.S. 946 (1966)
64. Benensohn H, Resnik HLP: Guidelines for "suicide-proofing" a psychiatric unit. Am J Psychother 26:204–211, 1973
65. 754 SW2d 75 (Tenn Ct App 1988)
66. Beahrs JO: Legal duties of psychiatric patients. Bull Am Acad Psychiatry Law 18:189–202, 1990
67. 215 NJ Super 484, 522 A2d 444 (1987), aff'd, Cowan v Doering, 111 NJ 451, 545 A2d 159 (1988)
68. Weinstock v Ott, 444 NE2d 1227 (Ind Ct App 1983)
69. Hirsh HL: The wrongful death action: a study in transformation—evolution not revolution. Medical Trial Technique Quarterly 30:410–451, 1984
70. Klein JI, Glover SI: Psychiatric malpractice. Int J Law Psychiatry 6:131–157, 1983
71. Drukteinis AM: Psychiatric perspectives on civil liability for suicide. Bull Am Acad Psychiatry Law 13:71–84, 1985
72. Tancredi LR: Emergency psychiatry and crisis intervention: some legal and ethical issues. Psychiatric Annals 12:799–806, 1982
73. Swenson EV: Legal liability for a patient's suicide. Journal of Psychiatry and Law 14:409–434, 1986
74. Stone AA: Suicide precipitated by psychotherapy: a clinical contribution. Am J Psychother 25:18–26, 1971

75. Kaye NS, Soreff SM: The psychiatrist's role, responses, and responsibilities when a patient commits suicide. Am J Psychiatry 148:739–743, 1991
76. American Psychiatric Association Legal Consultation Plan, Washington, DC, Fall 1985, pp 1–2
77. Ness DE, Pfeffer CR: Sequelae of bereavement resulting from suicide. Am J Psychiatry 147:279–285, 1990
78. TG Gutheil, personal communication, October 1989
79. MASS GEN LAW ANN ch 233, § 23D (West Supp 1990)

Chapter 13　　**Clinical Approaches to the Duty to Warn and Protect Endangered Third Persons**

Dr. Fowler has been treating Professor Harris, a 45-year-old nuclear physicist specializing in nuclear weapons development, with individual psychotherapy during the past 3 months. Professor Harris developed a reactive depression after the breakup of a love affair.

In treating her patient, Dr. Fowler learns that the patient's mother died when he was 3 years of age. His father suffered from alcoholism and physically abused the patient. Professor Harris remembers that as a child, he felt very rejected, hurt, and frightened by his own feelings of helplessness and storms of rage. Although his father remarried when the patient was 5, his stepmother was cold and distant. Professor Harris received much of his early sense of worth through the praise of teachers for his academic achievements. He was an honor student in college and graduate school, winning many academic awards. In his personal relationships, he remained aloof and was considered a loner.

After receiving his doctorate, he stayed with the physics department of his university until an argument with the chairman of the department forced Professor Harris to leave. He became depressed at that time, seeking the aid of a therapist. Dr. Fowler knows of this previous treatment but has not obtained the records from the therapist. The records would have revealed that Professor Harris lost control of his anger and attempted to choke the department chairman during their argument. Professor Harris had to be physically restrained by others.

Professor Harris's initial depression abated when he was asked to take an important research position with a prestigious institution engaged in the development of nuclear weapons. Although uncertain about whether to work in weapons development, he eventually decided to take the position. Professor Harris created a breakthrough with his discovery and development of low-yield tactical nuclear weapons. These weapons were found to be extremely valuable for use in military war games and against selected targets where highly circumscribed lethality was required.

While working on this project, he became enamored of his secretary. Twenty years younger than Professor Harris, she had worked for him about a year before their personal relationship developed. For the first time in his life, Professor Harris felt happy and close to another human being. Because his hobby is collecting guns, they spent many hours together firing his treasured weapons. Her family was vehement in their rejection of Professor Harris because they considered him cold and odd. Six months after the relationship began, it dissolved when she resigned her position as his secretary and refused to see Professor Harris. She was frightened away by his jealous rages and his desire for bondage and other sadistic practices in their sexual relationship.

Professor Harris was devastated and slipped back into depression. Dr. Fowler's diagnosis is reactive depression. There are no vegetative signs. Psychotherapy, three times per week, is begun. After 2 months of therapy, Professor Harris decides to cut back therapy to once a week. Professor Harris receives a major promotion that temporarily produces an improvement in his depression. Dr. Fowler is concerned that her patient has not dealt with his feelings of loss and anger.

Dr. Fowler also questions the possible transference meaning of her patient's decision to cut back appointments. She recalls that the patient's mother died when he was 3 years old and that his stepmother was a cold and distant figure. Does the patient fear his hostile feelings toward women? Is he afraid of getting too close and exposing vulnerable, tender feelings? Dr. Fowler feels that her patient cannot tolerate transference interpretations at this point.

Three weeks after his decision to cut back therapy, Professor Harris rapidly slips into a major depression and develops the delusion that death by cancer is imminent. Dr. Fowler is alarmed by Professor Harris's ideas that his former girlfriend, her parents, and his former department head at the university are gloating over his imminent demise. He has never been able to settle his guilt over developing nuclear weapons. Professor Harris now feels that his imminent death is a just punishment. He spends much time going over his gun collection, ruminating about whether death by his own hand is preferable to a slow, agonizing death by cancer. He tells Dr. Fowler that perhaps he should die by the very weapons he has engineered and "take some of these other worthless people with me." Also, during the past week, he makes threatening calls to his former girlfriend, her parents, and his former departmental chairman, fully identifying himself.

Dr. Fowler proposes that her patient return to three-times-a-week psychotherapy and begin taking antidepressant medication. He refuses both suggestions, stating, "I am going to die soon anyway." Professor Harris does not want medication to confuse his thinking or interfere with making his "final plans." Dr. Fowler's recommendation of psychiatric hospitalization is viewed by Professor Harris as a plot by his enemies to "foil me."

Dr. Fowler knows that Professor Harris has access to low-yield tactical nu-

clear weapons with a force of approximately 1,000 pounds of TNT that could kill anyone within 500 feet of ground zero. Radiation and heat are lethal up to 1,000 feet. The weapon is considered "clean" but could still cause radiation sickness to a significant number of people. Also, for the first time, Professor Harris is considering carrying a .38 caliber Beretta pistol. He is no longer eating, having lost 10 pounds in the past week. He spends much of each night "pacing and plotting."

Dr. Flower assesses her patient's risk of violence as high. This assessment is based upon the severity of Professor Harris' psychotic depression, threats of violence toward identifiable victims, access to weapons of mass destruction, a clear motive of revenge, and a deteriorating therapeutic alliance. Given the high risk of violence, immediate psychiatric hospitalization is the intervention of choice.

Because Dr. Fowler has done previous forensic work, she is reasonably familiar with the Tarasoff case and some of its progeny. She knows that in her jurisdiction, no Tarasoff-type duty to warn exists. Furthermore, a strict confidentiality statute, with few exceptions, prohibits disclosure of information without the patient's consent. Dr. Fowler is concerned that because of the patient's current state of delusional depression, he might attempt to kill the three individuals he has threatened, or perpetrate mass murder through use of a nuclear weapon. Dr. Fowler decides to test the therapeutic alliance one last time by urging Professor Harris to accept a voluntary hospitalization. He refuses. Dr. Fowler straightforwardly informs Professor Harris that she cannot allow him to remain untreated and dangerous to himself and others. She states that she will file for involuntary hospitalization if he refuses voluntary hospitalization. He shouts, "Traitor!" and rushes out of the office.

Dr. Fowler considers her options. She reasons that because no duty to warn exists in her state and because the three individuals threatened are fully aware of the threats made against them by Professor Harris, no duty to warn these three individuals exists. However, she decides that the danger to the public is so great that ethically, morally, and professionally she must inform the police, despite the existence of a strict state confidentiality statute. Dr. Fowler immediately signs medical certification papers for the involuntary hospitalization of Professor Harris, which permits the police to apprehend and take him to a designated psychiatric hospital. Dr. Fowler cancels her remaining appointments, knowing she cannot concentrate on her other patients. She wants to devote herself full time to following through on this case.

What duties have been created for therapists by the *Tarasoff* case and its progeny?

Generally, an individual is under no recognized duty to come to the aid of or to protect another who is in a position to be injured or killed (1). Thus, a passerby who spots a child drowning has no legal duty to come to the aid of the child and will not incur liability if the child's pleas for help are ignored, unless the passerby created the dangerous situation. Even if the passerby stops to watch the child drown and consciously refuses aid in order to induce the child's death, no liability is incurred (2). The exception to this rule occurs if a special relationship exists between the passerby and the drowning child. For example, if the passerby is the child's father, he has an affirmative duty to rescue the child. If he fails to attempt rescue, he will be legally responsible for his child's death. Other examples of special relationships are those between husband and wife, doctor and patient, employer and employee, public carrier and passenger, and innkeeper and guest.

In the *Tarasoff* case (3), the California Supreme Court noted first that a recognized duty to protect third parties was imposed only if a special relationship existed between the victim, the individual whose conduct created the danger, and the defendant. In *Tarasoff*, the court expanded this duty, stating "that the single relationship of a doctor to his patient is sufficient to support the duty to exercise reasonable care to protect others" from the violent acts of patients. The basis for this special relationship was the presumption of a predictive ability by the therapist as well as the ability to control the patient through involuntary hospitalization. Clinically, the duty to protect an endangered third person from a patient makes sense when the therapist possesses "insider information" about threatened violence to others arising from the treatment. Long before *Tarasoff*, psychiatrists attempted to protect others from the violence of their patients when having direct knowledge of such intentions.

In *Tarasoff*, Prosenjit Poddar, a student at the University of California, was under the treatment of a university psychologist who became alarmed that Poddar might try to kill his former girlfriend, Tatiana Tarasoff. After campus police were notified, they detained Poddar for a short time but released him after they declared him rational. Thus, the attempt to initiate involuntary hospitalization was aborted. On review of the case by the supervising psychiatrist, no basis for involuntary hospitalization was found to exist. The patient's records were inexplicably destroyed. Poddar, not unexpectedly, terminated his treatment. He stabbed and shot Tatiana Tarasoff to death 2 months later. Her parents sued the psychologist, the psychiatrist, and the university, claiming their daughter should have been protected from Poddar by, among other ways, warning her directly.

Both the trial court and the intermediate appellate court in the civil case ruled that a cognizable cause of action was not stated by the Tarasoff family. However, the California Supreme Court found in favor of the Tarasoff's, stating: "Once a therapist does in fact determine, or under applicable professional standards should have determined, that a patient poses a serious danger of violence to others, he bears a duty to exercise reasonable care to protect the foreseeable victim of danger." The court stated that the identity of the victim should be apparent on a "moment's reflection." The therapist is not required to conduct an investigation (4). The adequacy of the therapist's fulfillment of the duty to protect is to be measured by ordinary negligence rather than the professional negligence standard used in the assessment of violence (5).

Because of the trial court's sensitivity to the "dire consequences" of involuntary hospitalization and other forms of restraint, the decision focused on the duty to warn—not limiting this duty to readily identifiable victims. Because of the importance of the issues involved and the pressure applied by the American Psychiatric Association (APA), the California Supreme Court agreed to rehear the case (6). Thus, in *Tarasoff II* (3), the court created a duty to protect, rather than merely a duty to warn, the victim but was vague as to how this duty should be discharged. While *Tarasoff II* suggested that warning or calling the police might discharge the duty, conventional clinical interventions already employed by therapists in treating violent patients were left open as a possibility. Although *Tarasoff II* expanded the therapist's duty by requiring protection of endangered victims, the treatment interventions designed to protect endangered third persons are less in conflict with the duty to maintain confidentiality.

The requirement that there be a readily identifiable victim before a duty to warn can be imposed on the psychiatrist was thought to be settled in *Thompson v. County of Alameda* (7). In this case, a juvenile who had been recently released murdered a young boy in his own neighborhood. The juvenile had threatened to take the life of a child in his neighborhood if released but had not identified any particular child. The court found no duty to warn because the victim was not identifiable. Three years later, the California Supreme Court reopened this issue.

In *Hedlund v. Superior Court* (8), the court expanded *Tarasoff* liability by concluding that a psychotherapist had an obligation to protect a child who was apt to be in proximity to the threatened person. Steve Wilson, receiving outpatient treatment, threatened harm to another patient, Lanita Wilson. She was not warned. Lanita Wilson was subsequently shot and severely wounded in front of her young son. The young child suffered emotional trauma. The court held that the child was a "foreseeable and readily identifiable" victim who "will not be far distant" (8).

Other courts have issued their own *Tarasoff*-type rulings. In *McIntosh v. Milano* (9), a New Jersey Superior Court held that therapists are liable for failing to protect known potential victims from the violent acts of their patients but found the psychiatrist in the case under consideration not negligent. In *Lipari v. Sears, Roebuck & Co.* (10), a federal district court in Nebraska held that a duty to protect existed, even when the specific identity of the victim was unknown, if the therapist knew or should have known that the patient's dangerous propensities presented an unreasonable risk of harm to others.

Other courts have adopted elements of the *Tarasoff* ruling (11, 12). When confronted by the issue of whether psychiatrists have a duty to protect unidentifiable victims, a number of courts found no such duty but acknowledged that a duty may exist to warn identifiable victims (13). *Lipari* represents a minority view of courts litigating cases involving a duty to warn and protect. Nevertheless, some courts continue to expand the duty to protect beyond the more narrow identifiable threat–identifiable victim standard adopted by a majority of the courts (see *Washington v. Petersen* and *Schuster v. Altenberg* below). Beck (14) observes that most courts are explicitly rejecting the theory espoused by the court in *Lipari* that psychiatrists are liable to the world at large for patient violence. In negligent inpatient release cases, however, courts have generally found such a duty because greater control can be exerted upon an inpatient.

Prior to *Jablonski v. United States* (15), no legal judgment for failing to warn had ever gone against a therapist. Previous cases were settled out of court. In *Jablonski,* the Ninth Circuit upheld liability after a patient killed his common-law wife because the defendant's psychiatrist failed to record and pass on information to the evaluating psychiatrist, failed to obtain a prior medical record indicating violent behavior, and failed to warn the patient's common-law spouse that her husband was dangerous. One year after *Jablonski* was decided, the Ninth Circuit overruled the decision on other grounds (16). Nevertheless, the rationale of the case has not been overruled concerning the duty to warn.

In *Brady v. Hopper* (17), liability was not imposed on John Hinckley's psychiatrist by the federal district court because of a lack of foreseeability. Hinckley had not specifically threatened a victim. The decision was appealed. The Tenth Circuit Court of Appeals (18) affirmed the lower court decision after the Colorado Supreme Court declined to respond to the question certified to it by the appeals court.

Courts also have refused to impose a duty on a psychiatrist to warn the victim when the latter was aware of the danger. In *In re Estate of Heltsley v. Votteler* (19), the plaintiff had knowledge of the patient's previous aggressive behavior toward her but contended that a warning from the psychiatrist would have made her appreciate the significance of the threat. The Iowa Supreme Court rejected this argument. In *Jablonski* (15), the defendant's wife had received warnings about the patient from her priest, her mother, her attorney, and a psychological hotline. She had even voiced her fears to the psychiatrist, but, nevertheless, the court imposed liability.

The broadest application of *Tarasoff* liability occurred in *Petersen v. State* (20). The court extended liability for a psychiatrist's patient's *unintentional* harm of another. The patient involved had been recently discharged from a state hospital after expiration of a short-term commitment for emergency detention, even though the patient drove a car recklessly prior to release. The Supreme Court of Washington concluded that the psychiatrist had a duty to take reasonable precautions to protect any foreseeable person endangered by the patient's drug-related violent tendencies. The court established the broadest potential for liability by not distinguishing between intentional and unintentional foreseeable harm. The court also created the duty of involuntary hospitalization of patients who pose foreseeable danger to unidentified victims.

Two recent cases involving the duty to warn and protect have stunned the psychiatric community. In *Rotman v. Mirin* (21), a jury awarded $4.5 million to the estate of Ms. Rotman because she was murdered by the patient of the defendant psychiatrist. Dr. Mirin treated his patient, Mr. Gould, over a long period of time for paranoid schizophrenia. The individual who was killed was a former girlfriend of the patient. Both she and her parents were fully aware of his serious, chronic mental disorder and his proclivity for violence.

In 1975, the patient amputated his right arm by placing it on a subway track. Mr. Gould had numerous psychiatric hospitalizations before and after this incident. He made occasional threats to Ms. Rotman that he would have to kill her "to save the Jewish people." After a rehospitalization, Mr. Gould's threats to harm Ms. Rotman were communicated by his psychiatrist by telephone and letter. After his discharge, when Ms. Rotman was not home, Mr. Gould told her parents that he had to kill their daughter. Two months later, Mr. Gould stalked and stabbed Ms. Rotman 37 times.

The plaintiffs alleged that Dr. Mirin failed to adequately warn Ms. Rotman of his patient's ongoing intention to kill her and that this failure to warn was a deviation from the standard of care. Two psychiatrists testified for the plaintiff that the defendant's treatment of the patient was inadequate, stating that the patient should have been involuntarily hospitalized. In addition, the experts argued that the warning given Ms. Rotman was inadequate because it did not sufficiently express the seriousness of Mr. Gould's condition. The defendant denied liability, stating that Mr. Gould was not committable and no longer presented a danger to Ms. Rotman. The case was appealed.

In another controversial ruling, *Naidu v. Laird* (22), the Delaware Supreme Court found that an inpatient psychiatrist was negligent in failing to foresee a former patient's potential to commit a violent act $5\frac{1}{2}$ months after discharge. The patient had a very extensive prior psychiatric history. He was diagnosed as a severe paranoid schizophrenic in 1959 and was hospitalized 19 times between 1962 and 1977. The patient was noncompliant with neuroleptics and repeatedly relapsed into psychosis. On September 6, 1977, the patient, Mr. Putney, killed a man in an automobile accident. The last admission at Delaware State Hospital $5\frac{1}{2}$ months earlier was the seventh admission at that hospital.

The victim's wife claimed that the defendant and two other psychiatrists were grossly negligent in their treatment and decision to discharge the patient. A lower court found for the plaintiff, awarding $1.4 million. On appeal, the Delaware Supreme Court affirmed the verdict. The court rejected the defendant's two principal arguments that Mr. Putney was not committable and that no proximate cause existed between Dr. Naidu's treatment and the fatal accident because the latter was too remote in time to be legally sufficient. The court concluded that Mr. Putney met commitment criteria and was foreseeably dangerous. The court stated that the lapse of time, by itself, was not a bar to recovery, but one factor to be weighed by the jury.

Beck (23) observes that *Naidu* represents a system failure because a premium is placed on discharging patients on account of limited hospital resources. Only those patients who are acutely psychotic or grossly disturbed are retained. Beck feels that Mr. Putney should not have been in the community in the first place. Beck notes that courts are aware of the problems faced by public-sector psychiatrists, focusing rather on timely referrals and aftercare, which were missing in this case.

As the court noted in *Naidu,* time itself was not a bar to recovery. In two cases, *Novak v. Rathnam* (24) and *Phillips v. Roy* (25), the courts ruled that the violence occurring 14 and 19 months, respectively, after the alleged negligence could not be the proximate cause of the injury. Potential liability in these cases does not extend for an indefinite period. The statute of limitations for bringing a malpractice suit is unrelated to the issue of causation because the statute commences from the time of injury (violent act), not from the time of the alleged negligence.

The continuing expansion of the liability imposed on therapists for the violent acts of their patients raises the specter of the application of "strict liability" standards (i.e., when it is not necessary to prove negligence). As Stone (26) points out, the standard of negligence used in malpractice cases certainly makes little sense if a psychiatrist cannot make a reliable prediction of violence. Experts will second-guess the therapist's judgment. On the basis of 20/20 hindsight, they will declare that the harm to the third party was inevitable and that the patient was lethally dangerous. Mills (6) believes that the legal system, while unable to protect victims of violence, attempts to indemnify them financially through the insurance policies of mental health professionals. In this fashion, a creeping form of "strict liability" is being applied to therapists whose patients harm others (27). Under *Tarasoff,* the psychiatrist becomes an unarmed policeman with a deep pocket. Malpractice insurance becomes a compensation fund for victims (28).

Since *Tarasoff,* subsequent court rulings have been more complex and inconsistent. The *Tarasoff* principle has been applied differently by various courts. Felthous (29) has observed that the legal trend toward diversity and inconsistency in applying the *Tarasoff* doctrine undermines any real moral value that may be present. Given the conflicting social values reflected in the diversity of *Tarasoff* cases, Felthous feels that statutory law may be more suited to the expression of a consistent public policy.

In the clinical vignette, Dr. Fowler practices in a state with no *Tarasoff* duty to warn. She reasons that because no legal duty to warn exists, she is not compelled to issue any warnings. She believes that she is shielded from a *Tarasoff*-type action if Professor Harris harms others. Dr. Fowler's sense of legal invulnerability may be illusory. Although no *Tarasoff* ruling exists in her state, she conceivably could become the first defendant in a precedent-setting *Tarasoff*-type suit.

A court may find a therapist liable for harm inflicted on innocent third parties by his or her patient even if no duty to warn exists (30). With an ever-increasing number of states adopting *Tarasoff* in their court rulings, including some states by statutory provision, therapists cannot assume legal invulnerability from victim suits in states that have not yet adopted *Tarasoff* principles into law (31). Given this situation of ambiguity, the best policy in the treatment of potentially violent patients is to use good clinical practice, to be aware of statutory or case law in the state where one practices, or, if no state law exists, to be aware of national trends in the law. There is no guarantee, however, that what has legally transpired in other states will be recapitulated in similar form in one's own state.

Circumstances may impose a specific affirmative duty to warn a potential victim or conversely to impose a broader separate liability on a therapist for failure to detain, control, or hospitalize the patient. In *Duvall v. Goldin* (32), a motorist was injured in an automobile collision with a car driven by a psychiatrist's epileptic patient. The court of appeals held that the psychiatrist breached his duty to inform the patient not to operate a motor vehicle, raising the issue of whether the psychiatrist's negligence was the proximate cause of the accident.

A duty of reasonable care exists if harm is a reasonably foreseeable consequence of the therapist's failure to warn a patient not to drive. This duty exists even in the absence of a therapist-patient relationship with an injured third party. The duty is owed to persons in the foreseeable zone of danger (i.e., other drivers and pedestrians). No duty is imposed on the therapist to control the patient or affirmatively prevent patients from driving (33).

In *Schuster v. Altenberg* (34), a manic-depressive patient taking alprazolam and phenelzine crashed into a tree at 60 mph within an hour of her treatment. The patient died, leaving her 17-year-old daughter paraplegic. The psychiatrist was sued, with the plaintiff alleging negligent care and management of the patient. The trial court granted the defendant's motion for summary judgment. On certification from the court of appeals, the Wisconsin Supreme Court concluded that once negligence is established, the defendants are liable for the unforeseeable consequences of their acts to unforeseeable plaintiffs. Thus, in Wisconsin, one of the broadest *Tarasoff* duties is now the law. There is a duty to protect everyone, identifiable or not.

The Wisconsin Supreme Court ruled in the instant case that legal sufficiency for the following complaints existed:

1. Negligent diagnosis and treatment
2. Failure to warn the family of the patient concerning her condition and its dangerousness
3. Failure to seek commitment of the patient

On retrial, the psychiatrist was found not guilty. The trial court found the decedent 80% contributorily negligent, the plaintiff 20% negligent, and the defendant psychiatrist not negligent.

Felthous (35) provides an overview concerning the duty to warn or protect to prevent automobile accidents. The five major cases that are reviewed include *Hasenei v. United States* (36), *Petersen v. State* (20), *Naidu v. Laird* (22), *Cain v. Rijken* (37), and *Schuster v. Altenberg* (34). Felthous is critical of the collective inconsistency of courts in acknowledging nonclinical measures for protection, such as relying heavily on warning, that fosters confusing potential duties and liabilities. He suggests addressing the issue of warning or reporting legislatively, where clarity and consistency can be achieved statutorily.

In summary, a majority of courts have found no duty to protect absent a foreseeable victim. Despite the fact that the duty to protect is not the law in most jurisdictions and is subject to different interpretations by individual courts, the duty to protect is, in effect, a national standard of practice. Only Ohio has abrogated the duty to protect (38). For violent inpatients, the duty to protect others is usually met by the provision of customary care in controlling the patient. In the outpatient setting, the means of controlling a violent patient who threatens others are substantially limited. Given an identifiable victim and threat, outpatient psychiatrists must use a number of approaches to warn and protect persons endangered by their patients. The duty to protect is a major concern for therapists. Legislative efforts have been made to limit the *Tarasoff* duty. The APA has taken the position that it is quite proper to hold a psychiatrist liable for "flagrantly negligent" failures to protect other persons from harm (39).

Are psychotherapists other than psychiatrists liable under *Tarasoff*-type rulings?

The term *psychotherapist* is usually defined broadly by state regulatory statutes and licensing boards. The *Tarasoff* ruling technically applied only to psychologists and psychiatrists, specifically excluding all other mental health professionals. However, Mills (6) believes that if one holds oneself out to the public as a psychotherapist and is licensed by the state to practice psychotherapy, irrespective of credentials, the individual incurs *Tarasoff* obligations.

In *Peck v. The Counseling Service of Addison County, Inc.* (40), the parents of an outpatient who was treated by a mental health paraprofessional sued the clinic for negligent failure to warn them of the dangerous tendencies of their son. The plaintiffs contended that proper supervision of the counselor, who had a masters degree in educational psychology and a certificate as a psychological counselor, would have led to recognition of their son's dangerousness and a warning that he would commit arson. The Vermont Supreme Court reversed a judgment order of the Addison Superior Court that the counseling service was not liable for negligence to the plaintiffs.

The *Peck* case involved the plaintiffs' 29-year-old son, who burned down his parents' barn. Although the barn was completely destroyed, the plaintiffs were not hurt. At the time of the incident, John Peck was being seen as an outpatient at the counseling service. Peck told the therapist that he "wanted to get back at his father" after a heated argument. On further inquiry by the therapist concerning how he would get back at his father, Peck said, "I don't know, I could burn down his barn." After discussion of the consequences of such an act, Peck promised not to burn down the barn.

The Vermont Supreme Court, with two judges dissenting, held that "a mental health professional who knows or based upon the standards of the mental health profession should know that his or her patient poses a serious risk of danger to an identifiable victim has a duty to exercise reasonable care to protect him or her from that danger." The court based its findings on the fact that the therapist did not attempt to obtain the patient's most recent medical history and that the counseling service had no formal written policy governing interstaff consultation procedures for violent patients who endanger others.

Stone (41) points out that the lower court judge "apparently considered a counseling relationship in a clinic to be presumptively a special relationship." He adds that clinics that use therapists without advanced training may create liability for themselves in *Tarasoff*-type cases. It appears, therefore, that a special psychotherapist-patient relationship can be imposed on any counseling relationship, creating the attendant *Tarasoff* duties. Adequate supervision of other mental health professionals requires the imparting of legal information and the discussion of legal issues surrounding the care of patients requiring psychological interventions. Stone (42) states that there are three aspects of the *Peck* decision that adopt and extend the *Tarasoff* precedent. The decision imposes the *Tarasoff* duty on all "mental health professionals," permits a single standard of care to be applied, and creates liability for property damage as well as for personal injury.

What confidentiality problems are posed by *Tarasoff* and its progeny?

Trust is the cornerstone of psychiatric treatment. Without trust, no therapeutic alliance can develop, dooming the possibility of psychotherapeutic help. Whenever confidentiality is breached, trust is diminished or destroyed. Thus, therapists are understandably zealous in their protection of confidentiality. In the real world, confidentiality, like trust, cannot be absolute. Exceptions to the maintenance of confidentiality exist for the protection of both the patient and society.

In the clinical vignette at the beginning of this chapter, Dr. Fowler's decision to inform the police of Professor Harris's violent intentions may have breached the confidentiality statute in her state. In addition, it may have ruptured her treatment relationship with her patient. Faced with the possibility of a nuclear disaster with high casualties, she felt she had little choice but to break confidentiality to inform the authorities. Although respectful of the law, Dr. Fowler is firm in the view that her professional and moral duty to protect the patient and potential victims from his violent intentions supersedes blind adherence to a confidentiality statute that might prohibit such a disclosure.

If time had allowed, Dr. Fowler could have tried to contact an attorney who was knowledgeable concerning the state statute governing confidentiality. Although perceived as a strict statute, provision for an exception to maintaining confidentiality may exist if third parties are endangered by violent patients. Although the law is not clearly established in this area, a therapist who releases confidential information when a mental health confidentiality statute prohibits such a release would probably not be held liable for warning a victim or law enforcement authorities of a dangerous patient if acting in good faith (30). In fact, states that have enacted laws delimiting the responsibility of therapists for the violent acts of patients generally provide immunity from liability for therapists who make good-faith efforts to warn or protect endangered persons. The tenor of the law is to protect public safety over the confidentiality of individuals.

A case exists, however, in which a patient sued for a breach of confidentiality and contractual relation, alleging mental anguish and the incurring of a criminal record (43). The patient made death threats against President Reagan that the psychiatrist reported to the Secret Service. These threats were not a violation of the federal criminal code. The code does not provide immunity from legal liability for psychiatrists who report such threats, thus placing them in a difficult dilemma. The court ruled that before the suit could proceed, it must first be brought before the arbitration board for mandatory nonbinding arbitration as provided by Maryland law. One would expect the issue to be moot because the federal code requiring reporting threats against the president of the United States supersedes any confidentiality statutes.

In *Tarasoff*, the court was mindful of the importance of maintaining confidentiality in the therapist-patient relationship, stating that the warning to a victim should be done in such a way as to preserve confidentiality consonant with the prevention of threatened danger. The court made its position clear on the limitations of confidentiality by stating, "Protective privilege ends where public peril begins" (3). Nevertheless, a plaintiff may allege breach of confidentiality through the issuance of an "unnecessary" warning that causes a loss of a job, loss of a relationship, personal embarrassment with emotional distress, or defamation of his or her reputation.

The Principles of Medical Ethics With Annotations Especially Applicable to Psychiatry (44) states: "Psychiatrists at times may find it necessary, in order to protect the patient or the community from imminent danger, to reveal confidential information disclosed by the patient" (Section 4, Annotation 8). Thus, Dr. Fowler, in breaking confidentiality, is exercising an ethical duty and a professional choice that was promulgated by the APA at least 2 years before the legal imposition of the *Tarasoff* duty (45). The *Tarasoff* exception to confidentiality is part of the same exception established requiring the reporting of contagious diseases, suspected child abuse, and gunshot wounds. The exception exists for the welfare of the patient or society.

State statutes or common law may justify the maintenance of confidentiality over the *Tarasoff* duty. In *Shaw v. Glickman* (46), a Maryland court said that to disclose a patient's violent tendencies would violate state law concerning privileged communication, an extension from evidentiary privilege.

In *Hopewell v. Adebimpe* (47), a psychiatrist concerned about a *Tarasoff* ruling warned his patient's employer when she threatened harm. The patient sued for breach of confidentiality, and the psychiatrist claimed a *Tarasoff* defense. The court held that the psychiatrist had an absolute obligation under statute not to release confidential communications without the patient's written consent and that this law effectively eliminated the *Tarasoff* duty. The letter that was written by the psychiatrist to the patient's personnel director contained the following:

In the course of a psychiatric interview which took place in my office . . . the above-named reported feelings of being so enraged about her work situation that she will blow up and hurt somebody very seriously if the harassment does not stop!

This information is being related to you because there is a legal precedent requiring it and is not to be taken as an estimate of the probability that the threat will actually be carried out. It is, however, important that the person or persons at risk be notified. In this case, I believe that her immediate supervisor should know of this letter. . . .

The letter contained a stamped endorsement:

THIS INFORMATION HAS BEEN DISCLOSED TO YOU FROM RECORDS WHOSE CONFIDENTIALITY IS PROTECTED BY STATE LAW. STATE REGULATIONS PROHIBIT YOU FROM MAKING ANY FURTHER DISCLOSURES OF INFORMATION WITHOUT PRIOR CONSENT OF THE PERSON IN RESPECT TO WHOM IT PERTAINS.

Although it is difficult to say for certain, it appears that the psychiatrist was concerned with fulfilling a legal obligation rather than following the dictates of his clinical assessment about how to proceed. Clinical judgment must not be eclipsed when attempting to fulfill real or perceived legal duties. If possible, an attempt should be made to obtain the informed consent of the patient before embarking on warning others.

Statutes involving the duty to warn and protect usually contain immunity from liability provisions for mental health professionals who breach confidentiality in order to protect a third person endangered by the patient (48). Usually, a specific threat must be made against an identifiable victim or class of victims. Patients may sue for breach of confidentiality when information is disclosed to others in jurisdictions that do not have confidentiality provisions. If confidentiality statutes exist, suit may be brought for breach of contract that may incorporate the confidentiality provision of the statute (30). Mental health professionals must know the law governing confidentiality in their jurisdiction. Whereas the *Tarasoff* duty arises occasionally, the maintenance of confidentiality is a constant duty in clinical practice because the breach of confidentiality occurs frequently (49). Some states require that clinicians contact the authorities if patients inform them of intentions to commit a crime (50).

A few therapists give *Miranda*-type warnings to new patients about the therapist's duty to warn or protect third parties against violent threats. In most instances, starting a treatment on this note casts a pall on the fledgling therapeutic process. Patients already frightened of their own hostile fantasies may find such a warning confirmation of their projected fear that even the therapist is threatened by their anger. Secretive patients may seize upon such a warning to withhold further verbal expression of their violent propensities. Patients who need treatment the most may be frightened away. Mills (6) suggests that when the protection of others is necessary because of patient violence, utilizing appropriate clinical interventions often will allow for the preservation of confidentiality. In fact, Mills adds that making *Miranda*-type warnings to patients is a gratuitous gesture. Stock warnings to patients at the outset of treatment are a classic example of defensive psychiatry and may have destructive effects on the care of patients.

In an ominous twist, issuing a *Tarasoff* warning has been used by prosecutors in California as a wedge to obtain otherwise privileged patient-therapist communications (51). In *People v. William John Clark* (52), the California Supreme Court stated in dicta that when a *Tarasoff* warning discloses information to a third party, that information no longer remains confidential. In other cases, prosecutors have relied on *Clark* to obtain previously privileged therapist-patient information when a *Tarasoff* warning was issued. This legal strategy is being actively resisted by the California Psychiatric Association.

What statutory approaches have been enacted to limit the liability of psychiatrists for their patients' violent acts?

A number of states have passed immunity statutes limiting the responsibility of therapists for their patients' violent acts (53). The majority of statutes provide immunity for disclosures made to fulfill the duty to protect (48). The number of states passing such statutes grows every year (54). Other states are considering such legislation. Definitions vary considerably concerning when the duty arises and how to discharge it (48). Most statutes require an actual threat made against a clearly identifiable victim before a duty to warn or protect arises. Most often, discharging the duty involves warning the intended victim and law enforcement authorities (48).

Unfortunately, the duty to warn rather than protect is more often relied upon in these immunity statutes. Thus, the duty to warn may be defensively invoked as a risk-management tool. By itself, the duty to warn may be an insufficient psychiatric intervention. Sometimes, warning by itself may induce violence. Immunity statutes may encourage reflexive rather than reflective patient management (55). Appelbaum (56) decries the defensive hospitalization of patients solely because of a fear of liability and not because these patients actually require hospitalization on clinical grounds.

Clinicians should become knowledgeable concerning the language of such statutes if they exist. Unfortunately, some statutes contain contrary statements and confusing language. Frequently, multiple authorship and the forces of compromise encountered during the political process result in confusing statutory language. In California, a bill passed by the state legislature specifically defines and limits the *Tarasoff* duty (57). The statute reads as follows:

(a) There shall be no mandatory liability on the part of, and no cause of action shall arise against, any person who is a psychotherapist as defined in Section 1010 of the Evidence Code in failing to warn of and protect from a patient's threatened violent behavior or failing to predict and warn of and protect from a patient's violent behavior except where the patient has communicated to the psychotherapist a serious threat of physical violence against a reasonably identifiable victim or victims.

(b) If there is a duty to warn and protect under the limited circumstances specified above, the duty shall be discharged by the psychotherapist making reasonable efforts to communicate the threat to the victim or victims and to a law enforcement agency.

This law went into effect on January 1, 1986. Psychotherapists in California now have a specification of their duty toward endangered third parties. The duty to warn and protect can be discharged by making a reasonable effort to warn the identifiable victim and a law enforcement agency. Because the broader duty to protect is no longer required, retrospective second-guessing of treatment interventions by plaintiff's attorneys or courts will be considerably restricted. On clinical grounds, the full panoply of psychiatric interventions still should be considered with violent patients. The statute is referred to as a "civil immunity" law rather than a "duty to warn" law. Any duty to warn was established by the courts, whereas the statute merely limits the therapist's liability in suits brought by persons injured by the patient.

As Beck (14) points out, if professionals fail to exercise their clinical judgment and think they are excused from doing so by statute, serious risks may be incurred. If a patient seriously injures another person and the therapist failed to exercise due care, the courts will find a way to hold the therapist liable, even in the presence of an immunity statute.

Can psychiatrists be sued by their patients for failing to warn an endangered third person?

In *Cole v. Taylor* (58), the Supreme Court of Iowa reviewed a case in which a woman sued her psychiatrist for failing to prevent her from harming her former husband. The patient, Mary Kathleen Cole, was convicted of the first-degree murder of Alan Tyler. A suit for loss of consortium also was filed against the psychiatrist by the patient's current husband. The trial court held that the plaintiff's claim could be pursued. The Supreme Court of Iowa ruled that the plaintiff cannot maintain a civil suit based on her own criminal or immoral act. In other words, one cannot commit a crime and then attempt to ascribe civil liability to someone else.

A similar conclusion was reached in *Glazier v. Lee* (59). A patient convicted of voluntary manslaughter in the shooting death of his girlfriend sued his psychologist. The plaintiff started treatment 1 month before the shooting. The plaintiff claimed that the psychologist was negligent by failing to medicate or hospitalize him. The plaintiff argued that the failure to hospitalize encouraged the expression of aggressive feeling at his girlfriend, and that the therapist failed to warn the girlfriend of his potential violence. The theory of the plaintiff was that if a psychologist owes a duty to protect others from a patient's criminal acts, then as great a duty is owed to the patient by the psychologist to protect him from the harmful consequences of his own acts. The trial court denied a motion for summary judgment by the psychologist. On appeal, the appellate court reversed the trial court decision, granting the motion for summary judgment. Again, the court held that the psychologist's conduct did not relieve the plaintiff of criminal responsibility. The suit was based upon the illegal acts of the plaintiff and therefore was barred from proceeding.

Thus, suits against psychiatrists by patients who claim that potential victims should have been warned are unlikely to succeed. Felthous (60) discusses other "*Tarasoff* curiosities" arising from efforts to apply the *Tarasoff* doctrine to novel theories of litigation.

How is the concept of dangerousness defined in civil mental health law? What areas of psychiatric practice are affected by the concept of dangerousness when applied through civil mental health law?

Dangerousness is a legal status and not a psychiatric diagnosis or disposition (61). The concept of dangerousness has never been adequately explained by the courts. Courts tend to avoid precise meanings in defining dangerousness, preferring to keep it vague in the common law tradition so as to preserve applicability to specific situations (62). Legal scholars, however, have attempted to analyze dangerousness into components (63). Five components have been defined that may be useful as a decision-making guide for judges, jurors, probation officers, and mental health professionals. However, no direct formula can be derived for individual cases, nor can the components be quantified.

The five components of dangerousness are as follows:

1. *Nature of harm or conduct:* Does the individual threaten bodily harm, or is it harm to property or to individual sensitivities?
2. *Magnitude of harm:* Does the individual threaten murder, or is the threat a punch in the nose?
3. *Probability:* How likely is it that the feared harm will occur?
4. *Imminence:* When will the threatened action occur?
5. *Frequency:* How frequently will the threatened action occur?

A few civil commitment statutes contain the requirement that all five components be addressed. As a result, the requirement for the nature of the harm usually is serious bodily harm. Probability may require the statement of a reasonable probability that the harm will occur in the future. Imminence may be defined variably for the substantive criteria of danger to others but may specify a shorter time if self-harm is anticipated. Frequency usually refers to at least one violent incident having occurred. The barriers to the use of these components hinge on the fact that each component of dangerousness requires a public policy decision. Furthermore, the lack of validity for each component adversely affects the ultimate reliability of a prediction of dangerousness. Unfortunately, many of the components of dangerousness are themselves vague and undefinable.

In addition to involuntary hospitalization, other areas of psychiatric practice are affected by the concept of dangerousness. When considering the right to treatment, a proper assessment of dangerousness is necessary in determining appropriate treatment. In *Youngberg v. Romeo* (64), the United States Supreme Court determined that the patient was entitled to the provision of safe conditions and that restraint might be necessary to protect patients from harm perpetrated on themselves or others. In cases involving the right to refuse treatment, the patient's right to refuse neuroleptic medication is abrogated if the patient is dangerous to others or self.

The duty to warn endangered third parties turns on the concept of dangerousness. The standard requires that when the therapist determines or should have determined that the patient is dangerous to others, a warning to the victim must be made or the victim must be protected from harm. Finally, the decision to discharge a patient from the hospital requires dangerousness to be carefully assessed. In *O'Connor v. Donaldson* (65), the United States Supreme Court held that "[a] state cannot constitutionally confine without more a nondangerous individual who is capable of surviving safely in freedom by himself with the help of willing and responsible family members or friends."

The components of dangerousness that have been elaborated by legal scholars, particularly in relation to the legal issues surrounding involuntary hospitalization, do not take into account the specific individual suffering from a given mental disorder who is reacting to a unique environmental situation. Dangerousness reflects not a trait but rather a dynamic, time-limited interaction between the individual and the environment.

Mental health professionals have difficulty determining the threshold requirement for dangerousness before evoking the *Tarasoff* duty (66). Clinicians assess the risk of violence, not dangerousness, the latter being a legal construct. The courts have had little difficulty in imposing liability through hindsight analysis. Clinicians must evoke their duties when they know or should know their patient will be violent. The research literature states that this cannot be done with any degree of confidence. Therapists should not be held liable for failure to fulfill their *Tarasoff* duty unless the patient has engaged in violent behavior or made a recent threat of violence (66).

Many clinical indicators unique to specific patients may evoke the therapist's duty to protect. For example, a 28-year-old man with a passive-aggressive personality disorder became violent only when his stuttering stopped. The clinician noted that violent acts were always preceded by a period of 1–2 months in which the patient no longer stuttered but spoke very clearly. The clinician pointed this out to the patient and gained his cooperation for voluntary hospitalization when stuttering ceased. A variety of clinical indicators may evoke the *Tarasoff* duty, but it should not be prompted just by the fear of liability.

What do research studies indicate about the psychiatrist's ability to predict violent behavior?

Dangerousness, as asserted earlier, lacks legal definition. The parameters of dangerousness are very vague. As a result, the duty to warn endangered third parties is highly problematic. The term *foreseeability* also is open to many interpretations. When terms lack definition, reliability cannot be established and validity suffers. As long as the law persists in seeing dangerousness as a "trait" of mental patients, little accuracy of prediction can be expected.

The fit between mental illness and violence is a loose one. Generally, studies show that the dangerousness of psychiatric patients is equivalent to that of persons in the general population (67, 68). Only with certain mental disorders and under certain conditions does a tighter fit exist. Slovenko (53) points out that psychiatrists have had "little or no hesitation" in certifying persons for involuntary hospitalization who pose a danger to self or others. At the same time, psychiatrists claim that no professional standards exist for the evaluation of dangerousness.

For clinicians, dangerousness is a function of the dynamic interaction between a specific individual and a specific situation for a given period of time.

"Second generation" research on violence prediction shows that specific elements of the clinical situation contribute to the imminent dangerousness of the patient and allow for specific interventions to be made (69). Thus patients may be murderous for only a few seconds or minutes during their entire lives. Thereafter, the patient may never pose a danger again. Nevertheless, because of the lack of clinical standards for the prediction of violence in any context, the prediction of violence becomes an unreliable exercise (70).

Therapists may have no more skill than laypersons in predicting imminent violence according to "first generation" research studies on the long-term clinical prediction of violent behavior of offender populations (71, 72). In these studies, though methodologically flawed, the accuracy level has been roughly one out of three correct predictions over a 5-year period. These predictions have been limited by emphasis on certain traits of criminal offenders without the benefit of any situational analysis. However, the estimate that two out of three predictions of dangerousness are wrong underscores the problem of false positives as psychiatrists attempt to spread wide the dragnet and minimize liability.

More recently, a second generation of research and theory on the prediction of violence is emerging that emphasizes the limitations of existing research, points to the possibility of improved predictive methods, and evaluates public policy decisions that involve violence prediction (73). Tardiff (74) maintains that well-trained psychiatrists should be able to predict a patient's short-term potential for violence using assessment techniques similar to the short-term predictors of suicide potential. "Short term" is defined as a few days to a week. Research studies are presented to support this position.

Epidemiologic data containing known violence base rates are a risk factor for violence that should be considered by clinicians. In populations having very low base rates for violence, however, epidemiologic data may offer little advantage (75). Epidemiologic analysis has been of very limited use for outpatient populations because the base rate data have come from criminal offender populations. The base rate data for violence for nonhospitalized outpatients are not yet available.

Currently, therapists may consider national and local crime rate data with regard to age, race, and sex, although their usefulness is questionable for outpatients. Thus, because of the high false-positive prediction rate among psychiatrists and the low base rate occurrence for violence in outpatient populations (rare event with low specificity), predictability of violence to endangered third parties remains a fiction. Predictive accuracy may be improved when working with defined homogeneous populations having high base rates for violence. For example, a closed psychiatric unit treating very disturbed patients may have violence base rates of 25%–35%. Epidemiologic data containing known violence base rates for specific groups are an important assessment variable (76). More recent studies that focus on inpatient populations have demonstrated significantly improved predictability (77).

Personal, social, situational, and clinical variables are associated with violence. Monahan (78) has shown the association of violence with the following factors: male gender, black race, age 15–20, employment and residential instability, a history of alcohol or drug abuse, and a history of previous violence. Research studies have consistently found that a history of violent behavior is the single best "predictor" of violent behavior. In the United States, the rate of violent behavior in males is approximately 10 times higher than that in females. The violent crime rate in the United States is considerably higher among blacks than whites. This statistic refers to the prevalence, but not the incidence, of violence among individuals once they become violent (79). Tardiff, however, disputes race as a factor in violence (74). Situational factors associated with violence include an unstable family, a violent environment, a violent peer group, and available weapons and victims. Tardiff and Koenigsberg (80) reported on 2,916 patients evaluated by residents in the outpatient clinics of two large private psychiatric hospitals. Three percent had manifested recent assaultive behavior toward other persons. In over half the cases, a family member other than a child was assaulted. The patients more likely to be assaultive were young males who had a diagnosis of childhood and adolescent mental disorders or personality disorders.

Clinical risk factors associated with violence include soft neurologic signs, low intelligence, paranoid ideation, command hallucinations, anger and agitation, psychosis, and the stated desire to hurt or kill another (81). Lewis et al. (82) identified a "constellation of factors" in young persons that should alert mental health professionals to a high potential for future serious violence. These include serious violence as a juvenile, psychotic symptoms, major neurologic impairment and head injury, a history of child abuse, and psychiatric hospitalized or psychotic relatives. On the other hand, the presence of obsessive-compulsive defenses is likely to increase internal controls.

There is much clinical research suggesting that a lack of ability to control anger is, not surprisingly, related to violent behavior (79). Monahan (79) cites a large study of anger and aggressiveness conducted in California state mental hospitals over a number of years with tens of thousands of patients. The study found that anger during the first year of hospitalization was highly predictive of aggression during the second year, even after controlling for a number of factors including past violent behavior. In the clinical vignette, Professor Harris had a childhood and adult history of losing control of his anger.

Careful assessment and documentation of the pertinent clinical variables used in assessing the potentially violent patient may prevent allegations of negligent assessment. Even if the therapist should be tragically wrong in assessing the risk of violence, a mistake is not negligence if a reasonable standard of care (given the current state of the art) was used in assessing the risk of violence.

In the clinical vignette, Dr. Fowler did not attempt to make a prediction concerning whether Professor Harris would harm others. An assessment of a high risk of violence was made based on the severity of his mental condition, the threat of violence, and the enormous lethality of the weaponry available to the patient. Dr. Fowler correctly opts for the only sure course consistent with her patient's need for treatment: apprehension and involuntary hospitalization.

Beck (83) points out that despite scientific evidence to the contrary, most psychiatrists believe they can predict violence. Given this state of affairs, the best protection against allegations of negligence is to evaluate violence according to methods and procedures consistent with the highest standards. Included in these standards is the consideration of known risk variables associated with violence. Because predictions of violence by the psychiatrist will be wrong approximately two out of three times, humility dictates careful documentation of how the assessment of violence was conducted.

How do the courts generally view psychiatric testimony which states that the violent acts of patients cannot be predicted with any accuracy? Is a "strict liability" standard being applied in some cases involving the duty to warn and protect?

This question can be best answered by examining a 1983 decision of the United States Supreme Court. In *Barefoot v. Estelle* (84), a capital punishment case, the Supreme Court held that if jurors are authorized to bear responsibility for a death penalty based on predictions of future behavior, then psychiatrists are justified in testifying about dangerousness despite a predictive ratio of one out of three. The Court's support for the validity of psychiatric predictions of dangerousness in capital cases tends to give impetus to judicial expectations of psychiatric prediction in *Tarasoff*-type cases (85). If an accuracy of one out of three predictions of dangerousness is sufficient to justify execution, an even lower level of predictive accuracy may be found acceptable in litigation involving the duty to warn and protect.

The whole question of predictability may well become moot if courts expand *Tarasoff* liability toward a "strict liability" standard. A strict liability standard would provide that a mere occurrence of the harm will be enough to establish liability without regard to establishing negligence. In *Davis v. Lhim* (86), liability was found quite apart from the seriousness and the imminence of the threat made by the patient 2 years prior to the violent act. A mother was killed trying to restrain her son from firing a shotgun. The son had a long history of mental illness. He had been voluntarily hospitalized 2 months earlier. The only evidence that the patient posed a threat to his mother was a note in an emergency record 2 years earlier stating that the patient was "threatening the mother for money."

The Michigan Court of Appeals found that this was sufficient to support a jury finding that the defendant psychiatrist should have known that the patient posed a threat to his mother. In 1988, the Michigan Supreme Court overturned the Appeals Court decision under the state's governmental immunity laws. The court held that the decision to discharge a patient is a discretionary act (person exercises independent judgment), as opposed to a ministerial act (person follows policy), providing immunity from suit for a state hospital doctor (87).

Another case that raises serious questions about the application of a "strict liability" standard is *Naidu v. Laird* (22). In *Naidu,* the Supreme Court of Delaware held a psychiatrist liable for the violent act of a former patient that occurred $5\frac{1}{2}$ months following discharge of the patient from the hospital. The court ignored the lack of imminence of danger.

Psychiatrists evaluate and treat violent patients regularly and successfully. Furthermore, psychiatrists certify patients for involuntary hospitalization according to dangerousness criteria in the routine course of their practices. Courts, therefore, tend to be unsympathetic to the complaints of psychiatrists that they are unable to predict the violent acts of their patients. Therefore, psychiatrists need to inform the courts about the important clinical distinction between assessing and predicting violence. Although professional standards for the assessment of the risk of violence do exist, no such standards exist for the actual prediction of violent acts by patients. All the clinician can do is formulate and execute a clinical management plan based upon an assessment of the patient's risk of violence.

What clinical issues are created by the duty to warn?

The duty to warn is a favored intervention of the courts. The duty is of questionable value (6) and may be harmful under certain circumstances. In one study, violence did not decline as a result of warning compared with not warning (83). Prior to *Tarasoff,* hospital and staff members have been held liable for harm caused to other persons when patients were negligently released (87). In jurisdictions that have *Tarasoff*-type rulings, an obligation to warn may exist by itself or be part of a duty to protect. Even in non-*Tarasoff* jurisdictions, the possibility exists that the precedent to warn, established elsewhere, may be imposed at any time.

The problem for therapists is not to be blinded by the duty to warn from implementing other clinical interventions that may be more effective. Simply warning an endangered third party is rarely sufficient by itself. Other clinical interventions are usually required. One of the most useful clinical interventions is deepening the therapeutic alliance by seeing the patient more frequently. In most of the reported cases in which harm has occurred, psychiatric treatment was terminated (53). Most dangerous patients can be managed through good clinical practice.

Although it is important to seek consultation with an attorney in certain cases, the clinician should be aware that attorneys have a tendency to recommend following the letter of the law and issuing a warning. If followed reflexively, such a recommendation could be an invitation to practice defensive psychiatry, and also could abuse the patient's rights. This is not to imply that the duty to warn should be ignored when required or appropriate. The duty, however, may be only one of many interventions that can be used after consideration of the patient's needs and circumstances.

One major pitfall that therapists must avoid is the duty to warn in the service of defensive denial. Thus, the therapist must not act like a messenger who, after leaving a message, feels no further responsibility. Issuing a warning as a legal formalism is not an acceptable approach to managing the violent patient. Therapists must be reasonably certain that the threat of harm to others is real, and reasonable efforts to control the patient must be made before issuing a warning to the intended victim. If a warning is issued, reasonable follow-up should be attempted.

Whether the law mandates it or not, therapists have a moral, ethical, and professional duty to protect patients and their potential victims. The obligation is primarily professional. Legal imposition of this duty is incidental to the therapist's professional duty. When the duty to warn is implemented, every effort should be made to keep it a treatment issue. Beck (88) does this when he confronts potentially violent patients with the reality that the law has imposed a duty on therapists to protect society and that therefore the therapist and patient must work out a plan together that discharges this duty. Beck reports excellent results, although his sample is small. Wulsin et al. (89) reported helping an inpatient, whose voices commanded him to kill his mother, by assisting the patient in formulating a letter of warning to his mother. The therapeutic alliance was thus fostered and the crisis was managed without recourse to commitment or other interventions.

The *Tarasoff* duty may encourage the clinician to adopt a crisis family approach as an alternative to a "cold call" warning (90). When a patient threatens to kill a family member, the family relationships may be already beyond repair. If at all possible, when the psychiatrist determines that confidentiality must be broken to issue a warning, it should be done in the presence of the patient and with the patient's consent. After all, it is in the patient's, and everyone else's, best interest that violence be prevented. Although this may seem like an unrealistic recommendation, it should be remembered that the patient is probably ambivalent about the intention to harm someone else, or otherwise he or she would not be talking with the psychiatrist. People who unequivocally want to harm others go out and do it. It is the exceptional legal problem in psychiatric treatment that cannot be successfully addressed through common sense, good clinical practice, and a clear understanding of the relevant legal requirements (91). Thus, warning should be used primarily after other clinical interventions have been tried or appear inappropriate.

Warning endangered third parties is not without peril. Even if the victim is able to escape and evade the violent patient, predictability of violence is inaccurate to the extent that many individuals will be falsely warned. Receiving a letter or phone call from a therapist warning of serious violence may have a frightening psychological impact. Warned individuals may become severely distressed themselves and, in essence, become victims of the duty to warn. Will a posttraumatic stress disorder ensue followed by charges against the psychiatrist of negligent infliction of emotional distress? Furthermore, warning often becomes an empty gesture when police are reluctant to act before a crime is committed and preventive detention is not constitutionally permitted (6). What if the patient is out of town? Should a letter be sent? Should it be sent certified or by special delivery? How long will it take to be delivered? Trying to track down potential victims may, at times, seem to require the services of a detective agency. Finally, the therapist who attempts to warn others of danger may become a victim of violence at the hand of the patient or even be harmed by the endangered third person.

Generally, if the therapist decides to warn, a phone call is appropriate so that the potential victim can ask questions. Also, nuances and difficulties in communication can be appreciated by both parties. Sometimes, a trusted third party may act as a go-between. The warning should be made clearly. The clarity of the warning has been open to second-guessing by some courts. For example, in *Rotman v. Mirin* (21), two board-certified psychiatrists testified that the warning given by the psychiatrist to the victim's parents was inadequate. According to the plaintiff's experts, the warning communicated by telephone and letter was inadequate because it did not sufficiently express the seriousness of the patient's condition.

Unless done artfully and with great tact, warning may prematurely end a therapeutic relationship by breaching confidentiality, particularly if the patient's trust has been tenuous. The importance of this consideration may be nullified if danger of harm to others is imminent. Beck (92) reported that *Tarasoff* cases in office practice more often ended inexplicably in violence or a ruptured treatment relationship than *Tarasoff* cases in other settings. More subtly, *Tarasoff* concerns tend to skew the treatment process in the direction of scrutinizing violent fantasies for action potential rather than understanding their meaning (85). Introduction of the role of police officer disturbs the therapist's free-floating attention and position of neutrality by creating anxiety through role confusion. As a result, therapeutic effectiveness is correspondingly diminished. Many victims already know of the danger and may resent the intrusion of being warned (85). Other potential victims may not be able to take corrective action because of economic, social, or personal factors, which can then result in retaliatory violence toward the patient. This outcome could be legally actionable itself.

The psychodynamics of victim-victimizer psychology may be pertinent to a decision to warn. Threats of violence between husband and wife or other partner relationships may dictate attempting to move the victim toward a sheltered environment rather than warning the abuser that the abused partner is considering retaliatory violence. To do otherwise might seriously endanger the patient or precipitate mutual violence. Wexler (93) propounds the thesis that *Tarasoff* can be therapeutically advantageous if based upon the assumption that the majority of violent threat cases involve victim contribution. If victimological variables are considered when patients threaten others, Wexler feels that the patient-victim relationship is capable of being treated by an interactionist approach.

Beck (83) suggests that how a warning is given, not whether one is given, is the crucial factor. When the clinician discusses the warning with the patient prior to giving it, generally the result on therapy and the alliance is positive. Not discussing the warning with patients turns out almost uniformly badly for the therapeutic alliance and the therapy. This is also true for potential victims who are warned. If they feel evasive action can be taken and the therapist is acting responsibly and is genuinely concerned, the warnings are received positively. When potential victims appear to have no options at evasion and the therapist is perceived as not behaving responsibly, a profound negative reaction can occur.

In the clinical vignette, Dr. Fowler called the police because she had reason to believe that Professor Harris was about to commit mass murder. Because simply calling the police is often useless, she followed up the police call with signed medical certification papers for involuntary hospitalization that allowed the police to apprehend the patient in order to provide effective treatment for his psychotic depression.

Has the *Tarasoff* duty been applied to mental health care professionals and facilities to protect inpatients from harm?

Yes. For example, in *McCall v. Department of Health and Rehabilitative Services* (94), a Florida appellate court upheld a claim for failure to warn when a hospital patient was injured by another inpatient. The assaultive inpatient was known to be dangerous. There was a lack of evidence of any previous violence between the two inpatients.

In *Halverson v. Pikes Peak Family Counseling and Mental Health Center* (95), Evelyn Marie Halverson was sexually assaulted by another inpatient during her hospitalization. The other patient had a history of violence. Furthermore, the facility knew that the patient had specifically threatened Ms. Halverson. She sued the facility for negligently failing to control and supervise the patient who attacked her after the facility became aware of his violent proclivities toward her. The trial court dismissed her complaint, citing a state statute immunizing mental health professionals from liability for failure to warn or protect any person against violence from a mental health provider's patients except when a serious threat of imminent physical harm is made against a specific person or persons.

On appeal, the Colorado Court of Appeals reversed, ordering reinstatement of Ms. Halverson's complaint. The court found that Ms. Halverson's claim could fall within the statutory exception to the facility's immunity. Thus, the facility could have a duty to warn or protect Ms. Halverson under the Colorado statute. The court also found that continued hospitalization was not sufficient to discharge the facility's duty to warn or protect the threatened patient, who remained accessible to the other patient threatening the violence. The case was sent back (i.e., remanded) to the trial court to determine the adequacy of the facility's actions.

Freishtat (96), commenting on *Halverson* and another case (97) concerning the liability for employees' acts, states that when statutory duties have been created to warn or protect endangered persons from the violence of patients, courts will construe such statutes broadly. Even if legislatures have not created such a duty, courts may be inclined to create broad duties to warn or protect endangered third persons.

When a therapist-patient in treatment discloses sexual exploitation of his or her patient, or a patient discloses sexual exploitation by a previous therapist, does a *Tarasoff* duty arise toward the current patients of the exploitative therapist?

Eth and Leong (98) raise the question of whether a therapist has a *Tarasoff* duty to warn the potentially endangered patients of a therapist-patient who discloses patient sexual exploitation. When a patient makes such a disclosure, the accusation remains hearsay. Nevertheless, as noted elsewhere in this chapter, some jurisdictions require reporting of a sexually exploitative therapist unless the patient objects. Minnesota has a mandatory reporting requirement (99). Eth and Leong believe that a therapist-patient's disclosure of sexual misconduct confronts the therapist with a conflict involving confidentiality versus the duty to warn. Believing that the psychiatrist has an ethical and "perhaps legal responsibility to act," the authors recommend notification of an ethics committee or state licensure board.

The legal duty to warn or protect usually arises when serious, imminent *physical,* not psychological, harm threatens a clearly identifiable, endangered third person. Only under this circumstance is the obligation not to breach confidentiality overcome. Although some therapists feel that sexual exploitation is equivalent to or even worse than murder, such a position would go well beyond the most expansive *Tarasoff* holdings of a distinct minority of courts (100). Attempting to notify the patients who are thought to be at risk for sexual exploitation could be very traumatizing and largely unnecessary. Every patient of the offending therapist is not necessarily vulnerable to sexual exploitation. Furthermore, notifying an ethics committee or state licensure board is analogous to calling the police. Sexually exploitative therapists would be unlikely to come for treatment if treating therapists were under an expanded *Tarasoff* duty to report therapist-patient sexual misconduct to the authorities.

Therapists must decide whom they will serve: their patients or society. Ethical principles conflict on this issue. The psychiatrist is ethically required to report impaired colleagues while maintaining the confidentiality of the therapist-patient. (See Sections 2 and 4 of *The Principles of Medical Ethics* in Appendix 1). In the final ethical analysis, maintaining confidentiality should be given priority as long as further sexual exploitation ceases by the therapist-patient. Could a long-term treatment approach reduce the threat of patient exploitation while also fulfilling the duty to protect? The duty to warn, by itself, is usually an insufficient clinical intervention. Moreover, warning will probably end treatment as well as any hope of preventing continued patient exploitation. Fulfilling the duty to protect usually allows for a variety of clinical interventions with the therapist-patient. For example, it may be possible to bring the exploited patient into the therapist-patient's treatment in order to prevent further exploitation and initiate referral to another therapist (101).

The sexually exploitative therapist who comes to treatment is usually struggling with conflicts over sexual acting out. The therapist who finds the sexual exploitation of patients ego-syntonic does not consider the need for treatment. These individuals are predatory therapists who are likely to continue exploiting and psychologically harming their patients. Only when treatment efforts appear to be ineffective in preventing further patient exploitation should reporting be considered. In a number of states, vulnerable adult reporting laws exist that take precedence over the maintenance of confidentiality (102). In states that make therapist-patient sex a crime, failure to report the continuing sexual misconduct of a therapist-patient could also cause the treating therapist to run afoul of the criminal statute.

Reporting duties may also be owed to other mental health professionals or institutions who may be considering the exploitative therapist-patient for employment. For example, a Minnesota statute (103) requires divulging the therapist-patient's sexual involvement with his or her patients to prospective employers. The treating therapist is protected from liability when reporting is done in good faith. The use of signed wide-ranging release provisions in the hiring process would also permit reporting of therapist-patient sexual misconduct. If the treating therapist fails to pass on such information and the therapist-patient is hired and subsequently exploits other patients, the treating therapist may be held legally liable for injuries that are caused these patients.

Do psychiatrists have a legal duty to warn others endangered by a patient's human immunodeficiency virus (HIV) infection?

With the ever-increasing fear concerning the spread of acquired immune deficiency syndrome (AIDS), psychiatrists who treat HIV-positive patients face special ethical and possibly legal dilemmas (104). For example, how should the psychiatrist manage the HIV-positive patient who continues to have multiple sexual relationships, yet refuses to inform his or her partners? Consent between adults is a sham under these circumstances. Unlike other potentially dangerous patients, the promiscuous patient with concealed HIV infection constantly carries a potentially lethal weapon—HIV—with the occasion for harm commonly occurring within the unguarded embrace of a sexual or love relationship. Eth (104) notes four clinical situations in which violating confidentiality to protect life is ethically indicated: communicable disease, child abuse, threat of violence, and HIV seropositivity.

Psychiatrists who treat patients with HIV infections posing a continuing danger of infection to others should evaluate these patients in the same manner as other potentially dangerous patients. The patient's behavior, and not the HIV status per se, represents the immediate danger. The psychiatrist should focus the evaluation particularly on the following questions:

- What is the patient's diagnosis (Axes I and II)?
- Is the patient treatable by available psychiatric therapies?
- What is the motivation of the patient in not informing sexual partners of HIV-positive status?
- Can the endangering behavior be contained by and within the treatment?
- Can support groups or organizations be mobilized to help the patient?

Some HIV-positive psychiatric patients may be unemployable, shunned by society, alone, and terrified. Sexual contact with others may be motivated not so much by sexual interest as by the need for human contact, affection, and support. To expect these patients to be sexually abstinent without providing other sources of emotional sustenance is naive and insensitive. Support groups and organizations are critically important for these individuals.

On the other hand, the antisocial or borderline patient may be motivated to infect others out of malice or may display a callous indifference to the welfare of others. If this behavior cannot be managed clinically, the psychotherapist will need to consider issuing a warning if the identity of the endangered parties is known. When clinically feasible, the patient should be informed that a warning will be issued. A report to the health department also should be considered if the authorities will conduct contact tracing and notification. Case law suggests that simply warning public health authorities cannot satisfy the duty to warn (105). A full notation of all measures taken should be recorded in the patient's chart. Consultation with a colleague should also be considered.

Warning others of possible infection can be an important intervention. Warning, however, poses special problems. For instance, the patient may become permanently unemployable if his or her HIV-positive condition is made public. As in *Tarasoff*-type situations, warnings must be discreet, balancing the right of society to be protected from disease against the psychiatrist's duty to maintain patient confidentiality. Furthermore, the occasion for warning is a serious, imminent threat of infection to an identifiable victim. Currently, there is a lack of medical knowledge regarding the course of HIV infections on which to base a firm judgment. For example, the level of certainty about the likelihood of transmission of the infection is unclear. The number of exposures before an individual is put at risk is unknown (e.g., seroconversion after one exposure is rare). There is a wide variation in seropositivity even after repeated exposure to HIV-infected individuals (106). Also, wide variation exists in the infectivity of the HIV-infected individual.

Some states have enacted statutes forbidding the disclosure of HIV test results without a patient's consent. There is considerable uncertainty about the relevance of these statutes to situations in which third parties are being endangered by a carrier. Statutory situations regarding confidentiality and AIDS range from a majority of states that have no specific statutes addressing the issue to those states that have relatively strict confidentiality laws and states that allow breaches under broader circumstances. Case law in this area is quite limited but developing rapidly (107).

In regard to disease transmission, a physician can be sued for failure to warn family members or others close to the patient that the latter has a communicable disease (108). Before warning, a physician must assess whether the patient will likely be dangerous (40). The case law indicates that health care providers owe a duty to warn specific persons of the foreseeable danger of becoming infected by the physician's patient (109). Health care providers, however, have no duty to warn unforeseeable victims of communicable diseases (110). Psychiatrists may have a similar duty to warn sexual partners of HIV patients. The duty to protect the patients of HIV-infected health care providers under the care of psychotherapists has become an emerging issue (111). As with other communicable diseases, a statutory duty to warn of HIV infection eventually may be legislated by states.

Professional opinion will legitimately vary concerning psychiatric management of the AIDS or HIV-positive patient. This area is new, in flux, and extremely complex. The above discussion presents points to be considered rather than rigid guidelines to be followed. The APA has promulgated its AIDS policy concerning confidentiality and disclosure (112). Appelbaum and Appelbaum (107) endorse the APA guidelines while making additional recommendations for their implementation.

How should the therapist proceed in order to protect endangered third parties from violent patients?

The therapist should proceed *clinically* in the management of the violent patient. Above all, therapists must not get caught up in legal issues so that they become distracted from providing good clinical care. Although therapists must practice within the law, they do not have to become lawyers.

Tarasoff II (3) states that the therapist must exercise his or her own best judgment consistent with that reasonable degree of skill, knowledge, and care ordinarily exercised by therapists under similar circumstances in order to protect the victim from the foreseeable violence of dangerous patients. The court does not require perfect skill but only the skill exercised by therapists in similar circumstances. The court held: "The discharge of this duty may require the therapist to take one or more various steps, depending upon the nature of the case. Thus, it may call for him to warn the intended victim of danger, to notify the police, or to take whatever other steps are reasonably necessary under the circumstances" (3). Although vaguely defined, the duty to protect permits a more meaningful clinical approach to the management of violent patients. The duty to warn, by itself, is often a hollow legal formalism full of sound and fury but signifying little of clinical value. While warning may be part of a therapist's intervention strategy, it rarely should be relied on initially or exclusively. Gross et al. (113) provide a response guide for clinicians after hearing patients make violent threats.

Do professional standards of care exist for the assessment and prediction of violent acts?

Clinical methods for assessing the risk of violence are used regularly by psychiatrists in evaluating patients. The law requires that therapists exercise reasonable care in making such assessments. Predicting a violent act, however, is another matter. Professional standards do not exist for predicting violent behavior. Such predictions are judgment calls even when bearing a logical nexus to an adequate assessment of violence risk factors in a given patient.

Although psychiatrists must provide diagnosis and treatment according to a *reasonable* standard of care, successful results cannot be guaranteed. When a patient's risk for violence is assessed according to accepted clinical practices and the subsequent clinical interventions bear a logical nexus to the assessment, the treatment should fall within the professional judgment standard. The clinician must remember that the systematic assessment of the risk of violence is good clinical practice and only secondarily a risk management technique.

In *Littleton v. Good Samaritan Hospital and Health Center* (114), a patient administered a lethal dose of aspirin to her baby 2 weeks after discharge from the psychiatric unit. While hospitalized, the patient had discussed a plan of injecting her child "with something to kill it." The psychiatrist and hospital were sued in a survivorship and wrongful-death action. The trial court returned a verdict of $1,800,000 against the defendant. The case was appealed. The Ohio Supreme Court adopted a "professional judgment rule." Under this rule, a psychiatrist will not be held liable if, "after carefully examining all relevant data," he or she makes a "professional medical judgment" that the patient is not an immediate danger to others. The professional judgment rule would apply to both assessing the danger and deciding a course of action. The court added that it would examine the good faith and thoroughness of the therapist's decision according to "the competence and training of the reviewing therapist, whether the relevant documents and evidence were adequately, promptly and independently reviewed, whether the advice or opinion of another therapist was obtained, whether the evaluation was made in light of the proper legal standards for commitment, and whether other evidence of good faith exists." The case was remanded for a new trial under the professional judgment rule.

The use of reasonable professional judgment is a mainstay defense in malpractice suits (115). The credibility of this defense depends upon compliance with the standard of care as documented by the doctor's own records (116).

Can psychiatrists make short-term predictions of violent acts?

Tardiff (74) maintains that a competent psychiatrist should be able to predict a patient's short-term violence potential by using short-term assessment methods similar to those used in predicting suicide potential. He cites a number of research studies to support his contention. Short-term is defined as a few days or a week. In *Soutear v. United States* (117), the psychiatric expert testified that the prediction of violence is meaningless beyond 2–4 weeks. Although estimates vary, clinicians seem to question the validity of predictions of violence that exceed 1 month (53).

The courts have never specifically addressed the time limits of a therapist's duty to protect. Instead, it appears that the reasonableness of a therapist's evaluation of a patient's dangerousness plays a more important role in a court's finding of liability than the amount of time elapsing between the last therapy contact and the injury of a third party. In *Davis v. Lhim* (27), the court reached back 2 years to find a psychiatrist liable for a patient's murder of his mother. In *Naidu v. Laird* (22), the court found liability against the psychiatrist when the patient killed the plaintiff's decedent while driving in a psychotic state $5\frac{1}{2}$ months after discharge. Dr. Naidu contended that because of the lapse of time between his treatment of the patient and the accident, his treatment could not be considered the proximate cause of the death of the plaintiff's decedent. The court ruled that mere lapse of time was not sufficient to establish the remoteness of these two incidents because there was no demonstration of an intervening cause. Dr. Naidu presented no evidence that would break the "chain of causation."

Although prediction of violence may be possible when violence appears imminent, it is clinically more useful to assess the risk of violence rather than attempt to predict the actual occurrence of a violent act. Furthermore, patient violence toward others is a rare event with low specificity (high false-positive rates). The assessment of violence has been analogized to weather forecasting

(118). Because time attenuates predictive accuracy, the time-driven weather forecast model has applicability to the assessment of violence. The assessment of the risk of violence is a here-and-now determination. Probability determinations become progressively less accurate beyond the immediate short term (e.g., 24–48 hours). Like weather forecasts, assessments need to be updated frequently. Long-term forecasts are notoriously unreliable.

Assessing the risk of violence involves three separate steps (see Tables 13-1 and 13-2):

1. Identifying patients with risk factors associated with violence
2. Assessing overall risk of violence based on rating of specific risk factors
3. Making preventive interventions that bear a logical nexus to the overall violence risk assessment

TABLE 13–1. Assessment of violence risk factors

Risk factors	Facilitating	Inhibiting
Specific person threatened*		
Past violent acts*		
Motive		
Therapeutic alliance (ongoing patient)		
Other relationships		
Psychiatric diagnoses (Axes I and II)		
Control of anger		
Situational status		
Employment status		
Epidemiological data (age, sex, race, socioecocomic group, marital status, violence base rates)		
Availability of lethal means		
Available victim		
Syntonic or dystonic violence		
Specific plan		
Childhood abuse (or witnessing spouse abuse)		
Alcohol abuse		
Drug abuse		
Mental competency		
History of impulsive behavior		
CNS disorder		
Low intelligence		

Note. Rating system: L = low factor; M = moderate factor; H = high factor; 0 = nonfactor. Clinically judge low, moderate, or high potential for violence within 24–48 hours based upon assessment of violence.

*When a specific person is threatened and past violence has occurred, a high risk rating for violence is achieved.

Here-and-now violence risk assessment requires evaluating the patient frequently in regard to major clinical decisions (e.g., hospitalization, pass, discharge). Finally, a number of violence rating scales have been developed that are helpful in gathering important information about the potentially violent patient. No rating scale, however, can take the place of sound clinical judgment in the assessment of the risk of violence.

What risk factors do clinicians usually consider in the assessment of violence?

Therapists are on sounder clinical footing when assessing the patient's risk for violence rather than trying to actually predict violent acts. Approaching potential violence from the clinical side allows consideration of the possible connection between violence and mental disorders. Thus the therapist stays within the familiar province of clinical practice. On the other hand, legal definitions of dangerousness tend to be arbitrary and abstract concepts, not readily translatable into the diagnostic and treatment models used by psychiatrists.

A number of risk factors should be considered in clinically assessing the risk of violence (as noted earlier in this chapter in the section on violence research studies). Tables 13-1 and 13-2 are suggested for heuristic purposes only, encouraging a systematic approach to violence risk assessment. The therapist's clinical judgment concerning the patient remains paramount. Because violence risk factors will be assigned different weights according to the clinical presentation of the patient, these tables should not be followed rigidly. In Table 13-1, with the exception of *specific person threatened* and *past violent acts,* violence

Table 13–2.   Assessment of violence risk factors and psychiatric intervention options

Violence risk	Psychiatric interventions
HIGH	Immediate hospitalization if mentally ill and likely to benefit from hospitalization
MODERATE	Hospitalization Frequent outpatient visits Consider warning and calling the police Reevaluate patient and treatment plan frequently Remain available to the patient
LOW	Continue with current treatment plan

Tables 13-1 and 13-2 represent only one method of violence risk assessment and intervention. The purpose of these tables is heuristic, encouraging a systematic approach to risk assessment. The therapist's clinical judgment concerning the patient remains paramount. Given the fact that violence risk factors will be assigned different weights according to the clinical presentation of the patient, this method of assessment should not be followed rigidly.

risk factors are not listed in order of clinical importance. This determination depends upon the patient's clinical presentation. When time or circumstances do not allow for consultation, a systematic application of the approach recommended in these tables may prove useful (119). A complete discussion on the use of these tables in the clinical situation is found elsewhere (118, 119).

In the tables above, emphasis is placed upon clinical diagnosis and the assessment of interpersonal factors. Both Axis I and Axis II diagnoses should be reassessed if violence is threatened. Does the risk of violence related to an Axis I disorder abate when the disorder is successfully treated? Or is the risk of violence a chronic issue related to a severe character disorder? Patients with character disorders may make threats in therapy without intending to act on them. Rather, they may want to involve the therapist in taking responsibility for controlling their impulses. When threatened violence is related to this issue, the therapist must point this out to the patient while not becoming entrapped in the patient's psychodynamics. Identifying problems surrounding the patient's difficulty in assuming responsibility for his or her life then becomes the crux of the therapy.

The patient's specific life situation may contain elements that increase a patient's risk for violence. A smoldering antagonism between a boss and the patient may be rapidly heading for a violent confrontation. Can an intervention be made that introduces a third-party arbitrator? Certain angry patients are not continuously at a high risk for violence but may be so for only a few seconds or minutes when either a foreseeable or an unforeseeable life situation provides the trigger for the eruption of violence. The nature and quality of the patient's relationship with others are critical factors for evaluation. Is the patient isolated? Has the patient recently cut off relationships? Does the patient have current relationships in which the interaction is primarily hostile? What is the strength and condition of the therapeutic alliance?

Gutheil and Appelbaum (120) conceptualize aspects of the patient's mental functioning and environment into "risk factors" and "resource factors," subdividing each into external and internal categories. External risk factors include loss of significant relationships and supports. The more acute the loss, the greater the risk it represents. Internal risk factors include any condition that would decrease behavioral controls such as psychosis, drug or alcohol intoxication, and organic brain disorders. Resource factors include the availability of friends, family, therapist, protective settings, stable job situation, and specialized services such as social and homemaker services. Internal resources include higher intelligence, obsessional defenses, good relationships, social skills, and sustaining religious and ethical convictions.

Assessing the state of the relationship with the therapist is crucial. What is the status of the transference? If transference is negative, has it been persistently negative or changed recently? What is the reason for such a change? If the therapeutic alliance is intact and working, the patient is more likely to cooperate with treatment interventions. Therapists who are faced with violent patients may withdraw from fully evaluating the patient's violent tendencies because of anxiety, denial, or anger at the patient for placing them in a potential *Tarasoff*-type situation.

Unrecognized countertransference may lead to a subtle abandonment of the violent patient, causing increased separation anxiety and fears of loss of control that may precipitate violence. Clinical experience indicates that violent patients often feel very frightened and helpless, although their fears may manifest as morbid jealousy or as menacing behavior toward others. Therapeutic efforts directed at discovering and managing the patient's fear and helplessness may dramatically relieve his or her violent impulses.

After completing a violence risk assessment, how should the psychiatrist proceed in selecting a course of action?

Once the therapist determines that the patient is losing control, a number of specific interventions can be made. Selecting a course of action depends on the needs of the potentially violent patient and the clinical ingenuity of the therapist. Although the courses of action are numerous, a short list includes incorporating the potential victim into the therapy, seeing the patient more frequently to deepen the alliance, voluntary and involuntary hospitalization, and using social service interventions to improve the environmental situation. Table 13-2 illustrates some of the more common interventions that can be made according to the level of violence risk assessed.

The patient's violent tendencies should be discussed openly with the patient. If possible, every intervention should be handled as a treatment issue. If warning others is necessary, the patient's cooperation should be engaged whenever possible. Warning together may further enhance the therapeutic alliance as well as raise concern in the patient about the welfare of others. This outcome is more likely when the patient's violent impulses are dystonic. Rarely are the patient's violent impulses totally syntonic.

Family, if available, may be mobilized and medication changed or increased. The patient and the potential victim may be brought together in a protected situation to discuss their difficulties. Voluntary or involuntary hospitalization may be required. Involuntary hospitalization may shatter the treatment relationship, but this is an unavoidable risk that the therapist must be prepared to take. Environmental interventions may include removal of guns from the home, providing a companion, or, if substance abuse is present, hospitalization or enrollment by the patient in an alcohol or drug abuse program. The presence or absence of the patient's cooperation with these interventions provides an on-the-spot test of the therapeutic alliance. A panoply of treatment interventions are available, depending on the therapeutic ingenuity of the therapist and the particular condition and situation of the patient. Southard and Gross (121) have devised a useful decision tree for assessment and intervention with the potentially violent patient who may be dangerous to others.

Before a treatment intervention is attempted, a risk-benefit assessment should be conducted and recorded. Risk-benefit analysis permits an incremental, step-by-step approach to interventions with violent patients. Negligence usually is not assigned for clinical errors alone, but only when a significant departure from a reasonable standard of care leads directly to the harm of another. A documented risk-benefit analysis of important interventions with dangerous patients will be useful in demonstrating that, even though there was a violent outcome, reasonable care was taken with the patient. Categorical statements such as "The patient is no longer dangerous" are less legally defensible than notes that take into account the patient's clinical condition. The risk assessment of violence should be balanced against the benefits of a particular treatment intervention.

If involuntary hospitalization is considered, the risks of loss of control of violent impulses during outpatient therapy should be weighed against the benefits of attempting to maintain the therapeutic relationship, for both present and future care. The clinician also needs to consider the counterbalancing risks and benefits of involuntary hospitalization. Consultation with a colleague may be reassuring to both the patient and the therapist. If legal questions arise later, consultation may help establish that a reasonable standard of care was provided the patient.

Appelbaum (66), using the legally preferred term *dangerousness,* discusses the clinical implications of *Tarasoff* and presents a practical way to proceed clinically in meeting the duty to protect. The duty requires the therapist to assess the degree of the patient's dangerousness. In addition, the clinician must select a course of action to deal with the patient's threat and implement that course of action appropriately.

The assessment of dangerousness contains two separate parts: gathering information and making the prediction. Although the *Tarasoff* obligation is usually met by a careful clinical evaluation, Appelbaum (66) suggests that two questions be routinely asked: "Have you ever seriously injured another person?" and "Do you ever think about harming someone else?" These two questions often yield surprising information not obtained from taking a general psychiatric history. Areas that deserve particularly close assessment include the personal, social, situational, and clinical variables related to violence. The most common mistake made by clinicians is insufficient gathering of information upon which to base a later determination of dangerousness. Although standards of care do not exist for predicting dangerousness, clear standards do exist for gathering sufficient information for satisfying a reasonable standard of care. Because prediction is so problematic, careful documentation of the clinical reasoning behind the decision concerning dangerousness is essential. Written documentation that a colleague's views were obtained underscores that the clinician attempted to adhere to the standard of care.

Follow-up must be adequate but it is limited. If the patient stops taking medication or drops out of treatment, these issues should be addressed aggressively. A phone call should be made or a letter sent to the patient who precipitously terminates therapy. Clinicians must stoutly resist acting upon the almost inevitable countertransference feeling of being glad to be rid of these very difficult patients. Otherwise, inadequate follow-up may be given. Therapists should follow up their interventions to see if they are implemented. If the therapist recommends voluntary hospitalization, the therapist should arrange for the hospitalization and follow up to ensure the patient is hospitalized without delay. When the patient is involuntarily hospitalized, the therapist should contact the treating physician at the intake facility to discuss the case. In ongoing therapy, interventions must be revised if they have failed to alter the patient's tendency toward violence. If the patient is transferred to another facility, the assessment of dangerousness needs to be communicated. Reassessment for dangerousness must be made prior to discharge. There is, however, a limit to the duty to protect. Therapists are not police officers, nor do they have the training or resources to track down violent patients. Society must look elsewhere to fulfill those functions.

Do commitment statutes require involuntary hospitalization of persons under certain defined circumstances?

No. Commitment statutes are permissive (48). In other words, they enable mental health professionals and others to seek involuntary hospitalization for persons who meet certain substantive criteria.

The duty to seek involuntary hospitalization as a standard-of-care issue is another matter. Patients who are mentally ill and pose an imminent, serious threat of harm to themselves or others may require involuntary hospitalization as a primary psychiatric intervention.

In *Petersen v. State* (20), the court specifically acknowledged the psychiatrist's duty to commit patients *under certain circumstances* in the state of Washington. A patient was involuntarily detained when the hospital staff discovered that he was suffering from hallucinations and delusions. The patient had a history of abusing phencyclidine and other drugs. He was diagnosed as suffering from a schizophrenic disorder and given thiothixene. On expiration of the emergency detention period, the psychiatrist petitioned and obtained an additional 14 days of hospital stay. The psychiatrist testified that the patient was gravely disabled by drug abuse and remained a danger to himself. On the day before expiration of the last detention period, the patient was given a pass. He was observed that evening spinning his car in circles on the hospital grounds. The patient, nevertheless, was discharged the next day after the psychiatrist concluded that he had recovered from his drug-induced psychosis. Five days later, the patient struck the plaintiff's car while traveling at 50 to 60 miles per hour after running a red light. The patient was under the influence of drugs. The plaintiff claimed that the psychiatrist's failure to try to extend the commitment was the direct cause of her injuries. The jury awarded damages of $250,000.

The court scrutinized the steps the psychiatrist should have followed to protect the public from the patient. Stating that the psychiatrist "failed to petition the court for a 90-day commitment," the court made no mention of other interventions that could have been used. Thus, the court held that the psychiatrist was liable for not petitioning for commitment.

Although this case involves a psychiatrist practicing at a state hospital, it appears that the holding applies equally to psychiatrists at private hospitals in Washington State (122). *Petersen* places an increased burden on psychiatrists practicing in the state of Washington to initiate commitment proceedings. The case (20) represents a further extension of *Tarasoff* liability to a duty to protect unidentified victims, even when they are unintentionally harmed.

In 1986, the United States District Court in North Carolina held that "a psychotherapist judgment rule" would be applied to evaluate the "good faith independence and thoroughness" of a decision not to seek commitment (123). Liability would not be imposed for "simple errors of judgment." In this case, a patient seen in irregular outpatient treatment for posttraumatic stress disorder killed one person and wounded others in a shooting spree. Shortly before the shootings, 15 psychiatrists at a VA hospital staff meeting unanimously concluded that the patient could not be committed under North Carolina law despite threats of violence. The patient was subsequently convicted of first-degree murder. In the civil case, the court said, "What society in general desires and expects psychotherapists to do when considering whether a patient should be involuntarily committed is to actively consider the public interest and to use their professional judgment in light of that interest." The court ruled that the doctors did perform this duty.

On appeal, the Court of Appeals for the Fourth Circuit affirmed the lower court's summary judgment for the defendants (123). The court agreed with the psychiatrists who argued that controlling the patient through commitment would destroy the psychiatrist's potential for constructive influence over the patient "while warning to threatened third persons may well remain unknown to the patient or appear . . . as not necessarily attributable to the physician. Initiation of involuntary commitment proceedings threatens the patient's constitutionally protected liberty interest, while warnings to third persons . . . do not."

In *Schuster v. Altenberg* (34), the Wisconsin Supreme Court ruled that a complaint of failure to seek commitment of the patient raised a legitimate cause of action. The court stated:

> In the instant case, if it is ultimately proven that it would have been foreseeable to
> a psychiatrist, exercising due care, that by failing to warn a third person or by fail-

ing to take action to institute detention or commitment proceedings someone would be harmed, negligence will be established.

The opinion establishes in Wisconsin an affirmative duty to commit. In this case, a manic-depressive patient on psychotropic medication crashed into a tree at 60 miles per hour within an hour of treatment. The patient died, leaving her 17-year-old daughter paraplegic.

What risk management strategies are emphasized by attorneys regarding potentially violent patients?

Legal commentators (124), based on an analysis of *Tarasoff*-type cases, emphasize the following recommendations. In addition, they suggest a number of additional steps that can be taken, not only to improve the evaluation process but to reduce the risk of liability for patients' violent acts:

1. Obtain prior treatment records. The courts have held psychiatrists responsible for knowing what was in the patient's old records in four published cases (125).
2. Document the decision-making process, including risk-benefit assessments.
3. Consult with another therapist and/or attorney when management of patient is in doubt.
4. Issue all appropriate warnings to identifiable victims when danger is determined, even if victims are aware of danger of harm. This approach should be used if other clinical interventions fail or appear inappropriate.
5. If voluntary hospitalization is not possible and the patient appears to meet the criteria for involuntary hospitalization, initiate commitment proceedings if in serious doubt that the patient poses a danger to the public. Responsibility passes to the judicial system if the patient is not deemed committable by the court and ultimately harms someone. Nevertheless, the therapist should go on record as opposing dismissal of a violent, mentally ill patient. Involuntary hospitalization should be considered in the best interest of the patient and for the safety of others rather than as a defensive action by the psychiatrist solely to avoid liability.

What are some of the strengths and weaknesses in Dr. Fowler's clinical management of her potentially violent patient?

In the clinical vignette, Dr. Fowler's management of Professor Harris could have been enhanced by obtaining the patient's prior psychiatric record. With the information of prior violence, she might have better anticipated the patient's potential for violence. She also might have had more time to consult with a colleague, an attorney, or a forensic expert about the psychiatric-legal issues raised by this case. For instance, should a warning be given to potential victims by the psychiatrist even when they are aware of the threat? Does a warning from a psychiatrist have a greater impact upon a potential victim that will make it more likely that the warning will be heeded? Should the confidentiality statute be breached in order to issue a warning? Does the statute contain exceptions allowing for a duty to warn while also providing immunity from a breach-of-confidentiality action?

Because of her knowledge of Professor Harris's background of physical abuse and his hobby of collecting guns and developing weapons, should Dr. Fowler have explored therapeutically the possible connections between the meaning of weapons to his feelings of hurt, fear, helplessness, and anger? If the transference was turning negative, as she suspected, should not priority have been given to managing the negative transference therapeutically?

Although no *Tarasoff*-type duty to warn existed in Dr. Fowler's state, the absence of a statute or case law should not be a determinative factor. Dr. Fowler correctly reasoned that her ethical, moral, and professional duty dictated that she try to protect both her patient and other potential victims by calling the police. Similar reasoning was used in breaching the confidentiality statute. Also, Dr. Fowler did not call the police and then go about her practice as usual. She maintained her clinical role with the patient. Dr. Fowler medically certified Professor Harris for involuntary hospitalization to ensure further evaluation and treatment. She recognized that she was upset and distracted by the worries and fears raised by this case. She decided to cancel the rest of her patients so that she would be available to assist the police in trying to find Professor Harris. Following up on recommended interventions that have been implemented is very important. Therapists must be able to tolerate disruptions of their schedule, loss of time and money, and their own feelings of anger and frustration occasioned by the clinical and legal difficulties surrounding the management of violent, threatening patients. Finally, Dr. Fowler did not fall into the trap of trying to predict the occurrence of an act. Instead, a quick assessment of the risk factors for violence indicated a high risk requiring immediate intervention.

In summary, what are the salient aspects of the *Tarasoff* doctrine that apply to psychiatric practice?

Many therapists still misunderstand the *Tarasoff* decision because they believe that warning potential victims of patient violence rather than protecting endangered third parties from violence satisfies the legal duty.

Beck (23) presents an excellent summary of the current status of the duty to protect. He estimates that approximately 50 psychiatrists are sued each year for breach of the duty to protect. Of these, roughly two-thirds of the cases are settled before trial. Of the 17 trials, approximately two-thirds result in defendant verdicts. Six psychiatrists a year are found liable. Beck estimates that the odds for an APA member (35,000 members) to be sued for breach of duty to protect, go to trial, and be found liable are 5,800 to 1 in any one year.

Several conclusions can be drawn from the cases presented in this chapter. First, in about half of the outpatient cases, the courts have held that the therapist's control over the patient is not sufficient to establish a duty to protect without a foreseeable victim. In treating an outpatient, the *Tarasoff* duty operates when there is evidence, through either threats or acts, that the patient is dangerous to a specific, foreseeable victim. Second, the danger must be substantial, involving serious bodily harm or death. Third, if no threats or violent acts are uncovered after careful clinical evaluation, liability is unlikely even if violence should occur. Fourth, in inpatient release cases, the courts have held that there is a duty to control with or without a foreseeable victim. The duty to evaluate the patient for the risk of violence according to usual professional standards would obviate a *Tarasoff* duty because the continued high risk of violence would require further hospitalization. Litigation involving release of potentially violent patients who harm others will turn on whether the psychiatrist was negligent in evaluating the patient prior to discharge. If the court should release a patient deemed dangerous by the psychiatrist, the psychiatrist should go on record with his or her concern about the patient's potential for violence. The issues surrounding negligent discharge are discussed in further detail in Chapter 14.

The duty to protect the patient and endangered third parties is primarily a professional and moral obligation and secondarily a legal duty. Long before *Tarasoff*, psychiatrists acted to protect both patients and endangered third persons from violence. Thus, the therapist should attempt to integrate the *Tarasoff* duty into the clinical work with the patient. Reports of this type of approach have indicated a generally positive effect on the patient's treatment. Warning in a legalistic manner usually is counterproductive.

Beck (83) points out that once the clinical assessment is made that the patient is potentially violent, three basic options are open: *1)* deal with the violence in the therapy; *2)* discuss the problem with a third person such as the victim and/or the police; or *3)* voluntarily or involuntarily hospitalize the patient. Beck feels that if the therapist is satisfied after careful assessment that the patient will not commit violence before the next scheduled appointment, then the therapist can continue to treat violence as a purely therapeutic issue. If the therapist believes the patient will become violent within 24 to 48 hours, hospitalization is the treatment of choice. In most cases, when an intermediate position exists in which the therapist feels that violence is a distinct possibility but is not imminent, then the best course usually is discussion with some third person such as the potential victim. Warning also may be the intervention of choice when it appears likely that a patient will become violent before the next session but is not committable.

Finally, the maxim of forensic psychiatrist Dr. Jonas Rappeport—"When in doubt, shout"—is extremely important. Discussion with a colleague or a legal consultant may provide needed perspective as well as establish a reference to professional standards of care. Documentation of the rationale behind the assessment of the risk of violence is critical. What specific questions were asked? What answers were given? The conclusion about the patient's risk of violence should be noted, citing the clinical data used, the clinician's course of action, and the reasons behind choosing a particular course of action. The consultant should render a report, and the discussion with the consultant should be noted in the patient's medical record. If the therapist takes these steps, liability is unlikely even if violence occurs and another person is seriously harmed. Errors do not constitute malpractice when reasonable care has been taken in evaluation and treatment.

Finally, therapists who treat and manage violent patients should be adequately familiar with the current literature on the subject (126–129). As Appelbaum so aptly points out: "Clinicians have learned to live with *Tarasoff,* recognizing that good common sense, sound clinical practice, careful documentation, and a genuine concern for their patients are almost always sufficient to fulfill their legal obligations."

References

1. RESTATEMENT (SECOND) OF TORTS § 315 (1965)
2. Belli MM: Warning of the dangerous patient. American Journal of Forensic Psychiatry 2:7–14, 1982
3. Tarasoff v Regents of the University of California, 17 Cal 3d 425, 131 Cal Rptr 14, 551 P2d 334 (1976)
4. Tarasoff v Regents of the University of California, 33 Cal App 3d 275, 108 Cal Rptr 878 (1973)
5. Tarasoff v Regents of the University of California, 17 Cal 3d 439, 131 Cal Rptr 25, 551 P2d 345 (1976)
6. Mills MJ: The so-called duty to warn: the psychotherapeutic duty to protect third parties from patients' violent acts. Behavioral Sciences and the Law 2:237–258, 1984
7. 27 Cal 3d 741, 167 Cal Rptr 70, 614 P2d 728 (1980)
8. 34 Cal 3d 695, 194 Cal Rptr 805, 669 P2d 41 (1983)
9. 168 NJ Super 466, 403 A2d 500 (1979)
10. 497 F Supp 185 (D Neb 1980)
11. MacDonald v Clinger, 84 AD2d 482, 446 NYS2d 801 (App Div 1982)
12. Chrite v United States, 564 F Supp 341 (ED Mich 1983)
13. Cairl v State, 323 NW2d 20 (Minn 1982); Brady v Hopper, 570 F Supp 1333 (D Colo 1983), aff'd, 751 F2d 329 (10th Cir 1984); Furr v Spring Grove State Hospital, 53 Md App 474, 454 A2d 414 (1983)
14. Beck JC: Current status of the duty to protect, in Confidentiality Versus the Duty to Protect: Foreseeable Harm in the Practice of Psychiatry. Edited by Beck JC. Washington, DC, American Psychiatric Press, 1990, pp 9–21
15. 712 F2d 391 (9th Cir 1983), overruled, In re complaint of McLinn 739 F2d 1395 (9th Cir 1984)

16. Matter of McLinn, 739 F2d 1395 (1984)
17. 570 F Supp 1333 (D Colo 1983), aff'd. 751 F2d 329 (10th Cir 1984)
18. Brady v Hopper, 751 F2d 329 (10th Cir 1984)
19. 327 NW2d 759 (Iowa 1982)
20. 100 Wash 2d 421, 671 P2d 230 (1983) (en banc)
21. No 88-1562, Middlesex Cty Super Ct (Mass June 1988)
22. 539 A2d 1064 (Del Super Ct 1988)
23. Beck JC: Current status of the duty to protect, in Confidentiality Versus the Duty to Protect: Foreseeable Harm in the Practice of Psychiatry. Edited by Beck JC. Washington, DC, American Psychiatric Press, 1990, pp 9–21
24. 153 Ill App 3d 408, 505 NE2d 773 (Ill App Ct 1987)
25. 94 So 2d 1342 (La Ct App 1986)
26. Stone AA: Law, Psychiatry, and Morality. Washington, DC, American Psychiatric Press, 1984, pp 170–171
27. Davis v Lhim, 335 NW2d 481 (Mich App 1983), remanded on other grounds, 422 Mich 875, 366 NW2d 7 (1985), on rem, 147 Mich App 8, 382 NW2d 195 (1985), rvsd sub nom, Canon v Thumudo, 430 Mich 326, 422 NW2d 688 (1988); Jablonski v United States, 712 F2d 391 (9th Cir 1983), overruled, In re complaint of McLinn 739 F2d 1395 (9th Cir 1984)
28. Comment—the Tarasoff progeny: creating a weaponless policeman with a deep pocket. Capital University Law Review 15:699, 1986
29. Felthous AR: The ever confusing jurisprudence of the psychotherapist's duty to protect. Journal of Psychiatry and Law 17:575–594, 1989
30. Kamenar PD: Psychiatrists' duty to warn of a dangerous patient: a survey of the law. Behavioral Sciences and the Law 2:259–272, 1984
31. Appelbaum PS, Zonana H, Bonnie R, et al: Statutory approaches to limiting psychiatrists' liability for their patients' violent acts. Am J Psychiatry 146:821–828, 1989
32. 139 Mich App 342, 362 NW2d 275 (1984)
33. Gregory DR: Critical cases. Legal Aspects of Medical Practice 13:7, 1985
34. 144 Wis 2d 223, 424 NW2d 159 (1988), rev'd, Schuster v Altenberg, 86-CV-1327 (Cir Ct Racine Cty 1990)
35. Felthous AR: The duty to warn or protect to prevent automobile accidents, in American Psychiatric Press Review of Clinical Psychiatry and the Law, Vol 1. Edited by Simon RI. Washington, DC, American Psychiatric Press, 1990, pp 221–238
36. 541 F Supp 999 (D Md 1982)
37. 300 Or 706, 717 P2d 140 (1986)
38. OHIO REV CODE ANN § 5122.34 (Supp 1990)
39. Official actions: The Council on Psychiatry and Law. Am J Psychiatry 141:487–488, 1984
40. 146 Vt 61. 499 A2d 425 (1985)
41. Stone AA: Law, Psychiatry, and Morality. Washington, DC, American Psychiatric Press, 1984, pp 177–178; see p 178
42. Stone AA: Vermont adopts Tarasoff: a real barn-burner. Am J Psychiatry 143:352–355, 1986
43. Young v Sheppard and Enoch Pratt Hospital, No 139/328/82-L-598 (Cir Ct Baltimore City 1983)

44. American Psychiatric Association: The Principles of Medical Ethics With Annotations Especially Applicable to Psychiatry. Washington, DC, American Psychiatric Association, 1989
45. Quinn KM: The impact of Tarasoff on clinical practice. Behavioral Sciences and the Law 2:319–330, 1984
46. 45 Md App 718, 415 A2d 625 (Md Ct Spec App 1980)
47. 130 PHL J 107 (Pa Ct Com Pl 1981)
48. Appelbaum PS, Zonana H, Bonnie R, et al: Statutory approaches to limiting psychiatrists' liability for their patients' violent acts. Am J Psychiatry 146:821–828, 1989
49. Roth LH, Meisel A: Dangerousness, confidentiality, and the duty to warn. Am J Psychiatry 134:508–511, 1977
50. Melton GB, Petrila J, Poythress NG, et al: Psychological Evaluations for the Courts. New York, Guilford, 1987, pp 201–203
51. Wagner R: California psychiatrists challenge court's wide-open Tarasoff ruling. Psychiatric Times 7(11):35, 1990
52. 50 Cal 3d 583, 789 P2d 127, 268 Cal Rptr 399 (Cal), cert denied, Ill S Ct 442 (1990)
53. Slovenko R: The therapist's duty to warn or protect endangered third persons. Journal of Psychiatry and Law 16:134–209, 1988
54. ALASKA STAT § 08.86.200 (1988); ARIZ REV STAT ANN § 36-517.02 (Supp 1989); CAL CIV CODE § 43.92 (1987); COLO REV STAT § 13-21-117 (1986); 1987 FLA SESS LAW SERV ch 87-252 (West); IND CODE ANN § 34-4-12.4-2 (Burns 1987); KY REV STAT ANN § 202A.400 (Baldwin 1988); LA REV STAT ANN § 9:2800.1-2 (West 1986); MD CTS & JUD PROC CODE ANN § 5-315 (1989); MASS ANN LAWS ch 112, § 129A(c)(2) (West 1989); MINN STAT ANN § 329.31 (West 1987); TENN CODE ANN § 33-10-101-104 (1989); UTAH CODE ANN § 78-14a-102 (1988); WASH REV CODE ANN § 71-34-270(2) (1987); 1987 Wash Laws 212, 301
55. Mills MJ, Sullivan G, Eth S: Protecting third parties: a decade after Tarasoff. Am J Psychiatry 144:68–74, 1987
56. Appelbaum PS: The new preventive detention: psychiatry's problematic responsibility for the control of violence. Am J Psychiatry 145:779–785, 1988
57. CAL CIV CODE § 43.92 (Deering 1987)
58. 301 NW2d 766 (Iowa 1981)
59. 171 Mich App 216, 429 NW2d 857 (Mich Ct App 1988)
60. Felthous AR: The Psychotherapist's Duty to Warn or Protect. Springfield, IL, Charles C Thomas, 1987, pp 49–51
61. State v Hudson, 119 NH 963, 409 A2d 1349 (1979)
62. Meisel A: The concept of dangerousness in mental health law. Paper presented at the 15th annual meeting of the American Academy of Psychiatry and the Law. Nassau, Bahamas, October 1984
63. Brooks AD: Notes on defining the "dangerousness" of the mentally ill, in Dangerous Behavior: A Problem in Law and Mental Health (DHEW Publ No ADM-78-563). Edited by Frederick CJ. Rockville, MD, National Institute of Mental Health, 1978, pp 37–60
64. 457 U.S. 307 (1982)
65. 422 U.S. 563 (1975)
66. Appelbaum PS: Implications of Tarasoff for clinical practice, in The Potentially Violent Patient and the Tarasoff Decision in Psychiatric Practice. Edited by Beck JC. Washington, DC, American Psychiatric Press, 1985, pp 93–108

67. Monahan J, Steadman H: Crime and mental disorder: an epidemiologic approach, in Crime and Justice: An Annual Review of Research. Edited by Morris N, Tonry M. Chicago, IL, University of Chicago Press, 1983

68. Teplin LA: The criminality of the mentally ill: a dangerous misconception. Am J Psychiatry 142:593–599, 1985

69. Steadman H: A situational approach to violence. Int J Law Psychiatry 5:171–186, 1982

70. Wettstein RM: The prediction of violent behavior and the duty to protect third parties. Behavioral Sciences and the Law 2:291–318, 1984

71. Kozol HL, Bouchet RJ, Garofalo RF: The diagnosis and treatment of dangerousness. Crime and Delinquency 19:371–392, 1972

72. Dix GE: Clinical evaluation of the "dangerous" or "normal" criminal defendants. Virginia Law Review 66:523, 1980

73. Monahan J: The prediction of violent behavior: toward a second generation of theory and policy. Am J Psychiatry 141:10–15, 1984

74. Tardiff K: A model for the short-term prediction of violence potential and related research, in Current Approaches to the Prediction of Violence. Edited by Brizer D, Crowner M. Washington, DC, American Psychiatric Press, 1989, pp 1–12

75. Melton GB, Petrila J, Poythress NG, et al: Psychological Evaluations for the Courts. New York, Guilford, 1987, p 203

76. Simon RI: Concise Guide to Psychiatry and Law for Clinicians. Washington, DC, American Psychiatric Press, 1992

77. McNeil ED, Binder RL: Clinical assessment of the risk of violence among psychiatric inpatients. Am J Psychiatry 148:1317–1321, 1991; Janofsky JS, Spears S, Neubauer DN: Psychiatrists' accuracy in predicting violent behavior on an inpatient unit. Hosp Community Psychiatry 39:1090–1094, 1988; Blomhoff S, Seim S, Friis S: Can prediction of violence among psychiatric inpatients be improved? Hosp Community Psychiatry 41:771–775, 1990

78. Monahan J: The Clinical Prediction of Violent Behavior. Rockville, MD, National Institute of Mental Health, 1981

79. Monahan J: The clinical prediction of dangerousness. Currents in Affective Illness 10(June):5–12, 1991

80. Tardiff K, Koenigsberg HW: Assaultive behavior among psychiatric outpatients. Am J Psychiatry 142:960–963, 1985

81. Kroll J, MacKenzie TB: When psychiatrists are liable: risk management and violent patients. Hosp Community Psychiatry 34:29–37, 1983

82. Lewis DO, Aaronson BS, Restifo NP, et al: Children who later murder: a prospective study. Paper presented at the 138th annual meeting of the American Psychiatric Association, Dallas, TX, May 1985

83. Beck JC: The psychotherapist and the violent patient: recent case law, in The Potentially Violent Patient and the Tarasoff Decision in Psychiatric Practice. Washington, DC, American Psychiatric Press, 1985, pp 9–34

84. 459 U.S. 1169 (1983)

85. Beigler JS: Tarasoff v. confidentiality. Behavioral Sciences and the Law 2:273–290, 1984

86. 124 Mich App 291, 335 NW2d 481 (1983), overruled on other grounds, Davis v Lhim, 430 Mich 326, 422 NW2d 668 (1988)

87. Jones v State of New York, 267 AD 254, 45 NYS2d 404 (NY App Div 1943)

88. Beck JC: When a patient threatens violence: an empirical study of clinical practice after Tarasoff. Bull Am Acad Psychiatry Law 10:189–202, 1982

89. Wulsin LR, Bursztajn H, Gutheil TG: Unexpected clinical features of the Tarasoff decision: the therapeutic alliance and the "duty to warn." Am J Psychiatry 140:601–603, 1983

90. Appelbaum PS, Gutheil TG: Clinical Handbook of Psychiatry and the Law. New York, McGraw-Hill, 1982, p 195

91. Appelbaum PS: Tarasoff and the clinician: problems in fulfilling the duty to protect. Am J Psychiatry 142:425–429, 1985

92. Beck JC: Violent patients and the Tarasoff duty in private psychiatric practice. Journal of Psychiatry and Law 13:361–376, 1985

93. Wexler DB: Patients, therapists and third parties: the victimological virtues of Tarasoff, in Therapeutic Jurisprudence: The Law as a Therapeutic Agent. Edited by Wexler DB. Durham, NC, Carolina Academic Press, 1990

94. 536 So 2d 1098 (Fla Dist Ct App 1988)

95. 795 P2d 1352 (Colo Ct App 1990)

96. Freishtat HW: Forensic update. J Clin Psychopharmacol 10:426–427, 1990

97. Stropes v Heritage House Children's Center of Shelbyville, Inc, 547 NE2d 244 (Ind 1989)

98. Eth S, Leong GB: Therapist sexual misconduct and the duty to protect, in Confidentiality Versus the Duty to Protect: Foreseeable Harm in the Practice of Psychiatry. Edited by Beck JC. Washington, DC, American Psychiatric Press, 1990, pp 107–119

99. MINN STAT ANN § 147 (West 1989); MINN STAT ANN § 148B (West 1989)

100. Lipari v Sears, Roebuck & Co, 497 F Supp 185 (D Neb 1980); Jablonski v United States, 712 F2d 391 (9th Cir 1983), overruled, In re complaint of McLinn, 739 F2d 1395 (9th Cir 1984); Petersen v State, 100 Wash 2d 421, 671 P2d 230 (1983) (en banc); Peck v The Counseling Service of Addison County, Inc 146 Vt 61, 499 A2d 425 (1985); Naidu v Laird, 539 A2d 1064 (Del Super Ct 1988); Schuster v Altenberg, 144 Wis 2d 223, 424 NW2d 159 (1988), rev'd, Schuster v Altenberg, 86-CV-1327 (Cir Ct Racine Cty 1990)

101. Simon RI: Sexual exploitation of patients: how it begins before it happens. Psychiatric Annals 19:104–112, 1989

102. MINN STAT § 626.557 (Supp 1991)

103. MINN STAT § 148A.03 (Supp 1991)

104. Eth S: The sexually active, HIV infected patient: confidentiality versus the duty to protect. Psychiatric Annals 18:571–576, 1988

105. Tarasoff v Regents of the University of California, 17 Cal 3d 425, 131 Cal Rptr 14, 551 P2d 334 (1976); Lundgren v Fultz, 354 NW2d 25 (Minn 1984)

106. Cohen PT, Sande MA, Volberding PA (eds): The AIDS Knowledge Base. Waltham, MA, Medical Publishing Group, 1990, §§ 2.1–2.2

107. Appelbaum K, Appelbaum PS: The HIV antibody-positive patient, in Confidentiality Versus the Duty to Protect: Foreseeable Harm in the Practice of Psychiatry. Edited by Beck JC. Washington, DC, American Psychiatric Press, 1990, pp 121–140

108. Falk TC: AIDS public health Law. Journal of Legal Medicine 9:529–546, 1988

109. Hofmann v Blackmon, 241 So 2d 752 (Fla Dist Ct App 1970), cert denied, 245 So 2d 257 (Fla 1971)

110. Knier v Albany Medical Center Hosp, 131 Misc 2d 414, 500 NYS2d 490 (NY Sup Ct 1986)

111. Simon RI: AIDS dementia complex in healthcare providers: do treating physicians have an ethical and legal duty to protect endangered patients? Courts, Health Science and the Law 2:69–76, 1991

112. Official actions: AIDS policy: confidentiality and disclosure. Am J Psychiatry 145:541, 1988

113. Gross BH, Southard MJ, Lamab HR, et al: Assessing dangerousness and responding appropriately: Hedlund expands the clinician's liability established by Tarasoff. J Clin Psychiatry 48:9–12, 1987

114. 39 Ohio St 3d 86, 529 NE2d 449 (1988)

115. Simon RI: Clinical risk management of suicidal patients: assessing the unpredictable, in American Psychiatric Press Review of Clinical Psychiatry and the Law, Vol 3. Edited by Simon RI. Washington, DC, American Psychiatric Press, 1992, pp 3–63

116. Centeno v City of New York, 48 AD2d 812, 369 NYS2d 710 (NY App Div 1975), aff'd, 40 NYS2d 932, 389 NYS2d 837, 258 NE2d 520 (1976)

117. 646 F Supp 524 (Ed Mich 1986)

118. Simon RI: Concise Guide to Clinical Psychiatry and the Law. Washington, DC, 1988, pp 99–121

119. Simon RI: The duty to protect in private practice, in Confidentiality Versus the Duty to Protect: Foreseeable Harm in the Practice of Psychiatry. Edited by Beck JC. Washington, DC, American Psychiatric Press, 1990, pp 23–41

120. Gutheil TG, Appelbaum PS: Clinical Handbook of Psychiatry and the Law. New York, McGraw-Hill, 1982

121. Southard MJ, Gross BH: Making clinical decisions after Tarasoff, in New Directions for Mental Health Services: The Mental Health Professional and the Legal System. Edited by Gross B, Weinberger L. San Francisco, CA, Jossey-Bass, 1982

122. American Psychiatric Association Legal Consultation Plan Newsletter 3:2–3, 1984

123. Currie v United States, 644 F Supp 1074 (MD NC 1986), aff'd, 836 F2d 209 (4th Cir 1987)

124. Klein JI, Macbeth JE, Onek JN: Legal Issues in the Private Practice of Psychiatry. Washington, DC, American Psychiatric Press, 1984, pp 18–19

125. Jablonski v United States, 712 F2d 391 (9th Cir 1983), overruled, In re complaint of McLinn 739 F2d 1395 (9th Cir 1984); Peck v The Counseling Service of Addison County, Inc, 146 Vt 51, 499 A2d 425 (1985); Davis v Lhim, 124 Mich App 291, 335 NW 2d 481 (1983), overruled on other grounds, Davis v Lhim, 430 Mich 326, 422 NW2d 668 (1988); Bardoni v Kim, 151 Mich App 169, 390 NW2d 218 (Mich Ct App 1986)

126. Lion JR: Evaluation and Management of the Violent Patient. Springfield, IL, Charles C Thomas, 1972

127. Madden DJ: Clinical treatment of the violent person, in Psychotherapy and Other Traditional Clinical Treatment and the Management of the Violent Person. Edited by Roth L. Rockville, MD, National Institute of Mental Health, 1985

128. Tardiff K: Violence: the psychiatric patient, in Violence in the Medical Setting. Edited by Turner JT. Rockville, MD, Aspen, 1984

129. Tardiff K (ed): The Psychiatric Uses of Seclusion and Restraint. Washington, DC, American Psychiatric Press, 1984

Chapter 14

Preventing the Premature Release of Dangerous Patients

Mr. Artz, a 35-year-old chronic schizophrenic patient, is involuntarily admitted to a psychiatric hospital because of auditory hallucinations commanding him to kill his mother. He also has the delusional idea that his mother is poisoning him. The patient has never lived apart from his mother. Mr. Artz is involuntarily hospitalized for 90 days. During this time he is treated by Dr. Madison, who places the patient on thiothixene, 4 mg four times a day. Because Mr. Artz speaks only broken English, verbal interaction between the psychiatrist and the patient is minimal. Dr. Madison relies heavily on observation of the patient's behavior on the ward and consultation with the staff.

From the history given by the patient's mother, Dr. Madison learns that the patient has been involuntarily hospitalized three times in the past 10 years in another state. An assault preceded each of the previous hospitalizations. Prior to the second hospitalization, Mr. Artz stabbed a cousin. He was criminally charged but found not guilty by reason of insanity. Mr. Artz's mother provides this history, but she also speaks broken English. Dr. Madison feels he needs more information and initiates a written request for the patient's previous hospital records.

As the end of the 90-day involuntary hospitalization approaches, Dr. Madison reviews the clinical course of Mr. Artz with the staff. The patient stays to himself most of the time. There is no evidence of any violent behavior. Mr. Artz is described in the nursing notes as a "model patient." He fully cooperates with ward routine and regulations. Medication is never refused. After the first month of hospitalization, he denies any hallucinations or delusions. The staff informs Dr. Madison that the patient becomes sullen and withdrawn when his mother visits. No passes are requested by the patient.

A discharge conference is held with nursing and other ward personnel. The conference participants conclude that Mr. Artz is ready for discharge. Mr. Artz denies any intent to harm his mother or anyone else. Dr. Madison realizes at the discharge conference that the records he requested of the previous hospitalizations were never received. Because the patient has progressed so well, he decides to discharge Mr. Artz at the end of his commitment period. Dr. Madison

345

discusses the discharge with the patient's mother. She expresses some trepidation but agrees to have her son live at home. She hopes her son will be able to go back to his job as a laborer. Dr. Madison arranges an appointment for Mr. Artz at the community outpatient center for the first available session. His appointment is scheduled for 3 weeks after discharge. Mr. Artz is seen on the day of discharge and appears eager to leave.

Five days after discharge, Dr. Madison receives and reads Mr. Artz's previous hospitalization records. They reveal a diagnosis of paranoid schizophrenia on each admission. The history is consistent for each hospitalization. Mr. Artz would fail to keep his outpatient visits, stop taking his medication, and begin drinking. After some variable period of time, he would become delusional, hear voices, and then become assaultive. Dr. Madison has the records hand-carried to the outpatient center. No further follow-up is made.

Mr. Artz does not keep his outpatient appointment. He discontinues his medication and starts drinking again. Six weeks after discharge, while working as a laborer, he stabs the foreman to death. Mr. Artz believes the foreman cast a spell on him. The widow of the foreman brings a wrongful death action. She alleges that the patient was dangerous and suffered from severe mental illness when he was negligently released from the hospital. The patient's past history of severe mental illness, poor compliance with outpatient treatment, and subsequent violence is proffered in support of her claim.

Under what legal theories have psychiatrists been held liable for the premature release of violent patients who harm others?

Under general negligence law, there is no duty to control the conduct of third persons to ensure that they do not cause physical harm to others. However, the law states that if a patient is in custody, the doctor has a duty to prevent a patient from harming self or others (1). When under the "control" of the doctor and the hospital, the standard is how the similarly trained, ordinary practitioner would act (2). If actual practice differs from ordinary practice, liability is imposed for a breach of duty if the breach is the proximate cause of damage.

Although liability has been imposed on psychiatric facilities that had custody of patients who injured others outside the institution following escape or release, these cases are clearly distinguishable from the factual situation of *Tarasoff* (3). Duty-to-warn cases involve patients in outpatient treatment. Liability arises from therapists' failure to take affirmative measures to warn endangered third persons. In negligent release cases, however, liability may arise from the allegation that the institution's affirmative act in releasing the patient caused injury to the third party.

The *Restatement (Second) of Torts* (4) provides a basis for the imposition of liability on institutions in certain situations: "One who takes charge of a third person whom he knows or should know to be likely to cause bodily harm to others if not controlled is under a duty to exercise reasonable care to control the third person to prevent him from doing such harm." According to Reisner (3), the commentaries to the *Restatement* make clear that an institution may be liable to a third party injured by a patient if the facility *1)* released a patient when the facility knew or had reason to know that the patient was dangerous, *2)* failed to conduct an adequate predischarge examination of a patient with a history of previous violence, or *3)* failed to take adequate precautions in allowing the patient to escape.

Although the *Tarasoff* duty was originally applied to the outpatient setting, the same legal duty to protect individuals and society from harm by mental patients arises concerning the release of violent patients. Generally, the scope of the duty to warn is narrower than the duty not to release a violent patient. In cases involving failure to warn and protect an endangered third party, the violence was serious and imminent, and the victim was usually identifiable and foreseeable. The duty not to release a violent patient has a broader scope because these patients often may not express specific threats toward persons or groups, thus posing a threat to the general public. In release cases, courts have extended the therapist's duty beyond that owed to readily identifiable victims (5). The number of malpractice suits alleging negligent release exceed by at least five to six times the number of outpatient cases alleging a *Tarasoff* duty.

As a public servant, the physician has a general duty to protect other members of society. This duty is not new to the law. The physician often has "insider information" from the doctor-patient relationship concerning the potential for violence that no one else possesses. Thus, clinically, the duty to warn and protect arises from the concept of latent dangers to which the physician is privy but of which endangered persons may be unaware. To practitioners, this reasoning makes more clinical sense than the legal argument of a special relationship between doctor and patient creating the duty to protect endangered persons.

Mental health professionals are under great pressure to discharge institutionalized patients by deinstitutionalization initiatives and the doctrine of the least-restrictive alternative. Rein (6) observes that the evidentiary tools for making discharge decisions are contradictory, depending upon the interests represented. For example, he notes that in commitment cases patients' attorneys argue that psychiatrists cannot predict anything and that statements other than direct observation are hearsay. On the other hand, in wrongful discharge cases, plaintiffs' attorneys argue that psychiatrists can predict everything and that no aspect of the psychiatric history is hearsay. For the therapist, the greater the risk of patient violence toward others at the time of discharge, the greater the responsibility to take affirmative actions to warn and protect.

In *Bradley Center, Inc. v. Wessner* (7), a private mental hospital was held civilly liable when a patient was issued a weekend pass and killed his wife and her paramour. The patient attempted suicide 2 months after discharge from his first hospitalization and was admitted a second time. Before leaving on pass during the second hospitalization, the hospital record revealed that the patient was continuing to have marital problems. There were strong indications that he had an "explosive personality" and could cause harm to others. The children of the patient filed suit against the facility, arguing that their father's actions were reasonably foreseeable. Both the Georgia Court of Appeals and the Georgia Supreme Court held that if in the course of treatment of a mental patient, control is exercised over him by a physician who knows or should know that the patient is likely to cause bodily harm to others, an independent duty arises from the relationship. The duty falls upon the physician to exercise control with such reasonable care as to prevent harm to others at the hands of the patient.

In *Durflinger v. Artiles* (8), similar judicial reasoning was applied. After threatening to kill his grandparents with a hatchet and meat fork, the patient was involuntarily hospitalized. He was released after 10 weeks of hospitalization when it was determined that he did not need further care or treatment. He was sent to his parents in Oregon. He killed his mother and brother with a knife 1 week after discharge. A suit was brought against several psychotherapists who were involved in the release decision. The jury awarded $92,300 to the plaintiffs.

On review, the Kansas Supreme Court held that liability was "predicated upon the inherent duty of a physician in the ordinary course of treatment of his patient" following the "general rules of negligence and malpractice." The court, while distinguishing this case from *Tarasoff,* imposed on the therapist an affirmative duty to protect an endangered third party. The court held that the duty to exercise reasonable care in release extends to the general public and is not dependent on the existence of a special relationship with the therapist, patient, or victim.

Negligent release cases in which the victim is readily identifiable usually involve a wife, parent, sibling, or mother-in-law of the patient. In *Hicks v. United States* (9), the court heard testimony that when the patient's wife, Mrs. Morgan, visited him shortly before his discharge, the patient began "yelling that he was going to kill her when he got out because she was the reason for him being over there: it was her fault . . . . [W]e had to take my mother out of the visiting room." Mrs. Morgan was not notified of her husband's release beforehand, as she had requested of the hospital authorities, nor did she receive notice of his discharge court hearing. The patient shot and killed his wife while intoxicated 54 days after his discharge. The court awarded $100,000 in damages to the plaintiff for negligence on the part of St. Elizabeths Hospital in Washington, D.C. The court held that the hospital's failure to report all of the vital facts of the case in its report to the court prior to discharge of the patient was the proximate cause of the patient's negligent release and Mrs. Morgan's death.

In *Chrite v. United States* (10), a patient murdered his mother-in-law 6 months after he was released from a Veterans Administration (VA) hospital.

A wrongful death action was brought, alleging that the hospital personnel were negligent in failing to warn the mother-in-law that the patient was a threat to her. A note, apparently written by the patient and contained in the hospital record, read: "Was Henry O. Smith [the patient] here yesterday. He is wanted for murder. Mother-in-law." The court denied the defendant's motion for summary judgment when it ruled that questions of fact existed as to whether the mother-in-law was, in fact, a foreseeable victim. Because the mother-in-law was a readily identifiable victim, the 6-month interval between discharge and the murder was not seen as prohibitive. Nevertheless, at trial, the plaintiff was unable to prevail.

In *Davis v. Lhim* (11), 2 months after discharge, the patient had a struggle with his mother and a gun went off, killing her. The struggle may have been related to a possible suicide attempt by the patient. Very remote evidence relating to the *Tarasoff* duty was discovered in the emergency room record 2 years prior to the hospitalization. The document stated that the patient "pace[d] the floor and act[ed] strangely and [kept] threatening his mother." This evidence was sufficient to support a jury finding that the patient posed a threat to his mother. The psychiatrist appealed. The court of appeals affirmed the lower court decision. When the case reached the Michigan Supreme Court, it was remanded to the court of appeals to be reconsidered according to a recent ruling by the court delineating the application of specific tests for determining sovereign immunity.

The court of appeals held that the state hospital psychiatrist would be held to a standard of "a reasonable psychiatrist practicing medicine according to present day knowledge" with respect to making a decision to discharge the patient. The psychiatrist would not be accorded governmental immunity on the basis that the discharge decision was a discretionary act cloaking him with such immunity (11). Despite all scientific evidence to the contrary, the court of appeals nevertheless expected "a reasonable psychiatrist practicing medicine in the light of present day scientific knowledge" to predict dangerousness to the patient's mother 2 months after discharge when there was no indication, either at the time of admission or at discharge, that the patient was dangerous. In 1988, the Michigan Supreme Court overturned the appeals court decision under Michigan's governmental immunity laws (11). The court held that the decision to discharge a patient was a discretionary act (as opposed to a ministerial act) providing immunity from suit for a state hospital doctor.

In *Sellers v. United States* (12), the Court of Appeals for the Sixth Circuit found that a VA hospital psychiatrist owed no duty to a third person injured by a manic-depressive patient. Applying Michigan law, the court held that the psychiatrist had no duty to force a voluntary patient to remain hospitalized and no duty to warn the general public. In Michigan, the duty to warn arises only when violence is threatened toward readily identifiable potential victims. The patient had not mentioned or threatened the victim before the assault.

In *Petersen v. State* (13), the plaintiff was injured when her car was struck by a vehicle recklessly driven by a patient released from a psychiatric hospital 5 days earlier. The patient had been hospitalized for a schizophrenic disorder secondary to phencyclidine ingestion. Prior to the day of discharge, the patient was noticed driving his car recklessly on the hospital grounds. The Supreme Court of Washington held that the psychiatrist incurred a duty to take reasonable precautions to protect anyone who foreseeably would be endangered by the patient's mental problems. Thus, liability could be predicated on the doctor's failure to seek additional confinement or to take other necessary steps to protect the public.

In *Naidu v. Laird* (14), the court ruled against a psychiatrist when his patient killed the plaintiff's decedent while driving in a psychotic state $5\frac{1}{2}$ months after discharge. Dr. Naidu contended that because of the lapse of time between his treatment of the patient and the accident, the treatment could not be considered the proximate cause of the death of the plaintiff's decedent. The court ruled that the mere lapse of time was not sufficient to establish the remoteness of these two incidents, because there was no demonstration of an intervening cause. Dr. Naidu presented no evidence that would break the "chain of causation." (For a more complete discussion of this case, see Chapter 16.)

In *Littleton v. Good Samaritan Hospital and Health Center* (15), the plaintiff alleged that the psychiatrists had negligently released a voluntarily hospitalized patient who killed her daughter 2 weeks later. The jury found in favor of the plaintiff. Although the trial court reduced the amount of damages, the case was appealed to the Ohio Supreme Court. On appeal, the Ohio Supreme Court agreed with the defendant's proposal of the "professional judgment rule." Under this rule, a physician would not be liable for the release of a patient who later harmed another person if the decision was based upon a thorough examination of all the relevant data and represented a professional medical judgment that the patient was not an immediate danger to others. Applying the professional judgment rule, the court held that liability for discharging patients could be avoided in one of three ways:

1. If the patient did not display violent tendencies while hospitalized and there was no reason to suspect violence after discharge
2. If a thorough evaluation of the patient's potential for violence was performed, assessing all relevant factors, and the psychiatrist decides in good faith that the patient does not present a threat of violence
3. If a discharge treatment plan was formulated in good faith after making an assessment of the patient's potential for violence and the interests of potential victims

The Ohio Supreme Court ordered a new trial that would apply the professional judgment rule to the issue of the psychiatrists' liability.

When do psychiatrists who discharge potentially violent patients have a duty to protect in the absence of a specific foreseeable victim?

The requirement of a clearly foreseeable victim does not apply in a claim against an institution for negligent release of a patient if the staff knew or should have known that the patient was likely to harm others. If the patient is improperly released, the institution may be held liable even in the absence of a specific foreseeable victim (16). This conclusion was reached in *Lipari v. Sears, Roebuck & Co.* (17). In *Lipari,* a patient discharged from a VA hospital to a day treatment program purchased a shotgun and fired into a crowd in an Omaha nightclub. On the other hand, in *Soutear v. United States* (18), physicians at a VA hospital were found not negligent in releasing a patient who 3 months later killed his mother. The district court ruled that when uncontradicted testimony established that the physicians were unaware of homicidal intent, they could not be held legally accountable for failure to warn the victim.

When a duty of "foreseeability" to prevent random violence toward unidentified individuals among the public is imposed, warnings are no longer adequate. Police are reluctant to respond when no crime has been committed. If no identifiable victim exists to be warned, the psychiatrist must control the potentially violent patient in some manner and consider treatment decisions that include restraints, involuntary hospitalization, and conditional releases, or adopt treatments that might not have been otherwise contemplated (19).

In the clinical vignette, at the time of admission Mr. Artz suffered hallucinations commanding him to kill his mother. At the time of discharge, no hallucinations were present. Mr. Artz also denied any intention to harm anyone. Thus, no readily identifiable victim was endangered. Given the patient's past history of violent assaults, severe mental illness, alcoholism, failure to keep outpatient appointments, and noncompliance with medications, Mr. Artz was at high risk for committing some act of random violence. It was foreseeable that he would likely repeat an established pattern of violent behavior toward others unless closely supervised.

Are psychiatrists who practice in state and federal institutions protected from liability by governmental immunity?

Liability issues involving negligent release of patients are complicated by governmental immunity—the principle that the federal and state governments cannot be sued without their consent. This principle is based on English common law that the king or sovereign can do no wrong. Today, sovereign immunity is declining in use. Every state has enacted statutes waiving sovereign immunity in regard to certain types of cases. Under the Federal Tort Claims Act, damage suits can be brought against the United States for personal injuries, death, and damage or loss of property resulting from the negligence of government employees acting within the scope of their employment. Sovereign immunity still applies to intentional torts such as fraud, libel, slander, assault and battery, false imprisonment, false arrest, malicious prosecution, and abuse of process (20).

Courts often distinguish between discretionary and ministerial acts in determining immunity. Discretionary acts refer to those activities in which the person exercises independent judgment. Ministerial acts refer to those activities in which the individual follows policy and little independent judgment is required.

When therapists employed by the state and acting within the scope of their employment negligently discharge a patient, liability will not be imposed on the therapist or hospital if the court applies the doctrine of governmental immunity (discretionary act). The rationale behind the grant of immunity for discretionary acts establishes that a state official or officer is exempt from damages if his or her conduct does not violate statutory or constitutional rights that a reasonable person knew or should have known existed. In some states, statutory immunity exists for state-employed psychiatrists and psychologists who recommend release (21). No public officer, however, is absolved from liability for private and personal torts merely because of his or her status as an officer.

In *Clark v. State of New York* (22), an appellate court held that the state will lose its traditional immunity in tort cases involving dangerous patients if its physician-employees do not conduct careful examinations. The plaintiff successfully sued the state for injuries suffered when assaulted by an outpatient at a state mental health facility.

Two types of immunity exist: absolute and qualified. Judges are granted absolute immunity for their judicial actions, even if these actions are malicious or corrupt, in order to preserve the independence of the judiciary. Because immunity extends to all judicial branch members, psychiatrists appointed by the court are also protected under this doctrine. Mental health hearing officers who preside over commitment hearings are similarly protected. As an officer of the court, the psychiatrist who certifies a patient as part of the commitment process or who testifies at a commitment hearing has "absolute immunity" from liability (23).

Qualified immunity applies when officials or employees are not held liable for any act within the scope of their governmental duties that was performed in good faith. The psychiatrist employed by a state mental hospital who denies an involuntarily hospitalized patient release on the basis of a negligent determination would be immune from claims of false imprisonment. If the psychiatrist denies release of the patient while knowing the patient is qualified for release, the psychiatrist has acted in bad faith and qualified immunity will not be available for protection from liability (23).

In *Sherill v. Wilson* (24), a murder was committed by a patient who had been confined to a state mental hospital. The victim's mother brought a wrongful death action stating that the patient was negligently issued a 2-day pass from the hospital. The court rejected the claim, stating that detention and release of mental patients are "judgment calls." Moreover, the state statute authorized the release of patients if in their best interest. The court noted that patients are entitled to the least-restrictive environment consistent with the safety of the patient and the general public. In addition, the court did not want to raise any defensive fears among therapists about suits that might cause them to restrain their patients unduly.

Courts try to weigh the therapeutic and rehabilitative needs of the patient against the safety of the public. In an era of individual patient rights, civil liberties, and open-door treatment policies, society must accept a certain level of risk if it wishes to maintain these values. Compounded by the poor predictive capacities by psychiatrists of violent behavior, it is inevitable that violent patients will be released into the community.

What defenses may be available to psychiatrists against claims of negligent release of patients?

Courts have traditionally used certain legal rationales to exculpate governmental agencies and psychotherapists from liability emanating from third-party injury as a result of voluntary release from the psychiatric hospital. These legal rationales include the standard of honest error or professional judgment; governmental and official immunity; lapse of time between release and injury to others; the balance between public safety and treatment of the mentally ill; unforeseeable harm; and the absence of a special relationship to either the patient or the victim of the patient (25). Legal liability against governmental agencies and therapists is expected to increase as the trend toward deinstitutionalization continues and as courts find innovative ways to compensate victims of the violently mentally ill.

In *Sharpe v. South Carolina Department of Mental Health* (26), for example, the South Carolina Supreme Court affirmed the lower court's refusal to dismiss a complaint against the department and staff psychiatrists requesting damages for wrongful death of a person shot and killed by a patient released from a department facility. The case was remanded for trial. The defendants maintained that they were immune from liability according to the following section of the South Carolina Code: "Neither the superintendent of a mental health facility nor any other person legally participating in the release or discharge of a patient shall be liable either civilly or criminally on account of such participation" (27). Because the complaint alleged not only negligent discharge but also negligent treatment and the failure to notify the public that the patient was being discharged, the court held that although the statute immunized the defendants for releasing the patient, the defendants were not necessarily immune from all legal liability. Thus, the innovative construction of the complaint circumvented the statutory immunity code.

As noted earlier, in *Davis v. Lhim* (11), an alleged negligent release case, the Michigan Supreme Court did not rule on the substantive issues in this case. Rather, the court held that the decision to discharge a patient was a discretionary act providing immunity from suit for a state hospital doctor.

In *Karash v. County of San Diego* (28), the psychiatrist received sovereign immunity in a case involving a wrongful discharge and failure to warn. The psychiatrist was on notice that the inpatient he was evaluating was a "walking time bomb." The patient had been admitted to the county community mental health center after threatening to kill his wife. A shotgun and shells were discovered in his truck. About 1 month after discharge, the former patient shot his wife and himself. The California Court of Appeals determined that the psychiatrist was immune from suit for negligent release—and, by extension, failure to warn—subsequent to immunity provisions in several statutes governing 72-hour evaluation and treatment within a state facility.

Psychiatrists in outpatient settings who treat patients under much more ambiguous circumstances have to contend with the legal liabilities of the *Tarasoff* doctrine. On the other hand, psychiatrists who practice in certain inpatient settings may have immunity from suit for negligent release and failure to warn in discharging a clearly violent, dangerous person. In a growing number of states, immunity statutes exist that protect psychiatrists from liability who discharge the *Tarasoff* duty based on the requirements of the particular state statute (29).

What are some of the clinical and legal issues surrounding discharge decisions of potentially violent patients?

Patients who are admitted as informal or purely voluntary patients may leave the hospital at any time. Formal or conditional voluntary patients may be required, as part of their admission agreement, to stay a fixed period of time (usually 48 to 72 hours) after giving written notice of intention to leave the hospital. This provision allows time for the patient to reconsider the wisdom of premature discharge and gives the staff time to consider whether the patient presents a serious danger to self or others. At the end of a temporary stay, involuntary hospitalization may be considered for appropriate patients.

In some jurisdictions, statutes may prohibit the conversion of a patient's voluntary status directly to an involuntary status. The patient must first be discharged from the hospital. An ominously threatening patient should not be actually discharged in order to be converted to an involuntary patient except "on paper." In such situations, the requirements of the law may be met by escorting the patient to the emergency room of the hospital where he or she has been hospitalized and certifying the patient for involuntary hospitalization.

Voluntary patients may wish to leave the hospital against medical advice. If the patient is not a danger to self or others and is competent, the psychiatrist cannot do much more than try to deal with the discharge as a treatment issue.

Whether or not the patient signs an AMA ("against medical advice") form, a notation should be made in the record detailing the recommendations made to the patient about the need for further hospitalization as well as the possible risks of premature discharge. Voluntary patients who are incompetent but are not dangerous or gravely disabled cannot be kept in the hospital against their will, even if they have been adjudicated incompetent and a guardian gives consent for hospitalization. Under these circumstances, family or some other responsible party should be involved at the time of a premature discharge.

Patients protesting their involuntary detention in a hospital may obtain a writ of *habeas corpus*. The writ, which literally means "you have the body," is issued by the court requesting the immediate presence (same day or next) in court to review the reasons for detention. Although the review is procedural rather than substantive, the merits of the commitment are often reargued rather than the fairness of the involuntary procedures. The psychiatrist should attempt to work with the attorney and the patient to iron out differences (30). A writ of habeas corpus may deprive the patient of a therapeutic opportunity to examine the wish to leave the hospital. Recourse to legalistic measures by patients sometimes reflects an inadequate therapeutic alliance or its breakdown. Hospitals are likely to acquiesce when faced with a writ, rather than become legally entangled with the patient (31). This, however, may not be in the patient's best interest.

It is not unusual for psychiatrists and hospitals to discharge patients against their will (32). For a variety of reasons, patients may be unwilling to leave the hospital. Regressive dependencies, a breakdown in the therapeutic alliance in which the patient wishes to thwart the psychiatrist, fears of the demands and responsibilities of life outside the hospital, and severe separation anxiety cause some patients to cling desperately to the hospital. Although this is foremost a treatment issue, at some point, staying in the hospital becomes counterproductive for the patient. The patient's real mental health needs rather than his or her infantile wishes must be emphasized with the patient.

Good clinical care requires that patients not be summarily discharged. A time for discharge should be set well ahead to allow the patient an opportunity to work through feelings about leaving. A prearranged time will also give the patient an opportunity to schedule treatment after hospitalization.

Should serious harm befall the patient or others after a premature discharge, the psychiatrist will likely face a legal action for negligent treatment and discharge. Careful documentation of the reasoning behind any involuntary discharge decision should be entered in the medical record. Risk-benefit analysis is particularly important. Before a patient is involuntarily discharged, the balance should tilt in the direction of the rehabilitative and treatment benefits of the discharge versus the regressive risks of continued hospitalization. This is particularly true of the patient who, at the expiration of court-ordered commitment, does not want to leave. The original emergency reasons for admission, whether dangerousness or grave disability, should be sufficiently resolved.

When insurance coverage runs out, a private facility may no longer be able to care for the patient. Unfortunately, this is a fact of life and constitutes a sufficient reason for discharge. The psychiatrist and facility must be careful, however, not to abandon the patient. Arrangements for the patient's transfer to a suitable facility or to the care of a competent therapist willing and able to treat the patient should be in place before discharge. Some suicidal or dangerous patients requiring close supervision and care have been summarily discharged and given a clinic appointment 2 or 3 weeks away, not infrequently leading to a tragic result.

When a competent patient refuses treatment, the question of why he or she came to the hospital is immediately raised. Patients who refuse treatment and are not dangerous or gravely disabled but have been adjudicated incompetent may need to be discharged. Psychiatrists are not required to provide useless treatment when patients refuse clinically indicated psychiatric interventions. Careful documentation of the risk-benefit equation for these patients is essential, indicating how the benefits of discharge outweigh the risks.

For certain patients, conditional release has many advantages, particularly when facilities have adequate staffing to provide follow-up supervision. Conditional release allows for a transition period that permits the patient to become gradually acclimated to living outside the hospital. If the patient relapses, readmission of a known patient is easier for all concerned. Hospital services, such as social services and occupational therapy, may be available to the patient on conditional release. Patients who were originally admitted because of dangerousness have an opportunity to be more closely supervised as they make their transition into the community.

In *County of Hennepin v. Levine* (33), a lawsuit alleged the hospital's failure to comply with procedures established by law governing the granting of passes to individuals who are committed as mentally ill and dangerous. The court ruled that the pass program was a form of treatment, not a type of discharge, and thus similar to partial hospitalization. The court noted that civil commitment is based on a "prediction-prevention model," the purpose of which is, in large measure, to rehabilitate. The court seemed persuaded by testimony indicating that passes were "the most important part of the [treatment] program," providing social and recreational opportunities not available in the hospital and encouraging ties with the family and the community.

A patient who remains mentally ill and dangerous should not be discharged before the end of the commitment period. At the end of the commitment period, if the patient refuses to stay in the hospital and wants to leave against medical advice, the psychiatrist should go back to court and request a renewal or reissuance of a civil commitment order. The court must be informed of the patient's continuing dangerousness. As the time of expiration of a commitment order approaches, any doubt about the patient's condition and suitability for discharge should result in a consultation. If uncertainty still remains after consultation, the patient should be kept in the hospital until he or she improves or until the issue of discharge is litigated in the court. As Mills (2) points out, the courts, not psychiatrists, should be making policy decisions about the level of dangerousness that society will tolerate.

Clinically, the problem of the inability to predict violence in the outpatient setting carries over to release decisions. While patients who are clearly assaultive must not be allowed out of the hospital, passes nevertheless are sometimes inexplicably issued (7). The hospital and psychiatrists also must guard against elopement of dangerous patients.

Studies of patients released from mental hospitals, maximum security institutions, and correctional facilities show a low base rate for postrelease violence (34). These studies underscore the fact that prediction of violence at the time of release cannot be done with accuracy. Tardiff and Sweillam (35) studied patients who were admitted following assaultive or suicidal behavior. Schizophrenic patients' assaultive behavior was difficult to predict compared with nonpsychotic patients' behavior because the former was so often the product of disorganized and delusional thinking. This is an important clinical point to consider. Violence by patients with character disorders is often heavily weighted by situational factors. Although these factors may play some role in schizophrenic violence, the violence is often related to command hallucinations and paranoid delusions. Patients who still have these symptoms at the time of release must be carefully evaluated to see how compelling or syntonic these symptoms remain. The more unreachable, autistic, and disorganized the patient, the less the likelihood exists that the original assaultive behavior is under control.

In a study of assaults in the hospital and placement in the community, Tardiff (36) found that patients with the primary diagnosis of mental retardation, schizophrenia (nonparanoid type), or a psychotic organic brain syndrome "were more likely to be poor candidates for community placement and require secure environments or at least intensive inpatient treatment." In another study, Tardiff (37) found that paranoid schizophrenic patients directed violence toward others and self, having a higher level of interpersonal functioning than nonparanoid schizophrenic patients and mentally retarded patients. Kroll and MacKenzie (38) have developed a useful decision table for analyzing the risk of releasing potentially violent patients.

Families may be very concerned as the time approaches for the discharge of a formerly violent patient. The family is usually seen prior to the discharge of the patient. Families may try to exert pressure to keep the patient in the hospital. Their concerns about the patient should be carefully evaluated. Some discharge issues that should be explored with families include the following:

1. Will the family be supportive or rejecting to the patient?
2. Will the discharged patient be in any physical danger from frightened family members?

3. Can the family exert reasonable control over the patient?
4. What are the specific concerns of the family that can be usefully incorporated into the discharge planning?

The patient always should be seen on the day of discharge. It is not uncommon for some patients to regress rapidly as discharge time approaches. Patients may appear reasonably intact, only to decompensate on the day of discharge. Patients with malignant separation anxiety are the most likely candidates for a last minute relapse.

Hospitals generally have the power to discharge involuntarily hospitalized patients at their discretion and without court approval. In a number of states, statutes require that a patient with violent proclivities be discharged only with the written consent from the appropriate hospital authorities on examination and guarantee of supervision by a reputable person (31). However, a criminally committed patient, a mentally retarded patient, and a juvenile committed by a court order require an order for discharge from the committing court (31).

A federal district court in South Dakota allowed a wrongful death claim against the VA for negligently releasing a dangerous patient. The trial court said that the hospital knew of the patient's history of psychosis and violent behavior. He had been sent to the hospital by the county sheriff, and charges were pending on his release from the hospital. The VA had a duty to notify the local authorities of his release. His subsequent fight with plaintiff's decedent was foreseeable, and the hospital's negligence was the proximate cause of wrongful death. As a result, the court found the government liable under the Federal Tort Claims Act (39).

In *Semler v. Psychiatric Institute of Washington, D.C.* (40), the hospital violated a court order in transferring the patient to outpatient status. The patient had been previously convicted and sentenced to 20 years for abduction. As part of the sentencing agreement, the judge ordered close supervision of the patient. The patient killed a local schoolgirl on the premises of a private school. The Fourth Circuit held both the psychiatrist and the institute liable for the girl's death and awarded damages of $25,000. The court noted that by transferring the patient to outpatient status, the institute violated its duty to protect the public.

In *Grimm v. Arizona Board of Pardons and Parole* (41), the Arizona Supreme Court held that the state parole board has a duty to individual members of the general public to prevent the reckless or grossly negligent release of a highly dangerous prisoner. Furthermore, the court stated that parole board members could claim only qualified immunity for their administrative action.

The doctrine of immunity of the state and of its officials and employees is established by statute. The liability of therapists working in state hospitals depends on the scope of the immunity granted by the state legislature (42).

In the clinical vignette, the lack of adequate follow-up of Mr. Artz could have been obviated by a conditional release program or through outpatient commitment. Had the previous records of psychiatric hospitalization been available, Mr. Artz's posthospital clinical course in the past would have suggested the need for a closely supervised transition from the hospital to the community. Whenever possible, gradual rather than sudden discharges of patients with histories of violence should be attempted.

Who will be held legally responsible for harm resulting from managed care decisions that lead to premature patient discharge?

Important ethical and legal issues arise as a result of managed health care decisions (43). Psychiatric hospitals may be unable to provide long-term treatment to the dangerous mentally ill patient because of cost considerations. Psychiatrists may find themselves caught between the hospital wanting to discharge the patient for financial reasons and their professional and legal responsibility to provide appropriate patient care. The pressures for discharge under managed health care may lead to an increase in premature discharges of dangerous patients. Furthermore, as the length of hospital stays is reduced, the psychiatrist must become quite knowledgeable in the availability of community resources and the provision of quality aftercare.

In *Wickline v. State of California* (44), the treating physician, Dr. Polonsky, requested an extended stay of 8 additional days for his patient following surgery for Leriche's syndrome (occlusion of the abdominal aorta). The Medi-Cal reviewer granted 4 days. Mrs. Wickline suffered complications following the premature release, necessitating amputation of her leg. She sued Medi-Cal. The jury ruled in her favor, but a California appellate court decided that the treating physician was liable, not Medi-Cal.

In his testimony, Dr. Polonsky stated that he believed "that Medi-Cal had the power to tell him, as a treating doctor, when a patient must be discharged from the hospital." The appellate court noted that third-party payers of health care services can be held liable when appeals on the behalf of the patients for medical care

> are arbitrarily ignored or unreasonably disregarded or over-ridden. The physician who complies without protest with the limitations imposed by a third-party payor, even if his medical judgment dictates otherwise, cannot avoid his ultimate responsibility for his patient's care. He cannot point to the health care payor as the liability scapegoat when the consequences of his own determinative medical decision go sour. (44)

The lesson is absolutely clear. The physician is responsible for the medical care provided to his or her patient. The duty of the physician to exercise the best medical judgment on behalf of the patient is not dependent upon payment. Nor can this duty be abrogated to others.

In a subsequent case, *Wilson v. Blue Cross of Southern California et al.* (45), a California appeals court did not follow the specific language of *Wickline*. In *Wilson,* a patient was hospitalized at College Hospital in Los Angeles suffering from anorexia, drug dependency, and major depression. The treating physician determined that the patient required 3 to 4 weeks of hospitalization. After approximately $1\frac{1}{2}$ weeks, utilization review determined that further hospitalization was unnecessary. The patient's insurance company refused to pay for further inpatient treatment. The patient was discharged and committed suicide a few weeks later.

The Appellate Division of the California Court of Appeals held that third-party payers are not immune from lawsuits in regard to utilization review activities. The court determined that the insurer may be subject to liability for harm caused to the patient by premature termination of a patient's hospitalization. Though the fact pattern of this case differs from that of *Wickline,* the decision in *Wilson* signals that a third-party payer may be held legally liable for a negligent decision to discharge the patient either separately or along with the patient's physician, depending upon the facts of the case. Although both *Wickline* and *Wilson* are California cases, they offer insight and, perhaps, precedence concerning future reasoning by other courts who will be increasingly confronted by complex liability issues concerning utilization review decisions.

Should patients who assault hospital staff be considered for discharge and criminal prosecution?

When patients commit acts of violence on a ward, the staff must consider whether the unit is appropriately equipped and the staff thoroughly trained to handle such patients. Transfer to another facility may be an option. Appelbaum and Gutheil (32) recommend outright discharge of those patients who are not likely to be assaultive outside the hospital and who can care for themselves. Before this step is taken, an ombudsman or an impartial fact-finder may serve a useful mediating function. The patient should be given notice of discharge so that other arrangements can be made.

Patients who commit acts of violence unrelated to a psychotic disorder can be arrested by the police and criminal charges filed. Miller and Maier (46) discuss factors affecting the decision to prosecute mental patients. The hospital should not be used as a jailhouse for dangerous individuals who do not have a mental illness. Discharging such individuals should not be done without first notifying the police in order to protect the community. In all these circumstances, very careful documentation is necessary should allegations of negligent treatment or discharge be made.

Bringing criminal charges against assaultive patients is a controversial issue. The problem of viewing patients as "bad" versus "mad" always arises. Advocates for selective prosecution note that prosecution upholds the rights of staff members while also requiring patients to accept the responsibility for their aggressive acts (47). Other arguments proffered for prosecution include the deterrent of future aggression, the reality-testing value, and the creation of a public record to punish recidivists more harshly (48, 49).

The opposing position is that psychiatrists should maintain a clinical perspective on violent assaults. Presumably, assaultive individuals have been hospitalized for a diagnosable psychiatric disorder. Psychiatrists have successfully treated violent patients for decades. Violent assaults that are related to mental states require appropriate treatment, including the possibility of restraint and seclusion. A high index of suspicion for violence as well as preventive measures may preempt violent assaults upon the hospital staff (50). A patient's legal responsibility for the assault would turn on the question of competency. If substantial evidence existed that the patient possessed the mental capacity to conceive, plan, and execute the assault upon staff, then consideration should be given to prosecuting the patient. This view attempts to maintain the psychiatrist's clinical position. Nevertheless, ward patients who are competent should be held responsible for their acts.

What precautionary measures should be taken with potentially violent patients before issuance of a pass or discharge from the hospital?

Nothing seems to infuriate the public more than the release of a dangerous patient who kills or seriously injures another person. Before *Tarasoff*, no liability for violence to others by a discharged patient was assessed when the violence occurred at least 2 weeks after discharge (51). Legal experts in psychiatric malpractice recommend six steps that can be taken to minimize risk of liability for violent acts of patients (52). These recommendations can be applied to release decisions of previously violent patients and constitute good clinical practice as well as sound risk management techniques.

1. Records of previous treatments and hospitalizations should be obtained.
Patients and families may forget or intentionally withhold critical information for a variety of reasons. Writing to obtain records for prior hospitalizations is often inadequate. The patient may have been long discharged before the medical records arrive, because of brief lengths of hospital stays plus the time-consuming task of copying and mailing lengthy medical records. The FAX-ing of a discharge summary, however, may provide sufficient, timely information.

2. The clinical record should document clearly and completely the decision-making process surrounding release. Thorough risk-benefit analysis for both continued hospitalization and discharge considers all relevant sources of information and factors, permitting appropriate discharges and minimizing liability exposure should the decision be wrong. Errors alone are not legally actionable if reasonable care and skill were utilized in making the pass or discharge decision.

Rushing is the enemy of quality progress notes. Psychiatrists should allow sufficient time to record their decision-making process. Trying to write progress notes amidst the hurly-burly of a nurses' station may be inimical to adequate record keeping. Retiring to a quiet office or room provides the optimum setting for collecting and recording one's thoughts without the distorting effects produced by noise and interruptions.

Poythress (53) recommends the use of videotaped exit interviews with patients at the time of their release. By carefully structuring the interview, issues of concern surrounding release decision making and management can be addressed, presumably preempting second-guessing by plaintiff's attorneys. Presumably, a negligent release will not be unwittingly videotaped.

The record should be reviewed for discrepancies in diagnoses prior to discharge. Frequently, when interns and residents have been involved in the patient's care, a variety of diagnoses may have been entered into the patient's record. If the treating psychiatrist disagrees with these diagnoses, he or she should so state in the record as well as provide reasons for the disagreement. Should litigation arise later, unaddressed diagnostic discrepancies may be used by the plaintiff's attorney in an attempt to discredit the defendants.

3. If doubt exists over issuing a pass or discharge, a consultation with another psychiatrist and/or attorney should be obtained and documented. The psychiatrist's liability will be determined by reference to professional standards. Consultation may provide some extra protection. Consulting with an attorney will clarify the legal obligations and standards while determining whether due care was made in decision making.

4. When the psychiatrist determines that a patient poses the threat of violence to another, appropriate warnings should be made, even if the psychiatrist is certain that the potential victim is aware of the danger. When the patient who has previously been violent to identifiable persons is ready for discharge, the formerly endangered third parties often request notification prior to the patient's release. This is a complicated issue requiring careful clinical judgment on a case-by-case basis. Such requests may be honored when the patient, after discussion with the psychiatrist, consents to release of information.

Family members who previously have been threatened by the patient should be consulted as part of the process of deciding whether to release the patient. In many situations, it may be prudent for the psychiatrist to make such a warning. When a court-ordered commitment period has expired, if the psychiatrist feels that the possibility of harm may still exist to threatened persons, warnings may be advisable. In some situations, a warning might precipitate violence against the patient by volatile family members, raising difficult questions about the advisability of warning. A detailed discussion of warning endangered third persons is offered in Chapter 13.

As in *Hicks v. United States* (9) (see above), family members may request notification of the exact date and time of discharge so that they may make necessary arrangements and adjustments. Previous warnings of the patient's violent proclivities from relatives, friends, law enforcement officials, and judges place the mental health professional on notice that the patient considered for release may be dangerous (54). In *County of Hennepin v. Levine* (33), the court cited with approval a warning procedure to be invoked before issuing a pass. Before granting the pass, all interested persons, including the family, sheriff, committing judge, and other parties who petitioned for the commitment, would be made aware of the situation.

When a patient elopes from the hospital, the police must be notified immediately and warnings issued to identifiable, endangered third parties. Warnings should be given even if the endangered individual may have heard of the elopement from other sources. Liability to a third party for harm inflicted by dangerous patients who escape is closely related to legal concepts applied to negligent release or discharge cases (21). As a matter of fact, the duty to protect has been expanded from the inpatient to the outpatient setting. The duty to protect persons from patients who have been released or have escaped from mental hospitals goes back 75 to 100 years.

Beck (55) suggests that the *Tarasoff* duty seldom provides additional protection for the public beyond that which is provided by current standards governing release decisions. In most cases, the duty to use reasonable care according to professional standards is sufficient to safeguard a foreseeable victim and the general public. Thus, Beck feels that the duty to warn should be limited to patients who are thought to be still potentially violent and not committable and who have made threats or acted against a specific identifiable victim.

5. If any doubt exists about the danger to others posed by the release or discharge of the patient, involuntary hospitalization should be sought.   The judge is in the best position to determine how much risk of violence the community can tolerate. Moreover, the judge is immune from liability should the patient not be committed and harm someone. In these proceedings, psychiatrists do not commit patients but merely present medical findings for the court's consideration.

The commitment laws of a number of states allow institutionalized patients to receive convalescent leave or to be released on a conditional basis. Conditional release is provisional, allowing the patient, under appropriate circumstances, to be summarily readmitted (3). As a result, the usual commitment procedures are circumvented. Laws authorizing conditional release vest authority in the head of the facility where the patient was originally confined to revoke conditional release if he or she believes "the conditions justifying hospitalization continue to exist" (3). The authority to revoke conditional release is usually absolute, without the patient having a right to a hearing. The authority may be exercised for the period of the conditional release (usually 1 year). The provision of such laws giving summary revocation powers to the director of a facility is under increasing attack. In *In Re Application of True* (56), the court held that due process requires a hearing "before a neutral hearing body to be held as soon as reasonably possible following the patient's rehospitalization."

For some "revolving door" and potentially dangerous patients, outpatient civil commitment may represent a reasonable discharge disposition. All states permit some form of involuntary outpatient commitment (57). The states usually apply involuntary outpatient commitment in one of three ways: as a conditional release, as a dispositional alternative to hospitalization, or as preventive commitment.

Enforcing such an approach is a complicated problem. Miller (58), reporting on a national survey on the use of outpatient commitment, found that two-thirds of the jurisdictions that permit outpatient commitment use it as an alternative to inpatient commitment in fewer than 5% of commitments. Miller concluded that unless states obtain more input from both inpatient and outpatient practitioners in devising procedures for outpatient commitment, this procedure will continue to be ineffectively used.

Another means of assisting the "revolving door" patient is through newly enacted preventive commitment statutes (59). Although often included under outpatient commitment generically, preventive commitment is more specialized. The purpose of preventive commitment is to prevent predictable deterioration in an individual's mental condition that will lead to involuntary hospitalization. Lower commitment standards and fewer procedural protections exist than for involuntary hospitalization.

Preventive commitment differs from outpatient commitment by providing for less-restrictive alternatives to hospitalization. Preventive commitment also differs from conditional release, which requires the patient's compliance with an individual treatment plan in order to be released from commitment. Under conditional release, the patient remains on the hospital rolls until the commitment period has ended. The increasing popularity of preventive commitment appears related to concerns about the least-restrictive alternative treatment, the growth in the population of mentally disordered homeless persons, a backlash among mental health professionals over regulation of the mental health system, and demands by patient advocacy groups allied with mental health professionals for an easing of commitment standards.

Only relatively few states have enacted preventive commitment statutes, but more states are considering such legislation.

6. Before discharging a formerly violent patient, a postdischarge treatment and care plan should be developed. Frequently, patients do not make the initial follow-up outpatient appointment and stop taking medication. The psychiatrist should call the follow-up clinic to see if the patient keeps the initial appointment. Also, family members or caregivers should be entrusted with the duty to inform the psychiatrist if the patient is not taking medication or is acting in a manner that raises concern.

If the patient is being transferred to another facility, the assessment of the patient's current condition, including potential for violence, should be communicated to the staff at the new facility. In addition, the need for the reassessment of the risk of violence at the time of discharge also should be emphasized. Written communications are essential, but direct phone conversations with the new caregivers may be more effective in communicating problems and concerns about the patient. The failure to communicate relevant information to caregivers who may be unaware of the dangerousness of transferred patients can create liability problems for psychiatrists (60). The psychiatrist who discharges the patient is obviously not medically responsible for the patient forever, but should stay in contact with the patient until the latter is in competent treatment hands.

In *Desaussure v. New York* (61), the court held the hospital liable for the violent conduct of a released outpatient, even though the release was not negligent and there was no specific victim to warn. After being released to outpatient status, the patient missed six appointments. Although the psychiatrist had reason to believe that the patient would become uncontrolled without ongoing treatment and medication, he merely tried to reschedule appointments by phone.

The plaintiff's psychiatric expert testified that the correct procedures in the event of a failure to keep an appointment would have been *1)* to call and try to persuade the patient to come immediately; *2)* to enlist the help of a relative if unable to persuade the patient; and *3)* to send a treatment team to see the patient if the family is uncooperative. If all else fails, police assistance should be sought. The court and jury adopted this analysis.

Psychiatrists have been served a warning that special precautions must be taken with patients having violent proclivities, particularly at the time of release or discharge from a hospital facility or institution. The patient's willingness to cooperate is a crucial determinant in contact with follow-up treaters. A VA study of outpatient referral found that of the 24% of inpatients referred to the VA mental health clinic, approximately 50% did not keep their first appointment (62). The clinician's obligation is to structure the follow-up so as to encourage compliance. Limitations on the powers of psychiatrists to ensure follow-up treatment exist and must be acknowledged by both the psychiatric and the legal communities (63).

Poythress (53) makes specific risk management recommendations in avoiding negligent release litigation. To demonstrate due diligence in release decisions, he recommends the following:

1. The development of policies that govern release decision making in cooperation with knowledgeable legal consultants
2. Explicit documentation of an assessment of violence
3. Review of the written proposal to release by senior consulting staff or a review committee

Sparr and Drummond (47) describe a Department of Veterans Affairs referral procedure prior to the actual discharge of the patient. Discharge information forms are processed through referral coordinators. An aftercare appointment is made before the patient is discharged. Referral procedures must be coordinated meticulously or else the transition process to aftercare will break down.

In the clinical vignette, did Dr. Madison negligently discharge his patient?

Successful discharge planning is a process that begins with admission and includes the patient, the family, and the hospital staff (64). Clinical treatment and discharge planning are interdependent. Treating discharge as a last-minute event is antithetical to good clinical care. Records of the previous psychiatric hospitalizations of Mr. Artz should have been reviewed before discharge was considered. If the records were slow in arriving, a direct call to the hospitals should have been made.

The record of previous hospitalizations is particularly important because a language problem existed. Unless the patient speaks some exotic language, an interpreter is usually available at the hospital or in the community. Patients who speak rare languages usually are reasonably proficient in another tongue. Because verbal communication is essential to psychiatric evaluation and intervention, communication problems based on language differences should not be a problem if interpreters are available. This applies as well to foreign-born psychiatrists practicing in this country. Close supervision of foreign-born psychiatrists may be necessary if significant language difficulties exist.

Thorough risk-benefit analysis surrounding the decision to discharge Mr. Artz was not possible because of the lack of background information, the language barrier, and the apparent lack of any therapeutic alliance. Mr. Artz was described as a model patient by the nursing staff. Clinicians must be wary of patients described in this fashion. It is easy to be deceived concerning the patient's actual clinical status. The patient is living in a structured environment where physical needs are met, medications are administered, and stress from the outside world is minimized. Patients who cause little trouble to staff may be avoiding contact with the staff while continuing to suffer their illnesses under the cover of a "model patient." If no relationship or alliance exists between psychiatrist and patient, release decisions remain problematic. Patients cannot be expected to confide their thoughts and feelings about discharge in the absence of a trusting relationship.

Dr. Madison held a discharge conference with the staff. No consultation with another psychiatrist was sought, presumably because the patient did not seem to present a difficult discharge decision. Given the fact that the mother offered a history of three previous assaults, a consultation was entirely appropriate on this basis alone.

Dr. Madison did speak with the patient's mother prior to discharge. Conferences with families before discharge can be very useful for proper postdischarge planning. Moreover, the discharge concerns of the family usually are apparent, particularly if a family member has been the target of the patient's violence. If feasible, the patient should be included in the family conference. Some families may disavow any connection with the patient, refusing a predischarge conference and raising additional concerns about discharging the patient. Although Mr. Artz did not threaten his mother or anyone else at the time of discharge, command hallucinations to kill his mother were present at the time of admission. No other identifiable victims existed for Dr. Madison to consider notifying.

Mr. Artz was an ideal candidate for a conditional release program or for outpatient commitment. Mr. Artz's symptoms appeared to improve after the first month of hospitalization. To repeat, access to previous psychiatric records would have underscored the importance of conditional release. The concern that psychiatric hospitalization can obscure the violent tendencies of some patients can be addressed through a graduated program of weekend passes, trial visits, and trial job situations. Medication and treatment services can be supplied, either by the hospital or by community programs. A conditional release program can be tailored to the individual treatment needs of the patient. Furthermore, social services and other service agencies, as well as the psychiatrist, will have a basis to gather important information. Evaluation of the patient's outside relationships, job performance, and the ability to live with family or caregivers is critical to sound discharge decision making. Mr. Artz was discharged from a highly structured, supportive setting into a minimally supportive family and community situation without benefit of a transitional period.

Although a discharge may be entirely appropriate, follow-up care and planning may be deficient. Certainly, Dr. Madison was not careful enough about following up his patient to see that the postdischarge treatment plan was being adhered to by the patient. After Dr. Madison finally received Mr. Artz's prior psychiatric records, he discovered that the patient had a history of not keeping appointments, alcoholism, and noncompliance with medication. Dr. Madison was on notice that the past behavior of Mr. Artz would likely repeat itself.

An outpatient appointment scheduled for 3 weeks after discharge with a patient like Mr. Artz is too long a time without follow-up and care. Unexpected situations may arise that can destabilize a patient during the postdischarge period. Dr. Madison should have seen Mr. Artz as an outpatient until the clinic appointment time arrived, or he should have made alternate plans that would have provided for continuing supervision of the patient. Even if Mr. Artz had an appointment scheduled 1 week after discharge with another therapist, it would have been important for Dr. Madison to make contact with that therapist to ensure that Mr. Artz kept his appointment. Dr. Madison should have made sure that another mental health professional had assumed care for the patient. When Mr. Artz did not keep his outpatient appointment, Dr. Madison should have been in a position to know this information. He then could have attempted to contact the patient and family to assess the patient's noncompliance and consider his intervention options if the patient continued to refuse outpatient visits.

Mr. Artz had a long-standing alcohol problem. Before discharging a patient who has abused alcohol and drugs, anticipated problems and remedial actions concerning substance abuse should be discussed fully with the patient, and if possible with the family. Alcohol and drug problems tend to be recurrent and destabilizing. Violence is not an infrequent outcome. Careful planning for outpatient follow-up at alcohol and drug programs should be arranged well before discharge. If possible, the patient should be allowed to make direct contact with these facilities before discharge.

Finally, the discharge note should reflect the discussions and planning held with the patient and family. If the patient is not considered imminently dangerous, the note should indicate this as well as the improvements in the patient's condition that demonstrate that he or she is ready for discharge. Notes that make categorical statements about the presence or absence of risk of violence should be avoided. Instead, a careful risk-benefit assessment should be recorded.

References

1. RESTATEMENT (SECOND) OF TORTS, § 320, comment a (1977)
2. Mills JH: The so-called duty to warn: the psychotherapeutic duty to protect third parties from patients' violent acts. Behavioral Sciences and the Law 2:237–257, 1984
3. Reisner R: Law and the Mental Health System. St Paul, MN, West Publishing, 1985, p 106
4. RESTATEMENT (SECOND) OF TORTS, § 319, comment a (1977)
5. Recent developments in psychotherapists' liability for patients' conduct. Professional Liability Reporter, March-November 1984, pp 14–18
6. Rein WC, in Mental Health and Mental Retardation Quarterly Digest (Kansas Department of Social and Rehabilitation Services), Vol 4, May 30, 1985
7. 250 Ga 199, 296 SE2d 693 (1982)
8. 234 Kan 484, 673 P2d 86 (1983)
9. 511 F2d 407 (DC Cir 1975)
10. 564 F Supp 341 (E D Mich 1983)
11. Davis v Lhim, 335 NW2d 481 (Mich App 1983), remanded on other grounds, 422 Mich 875, 366 NW2d 7 (1985), on rem, 147 Mich App 8, 382 NW2d 195 (1985), rvsd sub nom, Canon v Thumudo, 430 Mich 326, 422 NW2d 688 (1988)
12. 870 F2d 1098 (6th Cir 1989)
13. 100 Wash 2d 421, 671 P2d 230 (1983) (en banc)

14. 539 A2d 1064 (Del Super Ct 1988)
15. 39 Ohio St 3d 86 529 NE2d 449 (1988)
16. Reisner R: Law and the Mental Health System. St Paul, MN, West Publishing, 1985, p 113
17. 497 F Supp 185 (D Neb 1980)
18. 646 F Supp 524 (E D Mich 1986)
19. Klein JI, Macbeth JE, Onek JN: Legal Issues in the Private Practice of Psychiatry. Washington, DC, American Psychiatric Press, 1984, pp 16–17
20. Keeton WP, Dobb DB, Keeton RE, et al: Prosser and Keeton on Torts, 5th Edition. St Paul, MN, West Publishing, 1984, p 1038
21. Bies EB: Mental Health and the Law. Rockville, MD, Aspen, 1984, p 229
22. 99 A2d 616, 472 NYS2d 170 (NY App Div 1984)
23. Reisner R, Slobogin C: Law and the Mental Health System, 2nd Edition. St Paul, MN, West Publishing, 1990, p 98
24. 653 SW2d 661 (Mo 1983)
25. Del Carmen RV: Civil liabilities of government psychotherapists and agencies for the release of the mentally ill. Journal of Psychiatry and Law 12:183–213, 1984
26. 281 SC 242, 315 SE2d 112 (1984)
27. S.C. CODE ANN (Law Co-op 1976)
28. Court of Appeal, Fourth Appellate District Division One, State of California Superior Ct, No 420863 (July 18, 1986)
29. Appelbaum PS, Zonana H, Retal B: Statutory approaches to limiting psychiatrists' liability for their patients' violent acts. Am J Psychiatry 146:821–828, 1989
30. Appelbaum PS, Gutheil TG: Clinical Handbook of Psychiatry and the Law, 2nd Edition. Baltimore, MD, Williams & Wilkins, 1991, p 105
31. Slovenko R: Psychiatry and the Law. Boston, MA, Little, Brown, 1973, p 213
32. Appelbaum PS, Gutheil TG: Clinical Handbook of Psychiatry and the Law, 2nd Edition. Baltimore, MD, Williams & Wilkins, 1991, pp 106–107
33. 345 NW2d 217 (Minn 1984)
34. Proess MG, Quinsey VL: The dangerousness of patients released from maximum security: a replication. Journal of Psychiatry and Law 5:292–299, 1977
35. Tardiff K, Sweillam A: Characteristics of assaultive and suicidal patients admitted to public hospitals. Bull Am Acad Psychiatry Law 7:11–18, 1979
36. Tardiff K: Assaults in hospitals and placement in the community. Bull Am Acad Psychiatry Law 9:33–39, 1981
37. Tardiff K: A survey of five types of dangerous behavior among chronic psychiatric patients. Bull Am Acad Psychiatry Law 10:177–182, 1982
38. Kroll J, MacKenzie TB: When psychiatrists are liable: risk management and violent patients. Hosp Community Psychiatry 34:35, 1983
39. Williams v United States, 450 F Supp 1040 (DC SD 1978)
40. 538 F2d 121 (4th Cir), cert den, Folliard v Semler, 429 U.S. 827 (1976)
41. 115 Ariz 260, 564 P2d 1227 (1977)
42. Reisner R: Law and the Mental Health System. St Paul, MN, West Publishing, 1985, p 109
43. Siebert SW, Silver SB: Psychiatrists' relationships with the general public, in American Psychiatric Press Review of Clinical Psychiatry and the Law, Vol 2. Edited by Simon RI. Washington, DC, American Psychiatric Press, 1990, pp 259–270

44. 183 Cal App 3d 1175, 228 Cal Rptr 661 (Cal Ct App 1986)
45. 222 Cal App 3d 660, 271 Cal Rptr 876 (Cal Ct App 1990)
46. Miller RD, Maier GJ: Factors affecting the decision to prosecute mental patients for criminal behavior, in Therapeutic Jurisprudence: The Law as a Therapeutic Agent. Edited by Wexler DB. Durham, NC, Carolina Academic Press, 1990, pp 369–377
47. Sparr LF, Drummond DJ: Risk management in Veterans Administration mental health clinics, in American Psychiatric Press Review of Clinical Psychiatry and the Law, Vol 3. Edited by Simon RI. Washington, DC, American Psychiatric Press, 1992, pp 67–97
48. Roth LH: A commitment law for patients, doctors, and lawyers. Am J Psychiatry 146:1121–1127, 1979
49. Phelan LA, Mills MJ, Ryan JA: Prosecuting psychiatric patients for assault. Hosp Community Psychiatry 36:581–582, 1985
50. Hoge SK, Gutheil TG: The prosecution of psychiatric patients for assaults on staff: a preliminary empirical study. Hosp Community Psychiatry 38:44–49, 1987
51. Appelbaum PS: Recent controversies in law and psychiatry. Presentation for the Council on Psychiatry and the Law Workshop at the 138th annual meeting of the American Psychiatric Association, Dallas, TX, May 1985
52. Klein JI, Macbeth JE, Onek JN: Legal Issues in the Private Practice of Psychiatry. Washington, DC, American Psychiatric Press, 1984, pp 18–19
53. Poythress NG: Avoiding negligent release: contemporary clinical and risk management strategies. Am J Psychiatry 147:994–997, 1990
54. Bies EB: Mental Health and the Law. Rockville, MD, Aspen, 1984, p 225
55. Beck JC: The psychotherapist and the violent patient: recent case law, in The Potentially Violent Patient and the Tarasoff Decision in Psychiatric Practice. Edited by Beck JC. Washington, DC, American Psychiatric Press, 1984, pp 9–34
56. 103 Idaho 151, 645 P3d 891 (1982)
57. McCafferty G, Dooley J: Involuntary outpatient commitment: an update. MPDLR 14(May-June):277–287, 1990
58. Miller RD: Commitment to outpatient treatment: a national survey. Hosp Community Psychiatry 36:265–267, 1985
59. Stefan S: Preventive commitment: the concept and its pitfalls. MPDLR 11(July-August):288–302, 1987
60. Underwood v United States, 356 F2d 92 (5th Cir 1966)
61. 4 Law Alert 144 (Feb 1985)
62. Zeldow PB, Taub HA: Evaluating psychiatric discharge and aftercare in a VA medical center. Hosp Community Psychiatry 32:57–58, 1981
63. Simon RI: Concise Guide to Clinical Psychiatry and the Law. Washington, DC, American Psychiatric Press, 1988, pp 119–120
64. Koch P: Discharge planning perspectives. Carrier Foundation Letter, No 143, May 1989

Chapter 15

Restraint, Seclusion, and the Least-Restrictive Alternative

Ms. Nelson, a 23-year-old college student, is admitted to the psychiatric ward of a general hospital at 1:00 P.M. for increasing agitation, confusion, and volatile mood swings following the ingestion of phencyclidine. Six hours after admission, she begins to scream incoherently, rips her clothes off, and swings wildly at patients and staff. Dr. Henry, the attending psychiatrist, begins rapid neuroleptization with intramuscular haloperidol as the patient starts to bang her head against the wall. Dr. Henry writes a seclusion order for the patient to be administered as needed. A male attendant is assigned to observe her full time. She is placed in a restraint garment. Her screaming and cursing becomes very disruptive to other patients, precipitating regressive behavior in some of them.

Eight hours after the patient is admitted, she is placed in seclusion. The restraints are removed, but an attendant stays with her because of concern that she will continue banging her head. Dr. Henry is called by phone and informed that the patient has been placed in seclusion. With rapidly increasing doses of haloperidol, the head banging does not recur. The patient, however, refuses to stay clothed. In addition, menstruation begins, but the patient resists any sanitary care. She starts to smear feces. A female attendant tries to stay with her. Due to the stench of the patient's continued refusal to be toileted, the attendant sits outside the door and checks Ms. Nelson frequently through a small window. Because the patient is not eating and drinking, the staff finds it difficult to determine the patient's fluid intake. When intramuscular haloperidol is given, three male attendants are required to hold her down. Attendants who perform this duty have to be rotated because of their great resistance to entering the room. Because of the summer heat and poor ventilation in the seclusion room, Ms. Nelson begins to sweat profusely.

At 11 A.M. on the next day, Dr. Henry visits the patient and is horrified when he sees her deteriorated condition. He calls the maintenance supervisor immediately, requesting improvement in ventilation and temperature control of the seclusion room. Within 2 hours, reasonable temperature and ventilation are achieved. He orders toileting procedures and has the patient dressed and placed in restraints. An attendant is stationed inside the seclusion room for constant supervision. Fluid intake is documented. The patient is fed initially by the attendant, but gradually she wants to feed herself. At meal times, she is taken out of restraints. The patient gradually becomes willing to take her medication by mouth. Dr. Henry attends to her at least twice a day. By the fifth day of hospitalization, the door can be left open and only 15-minute checks are required.

Ms. Nelson becomes particularly attached to a female attendant who has stayed with her in the seclusion room. This attendant accompanies the patient as she tries to make the transition to the open ward. Slowly, Ms. Nelson is able to participate in ward activities and no longer requires a seclusion room. She is integrated into ward activity before she is given her own room.

What are the legal origins of the least-restrictive alternative?

The concept of the least-restrictive alternative (LRA) derives from an area remote from the mental health field (1). As a result, the LRA is frequently used inappropriately in dealing with patients. The LRA principle was stated in *Shelton v. Tucker* (2), a 1960 United States Supreme Court case involving Arkansas' attempt to root out subversive individuals by compelling schoolteachers to provide a list of their memberships in outside organizations. The Court ruled that the state must seek the least possible interference with individual rights in order to constitutionally pursue its purpose. The language of the opinion, however, relates to political issues.

The principles of the LRA were applied to the mental health field in a 1966 D.C. Court of Appeals case, *Lake v. Cameron* (3). This case involved the care and disposition of an elderly, senile woman. Judge Bazelon stated: "Deprivation of liberty solely because of dangers to the ill persons themselves should not go beyond what is necessary for their protection." Thus, the court implicitly adopted the *Shelton* rationale. In other words, the court in *Lake* applied the LRA to mental health law by referring to treatments as more or less restrictive, although it did not establish any hierarchy based on restrictiveness.

Slovenko (4) states that a fundamental issue is whether the LRA should apply to involuntary hospitalization rather than outpatient treatment, or whether it should be applied in the establishing of treatment hierarchies. He asks: "Should the LRA be applied to seclusion, restraint, or treatment with neuroleptics?" Lawyers, concerned with individual liberties, have not always given full consideration to treatment consequences for patients when pursuing their legal goals. Although a patient may clinically benefit most from an involuntary hospitalization, any "less restrictive" alternative must be implemented that is consistent with minimally acceptable care. The LRA assumes that mental health services exist on a graduated level of equally efficacious restrictiveness, with the hospital being the most restrictive. In most jurisdictions, a one-dimensional view of the LRA has been resisted by making considerations of restrictiveness consistent with the treatment needs of patients. Thus, restrictiveness and therapeutic interventions are beneficially linked.

The LRA has been subsequently applied, through court-mandated guidelines, to procedures, treatments, and the physical environments of involuntary hospitalized patients. In *Lessard v. Schmidt* (5), the court used the LRA to develop procedural rights for mental patients who are undergoing involuntary hospitalization.

What are the clinical limitations of the LRA when applied to psychiatric interventions?

Empirical studies attempting to establish a hierarchy of restrictiveness demonstrate the difficulty of such an effort (1, 6). These studies indicate that classifications of restrictiveness are usually highly arbitrary and one-sided. The issue of restrictiveness is normally based on the staff's subjective perceptions of the modality used rather than the effect of the modality on the clinical needs of the patient. A risk-benefit analysis—which involves weighing the degree of restrictiveness for any given treatment or intervention against the degree of freedom from a disabling mental disorder—usually is not undertaken. On the other hand, Perr (6) has proposed "the most beneficial alternative" as being clinically more useful. The "optimal therapeutic setting" also has been offered as a substitute for the LRA.

Depending on state law and regulations, the clinician's judgment must be relied on for the choice of treatment best suited for the patient. The concept of the LRA, however, did not receive support in the important U.S. Supreme Court case of *Youngberg v. Romeo* (7). In *Youngberg,* a seclusion and restraint case, the Court expressed a clear preference for professional judgment. The Court stressed that "it is not appropriate for the courts to specify which of several professionally acceptable choices should have been made" and that "in determining what is reasonable, . . . courts must show deference to the judgment exercised by a qualified professional."

In the clinical vignette, the management of the patient throughout the course of her psychotic episode illustrates the inherent problems in arbitrarily establishing hierarchies of restrictiveness without regard to the patient's clinical needs. Which is more restrictive—seclusion, restraint, or treatment with neuroleptics? It is impossible to answer this question without knowing which modality of treatment will provide the patient the greatest freedom from her mental disorder. Although Ms. Nelson received high doses of haloperidol, she continued to regress. Placing the patient in the seclusion room by herself, while still administering high doses of medication, was not sufficiently effective. Restraining the patient in order to toilet and clothe her allowed the staff to stay with her, permitted a one-on-one sustaining relationship to develop. Although medication and seclusion were helpful and necessary, restraint of the patient permitted beneficial relationships to develop between staff members and a terrified, psychotic patient. Obviously, arbitrary hierarchies of restrictiveness must be avoided if they interfere with adequate clinical care of the patient.

How frequently is seclusion used in psychiatric facilities? What is the attitude of psychiatrists concerning the use of seclusion and restraint?

Studies indicate seclusion is used anywhere from 1.9% to 44% of the time depending upon the type of institution and its treatment philosophy (8). Hospitals serving busy urban areas tend to use seclusion more. Long-term care facilities tend to prefer neuroleptic treatment over seclusion. Geographical location also may be a factor. In a study of New York state hospitals, hospitals in New York City and in large towns had the highest rates of seclusion and restraint (9). However, an analysis by age group showed that New York City hospitals had the lowest rate of seclusion for patients under 35, even though the age group constituted the majority of patients secluded or restrained. Large towns had the highest rate of seclusion and restraint for this age group. The authors could provide no clear explanation for these findings.

Lion (10) observes that seclusion and restraint frequently evoke controversy and defensiveness among clinicians. He notes that many psychiatrists find physical restraint devices repugnant and prefer to deny their existence. Nevertheless, seclusion and restraint are extremely effective in the psychiatric treatment of certain patients.

What are the clinical indications for the use of seclusion and restraint of adults?

As a clinical management modality, seclusion and restraint have both indications and contraindications (11) (see Table 15-1). There are three main indica-

---

TABLE 15–1. Indications for seclusion and restraint

1. To prevent clear, imminent harm to the patient or others
2. To prevent significant disruption to treatment program or physical surroundings
3. To assist in treatment as part of ongoing behavior therapy
4. To decrease sensory overstimulation*
5. To respond to patient's voluntary reasonable request for intervention

---

*Seclusion only.

tions for seclusion and restraint: *1)* to prevent clear, imminent harm either to the patient or to others when control by other means is ineffective or inappropriate; *2)* to prevent significant disruption of the treatment program or damage to the physical surroundings; and *3)* to assist in treatment as part of the ongoing behavior therapy (11). The legal and clinical appropriateness of using seclusion and restraint explicitly for the purpose of behavior modification treatment is unclear. Seclusion and restraint may be legally treacherous when used with competent patients. Behavior therapy methods such as contingent restraint and locked time out may be used to deal with patients who are about to become seriously dangerous. Wexler (12) states that these programs appear to be similar to other emergency management methods sanctioned under the reasoning in *Youngberg v. Romeo* (7). Two other indications applicable only to seclusion are to decrease sensory overstimulation and to provide seclusion upon the patient's voluntary request.

In the vignette, the patient became unmanageable on the ward. She tried to violently strike both patients and staff. Her screaming and stripping behavior was so disruptive to other patients that it caused regression in some of them. It was necessary to provide a quiet seclusion room in order to decrease sensory stimulation for both Ms. Nelson and the other patients. Although the decision to seclude Ms. Nelson was colored in part by the competing interests of other patients, the decision was based primarily on her treatment needs. It is clear that Ms. Nelson met the first two criteria for seclusion and restraint.

Voluntary requests by patients for seclusion may be honored in order to provide support for weakening impulse control, to diminish seriously threatening contact with others, and to lessen the threatening experience of "flashbacks" and overstimulation for patients recovering from toxic or drug reactions. If the patient asks for seclusion, a viable therapeutic alliance with the staff probably exists. Manipulative patients, however, may try to use seclusion to avoid ward activities and treatment programs, to test staff resolve, or to draw the staff into sadomasochistic power struggles. Therefore, the motivation behind requests for seclusion must be considered.

Most states have freedom-from-restraint-and-seclusion statutes that should be familiar to mental health professionals who use these management modalities (13). States that do not have statutes governing the use of restraints usually have developed administrative regulations. Professional opinions as to the clinical use of physical restraints and seclusion vary considerably. Unless precluded by state law, there can be a variety of uses for seclusion justified on both clinical and legal grounds. Although statutory guidelines governing seclusion and restraint must be followed, they can never be a substitute for sound clinical judgment in the management of individual patients. As Perr (6) wisely observes: "Freedom from illness and disease is also a philosophical concept that needs to be treasured along with the right of physical freedom. In the long run, one without the other is not freedom at all."

What are the clinical contraindications to the use of seclusion and restraint?

Contraindications exist for the use of seclusion and restraint (see Table 15-2). Medical and psychiatric patients who are extremely unstable may require the close proximity of staff. Psychiatric units that have seclusion rooms some distance from the nursing station must carefully consider who they place in seclusion. Patients with delirium or dementia who cannot tolerate decreased stimulation (so-called "sundowners" among the elderly) may represent a group for whom seclusion is contraindicated. Patients with severe drug reactions or overdoses, those who require careful monitoring of their dosages, or extremely self-destructive, mutilating patients should not be placed in seclusion without very close supervision. For example, overtly suicidal patients should not be placed in a seclusion room. Instead, close and direct observation of the patient is necessary. The seclusion room usually does not lend itself to the implementation of a high level of suicide precautions. Also, patients who head bang should be kept in physical restraints, preferably in a bed or a wheelchair, where they can be observed by nursing staff.

In the clinical vignette, Ms. Nelson began to sweat profusely because of the poor thermoregulation induced by her rapid neuroleptization. Also, there was inadequate ventilation and temperature control of the seclusion room. Seclusion rooms that cannot be climatically controlled may present a contraindication for patients receiving high doses of neuroleptics. In addition, patients with circulatory or respiratory difficulties may present relative contraindications to restraint if circulation becomes obstructed or if these patients lie on their backs, increasing the possibility of aspiration.

Using seclusion as a punishment or for the sole convenience of staff is absolutely contraindicated. Secluding a patient to protect others is a clear indication, but the harm must be imminent. The mere expression of rude behavior is not by itself a legitimate reason for seclusion. With some patients who are well known to staff, the emergence of obnoxious behavior may be an early warning signal for an ultimate loss of control and physical violence. The staff may need to consider preemptively secluding the patient if it is known that other modalities

---

TABLE 15–2. Contraindications to seclusion and restraint

1. For extremely unstable medical and psychiatric conditions*
2. For delirious or demented patients unable to tolerate decreased stimulation*
3. For overtly suicidal patients*
4. For patients with severe drug reactions or overdoses, or those requiring close monitoring of drug dosages*
5. For punishment of the patient or convenience of staff

---

*Unless close supervision and direct observation are provided.

for management have not been effective in the past.

The potential for misuse of seclusion and restraint is always present and is a highly controversial issue. When staff anxiety leads to requesting seclusion of a patient, the psychiatrist must determine whether the request is a legitimate barometer of the patient's actual mental state. Seclusion is sometimes requested to gain a psychiatrist's attention when the staff feels a psychiatrist has been unresponsive to staff concerns about the patients (1).

The psychiatrist must closely supervise the use of restraint and seclusion. These procedures must be used only when clearly indicated and are never routine (14). Most state regulations do not comment on the type of prn order for seclusion and restraint left by Dr. Henry in the clinical vignette. Of the states with guidelines, only three allow prn orders for seclusion and two allow prn orders for restraints (15). The Joint Commission on Accreditation of Healthcare Organizations (JCAHO) does not allow prn orders for restraint and seclusion (16).

What are some alternatives to seclusion and restraint?

Before using seclusion and restraint in the management of Ms. Nelson in the vignette, the staff tried other interventions. For instance, neuroleptic medication and one-on-one supervision were attempted initially. With some acutely disturbed patients, verbal interventions as well as a tailored program of closely supervised socialization and recreation may also help to prevent loss of control. In some acutely psychotic patients, it may be clear at the time of admission that such patients cannot be helped by verbal and socialization techniques until some remission in their psychiatric condition takes place.

Bornstein (17) reports a 9-month prospective study of all patients who were restrained on the acute psychiatric units of two general hospitals. These patients were compared with a group of nonrestrained control patients. Restraint occurred more often in young, unmarried, seriously ill men with a previous history of violent behavior and psychiatric treatment. These characteristics were coupled with insufficient neuroleptic treatment and the perception by the patient of inadequate power authority on the unit. The incidence of previous violence was significantly higher in the restrained patients compared with the nonrestrained patients on the same unit.

One cannot make a prior judgment about which intervention—seclusion, restraint, or involuntary medication—is the least restrictive (1). The decision to use only one or a combination of these modalities depends on the clinical needs of the patient. In cases in which violence may occur (e.g., the paranoid schizophrenic patient driven by delusions), neuroleptic medication may be the intervention of choice. Using neuroleptics as a means of social control through "chemical restraint" is contraindicated when there is little connection between the violence and a treatable mental condition. For example, a developmentally retarded patient without psychotic symptoms may not respond behaviorally to neuroleptic medication. Furthermore, such medications may impair further learning. Temporary restraint and seclusion may be more appropriate for such persons.

In the vignette, Ms. Nelson was restrained before medication could be given, thus requiring the synergistic use of both modalities. Furthermore, the more intrusive intramuscular route was necessary because of her refusal to eat or drink. Patients receiving high doses of neuroleptics in seclusion must be observed carefully and frequently because of the possibility of oversedation or ominous, untoward adverse effects such as neuroleptic malignant syndrome. The JCAHO (16) standards state that "appropriate attention is paid every 15 minutes to a patient in restraint or seclusion, especially in regard to regular meals, bathing, and use of the toilet."

What are the guidelines for implementing seclusion and restraint procedures?

Initiation of emergency restraint and seclusion procedures by nursing and other professional staff in accord with established hospital policy for seclusion and restraint requires the psychiatrist's review and order for continuation (18). The psychiatrist should be notified immediately. Emergency implementation of restraint and seclusion should not exceed 1 hour without a physician staff member's oral order. After the initial implementation of seclusion and restraint, the psychiatrist should see the patient within 3 hours. Optimally, the psychiatrist should see the patient within the first hour. The psychiatrist must document his or her visit and describe the patient's condition, the need for restrictiveness, and any plans for further special monitoring or precautions to be taken by the staff. In the vignette, Ms. Nelson was not seen directly by Dr. Henry until 14 hours after her seclusion. When there is insufficient professional supervision of a secluded, acutely psychotic patient, a deteriorated condition—such as the one suffered by Ms. Nelson—is not uncommon.

Subsequent visits by the psychiatrist are a matter of clinical judgment. Although a patient may need to be seen more frequently, a minimum of one visit a day seems appropriate. The seclusion and restraint order should be reviewed on each visit and the need for continued restriction documented (18). A risk-benefit analysis should be conducted describing the benefits as reflected in improvement in physical states, mental status, and control of violence versus the adverse physical and emotional effects of seclusion. The ability of staff to handle the patient, with and without restriction, should be evaluated.

As stated earlier, the patient in seclusion or restraint must be observed every 15 minutes by members of the nursing staff. With some very violent patients, observation may be made only through a window. The patient may need to be observed continuously or, as in the case of Ms. Nelson, to have a staff member in the seclusion room. If a relationship can be established with the acutely disturbed patient, the time in seclusion may be significantly reduced, particularly when the relationship permits smooth transition to the open ward. If the door can be left open when the patient is quiet, nursing staff may not need to check more than every 30 minutes. The clinical observations made during these checks should be recorded and used in assessing the patient's progress and readiness to leave restraint or seclusion.

Toileting should be done at least every 4 hours. If the patient cannot use an adjoining toilet, then a bedpan will be necessary. Toileting can be one of the most difficult management problems in seclusion. Lion and Soloff (18) report that assaults by patients are most apt to occur concerning toileting. Considering that control, humiliation, and invasion of privacy issues are all intimately involved with toileting, this reaction is not surprising. If possible, patients should not be allowed to eat alone, because meals are important occasions for interaction with others. Assaultive patients may use food or utensils as weapons against themselves or others. Adequate administration of fluids is essential because of the possibility of profuse sweating and dehydration. The documentation of fluid intake is difficult but can be of critical importance.

In the vignette, Ms. Nelson's personal hygiene was allowed to deteriorate by permitting nudity and improper toileting to continue. She smeared herself with feces. She also was menstruating. Patients should not be allowed to become so hygienically offensive as to drive away staff. Once cleaned and dressed, the staff was able to interact with Ms. Nelson more comfortably. This facilitates her recovery. Allowing the patient to eat alone was a lost opportunity in helping her to resocialize.

The process of removal from seclusion and restraint occurs when the initial goals of restriction have been met. When the patient no longer poses a threat to others or self and is no longer a threat to disrupt the therapeutic setting of the ward, he or she may be removed from seclusion. The psychiatrist should use incremental steps in removing the patient from seclusion and restraint. As each step of a transition plan is successfully negotiated, the next step is taken. Introduction to ward routine can still be done while the patient is spending some time in seclusion. No one can be certain that the patient will not suddenly regress or become assaultive. Accordingly, a risk-benefit assessment should be made prior to final separation from seclusion. If the patient can form a reasonably stable relationship with a staff member, chances of successfully negotiating transfer to the open ward are maximized.

National guidelines for the proper use of seclusion and restraints have been established by the American Psychiatric Association (APA) Task Force on the Psychiatric Uses of Seclusion and Restraint (19). The Task Force report examines the indications for seclusion and restraint in three critically sensitive populations: children and adolescents, the elderly, and the developmentally disabled. The facility's legal counsel should review the recommended guidelines and techniques for compliance with state statutes and court decisions on the use of seclusion and restraint. Adherence to guidelines, state statutes, and court decisions should protect patients from abuse and practitioners from legal liability.

What are the judicial, statutory, and nongovernmental constraints placed on the use of seclusion and restraint?

Most states prohibit the use of restraint and seclusion except in an emergency when the patient threatens imminent harm to self or others (20). In Illinois, restraint and seclusion may be used only by a physician's order or in an emergency. The Illinois statute requires that after a patient has been placed in restraints or seclusion, the order must be reviewed, confirmed, and documented by a physician at least once every 24 hours (21). Where legislative enactment has been absent, courts have attempted regulation of seclusion and restraint through constitutional due-process protection.

Judicial and legislative guidelines for determining patients' behavior that warrants restraint vary from state to state. Most court cases have dealt with specific situations of alleged abuse of seclusion and restraint. In general, the courts have held that restraint and seclusion can be used only when a patient threatens harm to self or other and a less-restrictive alternative is not available to control the risk of danger (13). The constitutional standard was established by the U.S. Supreme Court in *Youngberg v. Romeo* (7). The Court held that mentally retarded, involuntarily hospitalized patients in state institutions "enjoy constitutionally protected interests in conditions of reasonable care and safety, reasonably nonrestrictive confinement conditions, and such training as may be required by these interests." The Court added that "in determining whether the state has met its obligations in these respects, decisions made by the appropriate profession are entitled to a presumption of correctness." The Court stated that the professional judgments of psychiatrists are to be given deference and that psychiatrists cannot be held liable for damages when inadequate budgets render them unable to meet professional standards.

Whereas most "freedom from restraint" cases involve involuntarily hospitalized mentally retarded patients, the principles enunciated in these decisions appear to apply to both voluntarily and involuntarily admitted psychiatric patients (19). State statutes generally do not distinguish between these three groups regarding seclusion and restraint. Many state statutes not only limit the use of mechanical and other restraints to situations of imminent harm or when necessary for the patient's medical needs, but also require a record of the reasons for restraint of all patients (13). Courts generally require assurance that professional judgment was exercised in the use of seclusion and restraint.

As alluded to earlier, the JCAHO has promulgated detailed national guidelines for hospitals regarding seclusion and restraint requirements (22). For instance, each restraint and seclusion order is time limited and shall not exceed 24 hours. Orders beyond 24 hours must be approved by the chairperson of the department. In addition, the JCAHO requires that a hospital have written policies and procedures governing the use of seclusion and restraint. Whenever a hospital violates its own rules and a patient in its care is injured, liability is likely.

Finally, the clinician must always recognize that mechanical restraints should be used only as clinical interventions. Tinetti et al. (23) found that the use of mechanical restraints in nursing homes for safety and behavioral management rather than for treatment of medical conditions is a prevalent practice. These findings confirm earlier data from the Health Care Financing Administration (24). Under guidelines from the Department of Health and Human Services, restraints should be limited to treating a nursing home resident's medical symptoms. In addition, a treatment plan must consider carefully less-restrictive alternatives, and specific informed consent must be obtained from the resident, family member, or legal representative (25).

Wexler (12) summarizes the legal aspects of seclusion and restraint by stating that *Youngberg v. Romeo* (7) allows psychiatrists considerable legal leeway in providing seclusion and restraint in emergency situations. Punitive uses of restraint "bristle with clinical, legal, ethical and policy difficulties and should not ordinarily be resorted to" (p. 123). Reisner (26) analyzes the current regulatory climate governing seclusion and restraint by stating that "as a result of *Youngberg* and in the absence of state statutes imposing additional regulation, institutions appear to have considerable latitude in the use of these devices so long as their use is authorized and closely monitored by a professional."

References

1. Gutheil TG, Appelbaum PS, Wexler DB: The inappropriateness of "least restrictive alternative" analysis for involuntary procedures with the institutionalized mentally ill. Journal of Psychiatry and Law 11:7–17, 1983
2. 364 U.S. 479 (1960)
3. 364 F2d 657 (DC Cir), cert denied 382 U.S. 863 (1966)
4. R Slovenko, personal communication, February 1985
5. 349 F Supp 1078 (E D Wis 1972), vacated, 414 U.S. 473 (1974), 379 F Supp 1376 (E D Wis 1974), vacated, 421 U.S. 957 (1975), on remand, 413 F Supp 1318 (E D Wis 1976)
6. Perr IN: The most beneficial alternative: a counterpoint to the least restrictive alternative. Bull Am Acad Psychiatry Law 6(4):iv–viii, 1978; see p vii
7. 457 U.S. 307 (1982), on remand, Romeo v Youngberg, 687 F2d 33 (3rd Cir 1982)
8. Gutheil TG: Review of individual quantitative studies, in The Psychiatric Uses of Seclusion and Restraint. Edited by Tardiff K. Washington, DC, American Psychiatric Press, 1984, pp 125–140
9. Carpenter MD, Hannon VR, McCleery G, et al: Variations in seclusion and restraint practices by hospital location. Hosp Community Psychiatry 39:418–423, 1988
10. Lion JR: Training for battle: thoughts on managing aggressive patients. Hosp Community Psychiatry 38:882–884, 1987

11. Gutheil TG, Tardiff K: Indications and contraindications for seclusion and restraint, in The Psychiatric Uses of Seclusion and Restraint. Edited by Tardiff K. Washington, DC, American Psychiatric Press, 1984, pp 11–18

12. Wexler DB: Legal aspects of seclusion and restraint, in The Psychiatric Uses of Seclusion and Restraint. Edited by Tardiff K. Washington, DC, American Psychiatric Press, 1984, pp 111–124

13. Brakel SJ, Parry J, Weiner BA: The Mentally Disabled and the Law, 3rd Edition. Chicago, IL, American Bar Foundation, 1985, pp 275–276

14. Greenblatt M: What have we learned from seclusion? Roche Report: Frontiers of Psychiatry, May 1, 1982, p 14

15. Tardiff K, Mattson MR: A survey of state mental health directors concerning guidelines for seclusion and restraint, in The Psychiatric Uses of Seclusion and Restraint. Edited by Tardiff K. Washington, DC, American Psychiatric Press, 1984, pp 141–150

16. Joint Commission on Accreditation of Healthcare Organizations: Consolidated Standards Manual. Chicago, IL, Joint Commission on Accreditation of Healthcare Organizations, 1991, p 147

17. Bornstein PE: The use of restraints on a general psychiatric unit. J Clin Psychiatry 46:175–178, 1985

18. Lion JR, Soloff PH: Implementation of seclusion and restraint, in The Psychiatric Uses of Seclusion and Restraint. Edited by Tardiff K. Washington, DC, American Psychiatric Press, 1984, pp 19–34

19. American Psychiatric Association: The Psychiatric Uses of Seclusion and Restraint (Task Force No 22). Washington, DC, American Psychiatric Association, 1984

20. Bies EB: Mental Health and the Law. Rockville, MD, Aspen, 1984, p 193

21. ILL REV STAT, ch 91 1/2, para 2-109 (1979)

22. Joint Commission on Accreditation of Healthcare Organizations: Consolidated Standards Manual. Chicago, IL, Joint Commission on Accreditation of Healthcare Organizations, 1991, pp 145–147

23. Tinetti ME, Liv WL, Marottoli RA, et al: Mechanical restraint use among residents of skilled nursing facilities. JAMA 265:468–471, 1991

24. Health Care Financing Administration: Medicare/Medicaid Nursing Home Information, 1987–1988. Washington DC, U.S. Department of Health and Human Services, 1989

25. Department of Health and Human Services: Medicare and Medicaid: requirements for long-term care facilities: final rule with request for comments. Federal Register, February 2, 1989, p 5322

26. Reisner R: Law and the Mental Health System. St Paul, MN, West Publishing, 1985, p 472

Section V:

Negligent Treatment

Chapter 16

Negligent Psychotherapy: Maintaining Treatment Boundaries With the Borderline Patient

The Therapist

Dr. Brown, age 45, has been in the private practice of psychiatry for the past 11 years. He treats mainly neurotic and character-disordered patients in two- to three-times-per-week psychotherapy. He finds hospital practice too time-consuming and demanding, usually referring patients who might possibly need hospitalization. Dr. Brown received personal psychotherapy three times per week for 2 years during his residency because of mood lability and angry outbursts that emerged after the birth of his son.

Dr. Brown is a middle child, having a brother 2 years older and a sister 1 year younger. His father was a very successful physician who also was politically active, rising to a high political position in state government. Dr. Brown's father was not at home for long periods of time because of the demands of his practice and political office. Dr. Brown's mother suffered severe postpartum depression after her first child was born. She suffered from recurrent episodes of depression throughout Dr. Brown's childhood.

In his own therapy, Dr. Brown remembered how unavailable his mother was during her depressive episodes. During these depressions, she would cling to him and confide her feelings of anger toward his father and the hopelessness of her life. He suppressed his anger toward his mother by trying to be her rescuer. He felt guilty and inadequate when he could not help her. He turned to his brother for emotional support but still experienced deep feelings of desolation and rejection. When his mother was not depressed, she doted on Dr. Brown, showering him with love and attention. She would tell him that he was a wonderful child. She would take him with her wherever she went, praising him to all her friends. These periods were very happy times, usually coinciding with the more active presence and participation of his father with the family.

Through his therapy, Dr. Brown also discovered that his self-esteem plummeted to very low levels during his mother's depression. He would feel "worthless, powerless, and castrated." When his mother was attentive, he felt "on top of the world; I knew I could do anything." As a child, Dr. Brown was able to buffer himself against his mother's mood shifts through academic achievement and consistent respect and praise from teachers and peers. As an adolescent, he was alternately rebellious and contrite toward his parents. He tried to establish more distance from his mother. When she was depressed, he busied himself with school activities and stayed away from home as much as possible. Much of his anger was directed at his father, whom he blamed for his mother's depression. During college and medical school, he distinguished himself academically. He poured himself into his work. He had time for only an occasional date, until Dr. Brown met the woman who later became his wife.

During the third year of medical school, he married. A son was born during Dr. Brown's internship year. When his wife became occupied with their new baby, he began to experience feelings of anger toward her. Episodes of depression and bewildering feelings of betrayal occurred frequently. He decided to seek treatment.

Dr. Brown soon discovered that the feelings of betrayal were emanating primarily from his relationship with his mother. The feelings also were related to his father's peripheral presence in his life. He began to fear that his anger would destroy his close relationships. He unconsciously turned the anger on himself, which resulted in depression. The birth of a son led to the surfacing of his childhood emotional traumas.

Now, years later, Dr. Brown finds it more satisfying to treat patients who do not suffer from affective disorders, or patients who do not develop intense transference reactions. He is most successful with less disturbed patients who make few demands and work collaboratively with him. He avoids inpatient psychiatry as much as possible.

The Patient

Ms. Gregory, a 24-year-old graduate student, seeks therapy because of increasing marital difficulties. Two years ago, she married a 46-year-old, twice-divorced businessman whom she met at a party. The courtship was intense and tumultuous, lasting 3 months. The couple decided to marry "on the spur of the moment." She describes him "jokingly" as "my good daddy." Ms. Gregory resents her husband's frequent absences on business trips. During the past 6 months, she has developed a sexual liaison with the chairman of her department, with whom she also feels rivalrous.

Ms. Gregory is an only child. Her parents were divorced when she was 9 years old. Her father, a very successful corporate executive, suffered from chronic alcoholism. Ms. Gregory was sexually abused by her father until the time of her parents' divorce. She greatly feared her father and felt powerless to extricate herself from the abuse. Feeling terribly humiliated about the abuse, she could not confide in her mother. Moreover, her mother seemed busy with her interior design business and was not physically present much of the time.

Although Ms. Gregory idealized her mother, her mother seemed distant and unconcerned about her needs. A succession of caregivers provided for her day-to-day care. Feeling abandoned, she would mercilessly torment them. When they tried to set limits, Ms. Gregory had explosive temper tantrums. Caregivers were dismissed when they complained to her mother about her behavior. The relationship between her parents was stormy. Ms. Gregory had the feeling that her mother was aware of the sexual abuse because it was alluded to in a fight between her parents.

Ms. Gregory had few friends in childhood and adolescence. She found it very difficult to trust anyone. She was very successful academically. Because of her striking beauty, she was actively pursued by young men. She showed little interest in them. She attended a strict denominational school and had strong desires to work as a missionary. When she competed in beauty pageants, she usually was a winner or at least a finalist. Ms. Gregory graduated high school at the top of her class and went to the college of her choice.

During her freshman year, she attempted suicide by slashing her wrists when she discovered she was pregnant. At that time, she expressed feelings of worthlessness, but she did not appear particularly depressed. After an induced abortion, she was hospitalized for 3 weeks because of suicidal ideation and depression. During the latter part of her freshman year, she began to abuse alcohol and use cocaine. Her grades dropped dramatically. She had to leave college.

After working a year as a secretary and receiving psychotherapy twice per week, she abstained from alcohol and drugs. She returned to college. Achieving excellent grades in her junior and senior year, she graduated with honors. Although she could initiate relationships with both men and women, a misunderstanding or personal slight inevitably would arise, leading to anger and rejection of the other person. The academic demands of graduate school provided a haven from these difficulties until her marriage and the affair.

The Therapy

During the initial visit, Dr. Brown is struck by the beauty and intelligence of Ms. Gregory. She discusses her marital difficulties, seeking an "opportunity to sort out my feelings about the marriage." Dr. Brown immediately decides to initiate therapy and see the patient three times a week.

During the first month of treatment, Dr. Brown gradually learns about his patient's past psychiatric history and personal difficulties. Ms. Gregory finds that Dr. Brown possesses an empathetic understanding of her difficulties. As

388 *Clinical Psychiatry and the Law, 2nd Edition*

she begins to trust Dr. Brown, Ms. Gregory shares her feelings of "respect and adoration" for her psychiatrist. Dr. Brown looks forward to her appointments. When he is forced to cancel her appointment because of an emergency, he notices a distinct sullenness and aloofness during her next visit.

Ms. Gregory is unable to make a decision about her marriage. She feels that her husband suspects an affair. Her husband gives her an ultimatum: either resign from graduate school or he will leave. She starts having difficulty falling asleep. She also notices that her appetite is decreasing. Ms. Gregory gradually slips into a major depression. She finds it increasingly difficult to leave the office upon the termination of her sessions. She begins to call Dr. Brown at home when suicidal ideas surface. During her sessions, she is clinging and whiny, constantly seeking Dr. Brown's advice and reassurance. After he attempts to interpret her dependent clinging as a quest for the good mother, she becomes more anxious and momentarily disorganized in her thinking. Ms. Gregory feels that Dr. Brown is no longer as attentive to her. Specifically, she senses an irritation and brusqueness in his manner when she calls him at home.

During a session, when Ms. Gregory beseeches him for advice, he recommends she break off the affair with her boss and try to work out her marriage. Dr. Brown is bewildered when Ms. Gregory responds in a towering rage, "I thought you would make such a recommendation—you're nothing but a moral prig. I don't want to hear such gratuitous comments from you again." Dr. Brown feels devastated, confused, and angry. Ms. Gregory continues to make demands for more time and attention. As these demands are inevitably frustrated, she begins to accuse Dr. Brown of abusing her like her father. This transference development flares unexpectedly with a compelling sense of reality for the patient. For brief moments during the session, she actually believes Dr. Brown is her father. Dr. Brown is alarmed at the rapid regression taking place. Interpretations aimed at improving her reality testing seem to terminate these brief psychotic episodes.

Dr. Brown no longer looks forward to seeing Ms. Gregory. Even though her suicidal preoccupations become more frequent, Dr. Brown tries to avoid hospitalization. Although Dr. Brown does have hospital privileges, he dislikes hospitalizing patients. When his patients require hospitalization, Dr. Brown refers them to other psychiatrists who have an inpatient practice. He is concerned that hospitalizing Ms. Gregory will break up the continuity of her therapy. The option of hospitalizing the patient is temporarily shelved. The patient alternates between feelings of adoring and hating Dr. Brown. She explodes into fits of rage when he is unable to meet the many demands she is making for extra appointment times and longer sessions. Whenever Dr. Brown tries to extend himself to the patient, she sabotages his efforts. She will not allow him to rescue her, leaving him feeling thwarted and helpless. She devalues his efforts. In an attempt to gain control over his mounting anger, he harshly reminds himself, "For god's sake—wake up! She is the patient, not you."

Emergency calls in the middle of the night are particularly upsetting to Dr. Brown. After such a call, he is unable to fall back to sleep. He begins to feel trapped and manipulated. Dr. Brown informs the patient that he cannot continue to treat her if she remains unable to control her need to call him constantly, particularly at night. He feels she is manipulating him out of a sense of entitlement. At her next session, Ms. Gregory appears very contrite and promises to try not to call. Three days later, she calls Dr. Brown again in the middle of the night, threatening to stab herself with a knife. He spends an hour on the phone and calms her down. He arranges an emergency appointment to see her the next day.

Dr. Brown is unable to fall back to sleep amid feelings of being controlled and suffocated by the patient. For the first time, he becomes concerned that she might make an actual attempt on her life. In addition, he is quite fatigued and feels very angry at Ms. Gregory the following day. During the emergency appointment, she rages at Dr. Brown's distance and lack of sensitivity, stating, "I will kill myself unless I can see you more often." Dr. Brown flies into a rage, screaming, "I have had enough of you and your manipulation—get out of here and never come back." The patient leaves in tears. After Dr. Brown composes himself, he is terribly chagrined at his outburst. He tries to contact the patient at home that evening but finds instead that she has been severely injured after jumping off the roof of her office building. Ms. Gregory suffers a permanent quadriplegia. Six months after her suicide attempt, Dr. Brown is sued for negligent psychotherapy and abandonment by Ms. Gregory.

What are the two most frequent types of malpractice suits encountered by psychiatrists who treat patients with borderline personality disorder? What factors contribute to these suits?

Therapists who treat patients with borderline personality disorder appear to be sued most frequently for suicide and sexual misconduct (1). Borderline patients typically demonstrate severe rejection sensitivity. Suits for sexual misconduct are *initiated* not so much by the fact of exploitation but rather as a reaction to feeling rejected and abandoned.

By far, the majority of suicides that occur are due to the borderline disorder itself rather than the negligence of the therapist. Failure to diagnose an intercurrent major depression or to appropriately assess suicide risk, however, may lead to allegations of malpractice. As in the vignette, inability to manage treatment boundaries can lead to allegations of negligence if suicide occurs.

The maintenance of treatment boundaries in the treatment of borderline patients and other psychiatric patients is a constant challenge. Boundary violations occur when therapists veer from a position of neutrality to a position of gratification of their own personal needs through the patient. Sexual misconduct begins in the context of gradual treatment boundary excursions until sex with the patient ultimately occurs (1).

Managing the transference of the borderline patient is crucial. Often, these patients want to live out or actualize their feelings toward the therapist. The therapist may feel constant pressure to make exceptions for the patient. Consultants frequently hear comments from therapists who treat borderline patients such as, "I ordinarily don't do this . . ." or, "While I don't usually do this with my patients . . ." or even, "Although I really don't think I should be doing this . . ." (2).

An exploitation index developed by Epstein and Simon (3, 4) can be useful to therapists who are experiencing treatment boundary problems. A survey of 532 psychiatrists using this exploitation index found that approximately two-thirds of the psychiatrists who achieved a high score were alerted and stimulated to make specific changes in their future treatment practices. A more complete discussion of boundary violations is presented in Chapter 17. A correct, initial diagnosis of borderline personality disorder will place the clinician on notice that strict treatment boundaries need to be maintained.

What clinical issues arising in the psychotherapy of patients with borderline personality disorder may have malpractice consequences for the therapist?

Patients with borderline personality disorder have a spectrum of clinical features that not only are difficult to manage therapeutically but also have potential liability consequences for the therapist. In addition, countertransference problems arise frequently in therapists treating borderline patients.

In the clinical vignette, Ms. Gregory presented many of the classic features of borderline personality disorder: good-bad splitting, devaluation, intense rage, narcissistic entitlement, rapidly developing psychotic transference, impulsivity, and projective identification (5). These clinical features were not apparent to Dr. Brown during the course of the initial interview. Frequently, borderline patients may make a good initial clinical impression, particularly if they possess high intelligence or other attractive qualities and personal accomplishments. Therefore, the therapist should allow for a period of evaluation that will permit an accurate diagnosis, differential diagnosis, and treatment plan. Patients who have had manifestations of severe psychopathology or regression in the past may develop these difficulties again in the course of therapy.

With accurate diagnosis, a reasonably predictable clinical course can be expected. Dr. Brown did not allow himself sufficient time to adequately evaluate and diagnose Ms. Gregory. Psychologically blinded by her intelligence and beauty, he was unable to see the severe psychopathology just beneath the surface. Because Dr. Brown relied heavily on intellect as one of his main psychological defenses, he overvalued its significance in assessing Ms. Gregory.

The importance of making a psychiatric diagnosis on each patient cannot be overemphasized. Psychodynamic formulations are important but do not have the prognostic significance of an accurate diagnosis. Psychiatrists are less likely to be surprised by the patient's clinical course if they take the trouble of formulating a working diagnosis. The *Diagnostic and Statistical Manual of Mental Disorders,* 3rd Edition, Revised (DSM-III-R) diagnosis of borderline personality disorder emphasizes chronically suicidal and self-mutilating tendencies as major characteristics of these patients (6). Diagnostic formulations should be made as a matter of course.

The various clinical aspects of borderline personality disorder pose special problems for therapists, sometimes creating opportunities for legal liability (7). The patient's good-bad splitting was very confusing to Dr. Brown. The patient's criticism of his treatment efforts as insufficient and insensitive angered him. He tried to control his anger and gain clinical perspective by reminding himself that she was the patient. He was alternately adored and hated. When Ms. Gregory beseeched his advice and he gave it, Dr. Brown was bewildered as the patient turned on him with intense rage. She projected on him a disavowed aspect of herself—"You're nothing but a moral prig"—and tried to control that aspect of herself by warning the therapist, "I don't want to hear such gratuitous comments again." The effect of this good-bad splitting and projective identification on the unwary or inexperienced therapist can easily engender bewilderment and even mounting anger. This can, in turn, lead to boundary violations in the therapist.

The therapist may be caught off guard as the idealization breaks down and the underlying angry feelings of the patient surface. Ms. Gregory's demands for extra appointments and longer sessions expressed her sense of entitlement. It was clinically appropriate to provide more appointments as her clinical condition deteriorated. Nevertheless, Dr. Brown felt manipulated, becoming involved in a power struggle with the patient.

The intense feelings engendered in the therapist by borderline patients may interfere with sound clinical judgment (7). Patients who demand special treatment may create angry, withholding reactions that lead to destructive power struggles between patient and therapist. Maintaining a position of flexible therapeutic neutrality with the borderline patient is important. In psychoanalytic terms, the therapist functions as a participant observer poised equidistant between reality and the patient's ego, superego, and id. Without reacting directly to the provocative patient, the therapist needs to ask, "What does it mean that the patient puts me in this position?" Mismanagement of treatment boundaries may lead to the provision of negligent psychotherapy.

Therapists also may become frightened by the rapid regression of a borderline patient. Psychotic transference can develop very rapidly, leading to overreactions by the therapist. Breaches of confidentiality, ill-advised interventions, or abandonment through inappropriate referral or discharge may result. Dr.

Brown was able to manage the psychotic transference therapeutically through interpretations aimed at strengthening the patient's defenses. However, he was unable to contain the patient's acting out, manifested by telephone calls at all hours of the night. Thus, he allowed himself to feel trapped and badgered by the patient, as he did with his mother when he was a child.

Patients cannot be effectively treated when they hold the therapist hostage at the point of a psychological gun because of destructive acting out. Acting out that cannot be controlled through usual treatment interventions may require the structured setting of a hospital, particularly if the acting out is destructive to the patient's treatment. Because Dr. Brown disliked hospital work, he temporized in hospitalizing Ms. Gregory. Mental health professionals who treat borderline patients must be prepared to hospitalize a patient who is in a crisis or should at least be prepared to refer the patient for hospitalization. Ideally, therapists should be able to hospitalize their own patients to maintain continuity of care. Psychological abandonment of borderline patients is not an uncommon countertransferential response by therapists. If the patient is harmed, a malpractice suit may be filed.

Dr. Brown failed to hospitalize a suicidally depressed borderline patient. Ostensibly, this critical intervention was not pursued because of Dr. Brown's preference for managing his patients outside of the hospital. Given the countertransference problems Dr. Brown was experiencing toward his patient, it appears that he had difficulties separating from her.

Dr. Brown did not distinguish between suicidal behavior as an emergency state and suicidal behavior as a chronic maladaptational life-style (8, 9). The acute suicidal state often presents itself in the context of a major depression with the associated vegetative features of sleep disturbances, anhedonia, and weight changes. With acute suicidal states, all efforts are made to assist the patient through the crisis until self-destructive impulses have passed. In the chronically suicidal patient, therapeutic interventions are aimed at enabling the patient to face and master conflicts rather than avoid or escape through the option of suicide. Rage rather than depression appears to underlie chronic, recurrent suicidal episodes. Paradoxically, the option of suicide is a solace to some patients who fear being overwhelmed by feelings and impulses. The idea of suicide may provide the patient with some feeling of control. Nevertheless, chronically suicidal patients may have life-threatening exacerbations of self-destructive impulses.

Dr. Brown felt that Ms. Gregory was attempting to extract entitlements through her threats of suicide. Dr. Brown's power struggle with his patient did not permit him to explore the motivations behind the patient's manipulation or allow him to see the acute crisis aspects of her suicidal depression. Missing the diagnosis of an intercurrent major depression in a patient with borderline personality disorder is a major clinical error fraught with potentially serious legal consequences.

What are some of the malpractice pitfalls that may accompany countertransference issues encountered by therapists who treat borderline patients?

Countertransference problems are inevitable in the treatment of the borderline patient. The ability to use these reactions for the benefit of the patient's treatment is critical. All therapists, being human, have certain vulnerabilities and limitations. Therapists who treat borderline patients should have a good working knowledge of their own conflicts and defensive operations. Vulnerabilities inevitably will be tested by the borderline patient. Those therapists who remain ignorant of their own professional limitations may become rudely acquainted with them in a court of law. Slovenko (10) states: "Good sense, the law, and professional ethics would all maintain that one should not undertake services in a matter outside of one's competence. If services are undertaken by a therapist who discovers that he or she cannot properly care for the patient, an affirmative duty exists to seek qualified help." Qualified help also may mean treatment for the therapist, if indicated. Additionally, a period of self-analysis, or "analytic toilet" (advocated by the English psychoanalyst Edward Glover), should be considered by a therapist who is experiencing consistent difficulties in the treatment of certain patients (11).

In *Hess v. Frank* (12), the psychiatrist treated the patient from 1961 to September 1969. On September 26, 1969, the patient alleged that during a regularly scheduled session, without just cause, the psychiatrist became abusive to the patient, uttering various words and phrases that the psychiatrist knew or should have known in his professional capacity would cause grave mental anguish and be injurious to the health of the patient. The alleged abusive statements were uttered during the course of an argument over fees as well as the appointment schedule. The patient sought $100,000 in damages.

The court dismissed the patient's case against the psychiatrist. The court held that the argument was outside of the professional treatment relationship. From the clinician's perspective, however, the court's position that discussions or even arguments about billing somehow exist outside the scope of therapy is unrealistic. All issues that arise in the course of therapy are grist for the therapeutic mill. The court stated: "The conduct complained of, however, was not part of the course of treatment and there is no claim or indication that defendant failed to provide medical services in accordance with accepted standards or that he did not exercise requisite skills in the treatment of the plaintiff." Apparently, the court did not consider the possibility of mismanagement of the countertransference by the psychiatrist, who, after treating the patient for 8 years, "without any just cause, became abusive to the patient."

Obviously, therapists who lose their temper with patients have lost control of the treatment. When the therapist screams at the patient, the therapy is invariably over. For example, the Washington Psychiatric Society reported an ethical violation by one of its members (13). A patient in individual therapy was transferred to group therapy with the same doctor but decided not to continue. At the session, the psychiatrist "made angry and denigrating comments about the patient." The psychiatrist refused to allow the patient to reply, ordering the patient to leave. The investigation revealed that the psychiatrist "allowed his anger at the patient rather than thoughtful therapeutic intent to govern in actions at the last group session." The psychiatrist was admonished for violating Section I of *The Principles of Medical Ethics,* which states, "A physician shall be dedicated to providing competent medical service with compassion and respect for human dignity." Gutheil's (7) axiom—that bad results plus bad feelings lead to malpractice suits—is particularly important to keep in mind when treating patients with borderline personality disorder.

Dr. Brown was limited in his effectiveness in treating patients manifesting depressive symptoms, manipulative tendencies, and intense clinging, dependent, angry transference reactions. Dr. Brown's early relationship with his mother contained many of these issues. Through therapy, he had some awareness of his vulnerabilities and confined himself to the treatment of less disturbed patients. The almost symbiotic relationship with his mother in which he was subjected to her intense mood swings and outpourings of anger and hopelessness was overwhelming to him as a child. The inconstancy of his mother's moods and her unavailability led to a deep sense of betrayal and distrust that mobilized his feelings of rage. In part, Dr. Brown's wish to rescue his mother was a defense against these angry feelings. His personal psychological problems, combined with the patient's intense affects and demands, interfered with his clinical judgment. His anger built up and finally exploded at the patient, precipitating her abandonment and suicidal plunge.

Can the therapist's childhood and personal psychodynamics be used as a defense in a malpractice suit? Can the limitations of therapists be used as a risk management technique?

A therapist's childhood and personal psychodynamics have no direct bearing in a civil case, nor can these issues be raised as a defense in a malpractice suit. Therapists should have a reasonably thorough knowledge of their personal strengths and weaknesses when treating and managing certain psychiatric patients. This facilitates good clinical practice as well as helps to avoid legal entanglements with patients.

Even the most experienced therapist cannot always effectively treat the borderline patient. Therapists are not born with the knowledge of how to treat these difficult patients. All therapists must begin from a state of ignorance and inexperience. Supervision and consultation with other therapists who have more training and experience should be considered when the clinician is having difficulties understanding or managing the care and treatment of any patient. Dr. Jonas Rappeport's maxim about consultation is extremely important to remember: "When in doubt, shout" (14). Therapists are liable for failure to refer if they knew or should have known that a clinical problem existed that they were not competent to manage (10). Dr. Brown should have diagnosed the patient's borderline personality disorder and considered his own limitations with such a patient, referring her elsewhere for competent help.

Because the treatment of borderline patients is replete with unexpected clinical twists and turns, careful documentation of the reasoning behind treatment interventions should be made. Sometimes the therapist is required to make a treatment intervention that appears contrary to a layperson's logic, such as a well-thought-out, clinically indicated discharge from the hospital that is complicated by regression (7). The discharge appears to fly in the face of the patient's regression, even though clinical assessment has been careful and indicates that the patient can tolerate the temporary anxiety surrounding discharge. The reasoning governing the clinical decision should be carefully documented. Good clinical documentation is the psychiatrist's best friend in court.

In treating borderline and other disturbed patients, therapists must be able to tolerate some degree of being "on call." Late night calls are not unusual. On occasion, the therapist must be prepared to give the patient his or her home phone. Therapists who cannot tolerate this type of intensity and involvement probably should not treat these patients. Dr. Brown is not psychologically prepared or able to make that type of commitment to his patient. Moreover, therapists must be able to withstand the uncertainty and calculated risks involved in the treatment of very disturbed patients. Therapists who find it difficult to tailor their treatment interventions to the needs of disturbed patients while maintaining treatment boundaries will inevitably provide ineffective or even harmful treatment, leading to possible allegations of negligent psychotherapy.

There is no shame in admitting limitations in treating certain patients. All therapists have limitations. Knowledge of these limitations can be used as a risk management technique in avoiding patients whom the therapist might have a tendency to treat negligently.

What are the legal difficulties in pursuing a claim of negligent psychotherapy?

Dr. Brown was sued for negligent psychotherapy and abandonment. (The topic of abandonment is discussed in Chapter 18.) To prove negligent psychotherapy, the plaintiff must show through expert testimony that Dr. Brown deviated from the standard of care of a reasonable and prudent psychiatrist. Moreover, the plaintiff must demonstrate by a preponderance of the evidence that the deviation in care was the direct cause of injuries sustained by Ms. Gregory, namely, quadriplegia.

With the exception of suits involving sexual misconduct, abandonment, and gross acting out by the therapist, malpractice suits alleging negligent psychotherapy are rare (15). Negligent psychotherapy suits are difficult to win because proving that a departure occurred from the standard of care is so problematic. For example, therapists disagree about the indications and effectiveness of the more than 450 psychotherapeutic modalities currently used. Proximate cause is equally difficult to establish, because so many factors can influence the course of an illness. Until relatively recently, courts did not allow for a determination of psychic injury apart from physical damage. Skepticism abounds regarding psychic injury alone. Furthermore, what one therapist considers symptoms of psychic damage, another may welcome as signs of progress. It is an axiom among therapists that progress cannot occur in therapy without some psychic pain.

In malpractice actions, the standard of care is the degree of skill and learning that is ordinarily possessed and exercised by members in good standing in the profession (10). The plaintiff must find an expert to testify to the standard of care and the deviation from that standard. A psychiatrist is judged according to his or her school and mode of therapy, even if that school represents only a respected minority of professionals. A single practitioner following his or her own theoretical principles does not constitute a respected minority. With so many schools of psychotherapy in existence, it usually is not difficult to find a supportive expert.

Can psychiatrists testify against psychologists and social workers or vice versa? According to Slovenko (10), the school rule is "one may testify about another school when the methods of treatment for a particular ailment are generally the same in both schools." In *Lundgren v. Eustermann* (16), a licensed psychologist with an extensive background in psychopharmacotherapy was found competent to give expert testimony challenging a physician's treatment of a patient with chlorpromazine. On appeal, the Minnesota Supreme Court held that a licensed psychologist was not qualified to give an opinion in a malpractice action on the standard of care required of a medical doctor (17). Also, in *McDonnell v. County of Nassau* (18), the court held that psychologists are not qualified to testify as expert witnesses in medical malpractice suits brought against psychiatrists or the hospitals with which psychiatrists are affiliated.

If statutes specify a standard of care, experts may not be required to establish a standard. The violation of a statute constitutes negligence per se under tort law (10). Experts may not be required when the issue at hand is within common knowledge, or when the act complained about itself indicates improper treatment. In the latter circumstance, the doctrine of *res ipsa loquitur* ("the thing speaks for itself") may be invoked. The standard of care may also be demonstrated by published standards, by package inserts, or through medical treatises.

Burgeoning efforts to standardize psychiatric treatment through the development of treatment manuals also may establish a standard of care. In the late

1970s, researchers began to develop treatment-specific manuals to form a basis for comparing the various psychotherapies (19, 20). The American Psychiatric Association has published a three-volume treatment manual describing the state of the art for treating 23 different disorders without endorsing any particular form of therapy (21). However, no official treatment manual or guidelines can substitute for sound clinical judgment as applied to a particular patient. Insurance carriers can be expected to expand standard setting for psychiatric treatments that may be eventually referred to as a standard of care in psychiatric malpractice cases. Standards of practice also will be influenced by the Health Care Financing Administration (22) and professional practice guidelines (23).

With over 450 different schools of psychotherapy in existence and the court's disinclination to judge the appropriateness or efficacy of competing reputable schools, determinations of standard of care become extremely difficult (24). On the other hand, when outmoded therapies are used but more effective therapies are available, the claim of negligent treatment may be more readily raised (10).

Did Dr. Brown deviate from the standard of care in his treatment of Ms. Gregory? Was he negligent in not initially making the diagnosis of borderline personality disorder? Mismanagement of countertransference feelings that led to the precipitous discharge of a suicidal patient who then attempted suicide would be considered clear negligence. Quite likely, an expert for the plaintiff would assert that Dr. Brown substantially departed from a reasonable standard of care in the treatment of Ms. Gregory.

In malpractice cases alleging negligent psychotherapy, causation is also very difficult to establish. The statement is often heard that psychotherapy does no good. Can it then be expected to do any harm? The natural course of an illness may be the reason for deterioration in the patient's clinical picture. How, then, does one determine the influence of the therapist on the patient for ill or for good?

To establish negligence, it may be necessary to establish a pattern of behavior. In *Roy v. Hartogs* (25), former patients of Dr. Hartogs came forward after reading about the case and testified against him, establishing the likelihood of negligence. A pattern may reveal abuse or incompetence. Obtaining such evidence must meet fairly rigid evidentiary rules, or it will lack probative value and be excluded (10).

Alleging suicide due to the negligence of a therapist in the treatment of a borderline patient may also be very difficult to prove. For example, a borderline patient becomes impulsively involved in a destructive relationship between weekly sessions. The patient agrees to a firm "contract" with the therapist to call if a crisis arises. The patient becomes acutely depressed and attempts suicide without calling the therapist. Even if the therapist improvidently relies upon a crisis contract, a legal argument can be made that the suicide was the product of a borderline personality disorder manifesting severe mood and interpersonal instability. Generally, the law regards an independent superseding variable as breaking the chain of causation. In the preceding hypothetical situation, the existing mental disorder would constitute a superseding variable, thus excusing the psychiatrist for unwisely relying on the "contract" (26).

What are some of the clinical-legal dilemmas surrounding termination of the stalemated patient?

The continued treatment of any patient in the face of deterioration or lack of improvement may raise the issue of negligent psychotherapy. The therapist has a duty to terminate treatment that is ineffective or harmful (27). Therapists have a duty to act in good faith toward patients by informing them, whenever necessary, that a certain treatment is of no benefit (28). The duty to terminate also requires that patients who need continued treatment be appropriately referred. Specialists should be consulted who can provide other or better treatment, especially if the psychiatrist knows or should know that the present treatment is not proving to be effective in relieving or curing the patient's condition (29). If termination is not considered feasible, at the very least a consultation should be obtained.

Patients who remain in long-term psychotherapy without improvement but then improve rapidly with psychopharmacological treatment may claim negligent treatment (30, 31). Some patients express a preference for psychotherapy over drug treatment, even though the latter might bring quicker results and is clearly indicated. This preference may be honored if the patient is properly informed of alternative therapies that may be more effective, and if psychotherapy is not contraindicated. Even though the patient competently consents, the clinician may not want to provide a less effective treatment. Under these circumstances, the patient should be referred.

Prolonged stalemates in psychotherapy are not unusual. Patients regularly produce infantile, dependent transference that may remain intractable to psychotherapeutic intervention over many years. Often, it is difficult to distinguish between the patient who requires years or even a lifetime of supportive therapy to function at a job, to remain in a family, or to prevent frequent hospitalizations, and a patient stalemated in a treatment relationship that has ceased to be therapeutic.

The former situation is similar to the diabetic patient who requires maintenance insulin therapy throughout life. On the other hand, the stalemated patient resists making any substantial internal or external changes, but rather lives in and for the therapy. Many of these patients have endured difficult families and deprived circumstances. Their best relationship often is with the therapist, so the temptation to replace life with therapy is very strong. Thus, the treatment itself becomes a defensive avoidance of life. Stalemated patients and patients who manifest negative therapeutic reactions to improvement should be considered for termination only after they prove intractable to concerted efforts at appropriate therapy. Consultation with another therapist is prudent. Consideration also should be given to obtaining supervision from a knowledgeable and experienced therapist before termination is implemented.

How should the therapist attempt to terminate the permanently stalemated patient? Even after thorough consideration of the psychological implications of termination with the patient, the therapist may fear that the patient will undergo a severe emotional crisis or psychotic episode. Termination and transfer to another therapist may have to occur within the hospital context. The fear that a patient will regress should not, by itself, prevent the therapist from transferring or terminating a patient who is permanently stalemated.

Therapists and patients often have a very different sense of time when it comes to evaluating the length of therapy. For some therapists, therapy is timeless. Often, stalemates that go on for years are rationalized until the therapist realizes, in a moment of agonizing recognition, that no substantial progress has been made after hundreds of hours and thousands of dollars have been spent. Moreover, the patient may have lost the opportunity to benefit from a more effective treatment. Diverting a person from therapy that may have provided a "substantial possibility of recovery" is malpractice (32). A disillusioned patient may seek legal redress for an alleged provision of negligent psychotherapy (29).

The psychotherapy of borderline patients increases the therapist's risk of liability because of the unique psychopathology of these patients. Certain of these patients pull a "gotcha" reaction, goading and provoking the therapist into a treatment faux pas. Then they feel, through the use of projective defenses, "Aha! My split-denied projective identification has worked! I can kill myself with a clear conscience, knowing that all the hostility and guilt lies on the therapist's side" (33). Dr. Brown was a recipient of this type of provocative behavior reflecting good-bad splitting and projection.

Abusive, provocative behavior needs to be interpreted immediately. If interpretation proves insufficient, direct confrontation with the consequences of the patient's behavior is required. The therapist cannot conduct therapy amid continuing abuse and threatening behavior. In these instances, consultation should be considered. Hospitalization of the patient may be necessary. Unfortunately, Dr. Brown allowed his patient's destructive acting-out behavior to go on to the point at which he lost control of himself and abusively, impulsively terminated Ms. Gregory. Acting-out behavior should be therapeutically engaged as soon as it emerges. Otherwise, this behavior can unleash acting out in the therapist that may become destructive to the patient's therapy. Strategies for structuring the outpatient treatment of borderline patients to limit acting out and to preserve the therapy are described by Kernberg (34). Malpractice allegations may develop from either the destructive consequences of the patient's acting out (often suicide) or the therapist's retaliation. Also, ethical complaints may be filed by patients.

It would not be difficult to establish that Dr. Brown's mishandling of his countertransference feelings, leading to the abrupt rejection and discharge of his suicidal patient, was the direct cause of her suicide attempt. Damage to Ms. Gregory is clear because of the physical injury (i.e., the quadriplegia). As stated above, proving emotional harm or psychic damage alone may be difficult. Few cases are reported (35). The above analysis shows, however, that the allegations of negligent psychotherapy against Dr. Brown meet the criteria for professional negligence, because a deviation in the standard of care was the direct cause of harm to the patient.

References

1. Simon RI: Sexual exploitation of patients: how it begins before it happens. Psychiatric Annals 12:104–112, 1989
2. Gutheil TG: Borderline personality disorder, boundary violations, and patient-therapist sex: medicolegal pitfalls. Am J Psychiatry 146:597–602, 1989
3. Epstein RS, Simon RI: The Exploitation Index: an early warning indicator of boundary violations in psychotherapy. Bull Menninger Clin 54:450–465, 1990
4. Epstein RS, Simon RI, Kay GG: Assessing boundary violations in psychotherapy: survey results with the Exploitation Index. Bull Menninger Clin 56(2):1–17, 1992
5. Kernberg O: Borderline Conditions and Pathological Narcissism. New York, Jason Aronson, 1975, pp 8–12
6. American Psychiatric Association: Diagnostic and Statistical Manual of Mental Disorders, 3rd Edition, Revised. Washington, DC, American Psychiatric Association, 1987, pp 346–347
7. Gutheil TG: Medicolegal pitfalls in the treatment of borderline patients. Am J Psychiatry 142:9–14, 1985
8. Olin HS: Psychotherapy of the chronically suicidal patient. Am J Psychother 30:570–575, 1976
9. Schwartz DA, Flinn DE, Slawson PF: Treatment of the suicidal character. Am J Psychother 28:194–207, 1974
10. Slovenko R: Malpractice in psychiatry and related fields. Journal of Psychiatry and Law 9:5–63, 1981
11. Glover E: The Technique of Psychoanalysis. New York, International Universities Press, 1968, p 92
12. 47 AD2d 889, 367 NYS2d 30 (NY App Div 1975)
13. Ethics alert. The Washington Psychiatric Society Newsletter, April 1990, p 7
14. R Slovenko, personal communication, January 1985
15. Simon RI: The practice of psychotherapy: legal liabilities of an "impossible" profession, in American Psychiatric Press Review of Clinical Psychiatry and the Law, Vol 2. Edited by Simon RI. Washington, DC, American Psychiatric Press, 1991, pp 3–91
16. 356 NW2d 762 (Minn Ct App 1984), rev'd, Lundgren v Eustermann, 370 NW2d 877 (Minn 1985)
17. Lundgren v Eustermann, 370 NW2d 877 (Minn Sup Ct 1985)
18. 129 Misc 2d 228, 492 NYS2d 699 (NY Sup Ct 1985)

19. Klerman GL, Weissman MM, Rounsaville BJ, et al: Interpersonal Psychotherapy in Depression. New York, Basic Books, 1984

20. Beck AT, Rush AJ, Shaw BF, et al: Cognitive Theory of Depression. New York, Guilford, 1979

21. American Psychiatric Association Task Force on Treatments of Psychiatric Disorders: Treatments of Psychiatric Disorders, Vols 1–3. Washington, DC, American Psychiatric Association, 1989

22. Psychiatrist must be aware of psychiatric quality screens. Psychiatric News 25(17):24–25, 1990

23. Work begins on practice guidelines. Psychiatric News 25(22)3, 28–29, 1990

24. United States v Klein, 325 F2d 283 (2d Cir 1963)

25. 85 Misc 2d 891, 381 NYS2d 587 (NY Sup Ct 1976)

26. Keeton WP, Dobb DB, Keeton RE, et al: Prosser and Keeton on Torts, 5th Edition. St Paul, MN, West Publishing, 1984, pp 301–319

27. Furrow BR: Malpractice in Psychotherapy. Lexington, MA, DC Heath, 1980, p 39

28. Malpractice: physicians' failure to advise patient to consult specialist or one qualified in a method of treatment which the physician is not qualified to give. 35 ALR 3d 349 (1971)

29. Simon RI: Psychiatric Interventions and Malpractice: A Primer for Liability Prevention. Springfield, IL, Charles C Thomas, 1982, p 57

30. Stone AA: The new paradox of psychiatric malpractice. N Engl J Med 311:1384–1387, 1984

31. Osheroff v Chestnut Lodge, 490 A2d 720, 722 (Md App 1985)

32. Hicks v United States, 368 F2d 626 (4th Cir 1966)

33. TG Gutheil, personal communication, April 1985

34. Kernberg OF: Psychotherapy with borderline patients, in Specialized Techniques in Individual Psychotherapy. Edited by Karasu BT, Bellak L. New York, Brunner/Mazel, 1980

35. Klein JI, Macbeth JE, Onek JN: Legal Issues in the Private Practice of Psychiatry. Washington, DC, American Psychiatric Press, 1984, p 5

Chapter 17 | # Undue Familiarity: The Sexual Misconduct of Psychotherapists

The Doctor

Dr. James is a 54-year-old psychiatrist who has practiced for approximately 25 years in the same community. He is married and has a teenage son and daughter. Dr. James spends long hours seeing patients in psychodynamic psychotherapy. He is board certified in his specialty and is respected for the clinical contributions he has made to the professional literature. During the last 5 years, his marriage has been troubled, but there is no thought of divorce. Dr. James and his wife take separate vacations and live, for the most part, separate lives. They have infrequent sexual relations.

Formerly quite active in the community and an avid golfer, Dr. James gradually has lost interest in these activities. He rarely sees colleagues or attends professional functions. He spends more time by himself. He no longer keeps in contact with his friends. Dr. James's teenage son is particularly difficult and constantly tests his authority. His teenage daughter had a brush with drugs. His wife is busy with her own social circle. She has been drinking more during the past 1 $\frac{1}{2}$ years. Dr. James himself requires a drink or two at night in order to fall asleep. Although Dr. James has been doing intensive psychodynamic therapy over the years, he has never had any personal therapy or analysis. He now finds his practice to be boring and the treatment responsibilities of patients burdensome.

The Patient

Ms. Wilson is an attractive 28-year-old woman who has been married for 3 years to a very successful 45-year-old businessman. They have no children. The patient comes to see Dr. James because of moderate to severe depression since the beginning of her marriage. She is sexually unresponsive and aloof from her husband, despite his being very solicitous of her. Recently, she has developed recurrent suicidal thoughts.

Ms. Wilson is an only child. At 3 years of age, her father died suddenly. Her mother became depressed and was psychologically unavailable to her after her

father's death. She remembers having frequent fantasies about being reunited with her father. Between the ages of 3 1/2 to 8, she experienced nightmares about her mother dying violently in an automobile accident. Ms. Wilson recalls that once the nightmares subsided, she was able to concentrate on her school-work and became an excellent student. She did not make many friends in school, describing herself as a loner. At age 18, she became pregnant during a brief adolescent love affair. She had an induced abortion. One week after the abortion, she became suicidally depressed. After cutting her wrists, she was hospitalized for 2 weeks of psychiatric care.

Ms. Wilson met her husband shortly after the failure of an important love relationship just over 3 years ago. In order to ease her feelings of loss and depression, she went on a cruise, where they met. They were married after 3 months of courtship, but she experienced very strong, ambivalent feelings about getting married.

The Therapy

Ms. Wilson undertakes three-times-per-week psychotherapy. Significant improvement in her depression occurs after 2 months of treatment. As she begins to idealize her therapist, her suicidal ideation disappears. The relationship with her husband, however, remains distant and strained. In due course, she begins to talk about feelings of "love" for Dr. James, which briefly disquiets her. She feels that he is omnipotent and will cure her. As time goes on, Ms. Wilson feels very safe in her sessions. The therapist attempts to interpret the idealized feelings toward him but stops when he sees that these interpretations are upsetting and angering the patient. She not only develops an idealizing transference toward Dr. James, but soon erotic feelings begin to color the transference. The patient makes solicitous comments like, "You seem aloof and depressed." Dr. James finds himself looking forward to the sessions with the patient.

The tenor of the sessions gradually shifts toward a social relationship, with the patient responding positively. Doctor and patient begin to address each other by their first names. Dr. James compliments the patient on her appearance. At times, uncharacteristically, he suggests how she might dress to maximize her attractiveness. Ms. Wilson complies with his suggestions. Dr. James divulges personal details about his marriage and frustrations. A handshake at the end of the hour progresses to a hug. The treatment sessions are rescheduled for the end of the day. Six months into the treatment, Dr. James moves from his chair, spending more time sitting with Ms. Wilson on the couch. Occasional hand holding and kissing occur. Dinner dates followed by a movie occur after therapy sessions.

Ms. Wilson now becomes frightened, wanting to cut back the frequency of her sessions. She wonders about obtaining a consultation. Dr. James realizes his overinvolvement but does not become alarmed because he feels he can extri-

cate himself by reestablishing treatment boundaries. He reassures Ms. Wilson that a consultation is not necessary and that the "therapy should be deepened." Her fears dissipate. About 1 year after beginning treatment, the patient begins to openly fantasize about having a "healing" sexual relationship with Dr. James. For the first time, Dr. James seriously considers acting on the patient's fantasy. He knows sexual involvement with the patient is unethical as well as malpractice. Dr. James, however, has never felt such "love" for anyone else before. He is transported by the fullness of her gaze, the richness of her smile, and the beauty and elegance of her hands. He cannot bear the prospect of foregoing a romantic relationship with his patient. He feels this is his last chance at happiness. Dr. James struggles with himself but finally decides that the relationship with the patient is an exception to the influence of transference and countertransference upon his clinical judgment. He feels truly in love. He further rationalizes that a sexual relationship might bring the patient out of her isolation and focus her more on the importance of relationships, acting as a corrective emotional experience for her sexual difficulties and her chronically low self-esteem. Dr. James admonishes his patient that if they undertake a sexual relationship, it must be kept absolutely secret. Dr. James stops billing the patient as they prepare for the "new phase" of treatment.

Ms. Wilson feels ambivalent about embarking on a sexual relationship with her therapist, but she is hopeful it will help. Secretly she expects this "new phase" to cure her depression and allow her to have a permanent relationship with Dr. James. Shortly after the initiation of the sexual relationship, her depression deepens and strong suicidal impulses reemerge. Frightened, she expresses rage at Dr. James, who then panics, terminating the relationship abruptly. He refers her to another psychiatrist for continued treatment. Ms. Wilson feels abandoned and betrayed. For the first time she feels intense rage mixed with feelings of love and yearning toward Dr. James.

Two weeks after beginning work with her new therapist, she hears the voice of Dr. James telling her to kill herself. She is found by her husband attempting to hang herself in the basement. She is immediately hospitalized, where she remains for 6 weeks. One year after her discharge, Ms. Wilson files a malpractice suit against Dr. James. She also investigates the possibility of filing criminal charges. Her husband sues the psychiatrist for loss of consortium after the patient files for divorce. In his defense, Dr. James asserts that the sexual relationship was considered part of the patient's therapy and that the patient had "freely given her consent."

Is it always negligence for a psychiatrist to have sex with his or her patient?

Yes. Sexual activity between a psychiatrist and the patient is negligence per se. The psychiatrist holds himself or herself out to the public as having standard professional skill and knowledge. The psychiatrist "must have and use the knowledge, skill and care ordinarily possessed and employed by members of the profession in good standing" (1). Since not even a respected minority of psychiatrists would state that sex with a patient falls within the standard skill and knowledge of good-standing psychiatrists, sex between psychiatrist and patient is an unquestioned and unchallenged deviation in the standard of care.

Illinois (2), California (3), Minnesota (4), and Wisconsin (5) make therapist-patient sex negligence per se by statute, creating a nonrebuttable presumption concerning the therapist's duty of care. To establish liability, the plaintiff need only prove that sexual contact occurred and caused him or her damage.

In legislation prohibiting therapists' sexual exploitation of patients, sexual behavior is defined in a variety of ways, some so vague as to invite constitutional challenges based on violation of the due-process clause in the United States Constitution and state constitutions (6). Most statutes define sexual activity as intercourse, rape, the touching of breasts and genitals, cunnilingus, fellatio, sodomy, and inappropriate or unnecessary examinations and procedures performed for sexual gratification. Obviously, statutory definitions cannot possibly encompass the wide range of sexual activities that constitute abuse of patients by therapists.

In *The Principles of Medical Ethics With Annotations Especially Applicable to Psychiatry* (7), sex with patients is unequivocally prohibited:

> The requirement that the physician conduct himself with propriety in his/her profession and in all the actions of his/her life is especially important in the case of the psychiatrist because the patient tends to model his/her behavior after that of his/her therapist by identification. Further, the necessary intensity of the therapeutic relationship may tend to activate sexual and other needs and fantasies on the part of both patient and therapist, while weakening the objectivity necessary for control. Sexual activity with a patient is unethical.

This ethical position has a venerable history. One version of the Hippocratic oath that dates back at least 2,500 years sets the following standard: "In every house where I come, I will enter only for the good of my patients, keeping myself far from all intentional ill-doing and all seduction and especially from the pleasures of love of women and men."

Presently, no psychiatrists can be found who will assert that sex with patients falls within an acceptable standard of care. Cummings and Sobel (8), after reviewing malpractice claims against psychologists, state that "only one person has been exonerated" of sexual misconduct in cases that have been filed. When the fact of a sexual relationship between psychiatrist and patient has been established, it is unlikely that the psychiatrist will escape liability (9). Perr (10) points out that American Psychiatric Association (APA) figures indicate that at least 15% of legal cases are related to sexual activities. Psychiatrists also run the risk of loss of licensure, criminal sanctions, and expulsion from professional organizations (11). Nonmedical therapists are equally vulnerable to malpractice for undue familiarity with patients.

Dr. James's admission of sex with his patient runs counter to the general finding that therapists who have had personal therapy tend to make such admissions. As a legal defense, Dr. James asserts that he was providing a "corrective emotional experience" through the sexual relationship with his patient and that the patient had "freely given her consent." The courts have consistently rejected claims of patient consent to a sexual relationship because transference phenomena have precluded a truly voluntary decision. Furthermore, the courts have stated that patients cannot consent to a professionally unacceptable treatment. As Gutheil and Appelbaum (12) state: "The claim that in no other setting would the physical expression of sexual longing be categorized as negligence on the part of one of the parties, though true, merely emphasizes the uniqueness of the psychotherapeutic dyad."

Do psychiatrists who see patients in consultation, evaluation, medication follow-up, or group therapy fall under the same ethical and legal prohibitions against sexual involvement with patients?

In an evaluation or consultation, the usual doctor-patient relationship may not exist. Whether the patient could bring a malpractice claim for undue familiarity is primarily a legal issue. The ethical issue remains unchanged, however, and sex during a treatment session is always potentially legally actionable.

Often, the most disturbed patients are the ones who are seen solely for medication appointments rather than for psychotherapy. Nevertheless, because of the extent of regression, powerful transference reactions may occur. The therapist is at a disadvantage in not having an ongoing therapy situation that permits assessments of the transference. Not surprisingly, some therapists who see patients infrequently espouse theoretical orientations that do not place much emphasis on transference phenomena. Moreover, in group therapy, intense patient transferences can become focused on the therapist without the benefit of the close scrutiny that a one-to-one therapy may provide.

Trainee therapists must also abide by the same ethical principles as fully trained therapists. Supervisors should be aware of sexual issues as they develop from the trainee's supervision. Ethical principles as well as the clinical management of sexual feelings in both the trainee and the patient need to be openly discussed.

Perr (10), on the other hand, feels that "psychotherapy occupies a special status" and that the same rules of sexual involvement with patients cannot be applied to evaluations, consultations, supportive therapy, and medication-oriented therapy. He counsels flexibility on a case-by-case basis rather than applying a mandatory rule. He states, "It does not seem reasonable to be absolutely rigid in this regard." No state codes or laws, however, make such distinctions. In fact, the existence of a prescription for medication can be sufficient to prove an ongoing relationship.

Is there a respected minority of psychiatrists who advocate sexual contact with patients as therapeutic?

No. Currently, a respected minority of psychiatrists does not exist that openly supports sex with patients under any guise.

In the early 1970s, however, there were advocates of the virtues of intimate therapy. Dr. James McCartney published an article in the *Journal of Sex Research* in which he averred that patients need to do more than talk about transference issues. He advocated nudity, touching, and intercourse with patients and admitted his use of such "treatment" (13). McCartney cautioned that the therapist should "remain objective and yet react appropriately in order to lead the immature person into full maturity."

In 1971, psychiatrist Martin Shepard published a book entitled *The Love Treatment,* in which he conducted interviews with patients who engaged in sex with therapists. Shepard concluded that "as many people are aided by intimate involvements with their therapists as are hurt" (14). Shepard examined 11 cases in which 6 clients labeled the sex as "useful," 3 as "harmful," and 2 as "a diversionary waste of time." Shepard found that some of the therapists had more severe sexual problems than the clients. He concluded that "such involvement is, generally speaking, not a good idea" (15).

A sequel, *The Psychiatrist's Head,* was published in 1972 (16) and subsequently republished as *Memoirs of a Defrocked Psychoanalyst.* Dr. Shepard denied that he had engaged in sexual relations with patients, stating that the characters described in his book with whom he was intimate were not in the context of the doctor-patient relationship. These publications created a flurry of interest at the time and were widely cited in legal articles. Dr. Shepard subsequently had his medical license revoked by the New York State Board of Regents (17). Dr. McCartney was expelled from the APA (18).

The use of sexual surrogates has not been fully litigated but appears to be largely a matter of prostitution between two consenting adults (18). Moreover, recommending extramarital affairs may lead to prosecution for promotion of prostitution. Therapists who advise patients to have sex in order to "emancipate themselves" or for other purported "therapeutic" reasons can be sued by a spouse. Damages for loss of consortium may also be available to the injured spouse of the patient (18). Therapists may also be violating criminal statutes that prohibit such advice to patients (19).

Are certain patients more vulnerable to sexual exploitation?

Generally, patients with borderline, dependent, and histrionic personality disorders are at increased risk for sexual exploitation (see Table 17-1). Kluft (20) points out that erotized behavior displayed toward a therapist is frequently the sequela of childhood sexual abuse. Thus, the patient's seductiveness must be viewed clinically as the manifestation of vulnerable, maladaptive behavior that should become the focus of treatment, not a means for therapist exploitation.

Victims of incest are particularly vulnerable to therapist-patient sexual exploitation. Twenty-three percent of incest victims who seek psychotherapy are sexually abused by the therapist according to an independent task force commissioned by the College of Physicians and Surgeons of Ontario (21). An additional 23% suffer other forms of abuse by the therapist. Less than 30% of these patients get any help from their first therapist. The average incest victim sees 3.5 therapists.

Pope and Bouhoutsos (22) describe three risk groups for therapist-patient sexual exploitation. Patients at low risk are high-functioning, maintain good interpersonal relationships, and demonstrate minimal fixed psychopathology. This group is at some risk during periods of intense stress, such as after the loss of an important relationship. At moderate risk are patients who are dependent and needy and have had previous difficulties with relationships. These patients usually suffer from a personality disorder. High-risk patients have histories of prior psychiatric hospitalizations, suicide attempts, major psychiatric illnesses, and alcohol and drug addiction. In contrast, Schoener (23) states that in his review of over 2,000 cases, no factors have been found that predict client involvement with therapists. Predictive characteristics were found for therapists only.

Forensic psychiatric review of cases of sexual exploitation reveals a high incidence of childhood sexual abuse in the victims (24). Childhood sexual abuse tends to create the need to master the original trauma through repetition, erotizes subsequent relations, distorts boundary maintenance in interpersonal relationships, induces low self-worth, and engenders guilt. Children who are

---

TABLE 17–1.   Some characteristics of patients vulnerable to therapist sexual
exploitation

1. Previously well-functioning patients with current depression and loss of a love relationship
2. Patients with dependent and other-directed personalities
3. Patients sexually and physically abused as children
4. Patients with previous hospitalizations, major psychiatric illnesses, suicide attempts, and alcohol and drug abuse
5. Patients with borderline, dependent, masochistic, and histrionic personality disorders
6. Attractive patients with low self-esteem

sexually abused may also be rewarded with attention and "love" for their sexual activities with adults. Sexually abused patients will frequently test boundary limits through seductive behavior to see if the therapist is safe. The exploitative therapist takes this opportunity to sexually abuse the patient.

Patients with borderline personality disorder (BPD) present special problems for therapists (25). These patients frequently attempt to manipulate and draw the therapist out of the treatment role. Therapists frequently find themselves making exceptions in the treatment of such patients. Patients with BPD often induce the greatest countertransference trap of all: the desire to do better than, or to undo the damage done by, previous parental figures. Thus a high level of vigilance for treatment boundary violations must be maintained by therapists who treat BPD patients (26). From a litigation perspective, suicide and sexual misconduct are the most common claims in malpractice suits against therapists treating patients with BPD.

In the author's experience, another group at risk for sexual exploitation includes the mentally retarded and patients who suffered chronic medical illnesses as children. The latter group experienced repetitive invasive medical and surgical procedures as well as frequent exposure of their bodies to a number of medical personnel. As a consequence, distortions during development occur involving body privacy boundaries that make these patients vulnerable to later sexual intimacies with therapists.

Are certain therapists at increased risk to sexually exploit patients?

Dr. James appears to be representative of a prototypical therapist who becomes sexually involved with patients (see Table 17-2). Middle-aged, tired, bored, and unhappily married, Dr. James has troubled teenage children, has practiced for many years, and has entered a sexual relationship with a young, attractive patient (27). Is there a constellation of other personality characteristics or profiles of therapists who are truly at risk? General profiles of sexually exploitative psychiatrists have been proposed by Stone and others (28). Schoener et al. (29)

TABLE 17–2. Personality profile of a "typical" sexually exploitative therapist

Age	40s to 50s
Sex	Male
Family constellation	Teenage children, troubled marriage
Medical symptoms	Chronic, not life threatening
Psychological symptoms	Depression, sleep disturbances, alcohol and drug abuse
Professional practice	"Burned out," ungratifying
Nature of patient	Young, attractive

have identified six distinct types: the seriously disturbed, the sociopathic, the impulsive, the isolated, those in crisis, and the naive. In the author's experience, five main groupings of exploitative therapists are found: 1) character-disordered predators, 2) sexually disordered (paraphilias) individuals, 3) incompetent individuals (usually poorly trained), 4) impaired individuals (alcohol, drugs, mental illness), and 5) situational reactors (recent major loss) (see Table 17-3). The first two groups tend to be "repeaters."

Dahlberg's (30) early review of nine therapist-patient sex cases found that middle-aged male therapists who became sexually involved with patients had less opportunity to meet young women except through their practices. He theorized that these therapists entered the field of psychotherapy as shy, withdrawn individuals who were found unattractive by the opposite sex. When they reached middle age, these therapists were unable to avoid acting out fantasies of having beautiful women "throwing themselves" at them without fear of rejection. Wood et al. (31) believe that a psychotherapist who engages in sex with a patient must be experiencing significant emotional distress that reduces impulse control and clouds judgment.

What is the reported rate of sexual contact between therapists and patients?

The percentage of therapists admitting sexual contact with patients was 7.7% in a survey of psychologists who answered positively to any questions regarding erotic contact behaviors or intercourse during treatment (32). A survey of physicians revealed that 10% engaged in erotic contact with clients and 5% reported having sexual intercourse (33). Another survey conducted by the Washington Psychiatric Society of its own members uncovered a self-report rate of 6.1% from 621 respondents (34). Pope et al. (35) found that 7% of their sample of psychologists conducting psychotherapy were engaged in sexual intimacies with their patients.

TABLE 17–3. Therapists at risk for sexually exploiting patients

Character disordered	**Impaired**
Borderline	Alcohol
Narcissistic	Drugs
Antisocial	Mental illness
Sexually disordered	**Situational reactors**
Frotteurism	Marital discord
Pedophilia	Loss of important relationship
Sexual sadism	Professional crisis
Incompetent therapist	
Poorly trained	
Has persistent boundary blindspots	

That "bad men do what good men dream" was confirmed in a more recent study by Pope et al. (36), who surveyed 575 psychotherapists and found that 87% (95% men, 76% women) felt sexually attracted to their clients but only 9.4% of men and 2.5% of women acted out such feelings; 63% felt guilty, anxious, or confused about the attraction. Tower (37), who termed these feelings as "countertransference anxieties," believed that virtually all therapists experience erotic feelings and impulses toward their patients. The vast majority of respondents in the study by Pope et al. (36) (82%) never seriously considered sexual involvement with patients. Reasons given for noninvolvement included that involvement was unethical, that it would be countertherapeutic and exploitative, that it was unprofessional, that it was against the therapist's values because of present commitment to a relationship, and that censure and loss of reputation might ensue.

The results of a nationwide survey of psychiatrist-patient sex were reported by Gartrell et al. (38). The report indicated that 7.1% of male and 3.1% of female respondents acknowledged sexual contact with their own patients. Eighty-eight percent of sexual contacts occurred between male psychiatrists and female patients, 7.6% between male psychiatrists and male patients, 3.5% between female psychiatrists and male patients, and 1.4% between female psychiatrists and female patients. While 38.4% were recidivists, none of the repeaters were female therapists. Only 40.7% of offending psychiatrists sought consultation because of their sexual involvement. Ninety-eight percent of the responding psychiatrists felt that sexual contact with patients was inappropriate and usually harmful. Twenty-nine percent reported that sexual contact after termination might sometimes be acceptable, and 17.4% believe that the APA ethical guidelines permit such contact. Sixty-five percent of psychiatrists reported treating patients who had been sexually abused by previous therapists. Forty-eight percent of the previous therapists were psychiatrists, 27% psychologists, 9% clergy, 7% social workers, and 6% lay therapists. Subsequent treating psychiatrists assessed that 87% of the patients were harmed. Only 8% of these psychiatrists, however, reported the abuse to a professional association or legal authority.

In surveys done after 1980, the percentage of therapists admitting sexual contact with patients has steadily declined. For example, as mentioned above, Gartrell et al. (38) reported in 1986 a rate of therapist-patient sex of 7.1% for male therapists and 3.1% for female therapists. In 1989, a survey of 4,800 psychiatrists showed a rate of therapist-patient sex of 0.9% for male therapists and 0.2% for female therapists (39). Although no clear reasons for this decline can be given, a conclusion that actual therapist-patient sex has declined by almost 10% since 1980 appears only overly optimistic. Even though responders remain anonymous, the threat of litigation may have caused offending therapists to forgo responding, further skewing the already unreliable data derived from surveys in the direction of underreporting therapist-patient sex.

The true incidence of therapist-patient sex is unknown. The empirical methods used to determine the incidence of therapist-patient sexual involvement are notoriously unreliable. Underreporting is a consistent flaw of self-report surveys. The actual incidence may be as high as 15% to 20%. Unfortunately, therapist sexual contact with child patients also occurs, but survey estimates of the incidence have not been reported (40). No reports could be found of sexual contact between a female therapist and a child (41). The professional literature is inconclusive concerning whether a higher incidence of therapist-patient sex takes place during therapy or after termination (42). The high incidence of therapist-patient sexual abuse does not appear to be higher than the incidence of sexual abuse found in the general clinical population. For example, Luepker and Retsch-Bogart (43) compared group members who were sexually exploited by therapists with the general population served by an agency and found no differences. The reality is that sexual abuse base rates are high in the first place.

All surveys of therapist-patient sexual contact have found a significantly lower incidence for female therapists. Among female therapists who do become sexually involved with their patients, heterosexual relationships appear to be the most common. A certain subset, however, develop what has been described as a "tea and sympathy" relationship with a female patient (44). These persons are usually heterosexual female therapists who become overinvolved and over-identified with their patients' problems, offering tenderness and closeness that may eventuate into hand holding, kissing, or even fondling the patient.

Can a reason for the infrequency of female therapists' sexual involvement with male patients be that the mother-son incest taboo is very strong for both parties? Other factors that may play a role in the lower incidence of female therapists' sexual involvement with patients are as follows:

1. The higher proportion of women and children in the professional practices of female therapists
2. The sexually inhibiting effects of maternal-child transferences and counter-transferences
3. Acculturation of woman into "nonpredatory" roles (e.g., nurturing, supportive); no "macho" equivalent
4. Gender differences in the biological basis of aggression (e.g., testosterone)
5. Gender differences in therapists' responses to desperate, needy patients of the opposite sex (nonerotic responses more likely from female therapists)
6. Gender differences with aging in the external and internal perception of the therapist as a sex object

What is the reported incidence of sexual contact between psychiatric residents and their educators?

A national survey of PGY-4 residents found that 4.9% of the 548 respondents reported sexual involvement with their educators. Additionally, 1.2% of the males and 0.4% of the females acknowledged sexual contact with patients (45). Pope et al. (35) collected data suggesting that students who engage in sexual intimacies with their educators are at a significantly higher risk to become sexually involved as therapists with their patients. It is not clear whether this is an identification issue or a continuation of boundary problems experienced by these students. The speculation of Pope et al. does not square with the fact that the vast majority of professionals who have sex with patients are male whereas graduate students who have had sex with professors typically are female. Sexual relations between a supervisor and a trainee, particularly if abuse of power exists, may be found to be unethical (46).

What legal actions can be brought against psychiatrists who are unduly familiar with patients?

Psychiatrists who indulge in sex with patients often become embroiled in civil, criminal, ethical, and professional disciplinary proceedings (see Table 17-4). The legal actions may include malpractice, intentional torts, contract actions, alienation of affection, seduction, criminal conversation, and violation of criminal statutes.

The consequences of therapist-patient sex are usually devastating for therapists as well as patients. Therapists stand to lose their reputations, professional licenses, families, and incomes following civil and criminal litigation. Ethical proceedings conducted by professional societies may lead to expulsion from membership and publication of the sexual misconduct, causing intense embarrassment and ostracism.

In *Walker v. Parzen* (47), an award for $4.6 million was granted by a San Diego Superior Court jury after the patient testified that she had been psychologically damaged when her psychiatrist seduced her during therapy sessions. She ultimately agreed to a settlement of $2.5 million to avoid further litigation on appeal. The complaint alleged that the psychiatrist had sexual intercourse

---

TABLE 17–4.   Legal and ethical consequences of therapist-patient sex

Civil lawsuit
  Negligence
  Loss of consortium
Breach-of-contract action
Criminal sanctions
Civil action for intentional tort (e.g., battery, fraud)
License revocation
Ethical sanctions
Dismissal from professional organizations

---

with her. He also had advised her to commit suicide after giving her drugs with which to do so. In addition to money damages, the psychiatrist lost his license for 1 year and was placed on probation for 10 years. On his return to practice, the California Board of Medical Quality Assurance prohibited him from treating female patients, working alone, or prescribing drugs that have potential for abuse during the probationary period (48). The plaintiff, Evelyn Walker, wrote a book about her experience, entitled *A Killing Cure* (49).

Anclote Manor Foundation v. Wilkinson (50) involved a breach-of-contract action in which the psychiatrist professed love to the patient and told her that he would divorce his wife and marry her. The court heard expert testimony on the proper management of transference and countertransference, noting that every expert asserted that the psychiatrist had engaged in "conduct . . . below acceptable psychiatric standards." The decision was founded solely on the theory of contract without allegations of sexual involvement. The husband brought suit after his wife's suicide and, under a contract action, recovered only the cost of her hospitalization and treatment.

In *Landau v. Werner* (51), a psychiatrist encouraged a patient to be emotionally involved with him, continuing social visits after she had "fallen in love." There were no allegations of any improper advances. The court held that medical testimony rejected the insertion of social visits into the treatment of an emotionally attached patient. The psychiatrist would be liable for any serious decline in the patient's improved condition if deterioration was proximately caused by negligent techniques. Thus, undue familiarity can be found in the absence of a sexual relationship.

In 1987, a psychiatrist was suspended from the APA and the district branch. He also was required to have weekly supervision by two colleagues for an ethical violation. The psychiatrist began a pattern of jogging with his younger female patient outside of treatment sessions. In addition, they shopped for clothing, played racquetball, and visited together in the patient's apartment. The ethics committee "found that the patient's wish for a close relationship with the psychiatrist was mishandled, with harmful blurring of the therapist/patient boundaries" (52).

Trust is the foundation of psychiatric therapies. Violation of trust by either the doctor or even the patient will usually ruin the prospect of beneficial treatment. The violation of trust can occur in many ways other than through sexual exploitation.

In the clinical vignette, Mr. Wilson brings suit for loss of consortium. A husband's standing to bring suit against a psychotherapist for sexual relations with his wife may be denied in states that have enacted "heart balm" statutes that bar civil liability for seduction, alienation of affection, and criminal conversations (adultery). In states having these statutes, although the patient may bring suit, the spouse has no cause of action. If the state does not have a heart balm statute, the spouse may have legal standing to bring suit (53).

In *Richard F. H. v. Larry H. D.* (54), a state statute abolishing an action for alienation of affection did not bar a lawsuit against a psychiatrist who had a sexual relationship with the wife of the patient. Courts may differentiate cases in which the spouse has had contact with the therapist. If the spouse has attended sessions, even a few, he or she may be able to argue a professional duty.

Under modern law, both husband and wife have an equal right to recovery for interference with their spousal relationship (i.e., loss of consortium) (55). Traditionally, the husband, not the wife, had the right to sue. Since 1950, most states have permitted both a husband and a wife to sue for damages for loss of consortium resulting from negligence or other injury to the spouse (56). In *Spiess v. Johnson* (57), however, a husband's claim for loss of consortium and alienation of affection was statutorily barred because it fell within the legislatively abolished tort of alienation of affection. But the claims for breach of contract and the intentional infliction of emotional distress were deemed properly pleaded.

In addition to civil litigation, the therapist may become involved in criminal proceedings. A number of states have passed statutes that make sexual activity by a therapist with a patient a criminal act (58). In addition, sexual exploitation of a patient, under certain circumstances, may be considered rape or some analogous sexual offense and therefore be criminally actionable under state sexual assault statutes. Typically, the presence of sexual assault is determined by one of three factors: the practitioner's means of inducement, the age of the victim, or the availability of a relevant state criminal code.

Sex with a current patient may also be criminally actionable if the state can prove beyond a reasonable doubt (i.e., with 90% to 95% certainty) that the patient was coerced into engaging in the sexual act. Typically, this type of evidence is limited to the use of some form of substance (e.g., medication) to either induce compliance or reduce resistance. Schoener et al. (59) also have described the use of anesthesia, electroconvulsive therapy, hypnosis, force, and threats of harm by some psychiatrists to coerce patients into sexual submission. To date, claims of "psychological coercion" via the manipulation of transference phenomena have not been successful in establishing the coercion necessary for a criminal case. In cases involving a minor patient, the issue of consent or coercion is irrelevant, because under the law, minors and incompetents (including adult incompetents) are considered unable to provide valid consent. Therefore, sex with a child or an incompetent individual is automatically considered a criminal act.

An increasing number of states have statutorily made sexual relations between therapist and patient a criminal offense when consent is not a defense (60). As an example, a Wisconsin statute holds:

> Any person who is or who holds himself or herself out to be a therapist and who
> intentionally has sexual contact with a patient or client during any ongoing thera-

pist-patient or therapist-client relationship regardless of whether it occurs during any treatment, consultation, interview, or examination is guilty of a class D felony. Consent is not an issue in an action under this sub-section. (61)

In one of the first cases decided under Minnesota's criminal statute, *State v. Dutton* (62), the Minnesota Appeals Court upheld the conviction of a pastoral counselor on four counts of psychotherapist-patient criminal sexual conduct. Halpern (63), after a recent review of sexual misconduct cases, believes that efforts at educating psychotherapists are not enough to eradicate sexual misconduct. Because between 90% and 94% of mental health professionals do *not* have sex with their patients, current educational effort appears to be quite adequate. He suggests that criminal sanctions should be pursued for their deterrent effect.

California, through a provision in the civil code, establishes that therapist sexual misconduct is a public offense prosecutable by the district attorney (64). A first-time offender who sexually exploits a patient is guilty of a misdemeanor. Second-time and subsequent violators may be prosecuted as having committed either a misdemeanor or a felony. The maximum penalty for a second offense of sexual exploitation is 1 year in prison and a $5,000 fine (65).

Therapists who become sexually involved with patients may run afoul of the law in those states that still proscribe adultery, sodomy, and fornication. Therapists who sexually exploit children also violate child abuse laws. Some states define sexual contact under the guise of treatment as rape (66). In Michigan, the criminal charge is rape "when the actor engages in medical treatment or examination of the victim in a manner or for purposes which are medically recognized as unethical or unacceptable" (67). A possible exculpatory argument can be made that these statutes do not apply if the therapist explains to the patient that sex is not therapy. In addition, Michigan law states that it is a crime to represent to a patient that sex with anyone except the spouse "is, or will be, necessary or beneficial to [his or] her health." As mentioned above, Wisconsin has passed a criminal statute that simply makes sexual activity by a psychotherapist with a patient a crime (61).

The Model Penal Code adopted in many states provides that an individual is guilty of rape when consent is defective because "[he] knows that she suffers from a mental disease or defect which renders her incapable of appraising the nature of her conduct" (68). Patients seeking psychological help may fit this definition. Nevertheless, rape may be difficult to prove when the patient who is initially told that sex is not treatment and is not forced gives consent. The number of states passing statutes making sex with a patient a criminal offense is expected to increase during this decade.

Regulations within licensure laws provide grounds for revocation of a psychiatrist's license by a state medical board for sexual misconduct. Disciplinary rules in a number of states specifically prohibit sexual contact between a psychiatrist and a patient (69).

What legal defenses have been asserted by defendants in sexual misconduct cases?

Defending sexual misconduct cases has not been a particularly successful area of litigation for attorneys. A review of recent sexual misconduct cases reveals an assortment of legal defenses asserted by defendant therapists. The most common defense is a denial of allegations of sexual involvement with the patient. This defense is fortified if no factual basis exists for the plaintiff's allegations.

Another frequently used defense is the statute of limitations. This argument suggests that suit should be barred after a period of time (usually 2 or 3 years after occurrence or discovery of injury). The issue of patient competency may "toll" (i.e., stop) the statute of limitations from running. For example, in *Riley v. Presnell* (70), the Massachusetts Supreme Judicial Court invoked the discovery rule that tolled the statute of limitations from running. The court rejected the defendant's defense that it was too late to bring a malpractice suit 7 years after the alleged sexual misconduct. The plaintiff successfully contended that he was unable to discover the psychological injuries resulting from the sexual misconduct because of the harm caused by the psychiatrist's behavior. In cases that involve exploitation of the patient, the therapist's negligence may impair the patient's ability to become aware of the psychological injuries that are produced (71).

Idealization of the therapist may prevent the patient from discovering his or her injury, thus permitting transference to toll the statute of limitations. Fradulent concealment of negligence by the therapist may also toll the statute. Fradulent concealment may occur in therapist-patient sex when the therapist informs

TABLE 17–5. Legal defenses asserted by defendants in sexual misconduct cases

1. Denial of plaintiff's allegations of sexual misconduct
2. Suit barred by statute of limitations
3. No doctor-patient relationship
4. Terminated patient—no legal fault under immunity statute
5. No causation of harm (psychological symptoms reflect inherent course of mental disorder)
6. No damages (no psychological harm caused by sex with patient)
7. Superseding intervening variable causing harm (not caused by sex with patient)
8. Contributory and comparative negligence (plaintiff's "contribution" to sexual misconduct)
9. Liability in supervision of offending therapist—sexual misconduct of supervisee beyond the scope of employment ("detour and frolic")
10. Marriage to patient
11. Improper pleading by plaintiff
12. Consent in cases claiming sexual assault

the patient that sex is therapy or when the therapist does not inform the patient that he or she is under the influence of transference.

Sex with a former patient may be legally defended in states that have enacted immunity statutes. These statutes prohibit a finding of legal fault for sex with a former patient if the sexual relationship begins within the immunity period. Table 17-5 contains a listing of some of the more common legal defenses asserted in sexual misconduct cases.

Legal defenses notwithstanding, the clinician must understand that sex with a current patient is *always* unethical. Even sex with a former patient is highly questionable ethically. Even though lawyers may attempt to fashion ingenious legal defenses in sexual misconduct cases, the fact that sexual involvement is unethical remains unchanged. In litigation, the victim may be blamed. Professionally, however, therapists are totally responsible for any sexual involvement with their patients.

What are other possible professional consequences of sexual misconduct?

Licensing boards are typically granted certain regulatory and disciplinary authority by state statutes to investigate allegations of professional misconduct. As a result, state licensing organizations, unlike professional associations, may discipline an offending professional more effectively and punitively by suspending or revoking his or her license. Because licensing boards are not as restrained by rigorous rules of evidence in trial procedures, it generally is less difficult for the abused patient to seek redress through this means. A review of published reports of sexual misconduct cases adjudicated before licensing boards revealed that in the vast majority of cases in which the evidence was reasonably sufficient to substantiate a claim of exploitation, the professional's license was revoked or suspended from practice for varying lengths of time, including permanent suspension (72).

Patients may bring ethical charges against psychiatrists before the district branches of the APA. Ethical violators may be reprimanded, suspended, or expelled from the APA. Ethical charges can be filed only against members of a professional group. All national organizations of mental health professionals have ethically proscribed sexual relations between therapist and patient. Obviously, this option is not available against therapists who do not belong to a professional organization.

Once sexually involved, some therapists have been blackmailed by their patients, usually for money. The exploited patient turns the tables and becomes the exploiter as the therapist desperately attempts to avoid the often severe legal and ethical consequences of sexual misconduct. Quite apart from the possibility of blackmail, sexual involvement with a patient is tantamount to committing professional suicide.

Finally, the harm to the psychiatrist, the psychiatrist's family, and even the psychiatrist's colleagues is also very great. The study of Brigham (73) shows that knowledge that a colleague has had sex with a patient is as great a stress on the clinician as having a suicidal patient.

What types of statutory remedies are provided for victims of patient-therapist sex?

A number of legislatures have enacted or are considering enacting statutes that provide civil or criminal remedies to patients who have been sexually abused by their therapists (74). Three types of statutory remedies exist.

Reporting statutes require the disclosure by the therapist to state authorities when learning of past or current therapist-patient sex. Minnesota is the only state that has a mandatory reporting statute. Other states with reporting statutes usually require consent from the patient before the therapist can report the patient's allegation of sexual exploitation by a previous therapist.

A few states (California, Florida, Illinois, Minnesota, and Wisconsin) have civil statutes proscribing sexual misconduct (75). Civil statutes, by incorporating the standard of care, make malpractice suits easier to pursue. For example, Minnesota has enacted by statute a specific cause of action against psychiatrists and other psychotherapists for injury caused by sexual contact with a patient (76). Some of these statutes also restrict unfettered discovery of the plaintiff's past sexual history.

In addition, criminal sanctions may be the only remedy for exploitative therapists without malpractice insurance who are unlicensed or do not belong to professional organizations. Colorado (77), Maine (78), Minnesota (79), California (80), North Dakota (81), Wisconsin (82), Florida (83), Michigan (84), New Hampshire (85), Wyoming (86), and Iowa (87) have criminal statutes governing doctor-patient sexual exploitation. A number of other states currently are considering enacting legislation that would criminally penalize a psychotherapist's sexual contact with a patient.

Statutes are created through the legislative process, which is sensitive to various political pressures and to the forces of compromise. Consequently, statutory language may be confusing, contradictory, and, sometimes, contrary to the original goals of the statute. For example, the California statute prohibits sexual involvement by a psychotherapist with a former patient for 2 years following termination of treatment (88). In 1989, Section 729 was added to the Business and Professions Code that made sex with a former patient a criminal event if the relationship "was terminated primarily for the purpose of engaging in sex" (89). If the patient obtains a referral to an independent and objective therapist for treatment, recommended by a third-party therapist, no criminal fault will be found, even if the referral was made in order to initiate a sexual relationship. Such an exception nullifies the intent of the criminal statute to protect patients from exploitation by their therapists. In effect, the new statute legitimizes post-treatment sex, in direct conflict with the ethical positions taken by most of the mental health professions. Nevertheless, therapists still are civilly liable for initiating sex with a former patient within 2 years of termination.

What is the significance of transference and countertransference in patient-therapist sex?

Transference is the primarily unconscious tendency of an individual to currently assign to others those feelings and attitudes originally connected with significant figures during the course of early development. In psychodynamic psychotherapy, the patient identifies the therapist with the parents or other significant early figures. The transference may be either positive (affectionate) or negative (hostile). Analysis of the transference feelings is a major therapeutic tool in individual and group psychodynamic therapy, enabling the patient to gain insight and understanding into the origins of personal difficulties and behavior (89).

Countertransference is the primarily unconscious emotional response of the therapist toward the patient. Greenson (90) contends that countertransference is a transference reaction to the patient. Grossman (91) defines countertransference as the therapist's reaction to the patient's transference. Although definitions do vary, countertransference is shaped by the therapist's inner needs and based on the conflicts and defenses that reflect the developmental psychological history of the therapist. For example, countertransference to the patient as a prohibited sexual object unconsciously may represent a compelling, early incestuous object for the therapist.

Unfortunately, countertransference feelings, particularly of the erotic variety, have become associated with mismanagement of the patients' treatment and are viewed with shame and embarrassment by some therapists. The work of Winnicott (92), Little (93), and Heimann (94) stimulated a significant literature underscoring that countertransference, when properly managed, can be used as a valuable therapeutic tool. The psychiatric literature on this subject underscores that ignorance of the countertransference may harm the therapeutic process and even the patient.

Transference feelings, in contrast to a transference neurosis, may be broadly described as primarily conscious feelings that the patient has toward the therapist. Transference phenomena, which are thought to be universal, may be particularly prominent in caregiving and service relationships such as in those involving doctor-patient, attorney-client, teacher-student, and priest-penitent. Depending upon whether an orthodox analytic view is taken or a more generic definition is used, transference and countertransference may hold very different meanings. For example, countertransference may simply mean disliking the patient.

Patients who come for psychiatric treatment are undergoing mental and emotional suffering that is painful and often debilitating. Thus, their decision-making capacity and judgment are usually impaired. Moreover, the therapist is viewed as a critically important source of help and hope. Under these circumstances, a transference involving the expectation of beneficent care and treatment occurs that is highly influenced by early, powerful wishes for nurture and care. The therapist is frequently idealized as the all-good, all-giving parent.

Combined with the fear of losing the newly acquired idealized parental figure, the beneficent transference leaves the patient vulnerable to exploitation by the therapist. The beneficent transference is a common psychological reaction, experienced to varying degrees by practically all patients. It should be distinguished from the transference neuroses that develop in a number of patients undergoing intensive, usually psychodynamic, psychotherapy.

An important aspect of transference is that it serves as a resistance to working through unresolved conflicts, losses, and yearnings. The mismanagement of transference and countertransference feelings is a key factor in the boundary violations that occur before sexual intimacy. Both therapist and patient who become sexually involved often unconsciously collude with each other to act out their mutual transferences as a way of avoiding confronting painful emotional problems. Whereas both therapist and patient may obviously *understand* the fact of their sexual involvement, very often they do not *appreciate* the largely unconscious, powerful emotional forces driving the creation of a therapist-patient sexual relationship. The patient may not *appreciate* that sexual involvement with the therapist will likely have devastating consequences on his or her current and future mental health as well as on therapeutic efforts to remedy the psychological injuries. Often, transference developments induce in the patient the desperate feeling that his or her therapist is utterly indispensable to personal survival. Such reactions, while not rendering the patient incompetent to consent to therapist-patient sex, do make it extraordinarily difficult for the patient to resist the exploitative therapist. Patient consent to sex with the therapist, however, is not the issue. It is the breach of fiduciary trust by the therapist who engages the patient in sex that is the appropriate focus of wrongdoing.

Quite apart from the issue of transference and countertransference, therapists with certain character disorders repeatedly exploit patients as a function of their personality defects. Gutheil (95) prefers the undue influence model in understanding sexual misconduct. He feels that transference and countertransference are demeaning, disrespectful, and unrealistic when used to describe the patient as a functional incompetent. Many patients enter into sexual relations in a competent manner, though misguided and usually unduly influenced. Gutheil observes that competent individuals may be unduly influenced in special relationships. Stone (96) has proposed the breach-of-fiduciary-trust model as another legal approach. This model does not require reference to the patient's transference or capacity to consent. Both of these models may have a certain applicability to behavioral or biological psychiatrists untrained in psychodynamic concepts.

What caution should the therapist observe when encountering "love feelings" or "love" transferences in patients during the course of therapy?

"Love feelings" or "love" transferences produced by patients in therapy are often not what they appear to be on the surface. Transferences, like dreams, have both manifest and latent content. Freud (97) emphasized that "transference-love" must be understood as a specific treatment phenomenon not identical to the experience of "falling in love" as it occurs outside of therapy. He states that the analyst

> must recognize that the patient's falling in love is induced by the analytic situation and is not to be attributed to the charms of his own person; so that he has no grounds whatever for being proud of such a "conquest," as it would be called outside analysis. (97)

The therapist who only considers the "love," or manifest, aspect of the patient's feelings will seriously misjudge the clinical situation. Most patients have felt deprived of warmth and affection in their important relationships. Behind powerful yearnings for a love relationship with the therapist may lurk deep feelings of rage and revenge. Moreover, the collusion of the therapist's and the patient's resistance to examining the deeper psychological meaning of "love feelings" may manifest itself in sexual behavior.

During her childhood, Ms. Wilson had conscious fantasies of being reunited with her lost father. She also had recurrent nightmares of the violent death of her mother. She unconsciously created a defensive split by idealizing her dead father and directing the anger over her loss toward her mother. In her treatment with Dr. James, she accomplished the same result by idealizing him while remaining estranged and angry with her husband. Dr. James accepted her manifest transference at face value, only to be surprised and frightened by the emergence of her anger toward him that precipitated a suicidal depression. The idealization of Dr. James, as is frequently the case, was a defense against the rage that she feared would destroy her important relationships.

"Love" transferences also contain deep, infantile expectations for a permanent fusion with the therapist. The patient believes the therapist will cure all past and current difficulties. This belief often reflects an attempt to deny pathological grief and repair losses and traumas that occurred at an early stage of development. What makes sexual intimacy with a patient so egregious is that these yearnings are exploited to meet the needs of the therapist rather than interpreted for the patient's benefit. The therapist abandons the duty to neutrality and the fiduciary trust position.

It is unethical for all physicians to engage in sex with their patients (98). Recently, the American Medical Association's House of Delegates adopted a report defining sexual contact within the physician-patient relationship as a breach of medical ethics (99). Psychiatrists, however, hold a special position. Unlike the general physician who intuitively works within the ambit of a positive transference and provides hope and succor for the patient, the psychiatrist often works directly with the transference as a therapeutic tool. As a therapeutic strategy, the therapist may encourage development of the transference but is expected to keep countertransference in check while protecting and working through the patient's transference. The very act of intently listening and caring is a very seductive process for both patient and therapist. Freud (97) warned against the temptation to act out the countertransference: "If the patient's advances were returned it would be a great triumph for her, but a complete defeat for the treatment." He goes on to say: "The love-relationship in fact destroys the patient's susceptibility to influence from analytic treatment. A combination of the two would be an impossibility." Thus, mishandling the transference and countertransference is a form of negligent psychotherapy.

In *Simmons v. United States* (100), the court addressed the consequences of mishandling the transference:

> The impact of sexual involvement with one's counselor is more severe than the impact of merely "having an affair" for two major reasons. First, because the client's attraction is based on transference, the sexual contact is ordinarily akin to engaging in sexual activity with a parent and carries with it the feelings of shame, guilt, and anxiety experienced by incest victims. Second, the client is usually suffering from all or some of the psychological problems that brought him or her into therapy to begin with. As a result, the client is especially vulnerable to the added stress created by the feelings of shame, guilt, and anxiety produced by the incestuous nature of the relationship, and by the sense of betrayal that is felt when the client eventually learns that he or she is not "special," as having been led to believe, and that his or her trust has been violated.

Courts, however, have not always found transference and countertransference to be mitigating factors for either the patient or the therapist. In a complaint filed in March 1977 for psychiatric malpractice, plaintiff Marcia Decker alleged that during the course of psychoanalysis Dr. Fink improperly manipulated the analysis for the purpose of engaging in sexual relations (101). Although the professional relationship between the parties apparently ended in December 1971, evidence indicated that the sexual relationship continued through the summer of 1975. The trial court ruled that Ms. Decker's claim was barred by the 3-year statute of limitations. The court also found that she was informed in 1973 by another psychiatrist that the defendant's conduct was improper.

On appeal, Ms. Decker argued that she had suffered from impaired judgment due to transference that tolled the statute of limitations. The court rejected this argument, refusing to add a new category, "impaired judgment," to the list of disabilities. Using a "reasonable man" standard, the court narrowly defined the criteria for incompetence, holding that mental incompetence tolls the statute only when the plaintiff is shown to have been "unable to manage his [her] business affairs or estate or to comprehend his [her] legal rights" (101). As a result, the court ignored the importance of transference as a powerful influence on the patient's judgment.

To maintain perspective, it should be stated that a significant number of sexual misconduct cases are not the result of a mishandling of transference or countertransference. Psychotherapists with malignant character disorders manifesting severe narcissistic, antisocial, or perverse character traits may induce patients to have sexual relations, quite apart from transference and countertransference issues. Analogously, a severely character-disordered patient may actively attempt to seduce or entrap his or her therapist into a sexual relationship. Nevertheless, the therapist is expected to maintain a treatment position with these difficult patients.

Will malpractice insurance cover the psychiatrist for sexual misconduct?

In a leading case, *Hartogs v. Employers Mutual Liability Insurance Company* (102), the court upheld the refusal of the insurance company to pay for damages when Dr. Hartogs attempted to treat his patient's fear of being a lesbian by initiating a sexual relationship with her. Dr. Hartogs claimed that the carrier should cover his defense because the jury found his actions to be malpractice, despite Dr. Hartogs's admission that he knew all along that what he was engaged in was "in no way pursuant to the doctor-patient relationship."

Most insurance carriers will not insure therapists for sexual misconduct, excluding it as an intentional tort or criminal action. The position is taken that what is not practice is not malpractice. As a matter of public policy, insurance usually does not cover for punitive damages either (103). In some malpractice policies, the psychiatrist may be able to obtain coverage for the costs of litigation but not for damages. Other carriers will only insure the therapist if the charges are denied. In *St. Paul Fire and Marine Insurance Company v. Mitchell* (104), the Georgia Court of Appeals held that the psychiatrist's mishandling of the transference and the romantic liaison with the patient were sufficient to bring a suit within the insurer's duty to defend.

According to Bisbing (105), the more than 20 legal opinions addressing the insurance implications of sexual misconduct malpractice suits have achieved quite different results. In a recent case, *St. Paul Fire and Marine Insurance Company v. Love* (106), the Minnesota Court of Appeals reversed a lower court decision in finding that an insurer was not relieved of its obligation to indemnify and defend claims in the provision of negligent psychotherapy arising from the professional relationship. The court of appeals found that the psychologist's malfeasance was not the sexual conduct per se but the mishandling of the patient's transference. The case was appealed to the Minnesota Supreme Court and affirmed (106). The court stated, "Psychotherapy purports to concern itself with emotional and sexual dysfunction, and the insurance company agrees to provide coverage for the risks inherent in the services provided by therapists. The occupational hazards attendant on transference are such a risk."

In the clinical vignette, if Dr. James held an insurance policy sponsored by the APA and the sexual misconduct occurred prior to May 1, 1985, he would be covered (107). The earlier version of the policy attempted to protect psychiatrists who might have been unjustly accused as well as to help compensate victims of sexual exploitation by spreading the cost to all policyholders. A change in the APA's position, ostensibly to discourage sexual misconduct, has led to the dropping of coverage for undue familiarity from its member malpractice insurance plan. As of May 1, 1985, the plan no longer pays claims for undue familiarity but continues to provide a legal defense of up to $100,000. In order for legal expenses to be covered, the charge of sexual involvement must be denied. Otherwise, no basis for a defense exists.

Nevertheless, therapists who work with patients intensively may allege that mishandling of the countertransference is a cause of their sexual misconduct. This may be deemed negligence and covered under some malpractice policies. Therapists who see patients infrequently or only for follow-up of medications may have difficulty alleging countertransference problems in order to stay within the negligence coverage of their malpractice insurance policy. An expert witness may be necessary in a legal action between the therapist and the carrier if the therapist asserts mishandling of the countertransference, because this allegation may be self-serving. Also, therapists may admit to having sexual relations with patients as "treatment" (as did Dr. James) in order to fall within the insurance coverage for treatment procedures rather than be excluded under nontherapy provisions.

Therapist-patient sex is usually preceded by progressive treatment boundary violations (26). As a consequence, patients are frequently psychologically damaged by the precursor boundary violations as well as the sexual misconduct of the therapist (108). Under these circumstances, the therapist's boundary mismanagement may fall under the negligence provisions of his or her professional liability insurance. Furthermore, the trend of decisions in sexual misconduct litigation favors compensation of victims.

What types of damages may the sexually exploited patient claim?

It is axiomatic that sexual misconduct never takes place in the absence of other deviations in the standard of care. But attorneys focus on the sexual misconduct because it appears to be the most damaging to the patient. The presence of other breaches in care may make the allegations of sexual misconduct more convincing in the absence of other evidence. Nevertheless, it is likely that if the patient has been damaged, all of the deviations in care have been contributory. For example, the progressive boundary violations that ultimately lead to a sexual relationship with the patient often produce psychic injury by interfering with the provision of care as well as causing regression in the patient's psychiatric condition. Frequently, the treatment boundary violations preceding the sexual act produce a significant degree of the psychological harm (108).

When the patient alleges a loss of treatment opportunity, it may be difficult to assess damages for such a claim. Patients are not continuously open to treatment throughout the course of their lives. Certain life events, often combined with the pain of distressing emotional symptoms, motivate patients to seek therapy. If the patient is sexually exploited, the treatment opportunity may be lost forever. Furthermore, the patient may be crippled in his or her ability to develop the trust necessary for any future therapeutic alliance. Thus, the patient may allege risk of future harm.

In *Greenberg v. McCabe* (109), a sexual misconduct case, the court denied $90,000 in damages awarded for future psychiatric treatment because "the plaintiff did not demonstrate that it was probable she would undergo future psychiatric care, based on her testimony that she would not undergo therapy and could not trust another doctor." However, the jury did award the plaintiff $275,000 for compensatory damages exclusive of the costs for future psychiatric care and $300,000 in punitive damages. Pope and Bouhoutsos (110) provide a guide to the assessment of psychological damage in patients who were sexually abused by therapists. Similarly, Schoener et al. (111) present excellent clinical guidelines for the expert witness responsible for assessing damages.

Frequently, patients seeking psychiatric treatment have been deprived of basic parental care or actually were physically and sexually abused as children. They often suffer from very low self-esteem. Currently, they may be abused by a husband or partner. The exploitative psychiatrist gives these earlier traumatic experiences an added reality that may overwhelm and disable the patient. In order for the exploiting psychiatrist to gain control over the patient, inappropriate and excessive amounts of medication are frequently prescribed. Initially, the exploited patient may feel special in receiving the therapist's attentions. As is often the case, the patient at some point is summarily dropped, leading to feelings of abandonment, betrayal, and rage.

In Table 17-6, the symptoms of a therapist-patient sex syndrome are described. This syndrome may reflect the existence of comorbidity so often seen in victims of therapist sexual misconduct. In forensic evaluations of these individuals, specificity of diagnoses according to the criteria found in the APA's *Diagnostic and Statistical Manual of Mental Disorders* will usually be required.

In the clinical vignette, Ms. Wilson lost her father at the age of 3. She was raised by a depressed and psychologically unavailable mother. The sexual relationship with Dr. James, whom she idealized in a father transference, reawakened overwhelming feelings of loss, sadness, and rage when she was suddenly terminated by him at a time of crisis. She subsequently turned this anger on herself in a suicide attempt. Therapists are liable in monetary damages for any harm they cause their patients.

Sexual misconduct cases are usually settled out of court when the psychiatrist confesses to the sexual relationship. Psychiatrists who lose in court may expect six-figure judgments for compensatory and punitive damages. Compensatory damages are awarded to replace the injury to the plaintiff that is caused by the defendant's wrongful acts. Compensatory damages may include damages for past and future loss of earnings, future medical and caregiving expenses, and intangible damages such as loss of normal life, inconvenience, humiliation, and pain and suffering. Courts may distinguish between general and special damages, the latter consisting of out-of-pocket losses, medical expenses paid, and lost wages (112). The purpose of punitive damages, if the defendant's behavior was intentional, willful, wanton, malicious, or extremely reckless, is to punish the offender rather than to compensate the victim. The punitive damage serves as a warning to the wrongdoer and others that wrongful conduct will not be tolerated by the community.

What monetary damages have been awarded by courts to victims of therapist sexual misconduct?

Prior to the 1976 decision *Roy v. Hartogs* (113), there was little precedent for legal claims of sexual involvement between a psychiatrist and patient. In *Zipkin*

TABLE 17–6. Psychological consequences of sexual intimacy with patients

Exacerbation of preexisting psychiatric disorders
Production of therapist-patient sex syndrome
    Ambivalence
    Guilt
    Feelings of isolation
    Emptiness
    Cognitive dysfunction
    Identity disturbances
    Inability to trust
    Sexual confusion
    Mood lability
    Suppressed rage
    Increased suicidal risk
Damage to personal relationships
Destructiveness to future treatment

Source. Adapted from Pope KS, Bouhoutsos JL: *Sexual Intimacy Between Therapists and Patients.* New York, Praeger, 1986

v. Freeman (114), the defendant was found to have manipulated the patient to his advantage by convincing her to become his mistress and to leave her husband. The patient alleged that she had sex with the psychiatrist and attended "group therapy" that involved nude swimming. The patient complained that the psychiatrist mishandled the transference, which a psychiatrist is expected to handle properly. The judge stated:

> Once Dr. Freeman started to mishandle the transference phenomena, with which he was plainly charged in the petition and which is overwhelmingly shown in the evidence, it was inevitable that trouble was ahead. It is pretty clear from the medical evidence that the damage would have been done to Mrs. Zipkin even if the trips outside the state were carefully chaperoned, the swimming done with suits on, and if there had been ballroom dancing instead of sexual relations.

The jury awarded plaintiff $17,000 in damages. The court subsequently reduced the award to $5,000. Since the mid-1970s, six-figure judgments in malpractice suits have not been uncommon.

In *Walker v. Parzen* (47), a $2.5 million settlement was agreed upon after an initial $4.6 million judgment was rendered by a jury. In this case, allegations of attempting to induce the patient's suicide, gross negligence in prescribing drugs, and the very poor psychological condition of the plaintiff were factors in the large settlement. In theory, at least, the monetary damage awards should be related to true psychic and physical injuries.

In *Mazza v. Huffaker* (115), a psychiatrist who was treating both husband and wife was discovered by the husband in bed with his wife shortly after they had separated. The husband was awarded $150,000 in compensatory damages for malpractice and criminal conversation and $500,000 in punitive damages. The court noted that there was expert testimony showing that "a patient who discovered his wife in bed with his psychiatrist would never again be able to form a trusting relationship with a psychiatrist which is necessary for psychiatric treatment and that such a discovery would harm the well-being of a patient." This case is unique in creating a third-party medical malpractice cause of action. The court allowed the plaintiff to recover on a malpractice claim arising from the treatment rendered by Dr. Huffaker to the patient's wife while she was a patient.

How does a therapist's sexual involvement with a patient generally occur? What clinically acceptable course of action was available to Dr. James when he found himself considering sexual involvement with his patient?

Usually, before sexual misconduct occurs, treatment boundaries are gradually eroded (116). The therapist will rarely become sexually involved with the patient all of a sudden. An excellent account of the gradual erosion of treatment boundaries leading to near loss of control with a client is given by Rutter (117). Unfortunately, professional ethics codes are usually silent concerning the specific boundary violations that often precede therapist sexual misconduct.

Sexual contact between therapist and patient usually is initiated in one of three ways: an affair with erotic sexual contact usually ending in sexual intercourse; covert or "sneaky" sex on the part of the therapist, usually involving varying degrees of erotic hugging; and sex represented as treatment to the patient (118). Schoener et al. (119) quote Valiquette's work indicating that 41.2% of therapist sexual contact began within 3 months of starting treatment. By 6 months, the cumulative percentage was 53%.

Many years ago, Freud enunciated the duty of neutrality based upon the principle of abstinence, which stated that psychiatrists must refrain from gratifying themselves at the expense of patients (120). Quite independently, a legal duty of neutrality also exists (120). Treatment boundaries are violated when the primary source of the psychiatrist's gratification is achieved from the patient directly rather than by engagement in the therapeutic process with the patient.

Epstein and Simon (121) have devised the Exploitation Index, which can be used by therapists as an early warning indicator of treatment boundary violations. A survey of 532 psychiatrists using the Exploitation Index revealed that 43% found that one or more questions alerted them to boundary violations; 29%

TABLE 17–7. Ten common scenarios of sexual exploitation

1. Role trading: Therapist becomes the "patient" and the wants and needs of the therapist become the focus.
2. Sex therapy: Therapist fraudulently presents therapist-patient sexual intimacy as a valid treatment for sexual or other kinds of difficulties.
3. As if . . . : Therapist treats positive transference as if it were not the result of the therapeutic situation.
4. Svengali: Therapist creates and exploits an exaggerated dependence on the part of the patient.
5. Drugs: Therapist uses cocaine, alcohol, or other drugs as part of the seduction.
6. Rape: Therapist uses physical force, threats, and/or intimidation.
7. True love: Therapist uses rationalizations that attempt to discount the clinical/professional nature of the relationship with its attendant responsibilities.
8. It just got out of hand: Therapist fails to treat the emotional closeness that develops in therapy with sufficient attention, care, and respect.
9. Time out: Therapist fails to acknowledge and take account of the fact that the therapeutic relationship does not cease to exist between scheduled sessions or outside the therapist's office.
10. Hold me: Therapist exploits patient's desire for nonerotic physical contact and possible confusion between erotic and nonerotic contact.

Source. Reprinted, with permission, from Pope K, Bouhoutsos J: *Sexual Intimacy Between Therapists and Patients.* New York, Praeger, 1986. Copyright 1986, Praeger.

made specific changes in treatment practices (122). When used as a heuristic device to aid students and clinicians in maintaining treatment boundaries, the Exploitation Index overcomes some inherent barriers to its usefulness. For example, exploitative therapists may be deaf to the consciousness-raising impact of the Exploitation Index, or unsophisticated therapists may not be able to effectively apply the instrument to individual case-to-case variability found in clinical practice. Tables 17-7 and 17-8 demonstrate common scenarios of patient sexual exploitation and therapists' rationalizations.

In the clinical vignette, Dr. James violated treatment boundaries along a rather typical, progressive path. The sessions gradually became social, and Dr. James shared personal information with the patient. First names were eventually used. Hugging at the end of the session occurred. The sessions were scheduled for the end of the day followed by dating. Finally, sex took place. Therapists having sexual intercourse with their patients frequently advocate and use nonerotic physical contact with patients more often than therapists who do not become sexually involved with patients (123). Self-disclosure, particularly about current problems or crises in the therapist's life, appears to be highly correlated with eventual sexual misconduct (23). Particularly noxious are disclosures about relationship problems, sexual frustration, sexual fantasies about the patient, and loneliness. Such self-disclosures also waste therapy time and promote care taking by the patient.

Theoretically, at least, therapist and patient have sufficient time and opportunity as treatment boundaries are progressively violated to back away from a sexual relationship. Therapists should be familiar with recommended treatment boundary guidelines and their underlying principles (124). When boundary violations begin and treatment boundaries cannot be reestablished, the patient should be terminated and referred. The therapist should seek personal help.

The duty of neutrality is also based on the legal concept of the fiduciary relationship. The psychiatrist-patient relationship is a fiduciary relationship in which the patient places a special trust in the psychiatrist to act in good faith and

---

TABLE 17–8. Rationalizations for therapists' sexual involvement with patients

1. Occurs outside of the therapeutic session.
2. Occurs after termination of patient's treatment.
3. Patient initiates sex or "seduces" therapist.
4. One's professor, supervisor, or colleague had sex with the patient with impunity.
5. Competent consent is obtained from patient.
6. Patient is not billed.
7. Patient is seen in consultation, for medications only, or in group therapy.
8. Sexual contact is for "therapeutic" purposes.

Source. Reprinted, with permission, from Pope KS, Bouhoutsos JL: *Sexual Intimacy Between Therapists and Patients.* New York, Praeger, 1986. Copyright 1986, Praeger.

in accordance with the best interest of the patient. Thus, the psychiatrist should be an unfailing patient ally who always attempts to place the patient's best interests first (125).

Clinically mature therapists realize that they cannot treat every patient. Although this realization may be a professional mortification to some therapists, it is a reality of everyday practice. For instance, therapists who are themselves depressed may have great difficulty working with depressed patients. A psychiatrist who has undergone serious financial reverses and feels that he or she has received bad business advice may have trouble maintaining treatment objectivity with an aggressive, acquisitive, acting-out business person. Even when not confronted with a personal crisis, a therapist will be most effective with only certain types of patients.

The assessment of the therapist's personal effectiveness and limitations in the treatment of problematic patients should be done during the period of initial evaluation. If the therapist has doubts about the ability to treat the patient adequately, the patient should be referred. It is usually very difficult for the therapist to step back and recognize an error after already accepting a patient for treatment. The administration of "analytical toilet," as recommended by the English psychoanalyst Glover (126), can be useful for therapists who experience personal difficulty with certain patients. A therapist must use self-scrutiny regarding personal reactions toward a patient for the benefit of the patient's therapy. Self-analysis, however, is often insufficient.

If the therapist initially experiences the feeling "Where have you been all my life?" toward a new patient, very serious consideration should be given to referring that patient elsewhere. This advice may prove very difficult to follow. Therapy is difficult enough without such added psychological burdens. Psychotherapists are human and should not knowingly tempt the fates. Self-scrutiny has its limitations. This is reflected in the professional joke about self-analysis evoking the therapist's own countertransferences. Therapists who are unable to understand and control their erotic feelings toward patients should at least consult with a trusted colleague as well as consider treatment for themselves.

When Dr. James became aware of his emotional overinvolvement, he should have informed his patient that he could no longer treat her and made a referral to another therapist. Boundary violations in the treatment of Ms. Wilson occurred gradually over time, beginning with emotional overinvolvement. The legal term "undue familiarity" has clinical value in describing the gradual development of emotional closeness that is unnecessary for treatment (e.g., excessive self-disclosure).

Dr. James had sufficient time to retreat within appropriate treatment boundaries or refer the patient long before the sexual relationship began. The patient probably would have experienced a strong negative reaction to the interruption of her therapy and the referral to a new therapist. This result, however, is far better than the outcome that Ms. Wilson suffered as a result of the sexual relationship with Dr. James. Paradoxically, Dr. James never had personal therapy or analysis despite the fact that he used intensive psychotherapy with patients. Thus, hidden vulnerabilities may have been present that could have been addressed much earlier in his career through his own treatment.

Although these recommendations for dealing with the therapist's powerful feelings appear to be reasonable, they are extraordinarily difficult to follow. Dr. James was highly respected in his profession and well established in the community. The sense of omnipotence and invulnerability that may arise after many years of reasonably successful work with patients may make an admission of failure regarding a particular patient's treatment almost impossible. Furthermore, the feeling of "being in love," particularly if the therapist is lonely and object hungry, can be so compelling that it blinds the therapist to the possibility of personal therapy. Impulses to sexually exploit a patient can be sufficiently powerful and ego-syntonic that the therapist is not susceptible to the idea of referring the patient and seeking personal therapy. Sometimes, advising such a therapist to seek personal treatment is as futile as advising a starving man shipwrecked on an island to avoid eating the poison flora that covers the island.

Dr. James was bored with his work, tired of his adolescent children's problems, and alienated from his wife. He slipped gradually into despair, becoming isolated and depressed. The prospects of a romantic relationship with a young, responsive, attractive woman appeared to be an irresistible antidote to his personal problems. In this respect, therapists who are isolated in personal relationships of their own seem to have a particular vulnerability when working intensively with young, attractive patients.

Should Dr. James have terminated the patient's therapy before initiating a sexual relationship with her?

Dr. James was motivated to initiate a sexual relationship with his patient and rationalize it as therapy. Psychiatrists have been advised in the past to terminate any relationship with a patient and refer him or her to another therapist if they wish to initiate a sexual relationship (127). Thus, both the therapist and the patient will have time to reflect on their desires for a sexual relationship with each other. Psychiatrists have also been advised that sexual intimacy with a consenting patient presents no legal jeopardy provided the psychiatrist is not treating or billing the patient (128). In other words, if one is planning to have a sexual relationship with the patient, terminate the patient and refer the patient elsewhere for therapy, but do not treat or bill the patient for any sexual encounter.

The critical word is "consenting." Although the psychiatrist may allege that the patient undertook the sexual relationship knowingly and without coercion, the patient may later contend that a clear choice was not possible because of the overwhelming powerful feelings created by the treatment situation. The patient may be so hungry for a relationship as to not be able to resist the sexual advances of the former therapist. Since this advice was given, the APA has subsequently formulated an ethical position concerning sex with a former patient.

The APA's Ethics Committee (129) reported an instructive case to the membership. A member psychiatrist was charged with engaging in sexual activities with his patient. There was never any dispute that the sexual activity had actually taken place. The therapist argued that the sexual relationship did not begin until several weeks after the therapy was terminated. The APA district branch, with jurisdiction over the psychiatrist, decided that the precise timing of the commencement of the sexual relationship was irrelevant. Even if the sexual relationship started after termination of therapy, the psychiatrist's sexual involvement constituted an exploitation of the "knowledge, power, and unique position that the psychiatrist held in the patient's life." The committee concluded that sexual involvement between a psychiatrist and a patient, even after the end of treatment, always raises concern about transference and countertransference. The termination of the formal doctor-patient relationship does not end the ethical concern. Also, the length of time between termination and the initiation of a relationship with a former patient is not determinative. The issue is whether an exploitation exists, particularly of transference.

Subsequently, the APA has taken the following ethical position: "Sexual involvement with one's former patients generally exploits emotions deriving from treatment and therefore almost always is unethical" (7). The hedge in this statement (e.g., "almost") is due to the complexity of this question. Some therapists marry patients. Furthermore, constitutional issues, especially interference with the right of association, may be raised by an absolute prohibition (130).

Similarly, the argument that therapy was terminated before the initiation of the sexual relationship was rejected in *Whitesell v. Green* (131). The plaintiff and his wife consulted a psychologist for marital counseling. Two weeks after termination of the treatment, the therapist and the wife began a sexual relationship. The plaintiff claimed a breach of duty, but the psychologist argued that no professional relationship existed. The plaintiff was eventually awarded $18,000 in damages.

In a more recent case, *Barnett v. Wendt* (132), an Ohio appellate court held that a psychologist's license was properly denied based upon his violation of the state licensure law forbidding sexual involvement with "immediate ex-clients." In *Barnett,* the psychologist had sex with the client 3 or 4 weeks after the termination of treatment.

On the question of when does the physician-patient relationship end, Perr (10) feels that "too many therapists have become involved with and even married to ex-patients for one to state that this is forbidden." However, positive transferences at the termination of therapy can sustain the recovery of patients for many years or even a lifetime. Contacts with patients after treatment, even if only social, can upset the transference. Furthermore, the inequality between therapist and patient tends to persist. In a post-termination relationship, most patients expect the therapist to be available as a caregiver as well as a friend. Because psychiatric patients frequently return for treatment during a period of crisis, the treatment relationship should remain unsullied and available to the patient. Therapists should consider a "closed door policy" that recognizes that once a patient walks through the therapist's door, it is closed forever to personal relationships. Gabbard and Pope (133) discuss the various clinical, ethical, and legal issues surrounding therapist sex with the terminated patient.

A few statutes limit the period of time after treatment ends for which a psychotherapist may be held legally liable for sexual involvement with a former patient. In California, a therapist will not be subject to civil liability for having a sexual relationship with a former patient 2 years after termination (134). In Minnesota, there is a 2-year post-termination period precluding therapist-patient sex (135). In Minnesota, also, it is a felony to have sex with a former patient without a time limit if the state can prove that the therapist used deception in therapy or the patient was so emotionally dependent as to be unable to resist his or her advances (136). Wisconsin (137) also has a civil statute making sex with a former patient legally actionable for seemingly an unlimited period of time. For example, the statute states: "Any person who suffers, directly or indirectly, a physical, mental or emotional injury caused by, resulting from or arising out of sexual contact with a therapist who is rendering or *has rendered* [emphasis added] to that person psychotherapy . . ." In essence, the statute states an absolute prohibition against sex with a former patient. Illinois (2) has a 1-year sexual prohibition period. In Florida, it is always actionable for physicians to have sex with a patient, current or terminated (138).

Although it may not be illegal in some states for the psychotherapist to have sex with a former patient, it still may be unethical. The patient may not have had a therapeutic termination but rather an interrupted therapy. The question of what constitutes termination always needs to be defined. Ethical violations often reflect significant deviations in care that may harm the patient. Therapists who entertain the possibility of post-treatment sexual relations usually communicate this attitude.

Frequently, sexual involvement by a therapist with a patient occurs at the termination of treatment (118). Therapist-patient sex during the conclusion of treatment is usually the result of mishandling the termination phase of therapy. This may be due to sexualizing the separation anxiety experienced by both therapist and patient. Moreover, the vast majority of sexual contacts with former patients occur within 6 months of termination (38). Statutes that prohibit sex by therapists with former patients for a specified period of time need to consider this fact.

Appelbaum and Jorgenson (139) have proposed a 1-year waiting period after termination that "should minimize problems and allow former patients and therapists to enter into intimate relationships." If adopted, this policy would likely disrupt treatment boundaries from the outset. What deviations in treatment boundaries will occur if the therapist from the very beginning of treatment entertains the prospect of the patient as a potential sexual partner? Will the therapy turn into a tryst and become a courtship? Will the course of therapy be prematurely shortened in order to get to the sexual relationship? Even if therapist-patient sex does not take place, maintaining the option of having sex with the patient will likely lead to boundary violations that harm the patient. Clinically, it is an oxymoron for a therapist to think that he or she can maintain appropriate treatment boundaries while, at the same time, holding out the possibility of having sex with the patient in the future. From the very beginning of treatment, the most credible therapist position remains "once a patient, always a patient."

Does marriage to the patient circumvent ethical and legal difficulties?

The marriage of patients to mental health professionals is not a rare event. A number of therapists have married former patients, and some have had quite successful marriages. Although anecdotal reports exist indicating that these marriages generally do not fare well, a higher divorce rate has not been reported. Success may depend on whether the marriage occurs immediately after treatment or long after treatment has been formally terminated. Marriages between therapists and patients that occur on the heels of an interrupted treatment may contain the seed for even greater difficulty later.

Freud's admonition that the therapist must recognize that the "patient's falling in love" is induced by the treatment situation and not the charms of the therapist is especially pertinent here. A literary classic on this topic is F. Scott Fitzgerald's *Tender Is the Night,* in which the psychiatrist who marries his patient deteriorates while she improves. If one believes in the successful analysis of the transference in the analytically terminated patient, then that patient should be on a reasonably equal decision-making footing with the therapist at the end of treatment. In real life, this rarely happens.

Coleman (140) proposes a "no harm, no foul" rule for post-termination relationships. With a focus primarily on transference, she argues that "when therapy has been properly terminated and the transference resolved . . . there is no longer a power relationship that can be abused." She concludes that sex with a former client should not be malpractice per se. Any such claim must show mishandling of the transference by the therapist that causes harm to the patient.

Although the marriage contract requires the least competency of the parties of all legal contracts, consent issues may arise if legal difficulties later develop between therapist and the former patient. Through residual transferences, the spouse-patient may still harbor powerful expectations of a cure by fusion with the spouse-therapist. Although transference "cures" do take place, they may be unstable and capricious. To the extent that exploitation is an aspect of the relationship between the therapist and the patient, a successful marital outcome may be highly doubtful. The psychiatrist's wish to marry and "equalize" his position with his former patient may not necessarily place both partners on an equal footing.

Would premarital sex be considered sexual misconduct? It is less likely that ethical charges or even legal claims will be made if there is a significant period of time between the formal termination of a patient and the initiation of a permanent relationship. If a divorce occurs, however, the patient may allege that he or she was at a significant disadvantage in competently consenting to marriage. Furthermore, the patient may claim that he or she has experienced significant pain and suffering during the marriage because of unresolved transference feelings that led to its dissolution. Moreover, what will prevent the therapist from continuing to choose future partners from patients?

Such an outcome occurred in a celebrated case in the District of Columbia. In *Carmichael v. Carmichael* (141), Fredrica Carmichael was awarded $1 million in damages by a Superior Court judge based upon her allegations that her husband, psychologist Douglas Carmichael, committed malpractice when he had sexual relations with her while she was his patient. Marriage cannot undo the original sexual misconduct.

In another ethics case that came before the APA, the Board of Trustees voted to expel a psychiatrist from membership when he was found guilty of unethical conduct for engaging in sexual relations with a former patient (142). The psychiatrist argued that he had immediately referred the patient when he became aware of his romantic feelings. He also stressed that his feelings toward the patient were genuine because he considered asking her to marry him. On appeal, the APA Ethics Committee reasoned that the prohibition against sexual activity is not limited to relationships with a current patient but also applies to a relationship with a former patient. The committee held that the psychiatrist's behavior was unethical despite his attempted termination of the treatment. The committee concluded that this kind of relationship is inherently exploitative even though the psychiatrist felt he was acting from pure motives.

In a survey conducted by Conte et al. (143), practicing psychotherapists on the faculty of the psychiatry department of a medical school were asked to rate various behaviors as falling in one of the following categories: grounds for malpractice, unethical, inappropriate, unacceptable, or acceptable. Of those surveyed, 74% were psychiatrists, 22% psychologists, and 4% social workers.

Although a number of questions concerning sexual contact with patients received a very low endorsement of acceptability (0 to 6%), questions concerning behavior areas related to marriage with patients received a higher endorsement of acceptability. The four behavior areas related to marriage with patients were:

1. Terminating treatment for the purpose of marrying a patient
2. Marrying a patient after proper termination of brief therapy

3. Marrying a patient you have seen once or twice for consultation only
4. Marrying a patient after proper termination of long-term therapy

The results of the 101 respondent psychotherapists for these four areas were: 9.2% found behavior 1 acceptable; 20.4% found behavior 2 acceptable; 23.7% found behavior 3 acceptable; and 29.6% found behavior 4 acceptable. Thus, a significant number of the surveyed psychotherapists believed marriage to patients was appropriate.

These findings may reflect the long-held belief that marrying the patient is much more acceptable than just having sex with the patient. Marriage to the patient, however, does not undo the original ethical or legal wrongdoing. Cases do exist in which the professional probably married the patient in order to head off a civil suit or licensure complaint (23). In states with mandatory reporting, such as Minnesota, if the couple comes for marital counseling at some future date, the therapist may be mandated to report the original therapist-patient sex to the licensing board (23).

Can sex between therapist and patient ever be therapeutic?

Some psychiatrists have questioned whether, in rare instances, a sexual relationship between a therapist and a patient may offer a corrective emotional experience to certain deprived, object-hungry or suicidal patients (144). Might a sexual relationship help a schizoid or a borderline patient focus more on the importance of relationships or provide a sense of being wanted, offering narcissistic repair for earlier emotional wounds? If this were the case, the sexual relationship with the patient would provide a "transference cure," although on clinical and theoretical grounds such transference cures are highly problematic and uncertain.

Psychiatrist Jay Katz feels that the ethics of therapist-patient sexual relationships deserve systematic study (145). He states: "I do not believe it to be a certainty that sexual intercourse with patients necessarily represents a conflict of interest. Do we know that sexual relations are harmful to therapy? Until we have gathered such knowledge, we need to ask what value preferences lead us to the conclusion that it is." Curiously, Leonard L. Riskin, a professor of law, recommends that as a matter of community policy "sexual relations between psychotherapist and patient are justifiable only if performed for research purposes under conditions that protect important interests of the patient, the therapist, the psychotherapeutic professions, and society" (146). Nevertheless, psychotherapists who have treated patients who have been sexually intimate with a previous therapist have little doubt that these patients are almost invariably psychologically damaged by the experience. Even if this sampling is skewed, the evidence of damage is incontrovertible.

Bouhoutsos et al. (147) surveyed 704 psychologists who had treated 559 patients reporting sex with a previous therapist. The respondents felt that 82% of the patients were adversely affected when the therapist initiated intimacies. When the patient initiated sexual intimacies, 39% were thought to be adversely affected. Twenty-nine percent of the patients had negative feelings about the sexual relationship; 16% reported positive effects. The disparity in the percentages between the therapist's assessment of adverse effects and patient responses of negative feelings is striking.

A survey conducted by the Washington Psychiatric Society of its own members revealed that 97% of female therapists felt that physician-patient sexual contact is always harmful, whereas only 79% of male therapists thought sexual contact is always harmful (34). Taylor and Wagner (148) analyzed the outcomes of patient-therapist sex. They found that, as reported by either the patient or the therapist, 47% had negative results, 32% mixed results, and 21% positive results! Butler and Zelen (149) reported that the potentially positive effects of sexual activity were more apparent for the therapist. Slovenko (150) observes that sexual relations have developed between female physicians and male patients. The relatively low number of suits resulting from these relationships could be, as Slovenko notes, due to differing assumptions about sexual roles— "It is just that a man does not think of suing a woman doctor for having sex with him."

Durre (151) concludes that "amatory and sexual interaction between client and therapist dooms the potential for successful therapy and is detrimental if not devastating to the client." A study by Bouhoutsos et al. (152) found that 90% of the patients were damaged by therapist-patient sexual intimacies. A distinct therapist-patient sex syndrome has been described by Pope and Bouhoutsos (22) that contains symptoms resembling those of both borderline personality disorder and posttraumatic stress disorder. Schoener et al. (153) challenge the existence of a distinct psychological syndrome following therapist-patient sex. They consider the harm to vary considerably.

It is not possible to see how a sexual relationship between therapist and patient can ever be beneficial when based on exploitation of the patient. Furthermore, any reasonable risk-benefit analysis based on clinical experience with patients who are sexually involved with therapists underscores the great risk to the patients' current and future mental health that eclipses any theoretical clinical benefit. The belief that a sexual relationship with a patient will repair his or her life deprivations is the singular triumph of therapeutic grandiosity over reason. The demands of many of these patients are endless. The inevitable frustrations of the patient's demands lead to escalating feelings of rejection and rage, dooming the relationship. There also remains the curious fact that these "corrective emotional experiences" usually are not provided to unattractive, obese, or physically disabled patients. Even if one assumes, for the purposes of argument, that the patient has not been damaged psychologically by the sexual experience, the patient nevertheless may have lost an important opportunity to obtain treatment. Some patients may be accessible to treatment at only certain critical junctures in their lives. An admonition against therapist-patient sex ascribed to Dr. Freida Fromm-Reichmann, a pioneering psychoanalyst, is helpful: "Don't have sex with your patients, you will only disappoint them."

Does the psychiatrist have an ethical and legal duty to report the sexual misconduct of other mental health professionals?

The Principles of Medical Ethics With Annotations Especially Applicable to Psychiatry (154) advises psychiatrists to "strive to expose those physicians deficient in character or competence" (Section 2). Only a few states have adopted reporting statutes designed to protect patients from therapist sexual abuse. In Minnesota, therapists who are informed by a patient of sexual involvement with a prior therapist are required to make a report to the licensing board even if the patient objects (155). The California "brochure" statute encourages a patient's reporting by requiring the subsequent therapist to provide the patient with information about patient rights and remedies (156). In California, however, there is no actual therapist reporting requirement.

A Wisconsin statute requires the therapist to seek the patient's permission to file a report (157). If the patient gives written consent, the subsequent therapist must file a report within 30 days. The patient remains anonymous. Strasburger et al. (158) feel that the Wisconsin statute embodies the most sensitive approach to both society and the victim by requiring a sexually abused patient's consent before reporting. This method empowers the victim, protects the right to clinical confidentiality, and extends some protection to future patients of an exploitative therapist. Nonmedically trained psychotherapists face similar dilemmas. Thus, clinicians are placed in a conflicting position when reporting is required because they must also maintain patient confidentiality under moral, ethical, and legal compulsion. Except for Minnesota, no state has mandated reporting over a patient's objections. A number of states provide a "good faith" shield from liability in reporting or testifying about another therapist (2).

One way sexual misconduct is discovered is through disclosure by a therapist who is in treatment. More commonly, disclosure may come from a patient's report to the new treating therapist. Not too long ago, such reports by patients were considered to be either transference distortions or outright psychotic transferences. Not only were patients disbelieved, but they were also blamed when they were sexually involved with therapists. Today, professional concern and awareness of the problem of sexual misconduct are very high.

Whereas some recommend that the discovering psychiatrist take a strong position as an advocate for the sexually abused patient because sexually exploitative therapists tend to be repeaters, a strong clinical argument can be made for the position of strict therapist neutrality (159). This attitude does not imply an avoidance of professional responsibility or a shunning posture toward the patient. The fact is that the patient has concluded a relationship with a therapist when both the therapist and the patient acted out their problems. The patient has been emotionally devastated and is now in even greater need of treatment. The new focus must be on the reestablishment of trust in a therapeutic alliance, or otherwise no treatment can take place. The patient needs to understand his or her perceptions, thoughts, and feelings about the sexual involvement with the former therapist. When psychiatrists become advocates for their patients, they engage the patient on an action level. From a treatment perspective, the patient may need less action and more time to think and reflect.

Whether the patient should take ethical or legal action against the former therapist should be a treatment issue. Therapist neutrality should not be viewed as an act of complicity to maintain silence. The patient may justifiably fear losing his or her marriage, profession, or children by reporting therapist sexual misconduct. The patient must be able to psychologically withstand the emotional burdens of an ethical complaint procedure or litigation, with its inevitable adversarial tone, financial strain, blame, and agonizing procedural delays. The patient may not wish to seek redress for a variety of reasons, including a sense of guilt or shame, or a continuation of feelings of protection, "love," and yearning for the previous therapist. On the other hand, the patient unconsciously may seek litigation as a way of continuing contact with the therapist. The wish is often to see the therapist again in the hope of being rescued from severe emotional pain.

Some patients have been repeatedly traumatized by a succession of therapists who insisted upon reporting the patient's accusations of sexual misconduct despite the patient's wishes to the contrary. Attempting to undo the exploitation of the previous therapist is a major countertransference trap that often leads to additional exploitation of the patient. Only when a therapist is found who is willing to honor the patient's request, will actual treatment begin. The patient should not be burdened with an adversarial procedure because of the therapist's need to vent personal outrage or the profession's need to police its own ranks. Moreover, a patient may be unable to express hostile feelings toward the new therapist when the latter undertakes an advocacy role for the patient. The new therapy should be kept as free as possible from double agent roles.

The therapist who acts as an advocate for the patient needs to ponder other critical issues as well. In a court of law, there is a presumption of innocence that must be overcome through the adversarial process that provides equal representation and other procedural safeguards. Hearsay evidence is not usually permitted. The Federal Rules of Evidence (160), however, provide an exception to the hearsay rule.

Unless there are several accusers, or there is corroborating evidence such as pictures, hotel-motel receipts, love letters from the therapist, or identifying anatomical features of the therapist, the reports of patients remain hearsay. In *State v. Haseltine* (161), the court of appeals held that in the absence of any indication that the defendant's 16-year-old daughter had any physical or mental disorder that might affect her credibility, admission of the psychiatrist's opinion that the defendant's daughter was an incest victim constituted an error that was prejudicial. This conclusion was based upon an opinion that she was telling the truth in her allegations of sexual contact by the father. The daughter's account of sexual assault was not corroborated by any independent evidence.

Clinicians who abandon the position of neutrality when given information about sexual misconduct run the danger of becoming both judge and jury. Clinical experience demonstrates that patients can develop powerful, erotized psychotic transferences that contain the delusion of sexual involvement with other individuals (erotomania or Clerambaults syndrome). Presumably, clinical judgment will differentiate fact from fiction. However, this is not always possible. There are vindictive, antisocial persons who may wish to malign the therapist with charges of sexual involvement because of an actual or perceived slight or insult (24). Some patients with borderline personality disorder may have serious problems in separating reality from sexual fantasies about the therapist.

Schoener et al. (162) note that the literature contains few instances of false claims of sexual misconduct against therapists. They expect the situation to change, however, because of greater awareness of therapist-patient sex in the community and because mandatory reporting has brought out some unsubstantiated claims. They note that a person without a legitimate grievance may find public accusation easier than an actual victim of therapist-patient sexual abuse. Thus, the false reporting of sexual accusations against therapists may follow the pattern of false accusations that have steadily increased in child abuse and rape cases.

Some therapists and attorneys believe that litigation serves important therapeutic ends (163, 164). Follow-up work with patients has demonstrated two factors that are key to their recovery: having taken action and having talked to others victimized in a similar fashion (23). The patient may feel vindicated when a jury of his or her peers finds the therapist guilty of negligence. In addition, overcoming feelings of helplessness, anger, and revenge may assist resolution of the trauma. The patient must be prepared to pay the high emotional costs of humiliation, public exposure of one's private life, and a further sense of assault and trauma inflicted by the legal system (11). Even after litigation is undertaken, victims of sexual misconduct may feel torn between prosecuting and wanting to protect the abusing therapist.

Stone (165) provides a helpful recommendation when he advises using a forensic consultant familiar with legal and ethical issues. Some patients may not be able to tolerate therapist neutrality, perceiving such a stance as condemnatory or rejecting. The forensic consultant may wish to take a more active advocacy position if this is acceptable to the patient. The extent to which a consultant may facilitate or hinder the patient's therapeutic progress remains problematic. Can the therapist and patient effectively work with feelings and conflicts triggered by the adversarial procedure, or will the litigation process mask feelings and conflicts that can be worked out only in the peace and quiet of an unperturbed treatment situation?

Ms. Wilson brought a suit against Dr. James. Can she concentrate on the therapeutic work at hand with the new therapist, or will she constantly be upset and distracted by the legal storm that will inevitably arise if Dr. James contests her claim? Unfortunately, some patients may have to choose between litigation and treatment. To complicate matters, the new therapist is rarely free from these conflicting issues.

California has created a reasonable alternative to mandatory reporting by adopting a brochure statute (166). The code requires psychotherapists whose patients allege sexual contact with a previous therapist to provide the patient with an informative brochure. The brochure gives a definition of therapist-patient sexual contact. It also describes common misconduct scenarios, a patient's bill of rights, instructions and options for reporting alleged sexual acts, complaint procedures, and available support services. Psychotherapists who fail to abide by the "brochure" law are guilty of "unprofessional conduct."

When a therapist-patient in treatment discloses sexual exploitation of his or her patient, or when a patient discloses exploitation by a previous therapist, does a *Tarasoff* duty to warn and protect arise toward the current patients of the exploitative therapist?

Eth and Leong (167) raise the question of whether a therapist has a *Tarasoff* duty to warn the potentially endangered patients of a therapist-patient who discloses patient sexual exploitation. When a patient makes such a disclosure, the authors feel that the accusation remains hearsay. Nevertheless, as noted elsewhere in this chapter, some jurisdictions require reporting of a sexually exploitative therapist unless the patient objects. Minnesota has a mandatory reporting requirement (155). Eth and Leong believe that a therapist-patient's disclosure of sexual misconduct confronts the therapist with a conflict involving confidentiality versus the duty to warn. They are of the opinion that the psychiatrist has an ethical and "perhaps legal responsibility to act," and recommend notification of an ethics committee or state licensure board.

The legal duty to warn or protect usually arises when serious, imminent *physical* (not psychological) harm threatens a clearly identifiable, endangered third person. Only under this circumstance is the obligation not to breach confidentiality overcome. Although some therapists feel that sexual exploitation is equivalent to or even worse than murder, such a position would go well beyond the most expansive *Tarasoff* holdings of a distinct minority of courts (168). Attempting to notify the patients thought to be at risk for sexual exploitation could be very traumatizing and largely unnecessary. Every patient of the offending therapist is not an equal target nor is he or she equally vulnerable to sexual exploitation. Furthermore, notifying an ethics committee or state licensure board is analogous to calling the police. Finally, sexually exploitative therapists would probably not come for treatment if treating therapists were under an expanded *Tarasoff* duty to report therapist-patient sexual misconduct to the authorities.

Therapists must decide whom they will serve—their patients or society. Ethical principles conflict on this issue. The psychiatrist is ethically required to report impaired colleagues while maintaining the confidentiality of the therapist-patient. (See Sections 2 and 4 of *The Principles of Medical Ethics* in Appendix 1.) In the final ethical analysis, maintaining confidentiality should be given priority so long as further sexual exploitation ceases by the therapist-patient. Might a long-term treatment approach reduce the threat of further patient exploitation while also fulfilling the duty to protect? The duty to warn, by itself, is usually an insufficient clinical intervention. Moreover, warning will probably end treatment as well as any hope of preventing continued patient exploitation. Fulfilling the duty to protect usually allows for a variety of clinical interventions with the therapist-patient. For example, it may be possible to bring the exploited patient into the therapist-patient's treatment in order to prevent further exploitation and initiate referral to another therapist (25).

The sexually exploitative therapist who seeks treatment is usually struggling with conflicts over sexual acting out. If the therapist who finds the sexual exploitation of patients ego-syntonic, he or she will not consider the need for treatment. These are the predatory therapists who are likely to continue exploiting and psychologically harming their patients. Only when treatment efforts appear to be ineffective in preventing further patient exploitation should reporting be considered.

In a number of states, vulnerable adult reporting law exists that takes precedence over the maintenance of confidentiality in therapy (169). In states that make therapist-patient sex a crime, not reporting the continuing sexual misconduct of a therapist-patient could also cause the treating therapist to run afoul of the criminal statute.

Reporting duties also may be owed to other mental health professionals or institutions who may be considering the exploitative therapist-patient for employment. For example, a Minnesota statute (170) requires divulging the therapist-patient's sexual involvement with his or her patients to prospective employers. The treating therapist is protected from liability when reporting is done in good faith. The use of signed, wide-ranging release of information provisions in the hiring process would also permit reporting of therapist-patient sexual misconduct. If the treating therapist fails to report such information and the therapist-patient is hired and subsequently injures someone, the treating therapist may have direct liability for future damages.

Prospective employers, however, do have other sources of information. In many states, abuse registries are maintained that list persons who have abused children or vulnerable adults.

What can be done to prevent sexual misconduct by mental health professionals?

In 1984, the APA established a work group to develop an educational program for reducing or eliminating sexual activities between psychiatrists and their patients (171). The prevention of physician-patient sex as a major problem is also being recognized beyond the United States. Recently, the College of Physicians and Surgeons of Ontario made sweeping, important recommendations in an effort to prevent the sexual abuse of patients by physicians (21).

A national survey of psychiatrists' attitudes on psychiatrist-patient sexual contact revealed disquieting results (172). Whereas 98% of respondents said that therapist-patient sexual contact is always inappropriate and usually harmful to the patient, 29.6% said that post-termination sexual contact may be acceptable. Seventy-four percent of psychiatrists acknowledging sexual contact with patients believed that sexual contact with a patient after termination could be appropriate. The ethical education of all psychiatrists must continue to receive high priority. *The Principles of Medical Ethics With Annotations Especially Applicable to Psychiatry* (173) should be read by all psychiatrists (see Appendix 1). For the psychiatric resident, it must be mandatory reading. Every psychiatrist must be as knowledgeable of current ethical practices as he or she is of clinical aspects of psychiatry. It is truly remarkable to discover in consultation and in seminars that so few psychiatrists have read this important document.

Although the ethos of medicine has always emphasized humanitarian concern for patients, intellectual capacity and performance currently seem to be given heavier weight than moral character in the selection of mental health professionals. Intellectual achievement does not guarantee mental health or the presence of sound character. The data from the study by Pope et al. (35) suggest that personal ethics and a regard for the patient's welfare are more compelling than fear of consequences in preventing sexual intimacies with patients. The ancient Greeks knew where to place their emphasis in recognizing that character is destiny.

Ironically, the word *therapist* contains two hidden words: the rapist. The line between treatment and exploitation of the patient can be very tenuous and easily crossed. Selection of prospective therapists must aim at uncovering potentially exploitative persons. In this regard, female therapists are not exempt from sexual misconduct. Female therapists are significantly represented among mental health professionals. Male therapists, however, are involved with female patients in 9 out of every 10 sexual misconduct cases (174). Tragically, children are not exempt from sexual exploitation by therapists either.

Individuals with severe narcissistic or antisocial personality disorder should be vigorously weeded out. The presence of one of the paraphilias should represent an absolute contraindication to training as a mental health professional. Psychological testing of all prospective candidates for training could strengthen the process of selection. There is resistance to this proposal by some educators who view psychological testing as "too intrusive" in the selection process.

The policy of mandatory therapy for prospective therapists that is implemented in psychoanalytic institutes deserves important consideration, particularly for mental health professionals who want to work intensively and psychodynamically with patients. Gartrell et al. (38) reported that offenders, as compared with nonoffenders, are more likely to have had personal psychotherapy or psychoanalysis as well as to have completed an accredited residency. Though this finding appears to be counterintuitive, surely it would be naive to think that personal therapy could prevent sexual misconduct in any absolute sense. Therapists with many years of analysis or therapy have not been immune from sexually exploiting their patients. Nevertheless, the incidence of sexual misconduct might be considerably higher without therapy. This issue deserves further study. Therapy for the therapist appears not to be as determinative as the type and degree of individual psychopathology of the therapist combined with the effectiveness of the particular therapy undertaken.

Adequate training is critical in learning how to recognize and manage the phenomena of transference and countertransference. Courses, seminars, and tutorials on the management of sexual feelings of therapists and patients should be an integral part of every therapist's training program. Because sexual misconduct is usually the end result of progressive boundary violations over time, therapists can be trained in early detection of boundary violations during the treatment of patients. Educational programs must provide an atmosphere in which therapists in training can acknowledge, discuss, and explore sexual feelings toward patients. Having therapists discuss sexual feelings, however, is not an easy matter, as verified by Searles (175). He described his "considerable anxiety, guilt, and embarrassment" over genital excitement during analysis of patients in addition to romantic and erotic dreams about these patients.

Some mental health professionals are not able to appreciate fully the existence and power of transference and countertransference feelings in the therapeutic situation despite many years of working with patients. For example, Dr. James took at face value his patient's wish for a sexual relationship with him while not fully recognizing the intensity of his own object hunger and depression, with predictable disastrous results. Mental health professionals need to know their own strengths and weaknesses. They should also have a good working knowledge of their coping mechanisms during personal crises. Managing transference and countertransference issues is a lifelong professional challenge.

In *Cosgrove v. Lawrence* (176), the court recognized that the mishandling of transference was a foreseeable occupational hazard. Although not leading to sexual exploitation in every case, the inability to handle transference and countertransference reactions may be the basis for providing substandard care and result in legal liability for the therapist. Furthermore, the personal consequences of mismanagement may lead to a chronic feeling of frustration and dissatisfaction with one's work.

Mental health professionals undergoing training primarily in psychopharmacology or behavior therapy may not be sufficiently trained in managing transference and countertransference. Such phenomena may be consciously denied or rejected. Nevertheless, *every* therapist, no matter what his or her theoretical treatment persuasion, must learn to manage the powerful feelings that frequently arise between therapist and patient. The Exploitation Index, developed by Epstein and Simon (121), may be a useful educational tool in helping therapists maintain treatment boundaries.

Therapists undergoing a personal crisis involving financial losses, malpractice litigation, or a disruption in their own personal relationships may be angry, lonely, and object hungry. For example, do patients seeing a recently divorced therapist themselves go through a divorce? To what extent do patients suffer this kind of iatrogenic effect? Prevention of iatrogenic effects or sexual involvement with a patient requires referral of the patient with whom the therapist cannot maintain a proper position of neutrality and ensure appropriate treatment boundaries.

Finally, research into the causes of sexual activities between therapists and patients is needed. Is there a significant difference between therapists who receive personal therapy and those who do not in determining which therapists will become sexually involved with their patients? What type of patient is more vulnerable to sexual exploitation? These are critical questions that need answers. The research conducted by Pope et al. (36) on the extent to which therapists are sexually attracted to patients, how they manage such feelings, and the extent to which their training is adequate in this regard represents an important start to an immensely important subject. In a recent study, Epstein et al. (122) surveyed 532 psychiatrists using the Exploitation Index (see discussion above). Approximately two-thirds of the psychiatrists who achieved a high score on the Exploitation Index were alerted and stimulated to make specific changes in their future treatment practices.

Can the sexual exploitation of patients by psychotherapists be reduced through consumer education?

The answer to this question depends upon the psychological strengths and susceptibilities of individual patients. Consumer education will help to some extent. Yet, it appears that the mental health professions have not done enough to educate the public.

As part of the increased education and consumer awareness of the public, prospective therapy patients need to be educated on the appropriate treatment boundaries that should exist between therapists and patients. This is occurring increasingly through radio and television as well as by books and special educational programs. Effective psychotherapy is a joint enterprise based on trust that is facilitated by mutually informed participants.

A study by Vinson (177) showed that sexually exploited female patients lacked knowledge of complaint procedures rather than motivation in taking action in their own behalf. Nevertheless, many patients who enter therapy, particularly for the first time, do not know what constitutes appropriate treatment, nor do they have clear ideas about treatment boundaries. Some patients simply may not know that sex with a therapist is unethical and that it constitutes malpractice. Patient ignorance combined with a powerful positive transference may lead to a blind trust that empowers the exploitative therapist. On the other hand, the patient who innately resists transference developments as part of his or her own unique psychodynamics may be less vulnerable to sexual exploitation than patients who want to live out their transferences.

Patients who sense they are being exploited often get an "Uh oh" reaction. Patients who are receiving benefit from their therapy, however, will often have an "Ah-ha" reaction to insight and psychological growth. The Wisconsin Task Force on Sexual Misconduct has published guidelines for patients who want to evaluate their therapy experience (178). The Task Force recommends a number of protective options for patients when exploitation threatens or occurs.

Recognition of two types of inappropriate therapist behaviors can be helpful in alerting patients, and even therapists, to the possibility that therapeutic boundaries are being crossed:

1. Is the therapist requesting or pressuring the patient to perform any personal task or join in any activity for the primary benefit of the therapist?
2. Is the therapist requesting to see the patient outside of therapy sessions in the absence of an actual psychiatric emergency or other compelling clinical reasons?

Are rehabilitation programs available specifically for sexually exploitative therapists?

Gartrell et al. (179) have described rehabilitative approaches to exploitative therapists. Minnesota has developed a program for the management and rehabilitation of sexually exploitative therapists (180). The Walk-in Counseling Center, a nonprofit agency in Minneapolis, evaluates exploitative therapists for rehabilitation potential. Pope (181) provides a format for the development of rehabilitation programs for the exploitative therapist. Generally, few programs exist for these individuals. They usually are lumped together with other impaired physicians and required to undertake some form of treatment.

References

1. Keeton W, Dobbs D, Keeton R, et al: Prosser and Keeton on Torts, 5th Edition. St Paul, MN, West Publishing, 1984, p 187
2. ILL ANN STAT ch 70, § 802 (Smith-Hurd 1989)
3. CAL CIV CODE § 43.93(b) (West Supp 1990)
4. MINN STAT ANN 148 A.02 (West 1986)
5. WIS STAT § 895.70 (1991)
6. Jorgenson L, Randles R, Strasburger L: The furor over psychotherapist-patient sexual contact: new solutions to old problems. William and Mary Law Review 32:645–732, 1991
7. American Psychiatric Association: The Principles of Medical Ethics With Annotations Especially Applicable to Psychiatry. Washington, DC, American Psychiatric Association, 1989, Section 2, Annotation 1
8. Cummings NA, Sobel SB: Malpractice insurance: update on sex claims. Psychotherapy 22:186–188, 1985
9. Klein JI, Macbeth JE, Onek JN: Legal Issues in the Private Practice of Psychiatry. Washington, DC, American Psychiatric Press, 1984, p 6
10. Perr IN: Sexual involvement with patients. Psychiatric Times 3(5):6, 1986
11. Simon RI: Concise Guide to Psychiatry and Law for Clinicians. Washington, DC, American Psychiatric Press, 1992
12. Gutheil TG, Appelbaum PS: Clinical Handbook of Psychiatry and the Law. New York, McGraw-Hill, 1982, p 153
13. McCartney JL: Overt transference. Journal of Sex Research 2:227–237, 1966
14. Shepard M: The Love Treatment: Sexual Intimacy Between Patients and Psychotherapists. New York, Peter H Wyden, 1971
15. Ibid, p 208
16. Shepard M: The Psychiatrist's Head. New York, Peter H Wyden, 1972
17. Shepard v Ambach, 68 AD2d 984, 414 NYS2d 817 (NY App Div 1979)
18. Hirsh HL: Loss of consortium. Medical Trial Technique Quarterly 30:84–110, 1983
19. Lange JE, Hirsh HL: Legal problems of intimate therapy. Medical Trial Technique Quarterly 29:201–208, 1982
20. Kluft RP: Treating the patient who has been sexually exploited by a previous therapist. Psychiatr Clin North Am 12:483–500, 1989
21. Task Force on Sexual Abuse of Patients: The Preliminary Report of the Task Force on Sexual Abuse of Patients: An Independent Task Force Commissioned by the College of Physicians and Surgeons of Ontario. Ontario, Canada, College of Physicians and Surgeons, November 25, 1991
22. Pope KS, Bouhoutsos JC: Sexual Intimacy Between Therapists and Patients. New York, Praeger, 1986, pp 45–56
23. Gary R Schoener, Executive Director of Walk-in Counseling Center, Minneapolis, MN, personal communication, February 1991; see also Borys DS, Pope KS: Dual relationships between therapist and client: a national study of psychologists, psychiatrists, and social workers. Professional Psychology: Research and Practice 20:283–293, 1989
24. Gutheil TG: Patients involved in sexual misconduct with therapists: is a victim profile possible? Psychiatric Annals 21:661–667, 1991

25. Gutheil TG: Borderline personality disorders, boundary violations, and patient-therapist sex: medicolegal pitfalls. Am J Psychiatry 146:597–602, 1989
26. Simon RI: Sexual exploitation of patients: how it begins before it happens. Psychiatric Annals 19:104–112, 1989
27. PF Slawson, personal communication, October 1984
28. Stone AA: Law, Psychiatry, and Morality. Washington, DC, American Psychiatric Press, 1985, pp 211–212; Olarte SW: Characteristics of therapists who become involved in sexual boundary violations. Psychiatric Annals 21:657–660, 1991
29. Schoener GR, Milgrom JH, Gonsiorek JC, et al: Psychotherapists' Sexual Involvement With Clients: Intervention and Prevention. Minneapolis, MN, Walk-in Counseling Center, 1989, pp 402–404
30. Dahlberg CC: Sexual contact between client and therapist. Contemporary Psychoanalysis, Spring 1970, pp 118-119
31. Wood B, Klein S, Cross HJ: Impaired practitioners: psychologists' opinions about prevalence and proposals for intervention. Professional Psychology: Research and Practice 16:843–850, 1985
32. Holroyd JC, Brodsky AM: Psychologists' attitudes and practices regarding erotic and nonerotic physical contact with patients. Am Psychol 32:843–849, 1977
33. Kardener SH, Fuller M, Mensh IN: A survey of physicians' attitudes and practices regarding erotic and nonerotic contact with patients. Am J Psychiatry 130:1077–1081, 1973
34. Women's Committee to the Washington Psychiatric Society: Result of questionnaire on sexual abuse between physicians and their patients. Washington, DC, May 24, 1985
35. Pope KS, Levenson H, Schover L: Sexual intimacy in psychology training: results and implications of a national survey. Am Psychol 34:682–689, 1979
36. Pope KS, Keith-Spiegel P, Tabachnick BG: Sexual attraction to clients. Am Psychol 41:147–158, 1986
37. Tower LE: Countertransference. J Am Psychoanal Assoc 4:224–255, 1956
38. Gartrell N, Herman J. Olarte S, et al: Psychiatrist-patient sexual contact—results of a national survey, I: prevalence. Am J Psychiatry 143:1126–1131, 1986
39. Borys DS, Pope KS: Dual relationships between therapist and client: a national study of psychologists, psychiatrists, and social workers. Professional Psychology: Research and Practice 20:283–293, 1989
40. People v Bernstein, 171 Cal App 2d 279, 340 P2d 299 (Cal Ct App 1959); State v Vonlock, 121 NH 697, 433 A2d 1299 (1981), overruled, State v Smith, 127 NH 433, 503 A2d 774 (1985); Anonymous v Berry, No 78-8182-CA, Duval Cty (Fla Cir Ct, March 14, 1979)
41. Simon RI: Sexual misconduct of therapist. Trial 21:46–51, 1985
42. Schoener GR, Milgrom JH, Gonsiorek JC, et al: Psychotherapists' Sexual Involvement With Clients: Intervention and Prevention. Minneapolis, MN, Walk-in Counseling Center, 1989, p 14
43. Luepker E, Retsch-Bogart C: Group treatment of clients who have been sexually involved with their psychotherapists, in Sexual Exploitation of Patients by Health Professionals. Edited by Burgess A, Hartman C. New York, Praeger, 1985
44. P Slawson, personal communication, October 1984
45. Gartrell N, Herman J, Olarte S: Psychiatric residents' sexual contact with educators and patients: results of a national survey. Am J Psychiatry 145:690–694, 1988

46. American Psychiatric Association: The Principles of Medical Ethics With Annotations Especially Applicable to Psychiatry. Washington, DC, American Psychiatric Association, 1989, Section 4, Annotation 14

47. Cal San Diego Super Ct (July 7, 1982), digested in 24 Atla L Rep 295 (1984)

48. Beis EB: Mental Health and the Law. Rockville, MD, Aspen, 1984, p 58

49. Walker E, Young PD: A Killing Cure. New York, Henry Holt, 1986

50. 263 So 2d 256 (Fla Dis Ct App 1972)

51. 105 Sol J 1008 (1961)

52. Washington Psychiatric Society: Ethics alert. Washington Psychiatric Society Newsletter, May 1987, pp 4, 7

53. Stone AA: Law, Psychiatry, and Morality. Washington, DC, American Psychiatric Press, 1984, pp 197–198

54. 198 Cal App 3d 591, 243 Cal Rptr 807 (Cal Ct App 1988)

55. Keeton W, Dobbs D, Keeton R, et al: Prosser and Keeton on Torts, 5th Edition. St Paul, MN, West Publishing, 1984, p 916

56. Oleck's Tort Law Practice Manual. New York, Prentice-Hall, 1982, Section 76

57. 89 Or App 289, 748 P2d 1020 (Or Ct App), aff'd 307 Or 242, 765 P2d 811 (1988) (en banc)

58. COLO REV STAT § 18-3-405.5 (1989); MINN STAT ANN § 609.344 (West 1989); MINN STAT § 609.344(g),(v),(h–j) (Supp 1985); ND CENT CODE § 12.1-20-06.1 (1988); WIS STAT ANN § 940.22(2) (West 1989); ME REV STAT Title 17-A, § 253(2)(I) (Supp 1989); CAL BUS & PROF CODE § 729 (Supp 1989); FLA STAT ANN § X (West 1990); IOWA CODE §§ 702.11, 709.15, § 614.1 (1991)

59. Schoener GR, Milgrom JH, Gonsiorek JC, et al: Psychotherapists' Sexual Involvement With Clients: Intervention and Prevention. Minneapolis, MN, Walk-in Counseling Center, 1989, p 331

60. Perr IN: Medicolegal aspects of professional sexual exploitation, in Sexual Exploitation in Professional Relationships. Edited by Gabbard GO. Washington DC, American Psychiatric Press, 1989, pp 211–227

61. WIS STAT ANN § 940.22 (West Supp 1984–85)

62. 450 NW2d 189 (Minn Ct App 1990)

63. Halpern AL: Sex with patients (letter). Psychiatric News 25(15):27, 1990

64. CAL BUS & PROF CODE § 729(b) (West 1990)

65. CAL BUS & PROF CODE § 729(b)(2) (West 1990)

66. NH REV STAT ANN § 632-A:2 (VII); COLO REV STAT § 18-3-403(h), 404(g) (1986); MICH COMP LAWS ANN § 750-520b(1)(f)(iv) (West Supp 1990); WYO STAT § 6-2-303(a)(vii) (1988)

67. MICH COMP LAWS ANN § 750.520b(1)(f)(iv)

68. MODEL PENAL CODE § 213 1(2)(b) (1962)

69. ARIZ REV STAT ANN § 32-2081 (5) (F) (1986); COLO REV STAT § 12-36-117(1)(r) (1985); DC CODE ANN § 458.331(1)(j) (Supp 1990); IND CODE 25-33-1-13.1(b)(5) (1985); KAN STAT ANN § 65-2837(b)(16) (Supp 1988); NEV REV STAT ANN § 630.304(5) (Michie 1986); WASH REV CODE ANN § 18.130.180(24) (1989 & Supp 1990); W VA CODE § 30-3-14(c)(8) (1986 & Supp 1989)

70. 565 NE2d 780 (Mass 1991)

71. Jorgenson L, Appelbaum PS: For whom the statute tolls: extending the time during which patients can sue. Hosp Community Psychiatry 42:683–684, 1991

72. Simon RI: Concise Guide to Psychiatry and Law for Clinicians. Washington, DC, American Psychiatric Press, 1992

73. Brigham RE: Psychotherapy stressors and sexual misconduct: a factor analytic study of the experience of non-offending and offending psychologists in Wisconsin. Unpublished doctoral dissertation. Cited in Schoener GR, Milgrom JH, Gonsiorek JC, et al: Psychotherapists' Sexual Involvement With Clients: Intervention and Prevention. Minneapolis, MN, Walk-in Counseling Center, 1989

74. Appelbaum PS: Statutes regulating patient-therapist sex. Hosp Community Psychiatry 41:15–16, 1990; see also Strasburger LH, Jorgenson L, Randles R: Criminalization of psychotherapist-patient sex. Am J Psychiatry 148:859–863, 1991

75. CAL CIV CODE § 43.93(b) (West Supp 1990); FLA STAT ANN § 458.329, 331 (West Supp 1986); ILL ANN STAT ch 70, § 802 (Smith-Hurd 1989); MINN STAT ANN 148 A.02 (West 1986); WIS STAT § 895.70 (1991)

76. MINN STAT ANN § 148A.02 (West 1989)

77. COLO REV STAT § 18-3-405.5 (1989)

78. ME REV STAT, Title 17-A, § 253(2)(I) (Supp 1989)

79. MINN STAT ANN § 609.344 (West 1989); MINN STAT ANN § 609.344(g,)(v),(h–j) (West Supp 1985); MINN STAT § 609.341 et seq (Supp 1990)

80. CAL BUS & PROF CODE § 729 (Supp 1989)

81. ND CENT CODE § 12.1-20-06.1 (1) (Michie Supp 1989)

82. WIS STAT ANN § 940.22(2) (West 1989)

83. 1990 FLA SESS LAWS SERV 490.0112 § 1(1) (tentative assignment) (West 1990)

84. MICH COMP LAWS ANN §§ 750.520b(1)(d)(i); 750.90 (West Supp 1984–85)

85. NH REV STAT ANN § 632-A:2 Part VIII (Supp 1986)

86. WYO STAT § 6-2-303 (1988)

87. IOWA CODE §§ 702.11, 709.15, § 614.1 (1991)

88. CAL CIV CODE § 43.93 (Deering 1987)

89. Karasu TB: Psychoanalysis and psychoanalytic psychotherapy, in Comprehensive Textbook of Psychiatry V, Vol 2. Edited by Kaplan HI, Sadock BJ. Baltimore, MD, Williams & Wilkins, 1989, pp 1442–1461; see pp 1446–1448

90. Greenson RR: The Technique and Practice of Psychoanalysis, Vol 1. New York, International Universities Press, 1967, p 348

91. Grossman CM: Transference, countertransference, and being in love. Psychoanal Q 34:249–256, 1967

92. Winnicott D: Hate in the countertransference. Int J Psychoanal 30:69–75, 1949

93. Little M: Countertransference and the patient's response to it. Int J Psychoanal 32:32–40, 1951

94. Heimann P: On countertransference. Int J Psychoanal 31:81–84, 1950

95. Gutheil TG: Patient-therapist sexual relations. Harvard Medical School Mental Health Letter 6:4–6, 1989

96. Stone AA: Law, Psychiatry, and Morality. Washington, DC, American Psychiatric Press, 1984, p 194

97. Freud S: Observations on transference-love (1915[1914]), in the Standard Edition of the Complete Psychological Works of Sigmund Freud, Vol 12. Translated and edited by Strachey J. London, Hogarth Press, 1958, pp 159–171; see pp 160–161, 166

98. Council of Ethical and Judicial Affairs, American Medical Association: Current Opinions of the Council on Ethical and Judicial Affairs. Chicago, IL, American Medical Association, 1989, Opinion 8.14, Sexual misconduct; see also Council on Ethical and Judicial Affairs, American Medical Association: Sexual misconduct in the practice of medicine. JAMA 266:2741–2745, 1991

99. House just says no to sex between doctors, patients. American Medical News, December 14, 1990, p 10

100. 805 F2d 1363, 1365 (9th Cir 1986)

101. 47 Md App 202, 422 A2d 389 (Md Ct Spec App 1980)

102. 89 Misc 2d 468, 391 NYS2d 962 (1977)

103. Slovenko R: Forensic psychiatry, in Comprehensive Textbook of Psychiatry IV, Vol 2. Edited by Kaplan HI, Sadock BJ. Baltimore, MD, Williams & Wilkins, 1985, pp 1960–1990; see p 1986

104. 164 Ga App 215; 296 SE2d 126 (Ga Ct App 1982)

105. Bisbing SB: Recent legal developments and psychiatry: 1989–1990, in American Psychiatric Press Review of Clinical Psychiatry and the Law, Vol 3. Edited by Simon RI. Washington, DC, American Psychiatric Press, 1992, pp 285–328

106. 447 NW2d 5 (Minn App 1989), aff'd 459 NW2d 698 (Minn 1990)

107. American Psychiatric Association: Professional Liability Insurance and Psychiatric Malpractice (Task Force Report No 13). Washington, DC, American Psychiatric Association, 1978

108. Simon RI: Psychological injury caused by boundary violation precursors to therapist-patient sex. Psychiatric Annals 21:614–619, 1991

109. 453 F Supp 765 (ED Pa 1978), cert denied McCabe v Greenberg, 444 U.S. 840 (1979)

110. Pope KS, Bouhoutsos JC: Sexual Intimacy Between Therapists and Patients. New York, Praeger, 1986, pp 39–55

111. Schoener GR, Milgrom JH, Gonsiorek JC, et al: Psychotherapists' Sexual Involvement With Clients: Intervention and Prevention. Minneapolis, MN, Walk-in Counseling Center, 1989, pp 133–145

112. Dobbs DB: Dobbs' Handbook on Remedies. St Paul, MN, West Publishing, 1973

113. 85 Misc 2d 891, 381 NYS2d 587 (NY Sup Ct 1976)

114. 436 SW2d 753, 761 (Mo 1968)

115. 61 NC App 170, 300 SE2d 833 (NC Ct App 1983)

116. Simon RI: Sexual exploitation of patients: how it begins before it happens. Psychiatric Annals 19:104–112, 1989

117. Rutter P: Sex in the Forbidden Zone: When Therapists, Doctors, Clergy, Teachers and Other Men in Power Betray Women's Trust. Los Angeles, CA, Torcher, 1989

118. Gary R Schoener, Executive Director of Walk-in Counseling Center, Minneapolis, MN, personal communication, April 1991

119. Schoener GR, Milgrom JH, Gonsiorek JC, et al: Psychotherapists' Sexual Involvement With Clients: Intervention and Prevention. Minneapolis, MN, Walk-in Counseling Center, 1989, p 43

120. Furrow BR: Malpractice in Psychotherapy. Lexington, MA, DC Heath, 1980, pp 33–36

121. Epstein RS, Simon RI: The Exploitation Index: an early warning indicator of boundary violations in psychotherapy. Bull Menninger Clin 54:450–465, 1990

122. Epstein RS, Simon RI, Kay GG: Assessing boundary violations in psychotherapy: survey results with the Exploitation Index. Bull Menninger Clin 56(2):1–17, 1992

123. Holroyd JC, Brodsky AM: Does touching patients lead to sexual intercourse? Professional Psychology 11:807–811, 1980

124. Simon RI: Treatment boundary violations: clinical, ethical and legal considerations, in Forensic Psychiatry: A Comprehensive Textbook. Edited by Rosner R. New York, Van Nostrand Reinhold (in press); Gutheil TG, Gabbard GO: The concept of boundaries in clinical practice: theoretical and risk management dimensions. Am J Psychiatry (in press)

125. Simon RI: The psychiatrist as a fiduciary: avoiding the double agent role. Psychiatric Annals 17:622–626, 1987

126. Glover E: The Technique of Psychoanalysis. New York, International Universities Press, 1955, p 92

127. Stone AA: Law, Psychiatry, and Morality. Washington, DC, American Psychiatric Press, 1985, p 212

128. Halleck SL: Law in the Practice of Psychiatry. New York, Plenum, 1980, p 103

129. Recent ethics cases. Psychiatric News 17(8):8–9, 1982

130. Schoener GR, Milgrom JH, Gonsiorek JC, et al: Psychotherapists' Sexual Involvement With Clients: Intervention and Prevention. Minneapolis, MN, Walk-in Counseling Center, 1989, p 275

131. No 38745 (D Hawaii Nov 19, 1973)

132. 33 Ohio App 3d 124, 514 NE2d 739 (Ohio Ct App 1986)

133. Gabbard GO, Pope KS: Sexual intimacies after termination: clinical, ethical, and legal aspects, in Sexual Exploitation in Professional Relationships. Edited by Gabbard GO. Washington, DC, American Psychiatric Press, 1989, pp 115–127

134. Cal Civ Code § 43.92(b)(2) (West Supp 1990)

135. Minn Stat Ann § 148A.01–.06 (West Supp 1989)

136. Minn Stat Ann § 609:345(h),(i),(j) (West Supp 1985)

137. Wis Stat Ann §§ 893.585, 895.70(2) (West 1989)

138. Fla Stat Ann § 458.329, 331 (West Supp 1986)

139. Appelbaum PS, Jorgenson L: Psychotherapist-patient sexual contact after termination of treatment: an analysis and a proposal. Am J Psychiatry 148:1466–1473, 1991

140. Coleman P: Sex between psychiatrist and former patient: a proposal for a "no harm, no foul" rule. Oklahoma Law Review 41:1–52, 1988

141. CV Nos DR-5289-88 and DR-37-89, DC Super Ct (October 29, 1989)

142. Recent cases of ethical violations reported. Psychiatric News 19(21):24, 32, 1984

143. Conte H, Plutchik R, Picard S, et al: Ethics in the practice of psychotherapy: a survey. Am J Psychother 43:32–42, 1989

144. Eyman JR, Gabbard GO: Will therapist-patient sex prevent suicide? Psychiatric Annals 21:669–674, 1991

145. Katz J: Designated discussion: Fritz Redlich's The Ethics of Sex Therapy, in Ethical Issues in Sex Therapy and Research. Edited by Masters W, Johnson V, Kolodny R. Boston, MA, Little, Brown, 1977, p 161

146. Riskin LL: Sexual relations between psychotherapists and their patients: toward research and restraint. California Law Review 67:1000–1027, 1979

147. Bouhoutsos J, Holroyd J, Lerman H, et al: Sexual intimacy between psychotherapists and patients. Professional Psychology: Research and Practice 14:185–196, 1983

148. Taylor GJ, Wagner NN: Sex between therapists and clients: a review and analysis. Professional Psychology 7:593–601, 1976

149. Butler S, Zelen SL: Sexual intimacies between therapists and patients. Psychotherapy: Theory, Research and Practice 14:139–145, 1977

150. Slovenko R: Sex in the office. Sexual Medicine Today, February 1979, p 6

151. Durre L: Comparing romantic and therapeutic relationships, in On Love and Loving: Psychological Perspectives on the Nature and Experience of Romantic Love. Edited by Pope KS. San Francisco, CA, Jossey-Bass, 1980, pp 228–243

152. Bouhoutsos J, Holroyd J, Lerman H, et al: Sexual intimacy between psychotherapists and patients. Professional Psychology: Research and Practice 14:185–196, 1983

153. Schoener GR, Milgrom JH, Gonsiorek JC, et al: Psychotherapists' Sexual Involvement With Clients: Intervention and Prevention. Minneapolis, MN, Walk-in Counseling Center, 1989, pp 159–176

154. American Psychiatric Association: The Principles of Medical Ethics With Annotations Especially Applicable to Psychiatry. Washington DC, American Psychiatric Association, 1989, Section 1, Annotation 1

155. MINN STAT ANN § 147 (West 1989); MINN STAT ANN § 148B (West 1989)

156. CAL BUS & PROF CODE § 728 (West 1990)

157. WIS STAT ANN § 940.22(3) (West Supp 1989)

158. Strasburger LH, Jorgenson L, Randles R: Mandatory reporting of sexually exploitative psychotherapists. Bull Am Acad Psychiatry Law 18:379–384, 1990

159. Stone AA: Law, Psychiatry, and Morality. Washington, DC, American Psychiatric Press, 1985, pp 211–212

160. Fed R Evid 803(4)

161. 120 Wis 2d 92, 352 NW2d 673 (Wis Ct App 1984)

162. Schoener GR, Milgrom JH, Gonsiorek JC, et al: Psychotherapists' Sexual Involvement With Clients: Intervention and Prevention. Minneapolis, MN, Walk-in Counseling Center, 1989, pp 147–155

163. Pope KS, Bouhoutsos JC: Sexual Intimacy Between Therapists and Patients. New York, Praeger, 1986, p 110

164. James Huegli, J.D., personal communication, October 1990

165. Stone AA: Law, Psychiatry, and Morality. Washington, DC, American Psychiatric Press, 1985, pp 210–211

166. CAL BUS & PROF CODE § 327 (West 1990)

167. Eth S, Leong GB: Therapist sexual misconduct and the duty to protect, in Confidentiality Versus the Duty to Protect: Foreseeable Harm in the Practice of Psychiatry. Edited by Beck JC. Washington, DC, American Psychiatric Press, 1990, pp 107–119; see p 116

168. Lipari v Sears, Roebuck & Co, 497 F Supp 185 (D Neb 1980); Jablonski v United States, 712 F2d 391 (9th Cir 1983), overruled on other grounds, In re Complaint of McLinn, 739 F2d 1395 (9th Cir 1984); Petersen v State, 100 Wash 2d 421, 671 P2d 230 (1983) (en banc); Peck v The Counseling Service of Addison County, Inc, 146 Vt 61, 499 A2d 425 (1985); Naidu v Laird, 539 A2d 1064 (1988)

169. MINN STAT § 626.557 (Supp 1991)

170. MINN STAT § 148A.03 (Supp 1991)

171. APA board sets up work group to assess sex problem between professionals, patients. Psychiatric News 19(15):4, 1984

172. Herman JL, Gartrell N, Olarte S, et al: Psychiatrist-patient sexual contact—results of a national survey, II: psychiatrists' attitudes. Am J Psychiatry 144:164–169, 1987

173. American Psychiatric Association: The Principles of Medical Ethics With Annotations Especially Applicable to Psychiatry. Washington, DC, American Psychiatric Association, 1989

174. Hale E: Sex with therapist harms most clients. USA Today, May 9, 1984, D1

175. Searles HF: Oedipal love in the countertransference, in Collected Papers on Schizophrenia and Related Subjects. New York, International Universities Press, 1965, pp 284–303

176. 214 NJ Super 670, 520 A2d 844 (NJ Super Ct 1986), aff'd, 215 NJ Super 561, 522 A2d 483 (NJ Super Ct App Div 1987)

177. Vinson JS: Use of complaint procedures in cases of therapist-patient sexual contact. Professional Psychology: Research and Practice 18:159–164, 1987

178. Wisconsin Task Force on Sexual Misconduct: Making Therapy Work for You. WTFSM, 121 S Hancock St, Madison, WI 53703

179. Gartrell N, Herman JL, Olarte S: Management and rehabilitation of sexually exploitative therapists. Hosp Community Psychiatry 39:1070–1079, 1988

180. Schoener GR, Milgrom JH, Gonsiorek JC, et al: Psychotherapists' Sexual Involvement With Clients: Intervention and Prevention. Minneapolis, Walk-in Counseling Center, 1989, pp 401–420

181. Pope KS: Rehabilitation of therapists who have been sexually intimate with a patient, in Sexual Exploitation in Professional Relationships. Edited by Gabbard GO. Washington, DC, American Psychiatric Press, 1989, pp 129–136

Chapter 18

Abandonment and the Psychiatrist's Duty of Care to the Patient

—————————

Mr. Quinn, a 42-year-old machinist, is hospitalized for depression and suicidal impulses by Dr. Wagner, who has treated him for the past 3 months with twice-per-week psychotherapy. Initially, Mr. Quinn came for treatment because of depression due to his recent acrimonious divorce and losing the custody battle for his two children. The patient worked very hard and steadily as a machinist since his graduation from high school. Because his parents had died in an automobile accident when he was 3 years old, he grew up in a series of foster homes until age 10, when he was "adopted" by an uncle. Because of Mr. Quinn's increasing depression and alcohol intake, he became nonfunctional at work and lost the job he had held for the past 24 years. This last loss precipitated the suicidal impulses and hospitalization.

After Dr. Wagner starts his patient on a tricyclic antidepressant, there is a moderate improvement in his appetite and sleep by the end of the third week of hospitalization. Although suicidal impulses are no longer present, occasional suicidal ideas persist. Dr. Wagner is notified by the hospital's business office that Mr. Quinn's insurance provides for only 30 days of hospitalization. The hospital's business office states that the patient must be discharged within 7 days. Because Mr. Quinn is no longer working, he cannot afford to pay for continuing psychiatric treatment.

Because the relationship between psychiatrist and patient is very good, Dr. Wagner is particularly reluctant to discharge his patient. However, he does not feel he can continue to treat Mr. Quinn without payment. Dr. Wagner discusses the problem with Mr. Quinn, who states, "I understand. I always believe in paying my own way." Dr. Wagner's clinical evaluation indicates that Mr. Quinn is only moderately improved. He feels encouraged, however, that suicidal impulses are being replaced by only occasional, fleeting suicidal ideas. He hopes that Mr. Quinn will be further improved during the remaining time before discharge. Transfer of the patient to the only available public psychiatric hospital facility under a voluntary admission is rejected because Dr. Wagner has heard stories that substandard conditions prevail at the public hospital.

As the time for discharge approaches, Dr. Wagner makes arrangements with a social worker at a community mental health center to see Mr. Quinn 10 days after discharge, the earliest appointment available. The patient's condition does not change appreciably during the last week of hospitalization. One week after discharge, Mr. Quinn throws himself in front of an oncoming subway car. He suffers multiple injuries and ultimately loses his left arm. Mr. Quinn is hospitalized 9 months for his physical injuries.

An unpaid balance of $1,500 is owed to Dr. Rose. All requests for payment go unanswered. After 6 months, Dr. Wagner files suit to recover his fee, even though he is aware of Mr. Quinn's suicide attempt. Shortly thereafter, Dr. Wagner is served with a $1,000,000 malpractice suit for negligent discharge and abandonment.

How is abandonment defined legally? Did Dr. Wagner abandon his patient by this definition?

Generally, a therapist in private practice has no duty to accept any person as a patient. Once the therapist agrees to treat the patient, however, a therapist-patient relationship is formed with the duty to provide treatment as long as necessary. When the therapist-patient relationship is unilaterally and prematurely terminated by the therapist without reasonable notice, the therapist may be liable for abandonment if his or her services are still needed by the patient (1). The patient must prove that the cause of the injury was the abandonment. If abandonment is proven, the burden of proving causation may be less rigorous than in other malpractice cases (1).

Abandonment may be either quite obvious or implied by a failure to attend, monitor, or observe the patient. Intentional abandonment can be confused with the negligent failure to follow the patient diligently (2). If the therapist uses poor judgment in terminating or does not diligently attend the patient, liability for negligence may ensue. On the other hand, if the therapist consciously terminates the patient while knowing that the latter needs continuing care, the therapist may be liable for intentional abandonment. In negligence cases, expert testimony will be required to determine the standard of care. If the abandonment is egregious, no expert may be necessary. Many courts have widened the concept of abandonment to those cases in which delay and inattention in providing care have caused injury (3). Until recently, suits for abandonment against mental health professionals have been infrequent (4). With pressure from third-party payers to limit psychiatric care, claims for abandonment may be the litigation of the future.

If no emergency or crisis exists, the therapist may terminate the patient when *1)* reasonable notice is given, *2)* assistance is offered in finding another therapist, and *3)* the patient's records are made available to the new therapist on request. In addition to verbal notification, written notice should also be given. Proper notice is essential in order for the patient to find a substitute therapist.

If an emergency or crisis exists, the therapist should see the patient through the current stressful situation. Termination, however, is an extremely difficult task with patients who seem to be in perpetual crises. On the other hand, terminating a patient with suicidal tendencies as an ill-advised risk management technique may backfire, causing the patient to suffer further regression or even to attempt suicide. Courts are less likely to find that a therapist adequately discharged his or her responsibility when the therapist ceases to attend the patient during a crisis or emergency. Although not always possible, terminating a patient who is undergoing severe psychological distress should be deferred until a more appropriate time clinically. Termination decisions must take into account ethical and professional concerns for the patient as well as legal considerations.

Therapists must realize that certain actions by the patient do not automatically terminate the therapist-patient relationship. Mere nonpayment of a bill, failure to be compliant, unilateral consultation with another mental health professional, or failure to keep an appointment are not causes for termination if the patient continues to need treatment (5). Furthermore, these issues should initially be taken up as treatment matters. For example, suppose the patient stops coming to regularly scheduled appointments. Does the therapist have a duty to contact the patient? The answer to this question depends on whether the patient's absence is a direct function of mental illness. The more severe the illness, the more the therapist should assume the responsibility for contacting the patient. Competent patients who merely stop coming to therapy should be sent a letter requesting clarification of their intention concerning their treatment status. If a response is not received within a specified period of time, the therapist can indicate that he or she will interpret the nonresponse by the patient as an expression of intent to terminate treatment.

In the clinical vignette, by terminating his patient solely because of lack of funds, Dr. Wagner abandoned him. The patient's clinical needs were improperly subordinated to monetary concerns. Mr. Quinn continued to be suicidal at the time of discharge, having improved enough to have the energy to kill himself. He had suffered a succession of devastating losses. The emotional effect of discharging him when his money ran out was not properly considered. The relationship between Dr. Wagner and his patient was described as "good" and could not have been quickly or easily replaced. Certainly, 7 days was not enough notice for Mr. Quinn to find another hospital, given his lack of financial resources and his continuing depressed, suicidal condition. For Dr. Wagner, Mr. Quinn's clinical condition should have been the primary consideration. Continued psychiatric hospitalization was the only reasonable option. Prematurely discharging a depressed suicidal patient into the community without any support or follow-up for 10 days was an egregious abandonment of Mr. Quinn.

The most prudent clinical course to have pursued would have been either to continue the hospitalization until Mr. Quinn improved enough to be discharged or to transfer him to another psychiatric inpatient facility. Dr. Wagner did not consider obtaining a consultation from the hospital social service for assistance in making an appropriate discharge disposition. Certainly, Dr. Wagner validly considered not transferring the patient to a facility where substandard care might be provided. However, Dr. Wagner's reliance upon anecdotal information does not replace the clinician's duty to adequately investigate the public facility's ability to provide reasonable care. Would the public psychiatric hospital, despite alleged deficiencies, still have been a better alternative than outright discharge of Mr. Quinn? Also, Dr. Wagner should have appealed both the hospital's and the insurance carrier's decision to discharge the patient through available procedures. Additionally, consultation with the chairman of the hospital department of psychiatry should have been pursued.

Finally, the patient's discharge was a critically important psychological event that was not sufficiently explored with the patient. Thus, Mr. Quinn was psychologically abandoned as well. When a patient is transferred from a private to a public facility, the psychological meaning of such a transfer should be explored with the patient.

What is the therapist's ethical and legal duty toward the patient who is unable to pay?

All professionals have a tradition of providing *pro bono* service to the economically disadvantaged. However, the ethical issues involved in continuing to treat a nonpaying patient are complex, particularly in the mental health field. In general, the therapist has no legal duty to treat patients who are unable to pay. The therapist must be careful, however, not to abandon the patient (6). The failure of the patient to pay a bill does not end the relationship, because the duty that exists is based on fiducial rather than financial responsibility (7). When treating a nonpaying patient over a long period of time, the potential for holding negative feelings toward the patient is very high. Private therapists do not usually have a large volume of patients and rely on the treatment of relatively few patients for their income. Treating a nonpaying patient may result in a significant loss of income. In fact, a nonpaying situation may eventually produce resentment in both the therapist and the patient, disrupting the therapy (8). On the other hand, there are patients who continue to need treatment but decide to terminate when their money runs out.

Therapists who see patients infrequently or only for medications may be able to handle the nonpayment issue more easily. The patient who runs out of money during the course of therapy presents more difficult problems. Terminating the patient may be very destructive to the unique relationship that develops-between the therapist and the patient. In fact, because the efficacy of a therapeutic modality may be founded on the unique rapport that exists between therapist and patient, it might prove quite difficult to find a workable substitute for the therapist. The therapist might decide to treat the patient for a token fee until the patient's financial situation improves, when a new fee can be negotiated. This option may be particularly pertinent to psychiatrists practicing in rural areas who have no place to refer nonpaying patients requiring continued treatment.

Free therapy may raise insurmountable negative transference and countertransference reactions, although Freud (8) found exceptions where free treatment was very successful. Freud (9) also advocated free treatment for the poor. Another option, permitting the patient to pay the money owed at a later date, places the therapist in the position of the patient's creditor. This may interfere with the therapist's efforts to maintain a position of neutrality. Similarly, entering into a barter arrangement with a nonpaying patient should be avoided. The therapist-patient relationship does not place both parties on an equal bargaining footing. The patient may not be capable of evaluating the value of what is exchanged. If others assume financial responsibility for the patient, the therapist may wish to formalize the arrangement with a written agreement. A model agreement form appears in Appendix 2.

Some psychiatric patients have the means to pay but do not do so for various, important psychological reasons. For example, a depressed patient may feel unreasonably impoverished, a narcissistic patient may feel entitled to free treatment, or a hostile and controlling patient may want to withhold money from the therapist. Money issues are always an integral part of therapy. The only "real thing" that the patient must give the therapist is money. Whenever possible, the treatment issues surrounding nonpayment should be thoroughly explored with the patient before collection efforts are initiated.

What are some common clinical situations in which therapists may run the risk of abandoning patients?

The patient has the right to leave treatment at any time and without notice. In some instances, the patient may terminate by simply not showing up for appointments. A patient who is mentally ill and a danger to self or others, however, may lack the mental capacity to make a competent termination decision. In such cases, the therapist's duty to care for the patient continues and requires that the therapist intervene. Moreover, a patient may need continued treatment. A letter confirming that the patient has terminated the services of the therapist should be sent to the competent patient. A sample confirmation-of-discharge letter is contained in Appendix 2.

In the hospital setting, a seriously disturbed patient may insist on leaving against medical advice. If such a patient has sufficient mental capacity to make a discharge decision and is not a candidate for involuntary hospitalization, the patient should be asked to sign a form stating that he or she is leaving against advice. If the patient refuses to sign such a form, the refusal should be documented in the chart. A certified letter should be sent to the patient confirming that he or she left against medical advice. When a patient discharges a psychiatrist or leaves the hospital against medical advice, the psychiatrist should be in a position to establish that no abandonment occurred (10).

Obviously, hospitalized psychiatric patients should not be summarily discharged when their money or insurance coverage runs out. Provisions for adequate continuing care must be made before the patient is discharged. In *Christy v. Saliterman* (11), a psychiatrist discharged a patient on termination of the patient's credit. On the morning of discharge, the patient had received electroconvulsive therapy. The psychiatrist prescribed paraldehyde over the phone but did not warn the patient of the possibility of soporific side effects. The patient fell asleep in a chair while smoking, setting fire to himself and suffering serious burns. The court held that the psychiatrist's negligent discharge and the failure to provide specific instructions about the medicine directly caused the injuries sustained by the patient.

Another area of concern to the psychiatrist is the initial visit and, in particular, the establishment of the doctor-patient relationship. Courts have concluded that it takes very little for a relationship to be established (12). Giving advice, making interpretations, and prescribing medications may serve to establish a therapist-patient relationship with all its obligations. As protection, therapists should attempt to limit the initial visit to strictly evaluative matters unless they wish to undertake the care of the evaluee immediately. The person who is seen only once may allege abandonment if treatment was provided and some damage ensued.

A person may come for an initial visit who is acutely psychotic, in need of treatment, potentially dangerous, and too disturbed to follow directions for referral elsewhere. Although the therapist is not legally obligated to actually treat such a person, it would be ethically and clinically proper to arrange for transportation to a hospital where the individual can be treated on an emergency basis. Although legal considerations are present, professional and ethical concerns must prevail in these clinical situations.

Often, the therapist's ethical and legal duties in terminating the patient depend on the circumstances (13). In *Brandt v. Grubin* (14), the court noted that when a physician is employed for a specific occasion or service, no liability for abandonment exists if treatment ceases after the performance of the specific purpose. In *Brandt,* a patient committed suicide after consulting a physician who prescribed some medication and recommended psychiatric help. The court rejected the plaintiff's expert's testimony that the physician abandoned the patient by failing to obtain a psychiatric consultation. The court held that if, after initial examination, the physician determines that he is not capable of treating the patient, he should not be held liable for "the actions of subsequent treating professionals nor his refusal to become further involved in this case" (14).

This type of reasoning also may apply to specialty clinics. For example, if a patient attends a phobia clinic for the sole purpose of being treated for specific phobias over a specified number of sessions, abandonment should not be an issue after treatment ceases. By special arrangements with the patient, psychiatrists may limit their engagement to treat the patient with one particular treatment or procedure or to provide treatment at a particular time or place (15). If the patient has reason to believe the physician has assumed a continuing treatment role as a "personal physician," however, then a special arrangement may not be possible.

Therapists who mismanage countertransference feelings may unwittingly abandon a patient when such feelings explode in the therapeutic situation. Angry outbursts may destroy months or years of therapeutic work. In *Hess v. Frank* (16), the court dismissed a suit for negligence brought against a psychiatrist who, during a regularly scheduled session, allegedly used abusive language toward the patient. An argument developed over fees and the appointment schedule. The psychiatrist had been treating the patient for over 8 years. The case was dismissed because the court viewed the argument as being outside of the treatment relationship, which is certainly not the case clinically. Although abandonment was not alleged by the patient, vitriolic arguments between a therapist and patient destroy the treatment relationship and leave the patient devastated and essentially bereft of the therapist's help. From a clinical perspective, the patient was abandoned.

In *Norton v. Hamilton* (17), a physician blew up at a distraught husband and wife who insisted that their baby was on the way. The physician insisted that it would be another 13 days before the baby was due. The physician told the husband he did not have to come back and would have nothing further to do with their case. The husband and wife sued. The physician brought a motion for summary judgment alleging that the action should be in contract, not tort. The court held for the expecting parents and noted that "if a physician abandons a case without giving such notice or providing a competent physician in his place, it is a failure to exercise that care required by law, which failure amounts to a tort."

In *Gillette v. Tucker* (18), a physician became enraged at the patient, ordering the patient out of his office and threatening to call the police unless she left immediately. The patient complained that her infected appendectomy incision had not healed as a result of the physician's poor job. The physician ultimately was found liable for failure to remove a cheesecloth sponge from the patient's abdomen.

Borderline patients who flit from crisis to crisis may sorely tax the therapist's energy and patience, leading to a countertransference-based, abrupt, and ill-advised termination eventuating in allegations of abandonment (19). Malignant narcissistic personalities and certain severe borderline patients may persistently act out destructively in order to manipulate the therapist. Because therapists cannot practice with a psychological gun to their heads, they may need to terminate such patients appropriately.

All therapists' difficulties with patients are not necessarily countertransference based. Some patients are genuinely difficult and demanding in their own right, often presenting unique problems that some therapists can handle better than others. Therapists must realize their limitations. Holding the grandiose notion that a therapist can treat everyone is the royal road to legal liability. Can a therapist effectively treat a patient whom he or she fundamentally dislikes? Whatever "dislike" may mean precisely, it may be reflective of countertransference that has not been properly resolved. If it is not possible to resolve countertransference reactions, the patient should be referred. Therapists must not terminate patients for capricious reasons. Patients must be given time to work through their termination.

The therapist's fiduciary relationship with the patient and the concomitant duty to neutrality demand that the therapist not continue to treat patients beyond the point of benefit. Certainly, therapeutic stalemates extending over years are not unknown. Patients may develop infantile, regressive dependencies that may persist for years and that are intractable to psychotherapeutic treatment. These so-called "therapeutic lifers" need to be distinguished from patients who, analogous to the diabetic patient, require years of maintenance therapy to function at a job or to stay out of an institution. On the contrary, the stalemated patient lives in and for the therapy, resisting efforts toward growth and independence. The treatment becomes a paltry substitute for living (20).

If a patient is allowed to remain stalemated for prolonged periods, the fundamental treatment goals of striving toward independence and autonomy are abandoned. Even though these patients may strenuously resist, it is not abandonment to refer them to other therapists who may be able to provide more effective treatment. Nor is it abandonment when the treatment is appropriately terminated. On the contrary, a corollary of the duty of nonabandonment is the duty to terminate ineffective or dangerous treatments (21). In *Ison v. McFall* (22), the court found that a physician has an explicit duty to inform the patient that the method of treatment will have no further therapeutic benefit.

During August, a vacation exodus among psychiatrists usually takes place. Patients may find that when they call a covering psychiatrist, they may be referred through a series of psychiatrists. On one such occasion, a psychoanalytic candidate was asked by a recently graduated psychoanalyst to cover his practice during the month of August. The candidate discovered later that other senior analysts, including his own, had signed out to the recent graduate. To his not unpleasant amazement, the candidate found himself unwittingly covering for his analyst, his fellow analysands, and himself! It is important not to subject disturbed patients to such a runaround. Feelings of discouragement and rejection may markedly inhibit the patient's efforts to obtain help and possibly lead to an allegation of abandonment if the patient is harmed.

When obtaining coverage, a psychiatrist should try to find another psychiatrist of similar experience and training. In addition, clinical information about patients who may call should be provided to the covering therapist. A covering psychiatrist should be carefully selected. The substitute psychiatrist must be competent and qualified (23). If difficulties arise between the patient and the covering therapist, the patient may allege that the psychiatrist was negligent in engaging an unqualified practitioner to cover his or her practice. If it can be shown that the covering psychiatrist was fully qualified and the patient was fully informed of the psychiatrist's absence, imposition of liability is unlikely.

A psychiatrist who uses a substitute is not liable for the substitute's negligence unless the substitute physician was acting as an agent in the performance of treatment or unless due care was not exercised in selecting the substitute psychiatrist (24). If a fixed stipend is paid to the covering psychiatrist, an agent (employee) relationship is established. If the patient is billed and the proceeds are shared with the covering psychiatrist after expenses, then a partnership is created. To avoid possible legal entanglements, the covering psychiatrist should bill independently for services rendered.

Another form of abandonment may occur when psychiatrists do not list a home phone number in the directory or with directory assistance. Instead, a nonforwarding answering machine collects overnight calls for the next day. Even for the psychiatrist with a quiet practice, this procedure is replete with untoward legal consequences, because emergencies can arise at any time with any patient. Hiding from patients significantly increases patients' anxiety and causes some of them to go to extraordinary lengths to find the psychiatrist. Ready availability appears to diminish the patient's anxiety, resulting in fewer phone calls to the psychiatrist and possibly lessening claims of abandonment if an emergency arises. No clear standards exist concerning how soon a patient's phone call should be returned. A good rule to follow is the sunset rule. This rule states that all calls from patients should be returned by the end of the psychiatrist's work day.

A creeping form of abandonment can occur from those two great enemies of the practicing psychotherapist: boredom and fatigue. Inattention, ennui, impatience, cutting back patient visits, and dissatisfaction with psychotherapeutic practice are all symptoms of therapist boredom and fatigue. When a crisis arises in a patient's life, the bored and tired therapist may consciously or unconsciously downplay its significance, providing either negligent treatment or abandoning the patient outright.

Failure to instruct the patient concerning side effects of medication, failure to stay abreast of the patient's condition, failure to admit the patient to a hospital when warranted, failure to follow the patient during hospitalization, premature discharge of the patient from the hospital, and improper referral of the patient may all constitute abandonment (5). When clinically appropriate, therapists who are unable to treat their own hospitalized patients should stay in contact with them through the admitting psychiatrist or by shifting temporarily into a consultative role.

What is the responsibility of the psychiatrist when a health care provider limits payment but the patient continues to need treatment?

When insurance benefits for psychiatric care are cut, patients may be abandoned if their benefits run out. Psychiatric hospitals and other health care providers, including health maintenance organizations, preferred provider organizations, and prepaid health plans providing psychiatric care, must be careful not to terminate patients summarily based strictly on financial considerations. The psychiatrist must always consider the treatment needs of the patient first. Mental health professionals working for such groups must be careful to resist any erosion of their professional duty to patients by financial and administrative pressures.

In *Wickline v. California* (25), the treating physician, Dr. Polonsky, asked for an extended stay of 8 additional days for his patient following surgery for Leriche's syndrome (occlusion of the terminal aorta). The Medi-Cal reviewer granted 4 days. Mrs. Wickline suffered complications following the premature release, resulting in amputation of her leg. She sued Medi-Cal. The jury ruled in her favor, but a California appellate court decided that the treating physician was liable, not Medi-Cal. In his testimony, Dr. Polonsky stated that he believed "that Medi-Cal had the power to tell him, as a treating doctor, when a patient must be discharged from the hospital." The appellate court noted that third-party payers of health care services can be held liable when appeals on the behalf of the patients for medical care

> are arbitrarily ignored or unreasonably disregarded or over-ridden. However, the physician who complies without protest with the limitations imposed by a third-party payor, when his medical judgment dictates otherwise, cannot avoid his ultimate responsibility for his patient's care. He cannot point to the health care payor as the liability scapegoat when the consequences of his own determinative medical decision go sour. (25)

The lesson is absolutely clear. The physician bears the responsibility for the medical care provided his or her patient. The duty of the physician to exercise the best medical judgment on behalf of the patient is not dependent upon payment. Nor can this duty be abrogated to others. In the clinical vignette, Dr. Wagner allowed the issue of money to interfere with his medical judgment, thus seriously harming the patient.

In a subsequent case, *Wilson v. Blue Cross of Southern California et al.* (26), a California appeals court did not follow the specific language of *Wickline*. In *Wilson,* a patient was hospitalized at College Hospital in Los Angeles suffering from anorexia, drug dependency, and major depression. The treating physician determined that the patient required 3 to 4 weeks of hospitalization. After approximately $1\frac{1}{2}$ weeks, utilization review determined that further hospitalization was unnecessary. The patient's insurance company refused to pay for further inpatient treatment. The patient was discharged and committed suicide a few weeks later.

The Appellate Division of the California Court of Appeals held that third-party payers are not immune from lawsuits in regard to utilization review activities. The court determined that the insurer may be subject to liability for harm caused to the patient by premature termination of a patient's hospitalization. Though the fact pattern of this case differs from that of *Wickline,* the decision in *Wilson* signals that a third-party payer may be held legally liable for a negligent decision to discharge the patient, either separately or along with the patient's physician, depending upon the facts of the case. Although both *Wickline* and *Wilson* are California cases, they offer insight and, perhaps, precedence concerning future reasoning by other courts that will be increasingly confronted by complex liability issues concerning utilization review decisions.

A related problem is patient "dumping." Patient "dumping" is defined "as the denial of or limitation in the provision of medical services to a patient for economic reasons and the referral of that patient elsewhere" (27). This problem increased dramatically in the 1980s because of rapidly rising health costs and the efforts to cut health care spending. The denial of appropriate medical care for economic reasons represents an egregious abandonment of the patient. Legal liability is likely to follow.

Managed care has restricted the therapeutic discretion of physicians while their professional and legal responsibilities to patients have continued unabated. When managed care guidelines conflict with the psychiatrist's duty to provide appropriate clinical care, he or she must be prepared to vigorously appeal managed care decisions that abridge necessary treatments. If the patient's hospital treatment is in jeopardy, the psychiatrist should initiate appeals with both the hospital and the insurance carrier. Once a treatment plan is recommended to the patient, the psychiatrist has a duty to complete the treatment or arrange for a suitable treatment alternative (28). The report of the Hastings Center conference on the impact of the new economics states: "Ethics is not free . . . once a patient is the medical responsibility of a practitioner or institution, he simply cannot be discharged when the financial resources are depleted" (29).

Psychiatrists may sign agreements and contracts with third-party payers that they do not sufficiently understand. Nevertheless, they remain professionally and ethically responsible for providing appropriate clinical care to the patient. For example, in *Varol v. Blue Cross–Blue Shield of Michigan* (30), the court ruled that when psychiatrists agree to a program's requirements and criteria, they are obligated to perform according to these contracts. The judge observed: "Whether or not the proposed treatment is approved, the physician retains the right and indeed the ethical and legal obligation to provide appropriate treatment to the patient." The judge then went on to decisively paraphrase their complaint:

> Irrespective of any obligation I have to my patients and to my profession, my judgment as to what is in the best interests of my patients will not be determined by the exercise of my medical judgment, but by how much I will be paid for my services. ... Since I am weak in my resolve to afford proper treatment, Blue Cross–Blue Shield of Michigan's preauthorization program would induce me to breach my ethical and legal duties, and the Court must protect me from my weakness.

Rachlin (31), in providing perspective on court rulings in managed care situations, aptly comments:

> Although these decisions are binding only in the jurisdictions in which they were rendered, a very clear message may be abstracted, one which is likely to have broad application: a practitioner is generally protected from liability of adverse outcomes resulting from economic constraints. Third-party payers and fourth-party reviewers have a right to decide against payment prospectively, concurrently, or retrospectively; physicians and other health care professionals will still be fully accountable for their clinical decisions, which must be made for the patient's benefit, not the dollar's.

What steps should the therapist take when terminating a patient?

The therapist has the right to withdraw from a case as long as proper notice is given so that the patient may find a suitable substitute. The termination of a patient, however, should be done under appropriate clinical circumstances and should be consistent with the best interests of the patient (32). Generally, it is better to inform the patient during a nonemergency. The patient should be informed verbally and a notation made in the patient's record. The patient's feelings and other issues surrounding the termination should be thoroughly discussed. Also, a certified letter confirming the termination should be sent and return receipt requested, even though courts presume first-class mail to be delivered (see Table 18-1).

The presumption that a first-class letter is delivered is based upon the "mailbox rule" that was first set forth in England in the case of *Adams v. Lindsell* (33). The rule essentially states that acceptance of an offer takes effect upon dispatch (i.e., upon being mailed). The overwhelming weight of authority in the United States supports the "mailbox rule." Thus, a letter sent by first-class mail that is legibly addressed to the addressee at the correct address and bearing sufficient postage is presumed to have been delivered to the addressee. There is no legal obligation to send a certified or registered letter to a patient. If the therapist wants to be sure that the patient *personally* receives the registered letter, then it should be sent restricted registered, return receipt requested.

The termination letter should indicate the reasons for termination or reflect that a thorough discussion of the reasons for termination was held with the pa-

---

TABLE 18-1.   Suggested guidelines for termination

1. Discuss termination with patient fully.
2. Indicate in a letter of termination:
   a. Fact of discussion of termination.
   b. Reason for termination.
   c. Termination date.
   d. Availability for emergencies (only until date of termination).
   e. Willingness to provide names of other appropriate therapists.
   f. Willingness to provide medical records to subsequent therapist.
   g. A statement of the need for additional treatment, if appropriate.
3. Allow the patient reasonable time to find another therapist (length of time depends on availability of other therapists).
4. Provide the patient's records to the new therapist upon proper authorization by the patient.
5. If the patient requires further treatment, provide the names of other psychiatrists or refer the patient to the local or state psychiatric society for further assistance.
6. If further treatment is recommended, a statement about the potential consequences of not obtaining further treatment should be indicated.
7. Send the termination letter certified or restricted registered mail, return receipt requested.

---

tient. However, the therapist is not required to state the reasons for the termination (34). In addition, the letter should include the date of termination, the availability of the therapist for emergencies up to the date of termination, and the willingness to provide names of other practitioners. (A sample termination form is included in Appendix 2.) The patient's record should be supplied to other therapists after receiving the patient's written permission. With certain patients, it may be appropriate to urge them to obtain further treatment.

The timing of termination is very important. Some psychiatric patients, particularly those suffering from borderline conditions, are almost perpetually in crises, and termination may appear to be impossible. Consultation may prove helpful. If termination is necessary, the therapist may need to see the patient on a daily basis, or even hospitalize the patient during the termination phase, until transition to a new therapist can be made comfortably.

How much time should be provided the patient to find another therapist?

The time allowed to find another therapist should be based on the severity of the patient's condition and the availability of alternative care. Sufficient notice also depends on the locality. If the nearest psychiatrist is 120 miles away, the rural patient will need more time than the patient living in a metropolitan center. The courts have used such normative words as "ample," "sufficient," and "reasonable" when referring to the time given the patient to find a substitute (5). The requirement that reasonable notice be given to patients before termination of treatment has been applied only to physicians. The principles underlying this rule, however, seem to apply to all mental health professionals (35).

Should the therapist bill the patient who suffers a bad treatment result?

Dr. Wagner doggedly pursued the collection of his $1,500 account, which apparently triggered a malpractice suit by his former patient. Therapists must weigh the risks and benefits of attempting to collect a fee from a patient who has suffered a bad result and is unhappy. The circumstances of the particular case will help the therapist determine the appropriate response. The therapist must assess the patient's pain and suffering, complications, additional therapy required, the extent of dissatisfaction and unhappiness, and the risk of potential damages. The therapist also must consider the expenditure of time and effort as well as the loss of income that results from defending a lawsuit. Such considerations may lead to closing the account and absorbing the loss. Moreover, in some jurisdictions, suing for nonpayment of a bill may extend or revive the statute of limitations on malpractice.

Alton (36) suggests that physicians wait until the expiration of the statute of limitations for the patient before filing a malpractice claim if they feel they must pursue payment. Usually, this is many years less than the statute of limitations for breach of contract. He also suggests that a bill must be sent for services rendered. Patients may feign dissatisfaction with services as an excuse for nonpayment. Even if a threat of suit exists or it is not likely that the patient will pay, the bill must be sent, because the receipt of a bill alone will not ordinarily trigger a lawsuit. More important, failure to send a bill may be considered an admission of fault. Alton feels that if a patient sues after receiving a bill, a suit was planned anyway. Similarly, the bill must be for a reasonable amount rather than an unusually low amount. The patient should never be told that no bill will be submitted, or that the bill will be reduced, because of complications or poor results. Failure to follow up on a bill that was sent, however, will not necessarily be considered an admission of fault. When normal billing procedures are carried out, negative inferences cannot be drawn. Alton observes that, in most instances, nonpayment will satisfy the patient's desire to punish the therapist.

Dr. Wagner's insistent pursuit of his bill appears to reflect an unfortunate attitude that places greater importance on money than on patient care. Two fundamental gratifications afforded therapists in the treatment of patients are a genuine, personal enjoyment of the treatment process itself and reasonable financial remuneration for services rendered. Emphasis on the latter, without the former, results in a perversion of the therapist's professional duty of devotion to the best interests of the patient.

What defenses can Dr. Wagner assert against the allegation of abandoning his patient?

A rather weak claim could be made that Dr. Wagner had little choice but to discharge the patient because the hospital recommended discharge of the patient. This defense will be given even less weight since *Wickline,* which affirms that doctors, not hospitals, are responsible for the discharge of patients. An absolutely clear-cut statement cannot be made on the question of whether the physician is always *solely* responsible for the patient's discharge. The answer depends on the situation presented and any relevant provisions set forth in the particular hospital's bylaws. Nevertheless, if a hospital decides to override the physician's decision in a situation in which the patient presents a high risk of danger to self or others, the hospital may be subjecting itself to liability if the patient is actually harmed (37). The court in *Wickline* made it quite clear that the physician is ultimately responsible for the care of the patient.

In general, circumstances dictate which defenses may be asserted against a claim of abandonment. If a competent patient unilaterally severs the relationship (e.g., failing to return), the therapist's duty is terminated. Proper notice is another defense against the claim of abandonment.

If a suitable substitute is provided, the therapist's intervening illness will not ordinarily be considered an abandonment of the patient. Section 6-C of the American Psychiatric Association's *Opinions of the Ethics Committee on the Principles of Medical Ethics With Annotations Especially Applicable to Psychiatry* (38) states:

Question: Because of ill-health, it has become necessary for me to retire. I have sent a written announcement to that effect to all my patients 90 days in advance. Full-fee patients have been accepted by other psychiatrists but I am having great difficulty placing my Medicaid patients. The local public clinics have long waiting lists. Will I be abandoning my patients?

Answer: No. Ninety days written announcement is quite adequate. It is unfortunate you are having such difficulty placing your Medicaid patients but you have done all you can be expected to do. Your colleagues might wish to consider their roles as ethical practitioners in assisting you and your patients in your time of need. See Opinion 8.11, AMA Council Opinions, 1989: "Once having undertaken a case, the physician should not neglect the patient, nor withdraw from the case without giving notice to the patient, the relatives, or responsible friends sufficiently long in advance of withdrawal to permit another medical attendant to be secured." (April 1978)

Proper preparation of patients who are likely to need assistance in the temporary absence of the therapist may avert a later legal claim of abandonment. For example, certain patients may require referral to emergency facilities if colleagues providing coverage cannot be immediately found. These patients should be informed about available emergency care facilities. Patients have sued for abandonment when the substitute is many miles away, making access to the therapist difficult or unduly burdensome (39).

Finally, a malpractice action by the patient against the therapist may allow the therapist to serve notice of termination (5). Although this course of action is not absolutely protected and legal opinion should be sought, termination of the patient appears appropriate in order to protect the interests of the therapist. Clinically, it seems inconceivable that a therapist could continue to treat a patient who is suing. The situation presents an insurmountable reality obstacle because any therapeutic alliance would almost certainly cease to exist.

In *Hammonds v. Aetna Casualty & Surety Co.* (40), the insurance company, fearing a lawsuit, induced the psychiatrist to abandon his patient. The court held that a physician, when threatened by a suit for malpractice, can terminate the physician-patient relationship, but only after "the claimant knows or suspects that he is the victim of medical malpractice and has expressed an intent to pursue his legal rights." The psychiatrist and insurance company complained that this stringent requirement would allow the "plaintiff an unfair advantage to fully prepare his case while the doctor is proscribed against the first defensive measure." The court disagreed, believing that the plaintiff rarely enjoys an advantage in any lawsuit.

Beis (41) describes a "professional will" that can be drawn up for a therapist who is concerned about his or her patients' care after he or she dies. The provisions include designation of a colleague who will inform patients about the therapist's death, the names of specific colleagues who will be available for prompt consultation and referral, retention of certain records, the request that certain patients not attend the funeral for good clinical reasons, and discussion with the new therapist of any continuing contact by patients beyond the expression of condolences to the family of the deceased therapist.

References

1. King JH: The Law of Medical Malpractice, 2nd Edition. St Paul, MN, West Publishing, 1986, p 23
2. Ibid, pp 25–26
3. Mains J: Medical abandonment. Medical Trial Technique Quarterly 31:306–328, 1985
4. Perlin ML: Disability Law: Civil and Criminal, Vol 3. Charlottesville, VA, Michie, 1989, pp 100–102
5. Hirsh HL: Abandonment: actual or constructive premature termination of the physician-patient relationship. Transactions and Studies of the College of Physicians of Philadelphia 6:207–222, 1984
6. Simon RI: Psychiatric Interventions and Malpractice: A Primer for Liability Prevention. Springfield, IL, Charles C Thomas, 1982, p 56
7. Ricks v Budge, 92 Utah 307, 64 P2d 208 (1937)

8. Freud S: On beginning the treatment (1913), in the Standard Edition of the Complete Psychological Works of Sigmund Freud, Vol 12. Translated and edited by Strachey J. London, Hogarth Press, 1958, pp 121–144
9. Freud S: Lines of advance in psychoanalytic therapy, in the Standard Edition of the Complete Psychological Works of Sigmund Freud, Vol 17. Translated and edited by Strachey J. London, Hogarth Press, 1958, pp 157–168
10. Pearson v Norman, 106 Colo 396 106 P2d 361 (1940)
11. 288 Minn 144, 179 NW2d 288 1970)
12. King JH: The Law of Medical Malpractice, 2nd Edition. St Paul, MN, West Publishing, 1986, pp 9–23
13. Klein JI, Macbeth JE, Onek JN: Legal Issues in the Private Practice of Psychiatry. Washington, DC, American Psychiatric Press, 1984, p 12
14. 131 NJ Super 182, 329 A2d 82 (1974)
15. McNamara v Emmons, 36 Cal App 2d 199, 97 P2d 503 (Cal Ct App 1939)
16. 47 AD2d 889, 367 NYS2d 30 (NY App Div 1975)
17. 92 Ga App 727, 89 SE2d 809 (Ga Ct App 1955)
18. 67 Ohio St 106, 65 NE 865 (1902), overruled, Oliver v Kaiser Community Health Foundation, 5 Ohio St 3d 111, 449 NE2d 438 (1983)
19. Gutheil TG: Borderline personality disorder, boundary violations and patient-therapist sex—medical legal pitfalls. Am J Psychiatry 146:597–602, 1989
20. Simon RI: Psychiatric Interventions and Malpractice: A Primer for Liability Prevention. Springfield, IL, Charles C Thomas, 1982, pp 96–99
21. Perlin ML: Disability Law: Civil and Criminal, Vol 3. Charlottesville, VA, Michie, 1989, pp 101–102
22. 55 Tenn App 326, 400 SW2d 243 (Tenn Ct App 1964), superseded by statute, Johnson v Lawrence, 720 SW2d 50 (Tenn Ct App 1986)
23. Tripp v Pate, 49 NC App 329, 271 SE2d 407 (NC Ct App 1980)
24. Graddy v New York Medical College, 19 AD2d 426, 243 NYS2d 940 (1963), appeal denied, 13 NY2d 1175, 197 NE2d 541, 248 NYS2d 541 (1964)
25. 183 Cal App 3d 1175, 228 Cal Rptr 661 (Cal Ct App 1986)
26. 222 Cal App 3d 660 (1990)
27. Ansell DA, Schiff RL: Patient dumping: status, implications, and policy recommendations. JAMA 257:1500–1502, 1987; see p 1500
28. Siebert SW, Silver SB: Managed health care and the evolution of psychiatric practice, in American Psychiatric Press Review of Clinical Psychiatry and the Law, Vol 2. Edited by Simon RI. Washington, DC, American Psychiatric Press, 1991, pp 259–270
29. American Psychiatric Association Ethics Committee: New mental health economics and the impact on the ethics of psychiatric practice: a report of the Hastings Center Conference on Psychiatric Ethics and the New Economics. American Psychiatric Association Ethics Newsletter 4(2):1–7, 1988
30. 708 F Supp 826 (ED Mich 1989)
31. Rachlin S: Perspectives on dual loyalties, in American Psychiatric Press Review of Clinical Psychiatry and the Law, Vol 3. Edited by Simon RI. Washington, DC, American Psychiatric Press, 1992, p 214
32. Sparr LF, Drummond DJ: Risk management in a Veterans Administration mental health clinic, in American Psychiatric Press Review of Clinical Psychiatry and the Law, Vol 3. Edited by Simon RI. Washington, DC, American Psychiatric Press, 1992, pp 67–97

33. 1 B & Ald 681, 106 Rep 250 (KB 1818)
34. Curran WJ: Breaking off the physician-patient relationship: another legal hazard. N Engl J Med 307:1058–1060, 1982
35. Reisner R: Law and the Mental Health System. St Paul, MN, West Publishing, 1985, p 69
36. Alton WG: Malpractice: A Trial Lawyer's Advice for Physicians. Boston, MA, Little, Brown, 1977, pp 44–46
37. American Psychiatric Association Legal Consultation Plan, personal communication
38. American Psychiatric Association: Opinions of the Ethics Committee on the Principles of Medical Ethics with Annotations Especially Applicable to Psychiatry. Washington, DC, American Psychiatric Association, 1989, p 36
39. Marco CH: A case of abandonment? Legal Aspects of Medical Practice 12:3, 1984
40. 243 F Supp 793 (ND Ohio 1965)
41. Beis EB: Mental Health and the Law. Rockville, MD, Aspen, 1984, p 65

Chapter 19

**Radical Therapies and
Intentional Torts**

During the past 10 years of practicing psychotherapy, Dr. Allen has used touching and hugging techniques in "innovative ways." He finds these techniques extremely useful in patients who were deprived of early warm, nurturing experiences, providing what he calls a "normative-restorative emotional experience." Dr. Allen explained his theory in a paper entitled, "The Therapeutic Aspect of Nonsexual Physical Contact With Psychiatric Patients." In this paper, Dr. Allen emphasized that touching techniques can make the relationship with the therapist "more of a human experience," particularly for emotionally deprived patients. Dr. Allen feels that touching techniques with selected patients allow the patient to focus on the importance of human relationships as a source of gratification rather than fear. Dr. Allen's paper was published in a reputable, but not peer-reviewed journal and presented before the local psychiatric society.

The paper is severely criticized because Dr. Allen's findings were based solely on his experience with only 16 patients. Moreover, the paper presented anecdotal case studies without any attempt at scientific analysis. Other critics questioned his assumption that the touching would not be perceived as sexual by the patient. Some therapists felt Dr. Allen's technique was not innovative or sufficiently sensitive to the possibility of breaching the patient's psychological defenses. Nevertheless, Dr. Allen continued to experiment with his touching techniques.

Mr. Lake, a 24-year-old single man, comes to treatment complaining of moderate depression, social isolation, and inability to get along with his boss. Mr. Lake manages the production and distribution of fashionable women's clothes for a prestigious manufacturer. His boss, the owner, is an extremely aggressive businessman. He is abusive toward Mr. Lake when production appears to be lagging. Mr. Lake tries to please his boss but becomes very "frustrated" with his constant demands, gradually becoming withdrawn and depressed.

Mr. Lake was raised by his father and an uncle after his mother died while giving birth to his sister. He was 2 years old at the time of his mother's death. Unknown to his father, who was busy and remote, the patient was sexually abused by the uncle from ages 5 to 9. Shortly after the patient's ninth birthday, the uncle left the home. Mr. Lake did well in school, although he had few friends. While in college, Mr. Lake began to experience recurrent mild to moderate depression, but by applying himself to his studies he "overcame" these episodes. He remained socially isolated but graduated with honors in business administration.

Dr. Allen treats the patient for 6 months with individual psychodynamic psychotherapy twice weekly. He notes that Mr. Lake is very lonely and isolated but yearns for closeness. In his work with Mr. Lake, Dr. Allen is not able to discern exactly what the patient's specific fears are about closeness, even though this issue is repeatedly explored. The patient does not consciously withhold memories of sexual abuse. He has repressed these memories and associated feelings. Dr. Allen, after careful consideration, feels that the patient might benefit from physical contact therapy. At the end of each hour, he shakes the patient's hand. All goes well for a month, with Mr. Lake appearing responsive to the warm handshakes. The handshakes progress to an arm around Mr. Lake's shoulder as patient and therapist walk to the door at the end of the hour. Dr. Allen is very careful to avoid any touching that might appear to be sexually seductive. When he uses this technique, Dr. Allen ceases the touching immediately if a patient objects or seems uncomfortable in any way.

The therapeutic alliance appears stronger. Mr. Lake's work relationship with the boss improves as well. Near the end of a therapy session in which Mr. Lake is talking about his father and uncle, he is overwhelmed by the sudden memories of the sexual abuse perpetrated by the uncle. Mortified, he becomes silent, wanting only to leave the session. As Dr. Allen places his arm around the patient and offers a handshake, Mr. Lake experiences severe panic. He hears his uncle's voice ridiculing him. Pushing Dr. Allen away, he tries to run out of the office. Because of the look of terror in the patient's eyes, Dr. Allen tries to restrain the patient physically. He shouts at Mr. Lake, "Control yourself. You are out of control. You will be alright. Don't force me to restrain you." Security men from the office building hear the commotion, run to the office, and lend physical assistance. The rescue squad is called, arriving within minutes. Because of his violent flailing, Mr. Lake is placed in four-point restraints and taken to a nearby hospital emergency room. He is voluntarily admitted to the psychiatric ward under the care of a staff psychiatrist.

Dr. Allen does not have hospital admitting privileges, but he wishes to visit the patient. Although Mr. Lake refuses to see him, Dr. Allen visits him anyway. After the patient vigorously protests, Dr. Allen finally leaves. Mr. Lake is diagnosed as suffering a brief reactive psychosis. He is released from the hospital 72 hours after admission upon signing a request for release form. He leaves against medical advice. One month later, he again is voluntarily admitted to a psychiatric hospital, where he is treated for a major depressive episode with psychotic features.

After discharge from the hospital 6 weeks later, he consults an attorney. A suit is brought against Dr. Allen alleging both intentional and negligent actions

*that have harmed Mr. Lake. The intentional torts claimed include assault and
battery, invasion of privacy, intentional infliction of emotional distress, and
false imprisonment. The negligence suit claims a lack of informed consent and
the provision of negligent psychotherapy.*

What are intentional torts?

In general, liability in psychiatric practice is predominantly a matter of negligence law. Intentional torts, however, play a significant secondary role in litigation (1). In contrast to negligence, the wrongdoer is motivated by the intent to
harm another person or realizes that such a result (harm) is substantially certain
to follow from his or her actions. Malice does not have to be proved. For instance, the wrongdoer may be acting with benevolent intentions and still cause
harm. Simply intending harm is not an intentional tort, but rather the person
must intend the consequences of a particular act or believe that the consequences are substantially certain to result from it (2).

"Intent," as used in the law of torts, refers to the consequences of an act
rather than the act itself. A typical law school example will be used to illustrate
this point. An individual fires a gun in a desert, intending to pull the trigger. But
when the bullet hits another person present at some distance in the desert without the knowledge of the person firing the gun, the result is not intended.

Certain acts may be both intentional torts and crimes, bringing forth civil and
criminal prosecution for the same wrongful act (3). In civil law, the psychiatric
assessment of suicide intent in insurance litigation requires knowledge of the
legal meaning of intent (4). The intentional torts are assault and battery, false
imprisonment, defamation, invasion of right of privacy, misrepresentation or
fraud, and the intentional infliction of emotional distress. An intentional rather
than negligent tort may be brought based on legal exigencies such as the availability of experts and the statute of limitations, which may differ according to
the type of tort. Expert witnesses are not required for intentional torts. Furthermore, intentional torts are not covered by most malpractice insurance policies.
If possible, mental health professionals should attempt to purchase a professional liability policy that provides coverage for intentional torts.

Under what clinical circumstances is the mental health professional most vulnerable to a suit for intentional tort?

Battery results from intentional, nonconsenting physical contact with the plaintiff that would be offensive to a reasonable person. An assault is simply the
apprehension that a battery will occur (1). As Prosser (i.e., Keeton et al.) (5)
states, assault and battery go together "like ham and eggs." In criminal law a
battery includes assault, but in civil law (torts) a battery may occur without an
assault, as in the case of an individual striking another from behind. In this situation, there is physical contact without apprehension (5).

An individual's right to prevent the unauthorized invasion of his or her physical integrity is vigorously protected by the law. In a famous 1914 case (6) enunciating the informed-consent doctrine, Justice Cardozo declared: "Every human being of adult years and sound mind has a right to determine what shall be done with his body." As a result, treatment without the patient's consent may constitute a battery. Whether the patient receives any benefit from the unconsented treatment is irrelevant. If there is no injury, there are no damages. When the patient consents to a particular procedure or treatment and the therapist does not sufficiently warn of risks that are likely to occur, liability for harm may be assessed on the basis of negligence due to a lack of informed consent. The legal term *offensive touching* generally applies to any invasion of the patient's physical integrity and not just the narrow act of physical touching.

The landmark psychiatric battery case is *Hammer v. Rosen* (7). Dr. John Rosen originated the innovative but controversial therapy—direct analysis— whereby schizophrenic patients were initially bombarded with id-type interpretations. The therapist also took the position of an all-powerful parent who would use physical methods to make contact with severely regressed patients. The court stated that the beatings Alice Hammer received over the course of 7 years of treatment with Dr. Rosen constituted improper treatment and malpractice. The case of a woman who was psychologically harmed and physically injured through a treatment called "rage reduction," or Z-therapy, is discussed in Chapter 20.

The tort of false imprisonment protects an individual's interest in freedom from restrained movement. In the decades before the 1970s, a number of spectacular cases involved psychiatrists who involuntarily hospitalized individuals out of spite or malice or for financial gain (8). False imprisonment may occur when the therapist threatens a patient with involuntary hospitalization knowing all along that the patient is not committable, thus causing the patient to stay in the hospital. False imprisonment and wrongful commitment are discussed further in Chapter 8.

Defamation refers to untrue statements made to a third party about another that tend to lower significantly that person's reputation and esteem in the eyes of the community. Communicating pejorative diagnoses to third parties that are incorrect and based on the mental health professional's malice or countertransference may be actionable. This subject is discussed in detail in Chapter 22.

Intentional misrepresentation (often referred to as deceit or fraud) occurs when mental health professionals seek to protect themselves by concealing negligence or by seeking to gain some economic advantage by misleading the patient (9). Because of the temptation to exploit that arises out of the close relationship between therapist and patient, the duty to neutrality is not always maintained by some therapists. Exaggerated claims about the benefits of idiosyncratic treatments may be made that have no basis in fact, in order to take financial advantage of the patient. For example, psychiatrists have misrepresented their own involvement with patients who, although actually seen by non-medical therapists, were billed for "services" as though provided by the psychiatrist. Some psychiatrists have billed for nonexistent sessions and have double and triple billed when seeing a couple or a family. Such claims are fraudulent and may invite both civil and criminal actions (10).

The right to privacy is really the "right to be let alone" (9). Actionable invasions of privacy include *1)* intrusion upon the seclusion of another, *2)* appropriation of one's name or likeness, *3)* publicity of the plaintiff's private life, and *4)* publicity placing plaintiff in a false light. Intrusion upon seclusion of another is a particular problem in teaching hospitals where patients are subject to the scrutiny of teaching rounds without their permission. Publication of a patient's private life without any attempt to disguise the identity of the patient or to leave out explicit sexual details resulted in the celebrated *Doe v. Roe* case (11).

The therapist who uses unorthodox techniques that cause great emotional distress to the patient may be liable for the intentional infliction of emotional distress or the *tort of outrage*. The clinical vignette in the chapter on outrageous behavior toward patients (see Chapter 20) describes how an idiosyncratic style of therapy severely damaged a patient emotionally.

Therapists using unorthodox or innovative techniques should ask the following questions:

1. What are my motives for using an innovative technique?
2. Is my therapeutic goal consistent with the patient's goal?
3. Is there support for the innovative technique in professional literature? Have at least a minority of respected (competent) therapists experienced positive results by using this technique, or is it strictly idiosyncratic?
4. Is it really necessary? Are there equally effective treatments that pose less risk?

In the clinical vignette, is Dr. Allen legally vulnerable to the claims of intentional and negligent harm made by his patient?

In his lawsuit, Mr. Lake alleges that Dr. Allen committed assault and battery by touching him without his consent. The assault and battery consisted of the actual physical touching, such as frequently placing an arm around the patient's shoulder and hugging him, but also using an innovative therapy without obtaining informed consent. Because Dr. Allen did not obtain consent at all, a legal action for battery is possible. The therapist's arm around the shoulder of any patient is highly questionable, but for a patient with sexual identity conflicts it could be quite offensive and frightening.

The patient also alleges assault. In particular, Mr. Lake argues that Dr. Allen put him in fear of imminent physical peril by shouting, "Control yourself. You are out of control. You will be alright. Don't force me to restrain you." Dr.

Allen counters this charge by stating that the patient unreasonably misinterpreted his comments, which actually reflected a concern that Mr. Lake might injure himself in the struggle. Furthermore, Dr. Allen maintains that the patient could have expressed an objection to physical contact at any time, which would have been immediately respected. Thus, Dr. Allen is alleging that the patient gave an implied or behavioral consent.

Psychotherapists who touch patients do so at their clinical and legal peril. Allegations of undue familiarity may be asserted. Plaintiff's experts will likely testify that Dr. Allen should have known that the touching of a male patient by a male therapist can trigger sexual identity conflicts involving both a covert desire for physical contact and a terrifying dread of such a wish. Because Mr. Lake's background of sexual abuse (of which Dr. Allen was unaware), the patient was particularly vulnerable to physical contact by a male therapist.

Patients frequently have deep concerns about closeness, autonomy, and sexual seduction. They can become sexually overstimulated and their symptoms exacerbated by therapists who are, either consciously or unconsciously, seductive in their interaction with patients. There is much clinical wisdom in confining physical contact to a friendly handshake at the first meeting, at congratulatory occasions, and at the termination of therapy, if the patient so desires.

Should the therapist never touch the patient? Touching requires definition. It may refer to a whole spectrum of physical contact from a simple pat on the shoulder to hugging involving genital rubbing. Situations may arise in which the human reaction of extending solace and comfort is appropriate. For instance, a teenage patient who just witnessed a fatal automobile accident before her hour of therapy was visibly shaken and on the verge of losing emotional control. An arm around the patient's shoulder by the therapist allowed the patient to regain control. Occasions will arise, perhaps on the occasion of a professional promotion, a marriage, or a birth, when a congratulatory handshake may be in order if the patient is receptive. Some patients need to shake hands at the beginning and end of each treatment session. This need should be addressed as a treatment issue if it appears to be overdetermined.

Dr. Allen's touching techniques raise questions about his motivations. Are the clinical indications that he proffers for commencing to touch patients supported by the psychiatric literature or a respected minority of therapists using similar techniques? Perhaps the touching is necessary only for the psychiatrist's own internal needs. A subset of sexually exploitative therapists are *frotteurs* who may consciously or subconsciously attempt to justify touching their patients as a form of therapy. Therapists who use innovative or radical techniques should be very clear about their personal motivations.

Forcefully restraining a competent, nonconsenting patient may lead to a legal action for false imprisonment. Unless performed under the most compelling threat of imminent harm to self or others, a claim of false imprisonment would be difficult to defend. In general, a recent overt act of violence or the presence of other clinical data indicating imminent danger should be present. In the clinical vignette, Dr. Allen decided to restrain Mr. Lake because of the look of terror in his patient's eyes. Unless there are other more compelling clinical reasons, preventing Mr. Lake from leaving the office based on the patient's appearance alone is hard to justify. Action-oriented therapists may be more prone to inviting intentional torts.

Because Dr. Allen persisted in visiting Mr. Lake in the hospital against the patient's objections, he invaded Mr. Lake's privacy by intruding upon his seclusion. Although therapists must not abandon their patients, a patient may discharge the therapist at any time. Unless the patient's act of discharging the therapist appears to result from impaired mental capacity to make health care decisions, the therapist must withdraw. While one frequently hears that patients are emotionally unable to let go of their therapists, sometimes intrepid therapists are unable to let go of their patients. Although the therapist may consider extratherapeutic measures to deal with a sudden interruption of therapy by the patient, he or she will usually be limited to verbal interventions with the patient.

Finally, Dr. Allen is charged with the intentional infliction of emotional distress. In other words, Mr. Lake argues that Dr. Allen knew or should have known that touching him without his consent could result in serious emotional harm. In order for Dr. Allen's conduct to reach the level of recovery for intentional infliction of emotional distress, the jury will have to find that Dr. Allen acted so outrageously that he intentionally or recklessly caused severe emotional distress to Mr. Lake. This subject is discussed in detail in Chapter 20.

In touching his patient, could Dr. Allen be successfully sued for negligent psychotherapy?

Proving negligence in psychotherapy is very difficult. Unlike intentional torts, negligence suits require expert testimony regarding the appropriate standard of care. There are currently over 450 different schools of psychotherapy, and the number is constantly increasing. Establishing a general standard of care among psychiatrists when so many disagree concerning the indications and effectiveness of the myriad therapeutic modalities now in existence is very difficult, if not impossible. Also, the legal requirement of proving the proximate cause of alleged psychic damage is equally difficult to establish when many factors can influence the course of an emotional illness. Furthermore, an outcome that one therapist considers to be psychic damage may be considered by another to be progress. In psychotherapy, little progress can be made without some psychic pain. In fact, a respected minority of therapists probably can be found asserting that the professionally discrete and therapeutically sensitive touching of patients does not represent an improper deviation from the standard of care and may actually be therapeutic for certain patients.

For example, John Bancroft, in his article "Ethical Aspects of Sexuality and Sex Therapy" (12), states:

> Should you ever touch your patient except for obviously clinical purposes? An arm around the shoulder or a hug to comfort distress might be construed as sexual and professionals are often advised to avoid even these basically caring gestures if only to safeguard themselves from the occasional histrionic manipulative patient. I would find such limitations to my therapeutic relationships unacceptable and am prepared to take the risk, providing that I am quite clear of my own motives.

Other mental health professionals, however, clearly hold different views.

What are some of the legal problems surrounding innovative or radical therapies?

"Therapies" involving physical or sexual abuse of patients appear to be negligence per se. The therapist is presumed to have deviated in the provision of reasonable care. Innovative therapies that solely benefit the therapist are a breach of the fiduciary relationship that exists with the patient and are legally actionable. Two legal issues that are applied to the use of innovative therapy are the doctrine of informed consent and whether the innovative therapy represents a departure from standard and accepted practice.

The legal measure for negligence liability relies on standards that determine what is customary. A treatment that is found not to be customary does not necessarily indicate liability. Proving that a treatment is customary usually precludes liability if the treatment was not negligently rendered. Customary treatment does not mean that a majority of therapists use it. In some jurisdictions, it is sufficient if a therapy is supported by a "respectable minority" of therapists (13). Unless egregious, even those forms of psychotherapy that would not be employed by most therapists probably fall within the "respected minority rule." This rule states that a therapist is free to choose from any of the available schools of therapy, even one that most physicians would not use, if a respected minority of therapists would employ the same therapies under the same circumstances (14).

As Slovenko (15) points out, "A single practitioner adhering to a certain theoretical framework would not constitute a school." Nevertheless, the number of practitioners may be very few. In *Hood v. Phillips* (16), the number of physicians in the world performing a highly controversial surgical procedure was six! Only two of the physicians were from the United States. Thus, the surgeon was not found guilty because of the respected minority rule even though the vast majority of the medical community found the procedure to lack medical justification and to be highly dangerous. Similarly, in *Leach v. Bralliar* (17), the physician was found not guilty of malpractice for a procedure used by a "respectable minority" of only 65 physicians in the United States. Prosser (18) states that "a 'school' must be a recognized one with definite principles, and it must be the line of thought of at least a respectable minority of the profession." By this definition, Dr. Allen's touching therapy may not represent a school operating with definite principles, but rather an idiosyncratic style of conducting psychotherapy.

When a therapist uses a novel or unique approach, it becomes more difficult to satisfy the standard of due care. For radical techniques, other criteria must be used to determine if the treatment is negligent. The reasonableness of implementing an innovative treatment approach will depend on *1)* current and future prognosis of the patient, *2)* the probability of success of a given treatment, and *3)* the type, severity, and probability of risks of the treatment. Radical departures from customary practice may be considered a lack of due care as a matter of law and may not be put before a jury (19). In malpractice actions involving innovative treatments, Hampton (20) suggests that if the therapy is both so unconventional and experimental as to fall outside of the practice of a respectable minority, it must first be determined whether the therapy is ethical and reasonable. He asserts that under these circumstances the burden of proof should rest upon the defendant to show that the standard of care was not breached.

Freiberg (21) suggests that the use of new and untested techniques poses a greater risk to the patient. Before using such a technique, the therapist "should be able to justify any unconventional treatment in terms of the patient's needs rather than his own, to establish that there is some foundation in psychiatric learning for his treatment, and to show that the conventional treatment has been unsuccessful."

Following traditional treatments merely out of fear of liability rather than using as a guide the best interest of the patient makes a mockery out of the therapist's professionalism. The need to protect the patient from harm must be balanced against the need to develop new, more effective treatment modalities. Otherwise, mental health professionals will be stifled in their quest for new discoveries that hold the promise of important breakthroughs. Innovative therapies that are developed on a foundation of research, presented to and studied by colleagues, peers, or supervisors and conducted by therapists with sound training and credentials, probably would lead to a more favorable review for professional usage by the courts.

In the clinical vignette, Dr. Allen published one article in a reputable, but not peer-reviewed journal. The paper also was presented at the local psychiatric society. Dr. Allen's paper drew severe criticism from his peers. In addition, Dr. Allen did not derive any of his conclusions from systematic research, but relied on his own experience with a few patients. The court would certainly take note of these shortcomings and peer criticisms.

For an example of the legal issues surrounding innovative therapies, Reisner and Slobogin (22) present an interesting discussion on the use of hemodialysis to treat schizophrenia and the liability of physicians who use dialysis as an experimental treatment. Although some researchers have suggested that pathogenic substances that produce schizophrenic symptoms may be removed through dialysis, this procedure is often stressful and associated with an increased incidence of depression and suicide. The authors pose the following questions about the liability of a psychiatrist who uses dialysis to treat a schizophrenic patient who subsequently becomes depressed and commits suicide: Should the fact that a small minority of physicians use dialysis to treat schizophrenia be determinative of a prima facie case of negligence? Would holding that the use of dialysis constitutes a lack of due care as a matter of law inhibit medical experimentation? Should the result depend on whether hemodialysis was offered as customary treatment rather than closely supervised medical experimentation?

What are the informed-consent requirements for innovative therapies?

When standard methods of treatment fail or are not indicated, innovative or radical therapies may be attempted. Therapists who use "intrusive therapies" should be aware of regulations created by judicial decisions and legislation that govern these therapies (23). Patients must be very carefully informed of all foreseeable risks. Alternative, less risky therapies must be explained. The patient should also be told that the treatment is untried and innovative and that it possibly contains unforeseeable risks. Both the therapist and the patient need to do a careful risk-benefit analysis. Also, consent should be obtained in written form. Perlin (24) notes that there is virtually no case law on the issue of nontherapeutic experimentation.

Roth (25) discusses informed consent in human experimentation. He states that if a psychiatrist seeks to enroll mentally ill persons in research, informed consent must be obtained. Psychiatric research is regulated by common law developments as well as by ethical guidelines, professional codes, requirements of regulatory agencies, scientific peer review, and the ongoing proceedings of local groups known as institutional review boards (IRBs).

Regulatory guidelines of the United States Department of Health and Human Services (DHHS) (26) currently have the most significant influence on research activities. The DHHS disclosure requirements include the fact and purposes of the proposed research; reasonably foreseeable risks; reasonably expected benefits; appropriate alternatives; a statement about the maintenance of confidentiality; an explanation about possible compensation if injury occurs in research involving more than minimal risks; information about the process of obtaining answers to pertinent questions; and a statement that participation is voluntary and refusal results in no penalties or loss of benefits. Informed-consent requirements surrounding biomedical and behavioral research are discussed in greater detail in Chapter 7.

In the vignette, Dr. Allen used his own brand of innovative treatment without the patient's knowledge and consent—a prime invitation for a battery suit. Although Dr. Allen's innovative therapy did not involve systematic human experimentation, he did use it with a number of patients. In part, his physical contact with patients was intended as research; however, it was idiosyncratic and did not employ any systematic research principles. In addition, no reference to outside guidelines governing procedure and consent was made by Dr. Allen. Finally, he did not obtain informed consent from his patients prior to implementing his touching technique.

References

1. King JH: The Law of Medical Malpractice, 2nd Edition. St Paul, MN, West Publishing, 1986, p 180
2. Keeton WP, Dobbs DB, Keeton RE, et al: Prosser and Keeton on the Law of Torts, 5th Edition. St Paul, MN, West Publishing, 1984, p 34
3. R Slovenko, personal communication, June 1985
4. Simon RI: You only die once—but did you intend it?: psychiatric assessment of suicide intent in insurance litigation. Tort & Insurance Law Journal 25:650–662, 1990
5. Keeton WP, Dobbs DB, Keeton RE, et al: Prosser and Keeton on the Law of Torts, 5th Edition. St Paul, MN, West Publishing, 1984, p 46
6. Schloendorff v Society of New York Hospital, 211 NY 125, 105 NE 92 (1914), overruled, Bing v Thunig, 2 NY2d 656, 143 NE2d 3, 163 NYS2d 3 (1957)
7. 7 NY2d 376, 165 NE2d 756, 198 NYS2d 65 (1960)
8. Halleck SL: Law in the Practice of Psychiatry. New York, Plenum, 1980, p 37
9. King JH: The Law of Medical Malpractice, 2nd Edition. St Paul, MN, West Publishing, 1986, pp 176–177
10. Slovenko R: Accountability and abuse of confidentiality in the practice of psychiatry. Int J Law Psychiatry 2:431–454, 1979
11. 93 Misc 2d 201, 400 NYS2d 668 (NY Sup Ct 1977)
12. Bancroft J: Ethical aspects of sexuality and sex therapy, in Psychiatric Ethics. Edited by Block S, Chodoff P. New York, Oxford University Press, 1981, pp 160–184
13. Reisner R, Slobogin C: Law and the Mental Health System, 2nd Edition. St Paul, MN, West Publishing, 1990, p 75
14. Malcolm JG: Treatment Choices and Informed Consent: Current Controversies in Psychiatric Malpractice Litigation. Springfield, IL, Charles C Thomas, 1988, pp 49–50
15. Slovenko R: Malpractice in psychiatry and related fields. Journal of Psychiatry and Law 9:5–63, 1981
16. 537 SW2d 291 (Tex Ct App 1976), aff'd Hood v Phillips, 554 SW2d 160 (Tex 1977)
17. 275 F Supp 897 (D Ariz 1967)
18. Keeton WP, Dobbs DB, Keeton RE, et al: Prosser and Keeton on the Law of Torts, 5th Edition. St Paul, MN, West Publishing, 1984, p 187
19. Ibid, p 76
20. Hampton LP: Malpractice in psychotherapy: is there a relevant standard of care? Case Western Reserve Law Review 35:251–281, 1984

21. Freiberg J: The song is ended but the malady lingers on: legal regulation of psycho-therapy. St. Louis University Law Journal 22:519, 1978

22. Reisner R, Slobogin C: Law and the Mental Health System, 2nd Edition. St Paul, MN, West Publishing, 1990, pp 83–84

23. Plotkin R: Limiting the therapeutic orgy: mental patients' right to refuse treatment. NULR 72:461, 479–481, 1978

24. Perlin ML: Mental Disability Law: Civil and Criminal, Vol 3. Charlottesville, VA, Michie, 1989, p 91

25. Roth LH: Informed consent and its applicability for psychiatry, in Psychiatry, Vol 3. Edited by Cavenar JO. Philadelphia, PA, JB Lippincott, 1985, pp 1–17

26. U.S. Department of Health and Human Services: Final regulations amending basic HHS policy for the protection of human research subjects. Federal Register 46:8366–8792, 1981

Chapter 20

The Legal Consequences of Outrageous Behavior Toward Patients

───────────────

Ms. Winters, a 24-year-old graduate student in psychology, seeks psychotherapeutic treatment because of her difficulty in making certain major life decisions. She sees Dr. Nichols, a psychotherapist, over the course of ten 45-minute sessions. Dr. Nichols uses an unorthodox style of psychotherapy aimed at accelerating treatment by directly circumventing the patient's defenses. He has discussed his technique with other psychotherapists. Dr. Nichols' method is abrasive, judgmental, demanding, and even insulting "to force the patient to face conflicts." His colleagues are uniformly unenthusiastic about his technique, expressing the concern that his confrontational style can produce serious regression in vulnerable patients. Furthermore, they warn that Dr. Nichols' treatment approach is controversial at best and is not practiced by any other credible practitioners. Dr. Nichols declines their advice, recalling that Freud faced strong opposition from colleagues and had to practice in isolation.

Ms. Winters finds the initial sessions helpful in clarifying areas of her life in which she experiences conflict. She is struggling between choosing a career path of academic work or placing more emphasis on trying to work out a troubled romantic relationship. She also expresses concern about her appearance, feeling she is physically unattractive and unappealing. Feelings of depression and occasional suicidal ideas are energetically explored by Dr. Nichols. As a means of dealing with her bouts of depression, her alcohol intake has increased. By the fifth session, Ms. Winters begins to resist the aggressive style of Dr. Nichols, expressing her own opinions and directly disagreeing with some of his recommendations. During the 10th session, upon having his therapeutic technique once again questioned by Ms. Winter, Dr. Nichols flies into a rage shouting, "You're stubborn and ugly. Who would want to live with you? You'll never get married. You're probably an alcoholic and will end up in the gutter. I wouldn't be surprised if you end up in the hospital and probably kill yourself along the way." Ms. Winters abruptly walks out of the session. She hears Dr. Nichols yell, "Good riddance. What a nut!"

Ms. Winters is severely emotionally distressed. She becomes increasingly depressed and preoccupied with suicide. She is unable to concentrate on her academic work and is forced to take a leave of absence. Because of her constant emotional turmoil, her romantic relationship collapses. Ms. Winters sees another therapist, who is outraged upon hearing of the abusive treatment she has received. The new therapist recommends that ethical and legal action be taken against Dr. Nichols. Ms. Winters is briefly hospitalized because she is assessed to be a serious suicide risk. She consults an attorney, who files a lawsuit for negligent psychotherapy and the intentional infliction of emotional distress.

What is the tort of outrage?

In recent years, courts have been addressing liability for the tort of "outrage" or the intentional infliction of emotional distress (1). Behavior is considered outrageous if it is "atrocious" or "intolerable" (2). As applied to health care providers, outrage is an extension of the strict liability doctrine involving intentional, deliberate, or reckless infliction of mental suffering with or without physical injury. According to the legal theory of strict liability, the injured person does not need to prove negligence but only that the injury was a result of the use of a product or service. The plaintiff may be the direct victim or a third party involved only indirectly.

Historically, when there has been no physical injury, recovering damages for emotional distress has been difficult. That trend, however, is changing. The emerging tort of outrage reflects two trends in the law (1). One trend recognizes that physicians are professionally responsible to identify reasonably foreseeable harm to patients; the other is an expansion of liability for emotional injuries.

How has the tort of outrage developed historically?

In 1861, the British jurist Lord Wensleydale stated: "Mental pain or anxiety the law cannot value, and does not pretend to redress, when the unlawful act complained of causes that alone" (3). The reluctance of the law to tackle the issue of mental pain alone was based on the view that it was too "metaphysical" to be measured, too variable and dependent on the individual concerned, and open to the possibility of fictitious and fraudulent claims. By the late 19th century, common law did not recognize an independent cause of action for the protection of one's peace of mind. Damage for mental suffering that accompanied injuries sustained as the result of commission of an established tort, however, was acknowledged (4). Damages that were permitted in this "parasitic" manner reflected a development toward establishment of the intentional infliction of mental distress as an independent tort.

As an independent cause of action, the intentional infliction of emotional distress first began to be recognized among "public servants" such as innkeepers and common carriers who were under a special obligation to the public because of their unique position to inflict harm. In this country, the tort of outrage was not available against ordinary defendants until the early 1930s. In *Great Atlantic & Pacific Tea Co. v. Roch* (5), a grocery man played a prank on a customer by wrapping up a dead rat and handing it to the plaintiff as a loaf of bread. Liability was imposed for the shock to the plaintiff. A transition period existed up to the mid-20th century, when the intentional infliction of emotional distress resulting in bodily harm was recognized as legally actionable, not so much from a right to be free from disturbance of one's mental tranquility, but rather from a right to be free from interference with one's physical well-being (6).

In *State Rubbish Collectors' Association v. Siliznoff* (7), a trend began that permitted recovery for emotional distress without physical harm. (The first American decision permitting recovery for emotional damage without physical injury occurred in 1905 [8].) In *Siliznoff,* a garbage collector was threatened with physical harm if he refused to pay another collector for a lost account. Currently, a majority of jurisdictions recognize the intentional infliction of emotional distress as an independent tort. Most of these jurisdictions have rejected the parasitic requirement of restricted recovery for actions accompanying a previously recognized tort or associated with physical injury (4).

What are the elements of the tort of outrage?

There are four elements to the tort of outrage (9). First, the conduct must be intentional or reckless. The wrongdoer must have the specific goal of causing emotional distress or must intend his or her specific behavior and knows, or should know, that emotional distress is the likely result. For example, in *Blakeley v. Shortal's Estate* (10), the defendant committed suicide in the plaintiff's kitchen by cutting his throat, knowing that it was likely that his body would be discovered by her. She was allowed to recover for the emotional distress caused by coming upon his body and the bloody scene. In *Chuy v. Philadelphia Eagles Football Club* (11), the plaintiff recovered for emotional distress when the team's physician announced to the press that the plaintiff suffered from a rare fatal disease. The physician's recklessness in rendering a conclusion that was false and without basis was sufficient to equate with intent.

Second, the conduct must be outrageous and intolerable, offending generally accepted standards of decency and morality. This requirement exists to limit frivolous outrage suits and to avoid claims when just hurt feelings, bad manners, and unpleasantness occur. Thus, in *Dowling v. Blue Cross of Florida, Inc.* (12), the dismissal of two employees based on false and unverified employee accusations that they had sexual relations in the ladies' lounge was held to lack the necessary outrageous character to support a claim of intentional infliction of emotional distress. In *Ford Motor Credit Co. v. Sheehan* (13), a case in which the plaintiff was successful, the creditor's employee posed as a hospital employee, falsely representing to the debtor's mother that her grandchildren were severely injured in an accident and that the hospital needed to know the debtor's whereabouts in order to inform him. Outrageous conduct was also found in *Sherman v. Field Clinic* (14) when the collection agency phoned the plaintiff 20 times a day, sent numerous letters, and called her husband at work threatening to embarrass him by informing his employer and co-workers of the unpaid bill.

Conduct may be considered outrageous if directed at mentally susceptible persons when it would not be considered so if directed at persons of ordinary susceptibilities. The defendant's knowledge of the weakness or susceptibility is an important factor in determining outrageousness. In *Nickerson v. Hodges* (15), the defendants buried a "pot of gold" for a mentally deficient, eccentric elderly woman to find. After she did find it, she was escorted in triumph to city hall, where she opened the pot and was exposed to public humiliation.

Third, there must be a causal connection between the wrongdoer's behavior and the emotional distress.

Fourth, the emotional distress must be severe. According to Merrick (4), courts have not found aggravation of a speech impediment, increased depression or embarrassment, and crying or experiencing sleep difficulties sufficient to recover for emotional distress. Headaches, loss of sleep and appetite requiring medical attention, or anxiety necessitating hospitalization met the requirement of severe distress. The American Law Institute notes: "Complete emotional tranquility is seldom attainable in this world, and some degree of transient and trivial emotional distress is part of the price of living among people. The law intervenes only where the distress inflicted is so severe that no reasonable man could be expected to endure it" (16).

Would Dr. Nichols' behavior toward his patient meet the legal criteria for the tort of outrage?

The first legal criterion appears to be met on at least two grounds. Dr. Nichols' behavior toward the patient appeared reckless because he failed to consider the damaging effect of his diatribe. Second, the treatment method developed and used by Dr. Nichols relied on deliberate confrontation as a means of eliminating the patient's defenses. Thus, the therapy had a high potential for producing regression and other foreseeable, untoward emotional effects. By any measure, Dr. Nichols' behavior toward Ms. Winters was vicious, humiliating, intolerable, and offensive beyond any generally accepted standard of decency and morality. Upon hearing of such behavior, most therapists would surely exclaim, "That's outrageous." The therapist stands in a fiduciary relationship with the patient, operating as an ally rather than an adversary.

Third, a causal connection clearly exists between Dr. Nichols' sadistic behavior toward Ms. Winters and her deepening depression and suicidal feelings that led to a disruption of her academic career and an important relationship.

Finally, her emotional distress was severe, requiring additional psychiatric treatment and psychiatric hospitalization.

Under what circumstances have physicians and hospitals been sued under the tort of outrage?

In a Tennessee case (17), the court allowed the plaintiff to recover compensatory damages when the hospital failed to dispose of her premature infant's body as promised. Moreover, the court also held that subsequently showing the plaintiff a jar of formaldehyde containing her child's shrunken body constituted outrageous conduct causing the mother severe emotional distress. The mother also recovered punitive damages against the hospital.

In *Molien v. Kaiser Foundation Hospital* (18), the plaintiff's wife went for a routine physical examination and was told that she had contracted syphilis. She was told to inform her husband so that he could be tested because he was now a suspected carrier. Although the diagnosis was erroneous, Mrs. Molien believed her spouse to be unfaithful, which lead to a disruption of their marriage. Mr. Molien was successful on appeal against the hospital for the negligent infliction of emotional distress. Other cases for emotional distress have involved unsuccessful sterilization procedures (19), refusing to provide for a dying woman (20), disfigurement by a plastic surgeon (21), exposing a pregnant woman to X rays (22), unnecessary hospitalization (23), wrongful detention (24), and invasion of privacy by hospital personnel (25).

In *Roberts v. Saylor* (26), the Supreme Court of Kansas awarded summary judgment in favor of the physician in an intentional infliction of emotional distress suit. Dr. Saylor was visiting the hospital to schedule his own wrist surgery when he saw Mrs. Roberts lying on a gurney. The plaintiff complained that the doctor told her prior to surgery, "I don't like you, I don't like you, I wanted to tell you that before you went in there." Dr. Saylor, however, testified that he only said, "Yes, I know Loretta Roberts. And, I don't like her anymore now than I have in the past." The court held that the physician's conduct was not sufficiently extreme or outrageous to incur liability for emotional distress.

In *Greer v. Medders* (27), Dr. Medders was covering for another physician who was vacationing. The patient was recovering from heel surgery. Because Dr. Medders failed to visit the patient for several days, Mr. Greer called his office to complain. Allegedly, Dr. Medders entered Mr. Greer's hospital room in an agitated state and said: "Let me tell you one damn thing, don't nobody call over to my office raising hell with my secretary. . . . I don't have to be in here every damn day checking on you because I check with physical therapy. . . . I don't have to be your damn doctor." Mrs. Greer, who was present, told Dr. Medders he need not worry because he was no longer her husband's doctor. Dr. Medders allegedly retorted, "If your smart ass wife would keep her mouth shut, things wouldn't be so bad." As a consequence, Mrs. Greer cried, while Mr. Greer allegedly suffered periods of uncontrollable shaking requiring psychiatric treatment. A suit was brought against Dr. Medders by both husband and wife for the intentional infliction of emotional distress.

The trial court granted the doctor's motion for summary judgment but was reversed by the Court of Appeals of Georgia. The court stated that Dr. Medders's statements could have been sufficiently abusive to support a judgment for the intentional infliction of emotional distress, particularly when made by a doctor to a postoperative patient lying in a hospital bed.

Stevens (28) notes that courts hesitate in applying the tort of outrage to health care providers when insulting words have been at issue. In the presence of the doctor-patient relationship, which creates a "special relationship" with authority over the patient, courts have been more willing to find outrageous behavior.

What areas of clinical practice hold the greatest potential for allegations of intentional infliction of emotional distress?

Radically innovative or wild therapies that overwhelm the patient either physically or emotionally are potential sources for a claim of outrageous behavior. As stated in the *Restatement of Torts*: "Generally, the case is one in which the recitation of facts to an average member of the community would arouse resentment against the actor and lead him to exclaim, 'outrageous'" (29). In fact, the tort of outrage is often attached to other, more conventional torts such as assault, battery, seduction, false imprisonment, and invasion of privacy.

Although not held to be a tort of outrage, the following cases could be so construed. Dr. Rosen, a psychiatrist, used physical methods of control such as wrestling to treat psychotic behavior using his pioneering but controversial "direct analysis" approach to severely disturbed, schizophrenic patients. In *Hammer v. Rosen,* the court held that Dr. Rosen assaulted the patient through a number of beatings and that Dr. Rosen's actions were intrinsically negligent, not requiring expert testimony to recover damages for malpractice (30).

In another case, a 22-year-old graduate student agreed to undergo an experimental treatment called "rage reduction," or Z-therapy, a form of treatment designed for autistic children. In this therapy, the patient is restrained, tickled, and poked when unsatisfactory answers are given to questions asked by the therapist. Ms. Abraham was continually poked and abused for 10 to 12 hours, suffering extensive bruising and acute renal failure. She was awarded $170,000 in damages (31).

In the clinical vignette, Dr. Nichols was the sole practitioner of an unorthodox treatment method. The defendant could not argue that there was a respected minority of practitioners exercising reasonable care that used this modality. In fact, he was not able to gain approval for his method of treatment from his colleagues. As a result, his "treatment" not only was unorthodox but appeared to be idiosyncratic.

On closer scrutiny, did his treatment approach rest on sound clinical and theoretical considerations, or did it reflect an irascible character and inadequate training? Was Dr. Nichols' obnoxious behavior toward his patient simply an example of unprofessional conduct toward a patient who disagreed with him, having nothing all to do with the clinical and theoretical merits of his therapeutic approach? Therapists do have an ethical and professional duty to control the expression of their baser impulses toward patients and to not dignify such expressions as methods of treatment.

Mental health practitioners who wish to develop radical therapies should not do so in isolation, but should subject their work to review by colleagues, peers, and research and investigational review boards. Treatment innovations must not be stifled, but such treatments must be carefully thought out with the patient's ultimate best interest in mind. A risk-benefit analysis for every subject might help temper overzealous innovations. Furthermore, unorthodox or radical therapies are often experimental, thus requiring the full and complete disclosure to the patient of all possible risks, side effects, and alternative treatments. Written consent is preferable. The therapist should also independently record the consent of the patient.

Other areas of clinical practice holding high potential for severe emotional distress claims include undue familiarity with patients, intrusion on the privacy of patients by staff not directly responsible for the care of the patient (such as in training institutions where the patient is unwittingly displayed at teaching or grand rounds), and involuntary hospitalization motivated by malice or deception. For example, one woman, suspected of insanity, was deceived into going to a hospital after being told that her husband and child were injured and taken to that same hospital (32). Halleck (33) notes that psychiatrists have been guilty of initiating commitment for financial gain, or to aid friends/relatives to get rid of difficult spouses. Some psychiatrists have also disregarded statutory requirements for involuntary hospitalization by not personally examining the patient.

Negative countertransference, particularly when malignant, can be unleashed on an unsuspecting, vulnerable patient, inflicting great emotional harm. Less egregious, harmful actions of therapists that damage patients may be litigated as claims of negligent psychotherapy or the negligent infliction of emotional distress. Health care providers such as health maintenance organizations, preferred provider organizations, and government insurance–sponsored programs must be sure that bureaucratic and financial considerations do not come before adequate treatment of patients, thus inflicting severe emotional distress.

What is the relationship between the tort of outrage and judicially imposed standards of care? What consequences do judicially imposed standards have upon clinical practice?

The tort of outrage, like the duty to warn endangered third parties, is an example of a judicially imposed standard of care (34). Another example of a judicially imposed standard of care occurred in *Canterbury v. Spence* (35). The court rejected the prevailing professional custom standard of informing patients in favor of a reasonable man standard in obtaining informed consent. In *The T. H. Hooper* case, Judge Learned Hand's opinion stated the principle underlying judicially imposed standards:

> [I]n most cases reasonable prudence is in fact common prudence; but strictly it is never its measure; a whole calling may have unduly lagged in the adoption of new and available devices. It never may set its own tests, however persuasive be its usages. Courts must in the end say what is required; there are precautions so imperative that even their universal disregard will not excuse their omission. (36)

The courts are rejecting the testimony of experts on accepted standards of care when they think such testimony to be inappropriate. Therefore, mental health professionals cannot always rely on what they or their colleagues do or think is best for the patient.

In *Osheroff v. Chestnut Lodge* (37), the plaintiff asserted that his depression was inappropriately treated by intensive psychotherapy alone, needlessly extending his hospital stay and causing him other emotional and financial harm. This case was settled but has generated considerable controversy between psychodynamic and biological psychiatrists (38, 39). When psychiatry is unable to settle its controversies internally, they may spill over into the courts as in *Osheroff*. The imposition of judicial standard of care upon psychiatric practice might unduly restrict the psychiatrist's full discretion in the diagnosis and treatment of mental disorders. Malcolm (40) observes that "the judicial tools exist for an innovative court to use should it decide to hold the use of an outdated medical practice negligent as a matter of law, even though it is espoused by a respectable minority or even a majority within the profession."

References

1. Hirsh HL: Medical malpractice predicated on the tort of "outrage." South Med J 71:818–820, 1978
2. Stevens GE: Negligent infliction of emotional distress by physicians and hospitals. Medical Trial Technique Quarterly 28:233–241, 1982
3. Lynch v Knight, 9 H.L. case 577, 11 Eng Rep 854 (1861)
4. Merrick RA: The tort of outrage: recovery from the intentional infliction of mental distress. Behavioral Sciences and the Law 3:165–175, 1985
5. 160 Md 189, 153 A 22 (1931)
6. RESTATEMENT OF TORTS § 306 (1934)
7. 38 Cal 2d 330, 240 P2d 282 (1952)
8. How v Chicago, Kalamazoo, and Saginaw Railroad, 139 Mich 638, 103 NW 185 (1905)
9. Agis v Howard Johnson Co, 371 Mass 140, 355 NE2d 315, 318–315 (1976)
10. 236 Iowa 787, 20 NW2d 28 (1945)
11. 595 F2d 1265 (3rd Cir 1979)

12. 338 So 2d 88 (Fla Dist Ct App 1976)
13. 373 So 2d 956 (Fla Dist Ct App), cert dismissed, Ford Motor Credit Co v Sheehan, 379 So 2d 204 (Fla 1979)
14. 74 Ill App 3d 21, 393 NE2d 154 (1979)
15. 146 La 735, 84 So 37 (1920)
16. RESTATEMENT (SECOND) OF TORTS, § 46, comment j (1965)
17. Johnson v Woman's Hospitals, 527 SW2d 133 (Tenn Ct App 1975)
18. 27 Cal 3d 916, 167 Cal Rptr 831, 616 P2d 813 (1980)
19. Bishop v Byrne, 265 F Supp 460 (S D W Va 1967)
20. Grimsby v Samson, 85 Wash 2d 52, 530 P2d 291 (1975)
21. Gluckstein v Lipsett, 93 Cal App 2d 391, 209 P2d 98 (1949)
22. Deutsch v Shein, 597 SW2d 141 (Ky 1980)
23. Larson v Lindahl, 167 Colo 409, 450 P2d 77 (1968)
24. Gadsden General Hospital v Hamilton, 212 Ala 531, 103 So 553 (1925)
25. Bazemore v Savannah Hospital, 171 Ga 257, 155 SE 194 (1930)
26. 230 Kan 289, 637 P2d 1175 (1981)
27. 176 Ga App 408, 336 SE2d 328 (1985)
28. Stevens GE: The physician's liability for abusive language: don't fuss or cuss, just huff and puff. Legal Aspects of Medical Practice 14(October):4–5, 1986
29. RESTATEMENT OF TORTS, § 46, comment g (Supp 1948)
30. 7 NY2d 376, 165 NE2d 756, 198 NYS2d 65 (1960)
31. Abraham v Zaslow, No 245862 (Cal Super Ct, Santa Clara Cty, Oct 26, 1970)
32. Savage v Boies, 77 Ariz 355, 272 P2d 349 (1954)
33. Halleck SL: Law in the Practice of Psychiatry. New York, Plenum, 1980, p 37
34. Hirsh HL: Judicially imposed standard of care: prophecy in medicine. Medical Trial Technique Quarterly 7:1–8, 1980
35. 6464 F2d 772 (DC Cir 1972)
36. 60 F2d 737, 740 (2d Cir), cert denied, 287 U.S. 662 (1932)
37. 490 A2d 720, 722 (Md App 1985)
38. Klerman GL: The psychiatric patient's right to effective treatment: implications of Osheroff v Chestnut Lodge. Am J Psychiatry 147:409–418, 1990
39. Stone AA: Law, science, and psychiatric malpractice: a response to Klerman's indictment of psychoanalytic psychiatry. Am J Psychiatry 147:419–427, 1990
40. Malcolm JG: Treatment choices and informed consent in psychiatry: implications of the Osheroff case for the profession. Journal of Psychiatry and Law 14:63, 1986

The Psychiatrist

Chapter 21

The Psychiatrist's Professional Relationship With Nonmedical Therapists

Dr. Rollins is a nonmedical therapist. Within the past year, court rulings enacted in Dr. Rollins's state permit certain nonmedical therapists to hospitalize and treat the mentally ill under the supervision of a psychiatrist. Dr. Rollins seeks and obtains hospital privileges to admit and treat patients on the psychiatric service of a general hospital.

In the course of outpatient practice, Dr. Rollins evaluates a 68-year-old widowed woman with symptoms of confusion, agitation, and paranoid delusions. The patient is brought to Dr. Rollins's office by her daughter, who also is the patient's legal guardian. Careful evaluation of the mental status indicates moderate cognitive deficits consistent with mild to moderate brain dysfunction. A presumptive diagnosis is made of primary degenerative dementia of the Alzheimer type with paranoid psychosis. Dr. Rollins decides that the patient needs immediate hospitalization and admits the patient to the psychiatric unit.

Dr. Sawyer, a psychiatrist and long-time friend of Dr. Rollins, agrees to act as a supervisor for all her hospital cases. For his fee, Dr. Sawyer initially considers an arrangement with Dr. Rollins whereby she will pay him directly a small percentage of her hospital billings. He realizes that this would be a form of fee splitting, and decides instead to bill the patient directly for actual hospital visits only. As required, Dr. Sawyer performs the initial workup, diagnosis, and treatment plan in collaboration with Dr. Rollins. An internist does the physical examination.

Dr. Sawyer prescribes thioridazine, 10 mg four times a day. The patient's daughter is not informed of the risks and benefits of major tranquilizers by Dr. Sawyer. He has full confidence in Dr. Rollins's professional abilities to manage the patient's daily psychological care and to make an appropriate discharge disposition when that time arrives. One week after starting the patient on thioridazine, agitation and confusion are dramatically improved. The paranoid delusions present at the time of admission are only occasionally present in the form of ideas of reference. Dr. Sawyer notes the excellent progress of the pa-

tient in the hospital record, stating he will see the patient again in 1 week. Because of the pressures of his own practice, Dr. Sawyer is unable to come into the hospital, but follows the treatment course of the patient through reports from Dr. Rollins.

Four weeks after admission, the patient develops wormlike movements of the tongue and pursing of the lips that are unnoticed by Dr. Rollins and the nursing staff. The tongue and face movements are noted in a medical student's work-up of the patient but are not communicated to Dr. Rollins or the staff. The patient does not complain of these symptoms and appears to be progressing very well. Discharge is planned, and the patient is to enter a nursing home. In preparation for discharge, Dr. Rollins calls Dr. Sawyer and inquires whether the patient's medication can be decreased. Dr. Sawyer suggests cutting the dose in half and observing the patient. Dr. Rollins agrees to this plan. Dr. Sawyer phones the order for the lower dosage of thioridazine.

Three days after the medication is decreased, the patient develops progressive dystonic movements of her arms and legs with swaying of the trunk. The patient and her daughter become alarmed. The nursing staff makes the diagnosis of tardive dyskinesia. After receiving an emergency call from Dr. Rollins, Dr. Sawyer sees the patient in the hospital. He orders an increase of the thioridazine to previous levels. The dyskinetic movements improve only slightly. The patient's daughter demands transfer of her mother to the care of another hospital. Four months later, a suit is filed against Dr. Rollins for lack of informed consent and negligent diagnosis and treatment. Dr. Sawyer also is named in the suit as vicariously liable for improper supervision and control of Dr. Rollins's treatment, lack of informed consent, and improper supervision and treatment of the patient.

What are psychiatrists' responsibilities in collaborative, consultative, and supervisory relationships with nonmedical therapists?

The American Psychiatric Association (APA) has formulated guidelines for psychiatrists when working with nonmedical mental health therapists (1). As mental health care delivery is provided more and more by a variety of nonmedical therapists, psychiatrists practice less in isolation and more within the framework of an organized health delivery system. Thus, the capacity to provide more extensive mental health care is enhanced. The cross-fertilization of different mental health disciplines fosters professional growth of the team members.

Psychiatrists should consider seeking collaborative, consultative, and supervisory roles with other mental health professionals that will enhance patient care (1). Kleinman (2) observes that the psychiatrist's relationship with nonmedical professionals broadened significantly during the last decade. Psychiatrists now must deal with the communication media, governmental agencies, attorneys and the legal system, managed health care personnel, and a myriad of other nonmedical professionals.

In a collaborative relationship, responsibility for the patient's care is shared according to the qualifications and limitations of each discipline (1). The patient should be informed of the separate responsibilities of each therapist. The responsibilities of each discipline do not diminish those of the other disciplines. Periodic evaluation by the psychiatrist and the nonmedical therapist of the patient's clinical condition and needs is necessary to determine whether the collaboration should continue. On termination of the collaborative relationship, the patient should be informed either separately or jointly.

When performing consultations, the psychiatrist does not have a treatment relationship with the patient and does not assume responsibility for care. The psychiatrist's relationship is with the nonmedical therapist, not the patient. The psychiatrist relies on information provided by the therapist. The risk of liability for the psychiatrist will arise only if the consultative advice provided is negligently based on inadequate or limited information. If the psychiatrist sees the patient directly, liability may be assessed for the negligent performance of the consultation (3).

Because treating therapists exercise independent professional judgment, the advice may be freely accepted or rejected. As a result, even negligent advice by the psychiatrist may not be the cause of harm to the patient (4). A nonmedical therapist may be judged less able to evaluate information provided than another psychiatrist. The psychiatrist must determine whether the nonmedical therapist has met professional standards of independent functioning in his or her discipline. Psychiatrists may also need to consult with nonmedical therapists, in order to provide more comprehensive care to patients (1).

In a supervisory relationship, greater liability risks exist. The psychiatrist must be sure that the supervisee carries sufficient malpractice insurance. According to the APA guidelines, the psychiatrist assumes direct responsibility for patient care and active guidance of the therapist (1). Psychiatrists also are directly responsible for the wrongful acts of their employees acting within their scope of employment (4). The employee may not be employed by the psychiatrist, but if he or she is under the direct control of the psychiatrist, a similar liability situation prevails. The psychiatrist employer or the psychiatrist who exercises control may be held vicariously liable for negligent acts of nurses or other employees, even when the psychiatrist is totally blameless.

Before the rise of vicarious liability, the "captain of the ship" doctrine was applied to surgeons who were held legally responsible for the complete control of other hospital personnel in the operating room. The surgeon was vicariously liable for the negligence of all the "borrowed servants." With the end of charitable immunity for governmental and charitable hospitals, the "deep pockets" of the surgeon were no longer the only source of compensation. The "captain of the ship" doctrine gradually sailed into the sunset (5). Today, courts apply a focused control analysis when evaluating vicarious liability claims rather than finding that the mere presence of borrowed servants is in itself sufficient to impose liability.

When supervising the treatment provided by nonmedical therapists, the APA guidelines advise that the psychiatrist is responsible for the initial workup, diagnosis, physical status of the patient, and development of a treatment plan (1). Thus, the psychiatrist establishes a treatment relationship with the patient. Informed consent is enhanced when the patient is able to meet the supervising psychiatrist and is given an opportunity to ask questions about the risks and benefits of treatment as well as the nature of the supervisory relationship. Appelbaum (6) recommends that "all responsibilities should be clearly specified, preferably in a written agreement among the patient, the psychiatrist, and the nonmedical therapist." As long as treatment continues under the psychiatrist's supervision, the psychiatrist is "ethically and medically responsible for the patient's care." Patients should be informed of any changes or termination of the supervisory relationship.

The APA "Guidelines for Psychiatrists in Consultative, Supervisory, or Collaborative Relationships With Nonmedical Therapists" is now over a decade old (1). Despite significant changes during this time, the guidelines have not undergone revision. Today, the relationship between psychiatrists and nonmedical therapists is infinitely more complex (2). Furthermore, an important caveat accompanies the guidelines stating "that they do not represent official policy but rather a 'living document' to be adapted to local custom and practice."

The practice of psychiatry has changed so much since the guidelines were created that certain guidelines may no longer be applicable. The guidelines are not particularly helpful in defining the psychiatrist's obligations in providing supervision to a nonmedical therapist. For example, the responsibilities of a supervisor differ from those of a psychiatrist who is directly treating the patient. Yet the guidelines suggest that a psychiatrist in a supervisory relationship "remains ethically and medically responsible for the patient's care." The meaning of this statement is unclear. Important distinctions that exist in the psychiatrist's responsibilities between supervisory and treatment roles appear to be ignored. Moreover, with the advent of biological treatments, the guidelines do not provide assistance in defining the scope of nonsupervisory responsibilities of psychiatrists who may provide medication backup for nonmedical professionals (7). The psychiatrist's liability in cases in which the nonmedical professional is found to have practiced outside of the scope of his or her practice will likely depend upon the nature and extent of the psychiatrist's relationship with the nonmedical professional and the patient.

In the vignette, Dr. Sawyer fulfilled his initial responsibilities for the evaluation, diagnosis, medical evaluation, and development of the treatment plan. He failed, however, to inform the patient's daughter, the legal guardian, of the risks and benefits of major tranquilizers. Moreover, he did not adequately maintain direct surveillance of the patient's treatment, relying instead on the verbal reports of Dr. Rollins.

Patients who are placed on major tranquilizers require regular supervision by psychiatrists. In particular, elderly women are at an increased risk for tardive dyskinesia and require careful monitoring. Dr. Rollins did not have the requisite medical training to maintain a heightened level of suspicion for the development and diagnosis of tardive dyskinesia. Dr. Sawyer did not fulfill his responsibility for adequate medical supervision of the patient. When a patient is hospitalized by a nonmedical therapist, the severity of the illness and the somatic treatments used require direct, active psychiatric supervision of the nonmedical therapist and the patient. In the vignette, supervision of the nonmedical therapist only without seeing the patient was not sufficient when somatic therapies are prescribed. Only the trained physician can adequately administer and follow up medical treatments. Even in states where nonmedical professionals are not required by law to obtain medical supervision of hospitalized patients, trained physicians should monitor treatment.

Psychiatrists should not undertake the supervision of nonmedical therapists unless they are fully prepared to assume medical responsibility for the patient. Psychiatrists must not be supervisors in name only, nor should they allow themselves to be used solely as a means for obtaining insurance payment for nonmedical providers. If a psychiatrist enters a collaborative, consultative, or supervisory relationship in which his or her role is being misrepresented, or the care provided by the nonmedical therapist is inadequate or inappropriate, the treatment may be unethical unless the purpose is to raise the quality of care. Psychiatrists should not continue in the above roles unless they are assured that they are being appropriately informed about the nature of the treatment and the clinical course of the patient. Otherwise, there is no assurance that the patient is receiving competent treatment. The frequency of collaboration, consultation, and supervision must be sufficient to fulfill the psychiatrist's medical, ethical, and legal responsibilities to the patient.

What is the ethical responsibility of psychiatrists when they are asked to provide a professional opinion during casual contact with a nonmedical therapist?

Psychiatrists must be very careful about rendering curbside consultations. In Section 5-A of the *Opinions of the Ethics Committee on the Principles of Medical Ethics With Annotations Especially Applicable to Psychiatry* (8), the circumstances for providing informal patient management advice are narrowly defined:

> *Question:* Is it ethical to teach counselling principles to clergymen? Is it ethical to give them advice in the management of specific cases?

Answer: It is ethical to teach counselling principles to clergymen. The second question is more complex. Section 5, Annotation 3 (APA) states: "When the psychiatrist assumes a collaborative or supervisory role with another mental health worker, he/she must expend sufficient time to assure that proper care is given. It is contrary to the interests of the patient and to patient care if he/she allows himself/herself to be used as a figurehead." Formal supervision of a pastoral counsellor would not differ from the supervision of other non-psychiatrist professionals. It is in the informal contacts that the problems arise. A clergyman might call a psychiatrist for advice or seek a "curbstone opinion." Perhaps a clergyman might bring up a specific case during a seminar with a group of clergymen. The ethical psychiatrist should refrain from giving specific patient management advice, assuming it is not an emergency situation, unless he [or she] is very much aware of the capabilities of the receiver of the advice and has sufficient information about the patient to make the advice reliable. The psychiatrist is both ethically and legally responsible for the advice he [or she] gives. (July 3, 1975)

Have courts addressed claims of negligent supervision by psychiatrists?

Cohen v. State of New York (9) addressed the issues of negligent supervision and institutional policies governing patient management. A 23-year-old married medical student was voluntarily hospitalized at Downstate Medical Center with a diagnosis of paranoid schizophrenia. The patient was treated by a first-year psychiatric resident. Four months after admission, the resident decided not to restrict the patient on the ward. He was placed on an open ward governed by a therapeutic community. The patient committed suicide on the very day of the transfer to the open ward. The admission record indicated that the patient was suicidal.

In addition to the question of whether a careful examination and reasonable care had been exercised, the factual issue centered on whether a qualified psychiatrist provided active supervision of the resident's care of the patient. The court of claims held that the resident "did not, at this point in his medical career, possess the requisite skill or trained psychiatric judgment to, essentially unsupervised, provide ordinary and reasonable psychiatric medical treatment and care to this decedent" (9). The court concluded:

> In [this] case, there was much more than a mere error of judgment. There was not one but many errors of judgment made by a doctor not qualified in an unsupervised status to make a judgment; made by those in supervisory capacity; and, all made without careful examination.

This reasoning applies to the supervision of nonmedical professionals who hospitalize mentally ill patients as well.

In *Peck v. Counseling Service of Addison County, Inc.* (10), the parents of an outpatient treated by a mental health paraprofessional sued the clinic for negligent failure to warn them of the dangerous proclivities of their son. The plaintiffs contended that proper supervision of the counselor should have led to a recognition of the danger of arson posed by their son and should thus have led to a warning. The Vermont Supreme Court imposed liability on the counseling service for property damage (son's burning down of the family barn) that occurred as a result of the mental health professional's failure to "take reasonable steps to protect third persons from threatened physical harm posed to them by his or her patient."

Clinics that use therapists who have not had advance training may create liability for themselves in *Tarasoff*-type cases (11). The counselor who was treating the patient in *Peck* had a master's degree in educational psychology. Adequate supervision of nonmedical therapists also requires imparting legal information and discussing the legal issues surrounding the treatment of patients requiring psychological interventions.

In *Andrews v. United States* (12), a federal appellate court in South Carolina ruled that when a psychologist induced a patient to engage in sexual intercourse, this action represented malpractice rather than assault and battery. The patient alleged that during counseling sessions with the psychologist, sexual advances were made, convincing her that the best course of treatment was to have sexual intercourse. As a consequence of such abusive treatment, the patient suffered severe depression and confusion about her self-worth. She also blamed the psychologist's conduct for the dissolution of her marriage. The trial court awarded the patient $70,000 in damages and her husband $30,000 for his claim of severe depression.

On appeal, the United States Court of Appeals for the Fourth Circuit found that the psychologist took advantage of his position as a counselor to induce a vulnerable patient to have sexual relations. The employer, the United States, could not be held liable for damages solely as a result of the psychologist's acts because they were outside of the scope of his employment. In monitoring the psychologist's treating activities, however, the supervising psychiatrists were acting within the scope of their employment. They were found negligent in carrying out their supervisory responsibility.

Private psychiatrists supervising other mental health professionals may incur liability if found negligent in their supervisory function. Thus, even though the supervisor could not be held directly responsible for the negligent acts of the supervised individual on a "frolic of one's own," the supervisor could be held responsible for damages resulting from negligent supervision (13).

The concept of negligent supervision is amorphous. Courts have defined it as failure to investigate the credentials or background of the individual to be supervised, failure to conduct the supervision in a reasonable and competent manner, failure to live up to the express or implied community supervisory standards, or failure to act on information provided to the supervisor (13). Slovenko (14) predicts that litigation involving supervisors may be the "suits of the future."

What is vicarious liability? How does it apply to the psychiatrist's relationship with nonmedical therapists?

Psychiatrists, in addition to being liable for their own negligence, can also be held liable for the negligence of others. The doctrine of vicarious liability developed from the "master-servant" relationship. If a "servant" negligently injured another while employed in the "master's" business (within the scope of his business), the servant ordinarily did not possess sufficient funds to pay money damages to the injured plaintiff. It was not considered just that the innocently injured person should bear the burden. Moreover, the injured plaintiff and his or her family could become a burden on others, including the local government. Courts reason that the master (i.e., employer) who benefited from the servant's efforts should bear the burden of paying when the servant cannot (15). Vicarious liability is defined as the responsibility of the person who possesses the right of control to pay monetary damages to the successful plaintiff. The Latin phrase used for this doctrine is *respondeat superior* ("let the master respond"). Eventually, the master may try to collect from the negligent servant, but this is often impractical. To cover vicarious liability, insurance is used instead (15).

Psychiatrists who employ nonmedical therapists are secondarily or vicariously liable for their negligent acts. The nonmedical therapist who negligently causes injury within the scope of his or her duties is directly liable. If the nonmedical therapist is not employed by the psychiatrist but is only supervised, the psychiatrist may be held liable for the negligence of the nonmedical therapist, because the psychiatrist retains some responsibility for the patient's care. The nonmedical therapist also may be held legally liable.

In *Marston v. Minneapolis Clinic of Psychiatry and Neurology, Ltd.* (16), the Minnesota Supreme Court refused to relieve a clinic from vicarious responsibility for the sexual misconduct of a psychologist who was an employee of the clinic. The court held that it was a question of fact whether acts committed by the psychologist were within the scope of employment. The court remanded the case for a new trial on the issue of liability.

Psychiatrists frequently see patients in a hospital or clinic setting where nonmedical therapists who are not employed by the psychiatrist are present to assist the psychiatrist in the treatment of patients. The "borrowed servant" rule (17) states that a servant directed or permitted by his master to perform services for another may become the servant of such others in performing the services. In other words, the nonmedical therapist may become the other's servant for some acts but not for other acts. The key question is whether a master-servant relationship between the psychiatrist and the nonmedical therapist is created when the latter is employed by persons or institutions other than the psychiatrist.

Courts have scrutinized the control issue more closely in borrowed servant cases than in the employee-master situation. In the latter instances, the requisite control is inferred from the existence of the employment relationship (18). Use of the borrowed servant rules does not necessarily mean that the psychiatrist is free from fault. The psychiatrist may be held vicariously liable under the borrowed servant rule and also may be found directly liable (19).

In the hospital setting, the psychiatrist may be directing a team using the concept and structure of the therapeutic community. Within the team, a variety of mental health professionals may have treatment responsibilities for the patient. Often nonmedical personnel may actually spend more time with the psychiatrist's patients than does the psychiatrist. When the psychiatrist is directing the team and the treatment of patients, he or she may be viewed as possessing the requisite level of control over other therapists. If a member of the team negligently harms the patient, the psychiatrist may be vicariously liable (20).

Even when not using a team approach, a psychiatrist may work closely with other mental health professionals in the provision of care and treatment to a patient. Psychiatrists have a professional and ethical duty not to delegate to any nonmedical professional any matter requiring the exercise of professional medical judgment (21). Thus, psychiatrists must monitor the care given to their patients by other mental health professionals. For example, a psychiatric nursing assistant decided to experiment with a psychotic patient by using an "adversive" therapy that she recently read about in graduate school. Whenever the patient disobeyed her order, she tied him to a chair for varying periods of time. Incredibly, this "treatment" was not discovered by the nursing staff until 4 days after it was initiated. The psychiatrist was totally unaware that the patient was being physically restrained. The family of the patient was outraged and threatened suit.

In the clinical vignette, Dr. Sawyer followed a court ruling in his state in acting as a supervisor for Dr. Rollins, a nonmedical therapist. More commonly, statutes may stipulate that a collaborative relationship be established between a psychiatrist and a nonmedical mental health professional in the care and treatment of psychiatric inpatients. As a result, the psychiatrist handles only the "medical" aspects of the treatment, such as prescribing medication and ensuring the physical and medical status of the patient. Even within this type of arrangement, Dr. Sawyer's follow-up care of the patient was inadequate. Whenever a psychiatrist works with a nonmedical therapist, either as a collaborator or as a supervisor, the provision of competent care by the psychiatrist is no different than when functioning alone.

What are acceptable billing procedures when psychiatrists supervise nonmedical therapists?

When a nonmedical therapist is directly employed by the psychiatrist, the services provided by the nonmedical therapist may be billed directly on the psychiatrist's letterhead. The bill should include the name of the therapist who provided the service, professional degree, number of visits, cost per visit, and the total fee (1).

Psychiatrists should not render bills to patients, third-party payers, or others in their own name for services not directly provided by them. Nor should the implication be allowed that services were provided by the psychiatrist when they were not. Supervised nonmedical therapists should directly bill the patient or third-party payer using their own name and letterhead at agreed-upon rates for the provision of services (1). In some situations, psychiatrists may bill for time provided on behalf of the patient's treatment even though the time was not actually spent with the patient. This may include extensive discussions with family members or other physicians and mental health professionals. Such charges should be discussed first with the patient.

Section 5-C of the *Opinions of the Ethics Committee* (8) states:

> *Question:* Is it ethical for a psychiatrist to bill for services provided by a nonmedical professional?

> *Answer:* Yes, as long as he indicates his role was supervisory and what the professional discipline of the nonmedical professional was. It would not be ethical, in fact it would probably be fraudulent, to bill for the services of another as if performed by the psychiatrist himself. (February 10, 1977)

This ethical opinion seems to be somewhat at odds with guidelines approved by the APA in 1980 (1). The statement would appear to be true only when the nonmedical professional is in the employ of the psychiatrist. Otherwise, the psychiatrist should not bill the patient for services not personally provided directly to the patient. Separate arrangements should be made with the supervisee for payment.

A personal interview of the patient by the psychiatrist in the course of a collaborative, consultative, or supervisory relationship should be billed directly to the patient or third-party payer on the psychiatrist's own letterhead for the time spent in providing services to the patient. Billing for consultation and supervisory services provided directly to nonmedical therapists that do not involve seeing the patient should be based on the financial arrangement between the two parties. The fee arrangement is usually based on time spent in consultation and supervision. The billing also may include additional costs if space and secretarial services are rented. The psychiatrist should not be a party to any arrangement whereby he or she receives a percentage of the nonmedical therapist's fee or is compensated directly or indirectly for referring patients (1).

In the clinical vignette, Dr. Sawyer considered a percentage fee arrangement for supervision but then realized that such an agreement would constitute fee splitting. Instead, Dr. Sawyer decided to charge only for services personally rendered to the patient. *The Principles of Medical Ethics With Annotations Especially Applicable to Psychiatry* (21) states:

> An arrangement in which a psychiatrist provides supervision or administration to other physicians or nonmedical persons for a percentage of their fees or gross in-

come is not acceptable; this would constitute fee-splitting. In a team of practitioners, or a multidisciplinary team, it is ethical for the psychiatrist to receive income for administration, research, education, or consultation. This should be based upon a mutually agreed upon and set fee or salary, open to renegotiation when a change in the time demand occurs. (Section 2, Annotation 7)

Written arrangements that specify the mutual obligations of both parties are preferable (1). The supervisor frequently is asked to provide documentation and to sign insurance forms so that the nonmedical therapist can receive payment. Psychiatrists must not allow themselves to be used as figureheads (*The Principles of Medical Ethics,* Section 5, Annotation 3). Psychiatrists who perfunctorily sign insurance forms for nonmedical providers without providing adequate supervision should realize that they are ethically, morally, and medically responsible for the care and treatment of the supervised patient (*The Principles of Medical Ethics,* Section 5, Annotation 4).

Another issue concerning monetary matters between psychiatrists and nonmedical professionals is boycotting by psychiatrists. Boycotting can invoke strict, unforgiving antitrust laws (22). For example, banding together informally with other psychiatrists to keep referrals away from nonmedical mental health professionals would likely be viewed as a blatant, illegal restraint of trade. Felony convictions and severe financial penalties may ensue if guilt can be established. Antitrust legislation is very complicated (23). Legal consultation should be sought if a psychiatrist's actions could be construed as limiting nonmedical professionals' ability to compete in the area of mental health care.

What are some of the ethical and legal problems that may arise when signing insurance and treatment plan forms for nonmedical providers?

Psychiatrists who work in multidisciplinary clinic settings or as private practitioners frequently are asked to sign insurance forms and treatment plans produced by nonmedical therapists. This request may involve either patients that are directly supervised by the psychiatrist or patients who have not been seen by the psychiatrist. The latter group may include patients for whom the insurance form is being signed, patients known only through staff conferences, and patients for whom a record review has been conducted. For psychiatrists working in clinics, considerable pressure may be applied by administrators to sign insurance and treatment plan forms.

Psychiatrists must understand that the signature of a physician is a formal statement that the physician is legally and ethically responsible for the action or consequences of the signed document (24). The psychiatrist's signature on a diagnostic formulation or treatment plan signifies review, agreement with the diagnosis, and approval of the plan. The psychiatrist's signature on an insurance or billing form signifies that the patient has received the treatment for which the third party is being billed. When signing a form for peer review, quality assurance, or other administrative review, the psychiatrist should indicate on the form that the evaluation was based upon review of a specific individual (also specify task and time).

Psychiatrists must be sure they understand the form they are signing. When a form contains a signature line for "supervising physician" or a treatment plan signature line for "reviewed and approved by," the psychiatrist must be certain that these services were provided. If the psychiatrist represents performing specific tasks on the form while not actually having done so, he or she is acting unethically and fraudulently (25). Moreover, the psychiatrist will be held liable if supervision is not provided (26). As emphasized above, the supervisory role of psychiatrists with nonmedical mental health professionals must not be perfunctory. On the contrary, such a supervisory role has specific responsibilities.

Fully disclosing the exact nature of the services provided by the psychiatrist is essential. Noting that a treatment plan was "reviewed and approved" but that the patient was not examined provides full disclosure. Similarly, if the purpose of the signature on the form is unclear, a complete explanation and description of the services rendered will help negate accusations of fraud for the care of an unseen patient. When signing an insurance form for therapy provided by the nonmedical therapist, the psychiatrist must indicate who actually performed the therapy to prevent charges of misrepresentation and fraud. Furthermore, if the psychiatrist has not examined the patient, stating so will undercut the argument that the psychiatrist is directly responsible for the care of the patient upon whose records or forms the signature appears (26).

References

1. Official actions: guidelines for psychiatrists in consultative, supervisory, or collaborative relationships with nonmedical therapists. Am J Psychiatry 137:1489–1491, 1980
2. Kleinman CC: Psychiatrists' relationship with nonmedical professionals, in American Psychiatric Press Review of Clinical Psychiatry and the Law, Vol 2. Edited by Simon RI. Washington, DC, American Psychiatric Press, 1991, pp 241–257
3. Hirsh HL: Duty to consult and refer. Legal Medicine Annual, 1977, pp 247–256
4. Klein JI, Macbeth JE, Onek JN: Legal Issues in the Private Practice of Psychiatry. Washington, DC, American Psychiatric Press, 1984, pp 29–33
5. Price SH: The sinking of the "captain of the ship": reexamining the vicarious liability of an operating surgeon for the negligence of assisting hospital personnel. J Leg Med 10:323–356, 1989
6. Appelbaum PS: General guidelines for psychiatrists who prescribe medication for patients treated by nonmedical therapists. Hosp Community Psychiatry 42:281–282, 1991; see p 282
7. Goldberg RS, Riba M, Tasman A: Psychiatrists' attitudes toward prescribing medication for patients treated by nonmedical psychotherapists. Hosp Community Psychiatry 42:276–280, 1991

8. American Psychiatric Association: Opinions of the Ethics Committee on the Principles of Medical Ethics With Annotations Especially Applicable to Psychiatry. Washington, DC, American Psychiatric Association, 1989

9. 51 AD2d 494, 382 NYS2d 128 (NY App Div 1976), aff'd Cohen v State, 41 NY2d 1086, 364 NE2d 1134, 396 NYS2d 363 (1977)

10. 146 Vt 61, 499 A2d 422 (1985)

11. Stone AA: Law, Psychiatry, and Morality. Washington, DC, American Psychiatric Press, 1984, pp 177–178

12. 732 F2d 366 (4th Cir 1984)

13. Kuder AV: Psychiatric supervision: a legal business. Washington Psychiatric Society Newsletter, September 1984, p 3

14. Slovenko R: Malpractice in psychiatry and related fields. Journal of Psychiatry and Law 9:5–63, 1981

15. Keeton WP, Dobbs DB, Keeton RE, et al: Prosser and Keeton on Torts, 5th Edition. St Paul, MN, West Publishing, 1984, Chapter 12, § 69

16. 329 NW2d 306 (Minn 1982)

17. RESTATEMENT (SECOND) OF AGENCY, § 227 (1957)

18. King JH: The Law of Medical Malpractice, 2nd Edition. St Paul, MN, West Publishing, 1986, p 240

19. King JH: The Law of Medical Malpractice. St Paul, MN, West Publishing, 1977, p 234

20. Cohen RJ, Mariano WE: Legal Guidebook in Mental Health. New York, Free Press, 1982, p 315

21. American Psychiatric Association: The Principles of Medical Ethics With Annotations Especially Applicable to Psychiatry. Washington, DC, American Psychiatric Association, 1989

22. Benedek E: Beware the antitrust trap. Psychiatric News 26(March 1):3, 1991

23. Brooten KE: How antitrust laws affect your medical practice. Private Practice 21:7–9, 1989

24. Official actions: guidelines regarding psychiatrists' signatures. Am J Psychiatry 146:1390, 1989

25. When not to sign insurance and treatment plan forms. American Psychiatric Association Legal Consultation Plan Newsletter, November 1985, pp 4–5

26. Treatment for Risk: A Newsletter for Members of the American Psychiatric Association Professional Liability Insurance Program 2(2):2, 4, 1990

Chapter 22

Defamation in
Clinical Practice

Dr. Wentworth, a 32-year-old psychiatrist who has been receiving insight psy-chotherapy three times per week for over a year, decides to terminate therapy because of a lack of progress. He entered treatment when panic attacks pre-vented him from working, requiring a leave of absence. Subsequently, he started a part-time practice but was unable to obtain many patients.

Dr. Wentworth feels stalemated in his personal therapy sessions and is con-vinced that the attitude of his therapist is cold, distant, and, at times, openly critical. No amount of psychotherapeutic work on this perception is able to re-solve this feeling. After seeking the services of another psychiatrist, he resumes therapy and treatment seems to progress quite well.

In the meantime, Dr. Wentworth decides to file a disability retirement claim with a former government employer. He gives permission for his new psychia-trist to turn over his records for review of his claim. After the disability board rejects his claim because "the psychiatric diagnosis is not related to the alleged work-induced disability," Dr. Wentworth asks his psychiatrist for a copy of the records sent to the disability board. His psychiatrist reluctantly prepares to turn over the records to Dr. Wentworth as required by state statute. Before ac-tually doing so, however, the psychiatrist reviews the records for the first time. He is shocked to see that he has written down a comment from a phone conver-sation made by Dr. Wentworth's previous psychiatrist that "the patient has a psychopathic personality and is a menace to patients." Realizing that Dr. Went-worth did not give consent to the previous psychiatrist for the release of any information, he considers excluding this line from the record but then remem-bers that the original record would be available from the disability board should Dr. Wentworth want to obtain it. He also does not want to tamper with the records.

When Dr. Wentworth reviews the record, he is shocked and furious over the comments made by his former therapist. He is outraged that his current thera-pist would record such a slanderous comment and pass it on to others without deleting this information or at least discussing it with him first. Dr. Wentworth abruptly terminates therapy and seeks the assistance of an attorney. He now feels that he understands why his practice has fallen off, as well as the reason for refusal of admission privileges by the local hospital. His first therapist sits *on the medical staff privileges committee. His suspicions are substantiated when a colleague informs him that his admitting privileges were blocked by his first psychiatrist, who apparently said, "Dr. Wentworth is unethical and dishonest." On advice of counsel, Dr. Wentworth brings a suit for defamation, breach of confidentiality, and lack of informed consent against both psychiatrists for $10 million.*

What is the legal definition of defamation of character?

The law of defamation is based upon the principle that persons should be able to enjoy their reputations free of derogatory and false attacks. Defamation of character is an intentional tort. An intentional tort arises from the deliberate interference with another person's rights. Defamation is defined as communicating false and malicious statements that are damaging to someone's reputation to a third person or persons. The plaintiff's reputation may be damaged by holding him or her up to hatred or ridicule, or the plaintiff, as a result of the malicious statements, may be shunned or ostracized (1). Slander is the oral communication (other than on radio and television) of such information; libel is the written or printed communication of defamatory material.

Formerly, libel applied only to damaging statements made in lasting form such as newspapers or, less commonly, pictures. Today, libel usually includes defamatory remarks broadcast on radio and television. Slander generally requires proof of financial damage as a result of defamatory comments. No such proof of "money damages" is required when injury to the plaintiff's reputation can be presumed (slander per se), as in damage to the plaintiff's business or profession. Statements are also defamatory per se if they state that the plaintiff suffers from a foul and loathsome disease or is guilty of a crime, or that a woman has been unchaste (2). The legal term *publication* is used when referring to both oral and written communication of defamatory material to a third party.

What defenses can be asserted against a claim of defamation?

There are a number of defenses or privileges to a charge of defamation. An absolute privilege is a complete defense to a charge of defamation, protecting even against a malicious untruth. When the plaintiff gives consent to publication by the defendant (i.e., authorization of release of information to third-party payers) or to publication of defamatory material in the course of judicial, legislative, or executive proceedings, statements made are covered by an *absolute privilege* (3). When the psychiatrist examines a patient for the court and makes statements in that capacity, he or she is protected under absolute privilege.

Defamatory statements made during civil commitment, if part of a judicial proceeding, are privileged unless the commitment was initiated with malice. Truth, of course, is a complete defense. In some jurisdictions, truth is a defense only as long as the true statements were published for good and justifiable ends. Although true, defamatory statements made by psychiatrists may be considered actionable if they constitute breach of confidentiality or invasion of privacy.

Qualified privilege is also designed to protect the important public interest in unrestrained speech while providing some measure of protection for the individual who is maliciously defamed. Some latitude for mistakes is provided by a qualified or conditional privilege. A qualified privilege exists in cases in which the publishing of otherwise actionable defamatory statements is communicated *1)* to protect the legitimate interests of the publisher (e.g., reputation), *2)* to protect the interests of others (e.g., safety), *3)* to protect common interests (e.g., exchange of information among professional societies), *4)* to communicate to one who may act in the public interest, and *5)* to function as fair comment on matters of public concern (e.g., quack medical services) (4). Thus, disclosures made in good faith in proceedings for involuntary hospitalization of a patient are protected under a qualified privilege. Entrusting a confidential report to the therapist's secretary also would be protected under the same privilege (5). One of the uncertainties about exercising the *Tarasoff* duty to warn endangered third parties is whether the reporting psychiatrist will be able to invoke a conditional privilege against a possible claim of defamation made by the patient.

Are there any legal merits to Dr. Wentworth's claims of defamation, breach of confidentiality, and lack of informed consent?

The legal merits of Dr. Wentworth's claims ultimately will be decided by a court of law. Certain actions by both psychiatrists appear to be egregious. The first psychiatrist released information without the patient's written or oral consent. If it can be shown that this unauthorized disclosure of information directly damaged the patient, then a successful suit for breach of confidentiality may be brought. If the first psychiatrist asserts the defense of truth to the slander charge, the issue would be whether the diagnosis was arrived at negligently.

The second psychiatrist wrote the defamatory comments of the first psychiatrist and republished these statements in his records to the disability board without prior review. Although he may wish to invoke the patient's consent as an absolute defense, problems will surely arise. Is the consent that was given by Dr. Wentworth an informed consent considering that he did not know of the presence of potentially defamatory statements in his record? Is the second psychiatrist negligent in recording the comments of the first psychiatrist and sending out the psychiatric record without properly reviewing and then informing the patient of its contents? Dr. Wentworth's attorney alleges that the second psychiatrist libeled his client by republishing the defamatory comments and committed malpractice by not obtaining an informed consent from the patient prior to sending out the defamatory record.

How can therapists avoid making defamatory statements about patients and nonpatients?

The therapist must be careful about what is written in the patient's records. Only information that is pertinent to the diagnosis, treatment, and general management of the patient should be recorded. All extraneous material should be excluded. Gratuitous comments made by previous therapists and comments made by patients about others have no place in the record. Although patients may properly consent to release of their records, records containing information about others may constitute defamation or an invasion of privacy (6). Even if therapists do not believe in the truth of the statements recorded, they may be liable for divulging an allegation by another. Thus Dr. Wentworth's second psychiatrist may have to bear the legal consequences of publishing "The patient has a psychopathic personality and is a menace to patients," even though he may not believe a single word of it.

The recorded comments of patients by physicians about nonpatients concerning their professions, businesses or trades, reputations, allegations of criminal behavior, sexual lives, and imputations of illness or diseases that carry social opprobrium may be defamatory per se (7). A statement may be defamatory per se even when the patient or nonpatient is no longer living. The dead or their survivors cannot sue for defamation or invasion of privacy because these are personal rights that die with the person, even if the individual was defamed while alive. On the other hand, words that independently reflect on and defame survivors, such as "by calling a man's dead mother a whore," may be actionable (6).

Before releasing any information from the patient's record, the therapist should obtain the patient's informed consent. Reviewing the record with some patients may be necessary, whereas others may not want to see their records. The patient has the right to refuse to see his or her record. The therapist should carefully document that the decision by the patient was made competently and without coercion. Furthermore, the therapist should note that the patient possessed the mental capacity to understand the possible consequences of forgoing review of the record. The therapist may have concerns about the possible psychological damage that reading the record might cause the patient in some instances. Of particular concern to the psychiatrist is the discovery of diagnoses such as schizophrenia or borderline personality disorder. The psychiatrist may choose to use only diagnostic codes, which offer more confidentiality when the record leaves the office. If the patient wants to review the record, diagnostic codes will give the patient the option of inquiring into the meaning of the codes, if so desired.

If the therapist suspects that the patient cannot tolerate review of the record, the patient should be informed of this opinion and the matter taken up as a treatment issue. However, the therapist may conclude that the patient lacks the necessary psychological capacity to understand and tolerate reading the information in the record. Therapists may not withhold information to serve themselves. Statutes in a number of states allow psychiatric patients full access to their medical/psychological records. Eventually, the patient may gain the capacity to competently decide whether to forgo reading the record. If time and circumstances do not allow for resolving the issue, an alternative is to paraphrase the record accurately, with the patient's sensitivities and disabilities in mind.

In what clinical settings are therapists more likely to make or be accused of making defamatory statements?

Writing an article or book about a patient holds the potential for actual or claimed defamation of character, especially if done without the patient's informed consent. Other potentially defamatory situations include warnings to endangered third parties, child custody evaluations, and the reporting of child abuse. Problems may arise when writing about research subjects and making public comments in the press, radio, or television concerning the mental history or diagnosis of patients or others.

A psychiatrist sued alleging that she was defamed by a movie of Sylvia Plath's novel *The Bell Jar*. The psychiatrist alleged that she was defamed by the creation of lesbian movie scenes depicting a character she said was based on her life and relationship with Sylvia Plath. The case was settled out of court for $150,000 (8).

In *Doe v. Roe* (9), the court stated that a "physician, who enters into an agreement with a patient to provide medical attention, impliedly covenants to keep in confidence all disclosures made by the patient concerning the patient's physical or mental condition as well as all matters discovered by the physician in the course of examination or treatment." The plaintiff, a patient of the psychiatrist and the unauthorized subject of a book that detailed her life and fantasies, allegedly verbally consented to publication of the book. The judge in that case stated, "I need not deal with the value of an oral waiver of confidentiality given by a patient to a psychiatrist during the course of treatment."

Mental health professionals must appreciate the importance of powerful transference feelings that can adversely affect the judgment of patients giving consent for public dissemination of their psychiatric histories. The clinician is in a particularly strong, potentially coercive position vis-à-vis the patient, even if not consciously intending to be. Consultation with a colleague may provide some objectivity for the therapist. An inherent danger when writing includes the reluctance of the psychiatrist to sufficiently disguise the identity of the patient in order to preserve the scientific accuracy and value of the work. Even when the patient gives a competent, informed consent to the publication of a psychiatric history, the author must be sure to maintain veracity by avoiding inaccuracies that might be construed as defamatory.

In *Gasperini v. Manginelli* (10), the father of a patient sued the psychiatrist for libel after the psychiatrist left the suffix "Jr." out of the patient's medical report. In another case, a psychologist was sued for describing a patient in the psychological report as "feeble-minded" and "a high grade moron" (11). In *Modla v. Parker* (12), the patient was told by the administrator just before her discharge from the hospital, "Do me a favor and see a psychiatrist." The patient brought suit for slander, but the court found the administrator was not liable because the patient failed to prove that her personality or profession was injured. Another court dismissed a libel suit against a school's clinical psychologist who reported a suspected case of child abuse (13). Whereas most child abuse statutes protect practitioners who report suspected cases, libel may be shown if the plaintiff proves that the reports were false and that the practitioner acted with malice or ill will. Such accusations were made against a physician when he reported a suspected child abuse case. The physician wrote about his ordeal in defending a slander suit (14).

In the classic defamation case *Berry v. Moench* (15), a letter was sent without the patient's consent by the treating psychiatrist to another physician who was acting as an agent for the parents of the plaintiff's girlfriend. The letter contained, among others things, a diagnosis of "manic depressive depression in a psychopathic personality" and such derogatory comments as, "My suggestion to the infatuated girl would be to run as fast and as far as she possibly could in any direction away from him. Of course if he doesn't marry her, he will marry someone else and make life hell for that person. The usual story is repeated unsuccessful marriages and a trail of tragedy behind." The court found that this disclosure by the psychiatrist was protected under the doctrine of qualified privilege. The court held that the father's concern for his daughter's welfare was a sufficient interest to protect, outweighing the doctor's responsibility to keep the information confidential.

In *Hoesl v. United States* (16), the plaintiff alleged that a psychiatrist negligently diagnosed the patient during the course of an employment examination. Relying on the report of the psychiatrist, the patient's employer suspended him and subsequently terminated him as medically disabled. The plaintiff claimed that as a result of the negligence of the psychiatrist in preparing the report, the plaintiff "has suffered permanent and irreparable harm to his professional reputation" that impaired his earning capacity. The trial court stated that the communication of an allegedly false report to another gives rise to an action for defamation. The court held, however, that the plaintiff was not entitled to relief because the psychiatrist's report "was privileged under qualified immunity for reports about an employee's fitness to his employer."

The problems caused by negative countertransference phenomena can lead to defamation of patients. Psychiatrists may actively dislike certain patients. This antipathy may emerge when submitting diagnoses to interested third parties such as insurance companies, employers, or various review committees.

Halleck (17) warns that the pejorative rather than the clinical use of diagnostic terms such as psychotic, alcoholic, or paranoid can bring suits for defamation. This seemed to be the case with Dr. Wentworth's first psychiatrist when he referred to the patient as a "psychopathic personality" (unless this phrase was clinically accurate).

Mature clinicians know that they cannot treat all patients who seek their help. Moreover, the problem may not necessarily reside in the patient. Some psychiatrists are quite effective in treating patients with depression, while others are particularly adept at working with paranoid patients. A psychiatrist must recognize his or her limitations. Obviously, a therapist who sustains a dislike for a patient cannot successfully treat that patient. The omnipotent practitioner who does not recognize his or her limitations with patients may become narcissistically injured with a hostile, difficult patient, perhaps lashing out in abusive or possibly defamatory ways.

Another trap that the unwary therapist must guard against is making critical statements to patients about the care provided by others. If the patient then files suit against a former therapist, the mental health professional making the critical statement may be subpoenaed as a plaintiff's expert. The privilege of confidentiality will no longer apply. Unless prepared to swear to the opinion under oath, the critical statements of the other professional then appear to be false and malicious, thus inviting a suit from the defendant.

When a patient who is unhappy about another therapist asks for an opinion about the quality of care rendered by the previous therapist, it is appropriate to state that one does not have all the facts concerning what may have transpired between the patient and the previous therapist. Instead, clinical attention should be focused on the most pressing problem at hand, namely, the current treatment needs of the patient. Patients are entitled, however, to a forthright explanation of their current condition. The patient's well-being must always come before any misplaced sense of professional loyalty that might lead to the withholding of factual information. Aside from ethical concerns, therapists who attempt to cover up for others may be included in a malpractice action for withholding essential information.

Some practitioners have an unfortunate tendency to refer to disliked colleagues as "paranoid" or "psychopathic" or to use some other diagnostic epithet. Among other things, psychiatric colleagues also have been called "certifiable lunatics" and "non compos." Such epithets may be particularly damaging and insulting to a fellow psychiatrist, who may respond with a defamation suit. Halleck (17) recognizes this tendency and wonders why there are not more suits against psychiatrists and other physicians for defamation.

In *Hoesl* the court opined in dicta (nonbinding opinion) that "like other courts, California courts have refused to hold defamatory on its face or defamatory at all an imputation of mental disorder which is made in an oblique or hyperbolic manner (statement made 'not to describe the plaintiff as a person who was mentally ill but as one who was unreasonable in his actions and his demands'); (letter implying that mental patient released by hospital should still be institutionalized is not libelous per se); (characterization of plaintiff as 'paranoid' and 'schizophrenic' constitutes nondefamatory hyperbole)" (16). Actually, psychiatrists now are more vulnerable to defamation suits by their fellow psychiatrists, particularly in relation to denial of admission privileges to hospitals and in peer review procedures.

Can psychiatrists be held legally liable for statements made during the course of participation in the work of professional committees?

Psychiatrists who make derogatory comments about colleagues in peer review meetings may be sued for defamation and tortious interference with business relations. The frequency of such lawsuits is expected to rise (18). Most state statutes provide a substantial degree of confidentiality to the peer review process, although care must be taken not to abuse the privilege. Currently, about half the states have laws making peer review reports privileged. The other half have "qualified" peer review confidentiality. Lawyers have access to factual materials but not to the opinions and conclusions of individual participants.

Problems arise when peer review committees are not monitored closely, thus preventing conflicts of interest among members that may lead to allegations of bias, conspiracy, and restraint of trade. In *Patrick v. Burget* (19), the United States Supreme Court unanimously ruled that a hospital peer review committee with the authority to grant privileges is not immune from antitrust laws. The Supreme Court, concluding that the state failed to actively supervise the peer review process, upheld the original trial decision. In a recent Supreme Court decision involving another antitrust case, the high court ruled 5 to 4 that an ophthalmologist had a right to sue peer reviewers who removed him from the staff of a Los Angeles hospital (20). This case, as in the earlier Supreme Court decision in *Patrick,* is expected to have a further chilling effect on peer review.

The sole purpose of peer review is to determine whether the clinician is professionally qualified. Comments that go beyond the identification of substandard care and the improvement of the quality of care may lose the qualified privilege of confidentiality. Statements made in bad faith, such as those in the vignette, may be legally actionable. Comments about the personality of the clinician are not considered appropriate criteria for staff appointments (21). Some degree of statutory immunity from civil suits is granted by all states as long as the statements are not malicious. Unsubstantiated comments made out of jealousy or resentment may invite a lawsuit. In the vignette, the comments made against Dr. Wentworth appeared to have a malicious quality. Psychiatrists involved in peer review must not reveal confidential information discussed in official meetings with anyone, including the physician in question.

Psychiatrists who are members of peer review committees on hospital staffs, medical societies, or state licensing boards (as well as medical staff credentialing, quality assurance, and disciplinary committees) should be familiar with the particular state statute that applies to their activities. State statutes differ as to which activities are covered and to the degree and extent they offer immunity. Some statutes cover only utilization review committees, whereas others offer immunity only to physician health care providers (22). Greater access to peer review records can be expected in the future as courts place greater emphasis on public versus private interests. Without this privilege, maligning a professional's qualifications can be "actionable per se," and the defamed person does not have to show monetary loss due to the libel or slander (23).

In *Kilcoin v. Wolansky* (24), statements made about the chief of services at a state mental hospital during the course of an official investigation became the basis of a libel and slander suit. The New York Court of Appeals reversed a lower court's decision and ruled that no malice was demonstrated. Furthermore, the court added that the acts complained of were well within the embrace of the statutory obligation to ensure humane treatment of patients.

The key to participation on committees is to act without malice. Professional committees are designed to further the vital interest of assuring quality care for patients. If statements made in this context are within the scope of this important interest, free from malice, and communicated in a proper manner, the conditional privilege will exist. Under the most scrupulous standards, recommending denial of hospital privileges, questioning a colleague's competence at staff meetings, or reporting an impaired colleague may not prevent a suit. However, good-faith reporting will almost certainly prevent its success.

The failure to report incompetent colleagues or a cover up of their negligence may result in a lawsuit against the supervising psychiatrist (25, 26). Psychiatrists who serve on credentialing and peer review committees should check their professional liability insurance to see if they are covered against legal actions brought in the line of such committee work.

Finally, in New Jersey, the protection of qualified privilege has been extended beyond hospital medical staffs and nursing homes to employees of state-operated residential facilities for the developmentally disabled. In *Fees v. Trow* (27), an employee (teacher) reported her observation of a resident patient seated on the lap of another employee (also a teacher). The employee was terminated. The New Jersey Supreme Court reversed the appellate court and reinstated the trial court's judgment of qualified privilege and immunity for the reporting employee against a suit for defamation. This decision appears to reflect the increasing tendency of courts to protect a variety of health care professionals who candidly report abuse of the mentally ill, the elderly, and other vulnerable groups who may not possess the ability or knowledge to protect their civil rights (28).

References

1. Keeton WP, Dobbs DB, Keeton RW, et al: Prosser and Keeton on the Law of Torts. St Paul, MN, West Publishing, 1984, p 773
2. Ibid, pp 778–793
3. Ibid, pp 816–820
4. Ibid, pp 824–832
5. Reisner R, Slobogin C: Law and the Mental Health System, 2nd Edition. St Paul, MN, West Publishing, 1990, p 265
6. Slovenko R: The hazards of writing or disclosing information in psychiatry. Behavioral Sciences and the Law 1:109–127, 1983
7. Prosser WL: Law of Torts, 4th Edition. St Paul, MN, West Publishing, 1971, pp 754–760
8. Psychiatrist receives settlement in suit: alleges defamation from movie portrayal. American Medical News, February 13, 1987, p 42
9. 93 Misc 2d 201, 400 NYS2d 668 (NY Sup Ct 1977)
10. 196 Misc 547, 92 NYS2d 575 (NY Sup Ct 1949)
11. Iverson v Frandsen, 237 F2d 898 (10th Cir 1956)
12. 17 Ariz App 54, 495 P2d 494, cert den, Modla v Southside Hospital, 409 U.S. NY App Div 1038 (1972)
13. Miller v Beck, 82 AD2d 912, 440 NYS2d 691 (1981)
14. French JD: Another threat in child-abuse cases: slander. Medical Economics, October 5, 1987, pp 51–56
15. 8 Utah 2d 191, 331 P2d 814 (1958)
16. 451 F Supp 1170 (ND Cal 1978); aff'd, 629 F2d 586 (9th Cir 1980)
17. Halleck SL: Law in the Practice of Psychiatry. New York, Plenum, 1980, pp 36–37
18. Cassidy R: Can you really speak your mind in peer review? Medical Economics, January 23, 1984, pp 246–262
19. 486 U.S. 94, on remand, 852 F2d 1241 (9th Cir 1988)
20. Summit Health Ltd v Pinhas, 59 U.S. 4493 (1991)
21. Rosenberg CL: Beware of the legal booby traps of hospital committees. Medical Economics, July 22, 1985, pp 110–114
22. Norman JC: So-called physician "whistle-blowers" protected. Legal Aspects of Medical Practice 11:3–4, 7, 1983
23. Alsobrook HB: When you can—and can't—badmouth a colleague. Medical Economics, April 2, 1984, pp 72–85
24. 52 NY2d 995, 420 NE2d 87, 438 NYS2d 289 (1981)
25. Darling v Charleston Community Memorial Hospital, 33 Ill 2d 326, 211 NE2d 253 (1965), cert denied, 383 U.S. 946 (1966)
26. Gonzales v Nork, 20 Cal 3d 500, 143 Cal Rptr 240, 573 P2d 458 (1978)
27. 105 NJ 330, 521 A2d 824 (1987)
28. Freishtat HW: Forensic update. J Clin Psychopharmacol 7:348–349, 1987

Chapter 23

The Impaired Psychiatrist

Dr. Wilbur, a 56-year-old psychiatrist, has been in private practice for 26 years. His practice consists mainly of outpatient work and the short-term hospitalization of patients. Dr. Wilbur is a very hard worker, seeing patients 12 to 14 hours a day in his office in addition to his hospital patients. Having obsessive-compulsive personality traits, he is perfectionistic and demanding of himself. He trusts his own judgment almost exclusively, persevering until his goals are accomplished.

Dr. Wilbur is the oldest of six children. He was raised in a close family. His father worked long, hard hours as a printer and later as a foreman of a printing plant. He imparted the values of hard work, self-sacrifice, and excellence to his son. Because of the family's difficult financial circumstances, Dr. Wilbur worked his way through college and medical school, graduating with honors from both. While in medical school, he graduated at the top of his class and was honored by election to a prestigious medical honor fraternity. As a psychiatric resident, his clinical and administrative abilities were recognized early. He was appointed chief resident.

After 2 years in private practice, he married a nurse whom he had met during the course of his hospital practice. Three children were born—two older daughters and a son. The marriage worked well except that his wife complained about the long hours he spent at work away from the family. Dr. Wilbur felt particularly close to his son, experiencing guilt about the time he spent away from him. About 10 years ago, Dr. Wilbur developed rheumatoid arthritis that became a source of constant moderate pain. His physical movement was restricted, curtailing a newly found interest in tennis. The arthritis first flared under the additional stress of pursuing his long-time ambition to create a new subspecialty board for psychotherapists.

Five years ago, his son died of leukemia. Dr. Wilbur was grief stricken. He tried to deal with his grief by working harder, denying his own needs and the needs of his family. Dr. Wilbur always looked on his own needs as unimportant compared with those of his patients. Marital difficulties ensued. Dr. Wilbur's wife began to abuse alcohol and had an affair with one of her husband's colleagues. Dr. Wilbur felt irreconcilably betrayed. One year ago, he divorced his wife. The divorce was uncontested. His daughters were off in graduate school.

Now, living alone is very difficult for Dr. Wilbur. He no longer has the energy to work long hours. In order to fall asleep at night, he starts to use alcohol. When this proves insufficient, he combines alcohol with benzodiazepines. The combination of alcohol and benzodiazepines is used initially at night. As time goes on, he uses alcohol and tranquilizers in the morning to alleviate feelings of depression. He withdraws from social relationships, just seeing patients and having only superficial contacts with colleagues during his hospital work. Dr. Wilbur recognizes that he is depressed and functioning marginally with the "help" of alcohol and drugs. He feels, however, that he has always been able to rely on himself at times of crises in the past. Dr. Wilbur is adamant about being able to handle his current problems on his own.

During the past 3 months, colleagues and nurses at the hospital have commented to each other about his unkempt appearance. Dr. Wilbur has always been a fashionable dresser. Irritation and mood swings alternating between depression and elation are also noted. On two separate occasions, the odor of alcohol has been detected on his breath by nursing staff during the course of his hospital rounds. Uncharacteristically, Dr. Wilbur begins to see his hospitalized patients only two or three times per week, whereas formerly he saw them every day except on Sundays. His patients are told that they will be seen the next day, but then Dr. Wilbur does not show up at the hospital until 2 or 3 days later. His office practice is falling off and the frequency of patient cancellations is rising. A malpractice suit is filed against Dr. Wilbur, claiming negligent abandonment of a hospitalized patient who developed serious side effects from a neuroleptic medication. The suit upsets Dr. Wilbur very much, increasing his depression.

Dr. Wilbur's behavior with hospitalized patients is finally reported by the nursing staff to the head of the department of psychiatry. The chief of the department makes an appointment to see Dr. Wilbur, but Dr. Wilbur cancels the appointment at the last minute because of the "flu." The department chief is concerned not only about Dr. Wilbur's health but also about a state licensing statute that requires investigation and reporting of physicians suspected of impairment. Moreover, the chief is aware of specific court decisions imposing liability on hospitals and staff members for harm to patients caused by impaired physicians.

Uncharacteristically, Dr. Wilbur had taken up the dangerous hobby of hang-gliding with reckless abandon that temporarily relieves his depression. Previously, he had no hobbies. He confides to a nursing supervisor whom he has known for 20 years at the hospital that he is thinking of increasing his life insurance coverage.

When Dr. Wilbur does not keep his second appointment with the department head, the latter becomes suspicious and calls Dr. Wilbur's office. When no one answers at his office, the department head goes to Dr. Wilbur's home and finds him unconscious. He is rushed to the emergency room and placed on life support systems. Two days later, Dr. Wilbur regains full consciousness. He admits

*to taking an overdose of 50 25-mg tablets of a tricyclic antidepressant in com-
bination with alcohol. Colleagues and nursing staff at the hospital are extremely upset but are not really surprised. Feelings of guilt are prominent
among staff members for not having intervened earlier.*

What is the definition of an impaired physician? What are some of the symptoms of impairment?

According to the American Medical Association (AMA), the impaired physician is unable to practice medicine with reasonable skill and safety because of
drug or alcohol abuse, physical or mental illness, or a combination of these disorders (1). The AMA defines impairment as "the inability to practice medicine
with reasonable skill and safety due to physical or mental disabilities including
deterioration through the aging process or loss of motor skill or abuse of drugs
or alcohol" (2). Thus, the impaired physician is defined solely in terms of the
deterioration of job performance, although many other aspects of his or her life
are adversely affected. Impaired physicians present three basic areas of concern: the maintenance of competent care for their patients, the welfare of impaired physicians and their families, and the need to uphold the reputation of the
medical profession (3).

As the clinical vignette suggests, some of the more common manifestations
indicating impairment include conducting hospital rounds with alcohol on the
breath, excessive cancellation of rounds or office hours due to the "flu" or other
nebulous and recurring illnesses, vague excuses for nonperformance, and unavailability to patients and colleagues. In addition, changes in the pattern of
regular activities such as dropping golf or other formerly gratifying activities,
avoiding colleagues, or withdrawal, irritability, loss of weight, forgetfulness,
and frequently appearing on the verge of tears, may be the first overt signs of
impairment.

Does the psychiatrist have an *ethical* duty to intercede with an impaired colleague?

*The Principles of Medical Ethics With Annotations Especially Applicable to
Psychiatry* (4) states: "A physician shall deal honestly with patients and colleagues, and strive to expose those physicians deficient in character or competence, or who engage in fraud or deception" (Section 2). It further states:
"Special consideration should be given to those psychiatrists who, because of
mental illness, jeopardize the welfare of their patients and their own reputation
and practices. It is ethical, even encouraged, for another psychiatrist to intercede in such situations" (Section 2, Annotation 4).

Psychiatrists who behave unethically as a result of mental illness are not automatically expelled from membership in professional organizations. Procedures for handling complaints of ethical violations are contained in American

Psychiatric Association (APA) publications (4) (see Appendix 1) or can be obtained from the local district branches of the APA. The APA (5) recommends that the psychiatrist be placed on inactive status and be encouraged to seek treatment.

The practice of medicine is not a right but a privilege. Return to active membership, therefore, requires reinstatement of a suspended or revoked license by the local licensing body. The goal of all these proceedings is rehabilitation.

Does the psychiatrist have a *legal* duty to report an impaired colleague?

In the clinical vignette, Dr. Wilbur's colleagues are aware of his increasing depression and deteriorating competence. At a late stage, his department chief is finally prepared to confront Dr. Wilbur about his deteriorating performance. Most physicians are loathe to report a colleague, based on a variety of concerns. The ineffectiveness of reporting often is cited as a reason. Also, the fear of being labeled as a troublemaker or being sued for defamation can inhibit the reporting of impaired physicians. Criticism from other physicians such as "no loyalty," "tattling," and "witch-hunt" may be heard. Physicians who contemplate reporting an impaired physician must ask themselves, "Do I care enough to take the criticism from others?" Loss of patient referrals is not an uncommon consequence of reporting an impaired physician. In summary, many reasons contribute to the ineffectiveness of voluntary reporting.

Until recently, the prevailing view was that physicians could be properly judged only by their peers. Discipline was a professional, not a public, matter. In fact, medical societies had little or no authority to enforce any disciplinary actions. George Bernard Shaw's statement that "every profession is a conspiracy against the laity" seems to be an apt commentary on self-policing by the medical profession.

Currently, courts are upholding the rights of medical societies to discipline, evaluate, and counsel errant, unethical, and impaired physicians (6). State licensing boards, through statutory authority, also possess disciplinary powers. The landmark ruling in *Darling v. Charleston Community Memorial Hospital* (7) held a hospital liable for an improper review of a staff member's credentials and established a hospital duty to furnish competent medical care. In essence, hospital staffs have been put on notice that failure to restrict privileges of negligent physicians may create legal liability for the staff if a patient is harmed.

In addition to case law, state statutes and the Joint Commission on Accreditation of Healthcare Organizations (JCAHO) standards define a medical staff's responsibility to monitor the qualifications and clinical abilities of its membership. For example, the JCAHO *Consolidated Standards Manual* provides for "documenting that each member is qualified for membership and encouraging an optimal level of professional performance of its members through the appointment and reappointment procedures, delineation of clinical privileges, and periodic reappraisals. . ." (8).

Hospitals can and will be held liable for failure to act against physicians who fail to report negligent physicians (6). Similarly, the entire medical staff as a separate entity may be held liable for failing to initiate positive action regarding a physician who is known to be incompetent, or for failing to exercise due care in selecting physicians for the staff (9).

Almost all states and territories have adopted statutes governing identification and discipline of impaired physicians (10). These statutes include *1)* mandatory reporting by one or more various health care providers and institutions; *2)* immunity from suit for good-faith reporting; *3)* due-process safeguards for the reported physician; and *4)* reinstatement opportunity. In addition, mandatory reporting of incompetent and impaired physicians has become the law through passage of the Health Care Quality Improvement Act of 1986 (HCQIA) (11).

Reporting requirements are most often imposed on health care institutions. The HCQIA and many states require the reporting of physician disciplinary actions by hospitals, medical staffs, medical societies, and review organizations. The HCQIA provides immunity for health care entities and providers who make peer review reports in good faith (12). A number of states place the duty to report the impaired physician squarely on other physicians, although the requirements vary greatly (1). Some laws provide an exemption from reporting when the impairment is discovered by the physician in the role of therapist (13).

Disciplinary organizations do not necessarily react therapeutically toward the impaired physician. Sargent (13) reports the case of a manic-depressive physician who attempted suicide by swallowing sample drugs. After a successful rescue, treatment, and return to practice, the physician was placed on probation for 2 years, and his name was published in the medical society journal as a drug violator. The only evidence of drug use was his suicide attempt. This type of reaction drives the impaired physician farther underground.

Enforcement of reporting requirements is problematic because it may be difficult to prove that a physician knew of a colleague's impairment. The requirement that a treating physician make such a disclosure presents special problems in psychiatry. The need to maintain patient confidentiality as well as the need to maintain a treatment position vis à vis the patient's disclosures complicate the issue of reporting. Perhaps a consultant can be used to handle administrative and reporting issues that arise in the psychotherapeutic treatment of the impaired physician (14).

Immunity from suit is granted by a number of states, provided the report of suspected physician impairment is made in good faith and without malice (13). Nevertheless, physicians must realize that immunity does not prevent a defamation suit from being filed. The physician may be subjected to defending a lawsuit brought by the physician who was reported. However, the law provides sufficient legal protection for the reporting physician (acting in good faith) to prevail against such an action (6). One commentator notes that as of 1985, no physician has been successfully sued for the good-faith reporting of an impaired colleague (15). Defamation and the defense against such allegations are discussed in Chapter 22.

Due-process protection is provided in state licensing statutes for procedures that restrict, suspend, or revoke a physician's license. These procedures must provide notice of charges, hearings, opportunity for representation by legal counsel, production of witnesses, the presentation of evidence on one's behalf, examination of evidence, and cross-examination of witnesses (1).

Presently, most states are attempting to place less emphasis on disciplinary action and more on rehabilitation programs. California (16), through the Medical Board of California, gives impaired physicians a choice of forgoing disciplinary actions by enrolling in statewide treatment programs. With the threat of discipline removed, self-referral is encouraged. In California, 75% of the treatment enrollees during the second year of the program were self-enrolled.

All 50 states have impaired physicians committees sponsored by the states' medical societies (17). These committees have been established to deal exclusively with the problem of impairment. Members of these committees consist of qualified physicians who have recovered from an illness or have appropriate training in substance abuse disorders and mental illness. The success of the work of medical societies with impaired physicians has been enhanced because programs exist that permit licensing boards to refer cases initially to the medical society for confidential investigation and intervention (10).

How effective have impaired physicians programs been in dealing with the impaired physician?

To the APA, an impaired physician program is considered a form of peer review (18). Many of these committees, however, are ineffective because of lack of funding and the almost exclusive reliance upon volunteers. Another problem is the recalcitrance of reported physicians who work with these committees. However, if a reported physician is uncooperative, he or she is typically offered the "choice" of treatment or a recommendation of loss of license (2).

A reasonable support and intervention system comprised of volunteers is extremely difficult to construct. Walzer (10) notes that the "apparent success of some impaired physician programs seems attributable, in part, to having a full time director." A reliable system adequately funded and given top priority by the employment of professional staff is required. Such a professional committee can provide a "first-aid kit" on how to intervene with the impaired physician, develop guidelines on how to interview and manage the impaired physician, and administer a personal audit to all physicians.

In the clinical vignette, the department chief acted when he received reports of Dr. Wilbur's impaired professional behavior. Colleagues and nursing staff, however, were aware of Dr. Wilbur's difficulties and the negligent performance of his duties for approximately 3 months before interceding. Hospital staffs and the administration have an individual and collective responsibility to monitor the quality of care rendered by everyone, including attending physicians in private practice. The failure of physicians or professional groups to maintain their responsibilities in ensuring that adequate treatment is provided to patients may make them liable to any patient harmed by the negligent acts of an impaired physician (6).

When a psychiatrist becomes aware of a colleague's impairment in the hospital setting, the chief of service should be informed. At the same time, a memo should be kept in the psychiatrist's file noting that the chief was informed of the colleague's impairment. To preserve confidentiality, reporting should be kept within the psychiatrist's chain of command rather than going directly to the risk manager or the hospital director.

Is there a central clearinghouse that will maintain data concerning disciplinary actions against physicians?

Yes. On September 1, 1990, the United States Government created the National Practitioner Data Bank containing the records of malpractice suits and disciplinary actions against physicians (19). The purpose of the bank is to centralize the reporting of disciplinary actions against physicians by state licensing boards and by hospital and state medical societies. As a result, interested parties (e.g., state licensing agencies, hospital review boards) can assess whether an applicant has ever had disciplinary actions or civil suits successfully brought against them, including settled cases. The National Practitioner Data Bank is a product of the HCQIA of 1986 (20). The purpose of the act is to restrict the ability of errant physicians to move from state to state without disclosure of negligent or unprofessional conduct, and to provide protection and incentive for physicians involved in peer review (19).

Hospitals, health maintenance organizations, professional societies, and state medical boards, as well as other health care organizations, are required to report any disciplinary actions against providers lasting longer than 30 days. Disciplinary actions include limitation, suspension, or revocation of privileges or membership in a professional society. Insurers who make malpractice payments on behalf of providers, including settlements, are required to participate. Immunity from liability is granted for health care entities and providers making peer review reports in good faith (10).

Hospitals must query the data bank for information about physicians who make application for hospital privileges. Every 2 years, the data bank must also be queried about physicians holding current staff privileges or the hospital will lose immunity for professional peer review activities.

An additional, and quite valuable, consequence of the National Practitioner Data Bank is that it prevents errant professionals from changing hospitals or leaving the state in order to avoid detection of this information. Undoubtedly, this will be very useful in rooting out incompetent professionals. Nevertheless, the mere fact of an adverse judgment against the doctor in a malpractice suit proves nothing. It does not necessarily mean that the physician is incompetent or that the physician committed malpractice. The accurate reporting of such a judgment or prior disciplinary action will provide an inquiring agency the opportunity to investigate the relevancy and significance of the prior judgment.

Nevertheless, the data bank is creating considerable controversy. Legal commentators fear that the National Practitioner Data Bank will discourage settlement of legal claims, discourage hospital peer review, encourage litigation against hospitals over privileges, and tend to lower standards of medical practice (21). Nuisance or frivolous suits will more likely be actively defended by physicians.

Any disciplinary actions or malpractice payments made by physicians must be reported to the data bank. Failure to report is subject to civil monetary penalties of up to $10,000 for each unreported incident.

The public will not have access to the data bank. Plaintiffs' attorneys can have access to the data bank only if they can prove that the hospital failed to query the data bank regarding the physician in question. The information obtained can be used only to sue the hospital for negligent credentialing (22). Physicians can request information from the data bank about their own files without paying the $2 standard fee per name.

What are some of the personality traits and behaviors that precede suicide attempts by impaired physicians? What are some of the remedies?

Studies show that approximately 10% of all physicians are impaired and their compromised quality of care is estimated to affect as many as 100 million patient visits per year (23). Of these physicians, a very significant number attempt or commit suicide—the tragic sequela of impairment. Every year, physicians that number the equivalent of the student body of an averaged-sized medical school commit suicide (24). The lethal legacy of the physician who commits suicide is staggering. The physician's spouse, children, friends, and even patients themselves become nine times more vulnerable to suicide (25).

Dr. Wilbur illustrates many of the personality traits and behaviors of a physician who has become impaired. Obsessive-compulsive life-styles, perfectionistic standards of performance, overachieving, and perseverance until success is obtained are commonly observed in the physician who becomes impaired. Gabbard (26) describes the role of compulsiveness in the normal physician, particularly the adaptive and maladaptive uses of the compulsive triad of doubt, guilt, and an exaggerated sense of responsibility. Feelings of invulnerability and limitless capacity foster denial of the physician's own needs and limitations in the course of caring for others. Intolerant of his or her own shortcomings, the physician may also be demanding and uncompromising with colleagues and family. As the physician ages, energy and capacity diminish, but the internal demands for perfection continue, leading to a sense of frustration and failure.

Dr. Wilbur placed most of his energy and interest in his work, ignoring leisure activities, plain relaxation, and family relationships. Although he valued his family, Dr. Wilbur did not find time to derive pleasure and support from his wife and children. Too much of his energy was spent on activities that fed his ambition and self-esteem. Usually, the distance and alienation in family relationships diminish the family's appreciation of the severity of the physician's mental illness or alcohol and drug abuse problems. Often, the more prominent the physician, the less the family may be aware of impairment. In addition, the family may feel helpless and fearful to come forward for help. Professional isolation allows problems to fester unnoticed. The camaraderie and companionship of colleagues, particularly for psychiatrists in solo practice, is often missing. General information on the topic of physician impairment is available to assist spouses (27) and colleagues (28).

Malpractice suits and allegations of ethical violations can be emotionally disruptive and may ultimately lead to suicide (29). Doyle (30) feels that being sued for malpractice is the most psychologically stressful event in a medical career. Cranshaw et al. (31), reporting on a suicide epidemic among impaired physicians in Oregon, revealed that when impaired physicians were disciplined by the Oregon Board of Medical Examiners, they committed suicide at a high rate, rather than seeking the track of diagnosis and treatment.

The AMA and the APA conducted a joint pilot study on physician mortality and suicide. In preliminary data, the study found that in 85% of 144 cases of physician suicides investigated, the physician had suffered a significant loss in the prior 2 years (32). Of the suicides, 33% were among physicians who had malpractice claims filed against them. Almost all of these physicians had lost their hospital affiliations or licenses. Other statistics revealed an incidence of 20% of incompetent practices in suicidal physicians, while none occurred in physicians dying of natural causes. Of physicians who committed suicide, 73% were described as being responsible toward their patients, compared with 97% of physicians dying of natural causes. The AMA-APA study also showed that physicians who commit suicide are less satisfied with the profession of medicine (32). Only 13% found their families to be a source of satisfaction, compared with 30% of physicians who died of natural causes. Nearly half of the suicide victims did not have satisfactory marriages.

Dr. Wilbur also displayed another common characteristic of a high-risk physician: a strong work ethic combined with the *singular* pursuit of professional status. Many of these physicians come from hard-working, blue collar backgrounds where self-denial, hard work, and sacrifice are emphasized. The physician is often the standard bearer for such families, justifying the sacrifices and hardships of the parents. Family life is sacrificed to professional duties. Many nights are spent away from the family at professional meetings. The drive to be prominent in professional societies or specialty organizations becomes crucial.

Personal losses such as divorce, recent death of a spouse or child, or failing health can precipitate suicide in a depressed physician. In California, divorced physicians have a staggering suicide rate of 662 per 100,000 compared with a rate of 82 per 100,000 for divorced white men in the nonphysician population (33). Although not life threatening, chronic nagging physical disorders may play an incremental role in the suicide. Even "minor" incidents can act as catalysts for suicide in the depressed physician. Problems such as marital arguments, physical injury, a house fire, a stolen car, or a professional misunderstanding with a colleague can summate to precipitate suicide in a vulnerable, depressed physician.

Women are highly represented in the specialty of psychiatry. While sharing all of the above characteristics, some also bear the full responsibility of managing a family. Conflicts over competition are not uncommon. In the male-dominated profession of medicine, few role models exist as a guide for women. Women physicians have a suicide rate that is comparable to that of male physicians, and the rate of suicide is three to four times that of nonphysician women (32). Female physician suicides usually occur when the women are in their late 20s and early 30s, whereas the average age for male physicians committing suicide is 48.8 years.

Behavior signaling the imminence of suicide may include mood disorders, irritability, and particularly the termination of personal and professional relationships. Problems with concentration and recourse to alcohol and drugs are serious indicators of impairment. Disillusionment with the practice of medicine, the sudden desire to change careers, chaotic office routines with irregular hours, and decreasing patient load are also signs of trouble.

In contrast, if the physician works long hours, coming home only to sleep, and repeats the same cycle day after day, he or she is probably not dealing with personal problems. Increasing the coverage of a life insurance policy, the presence of poor appetite, weight loss, sleep disturbances, and the giving away of prized possessions may also be done in contemplation of self-destruction. Compulsive gambling, buying expensive "toys," and extramarital affairs may represent a last-ditch effort to avert a deepening depression. The sudden interest in a dangerous hobby or life-style may be a suicidal equivalent.

Sargent has been quoted as suggesting some preventive measures (24):

1. Physicians must remind themselves that they are not perfect nor should they seek perfectionistic aims.

2. Physicians need vacations. New or past activities of interest can be pursued. A vacation is also a helpful remedy for physicians' omnipotent feelings that they are indispensable.
3. Physicians need to maintain friendships and supports. The ability to exchange feelings openly and honestly with a friend is extremely salutary.
4. If the physician is preoccupied with self-destruction, professional help should be sought.

Although these ideas appear simple and self-evident, many physicians are unable to avail themselves of these preventive measures. When psychiatrists schedule many hours of psychotherapy each day, the pace can become grueling. The personal isolation attendant to the solo practice of psychotherapy can become a significant risk factor for impairment. Both patient and psychiatrist need vacations from intensive psychotherapeutic regimens; otherwise the therapist's fatigue and ennui can destroy the gratifications of intense, one-to-one work with patients. The need for personal therapy of the impaired therapist may be denied, even in the face of intense emotional suffering and the impairment of professional functioning. Denial is a defensive phenomenon that is not used by the psychiatrist's patients alone.

Mental and physical stress is an unavoidable part of the practice of medicine. Stress alone probably contributes to suicide only in the subgroup of physicians who have affective disorders. Shore (34) feels that the national suicide prevention effort during the past two decades has followed a stress and crisis intervention model without any evidence that the effort has led to a decreased suicide rate among the general public. Doyle and Cline (35) report primary, secondary, and tertiary methods of impairment prevention. The unsolicited introduction of the topic of physician impairment into a continuing medical education course on pulmonary disease and hypertension appeared to significantly heighten and maintain sensitivity to impairment issues among 90% of the course participants even 9 months later (35).

What can be done to treat physician impairment?

When a physician admits that a problem exists and help is needed, an intervention team composed of family members, office co-workers, hospital personnel, and other colleagues should assist the physician in obtaining help. Treatment follow-up is essential because initial recognition and admission of impairment by the physician does not necessarily guarantee follow-through (24). In the AMA-APA pilot study (see above), half of all physicians who committed suicide were in treatment at the time, suggesting the lethality of the conditions treated in this group (32). Thus flights into health and spontaneous recovery should be viewed with great skepticism. Physicians, and particularly psychiatrists, possess sufficient knowledge about mental and physical illness to stage a convincing cover-up.

The AMA-APA study (32) has provided an initial profile of the suicide-prone physician:

- A physician at risk for suicide usually signals his or her intentions.
- The physician is usually aware of emotional difficulties and may seek help for coping with them.
- Suicide risk remains during treatment. It is an illusion to think that the physician-patient is less of a suicide risk than any other psychiatric patient.
- The desire to escape mental pain may motivate suicide.
- A major risk factor is depression.
- A history of mental and physical problems is common.
- A history of drug abuse may exist. The suicidal physician may self-medicate.
- Social problems secondary to alcohol abuse usually exist.
- The physician has had a troubled childhood and family of origin.

The AMA Council on Mental Health recommends that if impaired physicians cannot be persuaded to seek help voluntarily, the medical staff or appropriate committees of the county or state medical society should be consulted (36). When receiving an impaired physician report, a dispositional process is set into motion.

A specially appointed committee of a medical society receives and investigates a complaint of impairment. After examining the case, the committee has two options: *1)* determine that the alleged impairment is unfounded, or *2)* determine that impairment exists. If the latter determination is made, the committee can recommend either or both of the following: *1)* care, counseling, and treatment acceptable to the committee, or *2)* suspension or revocation of the physician's license to practice medicine. If the physician agrees to the committee's recommendations, the treatment plan, including the possibility of restricted practice, may begin. If the physician refuses, the matter is referred to the state licensing board for a formal hearing with due-process guarantees.

If the medical society is unwilling or unable to act, the matter must be referred to the appropriate state licensing authority. The emphasis on treating, rather than punishing, the impaired professional is frequently the initial inclination of state medical societies; however, it is by no means an easy endeavor. Families are usually ineffective in persuading the physician to seek treatment. Colleagues frequently withdraw, not wishing to become involved. Initially, coercion may be required. Confrontation by a committee of colleagues who share responsibility for shepherding the impaired physician through a difficult time is advised. Rotation of members on this committee may be necessary to diffuse the considerable stress engendered by the difficulty of the task.

Compassion and courage are required to intercede on behalf of an impaired colleague. The prognosis is likely to be good with early intervention and sufficient treatment. According to one account, as many as 93% of impaired physicians return to practice with adequate continuing treatment and monitoring (37).

When drugs and alcohol abuse are present, a 2- to 3-year program should be used with inpatient treatment if needed, followed by intensive postdischarge treatment, including mandatory attendance at meetings of Alcoholics Anonymous, Narcotics Anonymous, and other appropriate self-help groups. Self-help groups are known to be helpful and a popular form of intervention with impaired professionals (38).

When appropriate, the physician should be encouraged to return to work as quickly as possible. Even after treatment is ended and the physician is eligible to resume full practice, adequate aftercare is critical to maintaining recovery. Because most physicians will want to return to their practice as soon as possible, aftercare can usually be carried out on an outpatient basis (38). Individual psychotherapy, while important, ordinarily should not be pursued exclusively or allowed to conflict with participation in group programs for the impaired physician with substance abuse. One such group, International Doctors in Alcoholics Anonymous, is specifically designed for alcoholic physicians. Physicians who have recovered from their alcohol abuse can become valuable resources for the alcoholic physician and can provide a supportive environment for recovery.

Shore (34) compared a group of mentally impaired physicians with a group of chemically dependent physicians. Both groups did equally well when rehabilitation coupled probation with treatment. Although both groups had frequent relapses, extended treatment over 5 years resulted in 80% of the physicians in each group returning to practice and practicing competently. Thus, relapse did not predict a grave outcome.

In a later study, Shore (39) monitored for 8 years 63 addicted or impaired physicians who were on probation with the Oregon Board of Medical Examiners. Seventy-eight percent of these physicians were afflicted with problems of addiction. The most successful treatment outcomes occurred with addicted physicians, whose improvement was significantly associated with random urine monitoring to detect continued drug abuse.

The risk of drug addiction among physicians is estimated to be 30 to 100 times greater than that of the general population. Nace (40) questions the current validity of this estimate for the United States because data on which the estimate was based were obtained from the Federal Criminal Office in Germany for the years 1954 to 1957. Nace quotes sophisticated epidemiologic studies indicating the combined prevalence of substance abuse and dependency to be 5.9%. He states that data are not available to clarify whether physicians exceed this rate.

Alcoholism among physicians is at a rate comparable to that of the general population (41). Morse et al. (42) compared the treatment results of physicians and middle-class control subjects abusing alcohol and drugs. Morse's study confirmed Shore's (34) findings. In summary, favorable outcomes can be expected from physicians who complete treatment. Three years after completing treatment, 83% of the physicians, as compared with 62% of the control subjects, had favorable outcomes. Also, 89% of the physicians continued to practice medicine.

Morse et al. emphasize that the severity of abuse or addiction did not adversely affect outcome, prompting them to recommend that even the most difficult cases should be given an adequate trial of treatment. The authors attribute the favorable outcomes to compulsory programs of rehabilitation with a structured monitoring system. Any rehabilitation program must provide prompt diagnosis and treatment, upgrade skills atrophied through disuse, monitor the use of these skills, and speak on behalf of the physician who encounters resistance among hospitals and colleagues in his or her attempt to return to practice. The problem of treating the alcoholic physician may be significantly complicated by the presence of coexisting psychiatric disorders.

What are some of the special problems that arise in the psychotherapy of impaired physicians?

Psychiatrists who treat impaired physicians outside of a rehabilitation program encounter an even more difficult task. Logan (43) has described the role of the psychiatrist in evaluating impaired colleagues. Issues discussed include procedural information, typical questions posed, diagnostic dilemmas, treatment recommendations, and ethical and legal problems.

Impaired physicians will not fully use a treatment program unless it is confidential. Monitoring, therefore, is necessary. Once a physician is suspected to be impaired, hospitals may not be able to assess appropriately the physician's professional functioning. Because of the hospital's responsibility for the maintenance of quality of care for patients, reports from the treating psychiatrist usually are sought before the hospital considers reinstatement (44). In *In re Murawski* (45), the New York State Board for Professional Medical Conduct issued a subpoena for the psychiatric records of a physician charged with professional misconduct. The treating psychiatrist's motion to quash the subpoena on grounds of privilege was denied. The court held that the action of the board was authorized under the law permitting access to records in order to evaluate the quality of care provided to patients by doctors under investigation.

The Colorado Medical Practice Act of 1985 provides a new exception to the "duty to report" physicians who are undergoing treatment for a mental disorder or substance abuse to the board of medical examiners. The new law attempts to preserve treatment confidentiality when the physician-patient presents no danger of harm to self or others (46).

Because of the legitimate concern for the maintenance of confidentiality, might an unspoken collusion exist between the therapist and the impaired physician to hide the impairment? Furthermore, treating psychiatrists may find themselves experiencing a divided loyalty to a physician-patient, particularly when the latter is a psychiatrist and concerns arise about the impaired physician's patients who may be endangered by inept treatment (13). Also, a threat to persons other than patients may occur when seizures or blackouts go unreported to the Department of Motor Vehicles. Psychiatrists often try to convince the doctor-patient to take a leave of absence in order to circumvent reporting requirements. Legal liability as well as ethical violations may arise for not reporting the impairments of a doctor-patient if harm results to another person (47).

The problems of denial in the impaired physician can also unleash similar mechanisms in the treating psychiatrist. A mutual conspiracy of silence can develop. The fear of being labeled mentally ill, the stripping away of the illusion of physician invulnerability, and the presence of alcohol and drug abuse can promote a paralyzing denial in therapists who have not come to terms with their own vulnerability. As part of the unrelieved participation in being human, all physicians are at risk for becoming impaired. This is a reality that must be faced by all physicians and their families.

The physician who needs professional help presents special treatment challenges. There are special safeguards and warnings to be observed by the therapist. Nevertheless, the physician-patient must not be treated as a special patient. Special treatment is a trap and an evasion of the serious problems that are present. Accordingly, the assumption that the impaired physician, by virtue of being a doctor, has more responsibility in conjointly making treatment decisions must be strenuously resisted. The impaired physician should be viewed as a suffering human being whose medical skills have not provided immunization from illness or the need for adequate treatment. Patient and therapist roles must be clearly distinguished and maintained.

Psychiatrists who treat impaired physicians must be willing to speak to family members or other appropriate persons who have important information bearing on the physician-patient. Speaking to third parties should be done while maintaining confidentiality, avoiding collusive relationships with others, or withholding secrets from the physician-patient. All extratherapeutic contacts should be reported to the physician-patient, as long as disclosure of these contacts does not disrupt the therapeutic process and is viable within the treatment relationship. When contacted, the therapist should report the call to the physician-patient and obtain permission to speak to the person initiating contact with the therapist. If the physician-patient refuses, the refusal must become a priority treatment issue. If the therapist ignores information from others and the physician-patient commits suicide, then the therapist may indeed be open to legal liability. These safeguards and considerations are essentially no different from the responsibility of confidentiality and privilege that every psychiatrist assumes once a doctor-patient relationship has been established with any patient.

A legitimate form of "conspiracy" exists when the therapist works with the family, who often need help themselves. If the therapist is not comfortable with the family therapy model, some other method that allows for family involvement and input should be considered. The myth that once the physician-patient is in treatment, contact by significant others is "meddling" should be dispelled. If the therapist does not wish to talk directly to relevant others, referral of these individuals to someone with whom the therapist will speak is important. For example, a consultant can be used in some form of therapeutic-administrative split.

Webster (48) concludes that family involvement in the treatment of the impaired physician is strongly indicated but urges that clinical judgment must be applied according to the needs and circumstances of the individual patient. Psychiatrists treating physician-patients in drug clinics may be bound by specific regulations governing discussions with third parties. Webster feels that trust must be built over time based on the psychiatrist's handling of specific incidents. Furthermore, the conditions of therapy must be explicitly made. Such conditions include any limitations on confidentiality when the psychiatrist contacts others. Psychiatrists who refuse to speak to anyone having information about the physician-patient should seriously consider not taking such patients for treatment. Because half of the physicians who committed suicide in the AMA-APA pilot study were undergoing treatment, therapists must realize that impaired physicians can be especially difficult to treat (32). Secrecy, denial, and conscious withholding of important information by impaired physicians are not uncommon in psychotherapeutic treatment. Therefore, it behooves the treating psychiatrist to confront these possibilities and devise ways of effectively addressing them for the benefit of treatment.

Finally, many impaired physicians will not go to psychiatrists for needed treatment. Instead, they may seek the help of nonmedical mental health professionals in order to avoid the humiliation and embarrassment they feel in seeing a fellow physician. The experience and expertise of nonmedical mental health professionals in treating impaired physicians are badly needed. Not only do nonmedical professionals provide an important resource for improving treatment methods, but they also can help in designing programs for prevention.

References

1. Petty S: The impaired physician: a failed healer. Legal Aspects of Medical Practice 12:5–8, 1984
2. Robertson JJ: Legal aspects of impairment, in Proceedings of the Fourth AMA Conference on the Impaired Physician: Building Well-Being. Chicago, IL, American Medical Association, 1980, p 45
3. Linn L: Other psychiatric emergencies, in Comprehensive Textbook of Psychiatry IV, Vol 2. Edited by Kaplan HI, Sadock BJ. Baltimore, MD, Williams & Wilkins, 1985, pp 1315–1330
4. American Psychiatric Association: The Principles of Medical Ethics With Annotations Especially Applicable to Psychiatry. Washington, DC, American Psychiatric Association, 1989

5. American Psychiatric Association: Opinions of the Ethics Committee on the Principles of Medical Ethics With Annotations Especially Applicable to Psychiatry. Washington, DC, American Psychiatric Association, 1989
6. Hirsh HL: The medical-legal implications of the problem of the errant or sick physician. Case and Comment, July–August 1977, pp 23–30
7. 33 Ill 2d 326, 211 NE2d 253 (1965), cert denied, 383 U.S. 946 (1966)
8. Joint Commission on Accreditation of Healthcare Organizations: Consolidated Standards Manual, 1991. Oakbrook Terrace, IL, Joint Commission on Accreditation of Healthcare Organizations, 1990, PO.2.5.10, p 16
9. Spies F, Houston A: Medical staff liability for the acts of an incompetent physician. J Arkansas Med Soc 75:283–284, 1979
10. Walzer RS: Impaired physicians: an overview and update of legal issues. J Leg Med 11:131–198, 1990
11. 42 U.S.C.A. § 11101 (Supp 1991)
12. 42 U.S.C.A. § 11111(a)(1) & (2)
13. Sargent DA: The impaired physician movement: an interim report. Hosp Community Psychiatry 36:294–297, 1985
14. Stone AA: Law, Psychiatry, and Morality. Washington, DC, American Psychiatric Press, 1984, pp 210–213
15. Sargent DA: The Impaired Physician. Paper presented at the 138th annual meeting of the American Psychiatric Association, Dallas, TX, May 1985
16. The California experience with a diversion program for impaired physicians. JAMA 329:226, 1983
17. Borenstein DB, Cook K: Impairment prevention in the training years: new mental health programs at UCLA. JAMA 247:2700–2701, 1982
18. American Psychiatric Association: Guidelines to district branches for an impaired physician program. Washington, DC, American Psychiatric Association, 1980
19. Johnson ID: Reports to the National Practitioner Data Bank. JAMA 265:407–411, 1991
20. 42 U.S.C.A. § 11101 (Supp 1991)
21. Grad JD: Will national data bank encourage litigation? Va Med 117:343–344, 1990
22. Attorney limited in access to and use of information from malpractice data bank. Clinical Psychiatry News, August 1990, p 12
23. Arana GW: The impaired physician. Directions in Psychiatry, Lesson 33 [nd]
24. Preventing physician suicides. American Medical News, February 1, 1985, pp 3, 17–18
25. Victoroff VM: My dear colleague: are you considering suicide? JAMA 254:3464–3466, 1985
26. Gabbard GO: The role of compulsiveness in the normal physician. JAMA 254:2926–2929, 1985
27. American Medical Association: What Every Physician's Spouse Should Know About Impairment. Chicago, IL, American Medical Association, 1986
28. American Hospital Association: Physician Impairment: A Selected Bibliography. Washington, DC, Division of Medical Affairs, American Hospital Association, 1985
29. Wohl S: Death by malpractice. JAMA 255:1927, 1986
30. Doyle BB: The impaired psychiatrist. Psychiatric Annals 14:760–763, 1987
31. Cranshaw R, Bruce JA, Eraker PL, et al: An epidemic of suicide among physicians on probation. JAMA 243:1915–1917, 1980

32. Council on Scientific Affairs: Results and implications of the AMA-APA Physician Mortality Project. JAMA 257:2949–2953, 1987
33. Perr IN: Suicide in the young. Psychiatric Times 3(1):1, 16, 1986
34. Shore JH: The impaired physician four years after probation. JAMA 248:3127–3130, 1982
35. Doyle BB, Cline DW: Approaches to prevention in medical education, in The Impaired Physician. Edited by Scheiber SC, Doyle BB. New York, Plenum, 1983, pp 51–67
36. American Medical Association, Council on Mental Health: The sick physician: impairment by psychiatric disorders including alcoholism and drug dependence. JAMA 223:684–687, 1973
37. Psychiatrist gives guidelines for helping impaired colleagues. Psychiatric News 20(24):24, 1985
38. Robertson JJ: In-patient and out-patient treatment techniques, in Proceedings of the Third AMA Conference on the Impaired Professional. Chicago, IL, American Medical Association, 1978, pp 32–35
39. Shore JH: The Oregon experience with impaired physicians on probation: an eight-year follow-up. JAMA 257:2931–2934, 1987
40. Nace EP: The impaired physician: the need for psychiatric leadership. Psychiatric Times 5(12):8–9, 1988
41. Webster TG: Problems of drug addiction and alcoholism among physicians, in The Impaired Physician. Edited by Scheiber SC, Doyle BB. New York, Plenum, 1983, pp 27–38
42. Morse M, Martin MA, Swenson WM, et al: Prognosis of physicians treated for alcoholism and drug dependence. JAMA 251:743–746, 1984
43. Logan WS: The evaluation of the impaired physician, in Legal Implications of Hospital Policies and Practices. Edited by Miller RD. San Francisco, CA, Jossey-Bass, 1989, pp 33–53
44. Johnson v. Misericordia Community Hospital, 99 Wis 2d 708, 301 NW2d 156 (1981)
45. 84 AD2d 496, 446 NYS2d 815 (NY App Div 1982)
46. COLO REV STAT § 11, 12-36-118(J)(1) (1985)
47. Angres DH, Busch KA: The chemically dependent physician: clinical and legal considerations, in Legal Implications of Hospital Policies and Practices. Edited by Miller RD. San Francisco, CA, Jossey-Bass, 1989, pp 21–32
48. Webster TG: Psychotherapeutic issues in psychiatric treatment of physicians with alcohol and drug abuse problems, in The Impaired Physician. Edited by Scheiber SC, Doyle BB. New York, Plenum, 1983, pp 109–122

Chapter 24 # The Psychiatrist Must Survive: Understanding and Coping With Malpractice Litigation

---

Mrs. Powell, age 42, is admitted to a psychiatric hospital. Her chronic recurrent depression dramatically worsened 3 months ago. She is no longer able to work as director of a leading business establishment. Her work has been very stressful because of personality conflicts with certain members of the board of directors. She cannot concentrate, cries often, is very agitated, and has recurrent suicidal ideas. She has lost 30 pounds during the past 2 months and experiences great difficulty sleeping. She wakes up at 2:00 or 3:00 A.M. and finds it impossible to go back to sleep. She constantly expresses feelings of hopelessness. Her depression was precipitated by a sports injury to her son that left him temporarily disabled.

Dr. Jenkins evaluates the patient during the first week of admission. Physical and laboratory studies are normal. Suicidal ideation abates. Dr. Jenkins makes the diagnosis of dysthymic disorder based upon a 3-year history of chronic, recurrent depression exacerbated by a traumatic life event. The chronic depression appears related to an Axis II obsessive-compulsive personality disorder that has caused difficulties in her personal and work relationships. Dr. Jenkins interviews Mrs. Powell's husband, who appears to be very supportive. He feels that there is more reason for his wife's depression than their son's injury. He volunteers that Mrs. Powell's father and maternal aunt both suffered from serious depressions. Also, his wife has had difficulty getting along with her son and others because of her perfectionistic tendencies.

Dr. Jenkins is primarily psychodynamically trained. The hospital has an excellent reputation for providing very competent long-term psychodynamic psychotherapy in an inpatient setting. Dr. Jenkins's assessment is that the patient's basic depression is secondary to the obsessive-compulsive personality disorder, which should be the primary focus of treatment. Given the patient's diagnosis of dysthymia and obsessive-compulsive personality disorder, good work history, high intelligence, and verbal ability, Dr. Jenkins embarks upon a treatment plan of four-times-per-week insight psychotherapy, group therapy, and art ther-

apy. After 1 ½ months of this treatment regimen, no significant improvement is noted. Hopelessness still is a prominent clinical feature. Furthermore, Mrs. Powell continues to have an extremely poor appetite. Her weight is down from 135 to 90 pounds. Dr. Jenkins decides to see the patient five times a week and orders diet supplements for Mrs. Powell.

Two months after being admitted, Mrs. Powell is found hanging in her closet. She is rushed to the emergency room of a general hospital, where she is revived. After close observation and neurological evaluation on the intensive care unit, she is transferred to the psychiatric unit of the hospital with a provisional diagnosis of minimal brain damage. After evaluation, the new psychiatrist makes a diagnosis of major depression, recurrent, and begins immediate treatment with a tricyclic antidepressant and supportive psychotherapy. Within 6 weeks, Mrs. Powell's mood is remarkably improved, her sleep pattern approaches normal, and her appetite gradually returns. Suicidal ideation is entirely absent. Ten weeks after the initiation of antidepressant medication, Mrs. Powell is discharged without any evidence of depression. Because the level of her cognitive functioning is uncertain, she is referred for a neurological consultation. Neuropsychological testing shows mild brain damage.

Six months later, Mrs. Powell sues Dr. Jenkins and the original psychiatric hospital for $3 million, alleging negligent diagnosis and treatment.

What are the essential elements of psychiatric malpractice?

Psychiatric malpractice is medical malpractice. Psychiatric malpractice is defined as acts or omissions by the psychiatrist in his or her professional capacity that cause or aggravate an injury to the patient. The injury is the result of a failure to exercise that degree of care, knowledge, and skill ordinarily possessed and exercised in similar situations by a member of the profession in the same field (1). A plaintiff must establish by a preponderance of the evidence *1)* that a psychiatrist-patient relationship has been created that establishes a duty of care for the patient, *2)* that the psychiatrist has breached this duty by an act or omission not in accord with professional standards, *3)* that the patient was harmed, and 4) that the harm to the patient was proximately caused by the psychiatrist's breach of duty (see Table 24-1).

The psychiatrist must be able to survive professionally. A basic knowledge of medical negligence law is essential for practitioners in order to dispel unreal-

TABLE 24–1.   The 4 Ds of malpractice assessment

A doctor-patient relationship creating a **DUTY** of care must be present.

A **DEVIATION** from the standard of care must have occurred.

DAMAGE to the patient must have occurred.

The damage must have occurred **DIRECTLY** as a result of deviation from the standard of care.

istic fears and fantasies about psychiatric malpractice. Psychiatrists, in order to protect themselves, need to know the legal reality governing their professional practices. For instance, if a psychiatrist provides substandard treatment and the patient is not harmed, there is no malpractice. Even if the patient alleges damage from the provision of substandard care, no malpractice can occur unless the damage is proximally caused by the deviation in care. Furthermore, there can be no malpractice unless a doctor-patient relationship has been formed.

The therapist cannot guarantee correct diagnosis and treatment. Mistakes may be made without necessarily incurring liability, provided due care is used in diagnosis and treatment. Thus, risk-benefit notes in the patient's chart regarding treatment interventions may be critically important in averting liability. Clinical judgments that later prove to be wrong cannot be shown to be negligent when reasonable care is used and the reasoning documented. The law is not interested in punishing errors in judgment per se (2).

How is the standard of care determined in malpractice law?

Normally through the use of an expert witness, the plaintiff is required to establish a standard of care and the psychiatrist's deviation from that standard (3). Treatises and articles from professional journals may be used in lieu of expert testimony in states that have adopted the learned treatise exception to the hearsay rule. The plaintiff is relieved of his or her "burden of production" if the facts allow for laypersons to conclude there was failure to conform to the applicable standard of care, or if the case falls under the *res ipsa loquitur* ("the thing speaks for itself") rule. In the latter circumstance, no expert is necessary. The plaintiff presents evidence of the injury and the circumstances surrounding the injury. In the past, courts have applied standards from the defendant's locality, but most courts now judge the psychiatrist by national standards (4).

Psychiatric diagnosis and treatment is still an imprecise science despite the development of the *Diagnostic and Statistical Manual of Mental Disorders* (5). One therapist's definition of deviation in the care of a patient may be another therapist's cornerstone in managing that patient. Therapists disagree about the indications and effectiveness of the great number of psychotherapeutic modalities currently available. Even within the same school of psychotherapy, different opinions often exist. Two behavior therapists may treat phobias with very different methods. For example, one might prefer systematic desensitization, whereas the other might adhere strongly to implosion. Psychiatrists also differ concerning the use of biologic and psychodynamic treatments. Some prefer insight psychotherapy for phobias, while others are adamant about the use of tricyclic antidepressants or an appropriate benzodiazepine. Others advocate a combined approach. Psychiatry has a tradition of being hospitable to diverse and competing schools of thought. Currently, there are hundreds of different schools of psychotherapy.

Lazare (6) describes four separate conceptual models used in the treatment of patients in contemporary psychiatry: biological, behavioral, psychodynamic, and social. Today. biological and behavioral models are ascendant while the psychodynamic and social models are in decline (7). The eclectic psychiatrist is under pressure from subspecialization in these areas. Biological psychiatry has already gained credibility with the medical community. Behavioral principles appeal to pragmatic physicians because they allow for relatively direct, uncomplicated approaches to treatment. In these areas, standards of care are better defined. Courts, however, may be reluctant to find a psychiatrist negligent if he or she follows a method approved by at least a respectable minority of the profession (3). On the other hand, experts are less reluctant now to testify against colleagues. Attorneys can no longer complain about a "conspiracy of silence" within the medical profession.

The court usually derives the standards of the profession from expert testimony of psychiatrists and by evaluating how the ordinary and prudent practitioner of the profession would have acted under the same or similar circumstances (8). Essentially, the judge and jury have no role in evaluating a defendant psychiatrist's conduct directly. They only evaluate the persuasiveness of the expert testimony with all other evidence (9). The law takes the position that it does not prefer one form of treatment over another. The law simply measures therapists' care by the standard from their own school of treatment if that school is supported by a respectable minority of fellow professionals.

In *Lundgren v. Eustermann* (10), a Minnesota Court of Appeals held that a licensed psychologist was competent to give expert testimony in a medical malpractice case challenging the chlorpromazine treatment a physician prescribed. This case was overturned by the Minnesota Supreme Court, which held that a licensed psychologist was not qualified to give an opinion in a medical malpractice action on the standard of care required of a medical doctor (10).

In some instances, the applicable standard may be defined by statute, or by the court, as in *Tarasoff v. Regents of the University of California* (11). In *Helling v. Carey* (12), the court held that tonometry examinations were required by law on all patients below the age of 40 regardless of the infrequency of glaucoma. The intentional infliction of emotional distress is another example of a judicially imposed standard (13). In *Tarasoff* and *Helling,* the courts imposed their own version of professional practice standards, despite professional opinion to the contrary. Other examples of judicially imposed standards can be found in informed consent, in confidentiality, and in civil statutes defining therapist-patient sexual misconduct, as well as in immunity statutes involving the duty to warn and protect. In *Canterbury v. Spence* (14), the court imposed the "reasonable man" standard in informed-consent litigation even though the professional custom standard was the prevailing standard.

In many states, standards of care may also be derived from drug manufacturers' instructions and from medical treatises under the Federal Rules of Evidence (15). Governmental and nongovernmental regulatory agencies may specify standards of care. Informed-consent statutes and other legislative mandates setting standards for peer review and record keeping are increasingly more common (15). Third-party payers such as private, state, and federal insurance programs are establishing standards for treatment. Managed care firms also create practice guidelines. Long-term psychotherapy is being drastically limited as an "appropriate" treatment modality for a number of psychiatric diagnostic categories. Treatment manuals recently developed for the various types of psychotherapy provide standards for this very ambiguous area (16). Inevitably, the standard of care will be influenced and shaped by third-party decision-makers.

The doctrine of *res ipsa loquitur* may be invoked only under special circumstances. This doctrine will apply when *1)* the harm done would not normally have occurred without someone's having been negligent; *2)* the conduct or mechanism that caused the injury was under the exclusive control of the defendant; and *3)* the plaintiff was not contributorily negligent. The plaintiff has a prima facie case of negligence, placing the burden on the defendant to prove there was no negligence. In *Meier v. Ross General Hospital* (17), the court held that the doctrine of *res ipsa loquitur* applied when a psychiatric patient jumped to his death through an open window of a hospital room.

How are current federal regulations shaping psychiatric standards of care?

The Health Care Financing Administration (HCFA) has developed screens and guidelines to be used by peer review organizations in all states to evaluate the quality of psychiatric care provided to Medicare, Medicaid, and CHAMPUS beneficiaries (18). The screens are used to evaluate quality of care provided by freestanding psychiatric hospitals, psychiatric units of general hospitals, and individual practitioners. Penalties such as disciplinary action by state licensing boards exist for physicians exceeding 25 quality points for any quarter.

The Medical Care Quality Research and Improvement Act of 1989 will provide funding for the Department of Health and Human Services to coordinate research on effectiveness and outcome appropriateness of medical care and to develop medical practice guidelines (19). Practice guidelines for at least three clinical disorders that account for large Medicare payments or that have significant variation in the volume or type of treatment rendered were applied after January 1, 1991.

Federal governmental efforts to control medical payments and monitor quality of care to recipients of federal health care programs inevitably shape standards of psychiatric practice by defining and funding "appropriate" care. Nevertheless, no official approved standard of care can substitute for sound clinical judgment in the diagnosis and treatment of individual patients.

Nonmedical therapists who hold themselves out to be specialists in the treatment of emotional and mental illness will be held to the higher standard of the specialist. If diagnosis and treatment of medical disorders are undertaken, then medical standards will be used (20). Finally, specialists are held to a higher standard of care than nonspecialists, even in cases involving the same problem. Thus, psychiatrists who do psychotherapy should not represent their work as psychoanalysis nor themselves as analysts if they are not so trained. The use of the traditional couch in psychoanalysis should not be used routinely for psychotherapy or by therapists not prepared to handle the transference complications that may develop. The couch is not just a convention.

How are new developments in biological psychiatry influencing the standard of care?

Psychiatrists have an ethical and professional duty to stay abreast of new developments. *The Principles of Medical Ethics With Annotations Especially Applicable to Psychiatry* (21) states: "Psychiatrists are responsible for their own continuing education and should be mindful of the fact that theirs must be a lifetime of learning" (Section 5, Annotation 1). The law has also imposed a duty on all physicians to stay abreast of changing concepts and new developments (22). The duty to keep up with medical and psychiatric advances is much clearer for specialists than for general practitioners (23). Psychiatrists are held to the standards and advances in diagnosis and treatment commonly used throughout the country (23). Knowledge concerning treatment efficacy and adverse effects of drug therapy is burgeoning. Psychiatrists who prescribe drug therapy must also apprise themselves of current developments in psychopharmacology.

In the clinical vignette, experts for both sides will testify about the standard of care due to Mrs. Powell and whether Dr. Jenkins deviated from that standard. The plaintiff's experts will testify that Dr. Jenkins misdiagnosed her patient, making a diagnosis of dysthymia and obsessive-compulsive personality disorder while ignoring profound dysphoria, suicidal ideation, and prominent vegetative signs of depression that met the DSM criteria for major depression. A history of chronic, recurrent depression combined with a significant family history of depression also strongly favored a diagnosis of major depression. Furthermore, the plaintiff's experts will argue, clinical experience and research have demonstrated a clear superiority of antidepressant drug therapy over psychotherapy alone in the treatment of major depression. Focusing treatment on a personality disorder was inappropriate, because a severe depression that was highly treatable required immediate medical attention.

Stone (7) states:

> Psychoanalysts and other psychodynamic therapists have heretofore been almost totally immune from malpractice suits because of virtually insurmountable technical and legal reasons. Patients dissatisfied with the lack of improvement after prolonged psychodynamic treatment may have found a way around these legal

obstacles—a way provided by biological psychiatry. . . . They may sue for malpractice because biological treatments were not administered.

Defense experts may have a difficult time refuting this testimony. Dr. Jenkins is primarily trained in providing psychodynamic psychotherapy. Other psychiatrists may be proficient in providing drug therapy only. Combined treatment approaches are often required. Some therapists, proficient in only one or two forms of therapy, apply their treatments in a procrustean fashion to all patients who consult them. As a result, the specter exists of the analyst futilely, but intrepidly, treating the bipolar patient with five-times-per-week psychoanalysis, or the neuropsychiatrist who unleashes a pharmacopoeia of antidepressant drugs on the neurotically depressed patient. According to Klerman (24), the use of one type of psychotherapy or pharmacological intervention in treating affective disorders is not supported by the literature. Affective illnesses are highly heterogeneous in origin. Treatment decisions will depend on careful evaluation of the patient according to rapidly developing research data.

In *Osheroff v. Chestnut Lodge* (25), Dr. Osheroff asserted he was inappropriately treated with psychotherapy for a major depression, needlessly extending his stay at Chestnut Lodge for over 7 months and causing him further emotional and financial harm. In January 1984, the state of Maryland Health Claims Arbitration Board found Chestnut Lodge liable, awarding $250,000 to Dr. Osheroff (26). In essence, the arbitration panel imposed a quasi-judicial standard of care, rejecting the treatment of depression solely by dynamic psychotherapy as a respected minority position. Both sides appealed as permitted under Maryland statute. The case was eventually settled for an undisclosed sum (27).

Dr. Osheroff alleged that Chestnut Lodge "negligently failed to diagnose by appropriate means a biological depression." Also, he added that the Lodge "negligently failed to treat this biologic depression by appropriate means." Furthermore, the staff at Chestnut Lodge "failed to obtain informed consent of the patient by failing to disclose to and discuss with him alternative therapeutic modalities and the cost/benefits of each of these alternatives" (28).

The *Osheroff* case immediately became a cause célèbre for the proponents of biological psychiatry. A storm of controversy surfaced between biological and psychodynamic psychiatry. Legal commentators carefully analyzed *Osheroff* and its implications for psychiatry (29). Years later, the controversy raised by *Osheroff* continued to be debated by Klerman (30) and Stone (31).

What are *practice parameters*? How will they affect the standard of care?

In just a few years, an explosion in the development of practice guidelines has occurred. More than a 1,000 guidelines have been published (32). More than 30 organizations, including governmental and other agencies, are busy crafting additional guidelines.

In 1989, the Physician Payment Review Commission called for the development of clinical practice guidelines (33). In response, the American Medical Association (AMA) and the national medical specialty societies established a process called *practice parameters* to guide the development of strategies to assure high-quality, cost-effective care (34). Practice parameters encompass guidelines, standards, and other patient management strategies. The standards reflect generally accepted principles of patient management (35).

The AMA advises that practice parameters may be introduced into evidence at trial as proof of what the standard of care should be in a given case. The opposing counsel may introduce rebuttal evidence that the parameter was not applicable to the clinical situation encountered by the physician (34). Clinicians must never forget that no "official" standard of patient care can substitute for sound clinical judgment based on the special needs of a given patient. Individual professional judgment has been acknowledged by the AMA in formulating practice parameters. The guidelines are not intended to be followed rigidly but are available to establish a range of appropriate clinical care (36).

Once a practice parameter is admitted into evidence, the court is not obligated to apply it as a predetermined standard of care. The court maintains full discretion in considering other evidence concerning the standard of care. Moreover, the court may reach conclusions that are contrary to the practice parameter if it finds other evidence more persuasive (37).

The American Psychiatric Association (APA), through its Task Force on Treatments of Psychiatric Disorders, has published a complete, multivolume text on the treatment of psychiatric disorders (38). While the book is not an officially sanctioned publication of the APA, psychiatrists are concerned that the medical practice guidelines in this publication will be adopted by courts as an inflexible standard of care. Meanwhile, the APA has established the Work Group on Practice Parameters to begin work on developing practice guidelines (39). The APA practice guidelines will include a disclaimer that guidelines are not to be used as medical directives. Individual cases and circumstances differ and technologies continue to evolve (40).

How is harm to the patient determined?

Even if a deviation from a reasonable standard of care occurs, malpractice cannot be assessed when there is no harm to the patient. The courts rely on the testimony of expert witnesses to determine the presence or absence of harm to the plaintiff. Until the 1960s and 1970s, the courts generally denied liability in negligence actions causing emotional distress in the absence of physical injury or impact (15). (The first American decision permitting recovery for emotional damage without physical injury occurred in 1905 [41].) Slovenko (15) quotes the famous dissent of Justice Musmanno of the Pennsylvania Supreme Court protesting the continued application of the physical injury requirement in which a plaintiff suffered fright and shock after being chased by a straying bull. Because the bull did not strike the plaintiff, the suit was dismissed, arousing Justice Musmanno to say that he would "continue to dissent from [the logic of such cases] until the cows come home" (42).

In *Christy Bros. Circus v. Turnage* (43), a Georgia court stretched the injury requirement by finding harm when a horse in the circus show defecated on the lap of a lady spectator, causing her great embarrassment. Although the courts now are finding compensable psychic impairment without physical injury or impact, judges and juries remain skeptical of the claim of emotional injury in the absence of physical damage. The proof of psychic injury or its causes is considered highly speculative.

In allegations of psychiatric malpractice, the presence of emotional injury can be very difficult to determine because emotional difficulties may preexist. Furthermore, the emotional injury claimed may be a result of the natural progression of the emotional or mental disorder being treated rather than caused by the psychiatrist's negligent actions.

In the clinical vignette, emotional injury is much easier to prove because of the associated brain damage caused by the suicide attempt. The degree of brain damage is pertinent. If no brain damage occurred, the plaintiff could still allege physical and mental suffering associated with an unnecessarily prolonged hospital course and an improperly treated depression and subsequent suicide attempt and its ramifications. The plaintiff's attorney will state that if prompt, appropriate treatment of Mrs. Powell's depression had been implemented, her prolonged mental suffering and suicide attempt resulting in brain injury would not have occurred.

What is the legal meaning of proximate cause?

When a psychiatrist deviates from a standard of care in the diagnosis and treatment of a patient and the patient alleges damage, no malpractice can be assigned unless the damage is the result of the deviation from the standard of care.

The law divides causation into two categories: cause-in-fact and legal or proximate cause (44). Cause-in-fact is expressed by the "but for" rule and asks the question: But for the conduct of the psychiatrist, would the patient have suffered the injury? If the injury would have occurred without the psychiatrist's conduct, no causation exists. If there is more than one cause of injury, the "but for" test might deny recovery in multiple causation.

When several causes act together to bring about an injury of which any one alone would have been sufficient to cause the injury, courts apply the "substantial factor" test (45). For example, two fires meet at a warehouse and burn it down. Either fire alone would have destroyed the warehouse. Applying the "but for" test, one could conclude that neither fire was the cause of the damage because the warehouse would have been burned by the other. The courts avoid this conundrum by considering all the causes that were substantial factors in causing damage or injury.

When two or more individuals have been negligent but uncertainty exists about who caused the plaintiff's injury, the "alternative cause" approach may be applied. The plaintiff must prove that harm has been caused by one of the individuals, even though the plaintiff is uncertain as to which one. The burden of proof shifts to the defendants, and each must show that his or her negligence was not the actual cause. For example, two shotguns are negligently fired in the direction of the plaintiff, who is hit by a pellet. The plaintiff cannot determine which shotgun fired the shot. Under the alternative cause approach, the defendants who fired the guns will have to prove that the pellet did not come from their gun. If neither defendant is able to do so, both may be liable.

In addition to the cause-in-fact, the defendant's act or omission must be the proximate cause of the injury. Proximate or legal cause exists when an uninterrupted chain of events occurs from the time of the defendant's negligent conduct to the time of the plaintiff's injury. Intervening causes may occur after the time of the negligent act but combine with the negligent act to cause injury to the plaintiff. In short, the defendant is liable for harm caused by foreseeable intervening forces. For example, a physician who is initially negligent in harming a patient is usually liable for aggravation of the patient's condition caused by the negligent conduct of the subsequent treating physician.

A superseding intervening factor, on the other hand, breaks the causal connection between the initial wrongful conduct and the ultimate injury and becomes a direct, immediate cause of such injury. An intervening force is superseding when it is not foreseeable and relieves the first actor from liability. As an example, suppose a physician carelessly leaves samples of benzodiazepines lying about the office. A patient, prone to abusing drugs, takes a bottle of benzodiazepines without the physician's knowledge and begins self-medicating. The patient becomes drowsy while driving and has an accident, injuring another person. The patient's unforeseeable act is a superseding intervening factor cutting off liability for the physician's original negligent conduct.

The concept of proximate cause is extremely elusive. It has little resemblance to Aristotelian logic as applied to scientific inquiry. Proximate cause is used as a convenience for public policy considerations and a rough sense of justice (46). The law arbitrarily stops tracing the causes of a series of events beyond a certain point. Thus, proximate cause often refers to the last factor in a series of events, the straw that breaks the camel's back, rather than first or primary causes.

Causation of emotional and mental illness is imperfectly understood. To distinguish emotional harm allegedly caused by the psychiatrist's negligent act or omission from the natural course of the disorder or from other causes in the patient's life can be very difficult. Medical causation is quite different from the legal concept of proximate cause.

In the vignette, Mrs. Powell's attorneys will argue that "but for" Dr. Jenkins's negligent diagnosis and treatment, Mrs. Powell would not have suffered deterioration in her clinical condition, leading to a suicide attempt and brain damage. The attorney will further proffer that the negligent diagnosis and treatment were the direct and uninterrupted cause of harm to Mrs. Powell.

What standard of proof is required in malpractice cases?

When a malpractice case goes to trial, the jury is instructed on the standard of proof required. Malpractice cases are civil suits requiring plaintiffs to prove their allegations by a preponderance of the evidence. "Preponderance of the evidence" is defined as the weight of evidence (51% versus 49% for the plaintiff to prevail). Criminal proceedings require that a defendant's guilt be proven beyond a reasonable doubt (90% to 95% range of certainty). In *Addington v. Texas* (47), the Supreme Court determined that the level of evidence for civil commitment proceedings must be at least clear and convincing (75% range of certainty). Percentages are used merely to illustrate the legal concepts. The law does not attempt to assign percentages to these standards of proof.

Because malpractice cases are determined by a preponderance of the evidence, the outcome of these suits is somewhat difficult to predict. Thus defendants who perceive themselves as being vulnerable for heavy damages may often choose to settle for a given amount rather than risk open-ended liability.

What kinds of damages are assessed against the psychiatrist who is found liable for malpractice?

Damages are divided into three classes: compensatory, nominal, and punitive. Compensatory damages are based on the principle that the plaintiff should be restored to his or her preinjury condition (48). Compensatory damages include, among others, payment for impairment of work ability, past and future loss of earnings, care giving, medical expenses, and intangible damages such as physical and mental pain and suffering, loss of normal life, inconvenience, and humiliation.

The court may make a distinction between general and special damages. Special damages include medical expenses, past and future lost wages, and other out-of-pocket expenses (49). The cost of litigation and attorney's fees are borne by the litigants separately and are not part of the damages assessed, unless otherwise provided by law. Nominal damages are awarded in cases in which an actual or technical wrong has been suffered that cannot be translated into dollar terms, such as when certain rights are violated. The fact-finder may make a symbolic award of one dollar.

Punitive damages are awarded to punish the offender and serve as a public warning to others that certain actions or behavior will not be tolerated. Punitive damages are awarded when the defendant's conduct is reckless, malicious, willful, or wanton. The amount awarded is at the discretion of the judge or jury. Some states do not permit awards for punitive damages. Punitive damages may be awarded in civil rights actions when the psychiatrist acts with malice or reckless disregard of the patient's civil rights. The patient does not have to suffer an actual loss to recover damages. Because punitive damages are personal to the injured party, if the patient dies while the case is in court, these damages cannot be awarded to beneficiaries, except in certain states.

In the lawsuit against Dr. Jenkins, punitive damages will probably not be claimed. There are no allegations of wanton, malicious, or reckless conduct. Compensatory damages will be sought for medical expenses, loss of work capacity and income, and physical and mental suffering.

Under what legal theories may a psychiatrist be sued?

Psychiatrists may be sued by their patients, by injured third parties, by relatives of a deceased patient under wrongful death statutes, or by a group of patients in a class-action suit.

In addition to negligence suits, psychiatrists may be sued for the intentional torts of assault, battery, false imprisonment, defamation, fraud or misrepresentation, invasion of privacy, and the intentional infliction of emotional distress. If the plaintiff has difficulty establishing all elements of an action for malpractice, a claim for relief may be brought under breach-of-contract theory (50) or based on deprivation of civil rights. A claim based on an express contract theory may be successful if the plaintiff proves that the psychiatrist expressly guaranteed a result (51).

Psychiatrists may also be liable for constitutional claims. Public hospitals and their mental health professionals may be liable for violation of rights guaranteed patients by the United States Constitution, by state constitutions, or by federal civil rights statutes (52). Class action suits have been successfully filed by patients during the past decade under the Civil Rights Act alleging violation of the due-process clause of the Fourteenth Amendment in state admission standards and procedures (53), the right to protection and safety (54), the right to adequate treatment (55), and the right to refuse treatment (56). In *O'Connor v. Donaldson* (57), a right-to-treatment case, monetary damages were awarded the plaintiff but were overturned on appeal. Whereas a few patients have recovered damages, most have sought equitable relief, either *mandating* public officials to provide certain minimal constitutional rights, or *enjoining* them from violating such rights.

The Civil Rights Act states:

> Every person who, under color of any statute, ordinance, regulation, custom, or usage, of any state or territory subjects or causes to be subjected, any citizen of the United States or other person within its jurisdiction thereof to the deprivation of any rights, privileges, or immunities secured by the Constitution and laws, shall be

liable to the party injured in an action at law, as suit in equity, or other proper proceeding for redress.

Two essential elements must be established to maintain an action under section 1983 of the Civil Rights Act. The patient must establish that the conduct in question is committed by an individual acting "under color" of state or territorial law, custom, or usage and that the conduct deprived the patient of rights, privileges, or immunities secured by the Constitution or United States laws. Under civil rights statutes, two kinds of rights are protected: substantive and procedural rights. The Fifth Amendment creates due-process procedural rights that protect against deprivations of life, liberty, or property, and this protection has been applied to the states through the Fourteenth Amendment.

Constitutional torts against federal hospitals and their employees based directly on violation of the U.S. Constitution raise complex litigation issues. Civil rights claims against state and county hospitals and their employees for violations of civil rights based on 42 U.S.C. § 1983 are narrowly defined. For example, § 1983 actions are not applicable to private hospitals and their employees, even if the hospitals receive public monies and are regulated by state/local laws. Mental health professionals working in federal and state institutions should determine whether their malpractice insurance covers constitutional torts.

Hospitals have a level of control over patients that provides ample opportunities for violation of patients' civil rights (58). Denial of the patient's right to vote in a federal election or the right to practice his or her religion would be cause for a civil rights action against the responsible person. After *Gerrard v. Blackman* (59), monitoring the patient's calls to an attorney by the psychiatrist could be the basis of a possible civil rights action, provided that the plaintiff sufficiently establishes state action.

In *Jobsen v. Henne* (60), the patient was assigned uncompensated work for 16 hours a day that was not part of a therapy program or related to the patient's housekeeping needs. The court held that a cause of action existed based on violation of the Thirteenth Amendment guaranteeing the patient's right of freedom from involuntary servitude. In another case, a patient who was a vegetarian for religious reasons was denied a special diet. The court (61), although realizing that the patient may have stated a cause of action, refused to award damages for civil rights violation because the plaintiff was unable to prove physical injury.

When a mental health professional acts under color of law as a state executive official, he or she is entitled to qualified immunity that is similar to sovereign immunity. Although the U.S. Supreme Court has rejected absolute immunity for executive officers from civil rights actions, balancing of individual rights against the needs of decision-makers to be free to exercise discretionary judgments has led to "good faith" immunity for defendants (62).

Therapists, like other citizens, may be sued for ordinary negligence if patients are injured around or within the therapist's office. For this reason, therapists should carry an insurance rider or obtain a separate policy that provides office premise liability insurance. These insurance policies often cover only the key individual on the premises and may not provide coverage for suits brought by patients seen by colleagues renting or sharing office space.

What standard-of-care issues are raised when the psychiatrist enters into an agreement with managed health care providers?

Health maintenance organizations (HMOs), independent practice associations (IPAs), and preferred provider organizations (PPOs) may create additional ethical and legal dilemmas for psychiatrists. Such managed care systems will interject cost and contractual pressures into treatment and dispositional decisions. Psychiatrists must not allow themselves to be put in the position of choosing between patients' need for quality care and the economic and administrative requirements of the health plan (63).

In *Wickline v. California* (64), the treating physician, Dr. Polonsky, requested an extended stay of 8 additional days for his patient following surgery for Leriche's syndrome (occlusion of the terminal aorta). The Medi-Cal reviewer granted 4 days. Mrs. Wickline suffered complications following the premature release, resulting in amputation of her leg. She sued Medi-Cal. The jury ruled in her favor, but a California appellate court decided that the treating physician was liable, not Medi-Cal.

In his testimony, Dr. Polonsky stated that he believed "that Medi-Cal had the power to tell him, as a treating doctor, when a patient must be discharged from the hospital." The appellate court noted that third-party payers of health care services can be held liable when appeals on the behalf of the patients for medical care

> are arbitrarily ignored or unreasonably disregarded or over-ridden. However, the physician who complies without protest with the limitations imposed by a third-party payor, when his medical judgment dictates otherwise, cannot avoid his ultimate responsibility for his patient's care. He cannot point to the health care payor as the liability scapegoat when the consequences of his own determinative medical decision go sour. (64)

The obvious misunderstanding that the surgeon expressed in *Wickline* is probably shared by other physicians concerning their duty and the authority of the third-party payer. The *Wickline* case stands for the unquestionable responsibility that the *doctor* has for a patient's health care. Accordingly, when a physician's decision and the position of a third-party payer conflict, it is the doctor's duty to protest any compromise in patient care that might be presented by a third-party payer. All channels should be pursued to ensure that the doctor's medical judgment (e.g., continued hospitalization) is carried out. Only after a physician has exhausted all options in an attempt to act in the patient's best medical interests can an argument likely be made that no liability attaches to the physician or affiliate hospital.

In a subsequent case, *Wilson v. Blue Cross of Southern California et al.* (65), a California appeals court chose not to follow the specific language of *Wickline.* In *Wilson,* a patient was hospitalized at College Hospital in Los Angeles suffering from anorexia, drug dependency, and major depression. The treating physician determined that the patient required 3 to 4 weeks of hospitalization. After about $1\frac{1}{2}$ weeks, utilization review decided that further hospitalization was unnecessary. The patient's insurance company refused to pay for further inpatient treatment. The patient was discharged, committing suicide a few weeks later.

The Appellate Division of the California Court of Appeals held that third-party payers are not immune from lawsuits in regard to utilization review activities. The court determined that the insurer may be subject to liability for harm caused to the patient by premature termination of a patient's hospitalization. Although the fact pattern of this case differs from *Wickline,* it is clear from the *Wilson* decision that a third-party payer may be held legally liable for a negligent decision to discharge the patient either separately or along with the patient's physician, depending upon the facts of the case. Although *Wickline* and *Wilson* are both California cases, they offer insight and, perhaps, precedence concerning future reasoning by other courts who will be increasingly confronted by complex liability issues concerning utilization review decisions.

Before signing a contract, the psychiatrist must be aware of plan requirements that may interfere with the provision of good clinical care and the traditional doctor-patient relationship. Some plan agreements provide that medical records be made available to other providers in the plan. For patients using managed health care plans who see the psychiatrist in his or her office, it must be explained that the same confidentiality that exists for other patients does not exist for them. Patients also may know other providers in the plan, and they may not want to have psychiatric information disseminated. Some contracts clearly state that the psychiatrist must provide information to administrators that may lead to loss of medical services to the patient. Patients who act in self-destructive or violent ways while refusing to follow a treatment plan may be severed from the plan. All of these issues require the informed consent of the patient before embarking on treatment.

Psychiatrists must realize that their responsibilities to patients are not necessarily limited by the contractual services covered by a managed health care plan. Should the plan decide to limit services to the suicidal or dangerous patient, the psychiatrist's legal duty remains the same as if he or she were treating the patient independently. The psychiatrist must take whatever steps are necessary to care for the patient adequately. The majority of managed health care plans reserve the right to review all hospitalizations, refusing coverage even when the patient is admitted as an emergency, if the plan believes that further treatment is not necessary. If the patient suffers harm as a result and a suit is filed, the plaintiff's attorney can claim that, in order to save money, the physician did not provide the necessary care. Courts will not accept the argument that a plan prevents the physician from providing accepted treatments or from referring the patient to appropriate specialists outside of the plan.

Sometimes, plan contracts will state that the physician must not make any communication or take any action that may adversely affect the confidence of patients in the plan. This does not, however, supersede the psychiatrist's duty to report child abuse or to warn endangered third parties.

The treatment prerogatives of the psychiatrist may be limited by the conditions of a plan. Thus, a limit may be placed on patients requiring long-term hospitalization. The temptation to cut corners in patient treatment can become a malpractice trap. The plan may specify which hospital must be used or require that referrals be made to other providers in the plan. Psychiatrists must not suspend their judgment in making competent dispositions and referrals, because the psychiatrist may be held responsible for making a negligent choice. During periods when the psychiatrist is away, nonparticipating psychiatrists who cover must understand that they will have to accept the fees designated by the health care plan and abide by its review procedures.

Psychiatrists should determine whether the contract contains a "hold harmless" provision that will require indemnification of the plan for any liability arising out of the psychiatrist's practice. Many malpractice policies will not cover any liability assumed under an oral or written agreement such as a contract provision. If the plan is sued because of care provided by the psychiatrist, he or she may be held personally liable for any resulting judgment while having no malpractice insurance to cover it. Obviously, the psychiatrist should consult an attorney before signing any contract with a health provider organization. The liability issues mentioned above are more completely discussed elsewhere (63).

What steps should the psychiatrist take after receiving notice of a malpractice suit?

Most psychiatrists experience a strong emotional reaction upon receiving notice of a complaint or summons. Some psychiatrists report an initial feeling of panic, followed quickly by indignant anger, feelings of betrayal, and dread of the stress and possible publicity involved in a long, drawn-out litigation. Such feelings are natural but should be vented only privately. The need for legal and emotional support is great when the psychiatrist is sued for malpractice (66). With the prior approval of the psychiatrist's attorney, it may be personally helpful to discuss the case with a colleague.

Charles et al. (67) reported a study on the impact of malpractice litigation on physicians' personal and professional lives. Both sued and nonsued physicians reported changes in professional behavior and emotional reactions to both the threat of being sued and actual litigation. Sued physicians reported significantly more symptoms than nonsued physicians. In more than half of the cases studied, the symptoms included one of two clusters descriptive of depressive and stress-induced illnesses. Significantly more sued physicians reported that they were likely to stop seeing certain types of patients, were thinking of retiring early, and were discouraging their children from entering medicine. In a later study, Charles and colleagues (68) found that 23% of 51 physicians sued found the litigation to be the single most stressful period of their lives. In a powerful book entitled *Defendant,* Drs. Sara Charles and Eugene Kennedy describe the ordeal of a 4-year-long malpractice litigation and trial (69).

All records pertinent to the case should be collected and reviewed prior to interviews with the insurer and the attorney assigned to defend the psychiatrist. Insurance carriers request early notification when any unexpected or adverse medical result occurs, when any communication is received from an attorney, or when patients or their families threaten suit or if suit papers are received. A clear copy of the patient's record will be requested by the claims supervisor for the insurance carrier.

Obligations of confidentiality cease on initiation of a suit by the patient. The original record must never be released unless specifically requested by the insurer. The patient's record must never be altered in any way. Not only are there legal penalties for doing so, but also cases that are perfectly defensible from a medical standpoint may be lost because of implications involving the integrity of the defendant. The psychiatrist must never contact the claimant or the claimant's attorney without prior consultation with the insurer and its attorney.

In malpractice suits, plaintiffs have attempted to discover the names, addresses, and, on occasion, the case histories of other patients treated by the physician to establish a pattern giving credence to the complaint. Thus, a patient complaining of sexual exploitation may appear more credible if other patients of the physician come forward to testify of similar incidents. Generally, such discovery is not permitted on the ground of privilege or relevancy (70). In the future, malpractice plaintiffs may have greater access to medical records and peer review documents that today are considered confidential. More courts are placing the public interest ahead of private interests in liability cases.

The APA Legal Consultation Plan (71) recommends taking certain steps after an adverse incident such as a suicide. The psychiatrist has potentially conflicting concerns to ensure that the patient's records are complete, to assist grieving family members, to ensure that incidents similar in nature do not occur again, and to protect against a claim of malpractice.

The patient's records must be brought up to date. To avoid any suggestion of impropriety, all entries made after the incident should be so dated. Rough notes should be kept. Self-serving, exculpatory statements as well as lengthy entries where previously briefer notations were made must be avoided. Before litigation begins, if a conflict exists with the nurse's notes, a meeting with the nurse, supervisor, and other doctors involved in the case should be considered. At such a meeting, the conflict should be discussed to see if it can be honestly reconciled. If it can, the correction should be made and a jointly prepared memorandum fully describing the circumstances should be signed by all parties and placed in the files. The psychiatrist's attorney should be present.

Conversations with family members are appropriate and can allay grief and assist family members to obtain help. Care must be exercised not to reveal confidential information about the patient and to avoid making self-incriminating statements. Such statements may further distress the family and provide a spur to litigation.

The psychiatrist should consult with an attorney before making any oral or written statements to other providers. Information regarding the care and follow-up of a patient should be provided immediately. A detailed account of the incident in question or statements apportioning responsibility should not be made before consultation with an attorney. For instance, details revealed to the hospital about the incident may later be used against the psychiatrist if the hospital attempts to shift responsibility to the attending psychiatrist.

A complete and candid report about the adverse incident should be made to the malpractice attorney or carrier. The report is privileged and cannot be used against the psychiatrist in court. Rather than permitting the insurer to raise the psychiatrist's insurance premium, a detailed report will allow for the best possible defense or settlement, perhaps contributing by lowering adverse experience for the carrier.

Should the psychiatrist who is sued retain a personal attorney in addition to the attorney provided by the insurance carrier?

Psychiatrists who "go bare" (i.e., have no malpractice insurance) will need to hire their own personal attorney immediately. Hiring a personal attorney in any case may be wise. Most attorneys hired by the insurer to represent the psychiatrist are competent and scrupulously honest. Some attorneys, however, may not be particularly expert in malpractice litigation, let alone the unique aspects of psychiatric malpractice. Furthermore, the attorney hired by the insurance company may have a potential conflict of interest in representing both the insurance company and the defendant psychiatrist. This conflict may surface when the insurance company wants to settle a claim and the defendant psychiatrist wants to fight on to the bitter end. Psychiatrists should understand that because the attorney hired by the insurance company may feel dependent on business from the insurance carrier, a conflict of interest could develop in regard to pressing the defendant psychiatrist's case against the carrier's wishes.

Insurance policies may or may not allow for the psychiatrist's permission prior to any settlement. Some carriers permit the psychiatrist to make the decision about settlement but hold the psychiatrist responsible for any amount of the award beyond the settlement offer. When there is an opportunity to settle a case for less than the policy limit but the insurer's attorney demurs, a personal attorney can write to the insurer and demand that it accept the plaintiff's settlement offer. If the company refuses, a basis may exist for claiming a waiver of the policy limit should the verdict exceed the insurance coverage. For these reasons, the psychiatrist being sued for malpractice may want to retain the services of a personal attorney who is expert in the area of psychiatric malpractice and who will represent solely the interests of the defendant psychiatrist. Competent attorneys hired by the insurer should welcome the collaboration of the defendant's personal attorney.

Sanbar (72) states that certain "red flags" should cause the defendant physician to consider hiring a personal attorney in a malpractice suit. If the insurance carrier sends a reservation-of-rights letter to the insured physician indicating that insurance coverage is being withheld, a personal attorney should be hired. The personal attorney can also assist in settlement negotiations and in conflict-of-interest situations (i.e., multiple defendants). In the event that the insurer will not cover damages, a request may be granted by the insurer for retaining the attorney of the defendant physician's choice. A counterclaim for unpaid bills or countersuits should be handled only by the personal attorney. Approximately 14% of physicians involved in malpractice actions use personal attorneys.

Sanbar (72) also notes a little known practice among defense attorneys hired by the insurer that may present a conflict of interest. A secret report written about the incident by the defense attorney to the insurance carrier could contain derogatory statements about the insured physician. This letter goes into the physician's file and will never be seen by the physician. To guard against this practice, Sanbar recommends writing a letter to the defense attorney indicating that a copy of any correspondence to the carrier regarding the malpractice claim against the physician be sent to the latter.

Alton (73) disagrees with automatically retaining a personal attorney. He feels that it is unnecessary and possibly harmful to the physician's interests. He states that most personal attorneys are not expert in medical malpractice defense. Furthermore, the personal attorney feels compelled to participate, possibly interfering with the conduct of the case. If a malpractice defense expert is hired, Alton feels that it will be expensive, and that a battle of egos may ensue that will undercut the case. He states:

> Your defense must be consistent, clear, strong, honest, and smoothly presented. You cannot afford ill feeling and fighting between members of the defense team. There can be only one chief—one attorney who will take the responsibility for and make the decisions, often on the spur of the moment, that will constitute your defense.

Alton feels that an exception to this advice occurs when the insurance company has hired inferior counsel and refuses to make a replacement.

Are there any reassuring facts for the clinician about psychiatric malpractice litigation?

In most instances, the successful prosecution of a psychiatric malpractice suit is a difficult task. The burden is on the plaintiff to prove by a preponderance of the evidence that all four elements—duty of care, breach of the duty, causation, and damage—are present. In a study by Slawson (74), 50% of the claims against psychiatrists were dropped before legal action was initiated, 25% involved some litigation activity, 19% percent were settled out of court for an agreed-upon sum of money, and only 6% went to court. Thus, the psychiatrist may take solace in the finding that only 20% of the cases were favorably litigated by the plaintiff.

Slawson and Guggenheim (75) report that malpractice actions against psychiatrists between 1974 and 1978 represented only 0.3% of 77,788 claims against all physicians. This figure is significantly below the percentage of practicing psychiatrists among all practicing physicians, and the percentage of the nation's patients seen by psychiatrists. Even though the number of malpractice suits filed against psychiatrists over the years has steadily increased, the number still is relatively low compared with other medical specialties. Psychiatrists must now carry substantial coverage, because the size of damage awards has been increasing. Publicity is rare unless the case is notorious or involves sexual misconduct. Armed with these facts, Slawson and Guggenheim (75) feel that psychiatrists can continue to provide good clinical care without undue interference from fears and fantasies about litigation and its consequences.

What are the legal procedural steps in a malpractice suit that goes to trial?

Rules of procedure and evidence permit a judge and jury to hear all relevant facts that both parties present in a dispute. The following outline, adapted from Beis (76), proceeds from the initial summons through the post-trial motions.

1. **Complaint.**   A summons containing the complaint is prepared and served upon the therapist. The complaint sets forth the general allegations that support the cause of action.
2. **Motions.**   Motions are made to the court for various kinds of relief including clarification of the complaint. A motion to dismiss the complaint may be made by the defendant if the claim is not recognized by law.
3. **Answer.**   A written response to the specific allegations is made to the plaintiff's complaint. The answer may also assert affirmative defenses.
4. **Discovery.**   The formal investigation of the other side's allegations, including:

   a. Written interrogatories
   b. Oral depositions

    c. Production of documents

    d. Physical and mental examinations

    e. Request for the admission of facts

5. **Pretrial conference.** In some jurisdictions, a pretrial conference is required with the judge, attorneys, and, in some instances, the patient attending. Settlement is discussed as well as methods of expediting and simplifying the trial.

6. **Trial.** The following is a rough outline of the major stages of a malpractice trial:

    a. Selection of jury

    b. Opening statements

    c. Testimony of witnesses and the introduction of other evidence

    d. Motion for directed verdict by defendant's attorney

    e. Rebuttal evidence by plaintiff

    f. Renewal of motion for directed verdict

    g. Closing arguments

    h. Jury instructions

    i. Jury decision

    j. Post-trial motions

A more complete discussion of procedural matters in civil litigation can be found in Beis's excellent book.

As of this writing, a number of states have authorized some form of arbitration of medical malpractice cases, and other states are considering it. Arbitration first appeared in American medicine in 1929. In recent years, arbitration has been gaining favor. Psychiatrists must carefully consider the pros and cons of voluntary arbitration in malpractice cases. A 1975 California Medical Association brochure, cited by Carlova (77), states: "Arbitration, . . . like a prescription medication, may not necessarily be good for everyone, everywhere. Each physician should evaluate his/her own practice and decide whether or not to adopt the patient-physician arbitration agreement."

Should the psychiatrist file a countersuit in response to a patient's malpractice suit?

Even when patients file a frivolous or nuisance suit, the psychiatrist should forgo the temptation to retaliate with a countersuit (78). Few countersuits are successful, and legal fees may double. Insurance carriers do not pay the legal costs of a countersuit. Proving that the patient brought the suit maliciously is difficult, and the legal problems are prodigious (79). The filing of a countersuit will extend the psychiatrist's involvement with the litigation and its disruptive effect on family life, personal equanimity, and professional practice. Most psychiatrists require peace and quiet in their lives in order to perform their work properly. The legal arena is a boisterous and unfriendly place for the psychiatrist who wants to maintain the professional calm necessary in treating emotionally disturbed patients.

Is there a national clearinghouse that will maintain data on malpractice suits and disciplinary actions against physicians?

Yes. On September 1, 1990, the U.S. government created the National Practitioner Data Bank containing the records of malpractice suits and disciplinary actions against physicians, dentists, and other health care professionals (80). The data bank was mandated by the Health Care Quality Improvement Act of 1986 (81). The purpose of such a bank is to centralize the reporting of disciplinary actions by state licensing boards, hospitals, and state medical societies against physicians. As a result, errant physicians will be prevented from moving to other states in order to escape the consequences of negligent or unprofessional actions. Interested parties (e.g., state licensing agencies, hospital review boards) can assess whether applicants have ever had disciplinary or civil suits successfully brought against them, including all settled cases.

Hospitals, health maintenance organizations, professional societies, and state medical boards, as well as other health care organizations, are required to report any disciplinary actions against providers that last longer than 30 days. Disciplinary actions include limitation and suspension or revocation of privileges or membership in a professional society. Insurers who make malpractice payments on behalf of providers, including settlements, are required to participate. Immunity from liability is granted for those health care entities and providers making peer review reports in good faith (82). Any disciplinary actions or malpractice payments made by physicians must be reported to the data bank. Failure to report is subject to civil monetary penalties of up to $10,000 for each unreported incident.

Hospitals must query the data bank for information about physicians who make application for hospital privileges. Every 2 years, the data bank must also be queried regarding physicians holding current staff privileges or lose immunity for professional peer review activities.

An additional, and quite valuable, consequence of the data bank is that it prevents errant professionals from changing hospitals or leaving the state in order to avoid detection of this information. Undoubtedly, this will be very useful in rooting out incompetent professionals. Nevertheless, the mere fact of an adverse judgment against the doctor in a malpractice suit proves nothing. It does not necessarily mean that the physician is incompetent or that the physician committed malpractice. The accurate reporting of such a judgment or prior disciplinary action will provide an inquiring agency the opportunity to investigate the relevancy and significance of the prior judgment.

Nevertheless, the National Practitioner Data Bank is creating considerable controversy. Legal commentators fear that the data bank will discourage settlement of legal claims, discourage hospital peer review, encourage litigation against hospitals over privileges, and lower standards of medical practice (83). Frivolous or nuisance suits will more likely be actively defended by physicians.

The public will not have access to the data bank. Plaintiffs' attorneys can have access to the data bank only if they can prove that the hospital failed to query the data bank regarding the physician in question. The information obtained can be used only to sue the hospital for negligent credentialing (84). Physicians can request information from the data bank about their own file without paying the $2 standard fee per name.

What do national loss statistics show about the type and frequency of psychiatric malpractice suits?

Slawson and Guggenheim (75) examined the outcome of 217 malpractice actions against psychiatrists from 1974 to 1978 using the detailed analysis of the National Association of Insurance Commissioners' nationwide study of 71,788 malpractice claims filed against physicians in the United States.

Ten psychiatric procedures accounted for nearly 50% of all psychiatric claims: tranquilizers, 17; psychotherapy, 16; mental health evaluations, 16; electroconvulsive therapy (ECT), 13; general psychiatric examination, 13; general medical examination, 9; unspecified drug, 8; antidepressant drug, 6; neglect, 6; and other psychoactive drugs, 4. The most common complaint about psychiatric procedures was that they were improperly done or not indicated. The average indemnity paid to patients harmed by these procedures was $26,000. The average indemnity for tranquilizers was $5,000, and for ECT, $3,500. The largest average paid indemnity, $109,000, was paid for the general examination category. Both the patients and the psychiatrists involved in the malpractice litigation were middle aged. More often than not, the psychiatrists were board certified, and the majority were in private practice.

The 10 most frequent causes of injuries in psychiatric claims accounted for 95 (44%) of the total claims: diagnostic errors, 36; suicide or self-injury, 26; death, 7; medical complications, 7; inadequate physical examination, 6; surgical complications, 5; tranquilizers, 4; and antidepressants, 4. The average indemnity paid for the 10 most frequent categories was $21,500.

The 10 most frequently listed psychiatric diagnoses accounted for 112 (52%) of the claims: depressive neurosis, 32; other neuroses, 20; psychosis (type not specified), 13; paranoid psychosis, 13; schizophrenia, 14; anxiety neurosis, 5; major affective disorders, 4; general psychiatric examination, 4; schizoaffective disorder, 4; and depressive disorder not elsewhere classified, 3. The neuroses, which were the largest diagnostic group, were associated with 16 fatalities and 6 permanent injuries with an average indemnity of $44,000. The largest indemnity paid was $250,000, for injury leading to blindness that resulted from a homicidal assault.

Although underreporting of suits against psychiatrists may have skewed the figures, the claims against psychiatrists represented only 0.3% of the 71,788 claims against all physicians. Slawson and Guggenheim feel that the data indirectly support the inference that the psychiatrist's facility with interpersonal relationships is a significant factor in maintaining low malpractice rates.

Psychiatry claims closed by a medical protective company between 1980 and 1985 are listed in Table 24-2. Suicide attempts accounted for the highest percentage of claims and percentage of dollars paid.

Data from the AMA published in the December 14, 1987, issue of *U.S. News & World Report* indicated that for every 100 malpractice suits, claims against psychiatrists *before 1981* amounted to 0.6. This figure increased to 2.4 out of 100 in 1985 (85). These figures must be placed in proper perspective. From these AMA data, it is clear that lawsuits against psychiatrists remain relatively low compared with all other medical specialties. In another study, only the specialty of pathology was lower than psychiatry (86).

Psychiatry ranks eighth among medical specialties in relative frequency of malpractice suits (4). Normally, if liability was imposed, tangible physical injury was demonstrated. Suits usually arise in all medical specialties when an unexpected bad result occurs, a large bill is owed, and the relationship between physician and patient has been poor (87). Gutheil (88) notes that psychiatric malpractice suits are the result of bad results and bad feelings. Suits against psychiatrists have been primarily for negligent diagnosis and evaluation, improper certification for commitment, suicide, mismanagement of somatic therapies, breach of confidentiality, and undue familiarity with patients. In the author's experience, malpractice suits in psychiatry most commonly occur fol-

TABLE 24–2. Psychiatry claims closed, 1980–1985

	Percentage of claims	Percentage of dollars
Incarceration/suicide attempts	21	42
Drugs (overdose or addiction)	20	10
Miscellaneous (failure to diagnose physical condition, breach of contract, and other claims	18	8
Psychotherapy/depression	14	3
Failure to treat psychosis	14	5
Restraints (paralysis or fracture)	7	16
Sexual misconduct	6	16

Source. Adapted from "Psychiatric claims closed 1980–1985." *Medical Protective Co. Protector* (Ft Wayne) 3(3):2, 1986

lowing suicide, undue familiarity, and medical complications.

Halleck (89) points out that certain expectations of due care appear with regularity in malpractice cases. A lack of diligence rather than a lack of skill accounts for more lawsuits, but negligence is not just confined to carelessness. Therapists who diagnose and treat beyond their skills are vulnerable to lawsuits. Moreover, psychiatrists must have command of the English language. Although foreign medical graduates may have an excellent knowledge of grammar, idiomatic expressions may not be understood or may be misunderstood. Careful supervision is necessary for psychiatrists who are not fluent in English. Other deficiencies in due care include failure to seek consultation in areas of skill limitations, not obtaining previous records of treatment, failure to follow up a patient's progress, and, in particular, failure to warn of side effects and to give precautions in taking psychoactive drugs.

The number of suits against psychiatrists is said to be small because of the patient's reluctance to expose a psychiatric history, the difficulty proving that the treatment was the cause of injury, and the psychiatrist's skill in managing the patient's negative feelings. Judging by the steep rise in current premiums for professional liability insurance for psychiatrists, psychiatry's reputation as a litigation backwater may be rapidly changing. In an effort to combat the rising costs of malpractice premiums, the APA insurance affiliate Psychiatrists' Mutual Insurance Company has adopted an "experience rating" standard. A psychiatrist who is subject to a "significant" claim will incur a 50% rate increase for the 3 years following the claim (90).

How should malpractice statistics be evaluated by clinicians?

A review of published data over 30 years reveals few statistically valid data. Even though the number of lawsuits against psychiatrists has increased steadily over time, any other conclusion based on these data is speculative. Smith (91) discusses a number of reasons for this lack of confidence:

> The majority of this information is simply generalizations from the closed insurance files of a single insurance carrier or extremely limited sample pools. As a result, the total sample size is small. Moreover, the figures and supporting data published with these and other studies are poorly organized, lack operational definitions, and consistently fail to control for numerous contaminating and other variables that will skew the results. For instance, multiple law suits against a single doctor, settled cases that are unrecorded, suits that are filed but later dismissed are all *not* accounted for.

Simon and Sadoff (78) note that any reference to these studies should be done with caution. The value of these studies appears to be for purposes of illustration and gross generalization only. Any reliance on malpractice data to make finite cause-and-effect conclusions is risky. Unfortunately, the dearth of "hard data" forces individuals, groups, organizations, and agencies studying malpractice to speculate when developing prevention policies and professional education. It is likely, given the lack of alternative sources of information for more accurate data, that this speculation leads to underestimating the seriousness of psychiatric malpractice.

References

1. Klein JI, Macbeth JE, Onek JN: Legal Issues in the Private Practice of Psychiatry. Washington, DC, American Psychiatric Press, 1984, p 2
2. Simon RI: Psychiatric Interventions and Malpractice: A Primer for Liability Prevention. Springfield, IL, Charles C Thomas, 1982, p 7
3. Klein JI, Macbeth JE, Onek JN: Legal Issues in the Private Practice of Psychiatry. Washington, DC, American Psychiatric Press, 1984, p 3
4. Slovenko R: Forensic psychiatry, in Comprehensive Textbook of Psychiatry IV, Vol 2. Edited by Kaplan HI, Sadock BJ. Baltimore, MD, Williams & Wilkins, 1985, pp 1960–1990
5. American Psychiatric Association: Diagnostic and Statistical Manual of Mental Disorders. Washington, DC, American Psychiatric Association
6. Lazare A: Hidden conceptual models in clinical psychiatry. N Engl J Med 288:345–351, 1973
7. Stone AA: The new paradox of psychiatric malpractice. N Engl J Med 311:1384–1387, 1984
8. Colten RJ: The professional liability of behavioral scientists: an overview. Behavioral Sciences and the Law 1:9–22, 1983
9. Keeton WB: Medical negligence: the standard of care. Texas Tech Law Review 10:351–354, 1979
10. 356 NW2d 762 (Minn Ct App 1984), rev'd, Lundgren v Eustermann, 370 NW2d 877 (Minn 1985)
11. 13 Cal 3d 177, 118 Cal Rptr 129, 529 P2d 553 (1974), reargued, 17 Cal 3d 425, 131 Cal Rptr 14, 551 P2d 334 (1976)
12. 83 Wash 2d 514, 519 P2d 981 (1974), superseded by statute, Harbeson v Parke-Davis, Inc, 98 Wash 2d 460, 656 P2d 483 (1983)
13. Hirsh HL: Judicially imposed standard of care: prophecy in medicine. Medical Trial Technique Quarterly 28:1–8, 1980
14. 464 F2d 772 DC Cir, cert den, 409 U.S. 1064 (1972)
15. Slovenko R: Malpractice in psychiatry and related fields. Journal of Psychiatry and Law 9:5–63, 1981
16. Simon RI: The practice of psychotherapy: legal liabilities of an "impossible" profession, in American Psychiatric Press Review of Clinical Psychiatry and the Law, Vol 2. Edited by Simon RI. Washington, DC, American Psychiatric Press, 1991, pp 3–91
17. 69 Cal 2d 420, 71 Cal Rptr 903, 445 P2d 519 (1968)
18. Psychiatrists must be aware of psychiatric quality screens. Psychiatric News 25(17):24–26, 1990

19. Merril TS: Does psychiatry need standards of care? Practice guidelines are now available. Clinical Psychiatry News 17(7):1, 18, 1989

20. King JH: The Law of Medical Malpractice, 2nd Edition. St Paul, MN, West Publishing, 1986, p 58

21. American Psychiatric Association: The Principles of Medical Ethics With Annotations Especially Applicable to Psychiatry. Washington, DC, American Psychiatric Association, 1989

22. Holder AR: Failure to "keep up" as negligence. The Best of Law and Medicine 116:107, 1973

23. Weintraub A: Physician's duty to stay abreast of current medical developments. Medical Trial Technique Quarterly 31:329–341, 1985

24. Klerman GL: Depression related disorders of mood (affective disorders), in The New Harvard Guide to Psychiatry. Edited by Nicholi AM. Cambridge, MA, Harvard University Press, 1988, pp 309–336

25. 62 Md App 519 490, cert denied, Chestnut Lodge, Inc v Osheroff, 304 Md 163, 497 A2d 1163 (1985)

26. Malcolm JG: Treatment choices and informed consent in psychiatry: implications of the Osheroff case for the profession. Journal of Psychiatry and Law 14:9–107, 1986

27. Psychotherapy negligence suit settled privately. Clinical Psychiatry News 15(11):9, 1987

28. State of Maryland Health Claims Arbitration Board, Amended Statement of Claim HCA No 82-262

29. Malcolm JG: Treatment Choices and Informed Consent. Springfield, IL, Charles C Thomas, 1988

30. Klerman GL: The psychiatric patient's right to effective treatment: implications of Osheroff v Chestnut Lodge. Am J Psychiatry 147:409–418, 1990

31. Stone AA: Law, science, and psychiatric malpractice: a response to Klerman's indictment of psychoanalytic psychiatry. Am J Psychiatry 147:419–427, 1990

32. McIntyre JS: News from the Council on Research. Steering Committee on Practice Guidelines. Psychiatric Research Report. Washington, DC, American Psychiatric Association, March 1991, 6:12

33. Physician Payment Review Commission, Annual Report to Congress, 1989, p 219

34. Hirshfeld EB: Practice parameters and the malpractice liability of physicians. JAMA 263:1556–1562, 1990

35. American Medical Association: Attributes to Guide the Development of Practice Parameters. Chicago, IL, Office of Quality Assurance, American Medical Association, 1990

36. Kellie SE, Kelly JT: Appropriateness criteria: potential usefulness in practice parameters (background report). Chicago, IL, Office of Quality Assurance, American Medical Association, 1990

37. Hirshfield EB: Should practice parameters be the standard of care in malpractice litigation? JAMA 266:2886–2891, 1991

38. American Psychiatric Association Task Force on Treatments of Psychiatric Disorders: Treatments of Psychiatric Disorders, Vols 1–3. Washington, DC, American Psychiatric Press, 1989

39. From the President: work begins on practice guidelines. Psychiatric News 25(22)3, 28–29, 1990

40. APA's practice guidelines to reflect input from entire field of psychiatry. Psychiatric News 26(October 4):12, 1991
41. How vs Chicago, Kalamazoo, and Saginaw Railroad, 139 Mich 638, 103 NW 185 (1905)
42. Bosley v Andres, 393 Pa 161, 142 A2d 263 (1958), overruled, Niederman v Brodsky, 436 Pa 401, 261 A2d 84 (1970)
43. 38 Ga App 581, 144 SE 680 (1928), overruled, Ob-Gyn Associates of Albany v Littleton, 259 Ga 663, 386 SE2d 146 (1989)
44. Kionka EJ: Torts: Injuries to Persons and Properties. St Paul, MN, West Publishing, 1977, p 29
45. Multistate Bar Review: Torts. New York, Harcourt Brace Jovanovich, 1982
46. Slovenko R: Psychiatry and Law. Boston, MA, Little, Brown, 1973, p 278
47. 441 U.S. 418 (1979), remanded, State v Addington, 588 SW2d 569 (Tex 1979)
48. Halleck SL: Law in the Practice of Psychiatry. New York, Plenum, 1980, p 23
49. Reisner R: Law and the Mental Health System. St Paul, MN, West Publishing, 1985, pp 87–88
50. Johnston v Rodis, 251 F2d 917 (DC Cir 1958)
51. Salis v United States, 522 F Supp 989 (M D Pa 1981)
52. 42 U.S.C. § 1983 (1982)
53. In re Ballay, 482 F2d 648 (DC Cir 1973)
54. Youngberg v Romeo, 457 U.S. 307 (1982), remanded, Romeo v Youngberg, 687 F2d 33 (3rd Cir 1982)
55. Wyatt v Stickney, 325 F Supp 781 (MD Ala 1971), aff'd in part and remanded in part, Wyatt v Aderholt, 503 F2d 1305 (5th Cir 1974)
56. Mills v Rogers, 457 U.S. 291 (1982), remanded, Rogers v Okin, 738 F2d 1 (1st Cir 1984)
57. 422 U.S. 563 (1975), remanded, 519 F2d 59 (5th Cir 1975)
58. Reisner R: Law and the Mental Health System. St Paul, MN, West Publishing, 1985, pp 124–131
59. 401 F Supp 1189 (ND Ill 1975)
60. 355 F2d 129 (2d Cir 1966)
61. Jones v Superintendent, 370 F Supp 488 (W D VA 1974)
62. Reisner R, Slobogin C: Law and the Mental Health System, 2nd Edition. St Paul, MN, West Publishing, 1990, pp 95–100
63. Contracts with PPOs, PIAs, and HMOs. American Psychiatric Association Legal Consultation Newsletter, Winter 1985, pp 1–4
64. 183 Cal App 3d 1175, 228 Cal Rptr 661 (Cal Ct App 1986)
65. 222 Cal App 3d 660 (1990)
66. Usdin G: Physicians need legal and emotional support when sued for malpractice. Psychiatric Times 7(11):26–27, 1990
67. Charles SC, Wilbert JR, Franke KJ: Sued and nonsued physicians' self-reported reactions to malpractice litigation. Am J Psychiatry 142:437–440, 1985
68. Charles SC, Warnecke RB, Wilbert JR, et al: Sued and nonsued physicians. Psychosomatics 28:462–466, 1987
69. Charles SC, Kennedy E: Defendant. New York, Free Press, 1985
70. Slovenko R, Grossman M: Confidentiality and testimonial privilege, in Psychiatry, Vol 3. Edited by Cavenar JO. Philadelphia, PA, JB Lippincott, 1985, pp 1–18

71. American Psychiatric Association Legal Consultation Plan, Fall 1985, pp 1–2
72. Sanbar SS: Proving and defending psychiatric malpractice. Paper presented at the fall symposium of the American College of Legal Medicine, Albuquerque, NM, October 1985
73. Alton WG: Malpractice. Boston, MA, Little, Brown, 1977, pp 144–146; see pp 144–145
74. Slawson PF: Psychiatric malpractice: a California state-wide survey. Bull Am Acad Psychiatry Law 6:55–63, 1978
75. Slawson PF, Guggenheim FG: Psychiatric malpractice: a review of the national loss experience. Am J Psychiatry 141:979–981, 1984
76. Beis EB: Mental Health and the Law. Rockville, MD, Aspen, 1984, pp 19–20
77. Carlova J: How malpractice arbitration backfired on a doctor. Medical Economics, August 19, 1985, pp 48–52
78. Simon RI, Sadoff RL: Psychiatric Malpractice: Cases and Comments for Clinicians. Washington, DC, American Psychiatric Press, 1992
79. Hirsh HL: The pitfalls and perils of countersuits. J Fam Pract 5:811–813, 1977
80. Johnson ID: Reports to the National Practitioner Data Bank. JAMA 265:407–411, 1991
81. 42 U.S.C.A. § 11101 (Supp 1991)
82. Walzer RS: Impaired physicians: an overview and update of legal issues. J Leg Med 11:131–198, 1990
83. Grad JD: Will national data bank encourage litigation? Va Med J 117:343–344, 1990
84. Attorney limited in access to and use of information from malpractice data bank. Clinical Psychiatry News 18(8):12, 1990
85. American Medical News, February 13, 1987, p 17
86. Medical malpractice: characteristics of claims closed in 1984. Report to Congressional Requesters. Washington, DC, U.S. General Accounting Office, Tables 14, 15
87. Sommers PA: Malpractice risk and patient relations. Legal Aspects of Medical Practice 13:1–4, 8, 1985
88. Gutheil TG: Medicolegal pitfalls in the treatment of borderline patients. Am J Psychiatry 142:9–14, 1985
89. Halleck SL: Law in the Practice of Psychiatry. New York, Plenum, 1980, p 48
90. APA moves to "experience rating" standard. Psychiatric News 26(August 2):16, 1991
91. Smith JT: Medical Malpractice: Psychiatric Care, Supplement. Colorado Springs, CO, Shephards/McGraw-Hill, 1986, p 4

Epilogue:
We Are Belegaled

What are we to do? Today, as never before, the practice of psychiatry is fraught with legal controls, restrictions, and pitfalls. In ever-increasing numbers, psychiatrists have joined the ranks of those sued for malpractice. In attempting to adequately care for our patients, we are faced by increasingly complex and stringent commitment laws, laws regulating release, the right to refuse treatment, the need to warn known victims, and legal requirements before using electroconvulsive therapy, to name only a few.

When change occurs in the public and political arena, the pendulum at first may swing too far. Only recently have we seen the beginning of a return to a more reasonable position. The human rights movement has accomplished a great deal for many. However, for some it has been misguided. Because psychiatry has more to do with control of patients' freedom and because our patients' symptoms are displayed by thought and behavior, legal changes may seriously affect our efforts to treat. The law has had difficulty equating the freedom of thought with hallucinations and delusions seen in the mentally ill, so it does not allow us to prescribe if that will change the "sick" thoughts. The law has trouble with the concept of dangerousness as transferred from the criminal model, so it does not allow us to commit property offenders or those who cannot adequately care for themselves. The law has difficulty recognizing a proper standard of care when restraint, be it physical or chemical, is involved and when the chart cannot convey the degree of the patient's disturbance and our therapeutic limitations, so it finds the doctor liable for emotional damage caused by seclusion.

We are belegaled. We read court decisions and casebooks to learn more about the legal limits placed on our practice. We may be afraid to act, even when our clinical judgment dictates otherwise. It is important to know and understand the law, but can we ethically allow these decisions to keep us from furnishing proper medical care? There is a fine line to walk so that our patients do not suffer because we fear the law. Our lawyer may advise us about a court decision that could be applied to one of our medical problems, but we must use our medical judgment when making medical decisions. Good law may not be good medicine, and good medicine may not always avoid lawsuits.

In the short period of time since the first edition of *Clinical Psychiatry and the Law* was published, there has been some fine tuning of the effect of the legal system on psychiatry. For the most part the federal courts have taken a somewhat more liberal, or hands-off, view of the supervision of patient care. However, many of the state courts have stepped in and insisted upon closer supervision with more due process for the patient. Many of us still look upon this as being of only limited value to the patient in terms of improving patient care, while it has proven to be quite costly in dollars and cents and time lost for the adequate treatment of refusing patients. We look forward to the time when there can be a more efficient and effective relationship between law and psychiatry in many of the areas in which we have an interface.

In the end, the law, like medicine, does not want people to suffer. Unfortunately, law and medicine have their own agendas and concepts of what is best for mankind. We must therefore continue to help the courts and legislatures understand our patients' needs as well as our therapeutic efforts and limitations. We must learn to work within the framework of the law while not sacrificing good patient care. In the end, we hope for good law and good medicine, which should be able to live together.

Jonas R. Rappeport, M.D.
Clinical Professor of Psychiatry,
University of Maryland School of Medicine;
and Chief Medical Examiner,
Supreme Bench of Baltimore City

Appendixes

Appendix 1

The Principles of Medical Ethics With Annotations Especially Applicable to Psychiatry

THE PRINCIPLES OF MEDICAL ETHICS
With Annotations Especially
Applicable to Psychiatry

1989 Edition

In 1973, the American Psychiatric Association published the first edition of THE PRINCIPLES OF MEDICAL ETHICS WITH ANNOTATIONS ESPECIALLY APPLICABLE TO PSYCHIATRY. Subsequently, revisions were published as the Board of Trustees and the Assembly approved additional annotations. In July of 1980, the American Medical Association approved a new version of the Principles of Medical Ethics (the first revision since 1957) and the APA Ethics Committee[1] incorporated many of its annotations into the new Principles, which resulted in the 1981 edition and subsequent revisions.

FOREWORD

ALL PHYSICIANS should practice in accordance with the medical code of ethics set forth in the Principles of Medical Ethics of the American Medical Association. An up-to-date expression and elaboration of these statements is found in the Opinions and Reports of the Council on Ethical and Judicial Affairs of the American Medical Association.[2] Psychiatrists are strongly advised to be familiar with these documents.[3]

However, these general guidelines have sometimes been difficult to interpret for psychiatry, so further annotations to the basic principles are offered in this

---

[1]The committee included Herbert Klemmer, M.D., Chairperson, Miltiades Zaphiropoulos, M.D., Ewald Busse, M.D., John R. Saunders, M.D., Robert McDevitt, M.D. Serving as consultants to the APA Ethics Committee were J. Brand Brickman, M.D., William P. Camp, M.D., and Robert A. Moore, M.D.

[2]Current Opinions of the Council on Ethical and Judicial Affairs, Chicago, American Medical Association, 1989.

[3]Chapter 8, Section 1 of the Bylaws of the American Psychiatric Association states, "All members of the American Psychiatric Association shall be bound by the ethical code of the medical profession, specifically defined in The Principles of Medical Ethics of the American Medical Association." In interpreting the APA Constitution and Bylaws, it is the opinion of the Board of Trustees that inactive status in no way removes a physician member from responsibility to abide by the Principles of Medical Ethics.

document. While psychiatrists have the same goals as all physicians, there are special ethical problems in psychiatric practice that differ in coloring and degree from ethical problems in other branches of medical practice, even though the basic principles are the same. The annotations are not designed as absolutes and will be revised from time to time so as to be applicable to current practices and problems.

Following are the AMA Principles of Medical Ethics, printed in their entirety, and then each principle printed separately along with an annotation especially applicable to psychiatry.

PRINCIPLES OF MEDICAL ETHICS, AMERICAN MEDICAL ASSOCIATION

PREAMBLE

The medical profession has long subscribed to a body of ethical statements developed primarily for the benefit of the patient. As a member of this profession, a physician must recognize responsibility not only to patients but also to society, to other health professionals, and to self. The following Principles, adopted by the American Medical Association, are not laws but standards of conduct, which define the essentials of honorable behavior for the physician.

SECTION 1

A physician shall be dedicated to providing competent medical service with compassion and respect for human dignity.

SECTION 2

A physician shall deal honestly with patients and colleagues, and strive to expose those physicians deficient in character or competence, or who engage in fraud or deception.

SECTION 3

A physician shall respect the law and also recognize a responsibility to seek changes in those requirements which are contrary to the best interests of the patient.

SECTION 4

A physician shall respect the rights of patients, of colleagues, and of other health professionals, and shall safeguard patient confidences within the constraints of the law.

SECTION 5

A physician shall continue to study, apply, and advance scientific knowledge, make relevant information available to patients, colleagues, and the public, obtain consultation, and use the talents of other health professionals when indicated.

SECTION 6

A physician shall, in the provision of appropriate patient care, except in emergencies, be free to choose whom to serve, with whom to associate, and the environment in which to provide medical services.

SECTION 7

A physician shall recognize a responsibility to participate in activities contributing to an improved community.

Principles With Annotations

Following are each of the AMA Principles of Medical Ethics printed separately along with annotations especially applicable to psychiatry.

PREAMBLE

The medical profession has long subscribed to a body of ethical statements developed primarily for the benefit of the patient. As a member of this profession, a physician must recognize responsibility not only to patients but also to society, to other health professionals, and to self. The following Principles, adopted by the American Medical Association, are not laws but standards of conduct, which define the essentials of honorable behavior for the physician.[4]

SECTION 1

A physician shall be dedicated to providing competent medical service with compassion and respect for human dignity.

1. The patient may place his/her trust in his/her psychiatrist knowing that the psychiatrist's ethics and professional responsibilities preclude him/her gratifying his/her own needs by exploiting the patient. This becomes particularly important because of the essentially private, highly personal, and sometimes intensely emotional nature of the relationship established with the psychiatrist.

[4]Statements in italics are taken directly from the American Medical Association's Principles of Medical Ethics.

2. A psychiatrist should not be a party to any type of policy that excludes, segregates, or demeans the dignity of any patient because of ethnic origin, race, sex, creed, age, socioeconomic status, or sexual orientation.
3. In accord with the requirements of law and accepted medical practice, it is ethical for a physician to submit his/her work to peer review and to the ultimate authority of the medical staff executive body and the hospital administration and its governing body. In case of dispute, the ethical psychiatrist has the following steps available:

   a. Seek appeal from the medical staff decision to a joint conference committee, including members of the medical staff executive committee and the executive committee of the governing board. At this appeal, the ethical psychiatrist could request that outside opinions be considered.
   b. Appeal to the governing body itself.
   c. Appeal to state agencies regulating licensure of hospitals if, in the particular state, they concern themselves with matters of professional competency and quality of care.
   d. Attempt to educate colleagues through development of research projects and data and presentations at professional meetings and in professional journals.
   e. Seek redress in local courts, perhaps through an enjoining injunction against the governing body.
   f. Public education as carried out by an ethical psychiatrist would not utilize appeals based solely upon emotion, but would be presented in a professional way and without any potential exploitation of patients through testimonials.

4. A psychiatrist should not be a participant in a legally authorized execution.

SECTION 2

A physician shall deal honestly with patients and colleagues, and strive to expose those physicians deficient in character or competence, or who engage in fraud or deception.

1. The requirement that the physician conduct himself/herself with propriety in his/her profession and in all the actions of his/her life is especially important in the case of the psychiatrist because the patient tends to model his/her behavior after that of his/her therapist by identification. Further, the necessary intensity of the therapeutic relationship may tend to activate sexual and other needs and fantasies on the part of both patient and therapist, while weakening the objectivity necessary for control. Sexual activity with a patient is unethical. Sexual involvement with one's former patients generally exploits emotions deriving from treatment and therefore almost always is unethical.

2. The psychiatrist should diligently guard against exploiting information furnished by the patient and should not use the unique position of power afforded him/her by the psychotherapeutic situation to influence the patient in any way not directly relevant to the treatment goals.
3. A psychiatrist who regularly practices outside his/her area of professional competence should be considered unethical. Determination of professional competence should be made by peer review boards or other appropriate bodies.
4. Special consideration should be given to those psychiatrists who, because of mental illness, jeopardize the welfare of their patients and their own reputations and practices. It is ethical, even encouraged, for another psychiatrist to intercede in such situations.
5. Psychiatric services, like all medical services, are dispensed in the context of a contractual arrangement between the patient and the treating physician. The provisions of the contractual arrangement, which are binding on the physician as well as on the patient, should be explicitly established.
6. It is ethical for the psychiatrist to make a charge for a missed appointment when this falls within the terms of the specific contractual agreement with the patient. Charging for a missed appointment or for one not cancelled 24 hours in advance need not, in itself, be considered unethical if a patient is fully advised that the physician will make such a charge. The practice, however, should be resorted to infrequently and always with the utmost consideration for the patient and his/her circumstances.
7. An arrangement in which a psychiatrist provides supervision or administration to other physicians or nonmedical persons for a percentage of their fees or gross income is not acceptable; this would constitute fee-splitting. In a team of practitioners, or a multidisciplinary team, it is ethical for the psychiatrist to receive income for administration, research, education, or consultation. This should be based upon a mutually agreed upon and set fee or salary, open to renegotiation when a change in the time demand occurs. (See also Section 5, Annotations 2, 3, and 4.)
8. When a member has been found to have behaved unethically by the American Psychiatric Association or one of its constituent district branches, there should not be automatic reporting to the local authorities responsible for medical licensure, but the decision to report should be decided upon the merits of the case.[5]

SECTION 3

A physician shall respect the law and also recognize a responsibility to seek

---

[5]However, state and federal law may impose reporting requirements with which district branches and the APA must comply.

changes in those requirements which are contrary to the best interests of the patient.

1.   It would seem self-evident that a psychiatrist who is a law-breaker might be ethically unsuited to practice his/her profession. When such illegal activities bear directly upon his/her practice, this would obviously be the case. However, in other instances, illegal activities such as those concerning the right to protest social injustices might not bear on either the image of the psychiatrist or the ability of the specific psychiatrist to treat his/her patient ethically and well. While no committee or board could offer prior assurance that any illegal activity would not be considered unethical, it is conceivable that an individual could violate a law without being guilty of professionally unethical behavior. Physicians lose no right of citizenship on entry into the profession of medicine.

2.   Where not specifically prohibited by local laws governing medical practice, the practice of acupuncture by a psychiatrist is not unethical per se. The psychiatrist should have professional competence in the use of acupuncture. Or, if he/she is supervising the use of acupuncture by nonmedical individuals, he/she should provide proper medical supervision. (See also Section 5, Annotations 3 and 4.)

SECTION 4

A physician shall respect the rights of patients, of colleagues, and of other health professionals, and shall safeguard patient confidences within the constraints of the law.

1.   Psychiatric records, including even the identification of a person as a patient, must be protected with extreme care. Confidentiality is essential to psychiatric treatment. This is based in part on the special nature of psychiatric therapy as well as on the traditional ethical relationship between physician and patient. Growing concern regarding the civil rights of patients and the possible adverse effects of computerization, duplication equipment, and data banks makes the dissemination of confidential information an increasing hazard. Because of the sensitive and private nature of the information with which the psychiatrist deals, he/she must be circumspect in the information that he/she chooses to disclose to others about a patient. The welfare of the patient must be a continuing consideration.

2.   A psychiatrist may release confidential information only with the authorization of the patient or under proper legal compulsion. The continuing duty of the psychiatrist to protect the patient includes fully apprising him/her of the connotations of waiving the privilege of privacy. This may become an issue when the patient is being investigated by a government agency, is applying for a position, or is involved in legal action. The same principles

apply to the release of information concerning treatment to medical departments of government agencies, business organizations, labor unions, and insurance companies. Information gained in confidence about patients seen in student health services should not be released without the students' explicit permission.

3. Clinical and other materials used in teaching and writing must be adequately disguised in order to preserve the anonymity of the individuals involved.

4. The ethical responsibility of maintaining confidentiality holds equally for the consultations in which the patient may not have been present and in which the consultee was not a physician. In such instances, the physician consultant should alert the consultee to his/her duty of confidentiality.

5. Ethically the psychiatrist may disclose only that information which is relevant to a given situation. He/she should avoid offering speculation as fact. Sensitive information such as an individual's sexual orientation or fantasy material is usually unnecessary.

6. Psychiatrists are often asked to examine individuals for security purposes, to determine suitability for various jobs, and to determine legal competence. The psychiatrist must fully describe the nature and purpose and lack of confidentiality of the examination to the examinee at the beginning of the examination.

7. Careful judgment must be exercised by the psychiatrist in order to include, when appropriate, the parents or guardian in the treatment of a minor. At the same time, the psychiatrist must assure the minor proper confidentiality.

8. Psychiatrists at times may find it necessary, in order to protect the patient or the community from imminent danger, to reveal confidential information disclosed by the patient.

9. When the psychiatrist is ordered by the court to reveal the confidences entrusted to him/her by patients, he/she may comply or he/she may ethically hold the right to dissent within the framework of the law. When the psychiatrist is in doubt, the right of the patient to confidentiality and, by extension, to unimpaired treatment, should be given priority. The psychiatrist should reserve the right to raise the question of adequate need for disclosure. In the event that the necessity for legal disclosure is demonstrated by the court, the psychiatrist may request the right to disclosure of only that information which is relevant to the legal question at hand.

10. With regard for the person's dignity and privacy and with truly informed consent, it is ethical to present a patient to a scientific gathering, if the confidentiality of the presentation is understood and accepted by the audience.

11. It is ethical to present a patient or former patient to a public gathering or to the news media only if the patient is fully informed of enduring loss of confidentiality, is competent, and consents in writing without coercion.

12. When involved in funded research, the ethical psychiatrist will advise human subjects of the funding source, retain his/her freedom to reveal data and results, and follow all appropriate and current guidelines relative to human subject protection.
13. Ethical considerations in medical practice preclude the psychiatric evaluation of any adult charged with criminal acts prior to access to, or availability of, legal counsel. The only exception is the rendering of care to the person for the sole puipose of medical treatment.
14. Sexual involvement between a faculty member or supervisor and a trainee or student, in those situations in which an abuse of power can occur, often takes advantage of inequalities in the working relationship and may be unethical because: (a) any treatment of a patient being supervised may be deleteriously affected; (b) it may damage the trust relationship between teacher and student; and (c) teachers are important professional role models for their trainees and affect their trainees' future professional behavior.

SECTION 5

A physician shall continue to study, apply, and advance scientific knowledge, make relevant information available to patients, colleagues, and the public, obtain consultation, and use the talents of other health professionals when indicated.

1. Psychiatrists are responsible for their own continuing education and should be mindful of the fact that theirs must be a lifetime of learning.
2. In the practice of his/her specialty, the psychiatrist consults, associates, collaborates, or integrates his/her work with that of many professionals, including psychologists, psychometricians, social workers, alcoholism counselors, marriage counselors, public health nurses, etc. Furthermore, the nature of modern psychiatric practice extends his/her contacts to such people as teachers, juvenile and adult probation officers, attorneys, welfare workers, agency volunteers, and neighborhood aides. In referring patients for treatment, counseling, or rehabilitation to any of these practitioners, the psychiatrist should ensure that the allied professional or paraprofessional with whom he/she is dealing is a recognized member of his/her own discipline and is competent to carry out the therapeutic task required. The psychiatrist should have the same attitude toward members of the medical profession to whom he/she refers patients. Whenever he/she has reason to doubt the training, skill, or ethical qualifications of the allied professional, the psychiatrist should not refer cases to him/her.
3. When the psychiatrist assumes a collaborative or supervisory role with another mental health worker, he/she must expend sufficient time to assure that proper care is given. It is contrary to the interests of the patient and to patient care if he/she allows himself/herself to be used as a figurehead.

4. In relationships between psychiatrists and practicing licensed psychologists, the physician should not delegate to the psychologist or, in fact, to any nonmedical person any matter requiring the exercise of professional medical judgment.

5. The psychiatrist should agree to the request of a patient for consultation or to such a request from the family of an incompetent or minor patient. The psychiatrist may suggest possible consultants, but the patient or family should be given free choice of the consultant. If the psychiatrist disapproves of the professional qualifications of the consultant or if there is a difference of opinion that the primary therapist cannot resolve, he/she may, after suitable notice, withdraw from the case. If this disagreement occurs within an institution or agency framework, the differences should be resolved by the mediation or arbitration of higher professional authority within the institution or agency.

SECTION 6

A physician shall, in the provision of appropriate patient care, except in emergencies, be free to choose whom to serve, with whom to associate, and the environment in which to provide medical services.

1. Physicians generally agree that the doctor-patient relationship is such a vital factor in effective treatment of the patient that preservation of optimal conditions for development of a sound working relationship between a doctor and his/her patient should take precedence over all other considerations. Professional courtesy may lead to poor psychiatric care for physicians and their families because of embarrassment over the lack of a complete give-and-take contract.

2. An ethical psychiatrist may refuse to provide psychiatric treatment to a person who, in the psychiatrist's opinion, cannot be diagnosed as having a mental illness amenable to psychiatric treatment.

SECTION 7

A physician shall recognize a responsibility to participate in activities contributing to an improved community.

1. Psychiatrists should foster the cooperation of those legitimately concerned with the medical, psychological, social, and legal aspects of mental health and illness. Psychiatrists are encouraged to serve society by advising and consulting with the executive, legislative, and judiciary branches of the government. A psychiatrist should clarify whether he/she speaks as an individual or as a representative of an organization. Furthermore, psychiatrists should avoid cloaking their public statements with the authority of the profession (e.g., "Psychiatrists know that . . .").

2.   Psychiatrists may interpret and share with the public their expertise in the various psychosocial issues that may affect mental health and illness. Psychiatrists should always be mindful of their separate roles as dedicated citizens and as experts in psychological medicine.

3.   On occasion psychiatrists are asked for an opinion about an individual who is in the light of public attention, or who has disclosed information about himself/herself through public media. It is unethical for a psychiatrist to offer a professional opinion unless he/she has conducted an examination and has been granted proper authorization for such a statement.

4.   The psychiatrist may permit his/her certification to be used for the involuntary treatment of any person only following his/her personal examination of that person. To do so, he/she must find that the person, because of mental illness, cannot form a judgment as to what is in his/her own best interests and that, without such treatment, substantial impairment is likely to occur to the person or others.

Procedures for Handling Complaints of Unethical Conduct[6]

Complaints charging members of the Association with unethical behavior or practices shall be investigated, processed, and resolved in accordance with procedures approved by the Assembly and the Board.

If a complaint of unethical conduct against a member is sustained, the member shall receive a sanction ranging from admonishment to expulsion. Any decision to expel a member must be approved by a two-thirds affirmative vote of all members of the Board present and voting.[7]

PROCEDURES

1.   All formal complaints charging a member of the American Psychiatric Association (APA) with unethical behavior shall be made in writing, signed by the complainant, and addressed to the accused member's district branch or, if addressed to the APA, shall be referred by the APA to the accused member's district branch for investigation[8] and decision in accordance with

---

[6]Approved by the Assembly, 1989; approved by the Board of Trustees, 1989. Implementation date, October 14, 1989.

[7]Chapter 10, Sections 1 and 2, Bylaws, American Psychiatric Association, 1988 edition.

[8]As used in these procedures, the term "investigation" is meant to include both an information-gathering or investigatory phase of a case and a hearing phase. This term does not apply to the process by which a district branch initially determines whether or not a complaint merits investigation.

the procedures set out in paragraphs 4 through 9 below.[9] If the accused member is a member-at-large of the APA, the complaint shall be referred to an ad hoc investigating committee, as provided for in paragraph 2 below.

2.   If, after receiving a written complaint, the district branch determines that there are compelling reasons why it would not be the appropriate body to consider the complaint, the district branch shall write to the Chair of the APA Ethics Committee, requesting that it be excused and providing a detailed explanation of the reasons for its request. If the Chair of the APA Ethics Committee determines that the district branch should not be excused, the district branch shall proceed with the complaint. If the Chair of the APA Ethics Committee agrees that the district branch should be excused from considering the complaint, the Chair shall then appoint three Fellows of the APA to serve as an ad hoc investigating committee to conduct the investigation and to render a decision.[10] When possible, these Fellows shall reside in the same Area as the accused member and in no event shall any such Fellow be a member of the APA Ethics Committee, the APA Ethics Appeals Board, or the APA Board of Trustees.

3.   If the district branch finds it cannot determine that the complaint merits investigation under the ethical standards established by The Principles of Medical Ethics With Annotations Especially Applicable to Psychiatry, the district branch shall so notify the complainant, requesting additional information when appropriate. If the district branch determines that the charges do not merit investigation, it shall notify the complainant, stating the basis for the conclusion and informing the complainant that he/she may address a request for a review of this decision to the Secretary of the APA. If the Secretary determines that the complaint merits investigation, the complaint shall be referred to the Chair of the APA Ethics Committee, who will appoint an ad hoc investigating committee as provided for in paragraph 2 above. When an ad hoc investigating committee is appointed, the district branch shall be so notified by the Chair of the APA Ethics Committee.

4.   If the district branch determines that a complaint merits investigation under the ethical standards established by The Principles of Medical Ethics With Annotations Especially Applicable to Psychiatry, the district branch shall advise the Secretary of the APA as well as the complainant and the accused member that it will be conducting the investigation, and that it will notify the complainant and the accused member in accordance with the provisions of paragraphs 16–23 below. The district branch shall also send a copy of the complaint to the accused member, along with copies of The Principles

---

[9]Paragraphs 4 through 9, below, set out minimum requirements. Each district branch should comply with any additional or more stringent requirements of state law.

[10]Unless otherwise indicated, when these procedures refer to activities of a district branch, the same requirements shall apply to the ad hoc investigating committee when it performs an investigation.

of Medical Ethics With Annotations Especially Applicable to Psychiatry and of these procedures. The accused member shall further be informed that he/she has the right to be represented by counsel; that he/she has the right to a hearing; and that, at the hearing, he/she will have the rights set out in paragraph 8 below. The member will also be informed of his/her right to appeal an adverse decision to the APA Ethics Appeals Board in accordance with the provisions of paragraphs 18–22 below.

5. The district branch investigation shall be comprehensive and fair and conducted as provided herein. A hearing conducted in accordance with the provisions of paragraph 8 below shall be held unless the accused member has voluntarily waived his/her right to a hearing or the district branch, prior to the hearing, has determined that there has been no ethical violation. The accused member's waiver of a hearing shall not prevent the district branch from meeting with, and hearing the evidence of, the complainant and other witnesses and reaching a decision in the case.

6. The accused member will be notified of the hearing by certified mail, at least 30 days in advance of the hearing. The notice will include the following:

    a. The date, time and place of the hearing;
    b. A list of witnesses expected to testify;
    c. Notification of the member's right to representation by legal counsel or another individual of the member's choice;
    d. Notification of the accused member's right to appeal any adverse decision to the APA Ethics Appeals Board.

7. The initial, information-gathering stages of the investigation, which may include preliminary interviews of the complainant and the accused member, may be conducted by any single member or a subcommittee of the ethics committee. In all cases in which there may be a decision adverse to the accused member, unless the accused member has waived his/her right to a hearing, there must be a hearing before the district branch ethics committee or a specially constituted ad hoc panel of at least three (3) members, at least one (1) of whom must be a member of the district branch ethics committee.

8. The hearing shall provide fairness and respect for both the accused member and the complainant. The following procedures shall apply:

    a. The accused member may be represented by counsel or other person. The counsel or other person may answer questions addressed to him/her, advise his/her client, introduce evidence, examine and cross-examine witnesses, and make opening and closing statements. Counsel's participation is subject to the continuing direction and control of the Chair. The Chair shall exercise its discretion so as to prevent the intimidation or harassment of the complainant and/or other witnesses and with regard to the peer review nature of the proceedings. Questions addressed by members of the committee or panel to the accused member shall be answered by the member.

b. Except when the district branch concludes that it is prepared to proceed solely on the basis of extrinsic evidence,[11] the complainant must be present at the hearing unless excused by the committee or panel Chair. The complainant will be excused only when he/she has so requested and, in the judgment of the Chair, participation would be harmful to him/her.

c. Except when the district branch concludes that it is prepared to proceed solely on the basis of extrinsic evidence or the complainant is excused pursuant to paragraph 8(b) above, the complainant shall testify regarding his/her charges.

d. The accused member or his/her attorney may challenge material presented by the complainant or the complainant's witnesses: (i) by appropriate direct challenge through cross-examination; or (ii) if the complainant asked to be excused from such direct challenge and the Chair determined that such direct challenge will be harmful to the complainant, by written questions submitted by the accused member and posed to the complainant by the Chair, with answers to be provided orally or in writing as the Chair in his/her discretion determines is appropriate.

e. The accused member may choose not to be present at the hearing and to present his/her defense through other witnesses and counsel.

f. The accused member may testify on his/her own behalf, call and examine supporting witnesses, and introduce relevant evidence in support of his/her case. Evidence may not be excluded solely on the grounds that it would be inadmissible in a court of law.

g. Members of the hearing panel may ask pertinent questions during the hearing.

h. A stenographic or tape record shall be made of the proceedings and a copy shall subsequently be made available to the accused member at a reasonable charge.

i. The accused member may make an oral statement and/or submit a written statement at the close of the hearing.

---

[11]For these purposes, "extrinsic evidence" shall mean documents whose validity and accuracy appear to be clear on their face and which do not rely on the assertions or opinions of the complainant and/or his/her witnesses. Examples of such evidence include admissions by the accused member, formal judicial or administrative reports, sworn deposition or trial testimony that was subject to cross-examination, photographs, medical or hospital records, hotel or credit card receipts, etc. When the district branch decides to rely solely on such extrinsic evidence, it should take appropriate steps to ensure that members of the hearing panel do not take into account any information from the complainant or other witnesses and base their decision solely on the available extrinsic evidence.

9. All ethics committee or panel recommendations shall be in writing and shall include a statement of the basis for the recommendation. If the investigation has been conducted by a panel, the panel shall make a recommendation only as to whether there has been an ethics violation and the district branch ethics committee shall review this recommendation and add its recommendation as to sanction, if any.

10. Upon completion of the investigation and any internal review procedures required by the district branch's governing documents, the district branch shall render a decision as to whether an ethics violation has occurred and, if so, what sanction is appropriate. If the investigation has been conducted by an ad hoc investigating committee, the ad hoc investigating committee shall make the decision as to both violation and sanction. The district branch or ad hoc investigating committee decision shall be in writing and shall include a statement of the basis of the decision. In all cases, the district branch shall seek to reach a decision within nine (9) months from the time that the complaint was received.

11. The four possible sanctions are as follows:

    a. admonishment—an informal warning;
    b. reprimand–a formal censure;
    c. suspension (for a period not to exceed five years);[12]
    d. expulsion.

12. In addition to the above sanctions, a district branch may, but is not required to, impose certain conditions, such as educational or supervisory requirements, on a suspended member.[13] When such conditions are imposed, the following procedures shall apply:

    a. if the district branch imposes conditions, it shall monitor compliance;
    b. if the ad hoc investigating committee imposes conditions, the Chair of the APA Ethics Committee shall establish a means for monitoring compliance;
    c. if a member fails to satisfy the conditions, the district branch or the APA monitoring body established by the Chair of the APA Ethics Committee may decide to expel the member;

---

[12]A suspended member will be required to pay dues and will be eligible for APA benefits, except that such a member will lose his/her rights to hold office, vote, nominate candidates, propose referenda or amendments to the Constitution or Bylaws, and serve on any APA committee or component. Each district branch shall decide which, if any, district branch privileges and benefits shall be denied during the period of suspension.

[13]Personal treatment may be recommended, but not required, and any such recommendation shall be carried out in accordance with the ethical requirements governing confidentiality as set forth in The Principles of Medical Ethics With Annotations Especially Applicable To Psychiatry. In appropriate cases, the district branch may in addition refer the psychiatrist in question to a component responsible for considering impaired or physically ill physicians.

d. if it is determined that a member should be expelled for noncompliance with conditions, the member may appeal pursuant to the provisions set forth in paragraphs 18–22 below;

e. if a member expelled for noncompliance with conditions does not appeal, the APA Board of Trustees shall review the expulsion in accordance with the provisions of paragraph 17 below.

13. After the district branch completes its investigation and arrives at its decision, the decision and any pertinent information concerning the procedures followed or relating to the action taken shall be forwarded to the APA Ethics Committee for review in accordance with the provisions of paragraphs 14–16 below. If the Chair of the APA Ethics Committee determines that these review functions are best carried out by a subcommittee, he/she shall designate such a subcommittee (or subcommittees) which shall include at least three (3) voting members of the APA Ethics Committee, and which shall be authorized to undertake these review functions on behalf of the full APA Ethics Committee. The review proceedings shall be undertaken expeditiously, in no instance exceeding ninety (90) days from the receipt of the district branch's report before the district branch is informed of the APA Ethics Committee's opinion, conclusion, or need for clarification of the material received. If the APA Ethics Committee fails to act within ninety (90) days, the district branch may inform the accused member in accordance with paragraph 16 below.

14. In all cases where the district branch renders a decision, including those where the district branch finds that an ethics violation has not occurred, the APA Ethics Committee shall review the information submitted by the district branch to assure that the complaint received an investigation that was comprehensive and fair and in accordance with the procedures in paragraphs 4–9 above. If the APA Ethics Committee concludes that these requirements were not satisfied, it shall so advise the district branch, and the district branch shall remedy the deficiencies and shall make further reports to the APA Ethics Committee until such time as the APA Ethics Committee is satisfied that these requirements have been met. If, in the view of the APA Ethics Committee, the district branch is either unwilling or unable to complete the investigation in a satisfactory manner, the Chair of the APA Ethics Committee may appoint an ad hoc investigating committee to conduct the investigation and render a decision.

15. In cases where the district branch has found that an ethics violation has occurred, the APA Ethics Committee or subcommittee, after ascertaining that the investigation was comprehensive and fair and in accordance with these procedures, shall consider the appropriateness of the sanction imposed. If the APA Ethics Committee or subcommittee concludes that the sanction is appropriate, it shall so notify the district branch. If the APA

Ethics Committee or subcommittee concludes that the sanction should be reconsidered by the district branch, it shall provide a statement of reasons explaining the basis for its opinion, and the district branch shall reconsider the sanction. After reconsideration, the decision of the district branch shall stand, even if the district branch decides to adhere to the original sanction, except that the sanction may be modified as provided for in paragraphs 17, 20, or 22 below.

16. After the APA Ethics Committee or subcommittee completes the review process, the district branch shall notify the accused member of the decision and sanction, if any, by certified mail. The accused member shall be provided copies of the district branch ethics committee and/or panel recommendation(s) and of the district branch decision. If the decision is that no ethics violation has occurred, the case shall be terminated, and the district branch shall also notify the complainant of this decision by certified mail. If the decision is that an ethics violation has occurred, the accused member shall be advised that he/she has thirty (30) days to file a written letter of appeal with the Secretary of the APA. In such circumstances, unless the complainant is requested to appear before the Ethics Appeals Board as provided for in paragraph 19 below, the complainant shall not be advised of any action until after the appeal has been completed or until the Secretary of the APA notifies the district branch that no appeal has been taken or that the procedures provided for in paragraph 17 below have been completed.

17. If, after review by the APA Ethics Committee or upon a finding of noncompliance with conditions as provided for in paragraph 12(c), above, the decision is to expel a member, and the member fails to appeal the decision, the APA Board of Trustees at its next meeting shall review the expulsion on the basis of a presentation by the Chair of the APA Ethics Committee and the documentary record in the case. A decision to affirm an expulsion must be by a vote of two-thirds (2/3) of those Trustees present and voting. A decision to impose a lesser sanction shall be by a majority vote. If necessary, the APA Board of Trustees may request further information from the district branch before voting on the decision to expel.

18. All appeals shall be heard by the APA Ethics Appeals Board, which shall be chaired by the Secretary of the APA, and shall include the two immediate past Presidents of the APA, the immediate past Speaker of the APA Assembly, and the Chair of the APA Ethics Committee. All members of the Ethics Appeals Board, including the Chair, shall be entitled to one vote on all matters. If any of the above cannot serve, the President is authorized to appoint a replacement.

19. The accused member shall be entitled to file a written statement with the Ethics Appeals Board and/or appear before the Board alone, or accompanied by counsel. In addition, the Ethics Appeals Board may request any information from the district branch and may also request the complainant,

accompanied by counsel if he/she so requests, and/or a representative of the district branch, accompanied by counsel if the district branch so requests, to attend the appeal. The APA counsel and other necessary APA staff may also attend if the Ethics Appeals Board so requests. Time limits and other procedural requirements concerning the appeal shall be established by the Ethics Appeals Board.

20. After hearing the appeal and reviewing the record, the Ethics Appeals Board may take any of the following actions:

   a. affirm the decision, including the sanction imposed by the district branch;
   b. affirm the decision, but alter the sanction imposed by the district branch;
   c. reverse the decision of the district branch and terminate the case;
   d. remand the case to the district branch with specific instructions as to what further information or action is necessary.[14] In cases involving a remand, the district branch shall report back directly to the Ethics Appeals Board. After the remand (or successive remands, if more than one is deemed necessary) the Ethics Appeals Board shall reach one of the decisions set forth in subsections (a), (b), or (c) above.

21. After the Ethics Appeals Board reaches a decision as set forth in paragraph 20(a), (b), or (c), if the decision is anything other than to expel a member, the APA Secretary shall notify the district branch of the decision and that it is final.

22. If the decision of the Ethics Appeals Board is to expel a member, the APA Board of Trustees at its next meeting shall review the action solely on the basis of the presentation of the Secretary of the APA (or his/her designee) and the documentary record in the case. The Board of Trustees may affirm the sanction, impose a lesser sanction, or remand to the Ethics Appeals Board for further action or consideration. A decision to affirm an expulsion must be by a vote of two-thirds (2/3) of those Trustees present and voting. All other actions shall be by majority vote. Members of the Board of Trustees who participated as members of the APA Ethics Appeals Board shall not vote when the Board of Trustees considers the case. Once the Board of Trustees has acted or, in a case of a remand, has approved the action taken on remand, the APA Secretary shall notify the district branch of the decision and that it is final.

23. Once a final decision is reached, the district branch shall notify the complainant and the accused member by certified mail.

---

[14]Remands will be employed only in rare cases, such as when new information has been presented on appeal or when there is an indication that important information is available and has not been considered.

24. Except as described in paragraph 25 below, disclosure by members of the APA of the name of the accused member, the fact that a complaint has been lodged, the substance of the complaint, or the identity of any witnesses, shall be limited to persons who need this information to assure the orderly and effective administration of these procedures.

25. To assure proper protection of the public, there are times when disclosure of the identity of an accused member may be essential. Such disclosure is authorized in the following instances:[15]

   a. The name of any member who is expelled from the APA for an ethics violation shall be reported in PSYCHIATRIC NEWS and, at the discretion of the governing council of the district branch, in its own newsletter or other usual means of communication with its membership.

   b. The name of any member who is suspended from the APA for an ethics violation or who resigns from the APA or a district branch during the course of an ethics investigation may be reported as deemed appropriate by the district branch, after approval by the APA Ethics Committee, or the APA.

   c. The Board of Trustees or, after approval by the APA Ethics Committee, any district branch's governing council may report an ethics charge or a decision finding that a member has engaged in unethical conduct to any medical licensing authority, medical society, hospital, clinic, or other institutions or persons where such disclosure is deemed appropriate to protect the public.[16]

---

[15]State and/or federal law may impose additional reporting requirements with which district branches or the APA must comply.

[16]Chapter 10, Sections 1 and 2, Bylaws, American Psychiatric Association, 1988 edition.

Appendix 2

Sample Forms

Authorization for Release of Medical Information

Date:

I hereby authorize Dr. _____ to release the circled information for the following purposes: _____ _____ [Specify any limitations.]

A. Psychiatric and medical history including diagnoses.
B. Records of outpatient treatment.
C. Records of psychiatric hospitalization and treatment.
D. Limited psychiatric information as follows:

I understand that I have a right to inspect and copy any information authorized for release by me. I also have the right to revoke consent at any time. This is a [   ] one time consent or [   ] continuing consent [please check one]. I have been apprised of the possible problems of waiving the privilege of privacy. Please send this information to the following individual and address:

_____

_____

_____

Signature _____

Address _____

_____

Informed Consent for Treatment With Psychotropic Drugs

Patient:

Dr. _____ has determined that I am suffering from a _____ disorder and that I should receive _____ medication for the treatment of this condition. The doctor has explained to me, and I understand, the diagnosis, the nature and purpose of the proposed treatment, the risks and consequences of the treatment, the probability of successful treatment, other reasonable treatment alternatives and the anticipated consequences if the proposed treatment is not given.

I have been specifically informed of the risk of developing tardive dyskinesia when I am taking major tranquilizers. I understand that tardive dyskinesia is an involuntary, abnormal muscle movement disorder that may persist after treatment ends and sometimes may be disabling.

The doctor has explained the most common side effects of treatment, but I do understand that other side effects may occur, and that I should promptly notify the doctor or a staff member of any unexpected changes in my clinical condition.

Although the doctor believes that the above medication should help my condition, I understand that no guarantee has been made to me concerning any expected results.

I understand that I will not be forced to take this medication and that I can stop taking it at any time. Unless serious complications of treatment arise, I understand that discontinuation of prescribed medication without consultation with the doctor could cause my condition to remain unimproved or worsen.

All questions of special concern to me have been answered. Upon consideration of the information provided me, I authorize the doctor, and such qualified assistants the doctor may designate to administer the named medication as the doctor deems advisable. I make this decision to accept the recommended drug treatment voluntarily and freely.

Signature: _____

Date: _____

Witnessed _____

Informed Consent Brochure for Electroconvulsive Therapy

Description of Electroconvulsive Therapy

Electroconvulsive therapy (ECT) is an accepted form of treatment for certain types of psychiatric disorders. It has been used successfully in thousands of cases in this country and abroad since its introduction in 1938. It is one of the most effective ways of treating depression and certain other conditions in patients who might otherwise require prolonged hospitalization.

The psychiatrist himself gives the treatment in a specially equipped treatment room, using a calibrated electronic instrument. If the psychiatrist feels an anesthesiologist is necessary, one will be present. The treatment consists of passing a small, carefully controlled electric current between two electrodes applied to the patient's temples. Treatments are usually given in the morning before breakfast. Prior to each treatment the patient receives a hypodermic injection to reduce oral secretions. No special dress or gown is required. Once in the treatment room, the patient is given an intravenous anesthetic that induces sleep within a matter of seconds. The patient is then given a second intravenous medication that produces muscular relaxation. The patient experiences no discomfort or pain during the treatment, nor feels the electric current, and has no memory of the treatment. When the treatment is given, the patient, who is already asleep, has generalized muscular contractions of a convulsive nature. These contractions, which have been "softened" by the second intravenous medication, last approximately 60 seconds. Minutes later, the patient slowly awakens and may experience temporary confusion similar to that seen in patients emerging from any type of brief anesthesia. When ready, the patient is then returned to the hospital room. Following this, breakfast is given and the patient is permitted to be up and about. Headache, mild muscle soreness, or nausea sometimes occur, but these are infrequent and usually respond to simple treatment.

The number of treatments in any given case will vary with the condition being treated, the individual response to treatment, and the medical judgment of the psychiatrist giving the treatments. A typical course of therapy may consist of 4 to 10 treatments. In some cases more treatments may be required. Although the treatments are usually given every other day, or three a week, the frequency of treatment will also vary with each case.

Adapted with permission from the consent form of the Department of Psychiatry, Sibley Memorial Hospital, Washington, D.C.

Risks

Electroconvulsive therapy, like any other medical or surgical procedure, involves a certain amount of calculated risk. Careful medical evaluation will be carried out in each case to ensure that there are no overriding medical contraindications to the treatment. Fatalities are extremely rare, reported at the rate of 1 in 1,000 to 1 in 10,000 patients. These figures are roughly the same as the rate associated with brief general anesthesia itself. Complications, although infrequent, may include fractures and/or dislocations or adverse cardiovascular, toxic, or allergic reactions to intravenous medication. These may sometimes occur in spite of all precautions and must be looked upon as a recognized hazard of the treatment. Should such a complication occur, appropriate treatment will be instituted and the patient's family notified.

Some confusion and memory loss, particularly recent memory loss, is not uncommonly experienced after electroconvulsive treatments. When this occurs, the great majority of objective data indicate that memory and thought functioning return to baseline by 1 to 6 months following electroconvulsive treatment. However, some patients continue to complain of memory difficulties of a persistent nature. Though not objectively verifiable, continued mild, spotty memory losses may occur in some individuals. Unilateral placement of electrodes produces less short-term memory loss and confusion than bilateral placement, but as many as 25% to 30% of patients do not respond to unilateral electroconvulsive treatment. In such an event, a full series of bilateral electroconvulsive treatments may be necessary to achieve maximum therapeutic potential.

Alternatives

The availability of alternative treatments depends on the clinical condition of the patient and the patient's response to previously administered treatments. The alternatives to electroconvulsive therapy include various medications, given singly or in combination, and various forms of psychotherapy, or both. If medications and psychotherapy have been tried without success, the alternative of seeking no further treatment may cause the disorder to remain unimproved or worsen. Rarely, spontaneous improvements do occur in psychiatric disorders for which electroconvulsive treatment is indicated. Psychiatrists will generally, but not always, try one or more of the above alternatives before attempting to use electroconvulsive therapy. However, electroconvulsive therapy may be the initial treatment of choice for certain psychiatric disorders.

Convalescence

After the last scheduled treatment the patient begins a "convalescent period," the duration of which varies with each patient. During this period (usually 1 to 3 weeks), the patient must either remain in the hospital or be discharged under the supervision of a family member or some responsible person selected by the family. This precaution is necessary because of the temporary impairment of memory which is an expected side effect of the treatment. During the convalescent period, the patient should not drive an automobile, transact business, or carry on usual employment until so advised by the doctor. Alcoholic beverages are prohibited. A responsible person should remain with the patient until such time as convalescence is completed. The duration of the convalescent period is determined by the patient's progress in consultation with the psychiatrist.

Outpatient Treatments

In some instances outpatient treatment may be recommended; in other cases "maintenance therapy" may be more suitable. In neither case is hospitalization required.

Outpatient treatment generally consists of a full course of treatment over a 2- to 4-week period without the patient's having to enter the hospital as an inpatient. "Maintenance treatment" consists of a regularly scheduled series of electroconvulsive treatments given over a period of time as a prophylactic measure to prevent recurrence of certain illnesses. In either event, a member of the family or a designated responsible person accepts the responsibility for:

1. Seeing that the patient does not take any food or drink after midnight preceding each treatment;
2. Escorting the patient to the hospital or other setting for the appointed treatment; and
3. Escorting the patient home after the treatment has been completed.

During the period of treatment and for at least 2 to 4 weeks following termination of treatment, the patient should be under the close supervision and constant companionship of the family.

Results

Finally, a word about the results of treatment. Although the results in most cases are gratifying, not all cases will respond equally well. As in all forms of medical treatment, some patients will recover promptly; others will recover only to relapse again and require further treatment; still others may fail to respond at all.

The above information has been prepared to answer some of the most frequently asked questions concerning electroconvulsive therapy, and to inform the patient and family of the benefits and risks involved in this treatment. This brochure represents the views of those members of this facility who are most experienced in administering this treatment. The attending psychiatrist will be glad to answer any further questions that may occur to the patient or family.

Consent Form for
Electroconvulsive Therapy

Dr. _____ has determined that I am suffering from a
_____ disorder and that I should receive electro-
convulsive therapy for this condition. I have read or have had read to me the
"Description of Electroconvulsive Therapy." I understand the nature and purpose of the proposed treatment, the risks and consequences of the treatment, the
probability of successful treatment, other reasonable treatment alternatives, and
the anticipated consequences if the proposed treatment is not given. This consent is given only for this course of electroconvulsive therapy and may be revoked at any time. Unless serious complications of treatment arise, I understand
that not completing the recommended number of electroconvulsive treatments
could cause my condition to remain unimproved or worsen. The approximate
cost of this series of electroconvulsive therapy has been explained to me.

All questions of special concern to me have been answered. Upon consideration of the information provided me, I, _____ ,
a patient in _____ and I,

_____ , of _____
Address

being the _____ , and nearest relative of _____ ,
Relationship   Patient

do hereby authorize and direct Dr. _____ , or his
[her] designee, to administer electroconvulsive therapy. I make this decision to
accept electroconvulsive therapy voluntarily and freely.

_____	_____	_____
Witness	Patient's signature	Date

_____	_____	_____
Witness	Relative's signature	Date

Adapted with permission from the consent form of the Department of Psychiatry, Sibley Memorial
Hospital, Washington, D.C.
Note: Consent by relatives may be legally insufficient in those jurisdictions that do not permit
proxy consent by next of kin for electroconvulsive therapy.

Discharge Confirmation of Patient Requiring Additional Psychiatric Treatment

Date: _____

Dear _____ :
(Patient's name)

This will confirm our conversation today in which you discharged me as your psychiatrist. In my clinical judgment you continue to require psychiatric treatment. If you have not already sought the professional services of another psychiatrist, I suggest you do so without delay. Upon your written authorization, I will forward your clinical records to your new physician.

Sincerely,

_____
(Psychiatrist's name)

_____
Note: Letter to be sent certified or restricted registered, return receipt requested.

Termination of the Psychiatrist-Patient Relationship

Date: _____

Dear _____ :
                            (Patient's name)

    This letter is to confirm our discussion that I can no longer continue your professional care. The reasons for this decision have been discussed thoroughly with you. Accordingly, I will not schedule regular appointments with you, but I will be available for emergencies until _____. I suggest that you obtain professional care without delay.

    If you choose to continue to receive treatment, I recommend that you contact another psychiatrist before the above termination date. If you need the names of other psychiatrists for referral, please contact me as soon as possible. On your written authorization, I will forward your clinical records to your new physician.

                                    Sincerely,

                            _____
                             (Psychiatrist's name)

Note: Letter to be sent certified or restricted registered, return receipt requested. This sample form may need to be modified according to the clinical circumstances.

Payment Agreement for
Treatment of a Relative

I, _____ , agree to pay
Dr. _____ for professional services provided
upon my request to   _____ ,
my _____ [relationship], based on the following
fee schedule: _____ .

I accept the personal and legal responsibility for the cost of services rendered by
Dr. _____ in the State of _____ .

Signature: _____

Date: _____

Witness: _____

Note: In most instances, an oral contract is valid. A promise to pay the debt of another person must be in writing only if there is a condition, such as, "I will pay if he or she fails to pay." A simple offer, "I will pay his or her debt," need not be in writing to be enforceable.

Living Will Declaration

**INSTRUCTIONS:
Consult this column for
help and guidance.**

To My Family, Doctors, and All Those
Concerned with My Care

**This declaration sets forth
your directions regarding
medical treatment.**

I, _____ , being
of sound mind, make this statement as a
directive to be followed if I become unable to
participate in decisions regarding my medical
care.
If I should be in an incurable or irreversible
mental or physical condition with no
reasonable expectation of recovery, I direct
my attending physician to withhold or
withdraw treatment that merely prolongs my
dying. I further direct that treatment be
limited to measures to keep me comfortable
and to relieve pain.

**You have the right to
refuse treatment you do
not want, and you may
request the care you do
want.**

These directions express my legal right to
refuse treatment. Therefore I expect my
family, doctors, and everyone concerned with
my care to regard themselves as legally and
morally bound to act in accord with my
wishes, and in so doing to be free of any legal
liability for having followed my directions.

**You may list specific
treatment you do not
want. For example:**

I especially do not want: _____

_____

**Cardiac resuscitation
Mechanical respiration
Artificial feeding/fluids
    by tubes**

_____

_____

_____

**Otherwise, your general
statement, top right, will
stand for your wishes.**

_____

You may want to add instructions for care you <u>do</u> want—for example, pain medication; or that you prefer to die at home if possible.

Other instructions/comments: _____

_____

_____

_____

If you want, you can name someone to see that your wishes are carried out, but you do not have to do this.

Proxy Designation Clause: Should I become unable to communicate my instructions as stated above, I designate the following person to act in my behalf:

Name _____

Address _____

If the person I have named above is unable to act in my behalf, I authorize the following person to do so:

Name _____

Address _____

Sign and date here in the presence of two adult witnesses, who should also sign.

Signed _____

Date _____

Witness _____

Witness _____

Keep the signed original with your personal papers at home. Give signed copies to your doctors, to your family, and to your proxy.

_____

Reprinted by permission of the Society for the Right to Die, 250 West 57th Street, New York, NY 10107.

Durable Power of Attorney for Health Care

Information About This Document

This is an important legal document. Before signing this document it is vital for you to know and understand these facts:

- This document gives the person you name as your agent the power to make health care decisions for you if you cannot make decisions for yourself.
- Even after you have signed this document, you have the right to make health care decisions for yourself so long as you are able to do so. In addition, even after you have signed the document, no treatment may be given to you or stopped over your objection.
- You may state in this document any types of treatment that you do not desire and those that you want to make sure you receive.
- You have the right to revoke (take away) the authority of your agent by notifying your agent or your health care provider orally or in writing of this desire.
- If there is anything in this document that you do not understand, you should ask for an explanation.

You will be given a copy of this document after you have signed it, and a copy will be sent to each person you name as your agent or alternative agent.

Durable Power of Attorney for Health Care

I, _____

hereby appoint

_____   _____
Name   Home address

_____   _____
Home telephone number   Work telephone number

as my agent to make health care decisions for me if and when I am unable to make my own health care decisions. This gives my agent the power to consent to giving, withholding, or stopping any health care, treatment, service, or diagnostic procedure. My agent also has the authority to talk with health care personnel, get information, and sign forms necessary to carry out those decisions.

Reproduced by permission of the National Hospice Organization, Arlington, Virginia.

If the person named as my agent is not available or is unable to act as my agent, then I appoint the following person(s) to serve in the order listed below:

_____   _____
Name   Home address

_____   _____
Home telephone number

_____   _____
Work telephone number

By this document I intend to create a power of attorney for health care that shall take effect upon my incapacity to make my own health care decisions and shall continue during that incapacity.

My agent shall make health care decisions as I direct below or as I make known to him or her in some other way.

(a) STATEMENT OF DESIRES CONCERNING LIFE-PROLONGING CARE, TREATMENT SERVICES, AND PROCEDURES;

_____

_____

_____

_____

(b) SPECIAL PROVISIONS AND LIMITATIONS:

_____

_____

_____

BY SIGNING HERE I INDICATE THAT I UNDERSTAND THE
PURPOSE AND EFFECT OF THIS DOCUMENT.

I sign my name to this form on   _____
                                                        (Date)

at: _____

_____ [address]

                                        _____
                                               (You sign here)

WITNESSES

I declare that the person who signed or acknowledged this document is person-ally known to me, that he/she signed or acknowledged this durable power of attorney in my presence, and that he/she appears to be of sound mind and under no duress, fraud, or undue influence. I am not the person appointed as agent by this document, nor am I the patient's health care provider or an employee of the patient's health care provider.

First Witness

_____
Signature:

_____
Home address:

_____
Print name:

_____
Date:

Second Witness

_____
Signature:

_____
Home address:

_____
Print name:

_____
Date:

AT LEAST ONE OF THE ABOVE WITNESSES MUST ALSO SIGN THE FOLLOWING DECLARATION.

I further declare that I am not related to the patient by blood, marriage, or adop-tion, and, to the best of my knowledge, I am not entitled to any part of his/her estate under a will now existing or by operation of law.

Signature: _____

Signature: _____

Combined Living Will and Durable Power of Attorney

Know all men by these presents that I, _____ ,
the undersigned, of sound mind, do hereby, make, constitute, and appoint my

_____ , of _____ , as my
(Spouse, son, daughter, etc.)   (Address)

true and lawful attorney-in-fact for me and in my name, place, and stead for the
purpose of making decisions regarding my health care at any time that I may be,
by reason of physical or mental disability, incapable of making decisions on my
own behalf.

If he or she is unable or unwilling to serve as my attorney at the time decisions
regarding my health care must be made, I designate my _____
(Son, daughter, close friend,
_____ , _____ , of _____ ,
etc.)   (Name)   (Address)

as my true and lawful attorney-in-fact for me and in my name, place, and stead
for the purpose of making decisions regarding my health care at any time that I
may be, by reason of physical or mental disability, incapable of making decisions on my own behalf.

If he or she is unable or unwilling to serve as my attorney at the time decisions
regarding my health care must be made, I designate my _____
(Son, daughter, close friend,
_____ , _____ , of _____ ,
etc.)   (Name)   (Address)

as alternate attorney-in-fact for me and in my name, place, and stead for the
purpose of making decisions regarding my health care.

1. I grant to said attorney-in-fact full power and authority to do and perform
   all and every act and thing whatsoever requisite, proper, or necessary to be
   done, in the exercise of the rights herein granted, as fully to all intents and
   purposes as I might or could do if personally present and able, with full
   power of substitution or revocation, hereby ratifying and confirming all
   that said attorney-in-fact shall lawfully do or cause to be done by virtue of
   this power of attorney and the rights and powers granted herein.
2. If, at any time, I am unable or unwilling to make decisions concerning my
   medical care and treatment, by virtue of physical, mental, or emotional disability, illness or otherwise, my said attorney-in-fact shall have the author-

Reproduced by permission of the National Hospice Organization, Arlington, Virginia.

ity to make all health care decisions for me and on my behalf, including consenting, refusing to consent, or withdrawing consent to any care, treatment, service, or procedure to maintain, diagnose, or treat my mental or physical condition, subject to the provisions of paragraphs 3 and 4 hereof if I am suffering from a terminal condition.

3. If, at any time, I should have an incurable injury, disease, illness, or disability, certified to be a terminal condition, and two physicians who have personally examined me (one of whom shall be my attending physician) have determined that my death will occur whether or not life-sustaining procedures are utilized, and that application of life-sustaining procedures would serve only to prolong the dying process, I specifically direct my said attorney-in-fact to authorize the withholding or withdrawal of such procedures. It is my intention that I be permitted to die naturally, with only the medication and nursing procedures necessary to alleviate pain and to provide me with comfort, dignity, and supportive care.

4. I also direct my said attorney-in-fact to make arrangements for the treatment of my terminal illness under the auspices of a hospice, if I should qualify for such care. I understand that acceptance into hospice care entails forgoing curative treatment and life-sustaining procedures that might otherwise be performed, such as resuscitation in case of cardiac arrest, and that forgoing such procedures might hasten my dying. I hereby consent to hospice care under such conditions and direct my attorney-in-fact to make any and all necessary arrangements for me to receive such care, including the signing of such consent forms as may be required by the hospice, any third-party payer, and the federal government.

5. In the absence of my ability to give directions regarding my health care, it is my intention that my said attorney-in-fact shall exercise this specific grant of authority and that such exercise shall be honored by my family, physicians, nurses, and any health care facilities in which I may be treated (including ambulances by which I may be conveyed between my residence and a health care facility), as the final expression of my legal right to refuse medical or surgical treatment. I understand and accept the consequences of such refusal.

6. This instrument is to be construed and interpreted as a limited power of attorney.

7. This power of attorney shall not terminate on my disability of incompetence.

The rights, powers, and authority of said attorney-in-fact herein granted shall commence and be in full force and effect on this _____ day of _____ , 19____ , and such rights, powers, and authority shall remain in full force and effect thereafter until this power of attorney or any part thereof is revoked by means sufficient under applicable state law to cause revocation.

Dated: _____ , 19____ .

_____
Signature

_____
Address

_____

CAUTION: A few states require signing before a judge or notary. Check state statute.

The undersigned hereby attest to their belief that _____ was of sound mind this _____ day of _____ , 19 ____ at _____ A.M./P.M. when the said principal signed this power of attorney.

We further attest that we are not related to the principal by blood or marriage, neither are we financially or professionally responsible for his/her care or employed by any institution so responsible. To the best of our knowledge, we are not entitled to any portion of the principal's estate either under the laws of interstate succession of this jurisdiction or under the terms of any will or codicil thereto.

_____	_____
[Print or type name]	[Print or type name]
_____	_____
Address	Address
_____	_____
_____	_____
Signature	Signature

Health Care Proxy

(1) I, _____ hereby
appoint _____
                    (Name, home address, and telephone number)
as my health care agent to make any and all health care decisions for me,
except to the extent that I state otherwise. This proxy shall take effect when
and if I become unable to make my own health care decisions.

(2) Optional instructions: I direct my agent to make health care decisions in
accord with my wishes and limitations as stated below, or as he or she otherwise knows. [Attach additional pages if necessary.]

_____

_____

[Unless your agent knows your wishes about artificial nutrition and hydration (feeding tubes), your agent will not be allowed to make decisions about
artificial nutrition and hydration. See instructions below for samples of language you could use.]

(3) Name of substitute or fill-in agent if the person I appoint above is unable,
unwilling, or unavailable to act as my health care agent.

_____

(Name, home address, and telephone number)

_____

(4) Unless I revoke it, this proxy shall remain in effect indefinitely, or until the
date or conditions stated below. This proxy shall expire [specific date or
conditions, if desired]:

_____

(5) Signature _____

     Address _____

     Date _____

Statement by Witnesses (must be 18 or older)

I declare that the person who signed this document is personally known to
me and appears to be of sound mind and acting of his or her own free will.

_____

Reprinted by permission of the New York State Department of Health.

He or she signed (or asked another to sign for him or her) this document in my presence.

Witness 1 _____

Address _____

Witness 2 _____

Address _____

About the Health Care Proxy

This is an important legal form. Before signing this form, you should understand the following facts:

1. This form gives the person you choose as your agent the authority to make all health care decisions for you, except to the extent you say otherwise in this form. "Health care" means any treatment, service, or procedure to diagnose or treat your physical or mental condition.
2. Unless you say otherwise, your agent will be allowed to make all health care decisions for you, including decisions to remove or provide life-sustaining treatment.
3. Unless your agent knows your wishes about artificial nutrition and hydration (nourishment and water provided by a feeding tube), he or she will not be allowed to refuse or consent to those measures for you.
4. Your agent will start making decisions for you when doctors decide that you are not able to make health care decisions for yourself.

You may write on this form any information about treatment that you do not desire and/or those treatments that you want to make sure you receive. Your agent must follow your instructions (oral and written) when making decisions for you.

If you want to give your agent written instructions, do so right on the form. For example, you could say:

If I become terminally ill, I do/don't want to receive the following treatments: . . .

If I am in a coma or unconscious, with no hope of recovery, then I do/don't want . . .

If I have brain damage or a brain disease that makes me unable to recognize people or speak and there is no hope that my condition will improve, I do/don't want . . .

I have discussed with my agent my wishes about _____ and I want my agent to make all decisions about these measures.

Examples of medical treatments about which you may wish to give your agent special instructions are listed below. This is not a complete list of the treatments about which you may leave instructions.

- Artificial respiration
- Artificial nutrition and hydration (nourishment and water provided by feeding tube)
- Cardiopulmonary resuscitation (CPR)
- Antipsychotic medication
- Electroconvulsive therapy
- Antibiotics
- Psychosurgery
- Dialysis
- Transplantation
- Blood transfusions
- Abortion
- Sterilization

Talk about choosing an agent with your family and/or close friends. You should discuss this form with a doctor or another health care professional, such as a nurse or social worker, before you sign it to make sure that you understand the types of decisions that may be made for you. You may also wish to give your doctor a signed copy. **You do not need a lawyer to fill out this form.**

You can choose any adult (over 18), including a family member, or close friend, to be your agent. If you select a doctor as your agent, he or she may have to choose between acting as your agent or as your attending doctor; a physician cannot do both at the same time. Also, if you are a patient or resident of a hospital, nursing home, or mental hygiene facility, there are special restrictions about naming someone who works for that facility as your agent. You should ask staff at the facility to explain those restrictions.

You should tell the person you choose that he or she will be your health care agent. You should discuss your health care wishes and this form with your agent. Be sure to give him or her a signed copy. Your agent cannot be sued for health care decisions made in good faith.

Even after you have signed this form, you have the right to make health care decisions for yourself as long as you are able to do so, and treatment cannot be given to you or stopped if you object. You can cancel the control given to your agent by telling him or her or your health care provider orally or in writing.

Filling Out the Proxy Form

Item (1)   Write your name and the name, home address, and telephone number of the person you are selecting as your agent.

Item (2)   If you have special instructions for your agent, you should write them here. Also, if you wish to limit your agent's authority in any way, you should say so here. If you do not state any limitations, your agent will be allowed to make all health care decisions that you could have made, including the decision to consent to or refuse life-sustaining treatment.

Item (3)   You may write the name, home address, and telephone number of an alternate agent.

Item (4)   This form will remain valid indefinitely unless you set an expiration date or condition for its expiration. This section is optional and should be filled in only if you want the health care proxy to expire.

Item (5)   You must date and sign the proxy. If you are unable to sign yourself, you may direct someone else to sign in your presence. Be sure to include your address.

Two witnesses at least 18 years of age must sign your proxy. The person who is appointed agent or alternate agent cannot sign as a witness.

Appendix 3

Glossary of Legal Terms

Glossary of Legal Terms

Adjudication   The formal pronouncement of a judgment or decree in a cause of action.

Assault   Any willful attempt or threat to inflict injury.

Battery   The unlawful use of force by one person upon another.

Beyond a reasonable doubt (evidence)   The level of proof required to convict a person in a criminal trial. This is the highest level of proof required (90%–95% range of certainty).

Breach of contract   A violation of or failure to perform any or all of the terms of an agreement.

Brief   A written statement prepared by the counsel arguing a case.

Burden of proof   The obligation to prove affirmatively a disputed fact or facts related to an issue that is raised by the parties in a case.

Capacity   The status or attributes necessary for a person so that his or her acts may be legally allowed and recognized.

Case   An action or suit at law.

Case law   The aggregate of reported cases as forming a body of law on a particular subject.

Cause of action   The grounds of an action (those facts that, if alleged and proved in a suit, would enable the plaintiff to attain a judgment).

Civil action   A lawsuit brought by a private individual or group to recover money or property, to enforce or protect a civil right, or to prevent or redress a civil wrong.

Clear and convincing (evidence)   Evidence sufficient to establish the proposition in question beyond hesitation (75% range of certainty). For example, the miminum level of evidence necessary to civilly commit someone.

Common law   A system of law based on customs, traditional usage, and prior case law rather than codified written laws (statutes).

Compensatory damages   Damages awarded to a person as compensation, indemnity, or restitution for harm sustained.

Competency   Having the mental capacity to understand the nature of an act.

Consent decree   Agreement by defendant to cease activities asserted as illegal by the government.

Consortium   The right of a husband or wife to the care, affection, company, and cooperation of the other spouse in every aspect of the marital relationship.

Contract   A legally enforceable agreement between two or more parties to do or not do a particular thing upon sufficient consideration.

Criminal law   The branch of the law that defines crimes and provides for their punishment.

Damages   A sum of money awarded to a person injured by the tort of another.

Defendant   A person against whom a claim or charge is brought.

Due process (of law)   A constitutional guarantee protecting individuals from arbitrary and unreasonable actions by the government that would deprive them of their basic rights to life, liberty, or property.

Duress   Compulsion or constraint, as by force or threat, exercised to make a person do or say something against his or her will.

Duty   Legal or moral obligation that one person owes another. Whenever one person has a right, another person has a corresponding duty to preserve or not interfere with that right.

False imprisonment   The unlawful restraint or detention of one person by another.

Fiduciary   A person who acts for another in a capacity that involves a confidence or trust.

Forensic psychiatry   The branch of medicine dealing with disorders of the mind in relation to legal principles and cases.

Fraud   Any act of trickery, deceit, or misrepresentation designed to deprive someone of a right or to do harm.

Guardianship   The relationship existing between a guardian and his or her ward.

Immunity   Freedom from duty or penalty.

Incompetence   A lack of ability or fitness for some legal qualification necessary for the performance of an act (e.g., under age, mental incompetence).

Informed consent   A competent person's voluntary agreement to allow something to happen that is based upon full disclosure of facts needed to make a knowing decision.

Intentional tort   A tort in which one is expressly or implicitly judged to have possessed intent or purpose to injure another.

Judgment   The final determination or adjudication by a court of the claims of parties in an action.

Jurisdiction   Widely used to denote the legal right by which courts or judicial officers exercise their authority.

Malpractice   Any professional misconduct or unreasonable lack of skill in professional or fiduciary duties.

Miranda   Refers to the *Miranda v. Arizona* decision that requires a four-part warning to be given prior to any custodial interrogation or detention.

Negligence   The failure to exercise the standard of care that would be expected of a normally reasonable and prudent person in a particular set of circumstances.

Nominal damages   Generally damages of a small monetary amount indicating a violation of a legal right without any important loss or damage to the plaintiff.

Parens patriae   The authority of the state to exercise sovereignty and guardianship of a person of legal disability so as to act on his or her behalf in protecting health, comfort, and welfare interests.

Plaintiff   The complaining party in an action; person who brings a cause of action.

Police power   The power of government to make and enforce all laws and regulations necessary for the welfare of the state and its citizens.

Preponderance of evidence   Superiority in the weight of evidence presented by one side over that of the other (51% range of certainty). The level of evidence required in civil trials.

Privileged communication   Those statements made by certain persons within a protected relationship (e.g., doctor-patient) that the law protects from forced disclosure at the option of the person (e.g., patient) in a legal proceeding.

Proximate cause   The direct, immediate cause to which an injury or loss can be attributed and without which the injury or loss would not have occurred.

Proxy   A person empowered by another to represent, act, or vote for him or her.

Punitive damages   Damages awarded over and above those to which the plaintiff is entitled, generally given to punish or make an example of the defendant.

Respondeat superior   The doctrine by which the master (employer) is liable in certain cases for the wrongful acts of his or her servants (employees).

Right   A power, privilege, demand, or claim possessed by a particular person by virtue of law. Every legal right that one person possesses imposes a corresponding legal duty on another person.

Sovereign immunity   The immunity of a government from being sued in court except with its consent.

Standard of care (negligence law)   In the law of negligence, that degree of care which a reasonably prudent person should exercise under the same or similar circumstances.

Stare decisis   Policy of courts to adhere to precedents and not to unsettle things that are established.

Statute   An act of the legislature declaring, commanding, or prohibiting something.

Subpoena   A writ commanding a person to appear in court.

Subpoena ad testificandum   A writ commanding a person to appear in court to give testimony.

Subpoena duces tecum   A writ commanding a person to appear in court with a particular document or paper.

Tort   Any private or civil wrong by act or omission but not including breach of contract.

U.S.C.   United States Code. The compilation of laws derived from federal legislation.

Vicarious liability   Indirect legal responsibility (e.g., the liability of an employer for the acts of an employee).

Appendix 4

Common Abbreviations and Terms
Used in Legal Citations

Common Abbreviations and Terms Used in Legal Citations

Symbols and Abbreviations

aff'd	lower court decision affirmed
aff'g	affirming
App	appellate (higher court)
APP Div	appellate division (e.g., NY Court of Appeals)
App Term	period in which appellate court hears cases
cert	certiorari (discretionary device by a superior court to hear cases from a lower court). For example, when the U.S. Supreme Court grants *cert,* it means it has "voluntarily" decided to review a case.
cert den	a petition for certiorari is denied or rejected
Cir	circuit/Circuit
Civ	civil/Civil
Crim	criminal/Criminal
Ct	court/Court
Ct Cl	Court of Claims
D	District (U.S. District Court) (federal jurisdiction)
Dist Ct	District Court (state jurisdiction or court)
id	cite to the immediate preceding authority
infra	citation found in upcoming passages
J/CJ	judge or justice/chief judge or chief justice
mod	opinion was modified
nd	no date available
reh'g	opinion was reheard
rev'd/rvsd	lower court opinion was reversed
slip op	slip opinion (advance publication of a recent opinion, typically in abbreviated form)
supra	previously cited authority that is not the immediately preceding citation
Sup Ct	Supreme Court (typically refers to state court)
S Ct or U.S.	United States Supreme Court
Super Ct	Superior Court (trial-level court) (state)
Vac	lower court opinion was vacated on appeal/rehearing

Terms

In re	in the matter of (e.g., all nonadversarial matters such as juvenile proceedings)
en banc	heard by the entire appellate court
ex rel	on behalf of
ex parte	by one, or for one, party (e.g., judges may choose to hear a matter, ex parte, or for the benefit of one party, without notice or response by an adverse party)
per curiam	opinion of the entire sitting court rather than the written opinion of one judge writing for the majority
sua sponte	of his own will (e.g., judge voluntarily hears a case on his own without prompting or a petition from a litigant party)
sub nom	a different name of a party in a subsequent history of a single case (for example, the defendant in *Wyatt v. Stickney,* 344 F Supp 373 [MD Ala 1972], aff'd sub nom, *Wyatt v Aderholt,* 503 F2d 1305 [5th Cir 1974])

Table of Cases

Duke Sanitarium v Hearn, 13 P2d 183
(Okla 1932), **6**
Dunham v Wright, 423 F2d 940 (3rd Cir
1970), **221**
Durflinger v Artiles, 234 Kan 484, 673
P2d 86 (1983), **286, 348**
Duvall v Goldin, 139 Mich App 342, 362
NW2d 275 (1984), **186, 305**

Enberg v Bonde, 331 NW2d 731 (Minn
1983), **171**

Faigenbaum v Cohen, Wayne County
Circuit Court, No 79-904-736 NM
Michigan, May 1982, **220, 226**
Faigenbaum v Oakland Medical Center,
143 Mich App 303, 373 NW2d 161
(Mich Ct App 1985), aff'd, Hyde v
Univ of Mich Bd of Regents, 426 Mich
223, 393 NW2d 847 (1986), **227**Farber
v Olkon, 40 Cal 2d 503, 254 P2d 520
(1953), **112**
Fees v Trow, 105 NJ 330, 521 A2d 824
(1987), **521**
Feiler v New Jersey Dental Association,
199 NJ Super 363, 489 A2d 1161
(1984), **33**
Ferguson v Quaker City Life Ins Co, 129
A2d 189 (DC 1957), **56**
Ferguson v Wolkin, 131 Misc 2d 304,
499 NYS2d 356 (Sup Ct 1986), **12**
Ferrara v Galluchio, 5 NY2d 16, **152**
NE2d 249, 176 NYS2d 996 (1958), **129**
Festa v Greenberg, 354 Pa Super 346,
511 A2d 1371 (Pa Super Ct 1986), **221**
Fitrak v United States, No CU81-0950
U.S.DC (ED, NY 1985), **196**
Fitzer v Forlaw, 435 So 2d 839 (Fla App
1983), **185**
Ford Motor Credit Co v Sheehan, 373 So
2d 956 (Fla Dist Ct App), cert
dismissed, Ford Motor Credit Co v
Sheehan, 379 So 2d 204 (Fla 1979),
489

Frasier v Department of Health and
Human Resources, 500 So 2d 858
(La 1986), **228**
Furr v Spring Grove State Hospital, 53
Md App 474, 454 A2d 414 (1983), **302**

Gadsden General Hospital v Hamilton,
212 Ala 531, 103 So 553 (1925), **491**
Gary v Gary, 631 SW2d 781 (Tex Ct App
1982), **61**
Gasperini v Manginelli, 196 Misc 547, 92
NYS2d 575 (NY Sup Ct 1949), **518**
Gerrard v Blackman, 401 F Supp 1189
(ND Ill 1975), **553**
Giallanza v Sands, 316 So 2d 77 (Fla
Dist Ct App 1975), **10**
Gillette v Tucker, 67 Ohio St 106, 65 NE
865 (1902), overruled, Oliver v Kaiser
Community Health Foundation, 5 Ohio
St 3d 111, 449 NE2d 438 (1983), **463**
Gitlin v Cassell, 107 App Div 2d 636,
484 NYS2d 19 (1985), **192**
Glazier v Lee, 171 Mich App 216, 429
NW2d 857 (Mich Ct App 1988), **312**
Gluckstein v Lipsett, 93 Cal App 2d 391,
209 P2d 98 (1949), **491**
Gonzales v Nork, 20 Cal 3d 500, 573 P2d
458, 143 Cal Rptr 240 (1978), **521**
Gooden v Tips, 651 SW2d 364 (Tex App
1983), **185**
Gowan v United States, 601 F Supp 1297
(D Or 1985), **248**
Graddy v New York Medical College, 19
AD2d 426, 243 NYS2d 940 (1963),
appeal denied, 13 NY2d 1175, 197
NE2d 541, 248 NYS2d 541 (1964), **465**
Grand Jury Subpoena Duces Tecum, et al
v Kuriansky, 69 NY2d 232, 505 NE2d
925, 513 NYS2d 359, cert denied, Y v
Kuriansky, 482 U.S. 928 (1987), **85**
Gray v Wood, No F2-1670 Dane Cty
Patients Compensation Panel, (Wisc
Feb 1, 1984), **31**
Greenberg v McCabe, 453 F Supp 765
(ED Pa 1978), cert denied, McCabe v
Greenberg, 444 U.S. 840 (1979), **427**

In re Certification of William R, 9 Misc
2d 1084, 172 NYS2d 869 (NY Sup Ct
1958), **143**
In re Estate of Heltsley v Votteler, 327
NW2d 759 (Iowa 1982), **302**
In re Grand Jury Proceedings, 867 F2d
562, (9th Cir), cert denied, Dee v U.S.,
110 S Ct 265 (1989), **56**
In re Guardianship of Richard Roe III,
383 Mass 415, 421 NE2d 40 (1981),
100, 101
In re Lifschutz, 2 Cal 3d 415, 85 Cal Rptr
467 P2d 557, 829 (1970), **40, 58**
In re Matter of Alleged Mental Illness of
Kinzer, 375 NW2d 526 (Minn Ct App
1985), **245**
In re Murawski, 84 AD2d 496, 446
NYS2d 815 (NY App Div 1982), **536**
In re Schiller, 148 NJ Super 168, 372
A2d 360 (1977), **125**
Ingber v Kandler, 128 AD2d 591, 513
NYS2d 11 (1987), **10**
Ison v McFall, 55 Tenn App 326, 400
SW2d 243, (Tenn Ct App 1964),
superseded by statute, Johnson v
Lawrence, 720 SW2d 50 (Tenn Ct App
1986), **464**
Iverson v Frandsen, 237 F2d 898 (10th
Cir 1956), **518**

Jablonski v United States, 712 F2d 391
(9th Cir 1983), overruled, In re
complaint of McLinn, 739 F2d 1395
(9th Cir 1984), **302**
Jablonski v United States, 712 F2d 391
(9th Cir 1983), overruled, In re
complaint of McLinn, 739 F2d 1395
(9th Cir 1984), **304, 322, 327, 335, 443**
Jacobs v Taylor, 190 Ga App 520, 379
SE2d 563 (GA Ct App 1989), **170**
James v Brown, 637 SW2d 914 (Tex
1982), **171**
Jobsen v Henne, 355 F2d 129 (2d Cir
1966), **553**
Johnson v Misericordia Community
Hospital, 99 Wis 2d 708, 301 NW2d
156 (1981), **536**

Johnson v Noot, 323 NW 2d 724 (Minn
1982) (en banc), superseded by statute,
Enebak v Noot, 353 NW2d 544 (Minn
1984), **164**
Johnson v United States, 409 F Supp
1283 (MD Fla 1976), rev'd, Johnson v
United States, 576 F2d 606 (5th Cir
1978), cert denied, 451 U.S. 1018
(1981), **267, 281**
Johnson v Woman's Hospitals, 527
SW2d 133 (Tenn Ct App 1975), **491**
Johnston v Rodis, 151 F Supp 345 (D DC
1957), reversed on other grounds, 251
F2d 917 (DC Cir 1958), **248**
Johnston v Rodis, 251 F2d 917 (DC Cir
1958), **552**
Johnston v Sibley, 558 SW2d 135 (Tex
Civ App 1963), **12**
Jones v State of New York, 267 AD 254,
45 NYS2d 404 (NY App Div 1943), **318**
Jones v Superintendent, 370 F Supp 488
(W D VA 1974), **553**

Kaimowitz v Department of Mental
Health for the State of Michigan, Civil
Action No 73-19434-AW (Mich Cir Ct
Wayne Cty, July 10, 1973), **97, 220,
250, 251**
Karash v County of San Diego, Court of
Appeal, Fourth Appellate District
Division One, State of California
Superior Ct No 420863 (July 18,
1986), **354**
Katz v State, 46 Misc 2d 61, 258 NYS2d
912 (1965), **265**
Kearns v Superior Court, 204 Cal App 3d
1325, 252 Cal Rptr 4 (1988), **7**Keene v
Wiggins, 69 Cal App 3d 308, 138 Cal
Rptr 3 (1977), **12**
Kirk v Michael Reese Hosp & Medical
Center, 136 Ill App 3d 945, 483 NE2d
906 (1985), rev'd on other grounds,
117 Ill 2d 507, 513 NE2d 387 (1987),
cert denied, 485 U.S. 905, **46, 187**
Kilcoin v Wolansky, 52 NY2d 995, 420
NE2d 87, 438 NYS2d 289 (1981), **521**

Index

Page numbers printed in boldface type refer to tables or figures.